Gu Kaizhi
AND THE
Admonitions Scroll

顧愷頭

金陵初置瓦棺寺僧眾設會請朝賢鳴刹注疏其士大夫無過十萬者愷
之刹注一百萬後成僧請勾疏愷之日宜置一壁遂閉戶畫維摩一軀畢
將點眸子謂寺僧曰第一日開見者責施十萬第二日可五百萬任施乃開
戶光明照寺施者填咽俄而果百萬

GU KAIZHI
AND THE
ADMONITIONS SCROLL

Edited by Shane McCausland

THE BRITISH MUSEUM PRESS

in association with

PERCIVAL DAVID FOUNDATION OF CHINESE ART

Colloquies on Art & Archaeology in Asia No. 21
PERCIVAL DAVID FOUNDATION OF CHINESE ART

The Admonitions Scroll:
Ideals of Etiquette, Art and Empire from Early China

Held 18–20 June 2001

The Trustees of The British Museum
gratefully acknowledge the generous support of the
E. Rhodes and Leona B. Carpenter Foundation
and other sponsors

First published in 2003 by The British Museum Press
A division of The British Museum Company Ltd
46 Bloomsbury Street
London
WC1B 3QQ

in association with the
Percival David Foundation of Chinese Art
School of Oriental and African Studies
University of London
53 Gordon Square
London
WC1H 0PD

Frontispiece:
Shangguan Zhou (1665–c.1750), 'Portrait of Gu Kaizhi',
from *Wanxiaotang huazhuan* (1743)

Contents

Part 3: The Treasure of Empires

Colour Plates

Preface

This volume presents the proceedings of an international colloquy about a singular work of art: the Chinese scroll-painting in the British Museum entitled the *Admonitions of the Instructress to the Court Ladies*, attributed to the legendary early master, Gu Kaizhi (*c.* 345–406). A narrative painting, the *Admonitions* illustrates episodes of an eighty-line poem about Confucian ethical behaviour composed in 292 CE by the savant and courtier Zhang Hua (232–300) to admonish Empress Jia (*c.* 257–300), ruthless wife of the Western Jin emperor Huidi (r. 290–306). The extant object comprises the paintings and inscriptions of the last nine of the original twelve scenes into which the painter divided the text (the first three scenes and the text of the fourth were lost possibly as early as the eleventh century). Consummately painted in 'gossamer' ink-outline and colour wash in perhaps the fifth or sixth century CE, the scroll has been ascribed to Gu Kaizhi or a contemporary since at least the eleventh century. Since then it has passed through the hands of many imperial and private collectors, and bears impressions of their seals, and a number of their own paintings and inscriptions on attached lengths of silk and paper. While it is agreed to be, in short, one of the great relics of early Chinese art, understanding such issues as its date, authorship, rhetoric and provenance has proved much less straightforward.

In part, this is because simply describing the material object is not simple: its physical form as a mounted painting on silk has so often changed through a series of historical processes, of which 'preservation' is but the latest one. The marks and attachments tell one complicated but incomplete history of the scroll; there are lost others – a potent reminder of how the past can only be ordered by a current state of knowledge.[1] We may speak of the scroll's different incarnations – historical moments at which it embodies particular sets of values, which seem to be keyed to changes in ownership, ideology and technology. Its original format as a didactic narrative scroll, for instance, was shaped by the normative ideology of early dynastic times: Confucianism. Its lyrical outline idiom is linked to the appearance of both the artist and new media – brush and silk – in the same period.

More recently – to try to sketch out the discursive context of this volume – the scroll's entry into the imperial collection of the emperor Qianlong (r. 1736–1795) of the Manchu Qing dynasty (1644–1911) in about 1745 is another sea change in its history. In spite of the emperor's rhetorical appeals to Chinese antiquity and cultural continuity, the scroll assisted in an ongoing 'clarification' of Chinese culture by the Manchu imperium in the context of China's emergence as a modern nation-state. It was remounted, given a new outer wrapper and title-slip; inside, it was given a new title-piece, and imperial seals, a painting and inscriptions, and a courtier's colophon-painting was added. It was recorded in a new imperial catalogue, re-housed, and re-branded as the first of the emperor's premier grouping of paintings, the 'Four Beauties'. Interestingly, this occurred at about the same time as its present home, the British Museum, was founded in 1753 in an Act of Parliament during the reign of George II (r. 1727–1760), 'to promote universal understanding through the arts, natural history and science in a public museum'.[2] This is also the rough date of this book's frontispiece, a woodblock-printed design by Shangguan Zhou (1665–*c.* 1750) depicting Gu Kaizhi 'transmitting the spirit' to one of his most celebrated paintings.

It was, indeed, in its Qianlong mounting that an Indian Army cavalry officer, Capt. Clarence A. K. Johnson (1870–1937), who acquired it in the vicinity of Beijing in 1900, brought the *Admonitions* scroll into the Museum for evaluation in 1902. It was purchased by the Museum early the following year. This new institutional context immediately began to shape a new identity for the scroll: it was authenticated as a masterpiece of Gu Kaizhi in the fledgling *Burlington*

Magazine by the poet and scholar Laurence Binyon (1869–1943). The scroll had not changed format by the time it was replicated in 1912–1913 in a run of one hundred woodblock-printed scrolls produced for the Museum by Japanese craftsmen. But it was a transformed object that was copied in 1922 by two celebrated Japanese artists of the Nihonga school, Kobayashi Kokei (1883–1957) and Maeda Seison (1885–1977), in the thousand-year-old literati tradition of closely observed hand-copying. By then, the 'scroll' was more accurately two long panels, it having been remounted in this format in the mid-1910s in the Museum's conservation studios. One panel displayed what had now become the artwork itself, the painting believed to be by Gu Kaizhi; and the other, the remnants of the scroll's assemblage of circa 1746. Incidental, and hence separated altogether, were the legendary jade toggle (for a valuation of which Johnson is said to have originally brought the scroll to the Museum), the Qianlong blue-brocade outer wrapper, and the courtier-painter Zou Yigui's (1686–1774) colophon-painting (which would perhaps just have made the second panel too long had it been included).

The years 1966–1967 mark another turning point in the *Admonitions'* history. In spite of being mounted on two stiff panels, the *Admonitions* continued to be imagined, no doubt consolingly, as an ancient handscroll, and in 1966 it was actually replicated as such. The Museum's 1966 colour collotype replica, commissioned of the Kyoto publishing house Benridō, re-created the object in scroll format in a kind of historical and technological hybrid. The plain outer wrapper of this scroll was labelled with a facsimile of the Qianlong emperor's title-slip, while the interior included only the ancient end-panels (in half-tone) and the painting itself (in colour) – overall, its notional Northern Song dynasty (960–1127) form. The year 1967 also saw the last update of world scholarship on the scroll: Professor Kohara's pair of articles in the *Kokka*.

To call the *Admonitions* a scroll,[3] therefore, is both handy and loose. It is thought the *Admonitions* was originally created as a handscroll, but this was not the norm in the pre-Tang period, when screens predominated. But this flexible word 'scroll' is used throughout this book, as it is in general speech and, no doubt, thought. It may refer to the extant artefact or to the scroll at different stages of its historical transmission. It has not really been possible to refer to the *Admonitions* more precisely. Recently, however, the word 'scroll' has once again become the *mot juste*, for the *Admonitions* has been re-created virtually using digital technology, and one can now scroll through its contents as in the form of its mid-eighteenth to early twentieth-century scroll-mounting at the Museum's Compass website. This technological vantage point enables us to make a virtual reality of its historical incarnations as a scroll-painting, a radical ordering of knowledge that was unimaginable before now. In addition to information and communication technology, this order of knowledge continues to be shaped by such factors as the discipline of art history, British official collecting and museum practices, and British interest in world cultures. The exhibition, the colloquy and this volume are determined by it, but have a significant role to play in informing it too.

A unique artefact, the age and quality of the *Admonitions* make it quite worthy of study in its own right. But it is not just its origins – art historical, rhetorical or ideological – that are of interest: copies have been made of it and remarks about it recorded over the centuries. Especially in a culture like China's that has placed such emphasis on transmission, we need to understand this provenance of the scroll, its instrumentality, and the dispersal of ideas seen to be embodied in it. In Michel Foucault's (1926–1984) sense of the word, we might call this project-at-large an 'archaeology' of the scroll: an analysis of the organic unity of the object, of its part in history.

The *Admonitions* would command our attention as it is, but new evidence for its study also keeps appearing on the horizon, not just from ongoing discoveries of tomb murals and so on in China, but also in Britain. The descendants of Capt. Johnson have recently provided the Museum with unpublished details about its acquisition. According to family tradition, Johnson was given the scroll in gratitude by a 'lady of high birth' to whose family he provided safe passage during the Boxer Rebellion while he was billeted at the Summer Palace north-west of Beijing.[4] Seemingly near completion, this 'archaeology' of the scroll must remain a work-in-progress, a preface to future studies that will have to take account of this new information. It might seem odd to be introducing new information in the preface to the volume, but the preface is of course written last; and, as Jacques Derrida reminds us, it becomes, like every act of reading or viewing, prefatory to any future reading or viewing.[5]

The process of studying the *Admonitions* collectively has brought a variety of different assumptions and analytical methods into play. These responses to the unique characteristics of this complex Chinese scroll-painting have taken as their aim exposing new seams in the record, and suggesting insightful new ways of researching them. Most of the tools and expertise to be found in the contemporary discipline, from the visual experience of the connoisseurs to the manipulation of ICT and abstractions of post-structural theory, can be found here. As Craig Clunas has observed, the study of the *Admonitions* scroll can reflect the relatively young field 'Chinese art'; it is an area of art history that has had to go through all historical stages of the discipline in quick time: from iconology and iconography to contextual and social enquiry to post-structural relativism. In this volume, therefore, studies of an intercultural or deconstructive posture appear beside others that assume or claim cultural exceptionalism, but they are all part of the same 'archaeological' project.

With some changes, the outline of this volume largely follows the plan of the June 2001 colloquy. The papers, almost all of which have been revised or rewritten, appear in a roughly chronological order, from classical to medieval to modern and post-modern times, and are punctuated by the discussants' remarks. Unfortunately, transcripts of the discussion sessions are too lengthy for inclusion here.[6] Happily, we can include a new conservator's report on the scroll.

In the introduction, Wen C. Fong begins with a vigorous formal analysis of both the painting and the calligraphy. He explores the scroll's consummate artistic quality, the depth and subtlety of emotional states, of the human desires and aspirations depicted, of the body language and, in particular Gu Kaizhi's forte: the depiction of human eye contact. The observation of these figures combined with the artist's sophisticated understanding of pictorial form and manipulation of its expressive power also provide Fong with an entrée to a defining moment of theoretical discourse in the Six Dynasties (265–589). In correlating his findings to an historical state of artistic development in the mid- to late sixth century, specifically to a context of creation at one of the late Southern Dynasties courts, Fong is the first of a number of contributors to this volume to see the *Admonitions* as an early medieval antiquity. Although some others maintain it is a ninth to eleventh-century copy or pastiche of an early painting, the consensus of opinion in these pages appears to be that both the paintings and the inscriptions were made in the Six Dynasties period. Finally, in describing the dynamic role played by the *Admonitions* and Gu Kaizhi in Chinese art history up to the twentieth century, Fong maps out territory for studies of the scroll's later transmission.

Kingship, the Way and Art

The *Admonitions* scroll has been compared to the Sphinx, for its sense of mystery and grandeur.[7] But it has also long been looked at by – and presented to – emperors, empresses and lesser subjects alike as a mirror, a mirror of reality – in the Chinese sense, as an instrument for self-reflection. It could be an aspirational object for those converted to the pursuit of virtue, but also an object of admonition for the wayward, a tool for the sovereign to manage his household and empire, or for the

foolhardy minister to intervene in the running of either.

As a narrative illustration of Confucian social and ethical principles by which early dynastic society was normally governed, the format of the *Admonitions* scroll was determined by a text, as noted. The author of this text, the statesman and poet Zhang Hua, faced with a dynastic crisis precipitated by the despotic rule of the Empress Jia, had resorted to the role of 'court instructress' (*nüshi*, literally, 'female historian') from the classic *Book of Odes* to issue a stern warning to the empress to change her ways. The women in the historical narratives painted within the scroll present models of human beauty in situations that alert the viewer to winning acts realized through the perfection of moral beauty, to the continuing need for self-vigilance in this regard, and to the ultimate rewards of moral perfection. Rhetorically, Zhang Hua's 'Admonitions' relates natural principles such as good behaviour to Chinese creation myths for the universe, government and society. A key passage is in his introduction: 'Human society begins with husband and wife. Their relationship extends to that for emperor and subject.'[8]

As a text illustration, the *Admonitions* scroll issues several kinds of challenge to our basic thinking about its genre. Yang Xin, for instance, puts great emphasis on an originating context for the painting, assuming that the implied criticism of the 'Admonitions' text would have necessitated very high-level support for the illustration project. He has also made another assumption, based on his knowledge of style and media, especially silks, of Song and pre-Song scrolls in the Palace Museum in Beijing: that the *Admonitions* scroll predates the Song by many hundreds of years. He balances interpreting the scroll as an instrument of moral reform with an understanding of it as a work of artistic self-expression. Thus, in conjunction with studies of the landscape and calligraphic styles, he also searches for plausible political contexts in the pre-Sui era in which such an illustration would have been needed. He alights on the reign of the Northern Wei (386–533) emperor Xiaowendi (r. 471–499), close in date to Wen Fong, but in the quite distinct context of non-Chinese rule in north China.[9]

Wen Fong sees the *Admonitions* as a copy of a scroll in the style of Gu Kaizhi, whereas Yang Xin identifies it as an original work, and not a copy. In her essay entitled 'Creating Ancestors', Audrey Spiro also finds it to be an original later work, a parody of early painting style. She does so by tracing the ancestry of the painting and dating the *haute couture* of court dress, jewellery and hair fashions by comparison with material culture from burials. She also explores the place of genre painting in early artistic creation, asking how much the style of this scroll is geared toward manifesting ritual and ideological needs of the ruling aristocracy of medieval China, and how much it is the parody of those needs in another age. The mildly erotic subject – the imperial harem – and the art-historical allusiveness of the work to early painting, she argues, betray it as a pastiche, and one that would have found a sympathetic audience in the Five Dynasties or early Northern Song (tenth to eleventh century).

In his discussant's remarks on these three essays, Richard M. Barnhart highlights points of agreement and disagreement, and examines the bases used by the three essayists (and others) for distinguishing a copy from an original work, before proposing his own radical views about the authorship and date of the *Admonitions*. He agrees with Yang and Spiro that it is an original work and not a copy; he agrees with Fong and Yang that it dates to the Six Dynasties; he agrees with Spiro that it is parodic and erotic. Barnhart differs from all, however, when he asks why it should not also date to about the lifetime of Gu Kaizhi. He raises the possibility that the scroll could indeed be by Gu Kaizhi, if not by one of his distinguished precursors or followers, about whom we know very little.

One of the main concerns raised by the painting as a textual illustration is how to account for the ideological position of the painter of the scroll in relation to the text. How do we evaluate the pictorial abstractions of the extraordinary 'hairline' ink-outline idiom, for instance, or indeed the formal success of compositions as didactic illustrations, or the portrayal of emotional tension, court brinkmanship, and humour to enrich visual interest? Much has been made of the social status of the artist. Yang Xin has determined him to be an anonymous court painter, whereas Chen Pao-chen identifies him as an erudite member of the ruling class. Is it possible to determine his personal stake in the illustration process, did he seek to carve out a personal realm for self-expression within the picture, or are these signs of the intervention of a qualified individual intended to lend authority and interest to the subject – that is, to sugar the bitter pill of admonition for a jaded audience? In art history generally, the temptation might be to understand pictorial transformations as means by which artists subvert culture – and we would be encouraged in this thinking by Gu Kaizhi's reputation for ribaldry and practical jokes. The gravity of the *Admonitions* scroll's subject, averting dynastic crisis, however, warrants caution; or at least suggests that the development of a kind of formal abstraction in the *Admonitions* could also represent a genuine response to the rhetorical demands of the subject.

Wu Hung's 'revisit' to the study of the *Admonitions* scroll proceeds with little expectation of earth-shattering discovery about it: it has been too intensely analysed for that, he

believes, particularly its dating problem. Rather, his approach is synthetic: he sets out to integrate new and old evidence, textual references, comparative examples, archaeological discoveries, physical analysis, and critical and analytical methodologies in a more comprehensive manner with the aim of determining the scroll's historical position. Like Richard Barnhart and others, Wu Hung finds no strong evidence of its being a copy; like Yang Xin, he sees no real basis for a connection with Gu Kaizhi. His most likely historical position is in what he calls a transitional phase in Chinese art and society between the third and sixth centuries, and more specifically to the fifth century – most likely the third quarter. As Wu Hung was unable to attend the 2001 colloquy, this new synthesis of his work on the scroll is presented here for the first time.

Julia K. Murray raises questions about the meaning of the *Admonitions* scroll as a work of didactic illustration. Rejecting arguments that see it as parodic or satirical, Murray defines the work as an imaginatively painted tool for admonition. The more *risqué* illustrations, such as the 'bedroom' scene, Murray sees as being justified by the need to create striking images for a possibly reluctant audience, a striking lesson in *realpolitik*. Murray disabuses us of the idea that didactic art need be straight-laced. Importantly, she identifies Zhang Hua's 'instructress' figure with the first-century female historian Ban Zhao; she also raises questions about Zhang Hua himself, and reviews his career at the Western Jin court and his relationship with the target of his admonitions, the depraved Empress Jia.

Julia Murray's is one of a number of papers that highlight the interest of the concept of admonition: that as a positivistic mode of expression, it provides an outlet for real criticism, if not in fact satire of both immoral behaviour and conservative values, but that it also has the merit of positing a solution. Admonition also seems to call attention to the manner of its delivery. The 'bitter pill' can be sugared, as in the case of the witty, intimate portraits in the *Admonitions* scroll. In this sense, it is possible to see the painter of the scroll as playing a role akin to the medieval court jester or 'fool': someone whose insights both amuse and hurt, but whom those in power tolerate. That Gu Kaizhi, the archetypal Six Dynasties genius, is described in his biography as being the perfect 'painter, wit and fool' has helped satisfy a historical need to ascribe the *Admonitions* to a great artist like him.

The problem of text-image relations is again faced in the study by Eugene Y. Wang of how Gu Kaizhi-style pictures that ostensibly depict Confucian filial-piety scenes on late Northern Wei sarcophagi actually illustrate Daoist beliefs about transcendence and otherworldliness. In these images, Wang argues, the Confucian narratives of filial piety act as pretexts;

placement and sequences of images, and the subtle manipulation of iconography within them betray the workings of an altogether different agenda. Illustrations do not necessarily convey the message of the texts they purport to illuminate.

In the title of her remarks on these last three essays the sinologist Michael Nylan playfully assumes the role of the 'female historian' or 'instructress' from the title of Zhang Hua's 'Admonitions' (*nüshi zhen*), but the message of her text is both trenchant and sincere. She cautions today's scholars to be aware of contemporary dichotomies, such as male vs. female and Confucian vs. Daoist, which we unthinkingly impose in historical enquiry into the early dynastic period. Nylan introduces the concept of a 'pleasure quotient' – habits and foibles one must give up in order to reap greater ultimate reward – to explore the rhetoric in the *Admonitions*, and argues that its message, that virtue truly is worth perfecting, was addressed equally to the Six Dynasties men and women who were its original audience.

Gu Kaizhi and the Literati Tradition

Part II comprises a set of papers given on the second day of the colloquy that are largely concerned with the *Admonitions* and Gu Kaizhi in early literati culture – that is, between the mid- or late Tang and the Yuan (ninth to fourteenth century). This period evidences a new concern with the formal language of the painting as painting, and with the rhetorical function of the historical individual, Gu Kaizhi, in contemporary culture.

The essay by Chen Pao-chen treats three important aspects in the study of the scroll. In the first, she aims to determine the nature of the painting as an illustration of Zhang Hua's 'Admonitions' text. She explores the faithfulness of the pictures to the function of the 'Admonitions' text as a work of Confucian admonition, and the relationships between the inscriptions and pictures within the surviving scenes. Importantly, Chen has also included a transcription and translation of the 'Admonitions' text itself. She finds it plausible that Gu Kaizhi would have been chosen to paint the original scroll, having been well placed to execute it on behalf of a powerful patron. In the final part of her study, Chen argues for a date for the extant painting of between 845 and 1075, on the basis of extant records of its existence.

By late Northern Song times, a schism had opened up between the absolutist state and the new social class of the intelligentsia, or literati (*shi*), with its own humanist ideology founded on individual moral self-cultivation as both the source of social transformation and hence the qualification for participating in government. Before this time, the scroll's connection to Gu Kaizhi may have been obvious or unimportant, but it was neither now. Contemporary accounts of it offer reflections of what its viewers sought from culture: in the case of Mi Fu (1052–1107), whose record is the earliest extant written one, it was a retroactive association of painting with literary learning, and with the embodiment of that learning and selfhood in the trace. In the case of the late Northern Song emperor Huizong (r. 1101–1125), it was a celebration of a supernatural talent in Gu Kaizhi, and an attempt to retake the cultural initiative from the literati. A neo-Daoist, Huizong was aiming to create a super-realist style in his painting academy through observation of natural phenomena and taxonomy of the natural order. Huizong set up a subtle if calculated resonance with the romantic, Daoist figure of Gu Kaizhi, who, through intense observation, was said to have 'used form to transmit the spirit' (*yixing xieshen*) of his subjects.

Alfreda Murck concerns herself with the scroll's connection to Gu Kaizhi, and she approaches the problem through literature. She begins by giving an account of perceptions of Gu Kaizhi and of the topic of admonition in medieval literary history, but finds no evidence of a link between the two before the late Northern Song, when the attribution of the scroll to Gu Kaizhi was made by Mi Fu. In his record, Mi Fu placed the scroll in the possession of a distinguished palace eunuch of the late eleventh century, Liu Youfang. This leads Murck to examine the possible function of the object as a tool of admonition for palace women of the Northern Song harem.

With Mi Fu and Huizong, the scroll takes on added meaning as a work of art, as it seems to shift from being an object of admonition concerning the regulation of women in the inner quarters of the imperial city to being an object of artistic beauty attributed to Gu Kaizhi. It seems there is a kind of subversion of its role as an instrument of correction. The new sense of importance attached to ancient works of art meant that many ancient scrolls got copied at the late Northern Song court by artists such as Mi Fu's contemporary, the first great literati painter Li Gonglin (*c.* 1041–1106), who was renowned for his ability as a copyist. So well known was he, in fact, that many Song-looking ink-outline copies of ancient works, including the *Admonitions* scroll in the Palace Museum, Beijing, have long-standing attributions to him. In his essay, Yu Hui sets out to re-examine the date and context of the Beijing scroll. By analysing the calligraphy of the inscriptions and the *baimiao* style of the painting, Yu determines this copy to have been done collaboratively at the Southern Song (1127–1279) court in the late twelfth century by a calligrapher and a more lowly court painter. He speculates that the copy could have been made as a record of the London painting, which is known to have entered the imperial collection of the Jurchen Jin dynasty in north China by about 1190.

Finally for part II, a study by this writer pursues the transformation of Gu Kaizhi's style and subject matter in the art of the pivotal master of the early Yuan, Zhao Mengfu (1254–1322), specifically in a study of Zhao's recreation of Gu Kaizhi's fabled portrait of the 'court-recluse' Xie Kun (280–322). Entitled the *Mind Landscape of Xie Youyu*, and painted in the manner of Gu's consummate 'gossamer' ink-outline, this painting, it is argued, illustrates how Zhao remodelled his own art in Gu Kaizhi's image as he embarked on what would become a comprehensive critical reassessment of China's painting history. This pivotal shift is seen as marking the outset of *later* Chinese art history.

In his commentary Maxwell K. Hearn probes the arguments of these four papers in relation to what he sees as the evolving power of both Gu Kaizhi and the *Admonitions* scroll to generate meaning over time in early modern Chinese history. He describes how understanding the later impact of the artist and this theme, along with determining the scroll's date and its origination with Gu Kaizhi, present three of the most vexing problems we face. Hearn is in agreement with Chen Pao-chen's assessment of the painting as a later copy, and commends her clarification of its early date of composition and probable creation by Gu Kaizhi. He highlights Alfreda Murck's link between the transformation of Gu Kaizhi into a 'literati' painter in the Tang-Song transition and the rise of scholar painting itself in the late Northern Song. He observes that Yu Hui and this writer's studies identify how the process of formalistic reinterpretation, wedded to a new focus on the expressive value of calligraphic brushwork, transformed painting, both in theory and in practice, by the fourteenth century.

The Treasure of Empires

At each point in its history, owners have sought to frame it, physically, institutionally or otherwise; it has never been enough simply to own the *Admonitions* scroll. In China, as no doubt elsewhere, ownership of such an object falls within a long tradition of 'possessing the past', that is, possessing secret charts, maps, diagrams, and, from about time of Gu Kaizhi on, paintings and calligraphy. Ownership conferred legitimacy upon rulers, who could either learn or be seen to learn from these treasures, and who could manipulate them to deliver the right ideological message. The third part of this volume, in which we focus on its role as a supreme state treasure, comprises a collection of essays, most of them specially

undertaken for this project and presented at the colloquy, that write a 'cultural biography' of the scroll.

Wang Yao-t'ing's specialized study of the seals, inscriptions, colophons, borders and other often-overlooked features on the painting and its peripheries provides the raw material and methodology for understanding its transmission. Exploring the period from 618 to about 1742, Wang's essay is an important reference study that enables us to get a clearer idea of what we mean by the term, the *Admonitions* scroll, at various historical moments. In examining taxonomies and procedures of cataloguing and documenting ownership, Wang allows us to visualize early modern collecting, connoisseurship and trade practices. In examining the traffic of art and connoisseurly 'red tape', he goes beyond the usual classification of such practices as being in good or bad faith, to suggest how seals and inscriptions could evoke personal meanings of the object for its owners and the cognoscenti that saw it.

In a parallel study conducted via the literary record, Stephen Little presents a narrative biography of the scroll during its provenance from the time of Yan Song (1480–1565) to the Qianlong emperor. He demonstrates how the scroll was seen as an exemplary, original work by Gu Kaizhi, but that while it was accorded special status in the canon, it had very little impact on figure or landscape painting of the late Ming–early Qing era. According to Little, it was chiefly valued by such leading literati as Dong Qichang (1555–1636) as a talismanic relic of Jin dynasty (265–419) calligraphy.

Yin Ji'nan's study represents a post-historical analysis of the image of Gu Kaizhi and of the creation and use of knowledge about early painting by late Ming and early Qing collectors and connoisseurs. As well as considering problematic the whole question of knowledge and knowledge production, Yin tries to imagine the possible impact of the *Admonitions* and other early scrolls on the lives of the Ming women for whom didactic texts about female etiquette, chastity and female virtue were being increasingly produced. Yin's paper casts a chastening light on Ming connoisseurs' chauvinistic obsession with the calligraphy of the scroll, highlighted by Little.

In his commentary to these essays, Cary Y. Liu works the concept of 'boundaries' introduced by Wang Yao-t'ing. Wang's paper, he notes, foregrounds the physical traces of the scroll as primary evidence; Little's the literary remains. Yin's, he observes, questions the ideology of the male literary elite in whose hands lay the power to shape wider social perceptions of early painting – and hence visuality and values. Liu highlights what he sees as the balanced and radical sensibilities of the self within the late Ming world-order.

The final panel pursues this 'cultural biography' of the scroll from the time of its entry into the Qianlong imperial collection in the 1740s up to the proceedings of the 2001 conference itself and even looks into what the future might hold in store for the scroll and the field.

Nixi Cura writes the eighteenth-century section, examining the role the Qianlong emperor played in reshaping perceptions of the *Admonitions* scroll in the context of his desire to consolidate Manchu rule over China. Cura assumes the 'subject position' of the emperor to explore how his manipulation of the scroll, including remounting, the impression of dozens of seals, and the addition of a title-piece, an orchid painting and a colophon, was conjured up to effect symbolic control over the minds and bodies of his Chinese subjects. She argues that his manoeuvres with the scroll, his most treasured painting, masked the threat of imperial sanction, disciplining and/or punishment. A ruler of ruthless benignancy, he seemingly used the painting to co-opt and hence 'cancel' the visual rhetoric of remonstrance, while presenting himself as perfected beyond need of admonition.

Collectively these studies teach us that facing up to the politics of owning the *Admonitions* scroll is nothing new, and Zhang Hongxing's intelligent reconstruction of the scroll's 'biography', from the time of its acquisition for the Manchu imperial collection in about 1745 up to its acquisition by the British Museum in 1903, considers this problem for today. In such cases, charges of self-censorship are sometimes levelled at the British Museum, but Zhang Hongxing's essay is specifically addressed to the question of how, in the aftermath of the Boxer Rebellion in 1900, the *Admonitions* scroll came into the possession of Capt. Johnson in or near Beijing. Importantly, Zhang both asks about and is able to account for the movements and perceptions of the painting in the nineteenth century, and for what the Manchu imperial family did with it and what they thought about it. Informed by his extensive archival research in the palace records in Beijing, Zhang states that the circumstance of Johnson's acquisition of the scroll remains unknown, but he proceeds to give a vivid picture of how the late imperial art collection was valued, and of its partial dispersal via an 'economy' of imperial gift-giving, eunuch pilfering and destruction, and imperialist appropriation.

Whereas for the Qianlong emperor the ideals of beauty and art in the *Admonitions* were subordinate to classical Confucian notions of kingship, for the writers of this volume art history is the modern scholarly discipline through which we approach the object. Just as Qianlong's refitting short-circuited the late Ming vision of the scroll as a relic of Jin calligraphy, and reconnected the scroll with his political orthodoxy, so the early twentieth-century remounting of the scroll short-circuited, or displaced Qianlong's configuration. The painting slipped out of its cultural frame – in which it was surrounded by 'all that Chinese writing', as Craig Clunas has put it – and into another. Now, however, the field takes a more complex line of enquiry about 'that Chinese writing', for it is recognized that most of it was inscribed by the hands of two non-Chinese emperors, a Jurchen and a Manchu. Over the twentieth century the object was reduced to the painting, and then in modern books to individual scenes, with the focus on its consummate artistic quality and authorship. This reifies a new set of connections, to other artists and media, to origins, and to the historical discipline.

In the final paper of this volume, Charles Mason surveys the art-historiography of the scroll from the time of its purchase by the Museum in 1903 to the 2001 colloquy, and considers how the Museum's remounting during World War I began the remaking of the object into an old masterwork in the history of world art. He sketches the changes of European scholars' interests in the scroll from identification and attribution (1903–1912) to criticism and debate (1923–1967) to contextualization and interpretation (1950s–present). With his discussion based mainly on writings about the object in Western languages, Mason gives shape to a more institutional style of artefact biography, and offers sincere reflections upon the ethics of cultural possession by the Euro-American museum as a late-modern institution.

Although the last to comment on the proceedings of the *Admonitions* colloquy, Craig Clunas pointedly does not seek what he calls the fashionable closure, averring instead that the multiplicity of views now prevalent in the field can be neither reduced to nor contained by such a move. He remarks on the interweaving of the scroll's life in London and the formation of the field of 'Chinese art'; he is also intrigued by how in the last hundred years of Western book-form publications, individual scenes – most commonly the 'rejection' scene – have come metonymically to represent the object, as well as by how the object had come to represent the field. But he notes how, at the same time, each generation feels compelled to reinvent the *Admonitions*. It is through great works like it, but through this one in particular, that we are able to have ongoing conversations about culture that are without threat of foreclosure: this, he believes, would be the equal of any definition of the great work of art that is the *Admonitions* scroll.

For the reader's convenience, the Romanization of Chinese in this volume has been standardized using the Hanyu pinyin system. Other systems have usually been modified, except in personal names and some commonly used place names (e.g. Peking, Taipei). A fourth-tone mark is used to avoid confusion between the medieval Jìn 晉 (fourth tone) dynasties (265–419) and the later Jīn 金 (first tone) dynasty of the

Jurchen (1115–1234). Chinese characters, where they appear, are given in their historical, 'complex' form (*fanti zi*). The contributors' textual references in the notes have been adapted as far as possible to suit the house style, which makes use of the Harvard author-date system. Titles of texts cited by contributors and the – in some cases – various editions of them consulted are listed in a consolidated bibliography at the end of the book. A glossary of Chinese and Japanese characters has been incorporated into the index. Dates, titles, readings and translations of terms given there and in the chronology of Chinese dynasties are generally accepted; however, the dates, etc. provided by individual contributors have, wherever possible, been preserved in their texts.

I should like to express my sincere thanks as the editor of this conference volume to the scholars who have been involved in its production, including the contributors, speakers, discussants and delegates at the June 2001 colloquy, and in particular my fellow organizers in the Department of Oriental Antiquities at the British Museum: the Assistant Keepers Jane Portal, who organized the concurrent exhibition, 'Emperors and Court Ladies: Chinese Figure Painting', and Carol Michaelson, and the Keeper Robert Knox. Helen Glaister of the Museum's Education Department greatly assisted in the organization and running of the event; the Museum's photographers did likewise for the production of visual resources for research. Sophie Sorrendegui and the Museum Assistants installed the accompanying exhibition and have since helped in numerous ways with the production of this volume. Hiromi Kinoshita and Hwang Yin provided the accurate, idiomatic translations, which we include here, of Yang Xin and Yu Hui's papers, respectively. The colloquy publicity material was imaginatively designed by Joe Cho and Stefanie Lew of Binocular, and the conference website by Art of Memory. The colloquy itself was graciously sponsored by the Chiang Ching-kuo Foundation for International Scholarly Exchange, the School of Oriental and African Studies (the Research Committee and the Department of Art and Archaeology under Philip Denwood) and the British Academy, as well as the Department of Oriental Antiquities and the Percival David Foundation.

At the Foundation, where I was privileged to be Percival David Visiting Scholar from 1999 to 2002, I should like to acknowledge with thanks the support of the curator Stacey Pierson, the administrator Elizabeth Jackson, James Carlisle (caretaker from 1969 to 2002) and Glenn Ratcliffe (the photographer), as well as the chair and members of the Foundation's Governing Council, who accommodated my wish to remain at the Foundation during 2001–2002 to edit this volume.

The publication of this book was made possible by a generous subvention from the E. Rhodes and Leona B. Carpenter Foundation via the American Friends of the British Museum, as well as the support of the joint organizers of the colloquy, the Percival David Foundation and the British Museum. The imaginative design was created by Andrew Shoolbred Ltd. The text was sensitively copy-edited by Coralie Hood and latterly Colin Grant. At British Museum Press the credit goes to Sarah Levesley and the excellent production team, and the editor Nina Shandloff, who carefully guided the book to completion. Ming Wilson, Zhang Hongxing, Judy Inn and Zhang Yi all kindly helped at different stages of production. For their intellectual community I am indebted to colleagues in the Department of Art and Archaeology and elsewhere at SOAS – too many to name here – and not just those in East Asian art history. I owe a special debt of thanks to Robert Knox, Stacey Pierson and Jane Portal, as well as John Carpenter, Wen Fong and Sarah Wong for their support along the way.

Shane McCausland
Bloomsbury
Summer 2002

NOTES

1 I refer to Michel Foucault's notion of 'recurrent redistributions' which 'reveal several pasts, several forms of connexion, several hierarchies of importance, several networks of determination, several teleologies, for one and the same science, as its present undergoes change: thus historical descriptions are necessarily ordered by the present state of knowledge, they increase with every transformation and never cease, in turn, to break with themselves' (1972, p. 5).

2 Quoted (10 May 2002) from the mission statement at http://www.thebritishmuseum.ac.uk/visit/about.html.

3 Or 'handscroll', a modern gloss on the Chinese term *juan*.

4 See the essay by Zhang Hongxing in this volume, esp. pp. 285–6.

5 Derrida (tr. Spivak) 1974 (1967).

6 Reviews of the colloquy include Hwang Yin's (2001) and one by this writer (2003). James Cahill has transcribed and published his reasons for seeing the scroll as a tenth-century copy, which he presented in a discussion session (2001).

7 By Kohara Hironobu (1967, 2001).

8 Tr. Chen Pao-chen.

9 Yang Xin's paper has been published in full in Chinese (2001) and is presented here in abridged form.

Text and Translation of Zhang Hua's Poem, 'Admonitions of the Instructress to the Court Ladies' ('Nüshi zhen')

晉司空張華《女史箴》

1. 茫茫造化
   máng máng zào hùa
   In the beginning the Universe was created in a gathering of misty air.[1]

2. 二儀既分
   èr yí jì fēn [2]
   From that, two primal principles, *yin* and *yang*, developed.

3. 散氣流形
   sàn qì líu xíng
   The air cleared; it flowed with, and enlivened human beings,

4. 既陶既甄
   jì táo jì zhēn
   Shaped and modelled (by Nü Wa).

5. 在帝庖犧
   zài dì Páoxī
   Among the ancient emperors, there was Paoxi [Fu Xi],

6. 肇經天人
   zhào jīng tiān rén
   Who began to set regulations for ruling men under Heaven.

7. 爰始夫婦
   yuán shǐ fū fù
   Human society starts with husband and wife.

8. 以及君臣
   yǐ jí jūn chén
   Their relationship extends to that for sovereign and subject.

9. 家道以正
   jiā dào yǐ zhèng [3]
   A family should be maintained in a proper way.

10. 王猷有倫
    wáng yóu yǒu lún [4]
    Likewise, a kingdom should be ruled in good order.

11. 婦德尚柔
    fù dé shàng róu
    Among women's virtues, gentleness is valued first.

12. 含章貞吉
    hán zhāng zhēn jí
    A woman should be clear-minded, self-restrained, and behave properly.

13. 婉嫕淑慎
    wǎn yì shū shèn
    She should be gentle, obedient, elegant, and cautious.

14. 正位居室
    zhèng wèi jū shì
    She must always keep herself in her place.

15. 施衿結褵
    shī jīn jié lí
    She should always remember her mother's teaching while helping her dress for the wedding:

16. 虔恭中饋
    qián gōng zhōng kuì
    'You must be respectful in doing everything, including cooking daily meals for your family and preparing offerings for ritual purposes.

17. 肅慎爾儀
    sù shèn ěr yí
    You should watch your manners, remain cautious and serious always.

18. 式瞻清懿
    shì zhān qīng yì
    You should always make yourself look fresh and behave virtuously to earn others' respect.'

19. 樊姬感莊
    Fán jī gǎn Zhuāng
    Refusing to eat fresh meat for three years, Lady Fan eventually moved King Zhuang of Chu to give up hunting.

20. 不食鮮禽
    bù shì xiān qín

21. 衛女矯桓
    Wèi nǚ jiǎo Huán
    To help Duke Huan of Qi cultivate a taste for fine music,

22. 耳忘和音
    ěr wàng hé yīn
    Lady Wei refused to listen to the sensuous songs from Zheng and Wei.

23. 志厲義高
    zhì lì yì gāo
    These two ladies' strong will and noble principles

24. 而二主易心
ér èr zhǔ yì xīn

Made the rulers change their minds.

25. 玄熊攀檻
xuán xióng pān jiàn

Just as the black bear climbed out of the barred cage,

26. 馮媛趨進
Féng yuán qū jìn

Lady Feng hastily moved her body toward it.

27. 夫豈無畏
fū qǐ wú wèi

Was she not afraid of being hurt?

28. 知死不恡
zhī sǐ bú lìn [5]

Clearly, she knew that she might die, but she did not care about it.

29. 班妾有辭
Bān qiè yǒu cí [6]

Lady Ban had reasons to end

30. 割驩同輦
gē huān tóng niǎn [7]

Her pleasure in sharing the emperor's palanquin.

31. 夫豈不懷
fū qǐ bù huái

And yet it was not because she did not love him;

32. 防微慮遠
fáng wéi lǜ yuǎn

Rather, she was mindful of his small errors and thoughtful of his future.

33. 道罔隆而不殺
dào wǎng lóng ér bù shā [8]

In nature there is (nothing) that is exalted which is not soon brought low.

34. 物無盛而不衰
wù wú shèng ér bù shuāi

Among living things there is nothing which having attained its apogee does not thenceforth decline.

35. 日中則昃
rì zhōng zé zè

When the sun has reached its mid-course, it begins to sink;

36. 月滿則微
yuè mǎn zé wéi

When the moon is full it begins to wane.

37. 崇猶塵積
chóng yóu chén jī

To rise to glory is as hard as to build a mountain out of dust;

38. 替若駭機
tì ruò hài jī

To fall into calamity is as easy as the rebound of a tense spring.

39. 人咸知飾其容
rén xián zhī shì qí róng [9]

Men and women know how to adorn their faces,

40. 而莫知飾其性
ér mò zhī shì qí xìng [10]

But there is none who knows how to adorn his character.

41. 性之不飾
xìng zhī bú shì

Yet if the character be not adorned,

42. 或愆禮正
huò qiān lǐ zhèng

There is a danger that the rules of conduct may be transgressed.

43. 斧之藻之
fǔ zhī zǎo zhī

Correct your character as with an axe, embellish it as with a chisel;

44. 克念作聖
kè niàn zuò shèng

Strive to create holiness in your own nature.

45. 出其言善
chū qí yán shàn

If the words that you utter are good,

46. 千里應之
qiān lǐ yìng zhī

All men for a thousand leagues around will make response to you.

47. 苟違斯義
gǒu wéi sī yì

But if you depart from this principle,

48. 則同衾以疑
zé tóng qīn yǐ yí [11]

Even your bedfellow will distrust you.

49. 夫出言如微
fū chū yán rú wéi [12]

To utter a word, how light a thing that seems!

50. 而榮辱由茲
ér róng rǔ yóu zī [13]

Yet from a word, both honour and shame proceed.

51. 勿謂幽昧
wù wèi yōu mèi

Do not think that you are hidden;

52. 靈鑒無象
líng jiàn wú xiàng

For the divine mirror reflects even that which cannot be seen.

53. 勿謂玄漠
wù wèi xuán mò [14]

Do not think that you have been noiseless;

54. 神聽無響
shén tīng wú xiǎng

God's ear needs no sound.

55. 無矜爾榮
wú jīn ěr róng [15]

Do not boast of your glory;

56. 天道惡盈
tiān dào wù yíng

For heaven's law hates what is full.

57. 無恃爾貴
wú shì ěr guì [16]

Do not put your trust in honours and high birth;

58. 隆隆者墜
lóng lóng zhě zhuì

For he that is highest falls.

59. 鑒於小星
jiàn yú xiǎo xīng

Make the 'Little Stars' your pattern.

60. 戒彼攸遂
jiè bǐ yōu suì

Do not let your fancies roam afar.

61. 比心螽斯
bǐ xīn zhōng sī

Let your hearts be as the locusts

62. 則繁爾類
zé fán ěr leì [17]

And your race shall multiply.

63. 驩不可以黷
huān bù ké yǐ dú [18]

No one can please forever;

64. 寵不可以專
chǒng bù ké yǐ zhuān

Affection cannot be for one alone;

65. 專實生慢
zhuān shí shēng màn

If it be so, it will end in disgust.

66. 愛極則遷
ài jí zé qiān

When love has reached its highest pitch, it changes its objects;

67. 致盈必損
zhì yíng bì sǔn

For whatever has reached fullness must decline.

68. 理有固然
lǐ yǒu gù rán

This law is absolute.

69. 美者自美
měi zhě zí měi

The 'beautiful wife who knew herself to be beautiful'

70. 翩以取尤
piān yǐ qǔ yóu [19]

Was soon hated.

71. 冶容求好
yě róng qiú hào

If by a mincing air you seek to please,

72. 君子所讎
jūn zǐ suǒ chóu [20]

Wise men will abhor you.

73. 結恩而絕
jié ēn ér jué

From this cause truly comes

74. 職此之由
zhí cǐ zhī yóu [21]

The breaking of favour's bond.

75. 故曰翼翼矜矜
gù yuē yì yì jīn jīn

Therefore I say, be watchful: keep an eager guard over your behaviour;

76. 福所以興
fú suǒ yǐ xīng

For thence happiness will come.

77. 靖恭自思
jìng gōng zì sī [22]

Fulfil your duties calmly and respectfully;

78. 榮顯所期
róng xiǎn suǒ qí

Thus shall you win glory and honour.

79. 女史司箴
nǚ shǐ sī zhēn

Thus has the Instructress, charged with the duty of admonition,

80. 敢告庶姬
gǎn gào shù jī

Thought good to speak to the ladies of the palace harem.

NOTES

1   Lines 1–32 translated by Chen Pao-chen; lines 33–80 by Basil Gray after Arthur Waley (Gray 1966). The Chinese text follows the one recorded in *Wen xuan, juan* 56. Variant characters inscribed on the Beijing and London *Admonitions* scrolls are given in the footnotes.
2   既: Beijing scroll has *shǐ* 始.
3   以: Beijing scroll has archaic form 㠯.
4   Beijing scroll begins line with *ér* 而.
5   愻: Beijing scroll has 喜.
6   姜: London scroll has *jié* 婕.
7   驩: London scroll has 歡.
8   囹: unclear in London scroll; possibly *wú* 無.
9   飾: Beijing scroll has *xiū* 修; London scroll has variant 脩.
10 London scroll lacks 而.
11 London scroll lacks 則.

12 London scroll lacks 出.
13 London scroll lacks 而.
14 Lines 51–53: London scroll has *yōu mèi* 幽昧 and *xuán mò* 玄漠 in opposite order.
15 無: Beijing scroll has 毋. 爾: Beijing scroll has 尒; London scroll has 尔.
16 無: Beijing scroll has 毋. 爾: Beijing scroll has 尒; London scroll has 尔.
17 爾: Beijing scroll has 尒; London scroll has 尔.
18 驩: Beijing and London scrolls have 歡. 黷: London scroll has 瀆.
19 翩: London scroll has *fān* 翻.
20 讎: London scroll has variant 仇.
21 職: London scroll has *shí* 寔.
22 靖: London scroll has 靜

Introduction: The *Admonitions* Scroll and Chinese Art History

Wen C. Fong

Admonitions of the Instructress to the Court Ladies (Nüshi zhen tu), a handscroll in the British Museum attributed to the fourth-century figure painter Gu Kaizhi (*c.* 344–*c.* 406), is arguably the most important early Chinese scroll painting in existence.[1] A near contemporary of the Calligraphic Sage Wang Xizhi (303–361), and, like Wang, a product of the Eastern Jìn dynasty (317–420) in southern China, Gu Kaizhi has traditionally been described as a founding father of classical Chinese figure painting, which reached its peak in the works of the Painting Sage Wu Daozi (act. *c.* 710–760) of the Tang dynasty (618–906). The *Admonitions* scroll – recorded in Mi Fu's (1052–1107) *History of Painting (Hua shi)* and in the Northern Song (960–1127) *Catalogue of the Imperial Painting Collection During the Xuanhe Era (Xuanhe huapu)* of 1120, and bearing impressions of an authenticated imperial palace seal, 'Ruisi Dongge' (Palace of Sagacious Contemplation, East Wing), dated between 1075 and 1078[2] – has exercised a powerful influence on later Chinese painters. Since its acquisition in 1903 by the British Museum, the scroll has stood for the beginning of classical Chinese painting in all modern writings on Chinese art history.[3]

The 'Admonitions' Text

The fall of the Han empire (206 BCE–220CE), in the early third century, was followed by three and a half centuries of political disunity and social disintegration. During this period, known as the Wei (220–265), Western Jìn (265–316), and Southern and Northern Dynasties (317–589), China was divided into northern kingdoms controlled by non-Chinese nomadic invaders and short-lived southern dynasties ruled by Han-Chinese courts. The *Admonitions* scroll illustrates passages from a moralizing text of the same name composed in the year 292 by the Confucian scholar-official Zhang Hua (232–300), who lived under the Western Jìn dynasty, in northern China.[4] In the official history of the Jìn (*Jìn shu*), Zhang is described as one who, 'while serving a weak emperor and a tyrannical empress, nevertheless secured national stability'.[5] The 'tyrannical empress' refers to Empress Jia (d. 300), consort of the Western Jìn ruler Huidi (r. 290–306). In 291 the empress ordered the execution of the Grand Preceptor, Yang Jun, and the following year had the dowager empress of the Yang clan murdered. In late 299 or early 300 she arranged the assassination of her stepson, Yu, the emperor Huidi's heir apparent. Empress Jia was deposed in the year 300 in a coup led by Prince Zhao, a member of the Western Jìn imperial family.

Zhang Hua composed his 'Admonitions' to remonstrate with the empress, who treated him with a grudging respect. Written in the tradition of earlier Eastern Han (25–220) didactic texts, which present women as paragons of virtue and exemplary conduct, the 'Admonitions' reflects the official teachings of a Confucian state.[6] According to Confucian ethics, the so-called Five Human Relationships – duty between ruler and subject, love between father and son, respect between husband and wife, affection between brothers, and trust between friends – constituted the cardinal principles of a just society. In addressing the relationship between husband and wife, Zhang's 'Admonitions' alluded to the sanctity of the fundamental relationship between ruler and minister, the constant violation of which threatened the very existence of the empire at the time.

The British Museum's *Admonitions* scroll illustrates the last nine of twelve episodes in Zhang Hua's text (the illustrations of the first three episodes are lost).[7] These scenes and their accompanying texts can be read as an exhortation to uphold Confucian standards of correct behaviour and a warning against personal ambition and the misuse of power:

Scene 1 (pls 1–2): Lady Feng, an exemplar of courage, protects the Han emperor Yuandi (r. 48–33 BCE) from the advance of a wild bear.

Scene 2 (pls 3–4): As an example of moral rectitude, the consort Lady Ban declines to ride with the Han emperor Chengdi (r. 33–7 BCE) in the imperial palanquin lest her presence be seen to reflect adversely on his character.

Scene 3 (pl. 5): An archer readies himself to shoot a tiger, which stalks its prey on a mountain top. The text, a clear warning against Empress Jia's excesses, reads: 'There is nothing high that is not soon brought low … When the sun reaches its apogee, it begins to sink; when the moon is full, it begins to wane. To rise to glory is as hard as building a mountain from grains of dust. To fall into calamity is as easy as the rebound of a crossbow.'

Scene 4 (pls 6 right, 8): Two court ladies admire themselves. The text reads: 'People know how to adorn their person, but few know how to embellish their nature.'

Scene 5 (pls 6 left, 7): A man and a woman in bed regard one another with suspicion. The text reads: 'If you depart from the principle [of goodness], even your bedfellow will mistrust you.'

Scene 6 (pls 9 right, 11): Three generations of a family gather together, illustrating that the promise of a virtuous life is that 'one's progeny shall multiply'.

Scene 7 (pls 9 left, 10): An emperor rebuffs a fawning beauty, a reminder that 'Affection cannot be monopolized … It will turn to disgust.'

Scene 8 (pl. 12 right): A lady kneels in deference. The text reads: 'Fulfill your duties calmly and with respect.'

Scene 9 (pls 12–13): The court instructress copies out the 'admonitions', while two palace ladies engage in idle conversation.[8]

The Confucian concept of a well-ordered and just empire was predicated not only on the presence of an enlightened ruler, but also on an optimistic belief in the human capacity for moral goodness. According to the Confucian theory of the Mandate of Heaven, while a virtuous ruler had the mandate to rule all under heaven, it was the duty of the minister to remonstrate with the ruler should he deviate from the path of virtue. While the *Admonitions* scroll may have reflected such ancient utopian ideals, the painting itself was in fact the product of a time of trouble, when the very concept of ethical rule was severely tested. By invoking Confucian precepts as the normative principles of human relations, Zhang

Hua spoke with a bluntness that ultimately placed his life at risk. He was executed in 300, when he opposed Prince Zhao for toppling Empress Jia.

Why Gu Kaizhi?

In 316 the Western Jin was overrun by nomadic chieftains in north China. The following year, a Jin prince enfeoffed in south China declared himself emperor of a new dynasty called the Eastern Jin and established its capital in Jiankang (later known as Nanjing, or the Southern Capital), in the heart of the rich Jiangnan region (south of the Yangzi River). It was at this time that Han-Chinese society, under pressure from the nomadic invasions in the north and in response to interactions with Buddhism and Graeco-Roman influences from the distant West, turned to religion and art for solace and spiritual harmony. With the mystical philosophies of Neo-Daoism and Buddhism came the notion of the infinity of space and time and a belief in a plurality of worlds and cycles of time, which introduced the concept of the spirit (*shen*) or soul (*ling*) transcending physical and temporal boundaries, and stimulated an interest in expressing such ideas in the arts. Under the aristocratic rulers of the southern courts at Jiankang, the secular arts of *belles-lettres*, music, calligraphy and painting flourished. This, in turn, brought a new awareness of creative genius and provoked discussions of aesthetic standards and critical theories among artists, collectors and connoisseurs alike.

In the warm climate of the south and the more relaxed atmosphere of the Southern Dynasties, leading calligraphers and artists such as Wang Xizhi and Gu Kaizhi, disillusioned with politics, turned to nature, religion and art, often retiring to the mountains to paint, practise calligraphy and develop theories on art. Gu Kaizhi was a native of Wuxi, in modern Jiangsu Province, where his father, Gu Yuezhi, had served as a magistrate.[9] Gu Kaizhi was described by his contemporaries as a painter of genius, an eccentric (*chi*) and a wit.[10] It is said, for example, that in the early 360s the young artist made a pledge of one-million cash to the Buddhist Tile-Coffin Temple (Waguansi), then under construction in Jiankang, a gesture that at the time everyone took as a joke.[11] After requesting that a blank wall be prepared for him, Gu Kaizhi withdrew to the temple where he worked for a month to produce a portrait of the Buddhist layman Vimalakirti.[12] 'When the door was opened, radiance filled the entire temple, donors blocked the hallways, and in a short time a million-cash donation was collected.'[13]

From the late 360s through to the 390s, Eastern Jin rule fell into the hands of a succession of powerful military governor-generals, beginning with Huan Wen (312–373) and Yin Zhongkan (d. 399) and followed by Huan Wen's son, Huan Xuan (369–404). In 371 Huan Wen ousted the emperor Feidi (r. 366–370) and replaced him with Jianwendi (r. 371–372). During the succeeding reign of Xiaowudi (r. 373–396), Yin Zhongkan, then governor-general of three regions administered from Jiangling, formed an alliance with Huan Xuan, but was killed by Huan in 399. In 403, after deposing the emperor Andi (r. 397–403; 404–418), Huan Xuan declared himself emperor, only to be defeated and killed the following year by the future founder of the Liu Song dynasty (420–479), Liu Yu (r. 420–422).[14]

Gu Kaizhi served as artistic advisor to each of these three powerful Eastern Jìn warlords, all of whom were lovers of *belles-lettres* and ardent art collectors. Huan Wen reportedly stayed up long nights with Gu and the young Yang Xin (360–442), a budding calligrapher, to discuss the art of calligraphy. Gu also painted a portrait for Yin Zhongkan. Gu is said to have once entrusted a chestful of his finest works to Huan Wen's son Huan Xuan for safekeeping. Upon discovering that Huan Xuan had taken some of the works, Gu, rather than confronting him, merely joked, 'Since these paintings are supernatural marvels, they must have flown away like some humans who have become immortals!'[15] In about 405 Gu Kaizhi finally received an appointment at the Eastern Jìn court as Honorary Regular Attendant, but he died soon thereafter at the age of sixty-two.[16]

According to *New Account of the Tales of the World (Shishuo xinyu)*, compiled under the aegis of Liu Yiqing (404–444), the Grand Guardian Xie An (320–385), who was well known as a calligrapher, described Gu Kaizhi's work as revolutionary: 'Your painting is like nothing that has ever been seen before!'[17] Beginning in the late sixth century, leading critics – from Yao Zui (late sixth century) and Li Sizhen (d. 606) to Zhang Huaiguan (early eighth century) – unanimously proclaimed Gu a genius of the ancient world.[18] Zhang Huaiguan wrote:

Because Master Gu imagined his painting in such a fine and subtle way, the depths of his spiritual (*ling*) expression are unfathomable. Though he left his traces in brush and ink, his spirit flies high above the cloudy firmament, so it cannot be sought merely in his painting. In creating beautiful images, Zhang Sengyou [act. *c.* 500–550] captures the flesh, Lu Tanwei [act. *c.* 465–472] the bone, and [only] Gu, the spirit. It is in the incomparable marvels of his spiritual (*shen*) expressiveness that Gu's works excel. When compared to calligraphers, Gu and Lu must rank with Zhong You

[151–230] and Zhang Zhi [late second century], and Zhang Sengyou with Wang Xizhi. These are the best of the best, both past and present![19]

It was the ninth-century historian Zhang Yanyuan (act. mid-ninth century) who first saw the history of Chinese figure painting as a development from the archaic hairline brushwork of Gu Kaizhi, in the fourth century, to the more dramatic and calligraphically expressive brush style of Wu Daozi, in the eighth century. In his influential work *Records of Famous Paintings in Successive Dynasties (Lidai minghua ji)*, completed in 847, Zhang described Gu Kaizhi's drawing as

tight and sinewy, smooth and continuous; it circles around and disappears [into the painted image]. Its manner is as untrammelled and easy as a wafting breeze or quick lightning, always with an idea guiding his brush so that the idea remains even after his brush ends. This is why his paintings are full of a spiritual air (*shenqi*).[20]

Zhang compared the energetic, discontinuous brushstrokes and dots of the sixth-century Liang dynasty (502–557) painter Zhang Sengyou to calligraphic principles described in *Diagram of the Battle Formation of the Brush (Bizhen tu)*, traditionally attributed to the fourth-century calligrapher Lady Wei (272–349), and linked the even more dynamic thickening-and-thinning brushwork of Wu Daozi to the wild-cursive style of Wu's teacher, the 'mad calligrapher' Zhang Xu (act. *c.* 700–750). From this comparison, Zhang concluded:

The spiritual (*shen*) expressiveness of Gu [Kaizhi] and Lu [Tanwei] is boundless, because their drawings are always complete and finely finished, while the wonders of Zhang [Sengyou] and Wu [Daozi] lie in their ability to capture images with only one or two abbreviated brushstrokes … Although the delineations [of Zhang's and Wu's works] may be incomplete, the ideas they express are always perfectly realized. Only when we understand that [good] paintings can be either abbreviated or finely detailed, are we able to judge their true merits.[21]

Zhang Yanyuan's characterization of ancient representational styles by their brush techniques was followed by writers of the Song dynasty (960–1279), who further distinguished these styles by the different drapery patterns depicted. Thus Guo Ruoxu (eleventh century) described Cao Zhongda's (act. *c.* 550–577) figure style as 'robes hanging as if emerging from water' (*Caoyi chushui*) and Wu Daozi's as 'draperies blowing

Fig. 1 Painted lacquer basket, early 2nd century CE. Lelang, Korea.

Fig. 2 'A Female Deity'. Silk hanging, 3rd century BCE. Changsha, Hunan.

in the wind' (*Wudai dangfeng*).[22] For Mi Fu and his fellow Northern Song connoisseurs, the *Admonitions* scroll, with its hairline technique – described earlier by Zhang Yanyuan as 'tight and sinewy, smooth and continuous' – could only represent the style of Gu Kaizhi.

It is important to note that the *Admonitions* scroll was a product of the Southern rather than the Northern Dynasties. With the rapid expansion of Buddhism in China between the third and the sixth century, most northern painters were engaged in the decoration of public temples. Scroll paintings on silk, of the kind exemplified by the *Admonitions*, were part of the earlier Han imperial tradition of secretly treasured (*micang*) maps and documents (*tushu*) collected in imperial libraries.[23] After the establishment of the Eastern Jin in 317, this tradition of illustrating history and the classics on silk scrolls was carried on by the Han-Chinese rulers of the Southern Dynasties, who, as successors to the Han emperors, sought political and cultural legitimacy by collecting precious scrolls of calligraphy and painting.[24]

In his own writings Gu Kaizhi argued that a painter should 'capture the spirit [*shen*] through the form [*xing*]' (*yixing xieshen*),[25] meaning that through mimetic representation – 'form-likeness' (*xingsi*), or conformity to what the eye sees – an image becomes supernaturally 'real' (*shensi*). Gu noted that the secret of 'transmitting the spirit in portraiture lies in the eye', which he believed to be the site of animation.[26] This interest in the eye of the depicted image may be seen in a Han painted lacquer basket from Lelang, Korea, dated to the early second century (fig. 1),[27] in which the figures, as Gu wrote, seem to 'look, answer, and communicate with one another'.[28] Gu's view of achieving realism in painting reflects the prehistoric principle of magic realism, by which the

painted image, through sympathetic magic, or the Law of Similarity, was perceived as the prototype in reality.[29] It is said that Gu, in order to attract the attention of a young lady he admired, painted her in such a lifelike manner that he was able to awaken her feelings for him by pricking the heart of the painted image with a needle.[30] This story not only attests to the co-option of a popular witchcraft belief by elite culture, but demonstrates that in early Chinese painting mimetic realism, or 'form-likeness', was considered functionally 'real' – that is, magically or supernaturally alive.

Early literary descriptions of paintings by Gu Kaizhi and Wu Daozi, with their frequent references to the supernatural spirit (*shen*) and soul (*ling*), may seem stilted and formulaic to modern readers. Yet we must appreciate the wonder and awe that these works inspired at a time when painting appeared 'like nothing that had ever been seen before'. The archaic schema for representing a female deity, as seen in a third-century BCE silk banner from Changsha, Hunan Province (fig. 2), presents the figure in three additive parts: the face seen in profile, the upper body seen from the side with the out-stretched arm covered in a voluminous sleeve, and the lower body shown draped in a flowing gown that spreads out and rests flat on the ground like the broad base of stemware. This linear 'stemware' schema was followed with only gradual modifications until the fourth century when Gu Kaizhi (pl. 10), in capturing the 'spirit' of his figures through his hairline drawing, taught the viewer to see the figures not only moving in space but also, like calligraphy, as a diagram of human emotion.[31] Writing about the *Admonitions* scroll in a recent edition of the *Sunday Telegraph Magazine*, the British art critic Andrew Graham-Dixon seems as struck by Gu's ability to convey human feeling in his figures as were the earlier critics Zhang Huaiguan and Zhang Yanyuan. Here is how Graham-Dixon describes the scene 'An Emperor Rebuffs a Fawning Beauty' (pls 9 left, 10):

> The figure of the emperor embodies moral revulsion. Raising an eloquent, nervily reproving hand and casting a glance of cool but withering contempt in the direction of the lady who has so displeased him, he is on the point of turning away in disgust. The fragile expression that she wears on her porcelain face suggests the beginnings of a sullen pout.[32]

There are reasons to suggest that, in about the year 400, Gu Kaizhi was commissioned by the Eastern Jìn court in Jiankang to create the *Admonitions* scroll. In 396, the twenty-first year of the reign of Emperor Xiaowudi, a tragic incident occurred in the imperial inner palace. The emperor one day remarked jokingly to his favourite consort, Lady Zhang, 'Now that you are thirty years old, it is time to exchange you for someone younger', whereupon Lady Zhang, in a jealous rage, killed the emperor.[33] Although accustomed to the murder or removal of rulers by contending princes and ministers, the Eastern Jìn court was unprepared for and deeply shocked by this violent act by a female member of the court. This event, I believe, was the reason for Gu Kaizhi's illustration of Zhang Hua's 'Admonitions', which was intended as a warning to the court ladies.

As pointed out elsewhere, the scenes depicted in the *Admonitions* scroll have a subtle and complex psychological underpinning, which may be attributed to Gu Kaizhi's genius.[34] If we compare Scene 2, 'Lady Ban declines to Ride with the Han emperor Chengdi in the Imperial Palanquin' (pl. 3), with a similar scene on a painted lacquer screen from the fifth-century tomb of Sima Jinlong (d. 484), in Datong, Shanxi Province (pl. 19), the artistic superiority of the *Admonitions* painting is immediately apparent. Notice how, in evok-

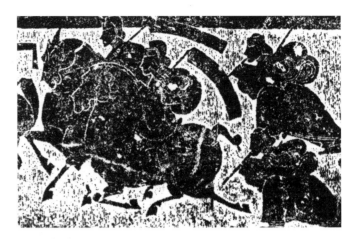

Fig. 3 'Flying Gallop', Wu Liang Shrine, 2nd century CE. Shandong Province.

Fig. 4 Ritual censer in the form of a cosmic mountain, 2nd century BCE.

Fig. 5 Rubbing of Gu Kaizhi,
*Admonitions of the Court
Instructress*, in Dong Qichang
(1555–1636), *Xihongtang fatie*.

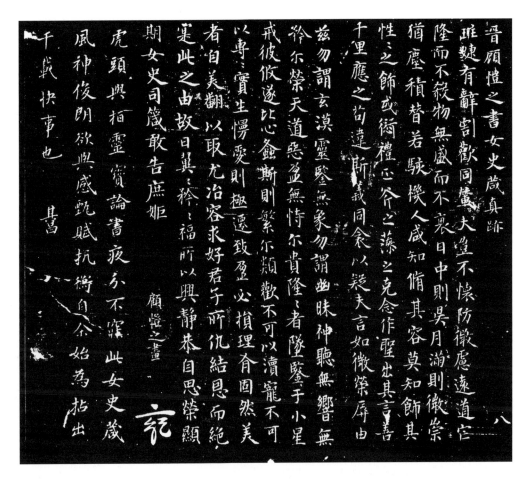

Fig. 5 Rubbing of Gu Kaizhi, *Admonitions of the Court Instructress*, in Dong Qichang (1555–1636), *Xihongtang fatie*.

ing the dancing rhythm of the litter bearers, the painter of the scroll borrows from the high-strutting gait of the Han dynasty archaic 'flying gallop' schema (fig. 3), the criss-cross pattern of the bearers' legs and feet in profile moving jauntily across the picture plane. By adding the young girl seated next to Chengdi in the palanquin, the painter also makes Lady Ban's own refusal to ride with the emperor suddenly seem irrelevant.

It is clear that in illustrating Zhang Hua's 'Admonitions' Gu Kaizhi was not merely affirming the Confucian ideals of womanhood, but also emphasizing the larger issue of human relationships, especially that between ruler and minister, the deterioration of which had placed the Eastern Jìn polity in mortal danger. In Scene 3 of the scroll (pl. 5), for example, the painter uses the motif of a Han cosmic mountain – borrowed from the form of a Han ritual censer (fig. 4) – to illustrate the text 'There is nothing high that is not soon brought low … When the sun reaches its apogee, it begins to sink; when the moon is full, it begins to wane.' The image of an archer preparing to shoot a tiger on the mountain, which illustrates the line 'the fall into calamity is as easy as the rebound of a crossbow', is fair warning to power-hungry warlords like

Huan Xuan and Liu Yu. And in Scene 5 of the scroll (pl. 6), mistrust between bedfellows, subtly described through the expression of the eyes and the physical rigidity of the seated couple, could easily allude to close military allies such as Huan Xuan and Yin Zhongkan who had turned on one another.

The Date of the *Admonitions* Scroll

If we accept the work as a copy of an original composition by Gu Kaizhi, should the British Museum's *Admonitions* scroll be dated to the pre-Tang or the early Tang period? When the leading seventeenth-century connoisseur and critic Dong Qichang (1555–1636) first examined the scroll, he was unable to compare its hairline drawing technique to any paintings known by him. Instead, he decided that the archaic style of the scroll's calligraphy related to the classic example of fourth-century small standard-script writing, the transcription of *Goddess of the Luo River (Luoshen fu)* attributed to Wang Xianzhi (344–388).[35] In his anthology of rubbings *Model Calligraphic Works in the Hall of Playing Geese (Xihongtang fatie)*, published in 1603, Dong reproduced the *Admonitions*

Fig. 6 Chu Suiliang (596–658), *Preface to Sacred Teaching (Shengjiao xu)*, dated 653.

Fig. 7 Chu Suiliang (596–658), the character *yong*, from *Copy of Preface to the Orchid Pavilion (Lin Lanting xu)*.

scroll's calligraphy as an authentic work (*zhenji*) by Gu Kaizhi (fig. 5), with the following comment:

> When Gu Kaizhi discussed calligraphy with [Governor-General] Huan Wen, they often stayed up nights without sleeping. This writing of 'Admonitions of the Court Instructress' [by Gu] possesses a bright and spirited quality that rivals [Wang Xianzhi's] *Goddess of the Luo River*. Since I was the first to point this out, it truly is a happy event for a thousand years![36]

Not everyone agreed with Dong's opinion. His friend and fellow connoisseur Chen Jiru (1558–1639), for example, attributed the scroll's calligraphy to the Southern Song (1127–1279) emperor Gaozong (r. 1127–1162).[37]

In order to resolve the question of the date of the scroll's calligraphy, which I believe is contemporaneous to the painting,[38] it is necessary to examine the calligraphy's brush technique and visual structure. After China was reunited, first, in 589, under the Sui dynasty (581–618) and then under the Tang dynasty, the Tang emperor Taizong (r. 626–649) brought together the finest calligraphers from the north and the south with the intention of establishing a common standard of writing.[39] This effort resulted in the development of a new monumental style of calligraphy, one that combined the formal epigraphic tradition of the north with the freer, more fluid style of the south established by Wang Xizhi. This so-called standard script (*kaishu*) reached its final artistic form in the writing of the Tang court calligrapher Chu Suiliang (596–658; fig. 6). Chu's writing is animated by individual brushstrokes that twist and turn, creating a three-dimensional effect, and by characters that are balanced and integrated into an organic whole.

In Chu's rendition of *Preface to the Orchid Pavilion (Lanting xu)*, the character *yong* (fig. 7) is composed of the eight brushstrokes that characterize the new standard script. Contemporary theorists described each of these strokes in the form of verbal metaphors: (1) the dot is like 'a stone falling from a high peak'; (2) the short horizontal stroke is like 'a cloud formation'; (3) the vertical stroke is like 'a withered vine'; (4) the bottom left-hand hook is like the 'sinews … of a mighty bow'; (5) the upward whip at left is like 'an arrow shot from a crossbow'; and (6) a downward thrust resembles 'a rhinoceros digging its tusk into the ground'; (7) another downward thrust at upper right represents this same movement; and finally, (8) an ending stroke is like 'a crashing wave or rolling thunder'. In describing calligraphy, early Tang theorists also referred metaphorically to the human body: physical terms such as 'flesh', 'bone', 'sinew' and 'vein', for instance,

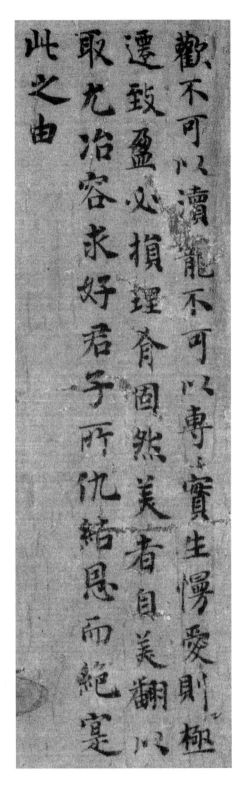

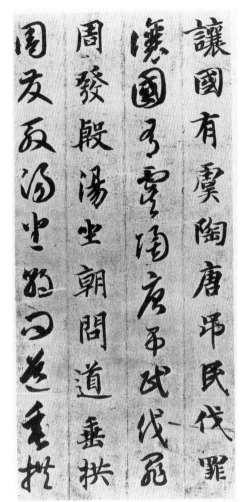

Fig. 8 (left) Detail of calligraphy from the *Admonitions* scroll.

Fig. 9 (above) Zhiyong (act. late 6th to early 7th century), *The Thousand-Character Essay (Qianzi wen)*. Ogawa Collection, Kyoto.

explained how the calligrapher allowed 'his idea to precede his brush' and 'his hand to be moved by his heart's desire', transforming the written character into an embodied image of the mind.[40]

In its brush technique and character composition, the calligraphy of the *Admonitions* scroll (fig. 8) shows none of the early Tang aesthetic and sophistication. It relates, instead, to the style of the leading late-Southern Dynasties calligrapher Zhiyong (act. late sixth to early seventh century; fig. 9), a descendant of Wang Xizhi and the principal exponent of the Wang tradition, and to late sixth-century manuscript and sūtra writings (fig. 10). The brush technique of these works, like

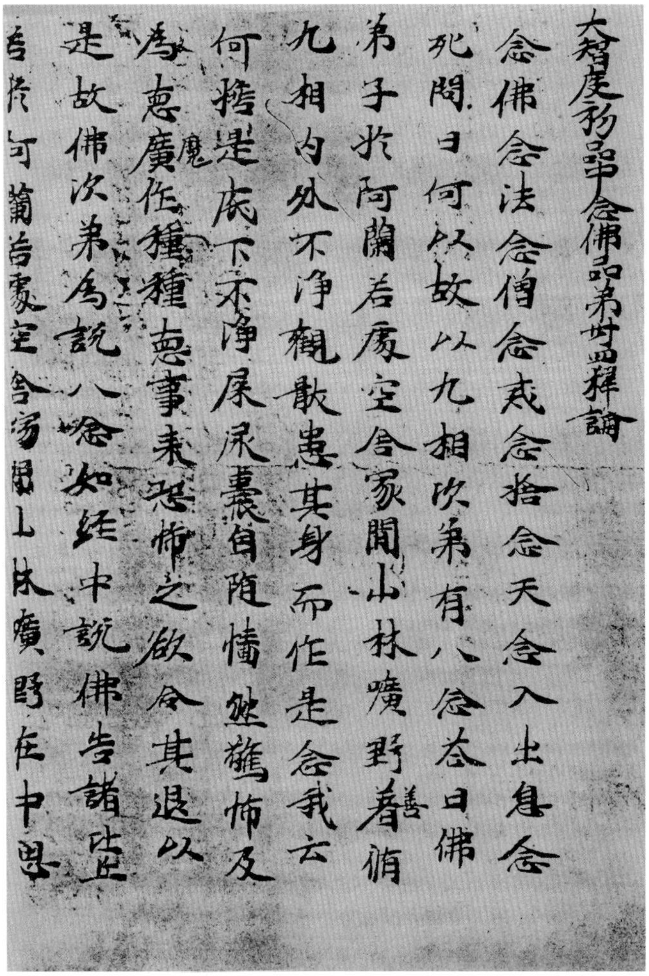

念佛念法念僧念戒念捨念天念入出息念

死問曰何以故以九相次弟有八念若曰佛

弟子於阿蘭若處空令家間小林壙野善循

九相內外不淨觀散其身而作是念我云

何捨是底下不淨屎尿囊自隨懍然雜怖及

為惡魔作穜穜惡事來恐怖之故令其退以

是故佛次弟為說八喻如經中說佛告諸比

冯惠廣作

何拾

念佛念法念僧念戒念捨念天念入出息念[...]

Fig. 10 Buddhist scripture, dated 510. (After *SDZS*, vol. 6, pls 104–105.)

strokes.'[41] In other words, Gu's and Lu's 'smooth and continuous' hairline drawings of the fourth and fifth centuries exemplified 'complete and finely finished' draftsmanship, while Zhang Sengyou's and Wu Daozi's increasingly bold and energetic abbreviated brushwork of the sixth through the eighth centuries became more and more calligraphically expressive. In its simplicity and apparent lack of self-consciousness, the *Admonitions* scroll's hairline brushwork compares more closely to the pure line drawing of the third-century BCE silk banner from Changsha (fig. 2) than the much later 'iron-wire' brush technique of the post-Song era (see pl. 22; pp. 172–173, fig. 5), which was a calligraphically inspired imitation of the archaic linear idiom.

From a representational point of view, the style of the *Admonitions* scroll also appears more advanced than Gu Kaizhi's archaic linear style of the fourth century. As pointed out by Yang Xin, the mountain form in Scene 3 (pl. 5) exhibits a sophistication that post-dates the period in which Gu Kaizhi lived.[42] The illusionistic effect of this scene may be compared with late Six Dynasties and early Tang depictions of mountains (fig. 11), in which overlapping triangular motifs are shown receding diagonally in three-dimensional space. The attenuated figures of the court ladies in the scroll (pl. 10) also compare closely with female figures depicted in sixth-century painted tiles from Dengxian, Henan Province (fig. 12); in both cases, the sideways movement of the standing figures

that of the *Admonitions* scroll, is relatively flat and one-directional, and the different parts of a character appear as separate additive components of a two-dimensional design. The British Museum scroll – which illustrates a third-century Western Jin text and is attributed to a fourth-century Eastern Jin painter – thus appears to be a Southern court work (its calligraphy probably executed in a court scriptorium) produced in the late sixth century before the Sui unification of China in 589.

Turning to the brushwork of the painting, the archaic hairline drawing of the *Admonitions* scroll, which fits Zhang Yanyuan's description of Gu Kaizhi's style as 'tight and sinewy, smooth and continuous; it circles around and disappears [into the painted image]', dates the painting to the pre-Tang period. According to Zhang, 'the drawings [of Gu and Lu Tanwei] are always complete and finely finished, while the wonders of Zhang [Sengyou] and Wu [Daozi] lie in their ability to capture images with only one or two abbreviated brush-

Fig. 11 Mirror with mountains, 7th century. Shoso-in Collection, Nara.

Fig. 12 (above) Filial piety scene. Painted tile, 6th century. Dengxian, Henan Province.

Fig. 13 (right) Buddha and Bodhisattvas, Cave 6, south wall, 480s CE. Yungang, Shanxi Province.

Fig. 14 (far right) Arhat or Bodhisattva, Sui dynasty, c.587 CE. Royal Ontario Museum, Toronto.

conforms to the archaic 'stemware' schema of the female image in the Changsha banner (fig. 2), while the billowing drapery folds and flying scarves of the figures begin to suggest volume and three-dimensionality. Likewise, the male figures in the *Admonitions* scroll (pls 2 right, 9 right) display three-dimensionally modelled faces and bodies more typical of the late sixth and seventh centuries. Among dated monuments, the closest comparison to the volumetric male figures in the *Admonitions* scroll is found on the back wall of Ning Mao's shrine, dated 529, in the Museum of Fine Arts, Boston.[43]

The new corporeality exhibited in the *Admonitions* scroll reflects developments in Buddhist sculpture of both north and south China in the late sixth century, in which there

occurred similar changes in the representation of the human figure, from the archaic schema of angular forms of the Northern Wei (386–534) in the first half of the sixth century (fig. 13) to the voluptuously round, illusionistic style of the Northern Qi (550–577) and Sui (589–617) after the mid-sixth century (fig. 14). In a major article, 'South Chinese Influence on the Buddhist Art of the Six Dynasties Period', published in 1960, Alexander Soper suggested that the impetus for this revolutionary change, which he ascribed to the renewed contact with Indianizing models introduced through Indonesian emissaries who travelled to China by the long-established southern sea route, came from the culturally sophisticated Chinese courts of the Southern Dynasties.[44]

Fig. 15 (left) Sogdian figures on Northern earthenware, 6th century.

Fig. 16 (right) Drawing of bas-relief carving on Yu Hong's sarcophagus, dated 592. Taiyuan, Shanxi Province. (After Wu Hung [ed.] 2000.7, p. 17, pl. 3.)

Soper cited Zhang Sengyou as a source of this new stylistic influence:

> The Indian mode was more readily available for study in the sixth century than ever before. [Zhang Sengyou's] familiarity with the Indian trick of painting in heavy chiaroscuro, for example, was undoubtedly gained through his contact with 'foreign' monk-artists at the Liang court, one of whom bore a name recognizable through the Chinese transliteration as Marabodhi.[45]

More recently we have learned that the momentous change in north China in the sixth century toward a more corporeal figural style was the result of Central Asian influences, specifically those transmitted from the West along the Silk Route by traders and emissaries from the distant kingdom of Sogdiana. The round, volumetric figures in Sogdian motifs can be found on northern Chinese earthenware of this period (fig. 15). Carvings on a recently discovered white marble sarcophagus from the tomb of Yu Hong (d. 592), a Sogdian chieftain who served as an ambassador to the Persian court and later as a Sui official in Taiyuan, Shanxi Province, show the distinctive Central Asian corporeal figure style (fig. 16).[46] Similar evidence of this style may be seen in wall paintings in north China, such as those in the tomb of Lou Rui, in Taiyuan (fig. 17), dated 570. In his study of the Lou Rui wall paintings, Jin Weinuo compares the figures with the volumetric forms of Northern Qi Buddhist sculpture (fig. 14), relating their style to that of Cao Zhongda, the well-known Sogdian artist and a leading Northern Qi court painter whose style was described as 'draperies as if emerging from water', and also that of Yang Zihua (mid-sixth century), another well-known Northern Qi court artist.[47]

This shift from schematic two-dimensional to round three-dimensional forms is readily apparent in sixth-century

Fig. 17 'Horsemen', mural in tomb of Lou Rui, dated 570. Taiyuan, Shanxi Province.

wall paintings at the Buddhist cave site of Dunhuang, in north-western Gansu Province. Located along the northern Silk Route between Central Asia and China proper and serving as a meeting ground of 'Western regions' (*xiyu*) and Chinese cultural influences, Dunhuang provides evidence of the importation from the fifth century onward of the Western chiaroscuro style, known as 'concave-and-convex painting' (*aotu hua*), and its gradual assimilation into the Chinese pictorial idiom.[48] The purpose of chiaroscuro modelling was to describe three-dimensional human figures, but as it travelled across Central Asia the technique became increasingly conventionalized and schematic. Dunhuang paintings, from the early fifth-century Caves 254, 272 and 275 show Indian models with patterned bands of shading similar to those seen in the Thousand Buddhas Caves at Kizil, near Kucha, in western Chinese Turkestan.[49] While flat bands of colour define the faces and bare-chested bodies, the figures themselves remain flat and two-dimensional, with little interest in the physical articulation of the body.

A new 'Chinese' Buddhist style of the late Northern Wei period – first exemplified by sculptures in Cave VI at Yungang, Shanxi Province (fig. 13), dating to the 480s – was introduced to Dunhuang by the early sixth century, as seen in 'Buddha and Bodhisattvas' in Cave 285, dated 539 (fig. 18). Professor Soper argued that '[this] new fashion used at Yungang was borrowed ready-made from southern practice, and in the South, prior to the transfer, had been familiar for a century.' He attributed the invention of this new sinicized Buddhist style to the Eastern Jin master sculptor Dai Kui (d. 396), whose style was influenced by the leading contemporary painting master Gu Kaizhi.[50] In place of the *samghati*, a shawl worn over the body in the Indian Buddhist tradition, the bodhisattva figures in Cave 285 wear a sinicized courtly robe, with long flowing sleeves and pleated draperies ending in a wide swallowtail, reminiscent of Gu Kaizhi's 'stemware' palace ladies (pl. 10).

The Dunhuang paintings can help us to understand the critical role that the early sixth-century southern painter Zhang Sengyou played in introducing the imported 'concave-and-convex' style to southern Chinese court painting. According to *A True Record of [the Southern Capital] Jiankang (Jiankang shilu)*, published in the eighth century:

The portals of Yichengsi [a temple in Jiankang, dedicated in 537], which are filled with 'concave-and-convex' flowers, were traditionally regarded as the work of Zhang Sengyou. Depicted in the Indian style, they are coloured red and blue-green. Viewed from afar, they appear to recede and project, but seen at close range

Fig. 18 Buddha and Bodhisattvas, Cave 285, north wall, inscription dated 539 CE. Dunhuang, Gansu Province.

Fig. 19 Concave-and-convex flowers, Cave 428, ceiling design, *c*.550s CE. Dunhuang, Gansu Province.

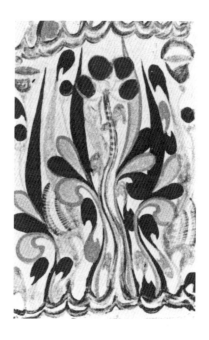

Fig. 20 Visnu, detail of the west wall, Cave 285, *c.*538–539. Dunhuang, Gansu Province.

they turn out to be flat. Considered a great rarity, the temple has been known as the Concave-and-Convex Temple.[51]

In Dunhuang Caves 288 and 428 (fig. 19), which date from the 540s and 550s respectively, the ceiling decorations display 'concave-and-convex' flowers whose twisting and turning designs, rendered with a knowledge of foreshortening and perspective, appear to 'recede and project' in space.

In the ninth century Zhang Yanyuan considered Zhang Sengyou's brushwork to be revolutionary, not so much because of its realistic 'concave-and-convex' style but because of its brilliant calligraphic quality:

Zhang Sengyou made his dots and dragging, hacking, and sweeping strokes in accordance with Madam Wei's *Diagram of the Battle Formation of the Brush*, so that

Fig. 21 'Running Bull', detail of north side of the ceiling, Cave 249, first half of 6th century CE. Dunhuang, Gansu Province.

every dot and stroke was an art in itself. His hooked halberds and sharp swords bristle like a great forest, and from these one can see that the use of the brush in calligraphy and in painting is the same![52]

Although Zhang saw both Zhang Sengyou's and Wu Daozi's brushwork as superb calligraphy, the paintings at Dunhuang suggest that the genius of these two painters lay in their ability to employ calligraphic techniques for representational purposes.

Indeed, most of the sixth-century paintings at Dunhuang typically show a mixture of the Western (Central Asian) chiaroscuro technique with Chinese linear style. For example, the painting of the Indian-style figure of Visnu in Cave 285 (fig. 20), dated to about 538–539, combines three-dimensional modelling of the human body with elegant calligraphic outline. In 'Running Bull' in Cave 249 (fig. 21), dating from the first half of the sixth century, the artist displays his mastery of three-dimensional representation of volume and movement through the thickening-and-thinning brush, without the enhancement of either colour or shading.[53] This interest in rendering three-dimensionality, expressed by the Chinese painter's transformation of the foreign 'concave-and-convex' modelling into a native calligraphic brush idiom, led eventually to the conquest of illusion in Chinese representational painting.

As a late sixth-century Southern court work disguised as a fourth-century original signed 'Gu Kaizhi', the *Admonitions* scroll appears to be influenced by Zhang Sengyou's realistic 'concave-and-convex' style. The hairline drawing technique, while remaining faithful to Gu's 'tight and sinewy, smooth and continuous' lineament of the fourth century, shows a keen sense of volume and three-dimensionality that reveals the painter's knowledge of both Lu Tanwei's 'bone' and Zhang Sengyou's 'flesh' of the fifth and sixth centuries.[54] To observe how the late sixth-century copyist merged his own style with that of Gu Kaizhi's, we may compare the *Admonitions* scroll's palanquin scene (pls 3–4) with the painting of horsemen from the sixth-century Lou Rui tomb (fig. 17), which has effectively transformed the archaic 'flying gallop' schema (fig. 3) into a group of rampaging northern warriors astride galloping ponies with a new three-dimensional corporeality. Yet the *Admonitions* palanquin scene, despite the billowing drapery folds of the litter bearers, which reflect the influence of the late sixth century, maintains the original Gu Kaizhi fourth-century linear pattern of criss-cross leg-and-foot motifs dancing laterally across the two-dimensional picture surface, which borrows from the archaic 'flying gallop' schema.

Gu Kaizhi in Chinese Art History

In his recent study of Chinese painting history, *Style and Changing Contexts (Fengge yu shibian)*, Shih Shou-chien explores different ways of interpreting artistic styles through their cultural and social settings.[55] Traditional art history begins with connoisseurship – that is, the determination of the 'When', 'Where' and 'Who' of works of art, and the different contemporaneous political and social circumstances in which the works were produced. It is the visual evidence of the art object that enables us to decipher what art can tell us about history. But the history of the *Admonitions* scroll attributed to Gu Kaizhi shows that the meaning of Gu Kaizhi always depended on the eye of the beholder rather than the object itself at the point of its creation. By focusing on the 'cultural biography' of the scroll, several papers in the present publication demonstrate how the scroll has enabled viewers through the centuries to both write and re-create Chinese art history. However, it is important to note, as Craig Clunas has pointed out, that the concept of the 'biography' of an object, which in its materialist approach and 'reception' aesthetic owes much to the disciplines of anthropology and ethnology, is relativist and therefore post-historical.[56]

An examination of the role of Gu Kaizhi in the history of Chinese painting must begin with the history of Chinese representational art. From the Han through the Song dynasty (third century BCE to the thirteenth century CE), a period that Max Loehr (1903–1988) called China's Age of Representational Art,[57] when the function of mimetic representation or 'form-likeness' (Gu Kaizhi's 'capturing the spirit through the

form') dominated the field of knowledge, supernatural realism (*shensi*) was a reflection of another, higher reality – that of the interdependent and correlative nature of the universe.[58] Although Chinese painters developed neither an anatomical approach to figural representation nor an approach to space based on linear perspective, they nevertheless incorporated in their work accumulated skills in mimetic representation that had evolved from the Western Han through the end of the Song period. In a process E. H. Gombrich (1909–2001) called 'schema and correction', early Chinese figural representation developed by 'making before matching [reality]'.[59] In the third-century BCE silk banner from Changsha (fig. 2), for example, we see the archaic 'stemware' schema from which the palace ladies of the *Admonitions* scroll (pl. 10) are 'corrected' and 'made' by matching a new sixth-century visual reality, the brush lines describing with precision the three-dimensional and volumetric drapery forms. Between the Han and Tang periods (third century BCE to early eighth century CE), Chinese representational art in sculpture and painting underwent a development similar to that of the Greek 'miracle of awakening' of the fifth century BCE, when the representation of the human figure evolved from one of archaic frontal rigidity to that of fully articulated natural movement in space. It was during the Song period (960–1279) that mimetic representation in Chinese painting finally reached its zenith before coming to an abrupt end following the Mongol conquest of 1279. From that moment onward, literati painters, turning back to art history, used a calligraphic idiom of art-historical styles to 'write ideas' (*xieyi*) or to express the artist's inner feelings.[60] This shift from mimetic to art-historical representation changed forever the function and meaning of later Chinese painting.

During the great flowering of *belles-lettres* and visual arts from the Wei, Jin and Six Dynasties to the Sui and Tang dynasties, creative innovation and originality were valued as primary assets in the arts. As noted earlier, it was Zhang Huaiguan, in the eighth century, who first saw Chinese figure painting as a progressive development from archaic linear evocation to latter-day realistic representation – with Gu Kaizhi seizing the 'spirit', Lu Tanwei the 'bone' and Zhang Sengyou the 'flesh'. Then, in the ninth century, Zhang Yanyuan described Chinese painting history as having evolved in three stages, from 'simple' to 'detailed' to 'complete':

In paintings of Early Antiquity, forms were simple and expressions calm and yet elegant and proper, as exemplified by the works of Gu [Kaizhi], Lu [Tanwei], and others. Paintings of Middle Antiquity were fine and detailed, exquisitely finished and exceedingly beautiful, as exemplified by the works of [the northern painters] Zhan [Ziqian; late sixth to early seventh century], Zheng [Fashi; late sixth to early seventh century], and others. Paintings of Recent Times are brilliantly executed, and they aim at [representational] completeness ... When we look at Wu Daozi's works, we can say that all Six Principles [of Xie He; act. *c.* 479–502] have been attained in like perfection, and the myriad phenomena are completely expressed. In Wu's work the divine has borrowed his hand, so profoundly does it fathom Creation itself.[61]

There is no doubt, however, that Wu Daozi, 'in [whose] work the divine has borrowed his hand', owed his success to the Han-Tang miracle of mastering illusion in mimetic representation. It is said that after seeing Wu's terrifying depictions of Hell at Jingyunsi, a temple in the Western capital Chang'an, 'people ceased wrongdoings and cultivated merits by choosing a vegetarian diet, causing the sale of fish and meat in the markets to plummet.'[62]

Zhang Yanyuan's progressive view of art history from 'simple' to 'complete' was in marked contrast to the retrospective view of Su Shi (1037–1101), the leading proponent of the scholar-official aesthetic (*shidafuhua lun*) in the late Northern Song period. For Su Shi, the state of completion described by Zhang implied a consummation of this progressive development:

> The learning of superior men and the skills of a hundred craftsmen, having originated in [antiquity] and developed during the Han and Tang periods, had reached a state of completion. By the time poetry had produced a Du Fu [712–770], prose writing a Han Yu [768–824], calligraphy a Yan Zhenqing [709–785], and [figure] painting a Wu Daozi, all possibilities for changes in the arts had been exhausted.[63]

Su Shi's statement bears a striking resemblance to twentieth-century Western discourse on 'the end of art history', specifically in the writings of Hans Belting and Arthur Danto.[64] For Su, the solution to what he perceived as the end of progressive art history was to turn back to earlier art history, to seek renewal through the revival of ancient styles rather than to create new modes of mimetic representation, which he considered neither meaningful nor possible.[65] Declaring that 'anyone who judges painting by form-likeness shows the insight of a child',[66] Su and his followers were more interested in the rhetorical and discursive language of persuasion in painting than its purely representational and descriptive role.

According to the philosopher and meta-historian Michel Foucault (1926–1984), a similar epistemological change from the representation of resemblance to that of the language of 'signification' occurred in European culture on the eve of the modern age. Before the nineteenth century, Foucault writes, there was a coherence 'between the theory of representation and the theories of language, [and] of the natural orders.' From the nineteenth century,

> the theory of representation disappears as the universal foundation of all possible order ... [and] a profound historicity penetrates into the heart of things ... Language loses its privileged position and becomes, in its turn, a historical form coherent with the density of its own past... [and] things become increasingly reflexive, seeking the principle of their intelligibility only in their own development, and abandoning the space of representation.[67]

In Chinese painting history we find Su Shi and his followers making an art-historical study of ancient representational styles, translating them into the abstract language of calligraphy, and using them to allude to history and to express other kinds of realities.[68]

The fall of the Tang dynasty in 906 marked a critical turning point in Chinese culture and politics. After more than a half century of disunity during the Five Dynasties (907–960) period, the reunified empire under the Song dynasty saw the beginning of urban development and a monetary economy. The dismantling of the hereditary military aristocracy of the Tang, which had forced China's rulers to adhere to the ancient Confucian ideal of an empire governed by 'public-mindedness' (*tianxia weigong*), led under the Song to a new absolutism in which 'the empire was ruled by one family' (*tianxia weijia*). The moral authority of the Confucian state was thus diminished, and during the late Northern Song, in the late eleventh century, a permanent schism developed between the ideology of the imperium and the private discourse of the literati-official class. In turning away from the official orthodoxy of a didactic narrative and adopting a new kind of art known as scholar-official painting, Su Shi advocated a new literati aesthetic that rejected mimetic realism in favour of calligraphic self-expression.

In his illustrations of *Classic of Filial Piety (Xiaojing tu)*, dating from about 1085 (fig. 22), Li Gonglin (*c.* 1041–1106), the leading late Northern Song figure painter and a protégé of Su's, created a new calligraphic, linear idiom in figure painting by reviving and reworking ancient styles. According to the *Catalogue of the Imperial Painting Collection During the Xuanhe Era* of 1120:

Fig. 22 Li Gonglin (*c*.1041–1106), chapter 15, 'Remonstration', from *The Classic of Filial Piety (Xiaojing tu)*. Datable to about 1085. Detail of a handscroll; ink on silk, 21.9 × 475.5 cm. The Metropolitan Museum of Art, New York. Ex coll. C. C. Wang Family, from the P. Y. and Kinmay W. Tang Family Collection, Promised and Partial Gift of Oscar L. Tang, 1996 (1996.479).

[Li] began painting by studying the works of Gu [Kaizhi], Lu [Tanwei], Zhang [Sengyou] and Wu [Daozi], and well-known works by [or attributed to] earlier masters ... Although he never plagiarized their work, he subtly modelled his paintings on their principles ... When he encountered famous works, he would keep copies of them; thus his home was full of well-known works of all kinds.[69]

Li Gonglin did not paint directly from life. Instead, in recreating the classical canon of ancient styles – from Gu Kaizhi and Lu Tanwei to Zhang Sengyou and Wu Daozi – he simplified the inherited imagery by reducing earlier representational techniques to calligraphic formulae. In shifting his focus from mimetic representation to the presentation of calligraphic action, Li considered his art not from the viewpoint of the spectator but only from that of himself, the painter. In literati paintings after Li Gonglin, the true subject of the calligraphic 'writing of ideas' with its emphasis on subjectivity and individual value was not mimetic representation but the artist's inner responses to the emergent new realities of the world.

According to his biographer, Li Gonglin always 'placed the idea or intent [*yi*] of a subject above all other considerations, making composition and decoration subordinate to it.'[70]

Li's painting of the 'intent', or mental image, parallels the lyric tradition in Chinese poetry, in which the operative principle is 'poetry speaks intent' (*shi yan zhi*).[71] The validation of the artist's intention, the notion that art reveals the artist's state of mind, was best expressed calligraphically by the seventh-century calligrapher-critic Sun Guoting (648?–703?), who wrote that 'the movement of [my] brush is never arbitrary; it is always purposeful.'[72] Li once said, 'I paint only as a grieving poet to express my own feelings. What can I do about people who do not understand and insist on treating my work as an object of entertainment?'[73]

As Richard Barnhart has pointed out, it was Li Gonglin who, above all other painters, was responsible for reviving Gu Kaizhi's archaic linear style in post-Tang Chinese figure painting.[74] Following Gu's archaic linear idiom, Li created a new calligraphic style known as 'white-drawing' (*baimiao*), which uses single brush lines, without colour or shading, to delineate forms in nature. We learn from Mi Fu's *History of Painting* that the *Admonitions* scroll was then in the possession of the collector Liu Youfang (act. late eleventh century). Mi himself owned a painting of a heavenly deva (a female deity from a Vimalakirti composition) attributed to Gu Kaizhi, which Mi believed to be a work described by Zhang Yanyuan and after which he named his study 'The Studio of Treasuring the Jin' (Bao Jìn zhai).[75] While we have no direct evidence that he actually knew of Gu's *Admonitions* scroll, Li Gonglin was, according to Mi, wildly enamoured of the heavenly deva painting in Mi's collection.[76] In re-creating early figure styles, Li focused on the well-defined hairline brush style of Gu Kaizhi and the thickening-and-thinning brushwork of Wu Daozi. By eliminating both colour and shading and communicating directly through calligraphic brushwork, Li imparts in his works a sense of physical movement and effort, through which the viewer is invited kinaesthetically both to experience and to merge with the image and the painter.

It was the Confucian discourse of 'remonstration' that joined Li's illustration of *Classic of Filial Piety* (fig. 22) with Gu Kaizhi's *Admonitions* scroll in their mutual expression of the 'idea' or 'intent' of loyalty and dissent. In Chapter 15, 'Remonstration', the text reads:

> In ancient times, if the Son of Heaven had seven ministers who would remonstrate with him, although he had not the right methods of government, he would not lose possession of All under Heaven ... The father who had a son who would remonstrate with him would not sink into the gulf of unrighteous deeds. Therefore, in the case of unrighteous conduct, a son must by no means refrain from remonstrating with his father, nor a minister from remonstrating with his ruler.[77]

Northern Song court politics was complicated by the frequent presence of power-wielding dowager empresses, who no doubt called to mind the infamous Western Jin empress Jia, the object of remonstration in the *Admonitions*. After the Northern Song emperor Renzong (r. 1022–1063) ascended the throne in 1022, his mother, the dowager empress Liu, ruled as regent for ten years. In the early 1060s, because the aged emperor Renzong was without an heir, the court was nearly torn apart, first over the question of succession and then by the ensuing debate over the status of Prince Bu, the natural father of the new emperor, Yingzong (r. 1063–1067). Upon Yingzong's succession to the throne in 1063, the dowager empress Cao (Renzong's wife) became regent. When Yingzong died suddenly in 1067, it was only through the courageous intervention of the chief minister, Han Qi (1008–1075), that the succession of the next emperor, Shenzong (Yingzong's son; r. 1067–1085), was secured. During the reigns of Renzong and Yingzong, remonstration with the throne was occasionally carried out successfully by able ministers. But under the imperial system, the monarch as absolute ruler was seldom a willing recipient of such remonstration, and a minister was more often than not severely punished for daring to criticize his master.

In Li Gonglin's illustration of 'Remonstration', we are witness to a scene of tense confrontation between the authority of the state and the power of moral virtue. The minister, bowing low, firmly stands his ground before the angry sovereign, who sits rigidly upright, his formidable empress standing beside him. This kind of confrontation not only often led to personal disaster but also carried profound dynastic implications. In the 'Remonstration' scene the attending officials at the upper right wear robes depicted in the subdued angular drapery pattern known as the 'iron wire' (*tiexian*) calligraphic style, while the two protagonists in the centre, the seated sovereign and his bowing servitor, are depicted with round, fluttering thickening-and-thinning drapery lines. The tremulous kinaesthetic movements, now both the site and the agent in language and moral action, create a vortex of emotional energy that forcefully communicate the spirit of the critical impasse between the opponents, the emperor ready to unleash his anger and his minister refusing to yield his ground.

In his recent book *A Cultural History of Civil Examinations in Late Imperial China*, Benjamin Elman examines the adoption of the Dao Learning (*Daoxue*) orthodoxy as the classical examination curriculum in the Song, Yuan (1272–1368), Ming (1368–1644), and Qing (1644–1911) dynasties from the perspective of 'the struggle between [Han-Chinese] insiders and [non-Han] outsiders in "China" to unite the empire'.[78] During the Southern Song (1127–1279) period, the ultraconservative Neo-Confucian thinkers known as the Dao Learning school, led by Zhu Xi (1130–1200), created an Orthodox Lineage of the Dao (*Daotong*) that positioned them as direct heirs of the legendary sage-kings Fuxi, Yao and Shun, the Zhou kings Wen and Wu, and the sage Confucius and his disciples.[79] Although it was at first banned as heterodoxy, in 1241 the Southern Song emperor Lizong (r. 1225–1264), in an attempt to demonstrate that the Song rulers, not the Mongols, were the legitimate heirs of the Confucian tradition, proclaimed the Dao Learning – now designated the school of Moral Principles (*Lixue*) – as the official state orthodoxy.[80] After the Mongol conquest of the Southern Song in 1279, the Mongol Yuan court, in 1313, adopted the Dao Learning as the official examination curriculum; but, as Professor Elman shows, 'the creation of a single-minded and monocular *Daoxue* [Dao Learning] orthodoxy, which built on Song and Yuan precedents, was principally a Ming dynasty construction.'[81]

In studying the works of Zhao Mengfu (1254–1322), the leading literati artist of the early Yuan period, in the context of the political and social contest between the Mongols and the southern Han-Chinese in Yuan China, we may observe Zhao's transformation of Chinese painting from Song mimetic practice to its post-Song discursive role.[82] In *The Mind Landscape of Xie Youyu (Youyu qiuhe)*, a handscroll dating to the early 1290s (see McCausland in this volume, pp. 168–182, fig. 5; pl. 22), Zhao recreates a lost composition by Gu Kaizhi by using the seal-script 'iron-wire' brush technique to evoke Gu's archaic linear delineation, now described as the 'archaic gossamer-like brush line' (*gaogu yousi miao*).[83] Through the example of the Eastern Jin courtier-recluse Xie Kun (Youyu; 280–322), who claimed to have preserved the purity of his mind in the mountains and valleys even while serving at court, Zhao Mengfu, a scion of the fallen Song imperial family who chose to serve at the Mongol court, argued for the age-old discourse on 'reclusion within the court' (*chao yin*).[84] In his landscape works, Zhao made a systematic study of classical Northern Song landscape styles, creating a new calligraphic vocabulary for what he called 'writing' (*xie*), rather than painting, a landscape.[85] By updating the official canon in calligraphy as well as in figure and landscape painting, and establishing an orthodox lineage of classical painters similar to the Orthodox Lineage of the Dao, Zhao thus achieved unprecedented Han-Chinese cultural autonomy under alien Mongol rule. In the process, he created an all-embracing grid of art-historical representation that imposed a central authority over all other forms of representation.

In the early seventeenth century the leading late Ming figure painter Chen Hongshou (1598–1652) used an 'iron-wire' brush idiom to create a decorative but highly charged archaistic figure style which, easily translated into a woodblock-printed idiom, led to the wide popularity of Chen's figure style in the growing mass culture of the late Ming and early Qing period.[86] In 'A Morning Drink' (fig. 23), from *Sixteen Views of Living in Seclusion* dated 1651, Chen portrays himself in the guise of the Northern Song scholar-artist Su Shi, who referred humorously to his habit of drinking in the morning as watering books (*jiaoshu*). In describing the billowing folds of the scholar's robe 'like the gossamer thread of a spring silkworm' – the Yuan critic Tang Hou's (early fourteenth century) description of Gu Kaizhi's style[87] – Chen's hairline brushwork conveys the essential expression of the subject with a masterly graphic sense of shape and space. A failed scholar turned professional artist, Chen became a popular designer of illustrations for woodblock-printed books and playing cards as well as large decorative paintings produced in multiple versions for the mass market in an expanding consumer economy.[88] It is in Chen's graphic idiom that we find a popular imaginary portrait of Gu Kaizhi (frontispiece) in Shangguan Zhou's (1665–*c.*1750) woodblock-printed *Wanxiaotang huapu (The Old-Age Laughter Studio's Painter's Manual)* published in 1743, which shows the legendary genius strutting away, with drapery lines flowing like 'gossamer threads of a spring silkworm'.

By the seventeenth and eighteenth centuries, such legendary artistic figures as Gu Kaizhi, Wang Xizhi and Wang Xianzhi lived only as myths and cultural heroes in the minds of

Fig. 23 Chen Hongshou (1598–1652), 'A Morning Drink', from *Sixteen Views of Living in Seclusion*, dated 1651. National Palace Museum, Taipei.

collectors, artists and critics, and the *Admonitions* scroll, as Stephen Little so aptly puts it, was 'a kind of talismanic relic of a long-lost golden age of Chinese painting and calligraphy'.[89] Nevertheless, it is instructive to see how the Qing emperor Qianlong (r. 1736–1795), an ardent devotee of classical calligraphy and painting and a voracious art collector, and his courtiers paid special tribute to the *Admonitions* scroll and its Song copy. In his titlepiece, 'The Beginning of Kingly Civilization' ('Wanghua zhishi'; pl. 23), to the Song copy, now in the Palace Museum, Beijing, Qianlong acknowledged the importance of Zhang Hua's 'Admonitions' as a perfect example of Confucian rulership by virtue ethic. One summer's day after viewing the *Admonitions* scroll attributed to Gu Kaizhi, the emperor 'painted a quiet branch of orchid to harmonize with the modest and retiring [female] virtues [depicted in the scroll]' (pl. 37).[90] The symbolic allusion of an orchid flower to 'modest and retiring' (*yaotiao*) female virtues comes from the ancient classic *Book of Poetry* (*Shijing*). Here, in one single stroke, the Qing emperor, through his knowledge of the classics and the possession of the ancient canon of Chinese painting represented by Gu Kaizhi, successfully unifies the theme of orthodox cultural transmission (*Daotong*) with that of political legitimacy (*zhitong*), and thus upholds the Dao Learning orthodoxy exalted in the official Qing imperial examination curriculum.[91]

Gu Kaizhi and Modern Chinese Painting

In the nineteenth and early twentieth centuries, political decline and the protracted struggle for modernization threatened to destroy forever the authority of China's artistic and cultural traditions. After the founding of the Republic in 1912, Chinese intellectuals, many of whom had studied in Japan and Europe, were intent on reforming China to build a modern nation-state. While many reformers of Chinese art looked to Western 'scientific realism' as a model for modernization, many others opposed learning from Western realism, pointing out that Chinese literati painting and calligraphy had since the times of Su Shi, Li Gonglin and Zhao Mengfu represented an essentially 'modern' artistic language.[92] Still others noted that ironically many Chinese artists had turned to European realism just as European art was heading in the opposite direction. For example, in his *History of Chinese Painting* (*Zhongguo huihua shi*) published in 1926, the painter Pan Tianshou (1897–1971), discussing the reasons why Western art had suddenly become essential to the development of Chinese painting, wrote that 'First, European painting in the last thirty to fifty years had developed a great [appreciation] for

the purity of line, tending towards the spiritual taste of the Orient.'[93]

It is important to understand that all leading Westernizers, including the artists Xu Beihong (1895–1955) and Lin Fengmian (1900–1991), saw and interpreted Western art from a Chinese perspective and through Chinese painting theories. While equating Western-style scientific realism with the Chinese term 'form-likeness' (*xingsi*), Xu Beihong, for example, used the term 'spirit-resonance' (*shenyun*) to describe artistic expression:

Both form-likeness and spirit-resonance are a matter of technique. While 'spirit' represents the essence of form-likeness, 'resonance' comes with the transformation of form-likeness. Thus for someone who excels in form-likeness, it is not hard to achieve spirit-resonance. Look at the relief sculptures at the Parthenon, carved some twenty-five hundred years ago in ancient Greece, and see how wonderful they are![94]

Xu based his theory of form-likeness and spirit-resonance on Gu Kaizhi's ancient dictum of 'capturing the spirit through the form' (*yixing xieshen*). In his famous galloping-horse paintings, which in the 1930s and early 1940s became a popular wartime symbol of China's resistance against the Japanese, Xu Beihong combines Western-style realistic, or 'scientific', rendering of form with the spontaneous and expressive Chinese calligraphic brush technique.

In *Goddess of the River Xiang* (*Xiang furen*; fig. 24), dated 1947, Fu Baoshi (1904–1965), who studied Western-style painting in Japan in the early 1930s, also combines Western modelling techniques with spontaneous Chinese brushwork. In his inscription on the painting, Fu quotes a line from the 'Nine Songs' by the tragic poet Qu Yuan (343–278 BCE), 'Gazing into the distance, how sad she looks'[95] – a description of the classical Chinese beauty yearning for her lover. Fu's interest in the theme of Qu Yuan dates back to his studies in Japan, where he would have known the famous painting by the leading Nihonga master Yokoyama Taikan (1868–1958) representing the slandered loyal minister Qu Yuan (fig. 25), who in 278 BCE, betrayed by his friends and banished from the court, wrote the immortal poem 'On Encountering Sorrow' before drowning himself in the Mile River.[96] In the early 1940s Fu, frustrated by wartime politics, frequently painted Qu Yuan and topics related to him.[97]

Fu Baoshi modelled his many portrayals of the Goddess of the River Xiang after palace ladies in the *Admonitions* scroll (pls 9 left, 10). Deprived of opportunities to study original ancient works, Fu and other early twentieth-century Chinese

Fig. 24 Fu Baoshi (1904–1965), *Goddess of the River Xiang*, 1947. Album leaf; ink and colour on paper, 26.7 × 32.7 cm. The Metropolitan Museum of Art, New York. Gift of Robert Hatfield Ellsworth, in memory of La Ferne Hatfield Ellsworth, 1986 (1986.267.277).

Fig. 25 Yokoyama Taikan (1868–1958), *Qu Yuan*, dated 1898. Ink and colour on silk, 132.7 × 289.7 cm. Itsukushima Shrine, Hiroshima.

painters had scant knowledge of early classical Chinese painting. Xu Beihong and Liu Haisu (1896–1994), both of whom were familiar with different schools of European painters, from Raphael, Rubens, Rembrandt and Delacroix to avant-garde masters, never mentioned whether they had seen the *Admonitions* scroll during their visits to the British Museum.[98] Fu Baoshi never travelled to Western Europe, and could only have known the *Admonitions* scroll through a reproduction. In representing a classical Chinese beauty yearning for her lover, Fu appears to follow the theme of the *Admonitions* scroll, which uses the female identity to allude to the equivocal relationship between man (the yearning lover) and the authority of the state. The Qu Yuan legend, as Laurence Schneider has noted, 'has served the modern Chinese as a medium for grappling with problems in the transformation of twentieth-century Chinese society … a forum for discourse, a stage for dramatically posing and answering questions, for expressing dilemmas.'[99] In analysing traditionalism in modern Chinese films, Jerome Silbergeld also writes:

> This [Qu Yuan] material suggests how far back in time one can trace the high literary tradition in China of appropriating female identity in the pursuit of masculine political ends. As early as the Han dynasty, poets had begun to combine elements of the *Odes* with gendered elements of Qu Yuan in political allegories whose indirect reference contemporary critics understood as

Fig. 26 Lin Fengmian (1900–1991), *Nude*, late 1970s. Hanging scroll; ink and colour on paper, 71.1 × 81.3 cm. The Metropolitan Museum of Art, New York. Gift of Robert Hatfield Ellsworth, in memory of La Ferne Hatfield Ellsworth, 1986 (1986.267.372).

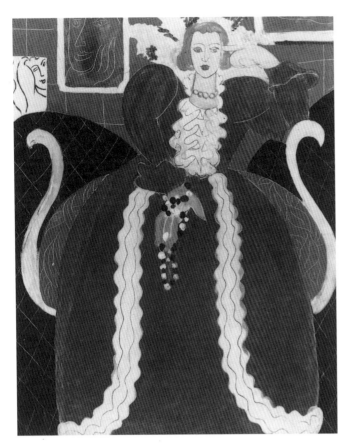

Fig. 27 Henri Matisse (1869–1954), *Woman in Blue*, dated 1937. Philadelphia Museum of Art.

brushstroke clearly marked on the paper surface, reflecting the Chinese belief that brushwork alone expresses the artist's emotion.

Matisse's methods of 'image construction', and his exploration of ideas about art and language that are bound up with Western emphasis on the primacy of language and linguistics, are irrelevant to the Chinese cultural experience.[102] As Professor Lang Shaojun points out, 'Matisse's special contribution lies in his ability to integrate pictorial representation with a new pictorial language ... [But] for the Chinese painter, the exploration and breakthrough of a new formal pictorial language has proven to be the most difficult task of the century.'[103] For the modern Chinese painter who had inherited from Li Gonglin and Zhao Mengfu a 'modern' calligraphic idiom, the proposition of inventing another pictorial language through a Western model must have seemed unduly complicated. In describing how Lin's paintings evoke poetry and musicality, Lang writes: '[Lin] uses a writing brush, absorbent paper and elegant colours to capture an illusory, intangible kind of beauty',[104] which, although influenced by Western models, remains distinctly Chinese in feeling. Lang's characterization of Lin's work echoes Gu Kaizhi's principle of 'capturing the spirit through the form'.

Because Chinese art is philosophically entrenched in life and in nature, there is no need for the Chinese artist to experiment with abstract, non-objective 'image constructions'. The modern painter Wu Guanzhong (b. 1919) has expressed this belief metaphorically, comparing his art to a kite tied by a string to the realities of the world. Wu writes:

designed to skirt possible political difficulties; by the Tang period, it was common to locate one's contemporary criticism in the Han.[100]

In his study of Lin Fengmian's female nudes of the 1970s (fig. 26), Lang Shaojun writes of Lin's search for a new formal pictorial language that paralleled Henri Matisse's (1869–1954) discourse on pictorial language and signs.[101] Matisse (fig. 27) began with a portrait from life and constructed his image of abstraction through dozens of preliminary sketches followed by successive stages of painting in oil, in which his working process is concealed as sketch improved on sketch and stroke concealed stroke. Lin, on the other hand, captured the image at once by 'writing' it calligraphically, with every

All forms and all phenomena, without exception, must originate with life ... I believe that non-objective art is like a kite with a broken string. The string that connects the kite to life has been severed; that which links it to emotion and to the karma of the world is broken off. Modigliani may have contributed to research and exploration ... but I shall always prefer my kite to a kite with a broken string.[105]

In other words, the dual emphasis on realistic representation and supra-real expression, as formulated by Gu Kaizhi in the fourth century, remains today the fundamental dialectic by which the Chinese artist shapes modernity.

NOTES

1   I am grateful to Judith Smith for editing the manuscript and helping with the notes, illustrations and glossary.

2   See Kohara 2000 (1967), pp. 24–29. For a detailed study of the collectors' seals on the scroll, see Wang Yao-t'ing, 'Beyond the *Admonitions* Scroll: A Study of its Mounting, Seals and Inscriptions', in this publication, pp. 192–218.

3   For a review of modern writings on the scroll, see Charles Mason, 'The *Admonitions* Scroll in the Twentieth Century', in this publication, pp. 288–294.

4   See Julia K. Murray, 'Who was Zhang Hua's "Instructress"?', and Alfreda Murck, 'The Convergence of Gu Kaizhi and *Admonitions* in the Literary Record', in this publication, pp. 100–107 and 138–145.

5   *Jin shu*, *juan* 35, 'Biography of Pei Wei'.

6   Zhang Hua's 'Admonitions' follows the tradition of earlier Eastern Han texts by Lady Ban Zhao (*c.*49–120), author of *Nü jie* ('Precepts for Women'), and Huangfu Gui (second century), author of *Nüshi zhen* ('Admonitions for the Court Instructress'), who wrote about paragons of female virtues.

7   See Yu Hui, 'The *Admonitions* Scroll: A Song Version', in this publication, pp. 146–167.

8   Translations of the texts are based freely on Arthur Waley's renderings (1923, pp. 50–51).

9   See Yu Jianhua *et al.* 1961, p. 1.

10 Gu Kaizhi was described by his contemporaries as possessing 'Three Excellences: painting, letters, and eccentricity'. See Zhang Yanyuan, 'Biography of Gu Kaizhi', in *Lidai minghua ji*, in *HSCS*, *juan* 5, p. 67.

11 Ibid., pp. 68–69; see also Acker 1954, pp. 378–379. Zhang Yanyuan cites from *Jingshi shita ji* (Notes on Temples of the Capital), a lost sixth-century work. According to Richard Mather (1964, p. 363, n. 2), 'The Wa-kuan Temple was originally an imperial mausoleum built on the site of an old kiln which had provided tiles for official buildings. About 363–364, by order of the fervently Buddhist Emperor Ai (r. 362–365) … it was converted into a temple.'

12 Gu Kaizhi's portrait of Vimalakirti was discussed at the 2001 colloquy by Liu Yang, 'Leaning Upon an Armrest: Gu Kaizhi's Vimalakirti and a Popular Daoist Iconographic Formula'.

13 Zhang Yanyuan, 'Biography of Gu Kaizhi' (*HSCS*), p. 69.

14 For biographies of Huan Wen, Yin Zhongkan and Huan Xuan, see *Jin shu*, *juan* 98, 84 and 99; see also Yu Jianhua *et al.* 1961, pp. 222–226.

15 See Zhang Yanyuan, 'Biography of Gu Kaizhi' (*HSCS*), p. 67.

16 Yu Jianhua *et al.* 1961, p. 130.

17 See Zhang Yanyuan, 'Biography of Gu Kaizhi' (*HSCS*), p. 67.

18 See quotations from Yao Zui, Li Sizhen and Zhang Huaiguan in Zhang Yanyuan, 'Biography of Gu Kaizhi' (*HSCS*), p. 69.

19 See ibid.

20 Ibid., pp. 21–22; see also Acker 1954, p. 177.

21 See Acker 1954, pp. 183–184.

22 Guo Ruoxu, *Tuhua jianwen zhi*, in *HSCS*, vol. 1, *juan* 1, p. 10; Soper (tr. & annot.) 1951, pp. 16–17.

23 According to Zhang Yanyuan, 'the emperor Wu [r. 140–88 BCE] of the Han dynasty established a secret pavilion for storing maps and documents (*tushu*), and the emperor Ming [r. 58–73 CE], who loved painting (*danqing*), opened a special painting studio (*huashi*). Furthermore, the emperor Ming founded the Hongduxue [Metropolitan Academy] in which to gather together rare works of art.' See Acker 1954, pp. 112–113.

24 See ibid., pp. 114–126.

25 Zhang Yanyuan, 'Biography of Gu Kaizhi' (*HSCS*), p. 71.

26 Ibid., p. 68. For the significance of the eye in painting, see Spiro 1988; see also Freedberg 1989, p. 86. The 8 July 2001 'Arts and Leisure' section of *The New York Times* reported how in the latest animated science-fiction film, 'Final Fantasy: The Spirits Within', the computer-generated heroine Aki Ross uses digitalized eyes to motivate soldiers, a technique, it is said, that is beginning to worry real actors.

27 Michael Nylan relates the Lelang basket to Shu culture (2001, p. 322, n. 91).

28 See Zhang Yanyuan, 'Biography of Gu Kaizhi' (*HSCS*), p. 71. Here, Gu Kaizhi seems to be speaking literally about how figures communicate in painting.

29 According to the Law of Similarity, image reproduces prototype. It was Sir James G. Frazer in *The Golden Bough*, part 1, *The Magic Art and the Evolution of Kings* (1913, p. 52), who first articulated the principle of sympathetic magic: 'First, like produces like … Second, things which have once been in contact with each other continue to act on each other at a distance after the physical contact has been severed. The former principle may be called the Law of Similarity, the latter the Law of Contact or Contagion. From the first of these principles, namely the Law of Similarity, the magician infers that he can produce any effect he desires merely by imitating it.' See Freedberg 1989, pp. 272–274.

30 Zhang Yanyuan, 'Biography of Gu Kaizhi' (*HSCS*), p. 68. See also Freedberg 1989, p. 264.

31 It goes without saying that stylistic development is not always a linear phenomenon. Nevertheless, we may trace naturalistic development in early Chinese figure painting from the Changsha silk painting (third century BCE), through Lady Dai's funerary banner from Mawangdui Tomb 1 in Changsha (early second century BCE) and the tomb paintings at Dahuting, in Mixian, Henan Province (early first century CE), to the shrine of Ning Mao (d. 527) in the Museum of Fine Arts, Boston. Already in the Mawangdui banner, figures and ritual utensils moving away from the strict register line begin to suggest front-and-back positioning in space.

32 Graham-Dixon 2001, p. 74.

33 See *Jin shu*, *juan* 9, 'Biography of Xiaowudi'; also *Zizhi tongjian*, *juan* 108.

34 See Kohara 2000 (1967), p.14.

35 See Stephen Little, 'A "Cultural Biography" of the *Admonitions* Scroll: The Sixteenth, Seventeenth and Early Eighteenth Centuries', in this publication, pp. 219–224, 241–248. For an illustration of Wang Xianzhi's *Goddess of the Luo River* manuscript, see *SDZS* 1954–1969, vol. 4, pls 90–91. It is also illustrated in Dong Qichang's *Xihongtang fatie*.

36 See Dong Qichang, *Xihongtang fatie*.

37 Chen Jiru, *Nigu lu*; see Yu Jianhua *et al.* 1961, p. 156. For other opinions, see Kohara 2000 (1967), p. 30.

38 In speculating that the scroll's calligraphy dates from the sixteenth century, Hironobu Kohara (2000 [1967], pp. 30–33) argues that the writing of Zhang Hua's 'Admonitions' text on the scroll was added after the impressions of the seal 'Ruisi Dongge' were made between 1075 and 1078. As proof of this assertion, he points to Scene 2 (pl. 3), where, according to him, the text is erroneously placed between the two standing ladies. This, however, is a misreading of the illustration. Earlier, Ise Sen'ichiro, in *Shina kaiga* (1922) had read the figure to the right of the text of Scene 2 as part of the preceding Scene 1. There is no doubt of the correctness of this reading, because the said figure, running to the left in order to escape the attacking bear in the middle of the scene, is beautifully balanced by two similar figures escaping to the right. See Chen Pao-chen, 'The *Admonitions* Scroll in the British Museum: New Light on the Text-Image Relationships, Painting Style and Dating

Problem', in this publication, pp. 126–137.

39 See Fong 1999, pp. 42–46.

40 Ibid., p. 41.

41 See above, n. 21.

42 See Yang Xin, 'A Study of the Date of the *Admonitions* Scroll Based on Landscape Portrayal,' in this publication, pp. 42–52. Max Loehr (1980, p. 18) also remarks that 'the mountain is treated in a manner incomparably more sophisticated than … any mountain scenery up to the sixth century if not the seventh.'

43 For an illustration, see Wu Hung 1995, p. 263, fig. 5.19.

44 Soper 1960.

45 Ibid., p. 90.

46 See Zhang Qingjie 2000. I am indebted to Professor Nancy Steinhardt for sharing a copy of the *Proceedings* in which this paper appears with me.

47 Jin Weinuo 1984, 2000.

48 Fong, Wen C. 1981.

49 See Fong, Mary 1976.

50 Soper 1960, pp. 48, 58.

51 Xu Song, *Jiankang shilu* (*SKQS* edition), *juan* 17, p. 24b.

52 Zhang Yanyuan, *Lidai minghua ji* (*HSCS*), p. 22; Acker 1954, pp. 178–179.

53 It is interesting to compare the sixth-century Dunhuang *Running Bull* with a similar *baimiao* (white drawing) rendering of a bull in a ceiling mural in Lou Rui's tomb in Taiyuan, Shanxi Province, dated 570. The latter is illustrated in Wu Hung 1997, fig. 34, p. 43.

54 See Zhang Huaiguan's quotation given above, p. 20; in Zhang Yanyuan, 'Biography of Gu Kaizhi' (*HSCS*), p. 69.

55 See Shih Shou-chien 1996, p. xi.

56 See Craig Clunas, 'The *Admonitions* Scroll in the Eighteenth, Nineteenth and Twentieth Centuries: Discussant's Remarks', in this publication, pp. 295–298.

57 Loehr 1964, p. 186, and 1972, p. 286.

58 Joseph Needham discusses the Han philosopher Dong Zhongshu's (*c*.179–*c*.104 BCE) correlative universe in 1956, pp. 281–283. Needham describes a symbolic correlative system of magical efficacy structuring a cosmos that is an 'ordered harmony of wills without an ordainer' (1956, p. 28).

59 See Gombrich 1960, pp. 116ff.

60 See Fong, Wen C. 1992, pp. 431ff.

61 Zhang Yanyuan, *Lidai minghua ji* (*HSCS*), p. 15.

62 *Taiping guangji*, *juan* 212; see also Huang Miaozi 1991, p. 14.

63 See the discussion of this passage in Peter Bol 1992, pp. 295–299.

64 See Belting 1987, pp. 46–48, and Arthur Danto in Lang 1984.

65 As Arthur Danto writes (in Lang 1984, p. 24), 'The history of Art now requires a totally different structure. It does so because there is no longer any reason to think of art as having a progressive history; there simply is not the possibility of a development sequence with the concept of expression as there is with the concept of mimetic representation.'

66 Bush 1971, p. 26.

67 Foucault 1973, p. xxiii.

68 Foucault writes (1973, p. 293): 'There is one major difference, however, between languages and living beings. The latter have no true history except by means of a certain relation between their functions and the conditions of their existence … Thus, to enable this history to emerge clearly, and to be described in discourse, there had to be … an analysis of the environment and conditions that act on the living being.'

69 See Chen Gaohua (ed.) 1984, p. 452.

70 Ibid.

71 See James J.Y. Liu (1975, pp. 67–70).

72 See Fong, Wen C. 1999, p. 37.

73 Chen Gaohua (ed.) 1984, p. 453.

74 See Barnhart 1972.

75 See Zhang Chou, in *Qinghe shuhua fang*, vol. 1, pp. 36r., 36v.

76 Ibid., p. 33v.

77 See Barnhart *et al.* 1993, pp. 137, 140–142.

78 Elman 2000, p. 621.

79 See Wen C. Fong, 'The Orthodox Lineage of Tao', in Fong & Watt 1996, pp. 257–259.

80 See Liu, James T.C.: 1973.

81 Elman 2000, p. xxv.

82 See McCausland 2000.

83 Shih, Shou-chien, 1984. See also Shane McCausland, '"Like the gossamer thread of a spring silkworm" – Gu Kaizhi in the Yuan (1271–1368) Renaissance', in this publication, pp. 168–182.

84 See Berkowitz 2000, p. 4, *passim*.

85 See Fong, Wen C. 1992, pp. 436–440.

86 See Fong, Wen C. 1976; Wang Cheng-hua 2001.

87 See Shane McCausland's paper in this volume (pp. 168–182), which takes its title, 'Like the gossamer thread of a spring silkworm', from Tang Hou.

88 See Fong & Watt 1996, pp. 411–413.

89 See Stephen Little, 'A "Cultural Biography" of the *Admonitions* Scroll: The Sixteenth, Seventeenth and Early Eighteenth Centuries', in this volume, p. 247.

90 The *Admonitions* scroll was considered the most important of the four works in the Qianlong emperor's collection known collectively as the 'Four Beauties' (*si mei*). The other three handscrolls, all attributed to Li Gonglin, were, like the *Admonitions*, mounted with a painting by the emperor and another by a court artist. See Zhang Hongxing, 'The Nineteenth-Century Provenance of the *Admonitions* Scroll: A Hypothesis', in this publication, pp. 277–287. Qianlong's choice of these four scrolls as the most valuable of his treasures is a subject worthy of future study.

91 For discussion of *Daotong* and *zhitong*, see Elman 2000, pp. 52, 62.

92 For statements by Chen Hengke (1876–1923) and Huang Binhong (1865–1955), see Fong, Wen C. 2001, pp. 14, 15, 175.

93 See Sullivan 1996, p. 25.

94 See Xu Beihong 1983.

95 See Owen (ed. & tr.) 1996.

96 See Fong, Wen C. 2001, pp. 76–78.

97 See ibid., pp. 111–113.

98 Yu Jianhua, co-author of *Gu Kaizhi yanjiu ziliao* (preface dated 1961), was the only scholar who wrote in the nationalistic vein typical of that period: '[The *Admonitions* scroll] is an art work of incomparable value. It is one of our national treasures. It is a monumental debt that we must recover someday from the British Imperialists.' (Yu Jianhua *et al.* 1961, p. 173).

99 Schneider 1980, p. 200.

100 Silbergeld 1999, p. 34.

101 Lang Shaojun 1995b.

102 For Matisse's ideas of art and language and constructional method, see John Elderfield, 'Describing Matisse' (1992, pp. 26–33, 64–69).

103 Lang Shaojun 1995b, pp. 213, 189.

104 Lang Shaojun 1995a, p. 107.

105 Wu Guanzhong, 'Fengzheng buduan xian' (Kite with Unbroken String) (1992, pp. 19–20).

Part 1
Kingship, the Way and Art

A Study of the Date of the *Admonitions* Scroll Based on Landscape Portrayal

Yang Xin

In Nature there is (nothing) that is exalted which is not soon brought low. Among living things there is nothing which having attained it apogee does not thenceforth decline. When the sun has reached its mid-course, it begins to sink; when the moon is full it begins to wane. To rise to glory is as hard as to build a mountain out of dust; to fall into calamity is as easy as the rebound of a tense spring.[1]

In order to depict the above passage of Zhang Hua's (232–300) text, 'Admonitions of the Instructress to the Court Ladies', the artist of the *Admonitions* scroll paints a mountain landscape dotted with rabbits, tiger, deer, a pair of pheasants in flight, and a sun and a moon in the sky (scene 3 of the British Museum scroll; pl. 5). To one side, a hunter clutches a drawn bow and takes aim towards the mountain.

In the painting, the hunter and the mountain appear to be divorced of each other and not in the least related. However, the reason the hunter draws his bow is to shoot the pheasants in the mountain. The artist had little choice but to depict Zhang Hua's warning 'to fall into calamity is as easy as the rebound of a tense spring'[2] in this creative way. He chooses the image of a drawn bow as a metaphor by which to admonish the imperial concubines; that is, if they do not conduct themselves in a proper manner, then they will come to no good end. The bow is the metaphor, not the hunter; however, the artist has to depict the hunter, as without him the bow cannot be drawn. That the artist successfully manages to depict the hunter in a landscape setting without overwhelming the all-important image of the bow demonstrates his resourcefulness and skill.

The aim of this paper is to explore when the *Admonitions* scroll was made, and to establish whether it is a copy or an original work. I will start by tracing the stylistic development of Chinese landscape painting in order to explore when

this piece was painted. I will then look at historical texts, painting techniques and finally calligraphy as a means of deducing whether it is a copy or an original. Through this approach, I will show that the *Admonitions* scroll is an original work of the late Northern Wei period (386–534).

I Early Landscape Painting

A moulded brick relief excavated from an Eastern Han (25–220) tomb in Zengjiabao, Chengdu, Sichuan depicting salt mining is probably the most successful landscape portrayal of life during the late Han (fig. 1). The picture is composed of overlapping undulating mountains scattered with trees, wild

Fig. 1 'Salt Mining' (Yan jing). Rubbing of a moulded brick relief excavated from Zengjiabao, Chengdu, Sichuan. Eastern Han Dynasty (25–220). Chengdu Museum, Sichuan. (Line drawing after *MSQJ, Painting*, vol. 18, fig. 239.)

Fig. 2 *Four Recluses of Nanshan (Nanshan si hao)*. Line drawing of a moulded brick relief excavated from a Southern Dynasties (420–589) tomb in Dengxian, Henan. Original in Chinese History Museum, Beijing.

animals and birds. Four figures operate a salt gantry in the foreground, whilst a fifth, in the lower right corner, kneels to stoke the fire of an elongated kiln. Two figures carrying heavy loads on their backs cross a bridge spanning two mountains.

Overlooking the rather primitive juxtaposition of figural and landscape scenes, as a pictorial whole 'Salt·Mining' is a highly successful landscape. The trees are simply rendered but are naturalistic. The artist uses simple curved lines to depict the mountain peaks, yet he is aware of the need to vary repeating elements; so the tall and lofty main peak is contrasted with the surrounding smaller peaks and ridges, thereby giving each mountain its own distinctive character. These same Han landscape elements are carried over into the Six Dynasties period (220–589) and are visible in the brick relief depicting *Four Recluses of Nanshan (Nanshan si hao)*, excavated from a Southern Dynasties (420–589) tomb in Dengxian, Henan.

The moulded brick depicts four hermits with hair untied and feet bare, seated on the ground in a relaxed manner (fig. 2). One plays the *qin* (zither), another the *sheng* (mouth organ), and one chants while the fourth engages in rhetoric. In the background, the mountain peaks act as a screen against which two fabulous birds fly entwined in a dance whilst a monkey perches on a rock. Curved lines form lofty and precipitous mountains both in the foreground and background. The mountains in a row recall the words of the famous ninth-century critic Zhang Yanyuan: 'In works [from the Wei and Jin dynasties] wherever landscapes are painted, then the aspect of the crowded peaks resembles [the teeth of] pearl-inlaid combs.'[3]

Most noteworthy is that the treatment of the rocks in the *Four Recluses* is markedly different from that of its mountains. The rocks are depicted as upright rectangular forms with the upper part tapering to a lozenge-shaped peak. A par-

allel line is drawn on each side of the rock which is joined to the main rock by a sloping line. Grass is then painted sprouting from the cracks. This particular rock form is very similar to that used in the Northern Wei engraved limestone sarcophagus panels depicting 'Stories of Filial Piety', in the Nelson-Atkins Museum, Kansas City (see p. 109, figs 1–2). The only difference is that the rocks in the *Four Recluses* are slightly rougher and simpler whereas those depicted in the 'Filial Piety' scenes are more articulated and complex. That they were produced during different time periods may explain this stylistic difference.

According to an inscription found in the Dengxian tomb, the deceased was a native of modern day Suzhou and the commander of an army, so archaeologists have dated the tomb to the Southern Dynasties period. Dengxian could well have fallen under the jurisdiction of his command during the Liu Song dynasty (420–479), therefore his tomb could well be Liu Song period, which corresponds to the early part of the Northern Wei dynasty in the north.

The mountain landscape in the *Admonitions* scroll

The rendering of the *Admonitions* mountain landscape (scene 3; pl. 5) is altogether more sophisticated than the mountains depicted in both the *Four Recluses* and 'Stories of Filial Piety'. For a start, the mountain peaks are depicted amassed together. Although they visually appear as a grouping of separate triangles, they are not simply stacked one on top of the other like building blocks, but have a sense of cohesiveness. The mountain contours are distinct and flow naturally, conveying a sense of volume. Snaking up from the base of the mountain is a path under which is an over-hanging cliff. The artist carefully depicts the rock texture of the cliff using parallel lines, however the line no longer just follows the outline of the rock, but is more dynamic, and changes with the rock form in a natural-istic manner. Between the peak in the foreground and the highest peak in the distance, trees and shrubbery are painted to indicate a valley and suggest distance between mountains. All these devices signal a new phase of landscape painting, indicating that the *Admonitions* landscape cannot possibly pre-date the *Four Recluses* or 'Stories of Filial Piety'; that is, it cannot be earlier than the Eastern Jìn (317–419), Liu Song or early Northern Wei.

Sixth-century landscapes

'Sūtra Stories' (Jingbian gushi), a line-engraved stone stele excavated from the Wanfosi site in Chengdu, Sichuan, illus-trating stories from the Buddhist sūtras, also depicts a very complete landscape scene (fig. 3). Looking at the landscape, it is clear that the artist has managed to resolve the proportional relationships between architectural elements, figures and land-scape. Moreover, unlike the figures in the Han 'Salt Mining' brick, the figures and landscape do not appear awkwardly jux-taposed like two overlapping 'photographic plates'.

Here, for the first time in Chinese painting, we see lines that give the illusion of recession to a horizon (*shi ping xian*) in the upper area of rivers and distant mountains. In order to convey a sense of distance, the artist not only enlarges the peaks in the foreground, but reduces those in the background and follows suit with the trees and figures. The peaks have a pulse, driving them forward and the main peak is conspicuous because of its placement in relation to the other peaks that surround and protect it in all directions. Between the moun-

Fig. 3 'Sūtra Stories' (Jingbian gushi). Line-engraved stone stele (*bei*) excavated from the Wanfosi (Myriad Buddhas Temple) site, Chengdu, Sichuan. Southern Dynasties (420–589). Sichuan Provincial Museum. (Line drawing after *MSQJ*, *Sculpture*, vol. 3, fig. 63 and detail, pp. 65–67.)

Fig. 4 'Sākyamuni Stele' (Shijiali foukan). Relief carving on the back of a stone stele with an inscribed date of 523, excavated from the Wanfosi site, Chengdu, Sichuan. Liang dynasty (502–557). Sichuan Provincial Museum. (Line drawing after *MSQJ*, *Sculpture*, vol. 3, fig. 54, pp. 54–55.)

tains, areas of level land are indicated by stands of trees, Bud-dhist shrines and pagodas. Lively figures dot the scene. It is evident that Chinese landscape painting has attained a new level.

Unfortunately the stele does not have a definite date. Comparing it, however, with a similarly carved stone stele (fig. 4) found from the same site, inscribed with the date 'fourth year of Putong of the Liang dynasty' corresponding to the year 523 CE, it is highly probable that 'Sūtra Stories' is either of the same period or a little later. Furthermore, the modelling of the trees, the clothing, hats and the coiffures of the figures are extremely similar. Even the bedchamber in the upper right corner is akin to that depicted in the *Admonitions* scroll.

The landscape style of the *Admonitions* scroll is more sophisticated than that of the *Four Recluses of Nanshan*, how-ever, next to 'Sūtra Stories' it appears conservative and prim-itive. Even though the handling of the mountains in the *Admonitions* scroll is more skilful than that in 'Sūtra Stories', the tiger perched on the mountain is awkwardly depicted. The artist composed the scene using a 'multiple-image method' to depict the landscape as two separate 'scenes'; therefore the tiger becomes larger than the mountain. Examining this awk-ward-looking tiger is in fact helpful to the study and under-standing of the development of landscape painting.

The tiger in landscape

The tiger is one of the oldest images in Chinese art. It is one of the animals of the four directions (*si shen*) and, as the White

Fig. 5 *Jātaka of Prince Sudāna (Saduo bensheng)*. Wall mural from Mogao Cave 254, Dunhuang, Gansu, and line drawing above. Northern Wei (386–534). (After *MSQJ, Painting*, vol. 14, fig. 18.)

Tiger, it symbolizes the West. In Han murals, the tiger is usually depicted with elongated body, outstretched limbs, extended tail and covered all over with long flowing fur. This image of the tiger was retained up until the Eastern Jin period.

In other works of art, however, when the tiger was portrayed as a hunter or as an animal of prey, it is depicted in a more naturalistic and sophisticated manner. The early Northern Wei mural *Jātaka of Prince Sudāna* in Mogao Cave 254, Dunhuang, depicts a scene of 'sacrificing one's life to feed the tiger'. Here, the tiger is not entirely realistic as it still retains the traditional elongated body-form (fig. 5), although it has evolved slightly from the White Tiger image and appears more naturalistic.

During the Western Wei (535–556), the tiger image undergoes a complete transformation. In the mural from Mogao Cave 258 at Dunhuang from this period (fig. 6), the tiger slinks forward with head lowered and tail extended, ready to pounce on the three small unsuspecting gazelles ahead. It is animated and full of life, and its feline form and striped patterning distinguish it from its antecedent, the White Tiger. Overall it appears much more realistic. The inscription, 'fourth year of Datong of the Great Wei', dates this tiger to the year 538 CE.

In the Northern Zhou (557–581) mural of the *Sujāta Jātaka* in Mogao Cave 296 (fig. 7), a crouching tiger in a landscape depicted on the ceiling is also very realistically rendered. What is singular is that the artist, in dealing with the relationship between the tiger, mountains and trees, has paid

Fig. 6 Line drawing of a tiger from a mural (below) in Mogao Cave 285, Dunhuang, Gansu. Western Wei (535–556). (After *MSQJ, Painting*, vol. 14, fig. 109.)

close attention to relative scales and proportion, so the tiger is no longer disproportionately large.

Very similar in style as well as time period to the feline depicted in the Western Wei mural is the tiger carved in relief on a Northern Wei stone stele of a Buddhist Triad donated by Zhang Lingfei with the dated inscription 'Da Wei Yongxi er nian' (second year of Yongxi of the Great Wei), corresponding to 533 CE, excavated from Shandong (fig. 8). The tiger slinks

Fig. 7 *Sujāta Jātaka (Xusheti bensheng)*. Wall mural from Mogao Cave 296, Dunhuang, Gansu Province. Northern Zhou (557–581). (After *MSQJ, Painting*, vol. 14, fig. 148 left.)

Fig.8 'Buddhist Triad donated by Zhang Lingfei' (Zhang Lingfei zao fo sanzun). Line drawing of a stone stele with the inscription 'second year of Yongxi of the Great Wei' (533 CE) carved on the back, excavated in Shandong province. Northern Wei (386–534). Baoli Museum, Beijing.

down the mountain slope, its eyes fixed on its prey, a small gazelle about to flee.

In the *Admonitions* scroll, the tiger is depicted seated in a similar pose as the feline in the Northern Zhou mural, and the modelling and patterning of its body, as well as the relative scale between animal and mountain are all comparable to the Northern Zhou and the Western Wei felines. Therefore, from the above analysis and comparisons of different Six Dynasties' modelling of the tiger in landscape, it is likely that the *Admonitions* scroll was produced during the late Northern Wei (471–534).

II Tracing the Provenance of the *Admonitions* Scroll

Some scholars have already pointed out that in Tang (618–907) and pre-Tang texts there are no written records verifying that Gu Kaizhi (c. 345–406) did indeed paint an *Admonitions* scroll. The earliest written record of the *Admonitions* scroll attributed to Gu Kaizhi is in the *Catalogue of Paintings in the Xuanhe Collection (Xuanhe huapu)*, edited during the reign of the Song (960–1279) emperor Huizong (r. 1101–1125). The Song scholar-painter and connoisseur Mi Fu (1052–1107) also records in *History of Painting (Hua shi)* that the Song emperor Taizong (r. 976–997) bought a scroll painted by Gu Kaizhi.[4] This piece of information is, in fact, not that illuminating as it fails to describe the painting, so we do not actually know *which* painting the emperor bought. However, examining the seal impressions proves to be more fruitful.

Authentication of seals and inscriptions

In the extant *Admonitions* scroll, there are three successively placed large square relief 'Ruisi Dongge' ([Palace of] Sagacious Contemplation, East Wing) seal impressions, which are virtually the same as the 'Ruisi Dongge' seal found on the Tang painting by Han Huang (723–787) entitled *Five Oxen (Wu niu tu)* in the Palace Museum, Beijing. This leads us to conclude that the extant *Admonitions* scroll is indeed the one recorded in the *Catalogue of Paintings in the Xuanhe Collection*.

The square relief 'Hongwen zhi yin' ([Academy for the] Dissemination of Culture) seal, however, is problematic. It does not share any similarities with the 'Hongwen zhi yin' seal on the Tang handscroll *Zhang Haohao's Poems (Zhang Haohao shi)* by Du Mu (c. 803–852) in the Palace Museum, Beijing. Furthermore, the placement of the seal is atypical and is not where one would expect it to be given its age. The

Admonitions seal is placed in the middle of the scroll, quite far away from the end of the painting. In contrast, the seal on Du Mu's handscroll is in the uppermost corner at the beginning of the scroll. The 'Hongwen zhi yin' seal on the *Admonitions* scroll is more like that on the Eastern Jìn manuscript *Mid-Autumn (Zhongqiu tie)*, attributed to the calligrapher Wang Xianzhi (344–386). Scholars have established that *Mid-Autumn* is a forgery by Mi Fu, so the 'Hongwen zhi yin' seal is undoubtedly spurious.

The end of the *Admonitions* scroll has a four-character inscription, 'Gu Kaizhi hua' (painted by Gu Kaizhi), which is clearly a later addition. When Mi Fu saw the *Admonitions* scroll in Liu Youfang's collection, he praised it but did not mention any such inscription, and Mi Fu always noticed inscriptions when he appraised ancient paintings. For instance, in *History of Painting*, he recorded that in a Li Sheng landscape hanging scroll which he bought, the inscription 'Shuren Li Sheng' (Li Sheng from Shu)[5] was written in tiny characters on a pine tree. In another instance, when a painting by Jing Hao (*c.* 870/80–925/35) belonging to the painter Wang Shen (*c.* 1046–*c.* 1100) was being re-backed, Mi Fu noticed the artist's signature on a rock, commenting that '[Putting an inscription in such a place] is not something a later person would do.'[6] If Mi Fu could pick out a tiny inscription on a pine tree, then he would have noticed an inscription in the *Admonitions* scroll, especially that of Gu Kaizhi. Therefore we can assume that when Mi Fu saw the *Admonitions* scroll, it did not have any such inscription.

During the Song, it was common among scholar-official collectors to buy and sell ancient calligraphy and paintings from each other, so artists often added spurious inscriptions and/or seal impressions – not least Wang Shen and Mi Fu. Therefore I suspect that the 'Hongwen zhi yin' seal mark and the signature 'Gu Kaizhi hua' are later additions, both added by Mi Fu.

Biographies of exemplary women

According to the *Jìn shu (History of the Jìn)*, Zhang Hua's 'Admonitions of the Instructress to the Court Ladies' was directly aimed at the Jìn empress Jia for her scandalous behaviour. Empress Jia is recorded as having 'a jealous nature', and 'behaved in a wicked and cruel manner, assisted members of her own family who sought power and formed a clique for her own selfish gain. She usurped power from the court, had licentious affairs in the imperial harem and had a base reputation outside.'[7]

The *Admonitions* scroll, inspired by Zhang Hua's didactic work, would have served as a means by which to admonish later generations of women. Ministers remonstrating with

emperors would also have cited it as historical precedent – what is called 'using the past as a mirror'. Such a work could not have been arbitrarily painted, but must have been specially commissioned by the emperor since no artist of the Jìn imperial court, including Gu Kaizhi, could possibly have dared paint such a controversial subject without specific orders from the emperor.

During the tumultuous period of the Northern and Southern Dynasties (386–581), China was divided into nine different imperial courts. Looking through the standard histories of these dynasties, it is apparent that the Northern Wei rule of Xiaowendi (r. 471–499) possessed the right cultural and political environment in which to create the *Admonitions* scroll.

Grand Empress Dowager Wenming

Xiaowendi was born in the first year of Huangxing (467 CE). When he was three, his mother (née Li) was forced to commit suicide according to the established decree,[8] so he was raised from a young age by Emperor Wencheng's (r. 452–465) Empress Wenming, the Dowager Empress, Lady Feng. After the death of Emperor Wencheng, his heir apparent Xianwendi (r. 466–470) was only ten years old, so the Dowager Empress Wenming ascended the throne to act as regent.

The *Wei shu (History of the Wei)* documents the reprehensible behaviour of Empress Wenming: 'The actions of the empress were not proper; she dishonourably doted on Li Yi so Xianzu [Xianwendi] sentenced Li Yi to death. The empress was not pleased. When Xianzu died suddenly it was said at the time that the empress was responsible for his death.'[9] Xiaowendi was only five years old when he ascended the throne. The Empress Wenming took the title of Grand Empress Dowager and continued ruling for the next twenty years.

Empress Wenming was indeed a force to be reckoned with. She consolidated her power by appointing family members to important positions, especially using her older brother Feng Xi, appointing him as General Commanding the Troops and ennobling him to a peerage of similar status to that of a marquis. When she became Grand Empress Dowager, he was promoted again. In order to further consolidate her status and power, she invested her two nieces (Feng Xi's two daughters) as concubines in the imperial palace, and both eventually became Xiaowendi's empresses. In the inner palace, she had affairs with officials and courtiers, often bestowing them with titles, great wealth and even immunity from death.[10]

Xiaowendi always respected and was filial towards the Grand Empress Dowager, treating her as if she were his real mother; however, his feelings were never reciprocated.[11] Even though Wenming mistreated Xiaowendì, he never complained, prompting historiographers to praise his 'benevolent understanding' and 'indulgent kindness'.

Xiaowendi

Xiaowendi was an extremely accomplished ruler. It was not until after the Grand Empress Dowager Wenming died in 490 CE that he ascended the throne and demonstrated his extraordinary abilities.[12]

Xiaowendi's ambition was to unite China. He reformed the palace system, implementing a sinicization policy prohibiting the use of non-Han Chinese language and clothing; but at the same time, he appointed both Xianbei and Han officials, considering them equally important. He adopted traditional Chinese rites and customs thus continuing Chinese traditions. Although his reforms were extremely ambitious, he oversaw all matters with a resolute hand. Thus under Xiaowendi's rule, the Northern Wei rapidly developed, flourished and strengthened its power.

However, Xiaowendi was less than satisfied when it came to the affairs of his imperial harem. The emperor took a liking to a particular concubine (née Lin) who eventually bore him a son and heir apparent, but according to the strict Northern Wei decree, her death was inevitable. Xiaowendi's first official empress was the second niece of the Grand Empress Dowager Wenming (the younger daughter of Feng Xi). The empress and her older sister both vied for the emperor's favour, jealously fighting one another in the harem. The empress was eventually framed by her older sister and demoted to commoner status. The older sister was enthroned as empress soon after. However, when her affair with the courtier Gao Pusa and her scheme to kill the emperor using witchcraft with her mother (née Chang) were revealed, she was forced to take a potion and kill herself.[13]

Xiaowendi and the *Admonitions* scroll

From the historical events described above, it is highly probable that Xiaowendi commissioned the *Admonitions* scroll for the following reasons: first, it is clear from written records, that the empresses and concubines had lost all morals and sense of virtue. They monopolized power, they were excessive, licentious and plotted to kill the emperor's descendants. Secondly, his first empress was demoted and the second killed, both for lack of merit and moral virtue. Therefore the *Admonitions* scroll might well have been commissioned as a didactic work of art, aimed at admonishing other palace women. Thirdly, during his reign, Xiaowendi was a staunch supporter of Han-Chinese customs and etiquette, and relied on ancient regulations and protocols to rule.[14] His policies sought to cultivate and balance both civil and military branches of government. He also practised Confucianism, familiarizing himself with its decrees and regulations so that he could implement them. It is most probable, therefore, that he would have commissioned a painting of Zhang Hua's 'Admonitions of the Instructress to the Court Ladies' in order to educate the women of the imperial harem.

Wang Rui: model for the *Admonitions* scroll?

The *Wei shu* records that in the second year of Taihe (corresponding to 478 CE), Gaozu (Xiaowendi), the Empress Wenming, hundreds of officials and guests from all over the country, assembled to watch a tiger display. A tiger escaped, scaled the gates of the enclosure and almost reached the imperial throne. The imperial bodyguards and attendants were all terrified but Wang Rui seized a halberd and warded off the tiger, causing it to back away.[15]

When Wang Rui died more than twenty years later, Xiaowendi and Empress Wenming both grieved deeply. They bestowed upon him an honorary lacquer coffin containing mirrors (*wenming miqi*)[16] and issued an imperial edict praising him. A portrait depicting him fending off the tiger was hung in all the palaces, and Gao Yun wrote a eulogy in his memory.[17] Even though Xiaowendi may have been too young to remember the tiger incident, he would have been about twenty-three or twenty-four years old when the painting of Wang Rui warding off the tiger was commissioned.

In a commemorative painting, Wang Rui would most likely have been depicted in a similar manner to Lady Feng warding off a black bear to protect her husband, the Han emperor Yuandi (r. 48–32 BCE) in the first scene of the British Museum scroll. By sheer coincidence, the Han exemplar Lady Feng had the same surname as the Empress Wenming. The depiction of Wang Rui and the tiger would have been quite ironic, however, for although Wang Rui was illustrated as an 'exemplary figure' warding off the tiger to protect the emperor, he was more likely to have been motivated to carry out such a courageous and virtuous deed because he was the secret lover of the Empress Wenming.

Xiaowendi believed in recording events truthfully. He once told his historiographers: 'Write the events of the period honestly; there is no taboo on the faults of the state. If the ruler thinks highly of himself, but the historiographer does not write about this, so people in the future will not have to fear anything.'[18]

If 'Wang Rui warding off the tiger' was indeed placed in 'many palaces' as the *Wei shu* records, then it follows that if Xiaowendi commissioned the *Admonitions* scroll, he too would very likely have been inspired to have many copies made to be placed in the different palaces of his empresses, concubines and other women of the court as a didactic reminder about their behaviour.

III The *Admonitions* Scroll: Original or Copy?

Several telltale signs distinguish a copy from an original. Since a copy is, by its nature, limited by the original work, the artist cannot freely depict what he wishes, so that figures, landscapes, trees and rocks will appear stiff and mechanical. Furthermore, if passages of the original were blurred or damaged in any way from age, the copyist would not see certain details clearly, and would have to resort to guessing; thus, misinterpretations and mistakes are common in a copy. The skill of the copyist is especially tested when working with an ancient piece from a much earlier time period. Examining particular aspects, such as the varied facial expressions of the figures and their costumes in the *Admonitions* scroll with all these points in mind, we discover that the painting does not possess any of these flaws.

Facial expression

In the 'toilette' scene of the *Admonitions* scroll (scene 4; pls 6, 8), the woman with her back to the viewer gazes into a mirror. By the expression in her eyes, we can see that she is admiring her own reflection. The other woman whose hair is being combed by an attendant has a different expression in her eyes, and a look of tranquillity is projected from her face. From her eyes, we can see that she is observing the attendant's actions and her own hair, and not using the time to admire her own looks, unlike her companion nearby. These minute facial details come directly from the artist's own observations and feelings, and a copyist would be hard pressed to replicate these same nuances.

The female figure

In figure 9 I have sketched four female figures, each from a different pictorial source, in order to compare their clothing and overall rendering, and thus illustrate the distinctions between original and copy. From left to right, the first female is from the 'rejection' scene of the *Admonitions* scroll. To her right is the nymph from the Song copy of *Nymph of the Luo River*; next is a young female attendant holding a box, from a Southern Dynasties painted tomb brick found in Jiangsu. The last figure is a female celestial from 'Stories of Filial Piety' on the Kansas City sarcophagus.

The female celestial from 'Stories of Filial Piety' and the rejected beauty from the *Admonitions* scroll appear to be from the same period, and from their exquisite modelling and similarity in costume they are clearly original works. However, where the *Admonitions* figure is clearly the artist's own creation – obvious from the clear and logical rendering of the figure which is free from any mistakes – the female celestial in 'Stories of Filial Piety' is visibly a copy because of its glaring misinterpretations. The portrayal of the 'Filial Piety' figure is meticulous: the artist must have traced the image directly onto the stone slab, before stone sculptors came in to carve it. The tracing lines may have faded or been rubbed off through carelessness – but it is evident that the carvers were not sure of what they were doing, and so misunderstood some details. Take the right shoe of the figure, for example. The original

Fig. 9 Line drawings of four female figures:
a) a beauty from the *Admonitions* scroll, British Museum;
b) the nymph from *Nymph of the Luo River (Luoshen fu tu)*, Song copy in the Palace Museum, Beijing;
c) a female attendant from a Southern Dynasties brick relief from Changzhou, Jiangsu;
d) a female celestial from the story of Dong Yong on the engraved sarcophagus, Nelson-Atkins Museum, Kansas City.

would have depicted the shoe peeping out from under the hem of her skirt. However, the engraver has interpreted her shoe as a ribbon. A quick look at the two large protruding shoes on the Southern Dynasties female figure is all that is needed to realize this. Also, in 'Stories of Filial Piety', there are some details which have been overlooked and not engraved at all. If artists from the same time and place could make such mistakes, then the probability of making mistakes will be even higher when copying something from a different period.

From the style of the nymph's clothing in *Nymph of the Luo River*, the figure, at first glance, appears to be from the same period as the three other examples. However, it is in fact a Song copy, which is corroborated by the numerous misinterpretations and mistakes in the rendering of her clothing – for example, where a ribbon of no definite origin emanates from her left sleeve. With the 'Filial Piety' and the *Admonitions* figures, the same ribbon is clearly painted as part of a shawl wrapped around the figure's shoulders.

Even though feet are hidden within the skirts of both the *Admonitions* and *Nymph* figures, the *Admonitions* beauty appears to glide forward in mid-step with her right foot forward, which is deftly suggested by the subtle rise of the hem and the folds of her skirt. The artists of both the *Admonitions* beauty and the lady in 'Stories of Filial Piety' skilfully manage to convey the female figures even underneath their full billowing clothing. On the other hand, no sense of movement or even of the body's form is gained from the *Nymph of the Luo River* figure. These points may seem trivial, but it is precisely these nuances that together convey a painting's 'spirit' and differentiate originals from copies. We can therefore say with certainty that the *Admonitions* scroll is an original work.

Calligraphy

The calligraphy in the *Admonitions* scroll is basically standard or block script (*kaishu*), with traces of running script (*xingshu*) appearing occasionally. For example, the section beginning 'ren xian zhi xiu qi rong' (people only know how to adorn their faces) has three 'zhi' (*'of/it'*) characters that are written in two different styles (the 'toilette' scene; fig. 10, pl. 6). The first 'zhi' (last character, first column) is written in strict *kaishu* – where the brush tip emerges as if to carve, like a knife slash. The second and third 'zhi' (eighth and tenth characters, second column) are written in running script so the brush tip makes sudden dots, producing a more rounded-off stroke. I will show that this type of calligraphy was in use at the end of the Northern Wei, further supporting my claim that the *Admonitions* scroll is from the late Northern Wei period.

The epitaph of Meng Jingxun records that Meng

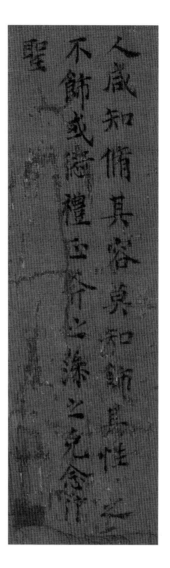

Fig. 10 (left) Detail of the inscription from the 'toilette' scene of the *Admonitions* scroll.

Fig. 11 (opposite) *Epitaph of Meng Jingxun*. Rubbing of the tomb epitaph of Meng Jingxun (d. 513), datable to 516 CE. Northern Wei (386–534). Palace Museum, Beijing.

Jingxun died in 'Yanchang er nian' (second year of Yanchang) during the Northern Wei and was buried three years later (fig. 11). Therefore the calligraphy on the epitaph dates to the first year of Xiping (516 CE), which is only eighteen years after Xiaowendi's death. The epitaph is written in regular script with traces of running script, as in the *Admonitions* calligraphy. However, by using a carving tool to engrave the calligraphy, some of the expressive quality of the running script has been lost; although where it was well carved, this quality comes through.

In the first and second lines of the main body of text, there are two 'zhi' (*'of/it'*) characters side by side (fifth from bottom). The first 'zhi' is the same as the first regular-script 'zhi' in the *Admonitions* scroll. In the second 'zhi', the marks left by the brush point, although not rapidly written dots, strongly suggest running-script style. Six lines from the end of text, the 'zheng' 正 character (fourth from bottom, in the phrase '… san nian zheng yue gengxu') is practically identical to the 'zheng' character written in running-cursive script in the *Admonitions* inscription (second column, sixth character).[19]

What is remarkable is that this epitaph helps solve a problem with the calligraphy in the *Admonitions* scroll. In the inscription to the landscape scene beginning 'dao wang long er bu sha' (in nature there is [nothing] that is exalted which is not soon brought low – see p. 16, line 33), only the upper part of the character 'wang' (not) is visible, because part of the silk medium is broken (pl. 5). If we check the original text by Zhang Hua, we find that the character should read 'wang', but looking at the mark left on the silk, it does not appear so; thus some scholars have concluded that it must be an incorrect character and hypothesize that it should read as 'jia' 家

(family). 'Jia' however, makes no sense at all in this context, debunking this theory. Only by examining this epitaph would one know that this character is in fact a 'wu' 無 (won't) character (fourth column of main text, eleventh character) written in running script. Although there is another 'wu' character written further down but in strict regular script (*zhengkai*) (eighth character), no one has ventured to guess that they are the exact same character, just written in different calligraphic styles. The meaning of the character 'wu' is no different from 'wang', just that there is a slight difference in literary flourish.

Conclusion

The *Admonitions* scroll is, without a doubt, an imperial palace painting from the Northern Wei period of Xiaowendi. That it cannot be attributed to Gu Kaizhi, however, is a great loss since it is the most highly commended of Gu Kaizhi's extant works and copies.

Since surviving literature from the Southern Dynasties is relatively plentiful, Chinese textbooks on painting history tend to expound in more detail about that period, neglecting other periods such as the Northern Dynasties (386–581), where few texts have survived. This painting will help to fill this void. It will also help to enrich our understanding of the historical significance of Xiaowendi's sinicization policy.

If accepted as a late Northern Wei painting, the *Admonitions* scroll will be only the third extant work – after the Palace Museum's *Pingfu tie* by the Western Jin calligrapher Lu Ji and *Boyuan tie* by the Eastern Jin calligrapher Wang Xun – to be acknowledged as from the Six Dynasties period. More importantly, it will be the first landscape painting from this early period.

Translated and abridged by Hiromi Kinoshita

NOTES

1   Tr. after Kohara 2000 (1967), p. 58, n. 6. This paper is an abridged translation of the Chinese original published in *Gugong Bowuyuan yuankan* (Palace Museum Journal) (Yang Xin 2001).
2   In the inscription on the painting, the character *fa* was incorrectly written as *hai* (line 38).
3   Chapter 1, section V 'On Mountains and Waters, Trees and Rocks' in *Lidai minghua ji*; tr. Acker 1954, p. 154.
4   '[Paintings of] *Vimalakirti, Heavenly Maidens* and *Flying Immortals* by Gu Kaizhi are in my collection. There is a horizontal scroll representing the *Admonitions of the Instructress to the Court Ladies* in Liu Youfang's collection ... In the *Veritable Records of [Song] Taizong (Taizong shilu)* it says: "I [the emperor] bought a scroll painted by Gu [Kaizhi]." Currently, there is a Tang copy of the *Biographies of Exemplary Women* painted by Gu in a literatus collection ...' (Mi Fu, *Hua shi* in *Meishu congshu* [*MSCS*], ser. 2, vol. 9, p. 4).
5   Ibid., p. 19.
6   Ibid., p. 17.
7   *Jin shu* 1930, *juan* 31, pp. 10a–11b.
8   During the Northern Wei, some members of the imperial harem suffered the consequences of a strict decree instigated by the politics of power. From the beginning of the dynasty, a harsh rule was implemented whereby 'when a member of the imperial harem gave birth to a son who was invested as Heir Apparent, his mother would have to die to ensure the future of the dynasty' (*Wei shu* 1930, *juan* 13, p. 5a). In this way, many empresses and imperial concubines were forced to commit suicide at a young age. The purpose of this rule was to eliminate the political influence of the future emperor's mother, thereby ensuring that the clan of a powerful consort did not become overly powerful. As a result,

many families were reluctant to offer their daughters to the imperial harem and the Northern Wei rulers sometimes had to take girls captive or take foreign brides.
9   *Wei shu* 1930, *juan* 13, p. 8b.
10 Wenley 1947, p. 6.
11 'Empress Wenming considered the emperor [Xiaowendi] too clever and in the future perhaps it would not benefit her, so she planned to have him dethroned. So in winter, wearing only a single layer of clothes, he was locked in a room, and starved for three days. She summoned the Prince of Xianyang to be installed...Officials first secretly concealed the emperor from the empress, the empress was enraged and beat the emperor several tens of strokes. The emperor suffered silently and did not complain.' (*Wei shu* 1930, *juan* 7 *xia*, pp. 34b–35a).
12 He drew praise from palace officials as he 'personally oversaw government affairs, could deal with countless matters in a day and in ten years he never had a break' (*Wei shu* 1930, *juan* 7 *xia*, p. 36b).
13 *Wei shu* 1930, *juan* 13, p. 16b.
14 See *Wei shu* 1930, *juan* 7 *xia*, p. 13b.
15 *Wei shu*, 1930, *juan* 93, p. 2b.
16 Literally 'posthumous and secret container of temperate brightness'; see Morohashi 1984, vol. 7, p. 17968.230.
17 *Wei shu* 1930, *juan* 93, p. 4b
18 *Wei shu* 1930, *juan* 7 *xia*, p. 35a.
19 Also, the 'shan' (mountain) radical written at the top of the character 'chong' (esteem, worship; eleventh column of text, second character) is written obliquely, as in the *Admonitions* calligraphy (e.g. 'family' scene, first column, fourth character). The 'chong' character in the extant Tang tracing copies of Wang Xizhi's *Orchid Pavilion Preface (Lanting xu)* is also like this.

Creating Ancestors

Audrey Spiro

I

The earliest-known mention of a scroll by Gu Kaizhi (c. 345–406) titled *Admonitions of the Instructress (Nüshi zhen)* appears in Mi Fu's (1052–1107/8) list of Jin dynasty paintings in *Hua shi (History of Painting)*. There it is said to be in a private collection.[1] The precise date for the composition of *Hua shi* is not known, but it had to be before Mi's death in 1107.

Not long thereafter a picture bearing the same title (format unspecified) was listed in the catalogue of the Northern Song (960–1127) imperial collection of paintings (*Xuanhe huapu*), the preface to which is dated 1120.[2] It is one of nine paintings attributed to the famous fourth- to fifth-century master; all nine are classified in the 'religious' (*daoshi*) section of the catalogue. Modern scholars have lamented the Song compilers' rule of only one category per painter, regardless of 'the fact that a number of artists produced more than one type of painting'.[3] The compilers may or may not have thought of a specific painter's oeuvre as separated into types, as we do; it is clear that this separation, if such it was, held no import for those charged with assembling the catalogue.

The category (that is, the genre) in which a painting is later classified, moreover, may have nothing to do with the way the painting was originally perceived by the maker and/or his audience. The acts of collecting and cataloguing inevitably redefine the genre. Although the categorizing of paintings burgeoned in the Song dynasty (960–1279), few uniformities of division or consolidation are discernible. Since genres and genre assignments affect our expectations and therefore our response to what we see, the question of Song classification has a bearing on the way we interpret the similarly named and attributed handscroll now in the British Museum.

We cannot know if the Museum's scroll is the one referred to in either or both Song dynasty texts noted above.

Nor can we know if the paintings referred to were authentic paintings (or even Tang dynasty [618–907] copies) of the early medieval period.[4] We can conclude, however, that Mi Fu and the compilers of the imperial catalogue had their own ideas about what a painting by Gu Kaizhi *should* look like, collecting, dealing, and discoursing on the basis of those ideas.[5]

I am not the first to suggest that this famous painting derives from a period considerably later than its putative date. In its present state, I contend, it is not a copy of an earlier painting, but an original painting by someone with sure knowledge of art of the early medieval period, if not specifically of the art of Gu Kaizhi, about whose work we also have no sure knowledge. So consistent with *attested* art of an earlier period is the painting, that its seemingly minor departures from that body of art now available to us are the evidence I will present to argue that it is a later painting, a parody of earlier art.

By definition, parody requires a pre-existent genre to play against. Without a concept of portraiture, for example, there can be no caricature. With that in mind, I shall briefly discuss the early medieval genre the present painting mocks; I will then note characteristics of the scroll demonstrably appropriate to art of that period and follow it with a discussion of some of its characteristics not found in early medieval art.

II

Although E. H. Gombrich (1909–2001) has argued that 'the first step on which everything else depends is the decision to which genre a given work is to be assigned',[6] logic suggests that, for the art historian, the first step on which all else depends must be to place the art object in time and space. If we know the genres of art prevalent in a given historical period, then the work of art in question must be seen to fit one of them; else it is likely to be dismissed as not appropriate to the period in question. Of course, there is the obverse danger of placing a painting in time and then determinedly shoehorning it into an existing genre. A problem with placement in time of the handscroll with which we are here concerned is that we do not know the painting genres of the Eastern Jin period (317–420). Genre theory is not the issue here; it is merely a question of how paintings were classified by makers and viewers. How, that is, did they perceive what they were doing?

It is useless for this purpose to turn to the earliest critical texts on painting in search of organizing principles. Lothar Ledderose, analysing early Chinese texts on painting, selected subject matter.[7] Although later texts might have enabled him to select other elements as the defining ones – ground, for example; format; site; purpose or function is another possibility – the earliest texts available to Ledderose (Xie He's [act. c. 479–502] and Yao Zui's [late sixth century]) restricted his choices considerably. Indeed, even there, subject matter is not mentioned in every instance (less than half the time by Yao Zui).[8] For the earlier periods, in fact, once we have made the generalization of figure painting (renwu) from the textual passages that mention subject matter, we are left with a generalization so broad as to be of little use except as a contrast to generalizations about later painting categories.

Judging from early texts, I would conclude that what mattered was function – exemplary, devotional, talismanic, commemorative, ceremonial, apotropaic; to delight, to terrify, to instruct, to punish, to appease, to heal, to legitimize. All these and more are discernible as functions of a single genre, figure painting. They are certainly not mutually exclusive; their complex permutations suggest that in this early period artists, artisans and audience saw these works in ways that do not readily fall into modern categories (as slippery as these also may be).

One example of categorizing by function includes depictions that today might be generically classified as portraiture, narrative or history – the Han dynasty (206 BCE–220 CE) evidence for interest in the depiction of filial, incorruptible, virtuous and wise mortals is incontestable. Textual evidence affirms the exemplary function of such art and further confirmation is found in the archaeological evidence. Art intended to promote emulation is also found in the period following the fall of the Han dynasty. Moreover, its subject matter expands. Therefore, a painting inscribed with an 'Admonitions' text by the third-century statesman and poet Zhang Hua (232–300) fits without blemish into a category of early art. What then of the painting itself?

Although much damaged and much repaired, the *Admonitions* scroll in its present state nevertheless conforms both broadly and in a surprising number of details to attested art of the period of Disunion (221–589) and even earlier. This conformity makes the anomalies all the more important for evaluation of the painting.

The format, for example, of a series of pictures or scenes accompanied by columns of brief text can be seen in Han art, for which the Wu shrine slabs serve as an obvious example.[9] In succeeding centuries, as new formats for pictorial narratives were introduced, these columns of text were often abandoned in favour of colophons, although wide frames that often separate individual scenes suggest that inscriptions may have been intended to accompany the events.

Although the *Admonitions* scroll is technically not a narrative, like many such it is indistinguishable in mode of presentation from narrative illustrations.[10] That is, function – in this case, rhetorical or hortatory – may determine the mode of depiction, regardless of 'genre' (i.e. 'narrative' or other).

Thus an excellent example for comparison with our scroll, and I shall revert to it more than once, is the well-known painted screen from the tomb of Sima Jinlong, dated to 484 CE. From the fragments remaining, it appears that the four-register format of picture plus text is an adaptation of the handscroll format (or vice versa) – see the four registers of a single panel of the Sima Jinlong screen in pls 16–19. Although no painted handscroll exists from this period, such sequences as the linear narratives on many tomb sarcophagi, for example, or the individual scenes from the life of the Buddha that wrap around the walls of Cave 6 at Yungang, also attest to its probable existence.[11]

As for the absence of setting and the emphasis on posture and gesture to establish spatial and psychological relationships between figures, we need only recall such Han dynasty paintings as the figures on the painted tiles now in Boston or those on the Lelang basket to conclude that the *Admonitions* scroll continues that early heritage – and in the same way as the pictures on the Sima Jinlong screen. This is not a format that disappears; it flourishes even in Buddhist narrative (fig. 1).

The material goods depicted in the scroll present no particular anomaly. The *chuang* or bed (pls 6–7), for example, has a long history,[12] while an engraving on a sarcophagus slab in Tenri University Museum confirms that the hinged screen and flat roof existed in Northern Wei (386–533) (fig. 2). The scroll's palanquin corresponds in precise detail to neither of the two known depictions of such vehicles from the early period. These two (from the Sima Jinlong screen [pl. 19] and a sixth-century Dengxian tile, respectively), however, are not identical, and there is no particular reason to doubt the authenticity of the scroll's depiction. Its flat canopy corre-

Fig. 1 Story of the Dīpaṅkara Buddha: cleaning the road (above) and the Bodhisattva teaching (below). Detail of a relief stele, 471 CE. The Xi'an Forest of Stone Tablets Museum.

Fig. 2 Detail of a rubbing from a stone relief sarcophagus. Northern Wei (386–533). Tenri University Museum, Nara. (After *MSQJ, Painting,* vol. 19.)

Fig. 3 Detail of a lacquer *pan* (basin). Tomb of Zhu Ran, 249 CE. Ma'anshan, Anhui Province. (After *Wenwu* 1986.3.)

sponds most closely to that of a wheeled carriage in a fourth-century tomb mural at Anak, Korea.[13]

The mirror-stand, like the cosmetic boxes accompanying it (pls 6, 8), also has its early examples. One is in the Field Museum in Chicago. Another is suggested by an iron dome-shaped base with an opening in the centre, excavated from a tomb in the north-east (Liaoning) datable to c. 415.[14] Since an iron mirror was also found in the tomb, the base is thought to have held its wood support. Even earlier is a predecessor to the *Admonitions* scene – a lacquer *pan* depicting a woman arranging her hair before a standing mirror was unearthed not long ago from a tomb datable to 249 CE (fig. 3). This miniature scene, far less sophisticated in its spatial organization than its descendant,[15] is nevertheless remarkable for the way the mirror is angled to display the daubs that represent the lady's reflection in the mirror.

As for that hallmark of Gu Kaizhi's art, the elegant lady of imperturbable mien, slender waist and ramrod back, of billowing hem and airy ribbons, I have elsewhere traced her rise to fame.[16] Here I shall briefly note that this noble creature appears on the scene no later than the mid-fourth century. By the fifth century she is all over the map (fig. 4), and by the sixth century she has achieved immortality (fig. 5). Those fluttering ribbons and undulating hems have become status markers, fit for only aristocrats and deities, wherever they may appear – in Buddhist art and most certainly in depictions of Confucian virtue (fig. 6, pl. 17). Style or fashion, in short, has become iconography.

Fig. 4 Donors. Detail of a line drawing of a mural, *c.*420 CE. North wall, Cave 169, Binglingsi, Gansu Province. (After *Heireiji sekkutsu*, Tokyo, 1986.)

Fig. 5 Devī from the *Vimalakīrtinirdeśa*. Detail of a mural. Northern Wei-Western Wei. Cave 127, Maijishan, Gansu. (After *MSQJ, Painting,* vol. 17.)

Fig. 6 'Story of Guo Ju' from 'Stories of Filial Piety'; (left) the wives of Shun. Detail of a rubbing from a stone relief sarcophagus, 62.2 × 223.5 cm. Northern Wei Dynasty (386–533). The Nelson-Atkins Museum of Art, Kansas City, Missouri (Purchase: Nelson Trust) 33-1543/1.

Fig. 7 'Ji of Wei Pleads with her Husband'. Detail of a rubbing from a stone relief tomb, late 2nd century CE. Yi'nan, Shandong. (After Zeng Zhaoyu *et al.* 1956.)

Fig. 8 Donor. Detail of a mural. Northern Wei (386–533). Cave 78, Maijishan, Gansu Province. (After *MSQJ, Painting,* vol. 17.)

It is therefore only to be expected that this epitome of decorous womanhood would figure in a Six Dynasties painting devoted to the illustration of proper behaviour for palace ladies. The evidence for paintings of *Virtue* – filial sons, exemplary wives, loyal ministers, faithful donors – is everywhere and uninterrupted from the Han dynasty on, donors being a post-Han innovation to the category.

It has been suggested that more than one genre of painting is apparent in the scroll.[17] The suggestion, however, is anachronistic in its assumptions. Although women are mentioned, for example by Xie He, there is nothing prior to the Tang dynasty to indicate that distinctions were made between exemplary women (*lienü*) and beautiful women (*meiren*) as subjects of painting. On the contrary, evidence suggests that, certainly by the fifth century, a new type of female exemplar was beginning to emerge, the worthy or the wise beauty (*xianyuan*), one who combined all the old Confucian virtues with a newly valued elegance and self-possession.[18] Note for example the youthful beauty of the virtuous mother of Qi, Yu's heir, in a scene formally close to one of the *Admonitions* scenes (pl. 14).

The earlier female exemplar can be seen on a relief from the late Han tomb at Yi'nan, where the virtuous Ji of Wei pleads with her husband, Duke Huan of Qi, to spare her father's state.[19] Shedding her jewels and loosening her girdle, her sashes and ribbons in disarray, the lady prostrates herself before her husband (fig. 7). Her successors, however, bred in a different climate, will present a new appearance. Regardless of provocation and however intense 'the mood of mourning and misfortune',[20] the aristocratic lady of Nanbeichao is not depicted prostrating herself and with loosened girdle. *Her* flying ribbons, whether intended as signs of physical motion, inner turmoil, or both, are carefully arranged, almost formalized, to reveal her elite status. So conventionalized are these adornments that their interpretation (motion, agitation, status, etc.) must rely solely on context. This, I would argue, is not an accident. The value of self-possession was of exceptional importance to Eastern Jin courtiers and to their descendants, as well. It is this grace under pressure that we see so clearly in the *Admonitions* scroll.

The scroll's male figures also conform to the period art, as demonstrated by the head of a male donor from Cave 78 at Maijishan, of likely Northern Wei date (fig. 8). The depiction of the male figure in the family scene of the scroll (pl. 9) is remarkably similar in outline to a kneeling figure (this one a woman) from the Sima Jinlong screen (pl. 18).

Fig. 9 'Seven Sages of the Bamboo Grove' (*Zhulin qixian*). Detail of a rubbing from a brick relief mural, *c.*5th century CE. Tomb at Xishanqiao, Nanjing. Provincial Museum, Nanjing.

Finally, I want to focus on the lone female figure to the right of the first inscription on the scroll (concerning the Lady Ban; pl. 2 left). Kohara Hironobu has convincingly demonstrated that the woman does not belong to the first scene. Arguing, however, against the suggestion that she stands in introspection (*kansan*), he rejects the notion that 'this [i.e. Eastern Jìn] was a world in which it was possible to occupy both these states (stillness [*sei*] and movement [*dō*]) at once'.[21] If by this Kohara means that he knows of no early composition that combines figures in action with figures in introspection, how would he characterize depictions of the Temptation of Śākyamuni by the Daughters of Māra? If, however, he is suggesting something of greater metaphysical (as well as psychological) import, as his language suggests, then I must also demur. We have only to remember the period of Division as the time of development of the concept of the recluse at court, one who remains in the world while emotionally withdrawing from it, to think that even here the scroll conforms to values and art of the period. This detail from a southern tomb is the evidence that movement and stillness can be combined in single images (fig. 9).

So much, then, for the authentically early characteristics of the *Admonitions* scroll. What are the characteristics that convince me it is of a later period?

III

Some anomalies, like the vermilion crescents on the women's foreheads that are known only from Tang times, or the 'shad-

ing' of the gauzy bedcurtains, are easily dismissed as later additions to a Nanbeichao original, of no great moment. Others, however, require more consideration, for they cannot readily have been added as afterthoughts or efforts at alteration. For example:

It is unnecessary to dwell at length on the oft-noted wit of the palanquin scene in which the lively, burlesqued porters, crowded and far too many for the vehicle, are a foil to the eye-contact between the dignified Lady Ban and her anguished (or perhaps merely astonished – note the raised eyebrows and open mouth) lord (pl. 4). Comparison with the same scene from the fifth-century lacquer screen drives home the differences between the two paintings. The screen's is a straightforward illustration of the lady's moral rectitude, which she, in her stance, retains in the scroll's depiction. In the latter, however, the ruler's expansive gesture of invitation is gone. By placing a beautiful lady at his side and altering his posture to a slight cringe, the artist compels the viewer to consider other possibilities for the open arms. The emperor may well be perturbed that Lady Ban has declined his invitation. On the other hand, he may be in anguish at having been caught out. Perhaps the antic movements of the porters are less exaggerated than they seem, since in this version quickstepping may be the better part of valour. The second figure in the palanquin may, of course, be a later addition to the scroll. However, Song dynasty copies of the *Nymph of the Luo River fu* also depict companions in the prince's vehicles. They are definitely female; they are not mentioned in Cao Zhi's *fu*.[22]

Consider the scene with a curtained bed (pls 6, 7). The

text reads, 'If the words that you utter are good, all men for a thousand leagues around will make response to you. But if you depart from this principle, even your bed-fellow will distrust you.' Arthur Waley's (1889-1966) comment that follows this translation, 'a very inadequate illustration to the text, but a most engaging design', is the key.[23] Zhang Hua's strictures may well refer to slander, but the visual composition implies that other activities may be at issue. The man, facing out but with his head turned towards the woman, sits on the bed. One leg is bent under him, a casual, relaxed posture. One slipper on the floor is thus unoccupied. A touch of delightful ambiguity is offered by the emperor's left foot, half in and half out of its slipper. Is the man coming or going? The object of his gaze sits erect against the lateral screen, her arm draped casually over its back. She is at ease as, her head fully raised, she meets the emperor's eyes directly. The emperor's hooded eyes and unsmiling face hint at sorrow (remorse?). But at what sorrow? Certainly, the lady's posture and open, direct gaze imply no shame, awkwardness, humility or other admission of transgression. The sorrow of longing or the sorrow of parting (perhaps both?) is a far likelier conclusion.

There are yet other elements of the scroll that suggest a later facture. For example, the Lady Ban, the Lady Feng, all the beauties are nearly identical (age indicated by hairstyle) save for their postures, the variations of which provide a liveliness, a veritable rhythm, to which the viewer responds. Otherwise, with faces all shaped alike, jewels alike, robes almost alike, ribbons curling and floating in the same way, we have the traditional, regulation Nanbeichao Beauty. I know of no early medieval work, regardless of format or site, in which all the females in the same composition are depicted in this uniform way. On the contrary, as I have noted, in these authentic early works the ribbons are clear status markers, separating the wearer from other figures (fig. 6).

There is another significant difference between the scroll and its predecessors. In every scene of the scroll it is possible to rationalize the presence of the floating ribbons, regardless of artistic intent. The pair of beauties hurry towards the preceptress, their lightweight garments appropriately floating as they sail (pl. 12 left); the charming beauty sinks to her knees, having just rushed in from the hall (pl. 12 right). And of course, in that most poignant of scenes, 'No one can endlessly please', the floating ribbons are the response to the emperor's apotropaic stance and gesture (pls 9, 10). The poor lady has rushed to approach him; she is quickly checked by the upraised, open hand confronting her. So quickly does she come to a halt that all her draperies whoosh behind her in echoing agitation. And so on. This rationality, it seems to me, fits with all we know of later painting – as we can observe the

effects of time and weather on the mountain in Song monumental landscape painting, so also we can observe the effect of movement on lightweight draperies in the figure paintings.[24]

I admit to a difficulty in rationalizing the male's floating ribbons in the family scene (pl. 9), which are so similar in placement to those of the seated woman on the lacquer screen. Perhaps he has just rushed in; perhaps they express his desire to get away, for a more miserable-looking group is rarely seen. Redrawn or not, the scene is surely another in the category of irony, although I cannot deny that examining the child for lice also qualifies as a scene of everyday life (for which, see below). Parenthetically, I can think of no other example like the compositional arrangement of this scene. The triangular, 'mountain' formation is unusual.

Short of a total reworking of an earlier scroll via a restoration process, the anomalies I have noted are unlikely to be the result of conservation efforts – that is, of serious efforts to reconstruct the painting as it might have been originally. Were it a matter of 'improving' on the original, surely it would have been easier – far less work than patching silk – to start afresh?[25]

In its present state the Admonitions scroll is a parody, a work that imitates the distinctive style and thought of another work of art, artist, or tradition for satiric or comic effect.[26] I am aware that there is no textual evidence for a painting genre of parody. Nor does there seem to have been a separate category in literature for the phenomenon, although it was presumably subsumed under such ideas of indirect remonstration as fengjian or fengci. In Western terminology, the intent of parody, like caricature, is satirical, often savage in its snap; just as often, however, its bite is gentler – a humorous, sometimes even affectionate, nibble often referred to as pastiche. It is in this latter sense that, on the basis of features not observable in extant art of the medieval period, I characterize the scroll as a parody. On the basis of these anomalies, I conclude that the British Museum painting is not a painting of the early medieval period; nor is it a copy of a painting of that period. It is an original painting that gently mocks the past, perhaps to comment on the present. It is possible that it was intended as a forgery, although the parodic effect suggests otherwise; it is more likely that it was intended to amuse, maybe even to alert, an audience knowledgeable about past art – and clearly male.

Kohara Hironobu classifies the scroll as a (copy of) a Nanbeichao genre painting (manners and customs; fūzokuga; fengsuhua).[27] He does so because of the anomalies he perceives and, I presume, because a concept of genre painting is found in Chinese texts – not, however, in those of Nanbeichao (it is known in Chinese literature, of course, as early as the Han dynasty). It is on the basis of some of the same anomalies that I conclude that the painting does not date from early medieval times and label it with a term I cannot find in the literature on painting, but which I shall try to substantiate with a body of visual material. I fully concur with Quitman E. Phillips's insight that the categories meaningful to literary men probably differed considerably from those of practising painters, particularly when the two came from separate social groups.[28] There can be no question that in later periods of Chinese painting, the separate social groups being sometimes one, the critical discourses of those learned men had exceptional influence on the practice of painting. This was certainly not the case for early medieval China, nor was it for the Song, the period when, as noted, categorizing of paintings proliferated.

'Paintings of customs and manners' are mentioned by Zhu Jingxuan in his ninth-century *Celebrated Painters of the Tang Dynasty (Tangchao minghua lu)* without further discussion.[29] It is not clear whether this phrase is the title of a painting[30] or a subject-matter category, since Zhu does not include it in his list of painting categories in his introduction. Similarly, Guo Ruoxu (act. 1070–after 1080) mentions four *fengsu* paintings, two of them dating, incidentally, from the fifth century. Although the titles are certainly suggestive, he fails to describe them, and with good reason: 'It is only my fondness for their fine titles that has [led to their inclusion here].'[31] Nor does the *Xuanhe huapu* include a category for genre paintings, which may mean only that none such was in the palace collection or that they were differentially classified.

All those Han dynasty scenes of spinning, farming, cooking, feasting, etc., can certainly be seen in some sense as depictions of customs and manners. In the following period, there are just as certainly scenes we may characterize similarly (fig. 2). The genre interest, however, was subsidiary to other, more significant functions served by the depictions. They were not there, that is, because of any social, political or humanitarian interest in viewing the life of the masses. On the other hand, the Song dynasty interest in scenes of everyday life as such is well documented, both textually and visually.

A group of paintings, many of controversial date, suggests that historical events of the tenth century were key to the production of many varieties of what Jerome Silbergeld refers to as anomalous painting, 'some of it helping to change future trends, some of it falling by the wayside in terms of historical influence'.[32] I propose that this tenth- to early eleventh-century period is where we may locate a rising interest in humorous paintings of various kinds, including that of parody.

Take, for example, the painting known as the *Palace Concert* or *Palace Ladies Drinking* and dated by various schol-

Fig. 10 *Ladies Playing Double Sixes.* Detail of a handscroll; ink and colour on silk, 30.7 × 64.4 cm. Freer Gallery of Art, Smithsonian Institution, Washington, DC: Purchase F1939.37.

ars anywhere from the eighth to the eleventh century.[33] This painting, little different in format from the Tang feasting scenes in tombs and religious art, has the quality that sets it apart from these earlier depictions – it is droll. Another example, I suggest, is the Freer Gallery's painting in the 'style of Zhou Fang', the tenth- to eleventh-century handscroll known as *Ladies Playing Double-Sixes* (fig. 10). Or that masterpiece of 'poignant *ennui*'[34] after Zhou Fang (act. 780–804, although on the other hand it might also be after Zhang Xuan, mid-eighth century), the painting now in the Nelson-Atkins Museum in Kansas City and known as *Tuning the Lute, Listening to Music, Turning the Lute and Drinking Tea*, etc. In composition – roughly one tree, one figure, absence of background, etc. – it harks back to Tang and pre-Tang tomb murals (figs 9, 11). The zigzag arrangement of the figures, however, is not known. Moreover, the focus on the *qin*, that hallmark of cultivated gentlemen, suggests this is no ordinary painting of palace ladies (fig. 12). The hint of gentle mockery

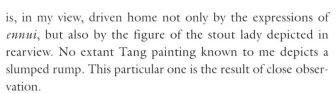

is, in my view, driven home not only by the expressions of *ennui*, but also by the figure of the stout lady depicted in rearview. No extant Tang painting known to me depicts a slumped rump. This particular one is the result of close observation.

In its present state the *Admonitions* scroll is an erotic painting. By erotic, I merely mean amatory, having to do with desire. The scroll, after all, is supposedly about the harem.

Mildly erotic paintings are known to us from the Song dynasty. Erotic art undoubtedly existed earlier, as did art of a more explicit nature. *Witty* eroticism, however, seems, on the basis of visual remains, to have been essentially a Song phenomenon. Consider, for instance, that most delightful example of sophisticated erotica, *Night Revels of Han Xizai*. Erotic interaction is evoked in this complex painting in many ways, but among the most important and subtle are eye contact and √

Fig. 11 (above left) 'Tuning the Lute'. Detail of a mural. Tang dynasty (618–907). Tomb at Nanliwang, Shaanxi Province. (After *MSQJ, Painting* vol. 12.)

Fig. 13 (above) *Night Revels of Han Xizai (Han Xizai yeyan tu)*. Detail of a handscroll; ink and colour on silk, 28.7 × 335.5 cm. Palace Museum, Beijing. (After *MSQJ, Painting*, vol. 2.)

Fig. 12 Copy after Zhou Fang (act. 780–804), *Palace Ladies Tuning the Lute (Gongji tiaoqin tu)*. 12th-century copy of a Tang (618–907) original. Handscroll; ink and colour on silk, 27.9 × 75.3 cm. The Nelson-Atkins Museum of Art, Kansas City, Missouri (Purchase: Nelson Trust) 32-159/2.

Fig. 14 *Night Revels of Han Xizai*. Detail of a handscroll; ink and colour on silk, 28.7 × 335.5 cm. Palace Museum, Beijing. (After *MSQJ, Painting*, vol. 2.)

Fig. 15 'Immortal with Herb of Immortality'. Detail of a rubbing from a stone relief tomb. Eastern Han (25–220). Suining County, Jiangsu Province. (After *Jiangsu Xuzhou Han huaxiangshi*.)

direction of gaze.[35] In the first scene, the gaze of most figures (the exceptions are not without interest) is not on the seated female performer, but on the negotiation between her and a male guest – a negotiation conducted primarily by eye contact (fig. 13).

Wu Hung has adroitly isolated a number of other pictorial devices that 'encourage the viewer to keep unrolling the painting, exploring the increasingly erotic images as he travels deeper inside' the mansion.[36] Comparing the scroll's ending with the *Admonitions'*, Wu emphasizes the similarities of the two handscrolls and their sophistication in holding the viewer's attention. Equally important here in enticing the viewer is certainly the activity implied by any number of complex negotiations within the scroll conveyed almost solely by eye contact. See, for example, the exchange between Han Xizai, undraped and seated on his chair, and a flautist – or is it two flautists? Look, too, at the exchange between the monk and the seated male (fig. 14).

This emphasis on gaze and glance seems to play a considerable role in Song figure painting in general. It is not only the varied groupings, but also the varied directions of glance and gaze of the figures that reward our close attention in the dispersed fragments known as *Ladies of the Court*, said to be a Song painting after Zhou Wenju (tenth century). A few examples of Southern Song (1127–1279) paintings in which the direction of gaze seems especially important to interpretation

are Ma Yuan's (act. *c.* 1190–1230) *On a Mountain Path in Spring* for decorum, Ma Lin's (*c.* 1180–after 1256) *Listening to the Wind in the Pines* for sly eroticism, Li Song's (1166–1243) *Knick-Knack Peddler* for apprehension, rage and an urge to mayhem.[37] Chinese art has always shown a regard for many kinds of visual wit (fig. 15), but the use of vision itself as a means of expression seems to be a Song phenomenon.[38]

My discussion has been based on the *Admonitions* scroll in its present state, text and illustration accompanying each other. It has long been noted that Zhang Hua's text bears little relation to the imagery of the scroll. If the painting were in fact a Six Dynasties creation, an important anomaly would be the style of the calligraphy, said to be of Tang provenance.[39] Their encroachment on the painting in several places, moreover, suggests that the inscriptions were not applied at the date of painting. Because of its peculiar placement in scene two, Kohara has argued that the text must have been added following the construction of the Palace of Sagacious Contemplation in 1075.[40] If so, the 'Tang style' calligraphy may have been intended as part of the antique flavour, the texts an enhancement of the ironies already present in the painting. Why it would be added at a later date is unclear. If, as another possibility, the intent was to lend respectability to a seemingly indecorous painting, it, like the rationalization proposed for *Night Revels* (Wu Hung's Creation Myth), does not succeed.[41] If Kohara's hypothesis is correct, then the scroll must date from before 1075.[42]

Patricia Ebrey has discussed the views of Sima Guang (1019–1086) regarding the education of women. At the age of nine, in addition to the *Analects* and the *Classic of Filial Piety*, girls should have the *Biographies of Exemplary Women (Lienü zhuan)* as well as Ban Zhao's *Admonitions for Women (Nü jie)* explained to them.[43] The issuance in the eleventh century of new editions of Liu Xiang's *Biographies* suggests a connection to Sima's dicta and a renewed interest in the subject.[44] It seems very likely that a number of illustrated and pictorial versions appeared as a consequence; at least one, with a preface dated 1036, claimed illustrations by Gu Kaizhi.[45] A handscroll with a similar title, now in the Palace Museum and said to be a Song copy of an original by Gu Kaizhi, has much in common with the *Admonitions* scroll (pls 29–30).[46] It is similar in composition, in delineation of its figures, in its multitude of flying ribbons. What it is not is a parody. The *Admonitions* scroll may well have been painted as a reaction to a host of repetitious, visually boring (albeit historically important) paintings.

A parody does not lack for conviction. Its creator is attacking either the values it mocks or the hypocrisy of those who parade those values. There is nothing in the *Admonitions* scroll to suggest that the parodist rejects the tradition of Ban Zhao, Zhang Hua, *et al.* Indeed, it may even be that exhortation was his intent, much as theatre (*zaju*) of the period is said to have shrouded criticism in the veil of comedy. 'Even when done in front of the emperor it brings no chastisement or punishment, for in an instant they [the performers] bring a smile to the sage's face.'[47]

I can no more prove that the *Admonitions* scroll is a product of the Song dynasty than I can prove it dates from any other. Short of new technology we can but search for plausibilities. The wit and delicacy with which the artist has manipulated old compositional and stylistic techniques, and without exaggeration (that is, without caricature), for any or all of several possible motives, is deserving of utmost admiration. The painting is a worthy homage to the past, and more.

NOTES

1   Mi Fu 1992–, vol. 1, p. 978.
2   *Xuanhe huapu* 1992–, vol. 2, p. 63.
3   Lovell 1973, p. 7.
4   The following comprehensive terms are here used interchangeably to include the dynastic periods from the late third century to the establishment of the Sui dynasty in the sixth century, regardless of technical distinctions: Nanbeichao (Northern and Southern Dynasties), early medieval China, period of Division, period of Disunion, Six Dynasties.
5   Zürcher 1955; Yang Xin 1989.
6   Gombrich, 'Aims and limits of iconology', 1972, pp. 1–22 (p. 21).
7   Ledderose 1973, p. 73.
8   The categorizing principle for both essayists, clearly, was not genre, nor even 'motif-level subject matter' (Murray 1998, p. 613); rather, it was quality.
9   Wu Hung 1989.
10   Murray 1998, pp. 608–609, 611–613.
11   Murray 1995; Chen Pao-chen 1995.

12   Chen Zengbi 1979; Handler 1992, 1993.
13   Chhae 1959, fig. 6.
14   Li Yaobo 1973, pp. 11, 23, figs 38, 39.
15   Wu 1994a, pp. 76ff.
16   Spiro 2003. The firm, tense, continuous outline strokes of the *Admonitions* figures are also attested by extant Nanbeichao art, as are the red inner contour strokes of some of the figures.
17   Kohara 1967, pt. 1, p. 20; 2000 (1967), p. 10.
18   Spade 1979; Nanxiu Qian 2003; Spiro 2003.
19   Zeng Zhaoyu *et al.* 1956, pp. 23, 39, pl. 53; Thompson 1998, pp. 348ff, figs A.3, 4.
20   O'Hara 1971, p. 51.
21   Kohara 1967, pt. 1, pp. 29ff; 2000 (1967), pp. 30–31.
22   On the highly relevant and vexatious issue of copies of paintings, see, e.g., Harrist 1999; Goodman 1983, esp. p. 100; Noel 1995.
23   Waley 1923, p. 51; also Kohara 1967, pt. 1, p. 20; 2000 (1967), p. 11.
24   In a similar vein, the floating ribbons of the goddesses of the Song dynasty Luo scrolls are entirely rational – the lady sails on water.

25   For the condition of the scroll, see Waley 1923.

26   Preminger & Brogan 1993, *s.v.*, adapted.

27   Kohara 1967, pt. 1, pp. 21–22; 2000 (1967), pp. 13–14.

28   Murray 1998, p. 614, n. 23.

29   Zhu Jingxuan 1992–, vol. 1, p. 167; Soper 1958, p. 206.

30   Yu Jianhua 1986, vol. 1, p. 22.

31   Soper 1951, p. 10.

32   Silbergeld 1999, p. 164.

33   Hearn & Fong 1999, p. 67; Cahill 1980, p. 53.

34   Lawton 1973, p. 202.

35   By gaze I refer specifically to the figures in the painting and their gazing at each other. For the viewer's gaze re this scroll, see Wu Hung 1996a, pp. 67–81 esp.; 1996b, pp. 321–324.

36   Wu Hung 1996a, p. 68.

37   All three versions are in the National Palace Museum, Taipei.

38   Save for the painting of two men in earnest conversation on a Han dynasty tile in the Museum of Fine Arts, Boston, I know of no paintings prior to the Song dynasty wherein eye contact plays such an important part in suggesting the relationship between the two figures.

39   Waley 1923, p. 52.

40   Kohara 1967, pt. 1, pp. 26ff; 2000 (1967), pp. 27, 31.

41   Wu Hung 1996a, p. 71.

42   Suzanne Cahill (personal communication) has suggested that the combination of earlier elements, the Nanbeichao painting style with Tang-style calligraphy, may be another indication of the scroll's late date – 'the best' calligraphy style paired with 'the best' figure-painting style.

43   Ebrey 1992, p. 652; see also Davis 2001.

44   O'Hara 1971, p. 10.

45   Carlitz 1991, p. 138, n. 48; Raphals 1998, Appendix 4.

46   *MSQJ, Painting*, vol. 1, pl. 94.

47   West 1977, pp. 7–8; see also Otto 2001.

66

Plates 1–13 Scenes from the *Admonitions of the Instructress to the Court Ladies (Nüshi zhen tu)*, painting attributed to Gu Kaizhi (*c*.345–406). Handscroll mounted on a panel; ink and colour on silk, 25 × 348.5 cm. Trustees of the British Museum (OA 1903.4-8.1 Chinese Painting 1).

Plate 1 (*previous page*) Detail of pl. 2.

Plate 2 Scene 1 – Lady Feng protects the Han emperor Yuandi (r. 48–33 BCE) from the advance of a wild bear.

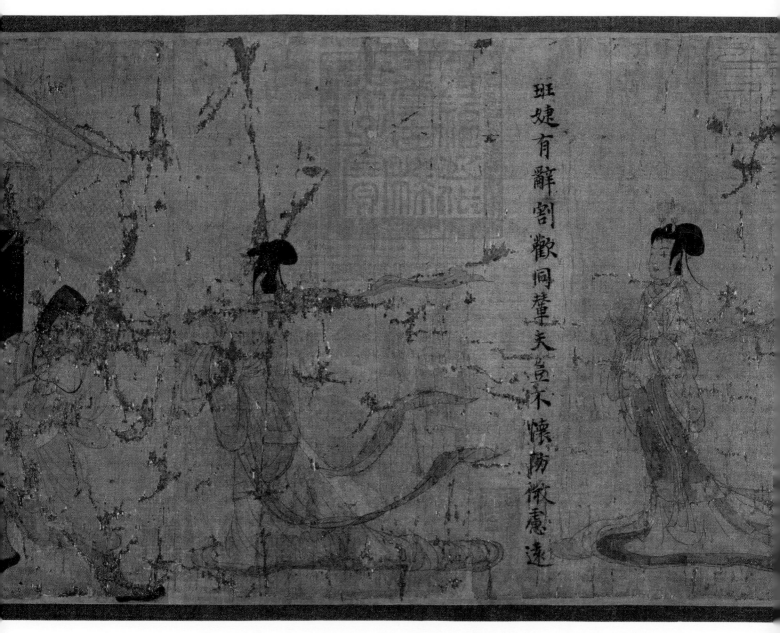

班婕有辭割歡同輦夫豈不懷防微慮遠

Plate 3 Scene 2 – Lady Ban declines to ride with the Han emperor Chengdi (r. 33–7 BCE) in the imperial palanquin.

Plate 4 *(following page)* Detail of pl. 3.

人咸知飾其容莫知飾其性
不飾或愆禮正斧之漆之克念作
聖

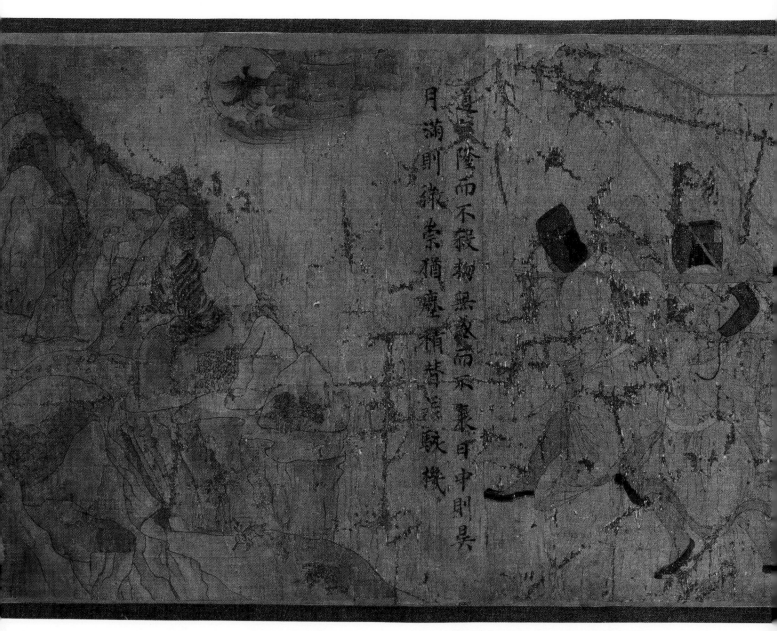

道具隆而不殺物無故而不衰日中則昃
月滿則徙崇猶塵積替若駭機

Plate 5 Scene 3 – an archer readies himself to shoot a tiger.

夫言如微　榮辱由茲　勿謂玄漠　靈鑒無象
勿謂幽昧　神聽無響　無矜爾榮　天道惡盈
無恃爾貴　隆隆者墜　鑒于小星　戒彼攸遂
比心螽斯　則繁爾類

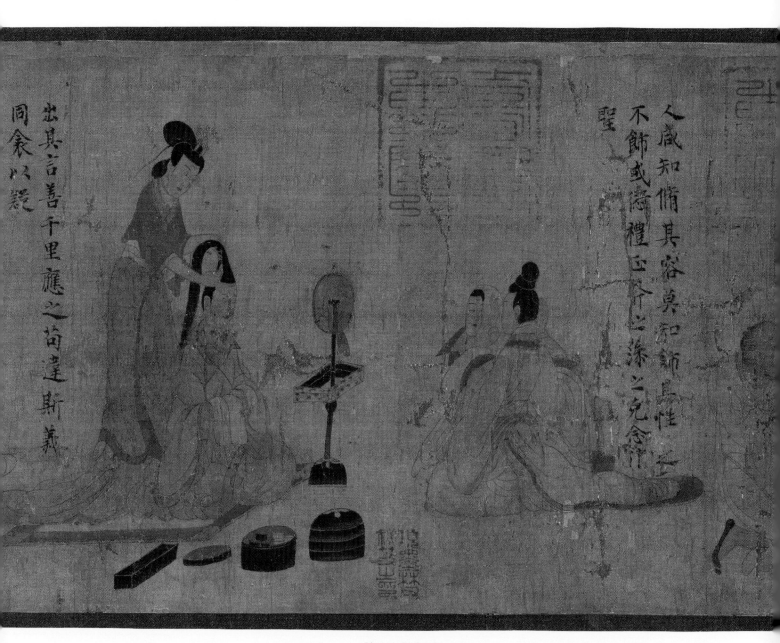

Plate 6 Right: Scene 4 – two court ladies admire themselves (the toilette scene).
Left: Scene 5 – a man and a woman in bed regard one another with suspicion (the bedroom scene).

Plate 7 *(following page)* Detail of pl. 6 left.

78

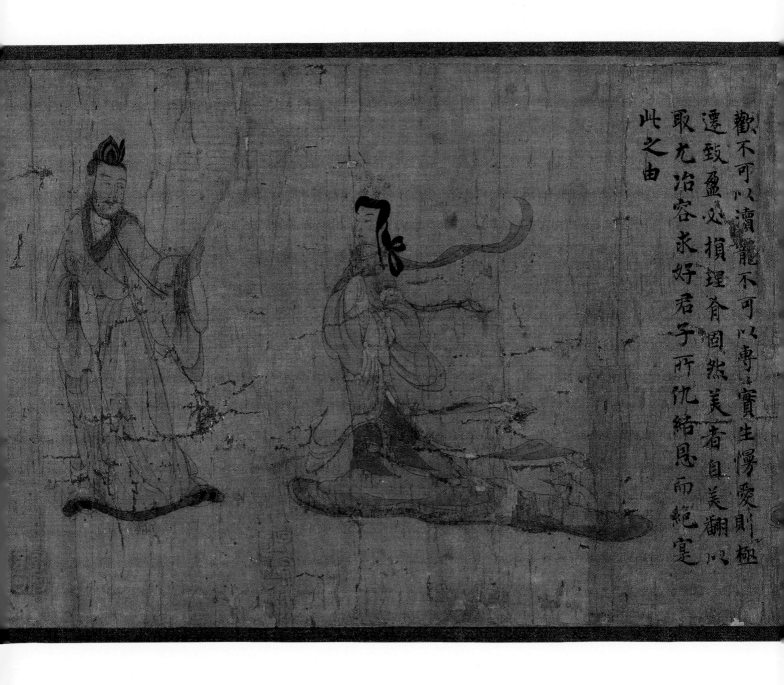

歡不可以瀆寵不可以專實生慢愛則極
遷致盈必損理之固然美者自美翻以
取尤冶容求好君子所仇結恩而絕寔
此之由

Plate 8 *(previous page)* Detail of pl. 6 right.

夫言如微榮辱由茲勿謂玄漠靈鑒無象
勿謂幽昧神聽無響無矜爾榮天道惡
盈無恃爾貴隆隆者墜鑒于小星戒彼彼
逐化心鑒斯則繁爾類

Plate 9 Right: Scene 6 – three generations of a family gather together (the family scene).
Left: Scene 7 – an emperor rebuffs a fawning beauty (the rejection scene).

Plate 10 *(following page)* Detail of pl. 9 left.

82

Plate 11 *(previous page)* Detail of pl. 9 right.

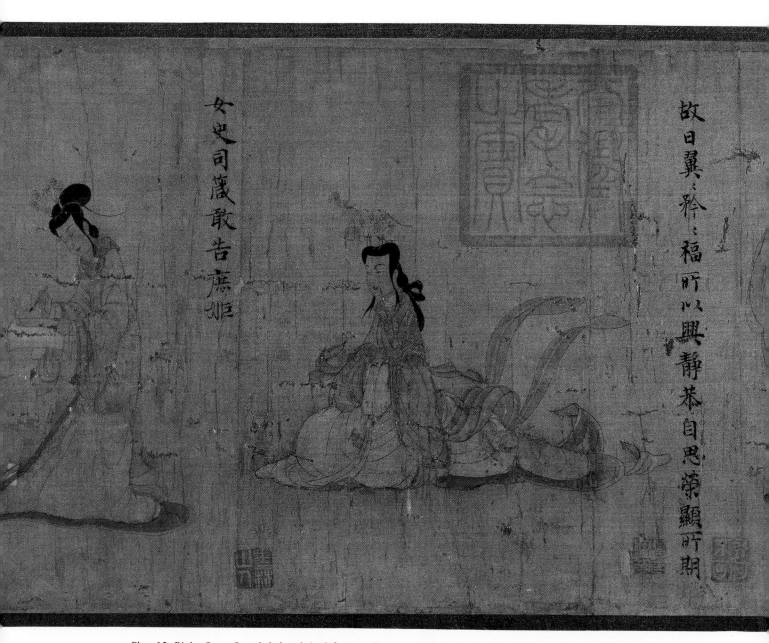

女史司箴敢告庶姬

故曰翼翼矜矜福所以興靜恭自思榮顯所期

Plate 12 Right: Scene 8 – a lady kneels in deference. Centre and left: Scene 9 – the court instructress copies out the 'admonitions'.

Plate 13 *(following page)* Detail of pl. 12 centre.

Concerning the Date and Authorship of the *Admonitions* Handscroll

Richard M. Barnhart

In a wide-ranging keynote address (Introduction, pp. 18–40) Wen Fong suggests that the author of the *Admonitions* scroll attributed to Gu Kaizhi (*c.* 345–406) was an unknown artist at a southern Chinese court in Nanjing around the end of the sixth century, long after the death of Gu Kaizhi and shortly before the Sui dynasty (581–618) was established. The famous scroll is described as a copy of an earlier work combining the art of Gu Kaizhi with elements associated with the leading Liang (502–556) court painter Zhang Sengyou. As to the essential historical character of the scroll, Fong notes, 'It is a work that could prove pivotal as a guide to late sixth-century Southern Chinese court painting.' The *Admonitions* in this view thus remains closely connected to Gu Kaizhi, Lu Tanwei (act. *c.* 465–472) and Zhang Sengyou, the great southern masters of the Six Dynasties period (265–589), and is understood to be physically a product of the late Six Dynasties period.

Yang Xin's understanding of the historical position of the painting differs slightly, but is not far from that of Wen Fong. Yang also regards the scroll as an anonymous product of the Six Dynasties period, but one made in the north and, specifically, at the Northern Wei (386–533) court at Luoyang. He further suggests that the scroll is a reflection of Emperor Xiaowendi's (r. 471–499) national campaign of promulgating Chinese language, art and culture throughout the Northern Wei realm. Although somewhat earlier than Fong's late sixth century date, perhaps by half a century, there is still much harmony here with Wen Fong's view. Both scholars find evidence in the *Admonitions* for the preservation of a classic Six Dynasties style of figure painting, and agree on a date of manufacture of roughly the sixth century. Both scholars also date the calligraphy, which may not be contemporary with the painting, to the sixth century.

Reasoned, balanced assessments from two leading authorities on Chinese painting, these are very welcome con-tributions to our understanding of a major monument. The relatively slight differences between the two only serve to emphasize a fact that I wish also to emphasize, and that is the limitations within which any historical assessment of the *Admonitions* must evolve: there is simply not enough evidence of any kind to prove or disprove the possibility either that the scroll was made in Luoyang in the early sixth century, such as Yang Xin proposes, or that it was made in Nanjing in the late sixth century, as Wen Fong suggests. Both are viable theories. And even they may provide too narrow a difference to indicate the actual parameters of the limitations that the available evidence places on our studies.

Yang Xin departs from most earlier scholarship known to me in suggesting that the *Admonitions* is not a copy of an earlier work at all, as almost all writers have generally assumed, but is an original painting, and, indeed, is the earliest such original painting extant. And – despite many fundamental differences with Fong and Yang – Audrey Spiro too argues that the *Admonitions* is not a copy: '[I]t is not a copy of an earlier painting, but an original painting by someone with a sure knowledge of art of the early medieval period', she observes.

In my personal commentary on these and other papers presented at the London conference let me note first that I agree with the view that the *Admonitions* gives little evidence of being a copy, although it can be very clearly shown to be based closely upon the practice of pictorial narrative maintained and developed by Gu Kaizhi's predecessors. The *Admonitions* bears none of the signs that are generally regarded as distinguishing a copy from an original painting, as Yang Xin notes. Against this new suggestion is summoned the prevailing view that the painting is a copy of the Sui or Tang (618–907) period, an assessment made on the basis of evidence of the kind presented in earlier publications by Kohara and in London by Chen Pao-chen.[1] In this widely accepted view it is held that 'incorrect' drawing of such elements as the canopy of the royal palanquin or the knots of the scarves worn by the elegant women of the scroll proves that the *Admonitions* is a copy. This argument is especially ironic in light of the fact that this supposed 'incorrectness' of drawing is established by comparison with works that are themselves in fact known and undoubted copies, works such as the Southern Song (1127–1279) *baimiao* copy in Beijing or the Sima Jinlong lacquer screen panels (before 484 CE), both of which are perfect revelations of the nature of copies and their characteristics. In these copies all 'mistakes' are corrected. This kind of comparison should therefore establish – if anything – that it is the copies that correct mistakes, leaving unresolved the question of what such 'mistakes' of drawing may mean in original works of art.

In fact, we have no reason at all to assume that Gu Kaizhi cared deeply about 'correct' representation of such things as beds or carriages, subjects which he himself noted held no interest for him. What concerned him was the quality of human spirit and personality revealed by social and human interactions among men and women, and the qualities of humanness and individual character and personality that he found in the painting of his teacher Wei Xie (mid-third to mid-fourth century), for example, and wanted to emulate. These are the qualities that distinguish the *Admonitions* most tellingly from all other Chinese paintings, and they are qualities that have nothing to do with realistic or 'correct' drawing, nothing to do with canopies or beds or even human anatomy. Wang Hui (1632–1717) repeatedly 'corrected' and improved Huang Gongwang's (1269–1354) *Dwelling in the Fuchun Mountains* scroll in Taipei, and the unknown Song copyist of the *baimiao* version of the *Admonitions* 'corrected' the London scroll. If that kind of correctness tells us anything at all about works of art it is that we need to look elsewhere for their essential historical qualities.

What can be said of the comparative visual material available to all of us is that there are intimate connections of many kinds between the *Admonitions* and the pictorial art of the Six Dynasties as we can otherwise know it, and no visible connection between the *Admonitions* and any post-Six Dynasties evidence. Much of the earlier material is associated with the Northern Wei, but evidence of any kind for the Southern Dynasties is extremely rare, and the sum total of available evidence is inadequate to evaluate more precisely the *Admonitions* on such a comparative basis. Placing the *Admonitions* somewhere within the span of the long and geographically wide Six Dynasties period clearly seems to me appropriate.

It is much easier to disprove the view that the *Admonitions* was manufactured anytime after the Six Dynasties. A Five Dynasties (907–959) or Song (960–1279) date has some-

times been suggested, and it was again at the London conference. But we have many Song paintings, far more than we have for all earlier painting together. We have, for example, Song copies of paintings attributed to Gu Kaizhi himself – several versions of the *Nymph of the Luo River*, perhaps the section of *Biographies of Exemplary Women* preserved in Beijing, even what is generally thought to be a Song copy of the *Admonitions* (the painting in Beijing). And we have deliberately classicizing paintings by distinguished artists such as Li Gonglin (c.1041–1106), including his *Classic of Filial Piety* (Metropolitan Museum), that actually emulate the art of Gu Kaizhi, among others.[2] It is unlikely that any Song artist knew more about Gu Kaizhi than Li Gonglin and the members of his circle such as Mi Fu (1051–1107), and there is no possibility, in my opinion, that Li could have made such a painting as the *Admonitions*. No Song painting known to me bears more than the most superficial resemblance in any particular aspect to the *Admonitions*.

And there are no Song parodies in existence of the kind recognized in the *Admonitions* by Dr Spiro. Such a parody would be as rare in the Song as it is in the Six Dynasties. To me, therefore, it is clear from the complete absence of evidence from a richly represented period that the *Admonitions* was not painted during the Five Dynasties or the Song period. Some details of repair and repainting were probably added over the course of the Song when the scroll was owned by the imperial court, but the painting was already ancient by that time.

By now too the Sui-Tang period is richly mapped and ordered by a dense sequence of wall paintings from Xi'an to Dunhuang, and nothing like the *Admonitions* has turned up anywhere, leaving its only physical, historical corollaries to be found in the period of Han (206 BCE–220 CE) to Wei.

Dr Spiro has offered a perceptive analysis of the relationship of these elements of style, composition and motif in the *Admonitions* to other art of the time. And I do want to express my complete agreement with nearly everything she has written about the visual qualities of the scroll, including her concept of parody, or ironic commentary as she finds it in the *Admonitions*, and with her description of the scroll as erotic in content. The *Admonitions* is surely a parody of court morality and of standard depictions of didactic subjects – and this parodic quality argues strongly against the kind of specific court sponsorship suggested by Yang Xin. Desire is surely a scarcely concealed subtext of the painting. The *Admonitions* presents a picture of female beauty, selflessness, virtue and desirability that only heightens by contrast the generally undistinguished self-satisfied male image the scroll offers. And as Audrey Spiro demonstrates, the painter gives us an entirely

Fig. 1. A woman at her toilet, from the *Admonitions* scroll in the British Museum.

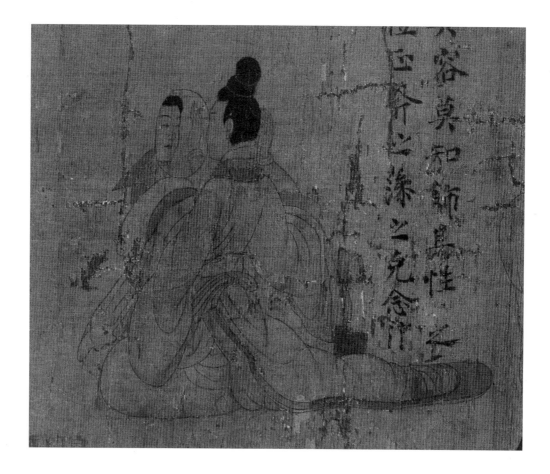

original reading and interpretation of Zhang Hua's (232–300) didactic text, creating the most striking image in all of Chinese art of the manifest virtues of women, and does this with wit, irony and humour (fig. 1).

It is also Audrey Spiro who notes in another insight I admire that the nearest equivalent to the sense of shared intimacy and human communication seen everywhere in the *Admonitions* is in the Boston Museum of Fine Arts' painted Han pediment, a work that also provides for me the nearest formal and stylistic equivalent for the *Admonitions*. Indeed, to me it is most striking that it is examples of Han art such as the Boston tomb tiles, the central, portrait level of the Feiyi from Mawangdui (second century BCE), the Wu Liang Shrine engravings in Shandong (second century CE), and the lacquer frieze of filial sons on the Lelang basket that suggest the simple and direct human interchange and limited compositional arrangements that we find in the *Admonitions*. Only nuances of representation and interaction and a fine elegance of line and gesture might indicate that centuries have passed between Western Han (206 BCE–9 CE) and the *Admonitions*. Clearly the painter of the *Admonitions* rooted his art in the immediate past, and perhaps if we attended more to these ear-

lier sources of the *Admonitions* rather than its later echoes we would see more clearly its historical position.

The *Seven Sages* from Xishanqiao in the vicinity of Nanjing of around 400, perhaps during the lifetime of Gu Kaizhi, suggest in somewhat crude form the level of individual characterization and nuance of representation that had become possible by the time of Gu Kaizhi; and the lacquer screen from Sima Jinlong's tomb, painted sometime before 484, in still cruder form contains so many obvious reflections of the style and subject matter of the *Admonitions* in debased form as to make intimate connections between them necessary. And this group of works defines the broad context within which the *Admonitions* takes its place most obviously.

By the time the Nelson-Atkins sarcophagus was made in the early sixth century the style of the *Admonitions* was already a fixed trope frozen into formulaic convention, like the later copies of the *Nymph of the Luo River*. And when we arrive at the wall paintings from the Lou Rui tomb and elsewhere in the Northern Qi (550–577) and Northern Zhou (557–580) periods we are at the end of the range of possibilities for the age of the *Admonitions*, in which, by contrast, nothing of this volumetric, Western-influenced figure style of the mid-sixth century can be found. Or, at least, I can see none of it in the *Admonitions*. What I want to suggest is that there is nothing in any of these or other known monuments of the time to suggest that the *Admonitions* must be dated to any later than the lifetime of Gu Kaizhi.

It then becomes truly only a small step, as Yang Xin noted, to re-establishing direct connections to that most foolish and romantic of painters, Gu Kaizhi, virtually the only traditional Chinese painter known to me whose love life and affection for jokes and humour is the very substance of his biography. The *Admonitions* is a romantic, erotic, humorous and deeply human work of art, rooted solidly in the art of the preceding Han dynasty, every detail of which bespeaks the personality of an individual voice, and the mind and life of a powerfully distinctive artistic personality. These are not features of an anonymous court production, and they are not features that can be associated with any known copy of any

Chinese painting, all of which immediately lose nearly every significant detail of individuality, nuance, subtlety and humour. This is shown to be true simply and thoroughly by the entire corpus of art we have from the Six Dynasties period, every other one of which is a copy or a replica, whether cut into stone, painted in lacquer onto wooden screens, or stamped with wooden moulds onto brick tiles. There is, finally, nothing with which to compare the *Admonitions*, and nothing to indicate that it was not painted by Gu Kaizhi – or his predecessor Wei Xie, or his followers Lu Tanwei or Zhang Sengyou, about whose art also we know virtually nothing, but who define the classical tradition of early secular figure painting in China of which the *Admonitions* is the complete embodiment.

The *Admonitions* may not be a masterpiece by Gu Kaizhi – who knows? – but it does seem to be the only masterpiece of Six Dynasties painting in existence.

NOTES

1   Kohara 2000 (1967), pp. 10–14. See Chen Pao-chen's essay in this
     volume, pp. 126–137
2   See, e.g., Barnhart *et al.* 1993.

The *Admonitions* Scroll Revisited: Iconology, Narratology, Style, Dating

Wu Hung

Earth-shattering discoveries can hardly be expected from a revisit to the *Admonitions of the Instructress to Palace Ladies*: this famous painting attributed to Gu Kaizhi has been so intensely analysed that it has generated a sub-field within the scholarship on Chinese painting. More realistically, a new study of the work should engage in three kinds of synthesis. The first kind is to bring historical evidence together in an increasingly comprehensive manner. While old textual references and comparative examples must be continuously employed and re-evaluated, new information – especially images and inscriptions found through archaeological discoveries – often problematizes previous conclusions and introduces new hypotheses.

The second kind of synthesis integrates different observations. While specialized research on the painting's physical and artistic properties – silk and pigment, inscriptions and seals, composition and drawing – will undoubtedly continue, it has become clear to most researchers that any credible opinion regarding the painting's dating, provenance, authorship and historical significance must rely on all such independent studies. The third kind of synthesis involves research methods and encourages a researcher to bring various scholarly concerns into a single focus. These concerns include formal analysis, iconography, connoisseurship, patronage, social and ideological context, and historical materiality. Different research methods inherent to these concerns are not necessarily contradictory but can complement one another to solve historical problems. One of these problems – the dating of the *Admonitions* – has dominated the scholarship on this painting. Conflicting dates have been proposed on the basis of pictorial and calligraphic styles, but in my view other factors, including changing ideology, taste and perception, should be incorporated to determine the work's historical position.

In what follows I attempt these syntheses, but add another one of my own: I have discussed this painting on various occasions but have never made it the focus of an independent study.[1] The current volume provides me with an opportunity to develop previous observations and bring them into a coherent interpretation.

Iconography/Iconology

In Erwin Panofsky's (1892–1968) formulation, an iconographic study uncovers *conventional meanings* of pictorial forms by consulting textual sources and/or traditional visual representations. An iconological interpretation, on the other hand, discovers *symbolic values* underlying specific motifs, images, stories and allegories.[2] Both iconography and iconology are text-based research methods, and are especially appropriate for studying a textual illustration like the *Admonitions* scroll.

Readers can find English translations of Zhang Hua's (232–300) text (which the scroll illustrates) and scene-by-scene descriptions of the painting in existing books and articles.[3] What I want to emphasize here is that in responding to Zhang's changing language and emphases, the painter of the *Admonitions* created different types of images and also related these images to written passages in different ways. One type of image can be termed 'narrative' or 'biographical': modelled upon conventional illustrations of the *Biographies of Exemplary Women*, the four scenes at the beginning of the scroll (including two missing scenes which are found in a Song copy of the painting in Beijing's Palace Museum[4]) depict particular historical figures and events. Thus we find Lady Feng who hastens to protect Emperor Yuan from a wild bear (pls 1–2) and Lady Ban who declines to sit in Emperor Cheng's palanquin to preserve sexual propriety (pls 3–4). The two heroines seen in the Beijing scroll are Lady Fan and a woman from Wei. The former, in the hope of persuading King Zhuang of Chu to give up hunting, stops eating the flesh of birds (pls 23 left, 24 right); the latter refuses to listen to the lascivious music enjoyed by Duke Huan of Qi (pl. 24 centre).

Because these four tales were all from Liu Xiang's (77 BCE–6 CE) *Biographies of Exemplary Women* and must have been illustrated since Liu's day, when depicting these subjects anew the painter of the *Admonitions* scroll would have had standard iconographic models at his disposal. This assumption gains validity from the Sima Jinlong (d. 484) screen, on which a scene depicts the story of Lady Ban in an identical composition, albeit in a much less refined style (pls 3, 19). This screen was a descendant of Liu Xiang's 'exemplary women' screen, which Liu created for a Han emperor and which must have been embellished with images of royal consorts like Lady Ban. It is therefore possible that the standard composition of the Lady Ban story, as attested to by the two scenes in the *Admonitions* scroll and on the Sima Jinlong screen, was transmitted from Liu Xiang's original work.

In illustrating the next six scenes, however, the painter of the *Admonitions* no longer had the privilege of standard iconographic models: he had to devise his own solutions to the unprecedented task posed by Zhang Hua's text. After citing the four royal ladies from the *Biographies of Exemplary Women*, Zhang's instructions on female morality turn abstract; the essay increasingly resembles a philosophical discourse that rejects a straightforward pictorial translation. In an effort to convert this discourse into images, the painter searched for anything tangible in the text as a visual stimulus. Sometimes this can be a place or a situation. The subject of the fifth scene, for instance, is the appropriateness of speech: 'If the words that you utter are good, all men for a thousand leagues around will make response to you. But if you depart from this principle, even your bedfellow will distrust you.'[5] The second sentence triggered the painter to imagine a couple conversing in a bedroom – an 'implied' situation which he then took as the subject of the illustration (pls 6 left, 7).

At other times, the painter singled out metaphors in a passage and converted them into visual images. This practice is exemplified by the third scene accompanying this passage:

> In nature there is [nothing] that is exalted which is not
>   soon brought low.
> Among living things there is nothing which having
>   attained its apogee does not thenceforth decline.
> Like the sun when it has reached its mid-course, it
>   begins to sink;
> Like the moon when it is full it begins to wane.
> To rise to glory is as hard as to build a mountain out of
>   dust;

> To fall into calamity is as easy as the rebound of a tense
>   spring.[6]

The painter illustrated *all* the images he could find in this passage – the sun, the moon, a man shooting a crossbow, and a layered mountain. The scene is therefore a conglomeration of literary metaphors made visible (pl. 5 centre). Divorced from the original text and reassembled into a picture, however, these images have changed their status from literary expression to pictorial motif.

Curiously, these and other scenes often invite responses that are at odds with the moral teachings they are supposed to reinforce. An uninformed viewer of the 'Bedroom' scene would hardly guess that the man sitting on the bed is disquieted by the words of his female companion. More likely the picture would arouse him to imagine the couple's intimate relationship in a private quarter. The 'Mountain' scene is a delightful portrayal of hunting game; and its naturalistic modelling of rocks and trees has attracted much attention from painting connoisseurs. What is important here is that these 'superfluous' interests beyond the text – whether the fascination with private life or an attempt at pictorial naturalism – reveal the *real* intent of the illustrations. This is not to say that the painter self-consciously championed such interests and placed them above the pictures' didactic function. Rather, the divide between the images' professed purpose and what they actually evoke is, in Panofsky's words, 'a symptom of something else'. For Panofsky, to discover this 'something else' is the object of iconology.[7]

The most complex scene in the *Admonitions* is the so-called 'Toilette' scene (pls 6 right, 8), which illustrates a passage inscribed to its right:

> People know how to adorn their faces;
> None know how to adorn their character.
> Yet if the character be not adorned,
> There is the danger that the rules of conduct be trans-
>   gressed.
> Correct your character as with an axe, embellish it as
>   with a chisel;
> Strive to create holiness in your nature.[8]

Once again the artist focused on a concrete image in the passage, which he found in the first line – 'People know how to adorn their faces.' Portrayed here are two elegant court ladies engaged in their toilette, each looking into a mirror mounted on a tall stand. One is having her beautiful long hair arranged by a maid. The other has had her hair arranged and is putting make-up on. Taking the illustration as a straightforward scene of daily life, no viewer would think there could be any harm in the women's behaviour, despite the writer's warning. On the other hand, the scene's focal image, the mirror, is heavily invested with symbolic meanings in traditional Chinese culture and invites the viewer to think about the scene's deeper implications.

Throughout China's imperial history, the mirror was a metaphor for any kind of self-reflection. For the Han (206 BCE–220 CE) scholar Li You, such self-reflection was about one's public appearance and conduct; he thus inscribed his own mirror with these words: 'Straighten your formal attire and tidy your official cap and robe' – a symbolic expression in Confucian rhetoric that meant maintaining good conscience and behaviour.[9] Also during the Han, Sima Qian (c.145–c.86 BCE) and Han Ying (act. c.150 BCE) analogized historical learning as looking into a mirror: by reflecting on the past one learns how to behave in the present.[10] Such positive symbolism of the mirror declined in the Wei-Jin period, however. Mirror reflections became increasingly synonymous with superficiality and were contrasted with more essential human qualities: character, emotion and thought. Zhang Hua's passage quoted above exemplifies this shift. His contemporary Fu Yuan made a mirror for himself with this inscription: 'Looking into a mirror one only sees one's appearance; looking into people themselves one finds real feeling.'[11]

It is possible that such scepticism was related to another new post-Han development in the mirror: this object was rapidly 'feminized' to become an *objet d'art* of the boudoir. 'Palace-style' poems collected in the *New Songs from a Jade Terrace (Yutai xinyong)* frequently employ the mirror this way, as we find in the 'Reflecting Mirror' by the Liang court poet He Sun (d. c.517):

The jade case open, she studies her image,
Over the jewelled stand she leans to apply make-up.
She faces her image full of lonely laughter,
Looks at a flower, idly twists sideways.
For a moment she creates cocoon-emerging eyebrows,
Cautiously glosses fresh peach tones.
Perhaps plumed hairpins would suit here?
May be the gold hairclasp is too close?
Her wayward lover travels without return,
Tearful cosmetics unbidden soak her breast.[12]

This is, of course, an aestheticized female icon conjured up by a male artist. And so is the 'Toilette' scene in the *Admonitions* scroll, which results from the same kind of aestheticization but in the visual realm. Looking at the picture, we sense little worry on the painter's part about the morality of the palace

ladies, but a great deal of concern about how to fashion the figures as serene images of female beauty. In other words, not only does the scene represent the target of Zhang Hua's criticism, but the painter's interests run totally counter to those of the writer. What we have here therefore is an illustration that rebels against its textual reference. This, in turn, means that the meaning of this illustration cannot be determined through a conventional iconographic exercise by referring to its textual source. Its significance must be sought in the broad cultural and intellectual transformation of the period in which the painting was created.

The last scene of the scroll signifies yet another word/image relationship: instead of illustrating moral instructions, it represents the Instructress herself (pls 12 centre, 13). The image's unique position at the end of the scroll leads us to examine the narrative technique and other stylistic attributes of the scroll.

Style/Technique

Among discourses on the concept of *style* in art history, the one offered by James S. Ackerman has the virtue of practical simplicity. To him, a style pertains to a mode of representation that is subject to both historical stability and transformation – a distinguishable ensemble of characteristics that are 'more or less stable, in the sense that they appear in other products of the same artist(s), era or locale, and flexible, in the sense that they change according to a definable pattern when observed in instances chosen from sufficiently extensive spans of time or of geographical distance.'[13] While this statement bears clear influence of historical evolutionism, we must agree that a style is a collective phenomenon associated with a particular historical moment. A discussion of the style of the *Admonitions* scroll thus necessarily links this painting with other examples in Chinese art that demonstrate similar modes of representation in terms of (1) narrative structure, (2) pictorial composition, (3) figurative type, and (4) methods of drawing and coloration.

The *Admonitions* can be considered a 'narrative' painting in two senses: first, some of its scenes depict events and stories. Second, the painting illustrates Zhang Hua's essay paragraph by paragraph and is viewed in a temporal sequence. This second aspect is in turn enhanced by two factors. The first factor is the painting's handscroll format, which makes the work literally a 'moving picture'.[14] The second factor is the image of the Instructress, which not only concludes the scroll but also frames the whole painting. Shown in the act of inscribing a scroll with a firmly held brush, this image depicts

Fig. 1 Frontispiece of the *Greater Sutra of the Perfection of Transcendent Wisdom (Mahaprajnaparamita-sūtra)*. Jin dynasty (1115–1234), 1149–1173. Collection of the National Library of China, Beijing.

the accompanying passage: 'Thus has the Instructress, charged with the duty of admonition, thought good to speak to the ladies of the palace harem.' She then is writing down the admonitions illustrated in the previous scenes in the scroll, and her image represents a narrator in a narrative painting.

But why did the painter end the scroll with the Instructress? A more logical way to represent a storyteller or instructor would be to show him or her at the beginning of a composition, as one finds in the image of the preaching Buddha in the frontispiece of a later Buddhist sūtra (fig. 1). The mode of narration in the *Admonitions*, in fact, conforms to a pre-Buddhist convention in written history, exemplified by the two greatest Han historical works, *Historical Records (Shi ji)* and *History of the Former Han (Han shu)*. After completing his survey of Chinese history up to his time, Sima Qian concluded *Shi ji* with 'The Self-statement of the Grand Historian' ('Taishigong zixu'). The last chapter of *Han shu* is likewise the autobiography of its author Ban Gu (32–92). This structure signifies the sacred mission of a historian: he is the witness of the vast panoply of events preceding him, and he 'ends' history.

As I have proposed previously, during the Han this retrospective mode of historical narration was not limited to

writing: the Wu Liang Shrine employed the same convention to frame a pictorial history.[15] Depicted on the three walls of the shrine, this history begins with the creation of mankind and ends at a representation of Wu Liang (78–151), a Confucian scholar who very likely designed the memorial shrine for himself. Other scenes in this history illustrate Confucian heroes and heroines: ancient sovereigns, loyal ministers, filial sons and virtuous wives. These scenes belonged to the tradition of Confucian textual illustration and were likely copied from scroll paintings. The *Admonitions* scroll emerged from the same artistic tradition, so it is logical that the painter would adopt the retrospective mode inherent to this tradition. We should also not forget that the original term for the Instructress is *nüshi* – a 'female historian'; her role is therefore similar to Sima Qian and Ban Gu, both court historians.

Created after the Han, however, this image renewed a traditional narrative device. While Wu Liang is still symbolized by an event in his life, the Instructress is depicted as an individual in action – what we find here is the first 'author' image in Chinese art history. Positioned at the end of the scroll, this image also plays an additional role in transforming the idle act of closing the scroll into a viewing experience. To roll the painting back up after viewing it, the spectator begins at the end of the scroll, with the image of the Instructress. The scenes glimpsed in reverse appear to illustrate the admonitions she has written on the scroll in her hand. We find a similar narrative technique in the *Nymph of the Luo River*, a scroll painting based on Cao Zhi's (192–232) poetic description of his

Fig. 2 Attributed to Gu Kaizhi; a 12th-century copy of a 6th-century painting. *Nymph of the Luo River*. Detail (final scene) of a handscroll; ink and colour on silk. Palace Museum, Beijing.

romantic encounter with the nymph. Here, Cao Zhi's image again concludes the painting: seated in a departing chariot, he looks back – a gesture that invites us to recall his vanished dream (fig. 2).

Shifting our focus from the scroll's narrative structure to its *compositional style*, we now consider how each scene is composed pictorially. Earlier I proposed that the pictures in the scroll reflect different degrees of originality. Some of them, such as the story of Lady Ban, derived their composition from existing prototypes; others were invented by the artist. But even those 'narrative' scenes in the first group show important development in terms of their composition. The four 'narrative' scenes at the beginning of the scroll (including the two found in the Beijing version) employ two compositional modes. In the cases of Lady Ban and the woman from Wei, only one picture apiece illustrates each of their stories; these two illustrations thus follow the 'episodic' or 'monocentric' mode typical of Han pictorial art (pls 2, 24 centre and 24 left–25 right).[16] In contrast, the story of Lady Fan is illustrated by two consecutive pictures: in the first picture the woman stands facing her husband as if appealing to him; in the second picture she is seated alone facing an empty table (see pls 23 left, 24 right)). The two pictures thus constitute a 'sequential' narrative. The story of Lady Feng may also be classified in this category: the main part of the composition is followed by a female figure moving in a leftward direction (see pl. 2 left). Although scholars have different opinions about

her identity, all agree that she does not belong to the scene to her right.[17]

Such a mixture of episodic and sequential representations also characterizes the Sima Jinlong screen. About twenty illustrations of Confucian tales on this screen have survived; the majority is shown in single pictures. Among a few sequential representations, the most elaborate one depicts Shun, an ancient sage-king who was also arguably the most eminent of all paragons of filial piety (fig. 3, pl. 16). The narrative sequence starts from a 'title scene', in which Shun stands facing his two loyal wives. The following pictures depict specific events in Shun's life. This sequence thus resembles that of the Lady Fan story in the Beijing *Admonitions* scroll, which also begins with the standing images of the woman and her lord (fig. 4, pl. 23 left). Unlike the Lady Fan story, which consists of only two scenes, however, Shun's story on the screen, though damaged, still includes three scenes. On a lacquered coffin excavated at Guyuan, Ningxia, Shun's story is illustrated by a series of eight pictures (see p. 113, fig. 12). Dated to 470–480, this coffin proves that elaborate pictorial cycles of Confucian tales had definitely come into existence by the late fifth century. But such cartoon-like picture-stories did not dominate narrative art after this time. As exemplified by the contemporary Sima Jinlong screen (before 484), late fifth-century artists could still mix different narrative modes in a single work. They could also use a 'minimum' sequential representation to tell a story: on an early sixth-century sarcophagus in the Nelson-Atkins Museum of Art, each of the

Fig. 3 Story of Shun. Detail of a painted lacquer screen. Tomb of Sima Jinlong, 484 CE. Datong, Shanxi Province.

eight Confucian tales is represented by two scenes, expertly integrated into a coherent landscape environment (see p. 109, figs 1–2).

The non-narrative passages in the *Admonitions* scroll are all illustrated by single scenes. I have suggested earlier that these compositions were likely created by the painter, not

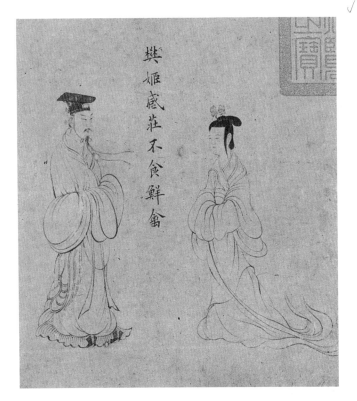

Fig. 4 Story of Lady Fan. Detail of the Beijing *Admonitions* scroll.

derived from existing models. Not coincidentally, these pictures convey a greater sense of three-dimensionality and reflect a variety of new compositional styles. In the 'Bedroom' scene, for example, a large roofed bed, painted diagonally in relation to the picture surface, provides a stage for the interaction of the husband and wife (see pls 6 left, 7). In the next scene, three groups of figures are organized in a pyramid-shaped composition never seen in Han art (pls 9 right, 11). At the bottom of the pyramid, a couple are watching two young women, possibly the master's concubines, tending two babies. Above them and forming the apex of the pyramid, a male tutor is educating two young boys. Osvald Sirén (1879–1966) has observed that because the figures in this last group are represented on a smaller scale, the picture generates the impression of foreshortening and gradual distance.[18] It is also possible, however, that the changing scale of the last group pertains to a different temporal order: the two boys represent the 'future' of the two babies. Indeed, we find that these two pairs of children have similar positions and gestures, which seem to indicate deliberate echoing.

Re-examining the 'Toilette' scene from a stylistic angle, we find that it signifies some of the most remarkable innovations in post-Han pictorial art (see pl. 6 right). The whole composition is divided into two equal parts, each with a lady looking at herself in a mirror. One lady turns inward; her face is reflected in the mirror. The other lady faces outward; her reflection in the mirror is implicit. The concept of a 'mirror image' is thus presented on multiple levels in this composition: each half of the picture contains a pair of mirror images, and the two halves together form a reflecting double.

I have termed this type of representation a 'front and back' composition, whose invention marked the beginning of an indigenous system for perceiving and depicting pictorial

Fig. 5 Story of Wang Lin. Carving on a stone sarcophagus from Luoyang. Northern Wei dynasty (386–533), early 6th century. Collection of the Nelson-Atkins Museum of Art, Kansas City, Missouri.

space. Dated examples of this perceptual/compositional mode come from the late fifth and early sixth centuries.[19] One of them, a picture engraved on the Nelson sarcophagus, illustrates the story of the Confucian paragon Wang Lin, who saved his brother from bandits (fig. 5). The scene is again divided into two halves. In the left half, figures are emerging from a deep valley and are shown in the frontal view. In the right half, figures are entering another valley and have their rear toward the viewer. Again, a perfect symmetry unites the two halves into a 'front and back' composition.

No picture like this existed in Han art. What we find on Han monuments are silhouettes 'attached' to the pictorial plane. Even pictures created during the fourth century do not substantially alter this traditional representation mode. (It is true that the portraits of the Seven Worthies in the Bamboo Grove [Zhulin qixian] from Xishanqiao, Nanjing, exhibit some new visual features: more relaxed and varying poses, spatial cells formed by landscape elements, and an emphasis on fluent lines. But these images are still largely attached to the two-dimensional picture surface, never guiding the viewer's eyes to penetrate it.) In this sense, the 'Toilette' scene in the *Admonitions* scroll and the Wang Lin picture-story on the Nelson sarcophagus marked a new stage in Chinese pictorial art, as they testify to a desire to see and represent things as they had never been seen and represented before.

Shifting the level of observation again, we now focus on the individual figures in the *Admonitions* scroll: their proportions and facial features, clothes and ornaments, gestures and movement. Related to the *figurative style* of the painting is its *style of drawing and coloration*: How are the figures painted?

The figurative type most frequently seen in the scroll is a court lady slowly walking toward the left or right. This image appears seven times, as Lady Feng protecting Emperor Yuan from the wild bear, as Lady Ban following Emperor Cheng's palanquin, as the Instructress writing on her scroll, and as anonymous court ladies on four other occasions. With an elegantly attenuated body, this graceful figure is shown consistently in profile or a three-quarter view (fig. 6a). The torso thrusts slightly forward at the waist – a gentle gesture that suggests movement. But the woman's upper body is held erect and flows into the sweeping curves of a conspicuous dress: the broad pendant sleeves, the floating draperies, and the very full train that widens dramatically at the bottom of the skirt. The most expressive elements of her clothes are the long, floating scarf and streamers, turning slowly behind her as if responding to currents of air. Poised, the woman glides effortlessly through space.

This figurative type is also seen in five other works: (1) the *Benevolent and Wise Women* (fig. 6b); (2) the *Nymph of the Luo River* (fig. 6c); (3) the Sima Jinlong screen (fig. 6d); (4) the Nelson sarcophagus (fig. 6e); and (5) the Dengxian tomb (fig. 6f). The first two items have been frequently discussed

Fig. 6 Female images: (a) the *Admonitions* scroll; (b) the *Benevolent and Wise Women* scroll; (c) the *Nymph of the Luo River* scroll; (d) the Sima Jinlong screen; (e) the Nelson-Atkins sarcophagus; and (f) the Dengxian tomb.

Fig. 7 King Qi of Xia and his mother (Qimu Tushan). Detail of a painted lacquer screen. Tomb of Sima Jinlong, 484 CE. Datong, Shanxi Province.

together with the *Admonitions* scroll to define a 'Gu Kaizhi' figurative style, but they are less useful in dating this style because both are later copies. In contrast, the other three items are authentic works from the Northern and Southern Dynasties (386–589); their dates indicate the historical temporality of this figurative type.

At least nine images painted on the Sima Jinlong screen conform to this type. Scholars have often contrasted this screen with the *Admonitions* scroll to show the latter's stylistic refinement. But in fact, more than one painter of differing artistic abilities may have decorated the screen. As evidence, some of the female images, such as the mother of King Qi of the Xia dynasty (fig. 7, pl. 14), are considerably better in artistic quality; the fluent yet precise brushwork reveals the hand of a capable artist. In comparison, the image of Lady Ban appears cumbersome; the streamers are stiff and the draperies are drawn in simplified parallel lines (see pl. 19). Regardless of such differences in artistic achievement, however, these images all belong to a single figurative type with similar costume, gesture, and movement. Also, like the ladies in the *Admonitions* scroll, these figures wear flower-like ornaments in their hair.

On the other hand, it is also apparent that the images on the screen, even the more skilled ones, have become formulaic and stereotypical. Some of them stand in a row in the same monotonous three-quarter view; the end of a scarf or streamer is always sharply folded in an unnatural manner. The tendency toward stylization becomes even more pronounced in the decoration of the Nelson sarcophagus and the Dengxian tomb, both dating from the early sixth century.[20] Once again we find the slender female figure in her conspicuous dress, but her features are further exaggerated and begin to lose representational purpose. Dong Yong's wife on the Nelson sarcophagus has become almost bodiless (fig. 6e). Guo Ju's wife in the Dengxian tomb wears a dress that dissolves into angular and tapered shapes; the bottom of her skirt turns into long streamers with sharply pointed ends (fig. 6f).

All these observations provide information for dating the *Admonitions* scroll, a task that I will attempt at the end of this essay. Before that, it is necessary to compare the painting's drawing style with some dated examples. Scholars have long noticed the distinct linear quality of the images in this scroll. In Sirén's words, 'the artist used a very fine brush, making lines as neat as the traces of a stylus, yet at the same time supple and elastic.'[21] These lines possess an aesthetic quality independent from the subject of drawing, dissolving substance and transforming objects into rhythmic structures that are nearly abstract designs. This linear style is shared by many works dating from the fourth to sixth century: the images of the Seven Worthies of the Bamboo Grove from Xishanqiao, Nanjing; the Sima Jinlong screen; the Nelson sarcophagus; the Ning Mao shrine in the Museum of Fine Arts, Boston; and murals in Dong Shou's tomb in Anak, Cui Fen's tomb in Shandong, and Lou Rui's tomb in Shanxi.[22]

The *Admonitions* scroll is not a monochromic drawing, however. The style and technique of coloration have attracted less attention from scholars because, again citing Sirén, 'the [paintings'] artistic expression is mainly dependent on the drawing, the colours are secondary.'[23] While this is certainly true, the minimal coloration in the painting results from a calculated decision and demonstrates some unambiguous rules. Several colours are found in the painting, but the painter's favourite one is clearly brick red, which he used throughout the scroll in three distinct ways. The first way is to colour some parts of the women's clothes and belongings solid red – scarves and streamers, mats and cosmetic boxes, edges of sleeves and skirts, and occasionally an entire blouse. The result is a series of disconnected 'blocks' of red accentuated in the

painting. Balanced with the ladies' black coiffures, these coloured blocks create visual tension with the linear structures of the images. The other two methods of coloration both serve to reinforce the three-dimensionality of drapery. The difference is that in one method, the red colour, now much diluted, is subtly applied along an ink line to emphasize a voluminous fold; while in the other method, the same colour is applied between two lines and makes the space a sunken one (see especially Emperor Yuan in the Lady Feng story; pl. 2).

Checking excavated tomb murals dating from the first century BCE to the tenth century CE, we find that the first method of coloration in the *Admonitions* scroll – that of creating scattered 'red blocks' in a composition – remained a popular technique throughout this long period. In the Bu Qianqiu tomb near Luoyang and in an Eastern Han (25–220) tomb at Anping in Hebei, for example, selected parts of figures' clothes are coloured solid red to contrast with fluent ink lines. This technique was employed with increasing sophistication in later tombs, such as a sixth-century Northern Qi royal tomb at Wangzhang and the tenth-century tomb of Wang Chuzhi at Quyang, both in Hebei.[24] The second method – that of applying the red colour along an ink line – became popular after the Han, as seen in a fourth-century tomb at Jiuquan in Gansu.[25] Because tomb murals were often created in a rapid and abbreviated manner, such shading was done in broad brush strokes. An exception is Li Xian's tomb at Guyuan, Ningxia. In this tomb dated to 569, shades of red are carefully applied along ink lines to depict round folds of drapery.[26]

The third method, that of colouring the space between two lines, is more specific and appears in much fewer excavated examples. One such example was found in 2000 in a Northern Wei (386–533) tomb at Datong in Shanxi. Two inscriptions in the tomb identify the deceased as a governor of Youzhou named Song Shaozu, who died in 477. The tomb contained an elaborate stone sarcophagus, originally covered with murals on its interior walls. But now only several images on the north wall, including two musicians playing a *qin*-lute and a *ruan*-guitar, are still recognizable (pl. 21). Although relatively sketchy, the lines used to depict the figures' faces, hands and clothes are precise and expressive. Even more significant, strips of red between ink lines represent folds of drapery, and thus provide a dated example of this particular method of coloration.

Dating

To date a work of art is to determine its historical position. To decide the historical position of a complex painting like the

Admonitions scroll we should consider multiple factors, including its artistic genre, iconography, narrative structure, composition, drawing and coloration, and inscription. My ongoing discussion has touched upon most of these aspects. Here is a brief summary of the findings as evidence for dating the scroll.

(1) The *Admonitions* scroll belongs to the tradition of textural illustrations in general, and to the genre of Confucian book illustrations specifically. Its content and style signify a particular developmental stage of this artistic genre. On the one hand, the painting retains many elements of Han representations of exemplary women; on the other, it demonstrates new tendencies in the post-Han period, including the interest in intellectual women and individual authorship, a more sophisticated use of the handscroll format, and intense attention paid to formal aspects of visual representation. By ending the scroll with the image of the Instructress, the painter utilized a traditional mode of historical narration to frame a series of individual scenes into a coherent pictorial composition.

(2) The 'narrative' scenes in the scroll are likely based on standard illustrations of stories of exemplary women, but other images reflect the painter's creative interpretation of Zhang Hua's text. Specific focuses of this interpretation signify a particular historical temporality. There is a strong interest in literary metaphors, which are translated into images and organized into pictures. Intense attention is also given to the figures' psychological states.[27] A third focus is private life, most notably the boudoir of court ladies. Similar interests can be found in Chinese literature during the Six Dynasties period, especially in 'palace-style' poetry that had its heyday in the courts of the Southern Dynasties from the late fifth to early sixth century. In particular, the mirror became closely associated with a specific type of femininity in 'palace-style' poems created during this period.

(3) Archaeological evidence demonstrates that large 'sequential' narrative representations of Confucian tales had appeared by the last quarter of the fifth century; such pictures were sometimes used together with more traditional 'episodic' compositions, as seen on the Sima Jinlong screen. The *Admonitions* scroll also mixes these two types of representations, but a 'sequential' narrative in this work only consists of two scenes and is therefore simpler than those found on the Sima Jinlong screen and the Guyuan coffin, both created around the 470s to the early 480s. Narrative illustrations on the early sixth-

century Nelson sarcophagus, though succinct, depict figures in a complex landscape and are akin to the *Nymph of the Luo River*, whose lost original has been dated to around the 560s.[28]

(4) Certain scenes in the *Admonitions* scroll reflect a heightened desire to represent a three-dimensional pictorial space. Some visual techniques developed to realize this desire are absent even in the best pictorial works of the late fourth and early fifth centuries, such as the images of the Seven Worthies of the Bamboo Grove from Nanjing. Among these new techniques, a 'front and back' composition enabled the artist to create an independent pictorial space inside the painting. Other manifestations of this visual mode in pictorial and calligraphic works are dated to the late fifth and early sixth centuries.

(5) In terms of figurative style, close parallels are found between the *Admonitions* scroll and the Sima Jinlong screen. But compared to the scroll, the figures on the screen appear more formulaic and stereotypical. Early sixth-century images of the same figurative types, as seen in the Dengxian tomb and on the Nelson sarcophagus, are even more stylized and so represent an even later stage of this image.

(6) The linear drawing style of the painting is a basic characteristic of early Chinese figurative art, and is less suggestive for dating the work. The 'block' colouring technique is also seen in many excavated tomb murals created from the Western Han to the Five Dynasties. But the method of applying the red colour between folds of drapery can be more precisely dated. Among the excavated tomb murals, the earliest one employing this technique is found in Song Shaozu's tomb dated to 573. But compared with the sensitive shading found in the *Admonitions* scroll, this mural shows a more schematized method, as the space between two lines is filled with colour and becomes a coloured strip.

(7) In addition to the painted images, the calligraphy of the written text provides important information for dating the *Admonitions* scroll. I have largely ignored this issue because of the limited length of this essay, and also because this is the subject of several learned papers in this volume. But here I want to mention that although some scholars have dated the scroll to the Tang or even the Song based on the calligraphy of the inscriptions, in my view these inscriptions are written in a style typical of the late fifth to early sixth century, as demonstrated by the inscriptions on the memorial steles of Xiao Dan, Gao Zhen, and Cao Wangxi, all created during this period.

None of the factors summarized here can alone determine the date of the scroll, but when considered together they become interconnected, supporting and supplementing each other. This study demonstrates that the painting mixes traditional ideology and pictorial formulas with new concepts, tastes, and artistic inventions. This heterogeneous or transitional quality is characteristic of the period from the third to sixth century, when Chinese society underwent a profound transformation and when the art of painting struggled to free itself from its traditional role in facilitating rituals and moral education. Comparisons between the *Admonitions* scroll and reliable archaeological materials further help us narrow down the time span of the painting's creation. In terms of narrative and compositional styles, it is more complex than pictures dating from the late fourth to early fifth century, but less complex than those from the 470s and the 480s. In terms of figurative and drawing styles, it has much in common with examples from the 470s and the 480s; but the latter appear formulaic and stereotypical. Works from the early sixth century are even more stylized. All this evidence leads me to propose that the scroll was created by a superb but anonymous artist in the fifth century. It is unlikely that this artist derived his model directly from Gu Kaizhi, because many images and representational modes in the scroll, as argued earlier, were invented after Gu's time. Since I do not find strong reason to identify this scroll as a copy, I consider it an original work from 400 to 480, most likely the third quarter of the fifth century.

NOTES

1 These writings include: Wu Hung 1994a, especially pp. 74–78; 1994b, especially pp. 55–57; 1995, pp. 265–76; 1996, pp. 62–68; 1997, especially pp. 47–56.
2 Panofsky 1939. A slight revision of the first chapter of this book ('Iconography and Iconology: An Introduction to the Study of Renaissance Art') appears in Panofsky 1955.
3 E. g. Gray 1966, pp. 3–5; Waley 1923, pp. 50–52; Shih, Hsio-yen 1976.
4 For a discussion of the Beijing scroll, see Yu Hui 2001. Although it is possible that this version preserves the complete composition of the *Admonitions* scroll, the copier must have made many changes. For example, the ancient vessels and musical instruments depicted in the first two scenes reflect a Song understanding of antiquity.
5 Unless noted, translations of Zhang Hua's text are from Gray 1966.
6 Translation based on ibid. (slightly modified).
7 Panofsky 1955, p. 33.
8 Here I have slightly modified Gray's translation.
9 Cited in *Gujin tushu jicheng*, vol. 798, p. 43.
10 See Wu Hung 1989, pp. 153–154.
11 Cited in *Gujin tushu jicheng*, vol. 798, p. 43.
12 Birrell (tr.) 1982, p. 153.
13 Ackerman & Carpenter 1963, p. 164.
14 For an analysis of the handscroll as a particular art medium, see Wu Hung 1996, pp. 57–68.
15 Wu Hung 1989, p. 217; also see pp. 148–156.
16 For a discussion of this composition, see ibid., pp. 133–134.
17 Among these scholars, Hsio-yen Shih (1976, p. 14) considers her the Instructress, and Kohara Hironobu (1967, part 1, p. 30) suggests that she is an attendant to Lady Ban (in so doing he takes the Beijing scroll, in which this figure is grouped with the Lady Ban scene, as a more authentic version of the painting). Another possibility is that this figure represents Lady Feng, who appears a second time, as Lady Fan does in the Beijing scroll.
18 Sirén 1956, vol. 1, p. 32.
19 Wu Hung 1994a.
20 Annette L. Juliano (1980, p. 74) has dated the Dengxian tomb to the late fifth or early sixth century. I think the early sixth century is more plausible.
21 Sirén 1956, vol. 1, p. 33.
22 For illustrations and brief discussions of these works, see Wu Hung 1997, pp. 34–58.
23 Ibid.
24 For colour illustrations of murals in these two tombs, see Hebei Provincial Institute 2000.
25 For colour illustrations, see Gansu Provincial Institute 1989. Typical examples include the images of the deceased master and a male zither-player on the west wall.
26 For illustrations, see *MSQJ, Painting*, vol. 12 'Mushi bihua', pls 60 and 61.
27 Sirén, for example, considers such interest in psychology the painting's 'actual soul' and the 'fascination of these scenes' (1956, vol. 1, p. 33).
28 Chen Pao-chen 1987, p. 171.

Who was Zhang Hua's 'Instructress'?

Julia K. Murray

In recent years, it has become increasingly common to describe the *Illustrations of the Admonitions of the Court Instructress (Nü shi zhen tu)* scroll in the British Museum as something other than what its title claims. A particularly influential characterization was made by Hironobu Kohara, who proposed that the paintings essentially were genre scenes of beautiful and alluring women, served up to gratify male viewers.[1] While granting that Zhang Hua (232–300) may have sincerely hoped to reform at least one palace lady, Empress Jia (*c.*257–300) by means of his elegantly worded admonitions, Kohara was convinced that the original painter made fun of the conventional moral precepts underlying Zhang's text by playfully inverting proper gender relations. In the nine scenes of the British Museum scroll, Kohara found 'a wonderfully satirical' treatment of 'indiscreet men and women',[2] replete with bold flirtation and innuendoes of sexual transgression. For example, the often-reproduced seventh scene depicts an encounter between an emperor and a lady, whose postures and gestures indicate that an interaction of some emotional charge is underway (pl. 9 left). The accompanying text reads:

> Favour must not be abused; and love must not be exclusive. Exclusive love breeds coyness and extreme passion is fickle. All that has waxed must also wane; this principle is sure. Admire your own beauty if you will, but that brings misfortune. Seeking to please with a seductive face, you will be despised by honorable men. If the bond of love is severed, this is the cause.[3]

According to interpretations that emphasize the first half of the passage, the confrontation shows the emperor in the act of rejecting a woman whom he had previously favoured. With his upraised palm, he literally puts a stop to their association, and she stands uncertainly before him, absorbing her change of fortune with decorous disappointment. However, focusing his reading on the next to last line, Kohara describes the composition as 'A woman of bewitching beauty advancing triumphantly upon a man who, surprised and embarrassed by her advance, shrinks back in disgust',[4] noting 'the woman's rather mocking expression and the caricature of a man vexed by unambiguous female flirtation'.[5] Commenting, 'This is a painter who flouts the conventions of didactic painting in a wonderfully satirical manner', Kohara relates the pictures to 'the spirit of the age'.[6] Elsewhere Kohara's visual analysis seems guided by his belief that the pictures constituted a genre parody. Interpreting the illustration of Ban Jieyu's (Beautiful Companion Ban) refusal to ride in Han Chengdi's litter (pl. 3), he described the consort standing behind the carriage as having a 'slovenly or sluttish appearance' and shamelessly lifting her skirt with one hand.[7] However, there is no such detail in the painting.

Other writers have gone a step further and characterized Zhang Hua's text itself as a parody, albeit one with a political intent.[8] This interpretation implies that the specific content of the text was relatively unimportant because it merely served as a vehicle for Zhang's expression of dissent. Such a suggestion has some basis in a line from Zhang's biography in the Jin dynastic history, which says, 'Hua feared the increasing power of Empress Jia's clan and wrote the *Admonitions of the Court Instructress* in order to *feng* 諷.'[9] The term *feng* sometimes does mean 'satire', but it may also mean to 'admonish in roundabout way', which seems the more likely here. The early Tang (618–907) commentator Li Shan truncated the explanation to, simply, 'Zhang Hua feared the increasing power of Empress Jia's clan and wrote the *Admonitions of the Court Instructress*.'[10] In her annotated translation of Zhang Hua's biography, Anna Straughair paraphrased the *Jin shu*'s comment into 'He wrote the *Admonitions of the Imperial Instructress* in order to draw attention to this danger.'[11] Straughair found it surprising that the empress did not retaliate against

Zhang, even though the powerful woman must have realized that she was the object of his admonitions. Her non-reaction affirms that the 'Nü shi zhen' was not a satire or parody, which would have been too insulting for her to ignore, but rather that it was a remonstrance, which the empress could disregard without consequence. In fact, the very next line of Zhang's biography in the *Jin shu* asserts that Empress Jia, despite being cruel and vindictive, respected and relied on Zhang and even promoted him to higher rank. Although he attempted to dissuade her more directly when she decided to depose the crown prince, Zhang continued to serve in her government. Ultimately, he paid with his life for refusing to participate in the plot that overthrew her in 300. Such a man seems unlikely to have written a parody or satire of the empress.

Another reason for thinking that Zhang Hua's 'Nü shi zhen' was not intended as a parodic text, at odds with its high-minded title, is that it came to be considered a model of the literary genre of admonition. In the early sixth century, Xiao Tong (501–531) selected the piece for inclusion in the *Wen xuan* anthology, where it served as the sole exemplar of admonitory writing. Slightly earlier, Liu Xie (*c.* 465–*c.* 520) had described the function of admonition as being 'to attack ill and ward off trouble'.[12] In the preface to his own anthology, Xiao Tong wrote, 'Admonition arises from repairing defects'.[13] His choice of Zhang Hua's 'Nü shi zhen' to represent the genre of admonition thus suggests that he understood its tone to be one of correction, rather than satire or parody.[14] Later commentators on the *Wen xuan* concurred in this evaluation.

In any case, Zhang presented his exhortations in the form of a lesson on ideal conduct for the ladies of the palace. He began by affirming the female role in the creation of social and cosmic harmony, offered four historical examples of intelligent women who exerted their influence appropriately, and devoted the rest of his tract to elegant epigrams conveying instructions of a more generalized sort. Underlying his homily is a framework of yin-yang cosmology in which all things wax and wane, and nothing lasts forever, perhaps a discreet way of cautioning Empress Jia that her ascendancy was impermanent. David Knechtges characterizes the text as 'a warning to the palace ladies, including the empress herself, not to be too complacent about their power and influence, which they could lose at any moment',[15] and as cautioning against 'the dangers that come from assuming prerogatives to which they are not entitled'.[16] In Straughair's crisp assessment, Zhang's 'Nü shi zhen' described harem politics, where fortunes were in constant flux; just when someone's power seemed greatest, it was already beginning to decline.[17] To survive in the treacherous currents of palace life, a woman needed to cultivate a strong inner core to sustain and guide her, and she had to conduct herself scrupulously in order to avoid arousing suspicion or resentment.

At the end of the piece, Zhang Hua identified his voice as that of a literate woman, the *nü shi*. By taking this subject position, he could write 'from the inside' about desirable female conduct, a safe and respectable theme, and his readers could intuit the contrast with the contemporary situation, which was too dangerous to mention directly. Although 'court instructress' has become the standard English translation of *nü shi* in the title of the British Museum scroll, the term has a certain range of meanings centring on the idea of a woman who could read and write. In fact, some scholars prefer to render it as 'female scribe' or 'lady recorder'.[18] According to the *Zhou li* (*Institutes of Zhou*), the Zhou (*c.* 1050–256 BCE) court appointed a literate woman, the *nü shi*, to manage the ritual obligations of the empress and advise her on the administration of the inner palace.[19] From the early Han period onward, the term *nü shi* has also been understood to designate a woman of the inner court whose duty was to document the merits and transgressions of the empress and consorts. A late Warring States-early Han commentary to the *Shijing* (*Book of Odes*) referred to the *nü shi* in explaining the significance of a red tube (*tong guan*), which was mentioned twice in the poem 'Jing nü' ('Chaste Girl').[20] The commentator Mao Heng and/or Mao Chang claimed that in ancient times, a female scribe kept records (with a red-tubed brush) to ensure that the empress and consorts would 'wait on' (*yu*) their lord in an orderly sequence.[21] Among other details, the commentary noted that women who became pregnant would be temporarily removed from the rotation. Thus the Mao explanation could mean that the *nü shi* was responsible for administering a regular and impartial procedure to provide the ruler with sex partners, which would maintain harmony in his household by preventing anyone from monopolizing his favour and arousing jealousy. For his part, the high-minded ruler was presumed to welcome a well-regulated system that selected his bed-mates and kept his sensual appetites in check. However, later writers did not dwell on the procedural details of this idealized ancient practice. Li Shan's notes to Zhang Hua's 'Nü shi zhen' in the *Wen xuan* cited the Mao commentary to 'Jing nü' and stated only that Zhang was referring to 'the principle of the lady scribe's red tube'.[22] Li's contemporary Liu Liang commented, 'The *nü shi* was a female official who wielded the red tube and documented the affairs of the empress and consorts. Zhang Hua feared the rising power of the empress's clan, so he borrowed the *nü shi* to write the *Admonitions* and thereby give precepts to the rear palace.'[23]

The institution of the *nü shi* as described in the *Zhou li* and the Mao commentary on the *Shijing* seems to have been long defunct by the Han period, if indeed it ever existed at all. Nonetheless, the name survived, and its meaning evolved into something more like 'instructress'. For example, a rhapsody written in the late first century BCE by Ban Jieyu, the famous consort of Han Chengdi (r. 33–7 BCE), contained the line, 'I look at the *nü shi* and ask about the *[Book of] Odes*.'[24] In the *Guafu fu (Widow's Rhapsody)*, a piece written circa 278 by Pan Yue (247–300), Zhang Hua's contemporary and colleague, a lamenting widow protested that she did not deserve her misfortune because, 'I modelled myself on the *nü shi*'s canons and precepts'.[25] Knechtges notes that the Jin court bureaucracy did not include an official post for a *nü shi* and suggests that the term had come to refer to a female tutor.[26]

All of these prior associations bore on Zhang Hua's appropriation of a *nü shi*'s voice to convey an admonitory but tactful message to Empress Jia.[27] Zhang owed his official position to the ambitious empress, who had brought him out of his premature retirement and given him major responsibility for running the government after Emperor Huidi (r. 290–306) succeeded to the throne in 290. Zhang was useful to the empress because he was an able administrator and did not belong to a great clan that could potentially rival her own. In 291, she consolidated her power by killing off the two official regents for the mentally deficient emperor, as well as most of the clan of Empress Dowager Yang and other rivals.[28] Zhang must have been appalled by her ruthless powerplay, in which he played a perhaps unwitting part. Nonetheless, he did not resign, and his 'Nü shi zhen' appeared soon thereafter. Was the *nü shi* whose voice he assumed just a generic figure, conjured up to enable a male author to circumvent the impropriety of addressing a woman directly, or might she have been modelled on someone specific? In my view, Zhang infused his *nü shi* with the persona of the eminent Ban Zhao (*c.* 45–*c.* 120 CE), a Han court instructress and the female scholar associated with the earliest didactic writings expressly for women.[29]

Ban Zhao was a member of a family of illustrious scholars and court officials, including her father Ban Biao (3–54) and older brother Ban Gu (32–92), the principal authors of the *History of Former Han (Han shu)*; and her great aunt was Ban Jieyu, the virtuous consort who refused to ride in the litter of Han Chengdi and also a woman of considerable literary accomplishment.[30] Ban Zhao herself received an unusually broad and thorough education for a woman and enjoyed the benefits of the family's celebrated library. Even more exceptionally, she was able to put her learning to conspicuous use after being widowed at a young age, eventually achieving a 'versatility of knowledge and skill in historical, philosophical,

and imaginative literature not surpassed by any woman of letters in later ages'.[31] As detailed in her official biography, she was summoned to court by the Han emperor Hedi (r. 88–105) and ordered to complete the *Han shu*, which Ban Biao had started, and Ban Gu continued but left unfinished when he died in prison.[32] Most unusually for a woman, she worked in the office for court historiography in the palace library (Dongguan cangshu ge) and gave instruction on the *Han shu* to Ma Rong (79–166) and his brother, among others.[33]

Ban Zhao's erudition proved useful to the emperor in other ways as well. For example, whenever an unusual object was submitted to the court as tribute, he reportedly commanded her to compose a rhapsody celebrating it. Moreover, the emperor also ordered his empress and palace consorts to consider Ban Zhao as their teacher. Although history does not record the content of their lessons, she undoubtedly used Liu Xiang's (77–6 BCE) *Lie nü zhuan (Biographies of Exemplary Women)*, whose anecdotal accounts of women of earlier times were grouped according to the specific virtues they demonstrated. The bibliography of the *Sui shu (Sui History)* listed an edition of the *Lie nü zhuan* containing Ban Zhao's annotations (*zhu*), which she may have written or used in an instructional context. Some sources suggest that she even composed additional biographies of recent women to supplement those in Liu Xiang's original compilation.[34]

Also indicative of the curriculum that Ban Zhao may have offered the palace women is her most famous work, the *Nü jie (Warnings for Women)*, which is considered to be the earliest instructional treatise written specifically for women.[35] The *Nü jie* was organized into seven chapters, entitled 'Humility', 'Husband and wife', 'Respect and caution', 'Womanly qualifications', 'Wholehearted devotion', 'Implicit obedience' and 'Harmony with younger in-laws'. In order for women to preserve their own positions and promote domestic harmony, the text relentlessly stressed the importance of self-abnegation and compliance. On one level, as Yu-shih Chen has recently demonstrated, it could be read as a survival manual for persons who found themselves operating in a treacherous environment from a position of weakness, whether they were women marrying into a large extended family or men and women at the court.[36] For the most part, however, the *Nü jie* served as a programmatic articulation of female virtues and ideals of conduct, based on the general principles outlined in the *Nei ze* (Domestic rules) chapter of the *Li ji (The Ritual Classic)*. As a foundational text in the Confucian construction of womanhood, the *Nü jie* became the model for many later works meant to instruct women in moral principles and mould their everyday behaviour.[37] One of these, the *Nü xiao jing (Ladies' Classic of Filial Piety)*, even took the form of a pedagogic dialogue between Ban Zhao and a group of young women.[38] Zhang Hua premised his 'Nü shi zhen' on values that the *Nü jie* explained in detail and echoed its basic propositions in his elegantly pithy phrases. Moreover, two of the four exemplary women that he singled out as especially suitable role models were Han women whose biographies in the *Lie nü zhuan*'s supplementary chapter were associated with Ban Zhao's authorship. And one of these paragons was none other than her great-aunt, Ban Jieyu.

In addition to affinities among these texts, as well as Ban Zhao's reputation as the eminent instructress to Han palace women and her central role in the formulation of 'idealized womanhood',[39] there are other reasons to think that Zhang Hua had her in mind as the ideal *nü shi*. Of particular significance is Ban Zhao's relationship with Empress Dowager Deng (*c.* 80–121), who was a dominant political force at the Han court from 106 until her death in 121.[40] An unusual woman who was said to be more interested in learning than in standard feminine pursuits, Deng Sui had begun her tutelage under Ban Zhao upon being presented to the palace in 96, when she was about sixteen years old. She soon became a concubine and attained the rank of *guiren* (Worthy Lady), rising quickly in the emperor's favour. Chen suggests that by practising humility and self-denial, and particularly by keeping other family members out of her relationship with the emperor, Deng gained a good reputation and made few enemies.[41] In 102, she was named empress after Hedi deposed Empress Yin on charges of plotting with her family against the throne, an abuse of power and position that contrasted with Deng's approach. She became Empress Dowager when Hedi died in 105, and until her own death in 121 she acted as regent to his heir, first to the short-lived emperor Zhangdi (r. 106) and then to Andi (r. 106–125).

Ban Zhao is thought to have produced the *Nü jie* in 106, just at the time that Empress Dowager Deng began wielding her significantly increased powers as regent. Chen suggests that Ban chose this strategic moment to advertise the empress dowager's support for conventional ideals of womanhood in order to forestall rumours that she and Ban might be seeking power for themselves.[42] Although Ban's preface to the *Nü jie* states that she wrote it to instruct her girls (*zhu nü*) in conduct that would be essential to success in their husbands' homes, the work appeared long after her own daughters would have been of marriageable age; and she framed its message for broader application in any case.[43]

Empress Dowager Deng continued to rely on Ban Zhao for advice and political counsel during her fifteen-year regency, and at times their relationship seemed very like that of emperor and minister. One of Ban Zhao's surviving writings is a memorial addressed to the empress dowager, urging her to grant the request of General Deng Zhi, her oldest brother, to retire after their mother died.[44] Despite Empress Dowager Deng's unambiguous and distinctly unfeminine prominence in governmental affairs, her posthumous reputation was extremely favourable, and her exceptionally long and full biography in the *Hou Han shu* praised her many exemplary qualities. Thus, Zhang Hua may well have had Empress Dowager Deng in mind as his *nü shi*'s ideal advisee, a model for Empress Jia to emulate. By adopting a Ban Zhao persona, Zhang Hua in effect was urging Empress Jia to play the role of Empress Dowager Deng. Unfortunately for all concerned, Jia did not accept the part and ignored his genteel admonitions. Even while encouraging Zhang with high positions and wealth, she disregarded his more pointed efforts to dissuade her from deposing the heir apparent, who was not her son. Although she succeeded in destroying the crown prince in 300, her triumph triggered the coup that brought about her own overthrow.

The circumstances described above lead me to believe that the 'Nü shi zhen' text represents the earnest and well-intended remonstrance of an official who, with the utmost loyalty, had 'turned all his energies to repairing the deficiencies in the government'.[45] But the illustrations present a much more ambiguous situation, because there is neither reliable information concerning their authorship, nor even an approximate date of creation accepted by most scholars in the field. Unlike the 'Nü shi zhen' text, which was securely attributed to Zhang Hua's authorship and confirmed as such by its inclusion in the early sixth-century *Wen xuan* anthology, the paintings were ascribed to a specific individual only in the late Northern Song (960–1127) period, without documentary support of any kind. Basing his judgement purely on visual impressions, Mi Fu (1051–1107) insinuated that the *Admonitions* scroll was by Gu Kaizhi (*c.* 345–*c.* 406), an odd choice in view of that artist's contemporary reputation as a convention-flouting free spirit.[46] Thus linked to the scroll, however, Gu's reputation for inspired foolishness has encouraged modern scholars to interpret the paintings as subverting the lofty-minded text.

If the paintings were made in Luoyang in the late Western Jin (265–316) period, they may well have been straightforward illustrations of Zhang Hua's treatise, sharing its admonitory intention. It is not impossible that the compositions originated in the late third-century Luoyang; advanced examples of late Eastern Han (25–220 CE) pictorial art suggest a trajectory that could have reached the sophistication of

Fig. 1 Banquet scene. Late Eastern Han period, end of 2nd century CE. Mural on north wall, main chamber, Tomb no. 1 at Dahuting, Mixian, Henan. (After *Wenwu* 1972.10, pl. 1.)

the *Admonitions* pictures by the late Western Jin period. For example, the spatial organization of the 'Toiletry' scene (pl. 6 right) is prefigured in a late second-century banquet scene in a tomb mural at Dahuting, Mixian, Henan (fig. 1). Arriving at a similar date by somewhat different reasoning, Kohara argues that the pictorial motifs in the British Museum scroll compare well with archaeologically recovered provincial works of the fourth century that preserved features typical of the art of more central areas about fifty years before Gu Kaizhi was active.[47] However, as demonstrated by other papers in this volume, many scholars find the compositions in the *Admonitions* scroll more compatible with considerably later periods. If the illustrations originated later and under different circumstances than Zhang's text, they might well have served some purpose other than admonition.

Without further pursuing the question of the scroll's date, I wish to suggest that its pictures were created in an era

when the activities of palace women (or a particular palace woman) were arousing concern.[48] I base this suggestion on what I perceive as an essential congruity between the text and illustrations – I do *not* find the pictures to be ironic or otherwise at odds with the admonitory treatise.[49] The disjunctures that others have pointed out seem to me merely to demonstrate that its ideas were sometimes very difficult to pictorialize. For example, the passage that accompanies the fourth scene in the British Museum scroll (pl. 6 right) contrasts the easy but unimportant task of ornamenting one's face (*shi qi rong*)[50] with the important but difficult task of polishing one's character (*shi qi xing*; lines 39–40). There is no question that the picture is directly based on the text, but because the scene shows women at their toilette (i.e. *shi qi rong*),[51] Kohara argues that it properly belongs to the genre of beautiful women rather than didactic painting.[52] In other words, he believes that it undermines the intent of the text, whether by pandering to a voyeuristic male gaze or simply by offering witty amusement. However, I would suggest that the illustrator opted to show women embellishing their external appearance because this was vastly more feasible than depicting the subjective and invisible process of inner cultivation. In scene

Fig. 2 'Filial Piety of the Empress'. Illustration of Chapter 2, *Nü xiao jing (Ladies' Classic of Filial Piety)*. Song dynasty (960–1279). Detail of a handscroll; ink and colour on silk, h. 26.4 cm. Reproduced with permission of the National Palace Museum, Taipei, Taiwan, R. O. C.

eight (pl. 12 right), the artist actually did attempt to portray a woman quietly and reverently reflecting on herself (*jing gong zi si*; line 77),[53] and the result is cryptic, to say the least.

Similarly, I would read the 'Bed Scene' (pl. 6 left) as the artist's straightforward attempt to capture the idea of the more easily represented part of the relevant text, rather than as a sly innuendo of eroticism. The excerpt says,

If one's words are good, [people as far as] a thousand *li* will assent to them; if one defies this principle, then even one's bedmate will harbour doubts.

Chu qi yan shan, qian li ying zhi; gou wei si yi, ze tong qin yi yi.[54]

Taking its inspiration from the latter half of this pronouncement, the painting offers a subtle mini-drama playing off the concrete image of 'bedmate'. As I analyse the scene, the emperor sits on a bench at the edge of a canopied bed, perhaps about to take leave of his consort. Twisting around to scrutinize her, he fumbles for a shoe with his bare foot, as if too preoccupied to put it on properly. The woman warily returns his searching gaze from inside the compartment. Sitting stiffly back against the low screen that surrounds the bed, she clutches the top as if to buttress herself against his reproach. From the viewer's perspective, a hanging tassel separates the two faces, signifying their discord. Their tense postures and strained expressions, set against the claustrophobic enclosure of the bed, masterfully convey the feeling of confrontation. By contrast, an attempt to illustrate the abstract concept of good words having an impact for 1000 *li* might look something like the scene from the *Ladies' Classic of Filial*

Piety depicting the filial piety of the empress (fig. 2), which is based on the lines 'Her virtuous influence reaches the common people and she is a model for all within the four seas' (*de jiao jia yu bai xing, xing yu si hai*). All we see here is a royal matron sitting decorously on a throne, presumably projecting unseen moral authority.

One final example of a scene that others have read as satire or parody is the depiction of Ban Jieyu declining to ride in the emperor's carriage (pl. 3). Here the argument that other scholars have made is that the sober moralizing of the accompanying text is undercut by the visual interest of the litter-bearers' grimaces and the lively rhythm of their feet. Also, the presence of another woman in the litter seems to mock the exemplary concubine's self-denying forbearance; after all, she wanted to ride but restrained her desire out of concern for the emperor.[55] However, genre touches are not necessarily incompatible with seriousness of purpose, and the larger context of the incident should be taken into consideration. In particular, we need to recall the exact reason for Ban Jieyu's refusal, which is detailed in her *Han shu* and *Lie nü zhuan* biographies. It is not simply that she wanted to avoid 'distracting his thoughts from affairs of state', as Waley and others explained it.[56] As a matter of fact, the emperor was already thinking of pleasure, because this outing was to the rear palace, where his ladies lived. Rather, in response to the emperor's invitation, Ban Jieyu pointed out that ancient pictures depicted wise and sagely rulers in the company of eminent statesmen, while the bad last rulers of the Xia, Shang and Zhou were shown with their favourite consorts. If she joined Chengdi in the litter, he would resemble those depraved rulers.[57] Although the emperor was impressed with her statement and gave up his request, he did not reform himself and become a wise ruler. Indeed, he was soon preoccupied with Zhao Feiyan and her sister, and court affairs became extremely chaotic; only a few years after his death, Wang Mang (r. 9–22 CE) usurped the throne. The encomium (*zan*) to Chengdi's official biography made the connection between his personal laxity and dynastic catastrophe crystal clear.[58] In other words, even if Chengdi rode without a companion on one particular occasion, he really was the kind of ruler who let his consorts lead him astray, to the detriment of dynastic fortunes. So, by depicting another woman seated beside the emperor in the sedan chair, the artist both portrayed Chengdi as one of those 'bad last rulers' and reminded the viewer of the ensuing debacle.

Based on such considerations, I would conclude that Zhang Hua's 'Nü shi zhen' text and the illustrations in the British Museum's handscroll share a serious, admonitory purpose and do not make fun of Confucian ideals of behaviour. Moreover, the echoes of Ban Zhao's ideas in Zhang's text and the relevance of her historical context for his own situation lead me to believe that she was the inspiration for his *nü shi*, a persona adopted by Zhang to make his message more compelling. Accordingly, it may not be entirely farfetched to identify the brush-wielding woman in the last scene of the scroll as an imaginary portrait of Ban Zhao (pl. 13). Her presence suggests an appropriate context and gives authorial coherence to the preceding sequence of pictures.

NOTES

1   Kohara 2000 (1967), pp. 10–14.
2   Kohara 2000 (1967), p. 14.
3   Tr. Shih, Hsio-yen 1976, pp. 11–12. See pp. 15–18 for the transcription of lines 63–74.
4   Kohara 2000 (1967), p. 12.
5   Kohara 2000 (1967), p. 13.
6   Kohara 2000 (1967), p. 14.
7   Kohara 2000 (1967), p. 13.
8   McCausland 2001, p. 23; British Museum 2001; Audrey Spiro, pp. 53–64 in this volume.
9   *Jin shu* 1974, *juan* 36, p. 1072: *Hua ju hou zu zhi sheng, zuo Nü shi zhen yi wei feng* (see glossary).
10 Xiao Tong 1936, *juan* 56, p. 1203.
11 Straughair 1975, p. 45.
12 Knechtges 1982, p. 80, citing *Wenxin diaolong* 3.194.
13 Xiao Tong 1936, p. 2: *zhen xing yu bu que*; tr. Knechtges 1982, p. 81.
14 Zhang's 'Nü shi zhen' was probably chosen for the anthology because of its literary polish, particularly its parallel prose, rather than because of its political or moral significance (Knechtges 1982, p. 51; and Jao, Tsung-i 1986, pp. 891–893). The 'classic' example of admonition was Yang Xiong's (53 BCE–18 CE) *Shier zhou, ershiwu guan zhen (Admonitions to the Twelve Provinces and Twenty-five Officers)* (Hightower 1957, p. 522).
15 Knechtges 1982, p. 80.
16 Knechtges 1996, p. 400.
17 Straughair 1975, p. 45, n. 63.
18 E.g., Knechtges 1996, p. 184 & Hightower 1957, p. 522, respectively.
19 Morohashi 1960, vol. 3, p. 2890, no. 6036–138. The commentary to the *Zhou li*, also cited by Morohashi, suggests that these women were literate slaves, sometimes of good family, who served as the inner palace counterparts to the male scribes in the outer court bureaucracy. It should be noted that the *Zhou li* was a utopian reconstruction of the early Zhou bureaucracy, probably written in the Warring States period (475–221 BCE; Boltz 1993, pp. 24–32).
20 Mao no. 42; see Kong Yingda 1968, vol. 1, *juan* 2 part 3, pp. 7b–8a.
21 Zhu Xi completely rejected Mao's interpretation and explained the red tube as a token given by the girl to her lover (Zhu Xi 1970, p. 104–106). Most Western translators follow Zhu's lead (e.g. Legge 1935, pp. 68–69). Bernhard Karlgren translates *tong guan* as "red pipe" and suggests that it was a plant that the girl picked (Karlgren 1974, p. 28).
22 Xiao Tong 1936, *juan* 56, p. 1205: *nü shi tong guan zhi fa*. Similarly, in glossing a reference to a *nü shi* in Pan Yue's *Guafu fu (Widow's Rhapsody)*, Li commented, 'Mao Chang's commentary to the *Odes* says that in ancient times, the empress or principal wife was supposed to have a *nü shi*' (Xiao 1936, *juan* 16, p. 338: *Mao Chang Shi zhuan yue guzhe hou furen bi you nü shi*).
23 Xiao Tong 1964, *juan* 56, p. 1a: *Nü shi, nü ren zhi guan, zhi tong guan shu hou fei zhi shi. Hua ju hou zu zhi sheng, gu jia nü shi zuo zhen yi jie hou gong ye.*
24 *Han shu* 1962, *juan* 97B, p. 3985: *Gu nü shi er wen Shi.*
25 Xiao Tong 1936, *juan* 16, pp. 336–341: *Xian nü shi zhi dian jie*; tr. Knechtges 1996, pp. 184–185. Pan Yue served in and out of Luoyang during the 270s–290s and, like Zhang Hua, was executed in 300 after Empress Jia's overthrow.
26 Knechtges 1996, p. 184.
27 Hightower (1957, p. 522) seems to be exceptional (and incorrect) in supposing that the admonition was directed *to* the *nü shi*.
28 *Jin shu* 1974, *juan* 31, pp. 963–966.
29 Various scholars differ in estimating Ban Zhao's life dates, with her birth ranging from *c*.45–49 and death from *c*.115–120. Her official biography appears in *Hou Han shu* 1965, *juan* 84, pp. 2784–2892. For useful discussions of Ban Zhao see Swann 1932; Hou, Sharon 1986, pp. 177–178; Chen, Yu-shih 1996; Mann 2000, pp. 845, 854–855; and Raphals 1998, pp. 236–246. Mann (2000, p. 854) notes that Ban Zhao's portrait replaced that of Confucius on the walls of girls' schools in China.
30 An account of the Ban family composed by its own members is in *Han shu* 1962, *juan* 100; biographies and some writings of Ban Biao and Ban Gu appear in *Hou Han shu* 1965, *juan* 40A, pp. 1323–1330 and *juan* 40A–40B, pp. 1330–1394, respectively; for Ban Jieyu's life and literary compositions, see *Han shu* 1962, *juan* 97B, pp. 3983–3988; virtually the same information appears in her entry in the supplementary chapter of *Lie nü zhuan* (*Lie nü zhuan jiaozhu* 1983, *juan* 8, pp. 6b–7a; tr. O'Hara 1971, pp. 230–235).

Useful discussions of the Ban family are given in Chen, Yu-shih 1996, pp. 241–244; Swann 1932, pp. 24–39; and Loewe 2000, pp. 4–7.

31 Hou, Sharon 1986, p. 182.
32 *Hou Han shu* 1965, *juan* 84, pp. 2784–2785.
33 Idem, p. 2785.
34 Raphals 1998, p. 108; Swann 1932, pp. 45–46.
35 An annotated English translation of the entire work appears in Swann 1932, pp. 82–99; selections are also available on the website of the UCLA Center for East Asian Studies at *http://www.isop.ucla.edu/eas/documents/banzhao.htm*. For discussion, see Chen, Yu-shih 1996; also Raphals 1998, pp. 236–246.
36 Chen, Yu-shih 1996, pp. 252–256. Chen finds the *Nü jie* strongly tinged with a Huang-Lao Daoist outlook and Militarist strategic thinking, based on comparisons with the *Dao de jing* and *Sunzi bingfa*.
37 Both Hou (1986) and Raphals (1998) describe numerous later texts inspired by or modelled on the *Nü jie*, including not only freestanding works but also sections of clan instructions relevant to women.
38 Murray 1988, p. 97.
39 Chen, Yu-shih 1996, p. 229.
40 Deng Sui came from a powerful Luoyang family; see her detailed biography in *Hou Han shu* 1965, *juan* 10A, pp. 418–430.
41 Chen, Yu-shih 1996, pp. 248–252.
42 Chen, Yu-shih 1996, pp. 244–245.
43 In her preface, Ban Zhao says that over forty years had passed since she had married into the Cao family at the age of fourteen *sui*. Because her husband died young, her children must have been born early in this period. Accordingly, Swann (1932, p. 91, n. 11) suggests that the preface to *Nü jie* referred to her nieces, and Chen (1996, p. 245) proposes that the text was written long before its 'publication' (whatever that actually meant in the Han dynasty). A problem with Chen's suggestion is Ban Zhao's preface refers both to her own relatively advanced age (at least fifty-four) and her concern for her unmarried girls.
44 *Hou Han shu* 1965, *juan* 84, p. 2785; tr. Swann 1932, pp. 76–77.
45 *Jin shu* 1974, *juan* 36, p. 1072: *Jin zhong kuang fu, mi feng bu que*; tr. Straughair 1975, p. 44.
46 Alfreda Murck explores the major features of Gu's 'persona' in the Tang and Song periods, which was based on literary rather than pictorial sources (pp. 138–145 in this volume).
47 Kohara 2000 (1967), pp. 48–49.
48 Accordingly, I am intrigued by Yang Xin's argument that the British Museum scroll was painted in the late fifth century, during the difficult period when Empress Dou Wenming dominated political affairs at the court of Northern Wei emperor Xiaowendi (r. 471–499), who moved the Northern Wei capital to Luoyang (pp. 42–52 in this

volume). In the discussion following his presentation at the 2001 colloquy, Yang further noted that Xiaowendi had wept upon seeing the ruins of the Western Jin palace and resolved that his dynasty would not suffer the same fate.
49 The visual evidence strongly suggests that the pictures were painted first and the passages of text were transcribed afterward, perhaps many centuries later. If the handscroll originally contained only paintings, it would be comparable to recorded Western Han (202–7 BCE) scrolls that contained illustrative matter for texts in a different format, such as bundles of written strips (*ce*); for examples, see *Han shu* 1962, *juan* 30, pp. 1701–1784. Once it became common for pictures and texts to share the same surface, a later owner of the *Admonitions* paintings may have wanted the relevant passages to appear next to their illustrations.
50 Unlike the *Wen xuan* version of the text, the British Museum and Beijing Palace Museum scrolls both have *xiu qi rong*. The Beijing scroll displays the standard form of the character *xiu* 修, while the British Museum scroll has a variant form 脩 that suggests greater informality.
51 Hsio-yen Shih (1976, p. 15) identifies the figure on the left, whose hair is being combed, as a man rather than a woman. This identification seems to me highly unlikely, because the proximity of an unambiguously female figure checking her coiffure in a hand-held mirror suggests that the scene is set in the women's quarters, and I know of no reason to think that the emperor went there to be groomed. Moreover, the person being combed is comparable in size to the lady holding the mirror, while the emperor (or any high-status male) would be likely to be portrayed on a distinctly larger scale.
52 Kohara 2000 (1967), pp. 8–10.
53 The British Museum scroll has the homophone and homonym *jing* 靜 instead of the *jing* 靖 used in the *Wen xuan* rendition of Zhang Hua's text and in the *baimiao Admonitions* scroll in Beijing. See *Jing gong zi si* in the glossary.
54 Lines 45–48; see the transcription on pp. 15–18.
55 Zhang Hua's allusion to the story emphasizes Ban Jieyu's desire to ride: 'Lady Ban declined, despite her desire, to accompany [the emperor] in the palanquin. How could she not have been sad? But, forfending the unseemly, she acted with prudence' (*Ban Jie you ci, ge huan tong nian. Fu qi bu huai, fang wei lü yuan*; tr. Shih, Hsio-yen 1976, p. 11; see transcription of lines 29–32, p. 16).
56 Waley 1958, p. 50.
57 *Han shu* 1962, *juan* 97B, pp. 3983–3984; tr. and discussed in Raphals 1998, pp. 78–81. The Song critic Guo Ruoxu also cites the story as an example of the efficacy of paintings for admonitory purposes; see Guo Ruoxu 1974, *juan* 1, p. 3.
58 *Han shu* 1962, *juan* 10, p. 330.

Refiguring: The Visual Rhetoric of the Sixth-Century Northern Wei 'Filial Piety' Engravings

Eugene Y. Wang

Connoisseurship and deconstruction make strange bedfellows. The former assumes the organic unity of things while the latter looks for internal wars. When the two join forces, the effect is to be savoured, such as one may find in Kohara Hironobu's meticulous connoisseurship on the *Admonitions* scroll. 'It is crucial to distinguish', he observes, 'between the meaning of the text and the agenda of the painter who selected and arranged the expressive forms.' The painter of the *Admonitions* scroll turned 'the textual content upside-down and inside out, a practice that is quite opposed to the thrust of the admonitions themselves.'[1] It would be edifying to try and substantiate this intuition. One could further ask, for instance, *what* 'agenda' is at stake, *how* the painting subverts the text, and under *what* historical circumstances? Unfortunately, uncertainty about the date and authorship of the original scroll makes such questions rather quixotic and fanciful. Bereft of dates, to parody David Hawkes, art historians flounder in aestheticism.[2]

While the scroll, contextually unmoored, does not allow us to substantiate Kohara's insight, its displaced 'twin' does. The scroll is often compared with the engravings on the Northern Wei (386–533) sarcophagus at the Nelson-Atkins Art Museum in Kansas City (figs 1, 2).[3] The august palace lady on the southern scroll and the elegant female figure on the northern sarcophagus make a striking match (figs 3, 4).

There are various ways we could make something of this. We could see it as a testimony to the existence of a pre-Tang (618–907) model upon which the scroll was based. We could use this evidence to recapitulate upon the familiar story of north-south cultural exchange. But for me, here is the opportunity to make good on Kohara's claim, emboldened by our knowledge of the sarcophagus' date – 520s – and its provenance, i.e. the Mangshan area to the north of the Northern Wei capital Luoyang.[4] There is a lot we can do with such specific knowledge of its original context.

The engravings are unusual in a number of ways. To begin with, this is the only surviving Northern Wei sarcophagus from Luoyang whose long sides *exclusively* feature filial piety scenes. The Yuan Mi sarcophagus at the Minneapolis Institute of Art, for instance, features engravings of filial images along with other motifs (fig. 5). Both designs were quite novel at the time. Most Northern Wei sarcophagi from Luoyang kept to the traditional design featuring the set of Four Directional Animals or variations thereof (fig. 6).

More notable, perhaps, is the integration of a lush landscape into the composition, a conspicuous departure from the Han (206 BCE–220 CE) convention. Scholars vacillate between seeing each panel as one composition and as three separate scenes.[5] They relieve the tension between compositional continuity and narrative discontinuity by affirming both: they *read* the human figures as players in the separate stories, and *view* the landscape as one picture. It is as if narrative content and pictorial logic, reading and viewing, could thus be neatly separated. But the compositional continuity is so palpable and its momentum so strong,[6] one suspects there is a coherent conceptual thread linking the three otherwise unrelated scenes.

A number of other things confirm this impression. It becomes clear that these particular filial piety stories are neither chosen nor arranged here randomly. We find structural correlations between the two slabs. To both short ends are assigned a scene of transportation or procession, and to both tall ends, a scene of a male/female encounter.

At this point, there is a block in our thinking that needs to be cleared out of the way. We usually group pictures in these engravings in several thematic categories: (a) Flight to Immortality (fig. 6); (b) Filial Piety stories (figs 1–2); and (c) a hybrid of the two (fig. 5). Too often, however, we take these categories for granted, and forget they are modern constructs, when in fact, such distinctions among them hardly existed in

Fig. 1 (above) 'Stories of Filial Piety' (right to left): Yuan Gu; Guo Ju; and Shun. Engraving on the side of a stone sarcophagus, *c*.525. Northern Wei Dynasty (386–533). Engraved grey limestone, overall 62.2 × 223.5 cm. The Nelson-Atkins Museum of Art, Kansas City, Missouri. (Purchase: Nelson Trust).

Fig. 2 (above right) 'Stories of Filial Piety' (left to right): Wang Lin; Cai Shun; and Dong Yong. Opposite side of the sarcophagus in fig. 1.

Fig. 3 (below) Palace lady from the rejection scene of the *Admonitions* scroll in the British Museum.

Fig. 4 (right) Goddess in the Dong Yong story. Detail of engraving on the Kansas sarcophagus.

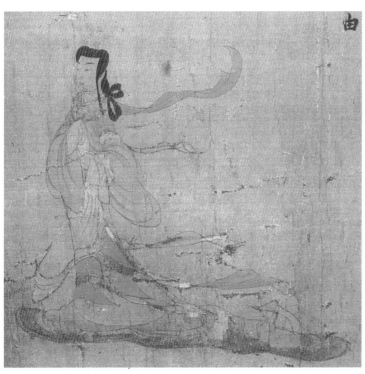

Fig. 5 Sarcophagus of Yuan Mi, or Prince Zhenjing, 524. Black limestone, h. 60, l. 223 cm. The Minneapolis Institute of Arts, William Hood Dunwoody Fund, 46.23.

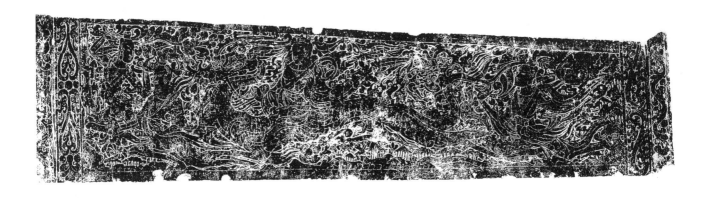

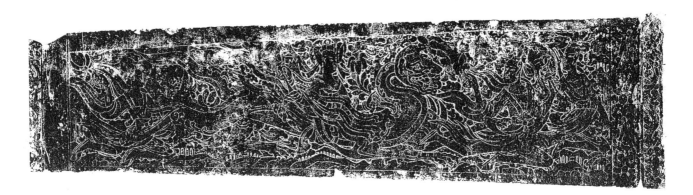

Fig. 6 'Flight to Immortality'. Two sides of a Northern Wei sarcophagus in the traditional design featuring the set of Four Directional Animals or variations. Ink rubbing of engraving on a sarcophagus from Haizi Village, Mangshan, Henan Province. Northern Wei dynasty (386–533). Limestone. Kaifeng City Museum. (After Wang Ziyun, *Zhongguo gudai shikehua xuanji* [Beijing, 1957], pl. 6.)

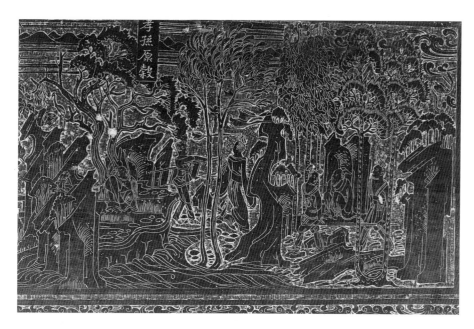

Fig. 7 (above) Line drawing of the decorative programme on the sarcophagus of Wang Hui. From Lushan County, Sichuan Province. Eastern Han, 212 CE. Stone, h. 101, l. 250, w. 83 cm. Lushan Museum. Drawing by Alice Tseng.

Fig. 8 (above right) Yuan Gu story on the Kansas sarcophagus.

the sixth century. The appearance of the so-called 'Filial Son' stories here is only a pretext for something else. The narrative content may cause us to lose sight of the funerary function of the object, whose purpose the 'decoration' must serve. It is necessary to reinstate this purpose. If we take the convention of coffin decoration seriously enough, we will be mindful of its emphasis on lateral development and spatial orientation within the panels.

From Han times on, sarcophagus design typically employs the set of Four Directional Animals, or its variations, because of its strong cosmographic associations (fig. 7). Since north is considered the region of *yin* and death, and south is associated with *yang*, birth and rebirth, the coffin's small end designates north, and often features the Dark Warrior, and the large end represents south, and is often occupied by the Vermilion Bird. The corpse's head is placed at the large end of the coffin, so that the design creates an imaginary scenario in which the deceased's disembodied spirit flies from north to south, hence, from the small/foot to the large/head end of the coffin. In this way, the deceased's spirit would be heralded by the Red Bird in front; the Dark Warrior behind; the Green Dragon on the left; and the White Tiger on the right.[7] We therefore speak of the 'left' and 'right' of the flying spirit

of the deceased, not of the body lying face-up in the coffin.

A typical Northern Wei sarcophagus design improves upon this scheme. It turns the Directional Animals into celestial mounts that transport either the deceased's spirit or the celestial ushers as they head toward transcendence. More innovative designs also came into being, such as on the Yuan Mi sarcophagus, made in 524,[8] where the Flight-to-Immortality shares space with filial paragons (fig. 5).[9]

The novel design of the Kansas City sarcophagus also appeared around this time (figs 1–2). Here the Flight to Immortality motif disappears altogether, and Filial Piety scenes take up the entire space. But a sarcophagus is a sarcophagus: we must assume that the quest for immortality remains the driving force behind its design. A lateral thrust from the short to the tall end still orders the images on the side slabs.

So, what is the connection between these scenes depicting unconnected tales of filial piety? Take the left slab first. The sequence begins from the short end with the story of Yuan Gu. When his father carries Gu's grandfather into the forest on a stretcher and abandons the old man there, Gu brings back the empty stretcher. Asked why, he replies that he intends to do the same to his own father in future. Upon hearing this, his father repents. Yuan Gu thereby earns the reputation of a filial paragon (fig. 8).[10]

The middle scene concerns Guo Ju, whose father dies when Ju is young. Ju supports his mother through hard labour. Soon his wife gives birth to a baby. Fearing that it might take away food from his mother, Ju resolves to bury the baby. While digging, he finds a cauldron with a cinnabar-

Fig. 9 Guo Ju story on the Kansas sarcophagus.

Fig. 10 (left) Shun story on the Kansas sarcophagus.

Fig. 12 (right) Shun story in a lacquer painting on the side of a coffin. From Guyuan, c.484 CE. (After Guyuan Museum and Sino-Japanese Archaeology Team, *Yuanzhou gumu jicheng* [Beijing: Wenwu chubanshe, 1999], pl. 18.)

coloured note in it saying: 'Guo Ju, the filial son: this cauldron of gold is a reward for you' (fig. 9).[11]

The final scene illustrates the story of Shun. Shun loses his mother when young. His father, Gushou, remarries and wants to get rid of him. He gets Shun to dig a well and buries Shun in it. Shun uses his ingenuity to escape. Bearing no grudge, he continues to attend to his father's needs with loving care, and earns the reputation of a filial paragon by the age of twenty. Recognizing his virtues, the sage-king Yao marries his two daughters to Shun and appoints him to a governorship (fig. 10).[12]

If we are guided by the textual narratives alone, we would remain convinced of the discontinuity between these stories – or, of their being related only insofar as they are all filial son stories. *Pictorially*, a different sequence of events unfolds.

First, keep in mind that the primary function of coffin design is to ensure that its occupant reaches the immortal land. Note the scenery in the Yuan Gu story (fig. 8): the forest has all the trappings of an immortal land. Michael Sullivan notes: 'The artist has emphasized the extreme age of the grandfather of Yuan Gu by placing him beneath an ancient pine tree on which perches a crane – both symbols of longevity.'[13] So, the point of this illustration is to depict the immortal land, and this is reinforced by the inclusion of significant details associated with it, such as the monkey and deer nearby. Thus, the act of carrying an old man on a stretcher into the forest, recounted in the filial piety tale, is transformed into a symbolic ritual of seeing off the deceased on a journey to a happy land, devoid of the overtone of desertion in the filial piety story.

A Northern Wei sarcophagus from Shangyao provides supporting evidence. Conventional images of the Flight to

Fig. 11 Fragment containing the Yuan Gu story reused on a Northern Wei sarcophagus from Shangyao, 6th century.

Immortality adorn its two long sides, but its rear slab recycles a fragment from another sarcophagus that contains various scenes of filial piety (fig. 11). From this 'repertoire', it is the Yuan Gu scene that was chosen as the appropriate piece for the foot end. This combination of the Flight to Immortality on the long sides and this filial piety story at the foot end has baffled scholars.[14] Now we see how this choice makes perfect sense.

So what we have here is a 'funerary narrative' in which a series of three unrelated filial piety stories are unfolding into a three-step symbolic process. The first stage is a departure scene, that of carrying the deceased into the immortal land (or graveyard). The second stage involves burial and making

Fig. 13 Engraving on the Ning Mao shrine, 527. Museum of Fine Arts, Boston.

offerings to the image of the deceased, which takes its cue from contemporary Buddhist funerary practice. Granted, the middle scene here (Guo Ju burying his baby) does not in and of itself support my argument. Analyses of both the opening and closing scenes, however, make a strong case, and will in turn shed light on the significance of the middle scene.

Much weight therefore hangs on the final stage. Its textual basis is the 'Shun cycle of myths',[15] a set of stories that had been in circulation since remote antiquity,[16] and were standardized in the Han.[17] Of the surviving Northern Wei illustrations of this subject, four are particularly notable: (1) the lacquer-painted coffin from Guyuan (c. 484 CE; fig. 12);[18] (2) the lacquer panel from the Sima Jinlong (d. 474 CE) tomb (entombed 484 CE; pl. 16);[19] (3) the engraving on the Ning Mao shrine (527 CE) in Boston (fig. 13); and (4) the engraving on the Kansas City sarcophagus (fig. 10).[20]

The surviving fragments of the Guyuan coffin, made around 484 or earlier,[21] contain illustrations of five filial piety tales. The Shun cycle takes up most of the space on the right side of the coffin, beginning with 'Shun's step-mother about to burn the granary shed to kill Shun', as indicated in the cartouche. Then follows a succession of scenes about Shun's relationships with his family members (fig. 12).

All other Northern Wei illustrations of the Shun cycle focus on two narrative strands: the ordeal that Shun goes through, and his conjugation with Yao's two daughters. The Sima Jinlong panel and the Kansas engraving are particularly alike in composition. In both cases, Shun escapes from perils on the left and meets Yao's two daughters on the right.

Differences between the two works register the change in taste that occurred in the intervening four decades (between 484 and 520s). The Sima Jinlong panel retains the Han compositional scheme: individual scenes proceed laterally; the entire composition is divided into different registers; all the figures, with little overlapping, are set against a void (pl. 16). By contrast, the Kansas engraving integrates figures into a richly textured landscape to create a somewhat different psychological effect (fig. 10). Then, the Sima Jinlong panel shows Shun as a stately figure, holding a tool, presumably to signal his regal stature and to illustrate a point made in the text that Shun 'tilled the soil on the Mount Li'. The panel merely fulfils its obligation to illustrate the text. This contrasts with the Kansas engraving, which shows a young Shun standing behind the portly and august King Yao, who introduces him to his two elegant daughters.

And what women these two are, especially the figure on the right shown with her back turned three-quarters to the viewer! With her trailing garments and scarves in a display of ethereal curvilinearism, she appears to be airborne, gliding gracefully in space (fig. 14). Our attention, throughout the scene, gravitates towards this pictorial flourish, the psychologically charged moment when a young man meets a young woman.

A literal adherence to narrative content would have had Yao aligned with his two daughters to meet Shun. Here, however, the engraving divides the figures strictly by gender, a choreography designed to highlight the *encounter*. Moreover, the woman with her back partially turned toward the viewer does not fully reveal her identity, which adds to her mystique and the dynamic of the encounter.

Now, compare the engraving with the illustration of the *Goddess of the Luo River* (pl. 20). Both set figures against a rolling landscape; moreover, both show a male group headed by a royal figure encountering an elusive, 'floating' female beauty with trailing robe and fluttering scarves. This similarity is most remarkable.

The painting is an illustration of Cao Zhi's (192–232) rhapsody (*fu*) entitled 'Goddess of the Luo River', which recounts how, when returning to the east coast from the capital in 223,[22] Cao Zhi encounters a nymph on the Luo River. 'She wore a gown of shimmering gauze' with trailing 'light sleeves of misty mesh ... Her form, swept along lightly ... She floated through air...' Though attracted to each other, the nymph sighs over the unbridgeable gap that intervenes between gods and men, which condemns them to 'dwell in realms set apart'.[23] The encounter leaves a lasting regret and sadness in the poet's heart.

Cao Zhi's rhapsody is an offshoot of a southern literary tradition about encounters with goddesses.[24] The subject derives from religious rituals in which a shaman invokes river deities to visit the world of men and laments his failure to make it happen. In Han times,[25] this tradition provided a framework for rhapsodies in which the speaker traverses the vast, misty, enchanted lakes-region of the south and meets an ethereal nymph. The encounter often ends with the infatuated speaker thwarted in his yearning, his passion for the river nymph unconsummated. Cao Zhi worked within this genre, as did many of his contemporaries. The tradition grew steadily over time.

In the fourth century, tales of Encounter with a Goddess became more involved and localized. They typically concern a young man who somehow chances to find a nymph. The encounter leads to a kind of one-night stand, after which the young man finds his way back into the mundane order. There are some new twists in this development. Unlike the early poetic scenario of an encounter against the backdrop of a vast imaginary panorama with hardly any topographic moorings, the medieval accounts are set in specific locations. Moreover, the character of the nymph has changed. She is now typically an *old* woman, even a thousand-year-old woman, who looks like a sixteen-year-old. They meet in a dream, or in the mountains, farming fields, and so forth. The goddesses reveal themselves to be female immortals (*xian*), so the ecstatic encounter and intimacy involves the couple's taking drugs, food, and wine.[26]

The Daoist overtones of such tales are obvious. The Daoist ritual of revelation, known as 'Descent of the Perfected' (*jiangzhen*), is set in identical narrative situations, except that the young man awaits the descent of the Perfected Person, a female immortal, in his own bed chamber.[27]

It was in this cultural context that the first recorded pictorial illustration of Cao Zhi's 'Goddess of the Luo River' appeared, painted, not by Gu Kaizhi, but by Sima Shao (299–325; r. 322–325), the second emperor of the Eastern Jin.[28] Sima Shao's personal circumstances reveal the symbolic investment he may have brought into the subject. His mother was initially a palace servant. Haunted by her humble social origin in a time of hardened attitudes to social mobility, she was often bitter and disgruntled. Her misgivings soured her relationship with the emperor who gradually became estranged from her.[29] This strained relationship caused by

Fig. 14 Yao's daughters in the Shun story on the Kansas sarcophagus.

social disparity must have had a telling effect on their son Sima Shao. It has been suggested that the increasing currency of the tale of encounter with a female transcendent in the fourth century was a sublimation of popular misgivings about social inequality, in an era when power was monopolized by prominent families of the hereditary nobility. The young men in such tales tend to be poor and of humble social origins.[30]

Two other historical figures had their share of influence on Sima Shao. Ruan Fang (fourth century), a National University Erudite, was one of the Mentors to the Heir Apparent. Ruan frequently lectured on the Daoist classics *Laozi* and *Zhuangzi* and neglected military affairs at a time when the latter was of pressing concern.[31] Wang Yi (275–322) was Sima Shao's painting instructor.[32] An uncle of the Calligraphic Sage Wang Xizhi (303–361), and regarded as the best painter of his time, Wang Yi was a native of Langya, which says much about his Daoist sensibility.[33] Both mentors to Sima Shao show Daoist orientations. His painting of the *Goddess of the Luo*

Fig. 15 Dong Yong story on the Kansas sarcophagus.

Fig. 16 Dong Yong story on the Wu Liang Shrine, Shandong Province.

River is accordingly to be seen in a similar light. It is driven by an anxiety over the gap between the transcendent realm and the human world, and uncertainty about how to navigate between them.

Likewise, Shun's meeting with Yao's two daughters in the Kansas engraving (fig. 10) is really an Encounter with a Goddess displaced into a Confucian narrative framework. The female figures with trailing garments are nymphs descending into the human world. Such an interpretation accords with the medieval Daoist appropriation of the Shun cycle.

The corresponding scene on the right slab (fig. 15) reinforces this impression. As a filial son story, the scene is about the poor Dong Yong finding ways of supporting his father

and, upon the latter's death, giving him a proper burial. In this Confucian framework the celestial maid in the guise of a mortal being who comes to his aid is only a *deus ex machina*, a heavenly reward for the filial paragon. Now, it is easy to see how the descent of the celestial maid in the Confucian story fits snugly into the alternative framework of Encounter with a Goddess.

The same story is retold in Gan Bao's (act. 317–322) *In Search of the Supernatural (Soushen ji)*; it is also grouped with other miracle tales whose primary interest is encounter with the supernatural. One tale concerns a young man who grows and feeds on fragrant grass, causing 'five-coloured divine moths' to produce silkworms on it. A 'goddess' arrives at night to help him make silk. The two then disappear into thin air. No one knows of their whereabouts. Another concerns a young man who receives two celestial maids sent by an immortal lady and is given special food for apotropaic purposes. Yet another tale regards a young man who repeatedly dreams of a goddess, a 'jade woman', descending to him. Their relationship extends even after his marriage to an earthly woman.[34] Placed in this textual setting, the Dong Yong story takes on new life; its thrust is about an earthling's miraculous encounter with the world of transcendence rather than about his human bonds and social-ethical obligations. This re-appropriation of a Confucian paragon into a Daoist framework is common in early medieval times.[35]

A comparison between the Han-period treatment of the Dong Yong story and its sixth-century counterpart clearly

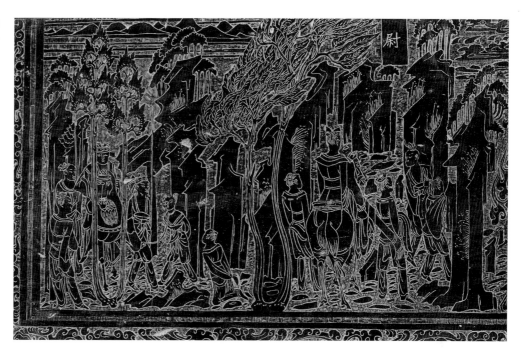

Fig. 17 Wang Lin story on the
Kansas sarcophagus.

demonstrates the shift of interest. In the mid-second-century Wu Liang Shrine engraving, the father-son relationship, pictured in massive form, fills up most of the space. The flying female figure on the right, above Dong Yong's head, is presumably the goddess, here marginalized (fig. 16).[36] The weight of emphasis is on human bonds solidly anchored in this world. In the Kansas engraving, Dong Yong walks away from his father and comes to a halt in front of the graceful goddess (fig. 15). Here, the dynamic is their encounter and its Daoist overtone is reinforced by the landscape and two deer near the old man signalling that this is an immortal land.

The Dong Yong scene alone does not clinch the argument, for we must also relate it to the two other scenes on the same slab. The sequence begins with the story of Wang Lin. Wang lost his parents as a teenager during the Red Brow insurgency. Although his neighbours all flee their homes, he and his brother stay by their parents' tomb. His brother ventures out and is captured by the insurgents who threaten to 'eat' him. Wang Lin gives himself up and offers to die in his brother's place. Moved by this bravery, the bandits set the two brothers free (fig. 17).[37]

Next is the tale of Cai Shun, whose father died when he was young. He takes good care of his mother, thereby earning a reputation as a filial son. His mother dies at the age of ninety. Before the burial takes place, a fire erupts in the neighbourhood. Cai throws himself on his mother's coffin and 'cries and wails to the heaven'. They are miraculously spared the fire (fig. 18).[38]

Now, the coffin scene is most explicitly self-referential: Cai's mother's coffin is shown lying in the same direction as the actual sarcophagus on whose side it is engraved. If it references the real-life funeral, what do we then make of the fire and execution scenes to the left? We can indeed relate the fire to the early Xianbei funerary practice of burning the deceased's body, his belongings, and his *dog* so that his soul could ascend to mythic heights. We could also speculate about its connection with Buddhist practice of cremation current at the time. We could relate the execution scene in the story of Wang Lin to contemporary filial piety accounts, such as one in the *History of Wei* about a man who accidentally beat his alcoholic wife to death in a rage. He was arrested and awaiting execution when his fifteen-year-old son, worried about the imminent orphanage of his four-year-old sister, begged the authorities to execute him in lieu of his father.[39] The event echoes the Wang Lin story.

But we have to establish some kind of connection between the execution and burning scenes. The Daoist belief in 'escape from the corpse' (*shijie*) provides a clue. According to accounts of this practice, upon a person's death his soul is said to escape the body and fly off to immortal realms, leaving behind an empty coffin. One may 'escape the corpse' by various means, chief among them *execution* and *fire*. Cases of 'escape from the corpse through execution' (*bingjie*) typically involve a Daoist adept who somehow runs into trouble with worldly authorities. He is then executed and his corpse is placed in a coffin. The execution turns out to be a blessing, for

Fig. 18 Cai Shun story on the Kansas sarcophagus.

it sets his spirit free from corporeal bondage, enabling it to roam the universe.[40]

Another means is known as 'escape from the corpse through fire' (*huojie*). The adept's body is subjected to fire which 'refines' it into a higher form of being; or, the adept's essence was believed to 'ascend with the smoke', a phenomenon known as 'ascent through glowing clouds' (*dengxia*).[41]

Here the Wang Lin scene, a potential execution, plays out an 'escape from the corpse through execution' (fig. 17). The burning scene fulfils the symbolic function of 'escape from the corpse through fire' (fig. 18). The spatial orientation of the coffin in the pavilion hints at the lateral development of the sequence. After the 'escape from the corpse' through execution and fire, the sequence ends with the immortal land, where deer are frolicking, the old man is supplied with wine, and the encounter with the goddess takes place.

One may wonder: why must the Daoist theme masquerade itself in Confucian trappings? Would not a straightforward Flight-to-Immortality design (fig. 6) express Daoist aspirations better? Indeed, coffin designs featuring the Flight to Immortality remained a popular option in the sixth century. The new design depicting Daoist transcendence in the guise of filial piety scenes is an outcome of the complex historical circumstances under the Northern Wei.

Confucianism under Northern Wei had a good run. The story of sinicization – by which non-Chinese in China are said to adopt Han-Chinese cultural practices – is too familiar to bear repeating here. I want to emphasize, though, that the imperial promotion of filial piety also was prompted by politi-

cal circumstances. Between 471 and 490, the Northern Wei was ruled by the so-called 'Twin Sages', namely, Empress Dowager Lady Feng and the young emperor Xiaowen (r. 471–499). Apparently, she was the real monarch and the child emperor a mere figurehead. In this context, the promotion of filial piety by the imperium comes as no surprise. The court revived the traditional Chinese practice of seeking exemplary filial sons from commanderies to fill government posts.

History shortly repeated itself. In 515, Emperor Xiaoming (510–528; r. 516–528) was enthroned at the age of six. His mother Hu Chonghua, the empress dowager, was really in control. The court issued a decree that filial sons across the country were to be publicly recognized and rewarded.[42] The court frequently held lectures on the *Classic of Filial Piety (Xiao jing).*[43] Of the fourteen filial paragons who received biographic entries in the *History of Wei*, eight were recognized for filial piety towards their mother.[44] That explains the centrality of filial piety toward a mother figure in the middle section on both sides of the Kansas sarcophagus.

However, official Northern Wei promotion of filial piety alone does not fully explain the sumptuous engravings. Coffin design exposes an inner tension in the Confucian system between its punctiliousness about ritual correctness and its ethical taste for austerity. Elaborate design may express hierarchical propriety and the depth of filial piety. The Confucian wariness of excess, however, counsels against extravagance. Registering this tension, coffin design oscillated between extravagance and austerity over time. From the third century on, the tendency was toward simple design.

This austerity continued into the early Northern Wei. Diao Yong (390–484), a distinguished Confucian scholar-official, specified to his sons that his coffin slabs were to be undecorated. He justified this decision through an essay titled 'On Filial Piety' (Xing xiao lun) in which he lambasted the two extremes of burial practices of the past, i.e. shabby and cursory disposal on the one hand and extravagant burial on the other.[45] Han Qilin, a general who died in 488, also made it clear in his will that he should be buried in a 'plain coffin' and that 'the funerary service should be frugal and simple'.[46]

Textual evidence suggests that up to the end of the fifth century, the plain coffin design remained the favoured type.[47] By the mid-510s, however, the decorative type had come back into vogue. The Diao family again provides us with a measure of this change. Diao Yong's teaching of austerity resonated with his son Diao Zun (441–516) who followed his father's example. By the time of his death in 516,[48] however, the undecorated coffin had become passé, so that even the local governor found the Diao's austerity 'too much out of touch with the [custom of the] time'. Diao Yong's descendants thought it no trivial matter and 'wrote to the National University to seek the Confucian academicians' opinions on the matter', only to find that the baffled scholar-officials 'did not know what to reply'![49] The sumptuous decoration of funerary paraphernalia had by this time become so prevalent that even the austerity-minded Confucian academics were resigned to its currency.

This growing taste for sumptuous coffin design, indicated by the Diao family's arrangements for Diao Zun's funeral in 516, coincided with an important event. In the same year, the court held discussions concerning the need to remodel the royal carriages for the imperial progress to 'the boundary sacrifice'. It was argued that the design should follow ancient models while 'reckoning with current circumstances'.[50]

The *History of Wei* describes the decorative programme on Northern Wei imperial carriages. The 'Cosmological Carriage' reserved for 'Grand Empress Dowager, the Empress Dowager, and the Empress' was most elaborate in design. It featured images of 'clouded mountains and forests, *immortals*, sages, loyal ministers, *filial sons*, chaste women, *roaming dragons, flying phoenixes*, the Red Bird, the Dark Warriors, the *White Tiger*, the *Green Dragon, fantastic birds* and *exotic beasts*'.[51] The description reads like an *ekphrasis* of the engravings on the Yuan Mi sarcophagus (fig. 5), and is but one step away from the Kansas sarcophagus (figs 1–2) which omits the White Tiger and Green Dragon.

The remodelling of the ritual carriages has additional significance for us. The carriages were deployed for imperial processions to the 'boundary sacrifices' (*jiaosi*) in the southern suburb of the capital city, where offerings were made to the spirits of ancient sages and ancestors. The suburban locale, therefore, signified a boundary between the human world and the realm of ghosts and spirits, while the excursion amounted to symbolic contact with the realm of the spirits.[52]

The occasion again highlights the tension in Confucian practice between deeply ingrained wariness about the 'otherness' of the world of ghosts and spirits, and ritual obligation toward ancestral authority. As such, it left room for other-worldly interests to thrive within the Confucian apparatus. The Empress Dowager Ling (d 528 CE), mother of Emperor Xiaoming, initially a Buddhist nun, had a strong interest in otherworldliness. She needed Confucian filial piety to maintain her authority; at the same time, her taste for the supernatural was not to be discounted. The result was a kind of Confucianism with otherworldly orientations – an oxymoron borne out of peculiar historical circumstances.

In fact, Confucianism under the Northern Wei was constantly appropriated for other purposes and aligned with other causes. The Celestial Master Daoism fashioned by Kou Qianzhi (365–448) that thrived under the Northern Wei in the fifth century, was Confucianism in disguise. The intense rivalry between Buddhism and Daoism further pushed Daoism into close alliance with Confucianism and vice versa. The most strident and stirring charge against Buddhism by its detractors was its adherents' lack of filial piety, and the sin of neglecting filial piety was gravest when one discontinued the '[boundary] offering'.[53] Confucian court-officials considered Buddhism a 'ghostly religion' that contradicted Confucius' teaching that 'not knowing life, how can one know death?' In their eyes, one should pursue daylight matters instead of the 'dark and obscure'. If, however, one must deal with the affair of spirits, one turns to those of the 'Three Thearchs and Five Emperors' of antiquity, who can be considered the proper 'ghosts'.[54]

Thus, to conduct the 'boundary sacrifice' was not only to fulfil Confucian ritual propriety, it was also a way of being in touch with the supernatural. 'Filial piety', a Northern Wei official argued, 'allows one to reach the deity' and eventually 'arrive at the other shore'.[55] This displacement of filial piety had been a common practice for some time. Since the late Han, the *Classic of Filial Piety* had been taking on extra-textual magical powers.[56] It was believed that, by quoting certain passages from the text, one could 'dispel evil spirits'.[57] This conviction formed the basis for a peculiar kind of funeral practice in which a dying man would hold the *Classic of Filial Piety* and *Laozi* in the one hand, and Buddhist sūtras in the other, in the hope that these talismanic texts would ensure his safe passage to the other world.[58]

Contemporary descriptions of the living environment of some Northern Wei court officials give us a clearer and more textured picture that matches the mood of the engravings. In *A Record of Buddhist Monasteries in Luoyang*, Wei Shou provides us with an account of a court official's residence in the Ward of Manifested Virtue in east Luoyang. Wei begins by setting up an opposition in lifestyle between a Confucian and a Daoist scholar-official. The Confucian official lived frugally, while Zhang Lun, Minister of Agriculture and a man with a Daoist disposition, is said to be 'extravagant'. But soon, hardened distinctions collapse, and claims and moral qualities with ideological labels become fictional or purely rhetorical. Terms such as 'simplicity and purity' are lavished on Zhang Lun, who, a moment ago, was described as 'extravagant'. The praise comes in the context of a rhapsody on the Mount Jingyang built by Zhang, presumably in his own residence. His garden landscape contained towering crags, deep chasms, cavernous gullies, tall forests with hanging creepers and dangling vines, winding stone paths, and the beds of torrents.[59] Many of these descriptive details match the scenery in the engravings.

Zhang Lun's Mount Jingyang embodies the dual aspects of the 'period notion' of transcendence (*xian*). First of all, it is a fictive space of eremitism that allows him to play the recluse away from the cares of officialdom while also donning the hat of the Minister of Agriculture. Secondly, it provides a means of transcending time and death (in Wei Shou's words):

> One of these pines could avert old age,
> Half a rock might prolong one's years.
> If you do not lie back beside them,
> Or wander among them in spring and summer,
> Your skeleton will rot in vain,
> And your heart will have nothing to remember.[60]

Mount Jingyang conflates eremitism with the quest for immortality. It involves a spatial reconfiguration. An eremitic life is normally to be sought in the less-trodden paths of deep mountains *out there*; immortality is traditionally to be sought *high above*. Now, with the artificial mount *nearby*, both can be had in the *here* and *now*. Temporally, one could 'enter the *past* as if it were the present'.[61] Spatially, '*nearby* gentlemen of the court' meet here with 'immortals from *afar*'.[62] One can indulge in imaginary roamings in distant realms of transcendence without stepping outdoors. One seeks 'the marvel of the gods' in his own backyard. The supernatural is hereby domesticated.

This changing notion of the quest for transcendence is registered in the varying designs of the Northern Wei sarcophagus engravings. The three designs – commonly characterized as Flight to Immortality, Filial Piety and a conflation of the two – are in fact of the same kind. The quest for transcendence remains their underlying theme. Even though we are not entirely certain about the chronological order in which they appeared, they plot a trajectory along which the notion of transcendence changed over time. In Han times, one yearned to fly to distant mythological lands, typically the Kunlun mountains, to reach the transcendence. Some time in the early fourth century, transcendence no longer needed to be sought in a place up on high; local mountains would suffice. It used to be that, of the three Daoist ways to 'ascend to transcendence' (that is, celestial, earthly and 'escape-from-the-corpse' transcendence), soaring into the sky in daylight was the best scenario. Now, from the fourth century on, this was no longer necessarily so. One may choose to linger on earth to have the best of the two 'worlds': one avoided the uncertainty of leaping into the vast unknown heavens by remaining in this world; yet, secluded in mountains, one was sufficiently far from the madding crowd. An encounter with a goddess could just as well happen in this world as the next.

Gradually, with the fashioning of a symbolic topography, such as Zhang Lun's Jingyang Mount, one could even feign 'going into the mountains' in search of transcendence by roaming in one's backyard. One may even see, in the figure of a local beauty, the semblance of the Goddess of the Luo River, or a celestial maid in the guise of the girl next door. Such are the workings of the visual rhetoric of the Kansas engravings, which represent the final stage of this historical process. If there is anything particularly or profoundly 'Confucian' about them, it is their success in bringing the supernatural – i.e. what Confucius called 'the disorderly, the powerful, the strange, and the spirits', which he chose not to deal with – into a harmonious intimacy with human mortals, as if these forces were just a part of us, part of this world.

NOTES

1 Kohara 2000 (1967), pp. 3 & 14.
2 Hawkes 1974, p. 42.
3 Gong Dazhong 1984, esp. p. 51. The sarcophagus engraving has attracted a sizeable scholarship; see, e.g., Okumura 1939, pp. 259–300; Soper 1948; Nagahiro 1969, pp. 181–184; Sullivan 1962, pp. 159–161; Sickman 1984, pp. 71–79; Wu Hung 1995, pp. 261–276.
4 According to Guo Yutang's documentation, a Shanghai dealer bought two Northern Wei sarcophagi with exquisite carvings, dated respectively 524 and 526. One of them may have landed in Kansas. See Gong Dazhong 1984, pp. 52–53. The 1933 acquisition record (no. 49) in the Nelson Art Museum indicates that the sarcophagus was purchased in Ta'er Lane in Beijing. The Beijing dealer claimed that the sarcophagus and the coffin came from the same tomb. Indeed, they were both sold in 1933. In any case, 520s would be a secure date. All Northern Wei sarcophagi date from the 520s or later.
5 See, e.g., Gao Wen *et al.* 1996, p. 127.
6 Sullivan 1962, pp. 160–161.
7 *Liji jijie* 1989, 4.84; tr. Legge 1967, 1.91.
8 According to the memorial tablet of Yuan Mi, Prince Zhenjing, at the Minneapolis Institute of Art, Yuan Mi was buried in 524 (Wang 1999, p. 58, fig. 2).
9 See Wang 1999, pp. 56–64.
10 *Taiping yulan* 1960, *juan* 519, p. 2360.
11 Gan Bao 1999, *juan* 11, pp. 362–363.
12 *Shi ji* 1959, *juan* 1, pp. 32–33.
13 Sullivan 1962, p. 160.
14 Luoyang Museum 1980, p. 230.
15 Birrell 1993, p. 75.
16 See, e.g., the account of Shun's career in *The Book of Historical Documents* (tr. Legge 1960, vol. 3, pp. 25–27, 29–51).
17 *Shi ji* 1959, *juan* 15, p. 31; Nienhauser *et al.* (eds & trs) 1994, vol. 1, pp. 11–12. A similar account exists in Liu Xiang's *Biography of Chaste Women*.
18 Guyuan 1984; Luo Feng 1990; Karetzky & Soper 1991; Sun Ji 1996, pp. 122–138.
19 Datong 1972.
20 The Yuan Mi sarcophagus in Minneapolis also contains a scene of the Shun story. The *mise-en-scène* of a filial son attending to his parent(s) is so formulaic that it could be exchanged for any other filial piety story simply by changing the title in the cartouche.
21 Sun Ji dates the coffin to 484–486 for a number of reasons. One concerns the costume style, which points to the period preceding the Taihe Reform instituted by the Northern Wei rulers in 486 (1996, p. 122).
22 Even though the poet's preface states the year to be the 'third year of the Huangchu reign', corresponding to 222 CE, according to Miao Yue's careful study (1947), Cao Zhi only went to the capital in 223.
23 Cao Zhi, 'The Goddess of the Luo', in Owen (ed. & tr.) 1996, pp. 194–197.
24 Hawkes 1974, p. 54.
25 The two prototypical works, 'The Rhapsody on Gaotang' and 'The Goddess', traditionally attributed to Song Yu, are most likely Han works. See Owen (ed. & tr.) 1996, p. 189.
26 Li Fengmao 1996, pp. 150–153.
27 See Bokenkamp 1996.
28 For a biographic account of Sima Shao, see *Jin shu* 1974, *juan* 6, p. 158.
29 *Jin shu* 1974, *juan* 32, 1974, p. 972.
30 See Li Fengmao 1996, p. 153.
31 *Jin shu* 1974, *juan* 49, p. 1367.
32 Wang Sengqian, 'Lunshu' (On calligraphy), cited in *Fashu yaolu* (Lu Fusheng *et al.* [eds] 1992–, vol. 1, p. 35).
33 He was Wang Xizhi's uncle and also known to have painted *Chaste Women of Virtue and Wisdom*, a subject Gu Kaizhi was also said to have painted. See Pei Xiaoyuan 1993 (639) (Lu Fusheng *et al.* [eds] 1992–, vol. 1, p. 174); Zhang Yanyuan, *LDMHJ* (Lu Fusheng *et al.* [eds] 1992–, vol. 1, p. 134).
34 Gan Bao 1999 (*c.*322), pp. 286–288.
35 The Lao Laizi cycle appears in both the *Biography of Chaste Women* and *Tales of Immortals*, with their respective distinct Confucian and Daoist overtones. In the Confucian account, he is the seventy-year-old acting as a child to please his parents. In the Daoist narrative, he is a man of Chu who escapes the turmoil of the world to 'south of Mengshan' where he builds a thatched hut, enjoys a simple existence, and declines the King of Chu's offers of official appointment. In *Baopuzi*, he is mentioned in the company of Zhuangzi as one of the Daoist paragons. *Baopuzi* (The Inner Chapters) (*ZZJC*, *juan* 8, p. 4).
36 There appears to be a bear on the left, presumably to show the celestial maid with the bear establishing her celestial identity.
37 *Hou Han shu* 1965, *juan* 39, p. 1300; *Dongguan Han ji*, cited in *YWLJ*, *juan* 21, pp. 388–389.
38 *Hou Han shu* 1965, *juan* 39, p. 1312. Other accounts of Cai Shun appear in *YWLJ*, *juan* 2, p. 35; *Runan xianxian zhuan*, cited in *YWLJ*, *juan* 35, p. 624; *YWLJ*, *juan* 80, p. 1377.
39 *Wei shu* 1974, *juan* 86, p. 1882.
40 Typical cases of 'escape from the corpse by way of execution' are the stories of Luan Ba, Liu Huo, and Wang Jia from the Daoist compendium *Yunji qiqian*, *juan* 85, 1996, pp. 526–527.
41 *Yunji qiqian*, *juan* 84, 1996, p. 520; *juan* 86, p. 533. For discussions of 'escape from the corpse', see Wen Yiduo, 'Shenxian kao' (Study of transcendents) (1949, *juan* 1, pp. 159–163); Robinet 1979.
42 *Wei shu* 1974, *juan* 9, pp. 222, 235.
43 *Wei shu* 1974, *juan* 9, p. 232; *juan* 20, p. 529; *juan* 36, p. 848; *juan* 38, p. 879; *juan* 77, p. 1703.
44 *Wei shu* 1974, *juan* 86, pp. 1881–1887.
45 *Wei shu* 1974, *juan* 84, p. 1858.
46 *Wei shu* 1974, *juan* 60, p. 1333.
47 When the Grand Empress Dowager Lady Feng died in 490, her will stipulated that 'the coffin and its outer encasement (*guo*) should be plain and sparing in form'; *Wei shu* 1974, *juan* 13, p. 330; *juan* 18, p. 2875.
48 *Wei shu* 1974, *juan* 38, p. 872.
49 *Wei shu* 1974, *juan* 84, p. 1858; *juan* 78, p. 1730.
50 *Wei shu* 1974, *juan* 180, pp. 2815–2816.
51 *Wei shu* 1974, *juan* 180, p. 2811 (italics mine).
52 See Li Shan's (d. 689) gloss on 'boundary sacrifice' (*jiaosi*) in his annotation of Yang Xiong, 'Rhapsody of the Sweet Spring', *Wen xuan*, vol. 1, *juan* 7, p. 321.
53 *Wei shu* 1974, *juan* 53, p. 1177.
54 *Wei shu* 1974, *juan* 53, pp. 1177–1178.
55 *Wei shu* 1974, *juan* 78, pp. 1737–1738. The line is derived from the *Classic of Filial Piety* and was often quoted in the praise of filial paragons. See *Wei shu* 1974, *juan* 86, p 1881.
56 In confronting peasant insurgents, some generals had their soldiers face north and recite *Classic of Filial Piety*, in the hope that 'the bandits would disappear of their own accord'; *Hou Han shu* 1965, *juan* 81, p. 2694.
57 *YWLJ*, *juan* 69, p. 1204.
58 *Nan Qi shu* 1972, *juan* 41, p. 729; Sun Ji 1996, pp. 126–127.
59 *Luoyang qielan ji*, *juan* 2, p. 90; tr. Jenner 1981, p. 189.
60 *Luoyang qielan ji*, *juan* 2, p. 95; tr. Jenner 1981, p. 192.
61 *Luoyang qielan ji*, *juan* 2, p. 91; tr. Wang, Yi-t'ung (tr.) 1984, p. 94.
62 'Afar, appreciated by immortals; nearby, be known to court officials', *Luoyang qielan ji*, *juan* 2, p. 93; tr. Wang, Yi-t'ung (tr.) 1984, p. 96.

Remarks of a Later Female Historian

Michael Nylan

The papers presented here by Julia Murray, Eugene Wang and Wu Hung are wonderfully rich, yet based in the strong presumption that a series of stark dichotomies shaped the classical age in China: male or masculine was supposedly pitted against female or feminine, and unConfucian activities associated with the cúlt of immortality against the Confucian (essentially reduced to filial piety), not to mention Daoist vs. Buddhist. Furthermore, the *Admonitions* scroll's frank acknowledgement of the heady pleasures of the hunt, the bedroom, and fine possessions is seen to undercut the didactic message of the admonitions. My own reading of Han (206 BCE–220 CE) and early Six Dynasties (265–589) texts and tombs has convinced me that such dichotomizing usually reflects the cultural expectations of our time more than those of the distant past.

Let me illustrate my point *vis-à-vis* two of the starkest dichotomies: male vs. female, and Confucian vs. unConfucian. Regarding male vs. female, Kohara Hironobu's text is quite revealing. In describing one scene (the 'rejection'), Kohara finds it impossible that a wise man would be 'surprised and embarrassed'; a man expressing such emotions, in Kohara's mind, becomes 'utterly ridiculous'.[1] I beg to differ. We who live in a highly genderized society, where the two sexes are said to be from Mars and Venus, easily overlook the obvious fact that sociopolitical rank, implying varying levels of cultivation and wealth, trumped gender distinctions in nearly every recorded case from the Han and Six Dynasties. The canonical texts, including the *Yi jing (Book of Changes)* and *Li ji (Book of Rites)*, describe the gentlewoman and the gentleman in the same way: both are to be humble, respectful, cautious and yielding. Both, by the way, are also to have a healthy sense of shame, for shame provides the primary motivation for moral change, according to the *Mencius (Mengzi)* and the *Xunzi*.

It is true that elite women must share their husband's bed with other women, and that they ideally sew and weave while their men direct the ploughing or serve in public office.

But elite women, like elite men, have the required capacity for self-cultivation and the solemn duty to instruct their children and protect their households. As Zhang Hua's (232–300) text accompanying scene 5 (the bedroom), puts it: 'If the words that you utter are good, all men for a thousand leagues around will respond to you. But should you depart from this principle, even your bedfellow will distrust you.' Men hearken to women – a woman's moral force is sufficient to command men's respect. And because the essential sameness between the sexes outweighs the differences, the real subject of much Chinese rhetoric about women is men. To take but one literary example, the chief object of Ban Zhao's (*c.*49–*c.*120) ire in her chapter on 'husband and wives' in *Nü jie (Instruction for Women)* is 'the gentlemen of the present age' who are so benighted as to think that they can rule the household without first winning their wives' respect. Didactic 'warnings to women' (whether literary or visual), in other words, serve as warnings to men – a point to which I will return. (Hence, it is futile to attempt to assign the scroll a date on the basis of reported back-palace intrigues.)

Turning to 'unConfucian' searches for immortality in potential conflict with 'Confucian' filial piety, let me put forth two propositions: first, that the term Ru (conventionally translated as 'Confucian') refers instead to a professional or proto-professional classicist, and second, that men trained in the classics, no less than others deprived of such training, want to ensure that they will 'live on' in some sense after death. One way to live on was through sacrifices made by one's descendants to the soul of the deceased, and this long predates Confucius (551–479 BCE), being traceable to the Shang dynasty (*c.*1500–*c.*1030 BCE). The rites texts[2] stipulate that as descendants worshipped their ancestors, they were not only to feed them, but also to visualize them in every detail, to make them come alive again before the pious descendants. That is the method of immortality to which the charming family scene alludes, whose legend says, 'Your race shall multiply'. The love and respect prevailing within the family circle constitutes the best assurance that sacrifices will be offered in perpetuity to the dead. But sometimes sons and grandsons are less than perfectly filial, and then they perform the sacrifices in a perfunctory manner – or not at all. For that reason, some men sought also to immortalize themselves through their writings, their deeds and the monuments erected to their memory. A third option – available only to those with vast resources – was to seek for personal immortality, in the hope that one might live as a material being in an afterlife realm on earth or in the heavens. All three ways to live on were embraced by the classically trained elites, the Ru, and all attempts to secure life beyond the grave represented the same search for personal welfare. With the elites of the Han and Six Dynasties, filial piety and alchemical drugs went hand-in-hand, with rare exceptions, as is clear from representative texts of the time. Only a few thinkers insisted that man's days were numbered and the only form of immortality that could be attained was one's good name.

I could continue such observations, but suffice it to say: there were no discrete 'schools' of thought in ancient China; there were only different 'ways' of conforming with the Dao that ideally allowed men and women to 'understand fate and take pleasure in Heaven's decrees'. It is important to note also that beauty, pleasure and possessions were not opposed by anyone called the Ru; they were, in point of fact, the rewards offered the discerning person in return for virtuous acts. Very much in the fashion of the ancient Greeks, the early Chinese assumed that the truly discerning person would undertake the search for the beautiful *and* the good. In an ideal state, arduous work on behalf of the common good or moral cultivation secured a person the conventional goals of high rank, great wealth, and physical ease. That good government operated to elevate the worthy was an axiom of faith. (By contrast, bad government failed to reward those who had made major contributions to the body politic.) It was only appropriate, then, that the legendary sage Emperor Yao rewarded Shun, the filial son, for his virtues with two absolute stunners, in the form of Emperor Yao's own daughters.

As works like the Nelson sarcophagus remind us, the most accomplished men of the time didn't consider life to pose a hard choice between history and beauty, but instead, probing questions about what role beauty and pleasure have played – appropriately and inappropriately – down through history. Nearly all the early major works of the Warring States (476–221 BCE) through to the Six Dynasties aim to clarify, I will argue in a forthcoming book, what I think of as the 'pleasure quotient': what one gives up to get something that yields

greater and more lasting pleasure. The great thinkers, in other words, are in serious discussion about the best means by which an enlightened state led by cultivated persons may utilize the inborn impulses to seek beauty and pleasure, inducing lesser humans to undertake and then persist in courses likely to maximize the chances for good. It is our own cultural biases projected upon antiquity that weigh the material against the immaterial, the body against the soul, and pleasure-taking against the ethical.

I have a further point to make, which is relevant to these fine papers. The *Admonitions* scroll, to my mind, fits perfectly in content and style with Liu Yiqing's (403–444) *Shishuo xinyu (New Tales of the World)*, the main literary compendium for the Six Dynasties. The essays by Kohara and by Wu Hung find in the *Admonitions* scroll the characteristic Six Dynasties irreverence toward strait-laced 'Confucian' values. Perhaps our reading of texts (visual and literary) ignores the underlying moral content of such works that focus on the huge gap between surface and reality. One scene in the *Admonitions* scroll explicitly takes up these issues: 'Men and women know how to adorn their persons, but few know how to embellish their souls.' Those who apply their fine cosmetics (and some Six Dynasties men used cosmetics, too) are contrasted with those who attend to their inner lives (the 'toilette' scene).

All this sounds serious enough – and I think it was. The great fear was that a preoccupation with pleasure in inappropriate contexts would consume, not sustain the body and the body politic. The *Admonitions*' painter, like the *Shishuo xinyu*'s author, surely recognized this. But 'didactic' need not mean 'naïve' or 'unsophisticated'. Admonition and aestheticism had long been combined in the *fu* (prose-poem) traditions of the day. (The received records have Gu Kaizhi expressing a particular fondness for these rhapsodies, which he considered far superior to the doggerel verses gaining popularity in his own age.) Therefore, I think it likely that the scroll is more than a straightforward rendition of morality tales. The very essence of 'indirect remonstrance', after all, is to be nuanced in one's rhetoric. One thereby plants a seed in another's mind, rather than delivering an unpalatable message that cannot be swallowed. And so the *Admonitions* painter, in conveying his meaning through highly flattering images, strengthened its rhetorical appeal to specific patrons. In that respect, the scroll represents a visual counterpart of the early prose-poems addressed to the emperors on the subject of their awesome authority.

Let us suppose for the moment that the original painter of the scroll was Gu Kaizhi or a near contemporary of like mind. The received literary sources of Gu's time say that Gu excelled his contemporaries in three ways – as a wit, a fool or jester, and a painter; in these roles, Gu displayed the pertinent allusions in his repertoire and an awareness that the ordinary platitudes collapse upon closer examination. Let us look at the scene where Lady Ban is shown refusing to ride with Emperor Chengdi in his litter, lest her emperor be regarded as like the worst rulers of the pre-Han period. However admirable Lady Ban's refusal, we see that the emperor – presumably because of that refusal – has already got another person to take Lady Ban's place, though he looks regretfully back on Lady Ban. (In the Sima Jinlong screen illustrating the same tale, the carriage is empty after Lady Ban's refusal.) Everyone knows how the story ends: the emperor hooks up, partly under eunuch influence, with the evil Zhao sisters, and the decline of the Han dates from his infatuation with these beautiful sisters, who supposedly killed Chengdi's rightful heirs. Thus, Gu's version hints that Lady Ban's upright refusal sets in motion the events that bring on the downfall of the dynasty she so rigorously serves. Lady Ban is no uncomplicated figure, for she warns us on two levels: dynasties rise or fall on the smallest of incidents and the unintended consequences of priggish behaviour may be disastrous, indeed!

My favourite tale about Gu has him describing his mourning for a patron, Huan Wen, one of the most powerful men of the day, in these terms: 'My nose was like the long wind over the northern plains; my eyes like a dammed-up Yellow River bursting forth.' While Gu much bemoaned the loss of his patron, he was not averse to using the most solemn occasion to parody the extravagant displays required by convention. It is this mastery of literary allusions touched by a waggish sense of humour that leads me to suggest a new interpretation for a scene over which art historians have long puzzled. Scene 7 supposedly illustrates this portion of Zhang Hua's text: 'It is the norm that there is nothing high which is not soon brought low … When the sun has reached its midcourse, it begins to sink; when the moon is full, it begins to wane. To rise to glory is as hard as building a mountain out of dust; to fall into calamity is as easy as the rebound of a tense spring.' In this scene, accordingly, a gigantic mountain suddenly looms. To the left of it is a hunter; above it, sun and moon. The scene seems so out of place in the scroll that some art historians have presumed the mountain must function in another way, perhaps as an allusion to a cosmic mountain. Kohara remarks that the picture is 'neither naturalistic nor realistic'. I think he is onto something; the scene is intended as metaphor. Literary allusions going back to the *Analects* (*Lun yu*) use the mountain as metaphor for the towering figure. Gu painted several patrons – the most famous men of the period – within mountain landscapes, so as to capture that association. So if the mountain = greatness, the hunter = a seeker after greatness. The first chapter of Yang Xiong's (53 BCE–18 CE) text on Confucian ethics, *Fa yan*, says, for example, 'When one hunts virtue, then one gets virtue. Then and only then will one get to savour the feast!' The sun and moon are symbols of enlightenment and wisdom. The two phoenixes also convey a cluster of auspicious meanings. The tiger may well be placed on the mountain as a playful reminder to patrons and viewers alike that it is ultimately Tiger-head (Gu Kaizhi himself) who establishes the very mountain-like qualities of the mountain, and so its justifiable fame.

Whether the painter is Gu or not, he intends (in a manner analogous with the Nelson sarcophagus' depiction of Shun with his two beauties) to make a strong rhetorical appeal: essentially, that all manner of pleasurable effects will ensue once a person follows virtue's path faithfully. Scene 7, like the family scene, was meant to persuade the scroll's viewers, who are as likely to have been men as women, that rich prizes – not the least of them social approbation – will come to those who heed the warnings conveyed by the scroll. Insofar as the viewers gain enlightenment and cultivation, it says, they may thus win keen pleasure, great renown, and historical immortality. After all, it is the mountain – the classic site of pleasurable hunts – that symbolizes what lasts forever. Such rhetorical arguments are calculated to appeal to the vanity of patrons and onlookers; by design, they induce viewers to undertake the arduous task of attaining virtue by assuring them that virtue's attainment enhances the continuity of the family and the ruling house. The mountain scene, like the contented family scene whose form it recalls, punctuates the otherwise prohibitory messages with positive appeals.

By way of conclusion, I note that in the European tradition, according to Terry Eagleton, aesthetics first functions as a discourse of the body.[3] The term refers, in its original German formulation, not specifically to art, but to the whole region of human perception and sensation associated with the material, in contrast to the realm of the immaterial, including the 'higher life' of art, of the life of the mind, and of the afterlife. In the Chinese context, beauty and pleasure are seen to be in tension with political obligation,[4] but beauty and pleasure never abandon their associations with the good life of virtue and wisdom, and the material rewards for such a life.

NOTES

1   Kohara 2000 (1967), p. 12.
2   *Li ji*, *Zhou li* (*Rites of Zhou*) and *Yi li*, and their early commentaries.
3   Eagleton 1990.
4   I owe this observation to Professor Li Wai-yee of Harvard University.

Part 2
Gu Kaizhi and the Literati Tradition

The *Admonitions* Scroll in the British Museum: New Light on the Text-Image Relationships, Painting Style and Dating Problem

Chen Pao-chen

Noted for its superb quality, the *Admonitions of the Instructress to the Court Ladies (Nüshi zhen tu)*, which was in the Qing (1644–1911) imperial collection before it left China during the Boxer Rebellion of 1900 and entered the British Museum in 1903,[1] is one of the most famous of Chinese paintings. This paper focuses on three aspects of the scroll: the text-image relationships, the painting style and the dating problem.[2]

The Text-Image Relationships

Attributed to Gu Kaizhi (*c*. 344–405),[3] the *Admonitions* scroll illustrates the rhymed prose-poem of the same title by Zhang Hua (232–300), an esteemed scholar and high-ranking official at the Western Jìn (265–316) court. The court was then dominated by Empress Jia (d. 300) and corrupt members of her maiden family; their abuse of power had precipitated the War of the Eight Princes (291–306), which jeopardized the stability of the empire.[4] Aware of the danger, and of his responsibility to advise the empress on her role and virtue, Zhang Hua wrote the 'Admonitions' as a memorial to her in the voice of an instructress. The text is short in length but rich in content: it comprises only eighty lines, generally of four characters each, in nineteen rhymes. Concisely and crisply worded, the 'Admonitions' is also a very musical text due to the complex play of rhythm and rhyme. Didactic in nature, it praises palace ladies of the past who acted meritoriously, and denounces behaviour that Zhang Hua deemed inappropriate for members of the imperial harem. A transcription and translation appear at the beginning of this book on pp. 15–17.

The extant *Admonitions* scroll consists of nine scenes proceeding from right to left, with each illustration following a passage of text in a sequence of 'monoscenic' compositions.

Illustrating Zhang Hua's entire text, the painting might originally have comprised twelve scenes.[5] The present scroll is incomplete, however: three scenes are missing at the beginning. As a later copy in the Beijing Palace Museum suggests (pls 23, 24), these include an introduction and two narrative scenes: 1) 'Man and wife', symbolizing the beginning of family structure, and the initiation of an ethical order in human society (lines 1–18); 2) Lady Fan refusing to eat the flesh of birds slaughtered by her husband, King Zhuang (r. 696–682 BCE) (lines 19–20); and 3) Lady Wei renouncing the music favoured by her husband, Duke Huan (r. 718–699 BCE) (lines 21–24).[6]

The British Museum's scroll opens with the fourth scene, which shows Lady Feng protecting Emperor Han Yuandi (r. 48–33 BCE) from attack by a black bear (pls 1, 2). The text, originally to the right but now missing, is in lines 25–28.

In the illustration, the emperor sits on a dais to the right. His eyes startled and his mouth open in alarm, he prepares to unsheathe a sword in self-defence. In the middle, Lady Feng interposes herself between the emperor and the bear, which two guards wearing tall black gauze hats (*longguan*) and armed with spears, hold at bay. At the same time, three other court ladies flee the emperor's side: the two *guiren* in light-coloured dresses cower to the right, and Lady Fu, in a red skirt, moves away at the left.

This dramatic scene, which shows the different reactions of various characters, obviously provides more detail than is indicated in the text. I believe this illustration is not based on lines 25–28 of the 'Admonitions' text, but on Lady Feng's biography in the *Han History (Han shu)*:

Lady Feng *jieyu*, like Lady Fu *zhaoyi*, became one of the emperor [Yuandi's] favourites. During the Jianzhao era (38–34 BCE), the emperor went to see an animal combat in the Tiger Enclosure. He and his concubines were all seated within the palace. A bear suddenly escaped over the fence. No sooner had the bear climbed the barrier and attempted to approach the palace than all the ladies, including the two *guiren* on both sides of the emperor and Lady Fu *zhaoyi*, ran away in panic. In contrast, Lady Feng *jieyu* moved hastily toward the bear, and stood her ground in front of it. Then, two guards came quickly and killed the bear.[7]

This biography evidently served as the textual source for the iconography. Thus, the artist deliberately put the scared Lady Fu at the left edge of the composition to sharpen the contrast with the brave heroine, Lady Feng, in the middle. Unaware of this, many scholars have mistaken the figure of Lady Fu for an attendant of Lady Ban (Ban *jieyu*) in the following scene, and have therefore had trouble 'punctuating' the text and images properly.[8] Similar mistakes also appear in the first and the third scenes of the Beijing version (pls 23–25), where the copyist, not fully understanding the alternating text-image principle of the composition, inserted text between two figures, thereby separating characters in the same episode.

The scene of Lady Feng functions not as an illustration of but as a pictorial reference to its inscription (originally to the right of the picture). This representational mode finds precedent in the illustrations of Emperor Xia Jie and Fuxi/Nüwa at the Wu Liang Shrine, Shandong, dated 151 CE,[9] which both refer to texts other than their accompanying inscriptions. In each of these cases, the artist had to have been not only a painter but also a scholar. Only a scholar-artist learned in history and literature could have created images drawn upon broad knowledge, rather than limited to references in the short inscriptions provided. The scene depicting the story of Lady Feng serves as a good example.

The fifth scene shows Lady Ban refusing to sit with Emperor Han Chengdi (r. 33–8 BCE) in his palanquin (pls 3, 4). The text, written in one column on the right (lines 29–32), alludes to Lady Ban's meritorious deed recorded in the *Han shu*:

As Emperor Han Chengdi was preparing to take an outing to the imperial garden, he invited Lady Ban to share his palanquin. But Lady Ban refused, saying: 'I have noticed that in ancient paintings wise rulers are always represented with their ministers at their sides, while the decadent emperors at the close of the Three Dynasties have favourites with them. If I accede to your request, will you not resemble these latter?'[10]

The illustration shows Lady Ban following the emperor, who sits by another concubine in the palanquin being carried by eight muscular servants. The worried-looking emperor peers back through the open window, and gazes at his beloved lady moving slowly behind. Her calm pose contrasts with the dynamic postures of the bearers, who are portrayed sparing no effort as they shoulder the palanquin; their legs are bent or braced against the ground, and their bodies push forward to the left.

The sixth scene shows a landscape (pls 5, 42), which is to be understood as a metaphor. The accompanying text, lines 33–38, is written in two columns.

This whole passage is conveyed emblematically as a landscape scene. A disproportionately large archer shoots towards a triangular mountain, with the sun and the moon on either side. The sun houses a three-legged raven, and the moon a hare, as attributes. The pyramidal mountain is dotted with shrubs and inhabited by a deer, a tiger, two hares and two pheasants; one of the birds flies up from the ground to escape the bowman's arrow.

In this scene, the artist employs both literal and metaphorical translation methods to pictorialize the text. Literal translation is evident in two cases: 1) the images of the sun and moon on both sides of the mountain, referring to the words, 'When the sun reached its mid-course, it begins to sink; When the moon is full it begins to wane'; and 2) the man holding a crossbow ready to shoot, referring to the words, 'To fall into calamity is as easy as the rebound of a tense spring.' Interestingly, the idea of a tense spring rebounding is further stressed by the image of the 'scared pheasant', which is a pun on 'rebound of a tense spring', as both are pronounced as *haiji* in Chinese.

Metaphorical translation can be found in the image of the mountain, which refers to the words, 'To rise to glory is as hard as to build a mountain out of dust.' In fact, the whole scene showing a man hunting in nature metaphorically represents the abstract notion in the text,

In nature there is (nothing) that is exalted which is not
    soon brought low.
Among living things there is nothing which having
    attained its apogee does not thenceforth decline.

This is a fundamental law of nature – things change constantly; nothing remains at its apex forever.

The seventh scene shows three court ladies attending to their make-up (pls 6 right, 8). The text, lines 39–44, runs in three columns.

Two ladies are seated on the floor. The one on the right, who is viewed from behind, paints on her eyebrows before a mirror. The figure on the left, seen in three-quarters view, sits on a mat by a mirror behind her toilet box, while another lady standing behind helps with her hair. This picture illustrates only part of the first sentence: '… women know how to adorn their faces'. While the rest of the text denounces superficial beauty, this picture ironically advocates it. That the treatment of the image contradicts the meaning of the text reveals the artist's intent to make the scene more interesting. As an artist, he was more concerned about aesthetic appeal than philosophical consistency. Still, he is clearly more than able to convert the abstract ideas of the text into a picture, as was just noted in the previous scene, and reappears consistently in most of the remaining scenes.

The eighth scene represents a man leaving a woman in a canopied bed (pls 6 left, 7). In two columns, the text is from lines 45–48.

The illustration shows a court lady dressed in a red garment sitting in a bed enclosed by a folding twelve-panel screen. Her arm hangs over the screen to the left. Meanwhile, an emperor wearing a 'golden-broad-mountain-hat' (*jin boshan shu*) sits on the side of the bed, putting on his shoes to leave. As such, the picture illustrates only the latter half of the last sentence: 'even your bedfellow will distrust you'. Abstract ideas conveyed in the remainder of the text are not represented.

The ninth scene depicts a prosperous family (pls 9 right, 11). The inscription is written in four columns (lines 49–62). The character *chu* (utter), originally the second in line 49, for an unknown reason is absent here.

The illustration shows an emperor and his family, including three concubines, five children and an old man, in a triangular composition. This group represents only the latter half of the last sentence: 'your race shall multiply'. Nothing else is illustrated, because the abstract ideas are too complicated to convey pictorially. This scene clearly demonstrates that a court lady's primary duty is to bear the emperor's offspring.

In the tenth scene, a woman begs in vain for a man's love (pls 9 left, 10). The accompanying four-column inscription contains the text of lines 63–74. The scribe has made two mistakes here, by transcribing the character *piān* 翩 (elegant) as *fān* 翻 (suddenly) (the second character from the bottom in the second column), and *zhí* 職 (naturally) as *shí* 寔 (truly) (the fourth character from the end).

The picture shows a court lady being rejected by an emperor, who raises his left hand in a gesture of refusal. The artist illustrates lines 71–72, 'If by a mincing air you seek to please, Wise men will abhor you.' Again, abstract notions are not represented.

The eleventh scene depicts a beautiful young lady (pl. 12 right). In one column, the text in part reads (lines 77–78): 'Fulfil your duties calmly and responsibly; Thus shall you win glory and honour.'

The illustration represents a court lady with a contented facial expression, kneeling on the ground facing left. Her happiness obviously derives from her obedience to the above teaching. As an emblem, this beautiful, cautious, obedient and satisfied young woman presents an ideal image to the court ladies for whom the doctrines were written.

In the last scene an instructress is represented in the act of writing (pls 12 centre and left, 13). In one column, the text states (lines 79–80): 'Thus has the Instructress, charged with the duty of admonition, Thought good to speak to the ladies of the harem.'

The artist shows her in a standing pose, writing the doctrines on a scroll and facing two smiling young women, who enter from the end of the painting. Their left-to-right movement contrasts with that of every other lady in the scroll, and implies that they are newcomers to the harem. This closing picture suggests that the preceding admonitions are so important that every lady in or entering the harem accepts them happily.

Overall, the artist has exercised great imagination in representing the Confucian values advocated in the text, particularly in his respect for the domestic ethical order – the foundation of harmony, stability and prosperity within the family. The artist reveals a strong urge to represent these values, particularly in his choices of subjects and in the way he represents figures of different classes. As for these subjects, we find that the meritorious deeds and the virtues of women – such as self-sacrifice, emotional suppression, prudence, sincerity and obedience – are emphasized, and feature in seven scenes ('admonitions' 2–5, 8 and 10), while unacceptable behaviour and attitudes – including admiring one's superficial beauty, speaking with evil intention, and seeking the love of a man – are not only denounced, but also represented sparingly in just three scenes ('admonitions' 6, 7 and 9).

Harmony, stability and prosperity are the most important values translated by the artist from the text to his painting. In the family scene (pls 9 right, 11), for instance, the imperial family is grouped in a wide-based triangular shape, a pyramidal composition that conveys a strong sense of stability. Moreover, each member of the family looks satisfied with his or her position within it. The static poses and peaceful countenances create a harmonious atmosphere. Court ladies are thus encouraged to foster the harmony and stability that make a family flourish, and to increase the size of the imperial family by giving birth to as many children as possible and raising them together.

The artist was aware that cultivating these values should not only be their guiding principle, but that the court ladies should also put them into practice in their daily lives, not just on special occasions. This is reflected in the artist's having represented all emperors and concubines dressed informally in everyday clothes. None is formally attired or elaborately made-up, suggesting that they are enjoying daily life in the imperial harem.

The hierarchy of Confucian ethics is also revealed in the forms of the figures, which are distinguished according to status. The sovereign is always larger than his subjects. Also, men appear larger than women of similar age, which communicates an assumed gender difference, not only in terms of biology, but also within the prevailing power structure, in which men were dominant and women subordinate.

Social distinctions are also made obvious. Imperial family members wear subdued and subtle facial expressions; they are dressed in large garments with billowing sleeves; their movements look fluid and elegant; and their body language is gentle and restrained. These formal characteristics bespeak their position as members of the well-educated upper class. In contrast, the guards and the palanquin-bearers appear rude and rough. They wear short garments, long trousers and flat-soled shoes, suitable for labour, and their hands are engaged in work. Their exaggerated facial expressions show uncontrolled emotions. These features make up the stereotype for the lower-class figures.

In order to convert the 'Admonitions' text into a series of interesting paintings, the artist evidently experimented throughout with different translation strategies, including literal, metaphorical and suggestive methods. Clearly, the relationships between the images and accompanying or related texts are complicated, but in his choice of subjects and his imaginative figural representations, the artist subtly – and most successfully – conveyed the Confucian moral teachings advocated in the text.

The Painting Style

From the perspective of representation, the *Admonitions* scroll demonstrates strong stylistic affinities with Han (206 BCE–220 CE) pictorial conventions of composition, figural style and spatial treatment. As far as composition is concerned, the formula used is an alternation of text (or mode A) and illustration (or mode B), and can be formulated diagrammatically, as follows:

Fig. 1 'Images of Ancient Emperors' (*Gu diwang xiang*). 151 CE. Detail of a rubbing of a stone engraving at the Wu Liang Shrine, Shandong Province. (After Wu Hung 1989, p. 158.)

Table 1: The compositional formula of the *Admonitions* scroll

B A	B A	B A	B A	B A	B A	B A	B A	B (A...)	← Mode
12	11	10	9	8	7	6	5	4 (missing)	← Scenes

The layout of the text passages (A) and the illustrations (B) is obviously formulaic and regulated. The device whereby two compositional units are repeated over and over in a lateral layout is a Han pictorial convention that remained in vogue during the early Six Dynasties (220–581) period; this can be seen in the stone relief, 'Images of Ancient Emperors', from the Wu Liang Shrine, dated 151 CE (fig. 1);[11] and in *Biographies of Exemplary Women: the Benevolent and Wise* in the Beijing Palace Museum, a Southern Song (1127–1279) copy of an early painting in the Gu Kaizhi style (fig. 8, pls 29–30).[12] While this Han compositional scheme was simple and understandable to the artist of the *Admonitions*, it was not to the later follower who added the three missing scenes in the Beijing Palace Museum copy: he broke up the alternating text-illustration pattern by inserting passages of text between two figures in the same scene, as noted above (pls 23–25).

In terms of figural style, the representation of the figures in the *Admonitions* scroll also shows a close relationship to Han pictorial conventions. Although they assume different poses in the scroll, the ladies are represented throughout by a figure with a triangular silhouette, cylindrical head, slender body, loose garments with billowing sleeves, and long skirts that end in a wide flaring hem (pl. 10). These characteristics find distant prototypes in the remote Chu (722–223 BCE) figural representations found at Changsha in Hunan, such as *Immortal on a Dragon (Xianren yu long)*, and *Lady with Phoenix and Dragon (Long feng shinü)* (see p. 21, fig. 2), datable to the fifth or fourth century BCE.[13]

Fig. 2 (left) 'The Filial Sons'. Detail of a painted lacquer basket, 2nd century CE. Lelang, Korea. (After *MSQJ, Painting*, vol. 1, p. 103.)

Fig. 4 (right) 'Jing Ke Attempting to Assassinate the King of Qin' (*Jing Ke ci Qinwang*). 151 CE. Rubbing of a stone engraving at the Wu Liang Shrine, Shandong Province. (After Wu Hung 1989, p. 316.)

Fig. 3 (below) 'Two Peaches Kill Three Warriors' (*Ertao sha san shi*). 48–47 BCE. Mural in Tomb no. 61, Luoyang, Henan Province. (After *MSQJ, Painting*, vol. 12, p. 3.)

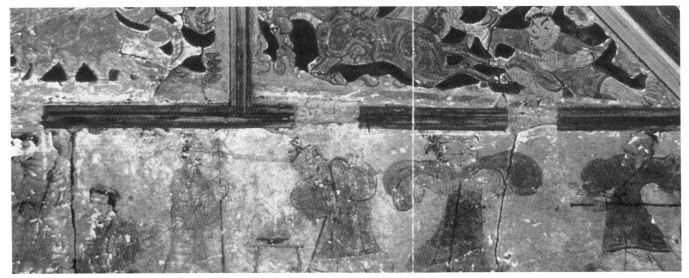

In terms of brushwork, each figure in the *Admonitions* is painted using thin, even, resilient brush-strokes – the so-called 'iron-wire' line (*tiexian miao*) or 'spring-silkworm-emitting-thread' line (*chuncan tusi miao*). The figures' heads are carefully depicted with a single outline that moves in and out along the contours of the faces, which are shown in three-quarters view (see the figures of the emperor in pl. 9 right and the instructress in pl. 13). The ladies' coiffures are beautifully decorated with hairpins in the form of standing golden birds called *jinque chai*. Their bodies appear pliant and their move-

ments gentle; long, flying ribbons elegantly adorn their billowing clothes and long skirts. The repetition of the curving lines of their clothing, ribbons and scarves creates a rich sense of rhythm. The use of colour in the painting is simple: primarily black and red are used; light purple and yellow are used sparingly, while white is suggested by simply leaving certain areas blank. Subtlety, serenity and simplicity are the scroll's aesthetic characteristics. Overall, the artist seems more concerned with depicting the formal beauty of the figures than with the three-dimensionality of the bodies underneath the

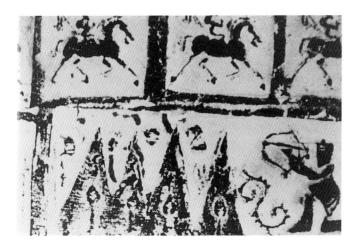

Fig. 5 Stamped tile design showing an archer shooting towards mountains. Western Han dynasty (206 BCE–8 CE). Zhengzhou, Henan Province. (Photo Archive, Far Eastern Art, Department of Art & Archaeology, Princeton University.)

clothes. In fact, depicting the face with care and the body only roughly is a Han pictorial convention, traceable to the 'Filial Sons' on the painted basket from Lelang, datable to the second century CE (fig. 2). Unsuccessful at representing the three-dimensionality of the human body, the Han artist emphasized the garments, adding shaded pleats to suggest indirectly the mass of the human torso. Such treatment also appears here in the *Admonitions* scroll.

Speaking of spatial treatment, in the *Admonitions* scroll all the figures are represented in large scale against a blank background. The scenes are like stage tableaux, and offer no sense of spatial depth. This treatment can be traced back to the Han depiction of figures in scenes such as 'Two Peaches Kill Three Warriors' (*Ertao sha san shi*) in tomb no. 61 at

Luoyang, datable to 48–47 BCE (fig. 3), and in the stone relief depicting 'Jing Ke Attempting to Assassinate the King of Qin' (*Jing Ke ci Qinwang*) from the Wu Liang Shrine (fig. 4).[14]

Even the *Admonitions* scroll's sole landscape scene, in which a man is seen drawing a bow beside a pyramidal mountain (pl. 5), derives from Western Han (206 BCE–8 CE) pictorial motifs, as seen in the hunting scene on a stamped brick from Zhengzhou, Henan (fig. 5), and on a bronze 'mountain' incense-burner (*boshan lu*) (see p. 22, fig. 4). Compared with its Han prototypes, the mountain motif in the *Admonitions* scroll shows more volume and spatial depth, which results from the artist's having used more intricate subdividing lines to describe the mass of the mountain and its interior space. Although the artist introduced some improvements upon the archaic Han style, he departed hardly at all from the basic Han schema.

The Dating Problem

Although a signature reading *Gu Kaizhi hua*, 'Gu Kaizhi painted this', appears at the end of the scroll, most scholars have taken it to be a later interpolation. The earliest record of a scroll by Gu Kaizhi entitled *Nüshi zhen* appears to be in the *History of Painting (Hua shi)* by Mi Fu (1051–1107).[15] No earlier historical document mentions either a scroll of this title or Gu Kaizhi's having painted a scroll entitled *Admonitions*. Most believe that the *Admonitions* scroll in the British Museum is a later copy of an original work related to Gu Kaizhi's style; but how late was this copy made? From as early as the Ming dynasty (1368–1644) through to modern times scholars have given disparate opinions from different perspectives. Those who have dated the scroll on the basis of studies of the calligraphy have suggested dates ranging from the Eastern Jin (317–420) to the Southern Song. Xiang Yuanbian (1525–1590) and Zhu Yizun (1629–1709), for example, believed the inscriptions to have been written by Gu Kaizhi himself; Dong Qichang (1555–1636) took them to be the calligraphy of Wang Xianzhi (344–386); Paul Pelliot (1878–1945), Basil Gray (1904–1989) and Tang Lan regarded the inscriptions as early Tang (618–907) in style, comparable to the calligraphy of Yu Shinan (558–638) and Chu Suiliang (596–658); Nakamura Fusetsu (1866–1943), Fukui Rikichirō (1886–1972) and Yu Jianhua (1895–1979) viewed the calligraphy as early Tang work in the sūtra-writing style;[16] Wen C. Fong dates it to the sixth century;[17] Taki Sei'ichi (1873–1945) dated it to the Northern Song period; and Chen Jiru (1558–1639) thought it was probably inscribed by the Song emperor Gaozong (1107–1187).[18]

Fig. 6 'Two Standing Ladies' (*Er linü tu*). 3rd century CE. Wuwei, Gansu Province. (After *MSQJ, Painting*, vol. 1, p. 107.)

Kohara Hironobu, however, has dated the painting and the inscriptions to two different periods.[19] He believes that the painting, which shows aspects of fourth-century style, was copied during the Tang period, but that the inscriptions were added later – sometime between 1075 (when the Ruisi Dongge or 'Eastern Pavilion of the Palace of Sagacious Contemplation' was built) and the beginning of the Yuan dynasty (1260–1368).[20]

Other scholars have focused their attention on the painting's style. Starting with Hu Jing (1769–1835), most art historians have accepted this scroll as a faithful Tang copy of an early painting probably by Gu Kaizhi.[21] This opinion sounds reasonable, but it needs solid supportive evidence to be convincing. In what follows, I shall take up this task and prove its probability by means of stylistic comparisons between the *Admonitions* painting and archaeological finds datable to the time of Gu Kaizhi.[22] I will also investigate historical documents related to the great artist.

To begin with the stylistic comparisons, the figural style of the *Admonitions* scroll is derived from an early tradition that can be traced back to the Warring States period, as was seen above in the comparison with *Lady with Dragon and Phoenix* (see p. 21, fig. 2). More specifically, both these works share a certain representational formula: throughout the *Admonitions* scroll, each standing lady is represented as a tall, slender, elegant form; her body is rendered in a curving shape.

While her head and upper torso move pliantly to one side, her long, broad skirt-hem trails behind in the opposite direction. She is well proportioned. The ratio between her head and her body is about 1:6, and her height approximately equals the maximum width of her skirt.

That this early representational formula remained prevalent during the Wei-Jin era (220–420) can be seen from 'Two Standing Ladies' (*Er linü tu*) from Wuwei, Gansu, datable to the third century CE (fig. 6), and from the 'Female Attendant' (*Shinü tu*) from Jiayuguan, also in Gansu, datable to the Wei-Jin period (fig. 7).[23] The iconography and colouring in these two paintings are close to those in the *Admonitions*. Similarities include: the ladies' hairstyles, especially the top-knotted hair-do with a short suspended tail (known as *chuixiao*);[24] the ladies' costume, consisting of a red blouse and long white skirt; the primary use of black-and-red colouring through most of the painting; the idea of reserving blank areas to suggest the colour white; and so on. Their iconographic similarities strongly testify to the fact that despite its being a copy, the *Admonitions* in the British Museum faithfully preserves some features of the original, and that the original version of the *Admonitions* was probably executed during the Wei-Jin period.

More precisely still, the date for the original version of the *Admonitions* should be prior to 484, as we shall see from a stylistic comparison between the *Admonitions* and the lacquer painting on a six-panelled screen excavated from the tomb of Sima Jinlong (d. 484) in Datong, Shanxi.[25] Plate 19 shows the Lady Ban narrative as it is depicted in the lacquer painting. In terms of both composition and iconography, it looks similar to the Lady Ban image in the *Admonitions* scroll (pl. 3). Their stylistic similarity strongly suggests either that these two scenes derived from the same prototype, or that one influenced the other. Since no earlier painting has been found that could have served as the prototype for these two narrative scenes, it is more likely that one served as the model for the other.[26] Moreover, since the Lady Ban narrative in the lacquer painting is artistically inferior to that in the *Admonitions*, it is probable that the former was stylistically influenced by the original version of the latter, and not the other way around. If this is the case, then the *terminus ad quem* for the execution of the original *Admonitions* scroll should be the year 484, when the lacquer painting was buried.

In addition to the Lady Ban narrative, other iconographic similarities between the Sima Jinlong screen paintings and the *Admonitions* are discernible, especially in the representation of the ladies' costumes. Since the iconographic details of the costumes in the screen paintings are relatively clear, they serve as important visual evidence with which to clarify certain related, yet misunderstood, passages of some of the ladies' costumes that are less clearly rendered in the *Admonitions*. Take the 'Three Meritorious Mothers of the Zhou Imperial Household' (*Zhoushi sanmu*), another painting on the same screen, for example (pl. 17). Each woman's costume consists of at least five articles in four layers, as follows:

1) The innermost layer comprises a blouse with a V-shaped collar and long sleeves, and a long skirt supposedly tied at the waist with a sash so long that its two ends trail and flow down through the air.

2) Over the skirt is an accessory with three triangular, banner-like components with long trimming ribbons that curl and flow through the air.[27]

3) Over that is a garment with long billowing sleeves; tied at the waist with a belt, it covers part of the skirt and the decorative accessory with the triangular components and its ribbons.

4) Over this garment is a large triangular scarf, whose two ends cross in front of the lady's bosom; two attached ribbons flutter in the air to each side.

Although some details of this costume are representationally ambiguous, it is still comprehensible through keen observation and analysis. This stylish ensemble must have been highly fashionable and widely prevalent in its time, but later artists

Fig. 7 'Female Attendant' (*Shinü tu*). Wei-Jin period (220–420). Jiayuguan, Gansu Province. (After *MSQJ, Painting*, vol. 1, p. 113.)

did not fully understand its original structure and would have made their own modifications, resulting in visual confusion. In the *Admonitions*, for example, the copyist modified these iconographic details in at least two places. The two ribbons supposedly attached to the scarf, fluttering up in the air on both sides of the lady's chest area (in the screen painting) become, in the scroll's rendering of Lady Ban (pl. 4), only one ribbon, and it is not attached anywhere, but comes out from her neck area. A similar mistake appears in the figure of the lady pursuing a man's love (pl. 10). These adjustments are structurally illogical and visually unnatural.

Moreover, the ladies' costumes in the *Admonitions* are extravagantly over-decorated with ribbons when compared with those in the *Biographies of Exemplary Women* (fig. 8), a Song copy of an earlier scroll that I believe is iconographically more faithful than others to the Gu Kaizhi style, despite the copyist's stiff and awkward brushwork. My research has shown that paintings in the Gu Kaizhi style often demonstrate such extravagance, by decorating the ladies' costumes with too many fluttering ribbons. Examples are the costumes in the

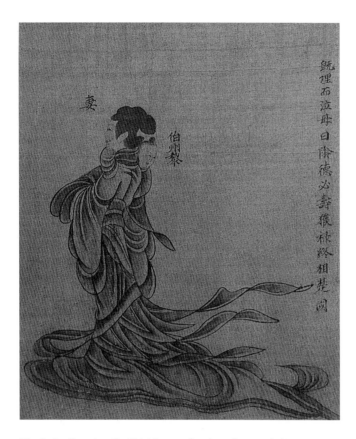

妻

伯州犂

銚理而流毋曰隆德必壽獲祿終相莫闋

Fig. 8 Attributed to Gu Kaizhi; copy, Southern Song period
(1127–1279). *Biographies of Exemplary Women: The Benevolent and Wise
(Lienü renzhi tu).* Detail of a handscroll; ink on silk. Palace Museum,
Beijing. (After *MSQJ, Painting*, vol. 1, p. 124.)

Guo Ju narrative from Dengxian, Henan Province, datable to
the early sixth century (see p. 27, fig. 12), and the figure of
the *Goddess of the Luo River* in the eponymous scroll in the
Beijing Palace Museum, datable to the twelfth century (pl.
31). In the *Admonitions*, although the fluttering movements
of the ribbons create an elegant visual rhythm and enrich the
aesthetic quality of the painting, most of these ribbons are
structurally unclear. This lack of clarity is likely to have
resulted from the copyist's misunderstanding or misinterpre-
tation of the original structure.

Other, similar problems are also discernible in the representation of the ladies' hairstyles and the structure of the
palanquin, and in the inscriptions. Beginning with the hairstyles, we find the ladies wearing their hair in two styles
throughout the scroll: one is the top-knotted hair-do with a
short suspended tail; the other consists of long trailing loops
of hair. A confusing feature appears in the hairstyle of the lady
second from the end of the scroll. While her long hair is
loosely tied in loops and trails down her back, as seen in the

portrayal of many other ladies' coiffures, an extra trace of hair,
supposedly the *chuixiao* (suspended tail), sticks out in an illogical manner from above her left ear (pl. 12). The copyist arbitrarily mixed the two different hairstyles into one, and made
this lady's hair-do appear strange and awkward.

Another copyist's error is discernible in the representation of the framework of the canopy for the palanquin in the
Lady Ban narrative, when it is compared with that in Sima Jinlong's lacquer painting (pls 3, 19). The framework of the
canopy in the lacquer painting shows its structure clearly: a
rectangular frame on the top is supported by six wooden bars,
four of which meet the frame at its four corners, while the
remaining two join the middle of the two longer sides of the
frame. However, the structure of this feature in the *Admonitions* is confusing. The lower supportive wooden bar at the
front, for example, which should have met the frame at the
corner nearby, has been moved up to the middle, and leaves
that corner unsupported. Such an adjustment is structurally
illogical, and must be regarded as the copyist's misunderstanding of the original feature. In addition, two mistakes
appear in the inscriptions, including slips of the pen (scene 10,
line 74) and the omission of one character (scene 9, line 49),
as noted above. All these iconographic modifications and textual mis-transcriptions effectively betray the *Admonitions* as a
later copy.

But when was this copy made? Since the Tang imperial
collection seal, 'Hongwen zhi yin', is considered dubious,[28]
the earliest reliable collection seal on the scroll is the 'Ruisi
Dongge' seal associated with the Ruisidian, which, according
to Kohara Hironobu, was built prior to 1075.[29] The year
1075 should, therefore, be regarded as the *terminus ad quem*
for this copy. However, I still believe that the *Admonitions*
scroll is a Tang copy since the mountain scene and the inscriptions demonstrate Tang style, as Kohara Hironobu and
Nakamura Fusetsu have pointed out.[30] Since no historical
documents of the Tang period, including *Lidai minghua ji
(Record of Famous Painters through the Ages)* by Zhang
Yanyuan (ninth century), mention any scroll entitled *Admonitions of the Instructress to the Court Ladies*, it is very likely
that this copy was made after 847, the year Zhang Yanyuan
completed his book. I therefore believe the British Museum's
Admonitions should be regarded as a copy, and that it was
probably made between 847 and 1075.

Still more importantly, who was the artist of the original
version of the *Admonitions* scroll? I believe that this probably
was Gu Kaizhi. As I have previously suggested, the *terminus
ad quem* for the execution of the original *Admonitions* is the
year 484, which is close enough to the time of Gu Kaizhi
(*c.* 344–405) for there to be a great possibility that the origi-

nal *Admonitions* scroll was by Gu's hand. Investigations into historical documents concerning Gu Kaizhi's life and times support this probability.

I have identified two important events in the *Jin History* (*Jin shu*), which occurred respectively in 375 and 396, that could have motivated the Jin emperor Xiaowudi (362–96; r. 373–96) or his successor, Andi (r. 396–418), to order a great artist like Gu Kaizhi to paint an *Admonitions* scroll. Both events occurred in the harem of Xiaowudi, a notorious alcoholic and womanizer. The first relates to his empress, Wang Fahui (360–380), a proud and jealous woman who was also addicted to drink. The second concerns his favourite concubine, Lady Zhang (c. 367/8–after 396), an insecure and jealous woman who eventually murdered him.[31]

The *Jin History* paints the following picture of Emperor Xiaowudi. Although only ten years old when he ascended the throne, he was, according to the Chief Minister Xie An (320–385), capable and shrewd, and was, at first, pleasant and tolerant for a man with absolute power. However, with time, he indulged himself more and more in liquor and women, eventually to the point that he was seldom sober. For the lack of righteous people to advise him, he never reformed.

His empress, Wang Fahui, the daughter of Wang Yun, was just sixteen in 375 when she became the empress to Xiaowudi, who was then thirteen years old. According to the *Jin History*, she was proud, jealous and a drinker, too. She annoyed the young emperor sufficiently for him to summon her father, Wang Yun, to the Eastern Hall (Dongtang) where he condemned her many acts of inappropriate conduct, and ordered Wang Yun to reprimand and tutor her. Thereafter, the empress did become more self-restrained and improved her conduct somewhat. She died in 380, at the age of twenty-one.

Lady Zhang, a favourite several years younger than the emperor, was worse. According to the *Jin History*, one autumn day in the year 396, when the emperor was thirty-five and she had reached her early thirties, they were residing in the new summer palace. He jokingly remarked to her, 'Judging by your age, you should have been abandoned by now!' Lady Zhang is said to have hidden her anger, and remained calm, but that evening the emperor died there quite suddenly. Xiaowudi was succeeded by the muddle-headed Emperor Andi, Sima Daozi, which allowed Yuan Xian to seize power, and as a consequence, no one was ever implicated in Xiaowudi's sudden death.

The alcoholic, jealous, and murderous behaviour of these court ladies in Emperor Xiaowudi's harem must have shocked the court, and would surely have reminded people of the terrible deeds of the notorious Empress Jia for whom

Zhang Hua had written the 'Admonitions'. It would be fair to assume that immediately after either event, the emperor and his officials took steps to prevent a recurrence. Xiaowudi – for the first event in 375 – or Andi – for the second event in 396 – and his officials are likely to have initiated programmes to re-educate the palace ladies using didactic doctrines: Zhang Hua's 'Admonitions' would have been a necessary and appropriate teaching material. They might also have considered that an illustrated version would be an ideal means to make the meaning of the text explicit and intelligible to these women. Under such circumstances, they could have asked a great artist like Gu Kaizhi to paint an *Admonitions* scroll.

There is no doubt that Gu Kaizhi was well known to members of the ruling class. His official biography relates that he was a genius in both literature and painting – in fact, he was an excellent poet, essayist, painter, theorist, and art critic.[32] While most of his literary works are now regrettably lost,[33] it is fortunate that some of his writings on art theory and criticism are extant today.[34]

Regarded as one of the greatest painters in Chinese history, Gu Kaizhi gained fame in his youth. Zhang Yanyuan records that Gu painted an image of Vimalakirti on a wall of the newly-built Waguansi (Clay Coffin Temple) in the Eastern Jin capital Jiankang (modern Nanjing), during the Xingning era (363–365) when he was only about twenty years old.[35] His *Vimalakirti* attracted thousands of viewers at that time and became an archetype for this image thereafter: we know of the existence of many copies during the Tang and the Northern Song periods from remarks by Zhang Yanyuan, Mi Fu and Ge Lifang (d. 1164).[36]

In addition to his versatility in arts, the many anecdotes about his behaviour recorded in *New Tales of the World* compiled by his younger contemporary Liu Yiqing (403–444), reveal Gu Kaizhi to have been a witty and tolerant man.[37] Gu's talents and personable character earned him fame and friends among the ruling class through several generations. He was very close to both the Grand Marshal Huan Wen (312–373), and the Chief Minister Xie An. The *Jin History* records Huan Wen, the most powerful man of his time, as having praised Gu's personality with the words:

Kaizhi's personality comprises folly and wit in equal measure. Integrated into one, these two elements perfectly balance each other.[38]

Huan Wen was so fond of Gu Kaizhi that he granted the young artist a position as aide-de-camp to the Grand Marshal (*Da sima canjun*) in 366, when Gu was about twenty-two years old.[39] For his part, the Chief Minister Xie An, who was the most powerful man after Huan Wen, had high praise for Gu's painting:

> There has never been a painter of such genius since the birth of man.[40]

Many of the younger, powerful generals who succeeded Huan Wen and Xie An, including Huan Xuan (369–404), Yin Zhongkan (d. 399) and Xie Zhan (381–429), also showed great favour towards Gu Kaizhi. Even Emperor Andi set sufficient store by Gu's talents to confer upon him an honorary post as cavalier attendant-in-ordinary (*Sanqi changshi*) at the beginning of the Yixi era (405–419), just before Gu's death. There is no doubt that Gu Kaizhi made friends with many high-ranking officials throughout his life. Extremely famous as a painter and very close to the ruling class, he might have been chosen as the ideal person to paint the original *Admonitions* through the recommendation of a high-ranking official close to Emperor Xiaowudi or Andi.

Be that as it may, the date for Gu Kaizhi's execution of the original *Admonitions* should, therefore, be some time after the first 'event' in 375, when he was thirty-one, or after the second in 396, when he was fifty-two.

It is my belief that the original *Admonitions* scroll would have been regarded as a rare work as soon as the artist had created it, and that it would have been treasured in imperial collections from the Eastern Jin to the Tang. For reasons unknown, the scroll was not recorded, so that even the great Tang art historian Zhang Yanyuan did not know about it or record it. It is likely that when, by the late Tang, the condition of the original scroll had deteriorated somewhat, the imperial house then ordered a skilled painter to make a copy. Overall, this Tang copy faithfully preserves the features of the original, but in a few places, where the copyist found the original too damaged to see clearly he 'invented' some features on his own. While the painting for the most part faithfully preserves the features of its original, the calligraphy of the *Admonitions* scroll betrays the period-style of the Tang.[41] It is, therefore, only after the Tang that this copy began its journey through the hands of numerous collectors, before it entered the British Museum in 1903.

NOTES

1   *SQBJ chubian* 1745 (*SKQS*, vol. 825), *juan* 36, pp. 429–430, & *juan* 44, pp. 642–643; see also Yu Jianhua *et al.* (comps) 1962, pp. 155–160, 167. For the scroll's history in London, see Binyon 1904, pp. 39–44; Gray 1966, p. 1; & Whitfield 1995, pp. 209–210. For studies of the historical provenance, see Kohara 2000 (1967), pp. 22–35; Toyama 1964, pp. 670–678; and Wang Yao-t'ing's essay in this volume, pp. 192–218. See also Ma Cai 1958; Jin Weinuo 1958, pp. 19–24; Tang Lan 1961, pp. 7–12; Yu Jianhua *et al.* (comps) 1962; Gray 1966, pp. 5–6; Kohara 2000 (1967); and Chen Pao-chen 1987, pp. 96–104.

2   This section is a revised version of part of my Ph. D. dissertation (1987, pp. 96–104; see also 2002). Unless otherwise noted, all translations are by the author.

3   There are some seven opinions regarding Gu Kaizhi's dates, ranging from 341 to 407; see Yu Jianhua *et al.* (comps) 1962, pp. 131–132 (this paper follows the chronology, 'Gu Kaizhi nianbiao', pp. 125–130).

4   See Wang Zhongluo 1980, vol. 1, pp. 209–219; *Jin shu* (*SKQS*, vol. 255), *juan* 31, pp. 580–582.

5   For a detailed description of the scroll, see Gray 1966.

6   The three scenes are reconstructed in this later copy, formerly attributed to Li Gonglin (*c.*1041–1106), in the Beijing Palace Museum. At the end are four colophons, by Bao Xilu (1345), Xie Xun (1370), Zhang Meihe (1390), and Zhao Qian (1392). For the scroll, see Yu Hui 2001; Kohara 1967, pt. 2, pp. 17–19. Most Chinese scholars date this copy to the Southern Song (1127–1279), but Kohara Hironobu suggests it was made by Liang Qingbiao (1620–1692) (2000 [1967], p. 40).

7   *Han shu* (*SKQS*, vol. 251), *juan* 97b, p. 29.

8   Including Ise Sen'ichiro, Taki Sei'ichi & Kohara Hironobu (see Kohara 1967, part 1, p. 29 & part 2, pp. 17–19; 2000 [1967], pp. 30–31, 37–39).

9   For these two pictures, see Chen Pao-chen 2000, pp. 92–93.

10 *Han shu* (*SKQS*, vol. 251), *juan* 97b, p. 10; Lady Ban's response tr. Gray 1966, p. 3.

11 For these images, see Wu Hung 1989, pp. 142–167; Chen Pao-chen 2000, pp. 87–94.

12 See Zhang Chen's entry on this painting in *MSQJ, Painting* (1986), vol. 1, p. 51.

13 See He Jiejun's entries on these paintings in *MSQJ, Painting* (1986), vol. 1, pp. 21–22.

14 For both, see Chen Pao-chen 1987, pp. 111–120.

15 Mi Fu, *Hua shi* (1982 [*c.*1103]), p. 188.

16 See Umezawa 1926, p. 100; Yu Jianhua *et al.* (comps) 1962, p. 173, pls 32–34.

17 Fong, Wen C. 2002, pp. 5–6, 38, 41.

18 Summary in Kohara 2000 (1967), p. 30.

19 Kohara Hironobu argues that the original scroll did not include accompanying texts, which were added later. I believe the original composition did comprise both images and texts, as seen in the *Goddess of the Luo River* scroll in Liaoning Provincial Museum. For the development of early Chinese narrative handscrolls, see Chen Pao-chen 1987.

20 Kohara (2000 [1967], pp. 14–33) takes 1075 as the *terminus a quo* for the 'Ruisi Dongge' collection seal, which appears in five places on the scroll (Kohara 2000 [1967], pp. 22–29).

21 See Hu Jing 1971 (1816), pp. 22b–23b. See also Ayers 1963, p. 1042. Yang Xin (2001; also, in this volume) has proposed that the scroll was probably executed in the late fifth century. Wen C. Fong believes that it was copied in the sixth century (2002, pp. 1–34; see also his Introduction to this volume).

22 Komai Katsuchika (1974, p. 382–399) carried out typological comparisons between various objects in the *Admonitions* and those unearthed in archaeological finds dating to the Han and Six Dynasties, but did not focus on the painting style.

23 See Zhang Mingchuan and Lin Sen's entries on these paintings in *MSQJ, Painting* (1986), vol. 1, p. 43 & p. 46, respectively.

24 For this unusual hairstyle, see Shen Congwen 1981, vol. 1, pp. 122 123.

25 See Xue Yong's entry in *MSQJ, Painting* (1986), vol. 1, p. 57.

26 Some scholars believe that the lacquer paintings in Sima Jinlong's tomb represent the northern style, this style having served as a model for the paintings which were made in the south (Hsieh Cheng-fa 2001; Zhi Gong 1972, pp. 55–59). I disagree with these views. Furuta Shinichi has suggested (1992, pp. 57–67) that the screen might have been made in the north rather than having been imported from the south, even though the painting style shows southern influence.

27 This accessory is probably the *feixian* or 'fluttering ribbons' mentioned in Sima Xiangru's (179–117 BCE) prose-poem; see Kohara 1967, pt. 2, p. 28, n. 3.

28 Huang Weizhong 1994, pp. 88–93.

29 Kohara 2000 (1967), pp. 22–29.

30 Kohara 2000 (1967).

31 For this and the following information, see 'Biography of Emperor Xiaowudi' in *Jin shu* (*SKQS*, vol. 255), *juan* 9, pp. 22–23; 'Biography of Empress Wang', *juan* 32, pp. 14–15.

32 'Biography of Gu Kaizhi' in *Jin shu* (*SKQS*, vol. 255), *juan* 92, pp. 43–45; see also Chen Shih-hsiang (tr. & annot.) 1953; & Ayers 1963.

33 Only seven prose-poems, some fragments of poems, and a few passages from his book, *Memoirs for Enlightening the Purblind (Qimeng ji)* survive in quotation in the *Jin History*, *New Tales of the World (Shishuo xinyu)*, and other texts (Zhuang Shen 1986; Yu Jianhua *et al.* [comps] 1962, pp. 215–221).

34 Including a 'Record of painting Yuntai Mountain' (*Hua Yuntaishan ji*), 'On painting' (*Lun hua*), and 'Comments on paintings of worthies by Wei and Jin artists' (*Wei-Jin shengliu huazan*), which were recorded by Zhang Yanyuan in his *Lidai minghua ji*, *juan* 5 (1974 [847], pp. 70–72).

35 Ibid., pp. 68–69.

36 See Yu Jianhua *et al.* (comps) 1962, pp. 142–146.

37 Cf. *idem*, pp. 119–122.

38 'Biography of Gu Kaizhi' in *Jin shu* (*SKQS*, vol. 255), *juan* 92, p. 45: *Kaizhi ti zhong, chi xia ge ban; he er lun zhi, zheng de ping er* (see glossary).

39 Ibid., p. 43; see also Yu Jianhua *et al.* (comps) 1962, p. 127.

40 'Biography of Gu Kaizhi' in *Jin shu* (*SKQS*, vol. 255), *juan* 92, p. 44: *Zi you sheng min yilai wei zhi you ye* (see glossary).

41 In later copies, the painting and inscriptions often show different degrees of faithfulness to the originals; see, e.g., my study of the *Goddess of the Luo River* scroll in Liaoning Provincial Museum (1987).

The Convergence of Gu Kaizhi and *Admonitions* in the Literary Record

Alfreda Murck

Over the last millennium the affiliation of Gu Kaizhi (*c.* 345–406) with the painting *Admonitions of the Instructress to the Court Ladies* has been as celebrated as it was obscure prior to the twelfth century. An attribution of an *Admonitions* painting to Gu Kaizhi was recorded around 1100, but before that moment, there is no mention in histories of Gu having illustrated the admonitory prose-poem by Zhang Hua (232–300). Furthermore, there is no other mention of Gu Kaizhi with the 'Admonitions' text. In the poetry of the Tang (618–907) and Song (960–1279) dynasties, scholars wrote about Zhang Hua and Gu Kaizhi in interesting ways but, as far as I can tell, never in the same poem. This paper reviews the literary evidence to see if light can be shed on the logic of the early twelfth-century attribution.

Another topic considered here is the Northern Song (960–1127) context for the use of painting to admonish. Since earliest recorded history, rulers and courtiers were sensitive to the messages conveyed by visual signs and representations, a phenomenon that still obtained in the Northern Song era. The rule of women during much of the eleventh century raises questions about how the scroll may have been appreciated in the period when the attribution was first recorded. A related subject is the identity of the early twelfth-century owner, a palace eunuch.

Finally, the role of the brilliant connoisseur Mi Fu (1052–1107) is considered in connection with the linkage of Gu Kaizhi and an *Admonitions* painting, for it was he who brought the two together in the first recorded attribution.

Zhang Hua

The author of 'Admonitions of the Instructress to the Court Ladies' had outstanding literary skills and was a charismatic speaker. Zhang Hua advised the Jin emperor Wudi (r.

265–290) on many problems including vital military strategy. In the administration of the following emperor, Huidi (r. 290–306), Zhang helped organize the Jin bureaucracy and was held in such high esteem that he was made Commander Unequalled in Honour.

Zhang Hua's poem 'Admonitions of the Instructress to the Court Ladies' was precipitated by the excesses of Empress Jia (d. 300). A concubine to the heir apparent since he was fifteen, Lady Jia became empress in 290 CE and efficiently usurped Emperor Huidi's power. She arranged the murders of those who opposed her, and, in at least one case, executed the hit man. Zhang Hua was one of the few courtiers who dared to remonstrate with her. In 292 he submitted his carefully worded poem on exemplary consorts and the negative consequences of grasping power or speaking ill of others.[1] Predominantly positive in tone, the poem nonetheless was considered slander. Zhang Hua was not punished, historians concluded, because Empress Jia needed his guidance. In the year 300, following his refusal to participate in a plot to usurp the throne, he was executed by a political foe.[2]

When Tang and Song dynasty poets referred to Zhang Hua, they did not mention 'Admonitions of the Court Instructress', and they rarely wrote Zhang's name. Rather they cited an allegorical tale in Zhang Hua's biography that features the idea of the natural world responding to human governance. The story relates that before Zhang Hua's state conquered the state of Wu, a purple ether was often visible between the constellations Ursa Major and Altair. Only Zhang Hua read it as Heaven's positive omen. He advised an attack on Wu, which was successful. The purple haze grew brighter. Zhang Hua solicited the help of an interpreter of signs, Lei Huan, who divined that the mist was caused by energy emanating from a magical sword. Zhang Hua saw this as a fulfilment of a prophecy given when he was a boy: at the age of sixty he would rise to high position and wear a precious sword. Lei Huan located the site, dug a deep hole, and found a stone box containing not one, but two swords. Lei understood them as magical objects with an ominous message: 'This dynasty will fall into disorder. Duke Zhang will be implicated in the disaster.'[3] Lei retained one sword and gave the one inscribed 'Dragon Spring' to Zhang Hua who treasured it. After Zhang Hua was executed, Dragon Spring disappeared. After Lei Huan died, the two swords were miraculously reunited. Lei's son was carrying the sword near a ford when, of its own accord, it leapt into the water. He ordered men to search for it. The sword was not found, but two dragons rose to the surface of the water. An essay was lodged in a coil. Coloured lights flashed and waves whipped the surface of the water. It was said that the two swords were thus transformed and reunited.

The allegory of the numinous swords and their subsequent transformation into dragons conveyed divine recognition of the loyal minister Zhang Hua. Heaven gave a sign in the form of the purple haze; the earth responded by yielding up the magical swords. The loyal service of Lei Huan spoke to co-operative action at a time of national crisis as well as life-long friendship. The allegory encapsulated Zhang Hua's fate: loyal efforts to aid his state and exceptional intelligence that, in the end, could not save him.

With such a complicated allegory, it is not surprising that later poets moulded allusions to meet their own aims. The Tang dynasty poet Li Bai (701–762) relished the heroism of swordsmanship and the swords' flashing beauty.[4] Bao Zhao (414–466) and Du Fu (712–770) were drawn to the idea of swords calling out from their stone tomb as a symbol of badly needed leadership.[5] The Dragon-Spring allegory was used to compliment a friend by implying that he was the prodigious talent that was needed. Reversing the message, poets could lament the lack of such a talent. Both implications are found in the poetry of Li Bai.[6] Du Fu flattered a minister by saying that he had a Dragon Spring sword at his waist.[7] The poet Bai Juyi (772–846), on the other hand, used the allusion to caution a friend to skip the heroics and discard Dragon Spring.[8]

The high official Chen Zi'ang (658?–699?) used the Dragon Spring allegory with good cause. Chen lived during the era of Wu Zetian (627?–705), the most notable woman in Chinese history to seize control of imperial power. Consort and empress to Gaozong (r. 650–683), in 690 she founded her own dynasty, the Zhou (690–704). In her climb to absolute power, Wu Zetian is said to have murdered her own baby daughter to incriminate a competitor, arranged the execution of two of Gaozong's sons, deposed her own son when he showed signs of independence, and ordered thousands of executions.[9] Chen Zi'ang bravely submitted memorials calling

for the cessation of harsh punishments. In his poetry he praised a fellow official for being like Zhang Hua, and urged a colleague to accept the astral signs and take up the light-emanating Dragon Spring sword.[10]

Not every poetic usage was political. Meng Jiao (751–814) likened a friend's precious calligraphy collection stored in a cave to the magical swords in the stone box, and the story of the dragons fated to be together contributed to a lament for his deceased wife.[11]

Allusions to Zhang Hua's Dragon Spring sword continued in the eleventh century. The statesman and poet Su Shi (1037–1101) complimented a fellow official that he was like the one who dug up Dragon Spring.[12] Caught in lethal factional politics, Huang Tingjian (1045–1105) was convicted of distorting a history of the Shenzong reign (1067–1085). In exile he reflected on the advantages of reclusion, but began a poem with an allusion to Zhang Hua that hinted at political activism: 'This path has been in thick fog for many years,/Happy that You observed the Dipper: dig up Dragon Spring.'[13] A friend had observed the Big Dipper omen – more likely observed it in metaphorical terms – and Huang Tingjian interpreted it as a sign to take action.

On the whole the poems that mention Zhang Hua are serious in tone. The main themes are the careers and duties of officials. By alluding to the Dragon Spring sword, poets urged friends to be like Zhang Hua, commended friends for having *been* like him, or admonished them to *avoid* being like him.

Gu Kaizhi

The poems that cite Gu Kaizhi by contrast are predominantly cheerful. He was admired for his brilliance and eccentricity, for his vivid personality, for his independence of mind, and creativity. The history of the Jin dynasty described Gu as having 'three perfections': literary talent, skill in painting, pure foolishness.[14] His foolishness, or blithe lack of inhibition, had enduring appeal. To praise a friend one had only to compare his behaviour with the bizarre behaviour of Gu Kaizhi by quoting the phrase 'pure foolishness'. Huang Tingjian teased a friend, writing, 'You really have become one perfectly foolish guy.'[15] His friend transcended – perhaps transgressed – normal social conventions.

Unlike other painters of his era, Gu was acclaimed a literary genius. Eleventh-century scholars admired Gu Kaizhi's outstanding poems, essays and epitaphs.[16] The iconoclastic official Su Shunqin (1008–1048) wrote a series of quatrains on issues of speaking out, entitling one pair 'Discussing or not discussing things thoroughly', a title which plays off a story about Gu Kaizhi. Gu gathered with friends to engage in conversation. Characteristic of the 'pure conversation' of their day, the gentlemen competed in topping each other with varied and witty similes. Attempting to define the concept of 'thorough discussion', one described it as speaking until you are bound by cloth wrappers and placed in a coffin. Another emphasized penetrating intellectual insights: 'thorough discussion' was like fish swimming into a deep spring or like a man releasing a bird to take flight. Gu Kaizhi defined it as a fire sweeping across a plain until nothing combustible remains. Su Shunqin's quatrains on Thorough Discussion implied political discord with playful and threatening images: 'Green water grass with one sweep cuts off a man's neck.'[17]

In the eleventh century, even fragments of Gu Kaizhi's poetry did not escape the interest of scholars. A favourite couplet was 'Spring waters fill the four marshes,/ Summer clouds [make] many strange peaks.'[18] When Su Shi and nine companions went on an outing, they chose this couplet to assign rhyme words as each participant prepared to write the requisite poem.

During the Tang dynasty, Gu Kaizhi's paintings that could still be seen elicited influential poetic comments. One of his most famous paintings was at the Tile Coffin Monastery near Nanjing. It was for this monastery that Gu Kaizhi had put his young reputation on the line. When monks were raising funds to repair the buildings, the largest pledge was one hundred thousand cash. The monks were incredulous when the impecunious painter promised one million cash. Gu asked them to prepare a wall where he painted a portrait of the Buddhist layman Vimalakirti. He instructed the monks to charge each visitor one hundred thousand cash on the first day, fifty thousand on the second day, and to accept any donation thereafter. His painting quickly attracted enough viewers to fulfil his pledge.[19]

The eighth-century poet Du Fu visited the Tile Coffin Monastery as a young man. Later he declared that he had not forgotten the region precisely because of the superb wall painting. Referring to Vimalakirti by the poetic name Golden Grain Shadow, he wrote:

> I looked at the painting until famished and thirsty,
> Pursuing the traces, one hates the vast waters;
> Tiger Head's Golden Grain Shadow,
> Miraculous and truly unforgettable.[20]

Much later in his life, Du Fu mentioned the same wall painting as inspiration for the study of Buddhism.[21] Du Fu's admiration could only have enhanced Gu's reputation with Northern Song scholars, the men who claimed they had dis-

covered Du Fu and praised him as the greatest poet of all time. Su Shi, for one, cited the line on Golden Grain Shadow and echoed the praise for the Vimalakirti portrait.[22]

Du Fu also used Gu Kaizhi's reputation to bestow praise. When Du Fu visited the Xuanwu Temple, he saw a landscape on a wall in the quarters of a Chan Buddhist monk. The poem he inscribed on the wall next to the landscape imagines a Daoist paradise and opened with a query on Gu Kaizhi:

> When did Tiger-head Gu
> Fill a wall with a painting of Cangzhou?
> Under a red sun, rocks and woods give forth vapour
> Beneath blue heavens, rivers and lakes flow.[23]

Du Fu probably was admiring a painting not by Gu, but by the monk who was his host, playfully 'mistaking' it for the work of the great master. Du Fu may have felt confident that his host would be pleased by the artful exaggeration. If we interpret the line as extravagant praise, we lose a reference to an otherwise unknown Gu Kaizhi landscape, but we gain the insight that, for Du Fu, Gu excelled at landscape painting as well as portraiture.

In 845 most Buddhist monasteries were to be destroyed. Before the Tile Coffin Monastery was demolished, the official Du Mu (803–852) commissioned artisans to make ten tracings of Gu Kaizhi's *Vimalakirti*. In the end, the original Gu painting was cut out of the wall and relocated to the protected Sweet Dew Monastery. Soon thereafter, a high official removed it to his home. Learning of this, the emperor sent a blunt inquiry, and the official quickly volunteered the wall fragments to the throne. The emperor showed the painting with pride, but it thereafter disappears from the historical record.[24]

In the eleventh century, Gu Kaizhi paintings were apparently no longer on display. In his light-hearted 'Song of Painting', the official Shen Gua (1031–1095) wrote of the absence of authentic Gu Kaizhi paintings and gave his low opinion of the copies circulating:

> The old traces of Kaizhi's *Vimalakirti* have been lost,
> We only see accumulated generations of commissioned
>   copies.
> Of Tanwei's authentic traces, one work is extant,
> On Sweet Dew wooden planks, a mythical beast is
>   shrivelled.

A painting by Gu's contemporary Lu Tanwei at least survived, but it was desiccated and distorted.[25]

The circulation of copies was stimulated not only by the imminent loss of great art, but also by an active art market. In both the fifth and eleventh centuries, zealous appreciation of painting led to shenanigans that were met with tolerance. Gu Kaizhi once placed some of his favourite paintings in a box, pasted a seal on the front, and gave the box for safekeeping to his friend Huan Xuan, who was delighted to be so entrusted. Huan is said to have enjoyed his own paintings at all hours, even viewing his treasures at mealtime, which led to oil stains from his fried cakes appearing on them. Huan surreptitiously opened Gu's box from the back, stole the paintings and had the box repaired, leaving Gu's seal intact. He returned the box to Gu as if it had been untouched. When Gu discovered that the paintings were gone, he expressed no suspicion of Huan Xuan, explaining their disappearance as a result of their miraculous spirituality. He concluded that they had transformed themselves and vanished like men becoming immortals.[26]

The story of Gu Kaizhi and Huan Xuan was cited by Su Shi in relation to his younger contemporary Mi Fu. Su suggests that Mi had a collector's passion akin to Huan Xuan's and that he too could make paintings disappear. As the most authoritative connoisseur of his era, Mi Fu borrowed fine works of art from private collectors to study and authenticate. When he could not bear to give them back, he carefully copied them, and returned the copies. Su Shi wrote:

> Strange, Sir; In what place did you come by this scroll?
> Formerly there was Huan Xuan who had oily fried cakes;
> Skilful stealing, bold snitching have occurred since
> antiquity
> I laugh: Who resembles the foolish Tiger Head?

Su Shi's poem was one in a jocular exchange of six poems. Mi Fu wrote three and Huang Tingjian contributed one.[27]

In the late eleventh century, Gu Kaizhi is linked with expressions of complaint in the poetry of Su Shi, Wang Shen (c. 1048–1103), and Huang Tingjian. For a poetic colophon to a landscape by the painter Guo Xi (c. 1000–c. 1090), Su Shi alluded to a phrase from Gu Kaizhi's biography and opened with a lament that suggested talented men were being wasted.

> When tree leaves fall, the poet already resents the
> autumn,
> And cannot bear 'level distance' provoking poetic
> sorrow.
> If you want to see where 'torrents vie in myriad valleys',
> Another day you'll have to impose on Tiger-head Gu![28]

The third line – where torrents vie in myriad valleys – quotes Gu Kaizhi's description of the mountainous scenery of Kuaiji (in modern Zhejiang Province). Su juxtaposed 'myriad valleys' with 'level distance' in the previous line to create a contrast that referred to serving and not serving in office: 'level distance' could be read as living in isolation on rivers and lakes while 'torrents vying in myriad valleys' hinted at the hierarchy of the court bureaucracy.[29]

Gu Kaizhi appears in another poem of complaint in 1088. Su Shi was under attack from his political enemies. Su Shi and Wang Shen exchanged poems in which they indirectly counter-attacked. Wang Shen lamented the ages-long absence of a character like Tiger Head: 'For lack of constraint, for a thousand years there has been no one like Tiger Head.' Wang Shen seems to imply that when officials were in conflicts, when they had to look over their shoulders and constantly be careful, Gu Kaizhi provided an image of freedom from social and political convention.

When Su Shi and Huang Tingjian were bidding farewell to their colleague Gu Lin, the surname he shared with Gu Kaizhi made comparison irresistible. Huang Tingjian wrote, 'This era's Tiger Head Gu / has inner qualities naturally strong and imposing.'[30] Gu Lin is said to have been portly; 'naturally strong and imposing' may have been one of the barbs that he reportedly disliked. Still, Huang Tingjian's line was meant to cheer Gu Lin as he was being demoted and expelled from the capital. At Gu Lin's departure, Huang wrote: 'Tiger Head's miraculous ink can always lodge [feelings].' 'Miraculous ink' may have referred to both the quality of his calligraphy and the content of his writing – in this case, Gu Lin's boldly critical memorials and essays.[31]

Finally, lest the above references create the impression of frequent citation, it is worth noting that Tang and Song dynasty poets did not often refer to Gu Kaizhi. Gu's contemporaries and near contemporaries Dong Fangshuo, Ruan Ji, Ruan Xian, Xie An, Wang Xizhi and Tao Qian are much more frequently cited. With few exceptions, the poems where Gu Kaizhi appears tend to be light-hearted. Beyond celebrating his paintings, mentioning Gu Kaizhi was a way of praising friends' creativity, eccentricity and individuality. Gu Kaizhi was cited for the colourful stories about his life, for his unrestrained and eccentric behaviour, for his transcendence of social norms.

Painting as Admonishment

Because of a cultural sensitivity to the messages in visual phenomena of all kinds, painting had the potential to criticise and admonish. Today we view the *Admonitions* handscroll much as the eighteenth-century Qianlong emperor did, as an incomparable masterpiece from the distant past. That probably was not the case in the eleventh century. Keeping the messages of Zhang Hua's 'Admonitions' prose-poem in mind, we can suppose that the circulation of its illustration could have been construed as criticism.

Whenever the *Admonitions* scroll was created, it is possible that during the eleventh century its function as a painting to instruct and rebuke became relevant again. The Northern Song witnessed a series of powerful women near the throne. Their participation in government was facilitated by a dynastic policy that curtailed the role of eunuchs in all official court business.[32] Although some female regents were prudent rulers, their influence was not always benign. Eleventh-century regencies for young or ill emperors combine for a total of more than a quarter of a century of female rule, which on many occasions generated criticism.

One woman whose behaviour caused alarm was Lady Liu (969–1033), the primary consort of Zhenzong (r. 997–1022). Toward the end of his reign, Zhenzong was incapacitated with illness. With the aid of eunuchs, Empress Liu usurped his authority. After his death, she served for eleven years as regent for emperor Renzong (r. 1022–1063). In 1033 when he was to assume full authority, she donned the emperor's robes to conduct an important sacrifice at the clan temple. The only precedent for this was the conduct of Wu Zetian who wore imperial robes and established her own dynasty in 690. Fearing that Liu was arrogating imperial power, the official Cheng Lin (988–1056) presented her with a portrait of Empress Wu Zetian. The message was instantly registered: throwing the painting to the ground, she denied any such ambition.[33] Cheng Lin's biography in the *Song History* ends with this incident and with the comment that people thought less of him for it. The admonition had been too blunt and had caused offence. It is worth noting, however, that Emperor Renzong could have ruled independent of his regent from 1028. That Empress Dowager Liu was still regent five years later suggests that she was reluctant to give up her role.

Two other women may have inspired a reproving use of the *Admonitions* scroll. Empress Dowager Cao earned praise from historians for assisting her husband Renzong when he was incapacitated with illness and for saving his life during an uprising of palace guards.[34] For the latter, she might have been compared to the exemplary Lady Feng Wan in the *Admonitions* scroll who protected her husband from a ferocious bear (pls 1–2). When their adopted son Yingzong (r. 1063–1067) ascended the throne at the age of thirty-two, his poor health led him to rely on his adopted mother, who served as regent and co-ruler from behind the curtain. Officials initially welcomed Empress Dowager Cao's participation in government. However, when Yingzong recovered and wished to take full charge, she refused to step down. Finally, one of the boldest critics of the empress had the curtain removed while the court was in session forcing the Empress Dowager to withdraw.[35]

Another woman who inspired criticism was Supreme Empress Dowager Gao (d. 1093). After her son Emperor Shenzong died, Gao served as regent for her grandson, Emperor Zhezong. During her regency from 1085–1093 the major political and economic policies that had been established by her son were abolished, infuriating the Reformers who were gradually eliminated from government. She was accused of favouring eunuchs, whose help she needed to rule, and of strictly disciplining members of the imperial clan.

In contrast to Cheng Lin, who was merely less well regarded for submitting a painted admonition, the scholar Zheng Xia (1041–1119) was severely punished. In his case no female regent was involved. In 1074 Zheng submitted a memorial to Emperor Shenzong on the consequences of choosing the wrong ministers. The text was accompanied by portraits entitled *Pictorial Record of the Careers of Proper and Upright Gentlemen and Heterodox Crooked Petty Men*. Zheng's portraits were analogous in concept to the *Admonitions*: they provided negative examples to be avoided and exemplary models for emulation. By suggesting a correlation between the evil officials of history and contemporary ministers, Zheng implied that Emperor Shenzong had made bad choices.[36] Both Shenzong and his officials took offence. Zheng Xia was convicted of the capital offence of slandering the court and of forming a faction. Emperor Shenzong spared him his life, instead confining Zheng to a hamlet in south China for eleven years.[37]

Northern Song reactions to admonitory paintings are a reminder that then, as in later dynasties, images and their implications were taken seriously. The sensitivity to pictures made a scroll like the *Admonitions* a political asset and a risk: an asset because its antiquity camouflaged the pointed lessons in the paintings; a risk because showing a painting with implied criticism could easily cause offence.

Liu Youfang

The man whom Mi Fu identified as the keeper of the *Admonitions* scroll was a eunuch in the Palace Domestic Service. Liu Youfang personally attended the emperor and his family in the innermost quarters of the palace. Through political reversals and intense factional politics, Liu Youfang sustained a long career. He served in the imperial pharmacy and rose to

Deputy Office Manager of the Palace Domestic Service. In the spring of 1075, when Wang Anshi (1021–1086) was called back to court to resume duties as prime minister, Liu Youfang escorted him from Jiangxi to the capital.[38] In 1082 Liu Youfang was made an Administrative Aide in the Palace Domestic Service which allowed him to be posted outside the capital. He was called back to the capital, and in the third month of 1085 was authorized to enter the innermost rooms of the palace.[39] When Emperor Shenzong died later that month, Supreme Empress Dowager Gao became regent for the young Zhezong, and it must have been she who approved Liu Youfang's selection for the Capital Security Office, a secret service agency that was responsible for keeping order in the capital.[40] Liu Youfang was soon sent out of the capital, but was instructed to continue serving the Capital Security Office.[41]

In the mid-1080s Su Shi drafted an imperial edict for Liu Youfang who was then an Administrative Aid in western Sichuan. Su praised Liu for having transcended his eunuch condition: 'Although you are what you are, you have the quality of a scholar-gentleman.' The citation describes Liu Youfang as genial, amicable, resolute, and thoroughly disciplined, and one who in leisure took an interest in books and historical records.[42]

The elderly Liu Youfang was given a series of sinecures. In 1090 he was made Congratulatory Commissioner, which presumably required him to deliver congratulations to imperial kinsmen on occasions such as birthdays.[43] Although Liu was not given a biography in the eunuch section of the official history, he was favoured in ways that other eunuchs were not. Liu once received imperially bestowed tea medicine along with thirteen gentlemen of the court, including consorts of imperial princesses (among them Wang Shen).[44] In the autumn of 1099 Liu Youfang was permitted to retire with warm thanks: 'In recognition of his years of service, Congratulatory Commissioner, Defence Commissioner of Xiongzhou, and Eunuch Affairs Deputy Office Manager Liu Youfang is given the honorific title Commissioner of the Hall of Abundant Happiness.'[45]

How did Liu Youfang come to be in possession of the *Admonitions* scroll? The question, although unanswerable, is interesting both because of the involvement of powerful women in Northern Song politics and because of the unusual recognition given to eunuch Liu by the imperial family. Did someone, wanting to send a message to a palace woman, designate Liu as the messenger? Or, perhaps the *Admonitions* scroll had been in the hands of an empress who presented it to the eunuch in recognition of his loyal service. Whatever the situation, Liu Youfang's stewardship of the scroll suggests that the painting circulated in the inner palace.

Mi Fu's Attribution to Gu Kaizhi

An eccentric character, Mi Fu reputedly was descended from Sogdian ancestry. The men of his family were not scholars but soldiers and generals.[46] Because his mother was a servant to the woman who would become Yingzong's empress, as a young boy Mi Fu played with children of the Song imperial clan. Fascinated with the past to the extent that he wore ancient costumes, Mi Fu assembled an outstanding collection of calligraphy and gained fame for his own brush writing. His official career was modest, but wherever he was posted he sought out private collections to study antique scrolls and objects. When closer to the capital, he regularly met with other collectors and swapped treasures with them. Mi frequently copied fine scrolls before returning them and, as noted above, sometimes returned the copy instead of the original. An expert connoisseur and forger, he was adept at mounting silk and paper scrolls, could distinguish old from new paper and silk, and was attuned to nuances of seals and brushwork. His notes on painting and calligraphy reveal a discriminating mind. He noted down small details and recorded when he had seen a scroll himself and when he was reporting someone else's comments. His critiques of works were informed by a thorough familiarity with the literary tradition and with the records of painters and collections. While he worked without benefit of photographic archives and archaeologically excavated material, he undoubtedly saw as many original works as any contemporary, including many not available to us. He had little concept of period style or theory of the development of representation; he focused instead on apprehension of the hand and personality of individual masters.

The attribution of a painting of the *Admonitions* to Gu Kaizhi first appears in Mi Fu's *History of Painting (Hua shi)*:

> *Admonitions of the Imperial Instructress*, a horizontal scroll at the home of Liu Youfang, superior brushwork and colour is lively, beautiful and smooth coiffures. The *Veritable Records of Taizong* notes the purchase of a Gu scroll. Today a scholar-official family has a Tang dynasty copy of Gu's *Biographies of Eminent Women*, which they had carved into wood panels to make a screen. The figures, all more than three inches high, are just like Liu Youfang's *Admonitions of the Imperial Instructress*.[47]

He did not say when he saw the painting; a *terminus ad quem* of 1103 is provided by the publication date of the text. The formulation of these remarks suggests that Mi Fu was ruminating on the attribution. He first wrote the title (not the painter's name as in some other entries), gave the painting's whereabouts, noted its qualities, mentioned related works, and singled out the similarity in the proportion of the figures to a Tang copy of a Gu Kaizhi painting. If Mi Fu did not himself make the attribution to Gu Kaizhi, he certainly found it acceptable. What were the factors that predisposed Mi Fu and his contemporaries to find plausible the association of Zhang Hua's 'Admonitions' with Gu?

Assuming Mi Fu was viewing the version of *Admonitions* now in the collection of the British Museum, he may have been encouraged by the evident humour in the painting to link the images to Gu's reputation for mischievous fun. For example, the sedan chair scene has the emperor Chengdi wistfully gazing back at his beautiful Lady Ban walking behind (pls 3, 4). Illustrating the decision of Lady Ban to walk rather than give rise to evil talk, the vignette is entertaining in the pathos of his gaze and the rhythmic patter of the litter bearers' feet. The flashes of playfulness in the *Admonitions* scroll reflect a lively mind and irreverent sense of humour that meshes well with the stories of Gu.

Style played a large role in the attribution. The superb quality of the drawing and its apparent antiquity called for an artist known to have excelled in figure painting. Gu not only painted figures, he is described as painting subjects that featured women, such as the *Goddess of the Luo River,* the *Ladies of the Xiang* and *Biographies of Eminent Women.* Mi Fu appropriately compared the *Admonitions* scroll at Liu Youfang's home to Gu Kaizhi attributions with female figures. He considered both style and Gu's propensity for painting women with fluttering drapery.[48]

Another attraction of the Gu Kaizhi attribution is suggested by the mindset of scholars who wrote poetry. To write a good poetic couplet, authors had to find appropriate juxtapositions of words in any given category. This matching of words was done for verbs, adjectives, nouns, pronouns and even proper names. Because the tiger and the dragon had been juxtaposed in Chinese thought since Neolithic times, Gu Kaizhi's nickname, Tiger Head, was a satisfying match for Zhang Hua's nickname, Dragon Spring. This is not to reduce the attribution to something as trivial as a good poetic match,

only to say that we should not dismiss the contribution that this kind of aesthetic balance made to the attribution's feeling of rightness.[49]

Finally an attribution to Gu Kaizhi may have been attractive because of his status as a literatus. He was not just an early painter, he was an erudite scholar and a brilliant poet and essayist. In the late eleventh century when some scholars were profoundly interested in the expressive potential of painting and likened it to the art of poetry, Gu was an example of a painter who excelled in literary arts. When Mi Fu sought a satisfactory attribution for an old painting, a rigorous methodology is likely to have mattered less than a sense of rightness and harmonious aesthetics. Attuned to history and refined through years of looking, his connoisseurship was ultimately based on a highly cultivated intuition.

Conclusion

In contrast to large wall paintings that were on display in monasteries, the British Museum scroll is a small work designed for individual viewing. As a private treasure, it may have escaped the attention of poets. Although the absence in the literary record of any link between Gu Kaizhi and Zhang Hua does not disprove the attribution to Gu, the silence should encourage caution.

The convergence of Gu Kaizhi and the *Admonitions of the Instructress to the Court Ladies* in the written record occurred at a cultural watershed when a leading literary circle dominated by Su Shi, Huang Tingjian and Mi Fu intersected with an inner court circle of palace women, imperial clansmen, and eunuchs. The tension between powerful palace women and Confucian officials during the eleventh century created opportunities for officials to use a painting like *Admonitions* to criticise and instruct. The growing admiration for Gu Kaizhi as a literatus and painter and the lack of prior association of his name with the illustration of Zhang Hua's poem makes it plausible that the attribution of the *Admonitions* scroll to Gu Kaizhi was an insight by Mi Fu.

NOTES

1 Kohara 2000 (1967), pp. 4–7.
2 *Jin shu* 1974, Zhang Hua's biography, *juan* 36, pp. 1068–1077.
3 *Jin shu* 1974, *juan* 36, p. 1075.
4 Li Bai, 'Ancient Airs', *QTS* 1960, *juan* 161, p. 1673; 'Sending off General Yu Lintao', *QTS* 1960, *juan* 176, p. 1796.
5 Bao Zhao 1980, 'Presenting six poems to my friend Ma Ziqiao', *juan* 5, p. 282; Du Fu, 'Autumn Day in Kui Prefecture, a song submitted to Supervisor Zheng and Adviser Li, in one hundred rhymes', line 5, *DSXZ* 1980 (1703), *juan* 19, p. 1699.
6 Li Bai used the allusion as a lament in 'Song of Liang Fu', *QTS* 1960, *juan* 162, p. 1682, and as a compliment in 'At a naval banquet, presented to secretary to the commander, attending censor', *QTS* 1960, *juan* 170, p. 1749.
7 Du Fu, 'Ten rhymes sent to Minister Dong Jiarong', *DSXZ* 1980 (1703), *juan* 14, pp. 1167–1169.
8 Bai Juyi, 'Upon hearing that Minister Li called on the Grand Councillor, sending long lines to He Weizhi', *QTS* 1960, *juan* 440, p. 4904.
9 For the events of Wu Zetian's reign, see Twitchett & Loewe (eds) 1979, pp. 290–332, and Ho, R. M. W. 1993, pp. 3–5.
10 Chen Zi'ang, 'Preface to "Luxuriant Bamboo" for Left Chronicler Dongfang Qiu', *QTS* 1960, vol. 3, *juan* 83, p. 896, and 'Summer day presented upon parting with Administrator Li Chongsi', *QTS* 1960, *juan* 83, p. 900.
11 Meng Jiao, 'Inscribing Wei Shaobao's cave for storing calligraphy at the Studio of Quiet Reverence', *QTS* 1960, *juan* 376, p. 4221, and 'Mourning', *QTS* 1960, *juan* 381, p. 4273.
12 Su Shi, 'Sending off Song Xiyuan at Taitou Monastery', *Su Shi shiji*, *juan* 18, p. 92.
13 Huang Tingjian 1979, 'Playfully using the rhymes in Wang Zhouyan's inscription for Master Yuan's "Poem on This Gentleman's Hall"', p. 2087.
14 *Jin shu* 1974, *juan* 92, pp. 2404–2406.
15 Huang Tingjian 1979, 'Sending ten poems to Chao Yuanzhong', p. 1717.
16 For a survey of Gu's literary works, see Zhuang Shen 1986.
17 Su Shunqin, 'Speaking or not speaking fully', *QSS* 1992, *juan* 309, p. 3897.
18 Gu Kaizhi, 'Numinous feelings', in *Xian Qin* 1988, *juan* 14, p. 931. For Su Shi's poem see *Su Shi shiji*, *juan* 18, p. 922. My thanks to Stuart Sargent for this reference.
19 Zhang Yanyuan in Acker 1954, pp. 378–379.
20 Du Fu, 'Sending off Reminder Xu Ba who is returning to Jiangning', *DSXZ* 1980 (1703), *juan* 6, p. 457.
21 Du Fu, 'Autumn Day in Kui Prefecture', lines 193–194, *DSXZ* 1980 (1703), p. 1715.
22 Su Shi, 'Master Pang', *Su Shi shiji*, vol. 8, *juan* 47, p. 2551.
23 Du Fu, 'Inscribing the wall in Chan Master's room at Xuanwu', *DSXZ* 1980 (1703), *juan* 11, p. 929.
24 Acker 1954, pp. 366–372, 376–380.

25 Shen Gua, 'Song on painting', *QSS* 1992, *juan* 686, pp. 8015–8016.
26 *Jin shu* 1974, Gu Kaizhi's biography, *juan* 92, p. 2405.
27 Su Shi, 'Two poems matching rhymes in Mi Fu's colophon to the Two Wang's calligraphy', *Su Shi shiji*, *juan* 29, pp. 1536–1538, where all six poems are recorded.
28 Su Shi, 'Second of two poems on Guo Xi's *Autumn Mountains in Level Distance*', *Su Shi shiji*, *juan* 29, p. 1540; tr. (slightly modified) from Sargent 1992, pp. 274–276.
29 See discussion of these literary tropes in Murck 2000, pp. 117–124.
30 Huang Tingjian 2001, 'Second of two poems matching Su Shi's rhymes sending Gu Zidun to Duyun Hebei', *juan* 2, pp. 29–30. For the background of Gu Lin's demotion see *Su Shi shiji*, *juan* 28, pp. 1494–1496.
31 Huang Tingjian 2001, *juan* 7, p. 157. For Huang's linking ink and meaning, see Murck 2000, pp. 185–187.
32 Chung, P. C. 1981, p. 3. This paragraph is based on Chung's study.
33 *Song shi jishi benmo*, *juan* 24, p. 190.
34 Chung, P. C. 1981, p. 74.
35 Chung, P. C. 1981, p. 75.
36 *Song shi*, *juan* 321, p. 10436.
37 On Zheng Xia's exile, see *XCB*, *juan* 254, pp. 6207–6208 and *juan* 259, pp. 6310–6315.
38 He is not to be confused with the official Liu Youfang (act. early 11th century) from Quanzhou whose father, Liu Changyan, lived from 942 to 999; *Song shi*, *juan* 267, p. 16. Eunuch Liu Youfang is mentioned in *XCB* 1986 (1134), from the years 1074 to 1099.
39 *XCB* 1986 (1174), *juan* 353, p. 8460.
40 *XCB* 1986 (1174), *juan* 361, p. 8. The Capital Security Office was headed by a military officer or a eunuch having the personal trust of the emperor, or in this case, Empress Dowager Gao (Hucker 1985, item 2833; other translations of titles also follow Hucker).
41 *XCB* 1986 (1174), *juan* 375, p. 9086.
42 Su Shi, 'Draft to Liu Youfang, Deputy Office Manager for the Right Duty Group of the Palace Domestic Service', *Su Shi wenji*, *juan* 39, 1119.
43 *XCB* 1986 (1174), *juan* 443, p. 10666. Hucker 1985, item 2656.
44 Fan Zuyu, *juan* 33, p. 5 (*SKQS*, vol. 1100, p. 366).
45 *XCB* 1986 (1174), *juan* 513, p. 12199.
46 This biography is drawn from Ledderose 1979, pp. 45–49.
47 Mi Fu, *Hua shi*, in Yang Jialuo (ed.) 1962, p. 4.
48 These themes are analysed in Chen 1987, and Murray 1990, pp. 27–53.
49 Other paired names could be cited. For example, the Southern Song poet and patriot Xin Qiji (1140–1207) admired dozens of historic heroes, but later authors linked Xin with the Han general Huo Qubing (140–117 BCE) because of the symmetry of their names: Qiji (discarding illness) neatly parallels Qubing (eliminating disease). My thanks to Hu Chirui of Peking University for this example.

The *Admonitions* Scroll: A Song Version

Yu Hui

There are presently two extant versions of the *Nüshi zhen tu (Admonitions of the Instructress to the Court Ladies)* handscrolls depicting a Western Jìn (265–317) text by Zhang Hua (232–300). One is the world-renowned British Museum scroll, believed to be a Tang dynasty (618–906) copy of an original work by Gu Kaizhi (*c.* 345–*c.* 406) (the 'Tang version'). The other lesser-known scroll, in the collection of the Palace Museum in Beijing, is believed to be a work of the Song period (960–1279) and has traditionally been attributed to Li Gonglin (*c.* 1041–1106; the 'Song version'; figs 1–2, pls 23–28). The latter, which has yet to be studied in any great detail, is the subject of this essay.[1] Important issues discussed here pertain to its dating, authorship and the circumstances of its creation. Moreover, as similarities may be detected between the two versions, is there a connection between them?

The Song version was painted on *jian* (silk-cocoon) paper in the *baimiao* (plain outline) manner. Although it bears no artist's signature or seals, it was recorded as a work by Li Gonglin in *Shiqu baoji (Precious Cases of the Stone Gully)*, the catalogue of the Qianlong emperor's (r. 1736–1795) painting collection.[2] The complete handscroll (including the title-piece and colophons) is 28.9 cm in height and 877 cm long. The painting itself is 27.9 cm by 600.5 cm. During remounting, about 0.5 cm had been lost from the top right corner where an imperial seal had been fixed. There are twelve scenes, each accompanied by text; three more than in the Tang version. They may be titled as follows: (1) 'feminine virtue yields honour', (2) 'Lady Fan abstains from meat', (3) 'Lady Wei puts aside her love for music', (4) 'Lady Feng confronts the bear', (5) 'Lady Ban humbly follows the emperor's palanquin', (6) 'happiness and sadness in human life', (7) 'comportment and deportment', (8) 'the suspicions of bedfellows', (9) 'words that honour and disgrace', (10) 'a warning against wanton behaviour', (11) 'prosperity is fostered with caution' and (12) 'the instruction of concubines'.

'Li Gonglin Nüshi zhen tu zhen ji' ('Li Gonglin's painting *Admonitions of the Instructress to the Court Ladies*, a true work') was written on the protective wrapper by the Qing collector Liang Qingbiao (1620–1691) in *kaishu* (regular script). The Qianlong emperor wrote the title-piece 'Wanghua zhi shi' ('the beginnings of kingship') in *xingkai* (running regular script) (pl. 23 right). The upper seal is from a face which has been carved in relief and reads 'Qianlong chenhan' ('calligraphy of the Qianlong emperor'). The lower seal 'Hanjing weidao' ('redolent with the scent of didacticism') is in intaglio. At the end of the painting, the emperor has also inscribed 'Qianlong *jiazi* (1744), autumn, the eighth month, lovingly examined and copied for a week'. The lower intaglio seal reads 'Neifu tushu zhibao' ('Treasure of the Imperial Household Library').

This is followed by several colophons from the fourteenth century (fig. 2). They were written by Bao Xilu in 1345, Xie Xun in 1370, Zhang Meihe in 1390 and Zhao Qian in 1392. There are also thirty-nine connoisseurs' seals. The earliest dates from the Ming period (1368–1644) and belonged to a gentleman named Yan. They read 'Migu wenyi zhi yin' ('artefact of secret antiquity' seal) and 'Yan XX shending zhenji miwan' ('Yan XX examined and approved this genuine secret plaything'). When compared with the disparate seals of later owners like Liang Qingbiao and the Qianlong emperor, these two seals must have belonged to the same person. Both were carved in relief in a similar style and had been fixed on with the same vermilion ink.

Taking their cue from the fourteenth-century colophons, both Liang Qingbiao and the Qianlong emperor continued to attribute the work to Li Gonglin. Without taking into consideration other important clues such as the presence of 'taboo' characters, there was a tendency for connoisseurs of the past to attribute any *baimiao* work of some age to this legendary master. One of the earliest modern stud-

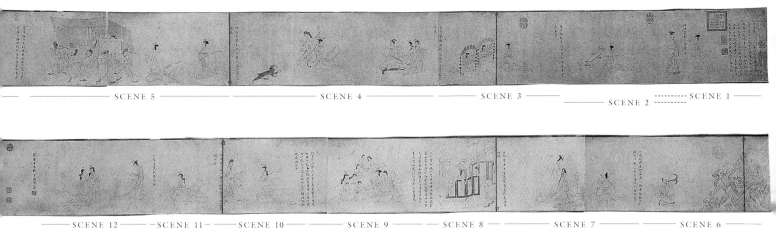

Fig. 1 *Admonitions of the Instructress to the Court Ladies.* Southern Song period, late 12th century.
Handscroll; ink on paper, 28.9 × 877 cm. Palace Museum, Beijing.

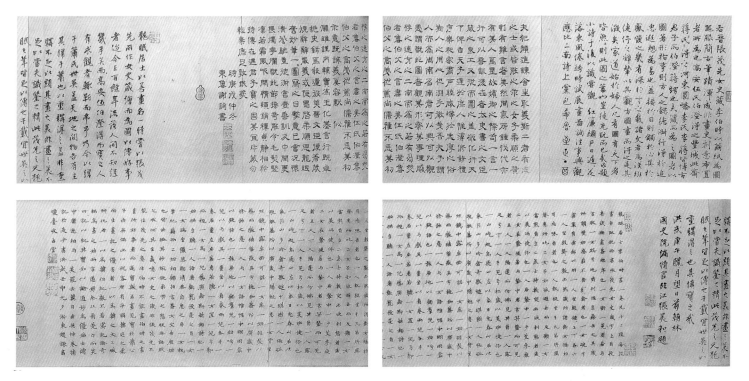

Fig. 2 Colophons to the *Admonitions* scroll in the Palace Museum, Beijing.

ies on the Song version is to be found in an article discussing the work of Gu Kaizhi by Tang Lan, a former director of the Palace Museum.[3] He referred to it as a Southern Song (1127–1279) facsimile. Based on the presence of taboo characters in the 'Nüshi zhen' text on the painting, Xu Bangda is also of the view that it is a Southern Song work and his subsequent analysis has proceeded from this starting point.[4] Li Yu, a professor at the Lu Xun Academy of Fine Arts in Shenyang, Liaoning Province, thinks that the Song version was a replacement for the incomplete Tang scroll.[5] However, the Japanese scholar Kohara Hironobu categorically rejects the artistic merits of the Song version and its value to scholarship. Moreover, he has expressed doubts over Li's view that the three opening scenes of the Song version may be seen as replacements to the Tang version.[6]

There are references in Song textual sources to the existence of paintings known as *Nüshi zhen tu* which were attributed to Gu Kaizhi. *Xuanhe Painting Manual* (catalogue of the Song emperor Huizong's collection) contains a reference to the Tang version under the section on works by Gu Kaizhi.[7] In *Hua shi (History of Painting)*, Mi Fu (1052–1107) records that he saw a painting with the same name in the possession of Liu Youfang. He further compares it to *Lienü tu (Illustrations of Exemplary Women)*, another Tang facsimile of a work by Gu, and notes that the figures in both paintings measured three *cun* (approximately 7.5 cm).[8] Since these measurements do not correspond with the scale of figures in the Tang version, Mi must have been referring to another painting. As there is no subsequent record of this work, it was probably destroyed in 1126 or 1127 when Kaifeng was conquered by the Jurchens and the Song imperial family retreated south. In the Runzhou region (modern Zhenjiang, Jiangsu Province), site of a decisive victory over the Jurchens, several families owned paintings by Gu Kaizhi during this period, but there are no references to works titled *Nüshi zhen tu*.[9] It is therefore likely that by the Southern Song period, the Tang version was the only extant work of its kind.

The Song version exceeds the Tang by a width of 3.6 cm and a length of 252.3 cm. Differences in dimensions and the scale of figures in the painting mean that the Song version is not a facsimile (*moben*). Can it then be considered a copy (*linben*)? An overall comparison of the composition, the stylistic rendering of figures and landscape elements, and the expressive technique indicate very close similarities between the two works. It is clear that the last nine scenes of the Song version have been directly copied from the Tang. Judging from the accuracy of modelling, it is highly improbable that it could have been copied from elsewhere.

While only nine scenes remain in the Tang version, there would originally have been twelve. There are, in fact, three and not two missing scenes as commonly believed. The constant reference to 'two missing scenes' is misleading and came about because only even numbers were counted in the traditional Chinese system of numbering sections or paragraphs. This misunderstanding has been compounded by the confusing composition of Scene 1 in the Song version (fig. 1, pl. 23 left). It is evident from a comparison of the Song version's first three scenes with its later nine scenes that the 'mother copy' for the former cannot have been the Tang version. The placement of seals from the Zhenghe reign period (1111–1118) at the beginning of the Tang version suggest that the three sections were already missing at the beginning of the twelfth century. The 'copyist' of the Song version probably had to 'create' these additional sections to complete the illustrations to Zhang Hua's entire text.

The copyist was confronted with several difficulties in the conception of these additional scenes. He strove hard to make the scenes appear seamless, as if they had belonged to the original narrative. Superficially, the style of clothing and the construction of the figures in these three scenes are based on the Tang version. However, when compared with the nine copied sections, the rendering of garment folds appears conceptually suspicious and the scenes are not cohesively organized. They also lack the 'brushstrokes of Gu Kaizhi [which] are strong in firmness and uninterrupted in continuity, circling back upon themselves in abrupt rushes; the tone and style [which] are untrammelled and varied, [and] the atmosphere and flavour [which are] sudden as lightning'.[10]

The depiction of material objects in Scene 2 also betrays some weaknesses and flaws (pl. 24 right). When early artists painted historical narratives, examples from contemporary material culture would be used. An artist from Gu Kaizhi's time would have used pottery and lacquer vessels to illustrate his painting. However, the Song copyist had reached further back into history. The bronze *dou*, *gui* and *ding* in this scene were food vessels used by the upper classes before the Qin period (221–206 BCE). This was not a coincidence. During the late Northern Song period (960–1127), the literati developed a taste for archaism along with an interest in antiquities. It remained the prevailing aesthetic preference during the Southern Song. The copyist appeared knowledgeable about ancient bronzes and to have access to collections of the imperial family and the upper classes – important clues to his identity which shall be discussed later.

The avoidance of 'taboo' characters was more strictly enforced during the Song dynasty than in any other preceding period.

Plates 14–19 Scenes from a lacquer-painted wood screen. Tomb of Sima Jinlong, 484 CE. Datong, Shanxi Province.

Plate 14 Tu Shan and her son Qi.

Plate 15 Duke Ling and his wife.

Plates 16–19 The four consecutive registers of a single panel of the Sima Jinlong screen (arranged vertically with pl. 16 at the top)

帝舜 帝舜二妃娥皇女英 舜父瞽瞍 与象敖焚廩井

Plate 16 Stories of Shun.

太姜 太任 太姒

Plate 17 Three meritorious mothers of Zhou.

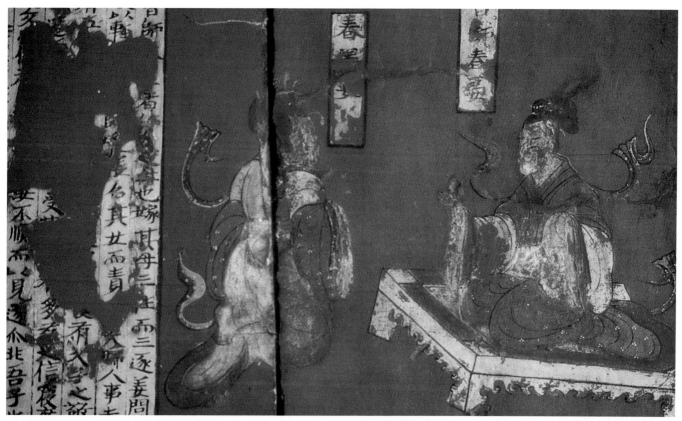

Plate 18 Chun Jiang, teacher of the State of Lu, and her daughter.

Plate 19 Lady Ban rejecting the emperor's invitation.

Plate 20 (above) Opening scenes from the *Nymph of the Luo River (Luoshen tu)*, traditionally attributed to Gu Kaizhi; copy, Song period (960–1279). Detail of a handscroll; ink and colour on silk. Palace Museum, Beijing.

Plate 21 (below) Mural inside the stone sarcophagus. Tomb of Song Shaozu, Northern Wei dynasty, 477 CE. Datong, Shanxi Province.

Plate 22 (right) Zhao Mengfu (1254–1322), *Mind Landscape of Xie Youyu (Youyu qiuhuo)*. Detail of a handscroll; ink and colour on silk, 27.4 × 117 cm. The Art Museum, Princeton University. Edward L. Elliott Family Collection. Fowler McCormick, Class of 1921, Fund (84-13).

Plates 23–28 Scenes from the *Admonitions of the Instructress to the Court Ladies (Nüshi zhen tu)*, traditionally attributed to Li Gonglin (*c.*1041–1106); copy, Southern Song period, late twelfth century. Handscroll; ink on paper, 28.9 cm × 877 cm. Palace Museum, Beijing.

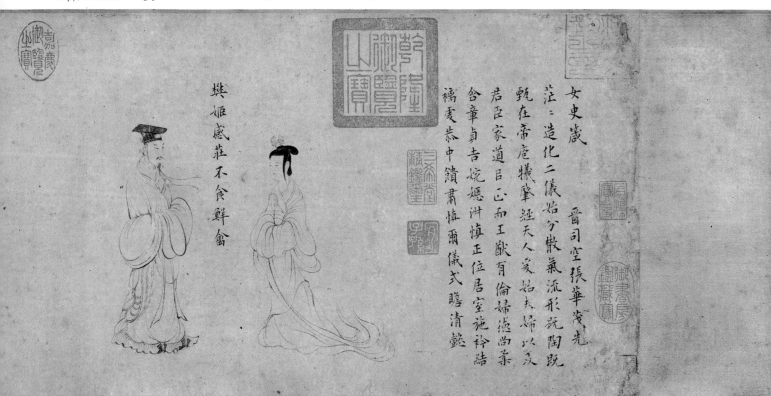

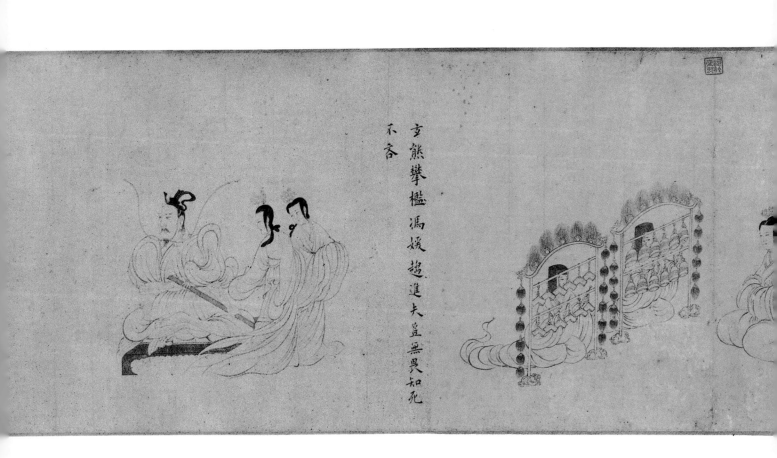

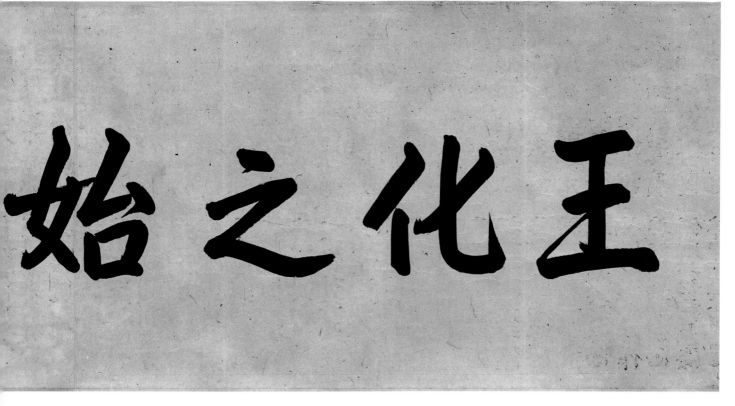

Plate 23 Right: 'Wang hua zhi shi' (the beginning of kingship), title-piece by the Qianlong emperor (r. 1736–1795). Left: Scene 1 – introduction.

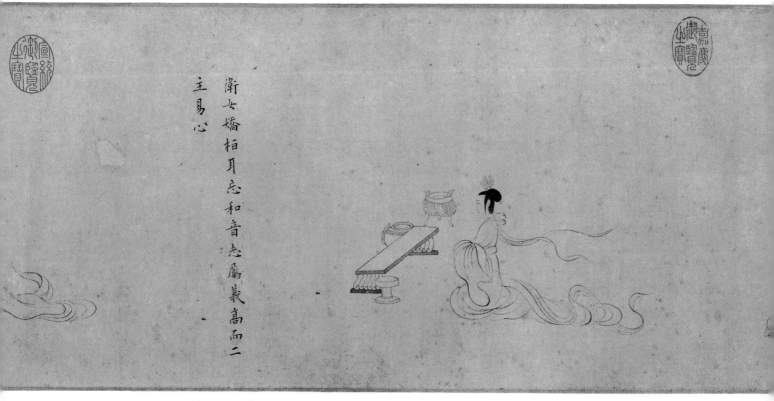

Plate 24 Right: Scene 2 – Lady Fan refusing to eat the flesh of birds slaughtered by her husband King Zhuang of Chu.
Centre: Scene 3 – the lady of Wei refusing to listen to the licentious music favoured by her husband Duke Huan of Qi.
Left (continued to pl. 25 right): Scene 4 – Lady Feng protects the Han emperor Yuandi (r. 48–33 BCE) from the advance of a wild bear.

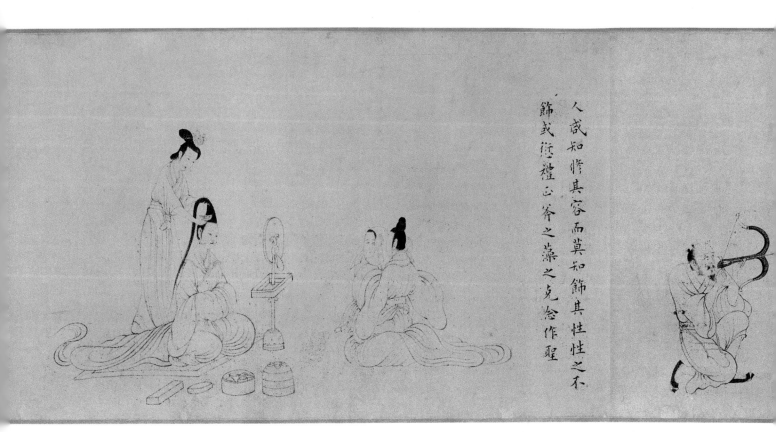

人咸知修其容而莫知飾其性之不
飾或愆禮正斧之藻之克念作聖

Plate 25 Right (continued from pl. 24 left): Scene 4 – Lady Feng protects the Han emperor Yuandi (r. 48–33 BCE) from the advance of a wild bear.
Left: Scene 5 – Lady Ban declines to ride with the Han emperor Chengdi (r. 33–7 BCE) in the imperial palanquin.

Plate 26 Right and centre: Scene 6 – an archer readies himself to shoot a tiger.
Left: Scene 7 – two court ladies admire themselves (the toilette scene).

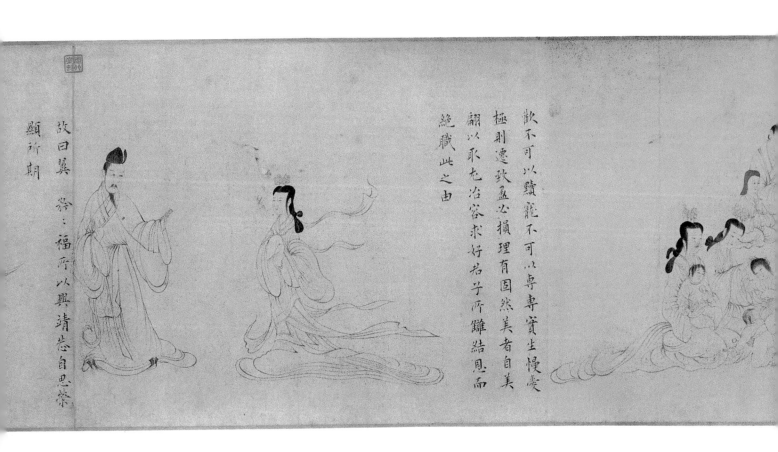

故曰翼　欸∴福所以興靖恭自思榮

顯所期

歡不可以瀆寵不可以專實生慢憂

極剭遷欽盈必損理有固然美者自美

翻以取尤冶容求好君子所讎結恩而

絶歳此之由

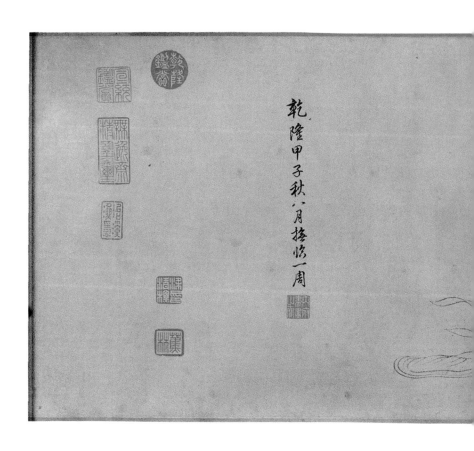

乾隆甲子秋八月捨臨一周

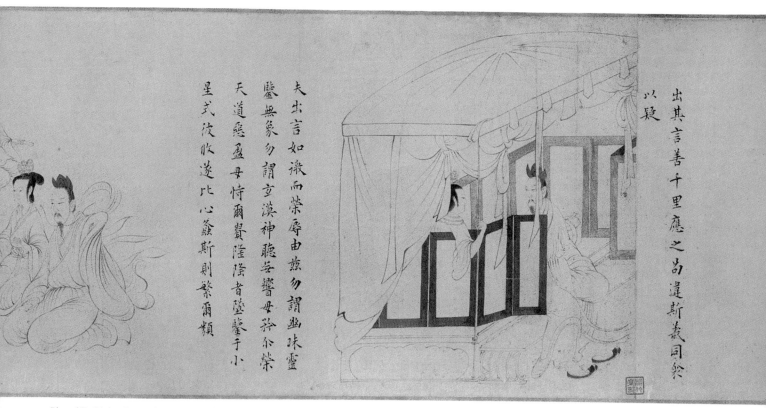

夫出言如微而榮辱由茲勿謂幽昧靈鑒無象勿謂玄漠神聽無響無矜爾榮天道惡盈無恃爾貴隆隆者墜鑒于小星式彼收遂此心蠆斯則繁爾類

出其言善千里應之苟違斯義同衾以疑

Plate 27 Right: Scene 8 – a man and a woman in bed regard one another with suspicion (the bedroom scene). Centre: Scene 9 – three generations of a family gather together (the family scene). Left: Scene 10 – an emperor rebuffs a fawning beauty (the rejection scene).

女史司箴敢告庶姬

故曰翼翼矜矜福所以興靖恭自思榮顯所期

Plate 28 Right: Scene 11 – a lady kneels in deference. Centre: Scene 12 – the court instructress copies out the 'admonitions'.

160

Plates 29–30 (above) Scenes from *Biographies of Exemplary Women: The Benevolent and Wise (Lienü renzhi tu)*, attributed to Gu Kaizhi; copy, Song period (960–1279). Details of a handscroll; ink on silk. Palace Museum, Beijing.

Plate 31 (right) Detail of pl. 20, showing the nymph from the *Nymph of the Luo River*, traditionally attributed to Gu Kaizhi.

Nearly all the emperors' names – more than fifty characters – were considered taboo. The characters were avoided either by excluding a stroke or by first substituting a character, then excluding a stroke. The first member of the Song imperial family whose name constitutes a taboo is the founding ancestor Zhao Xuanlang (*xuan* 玄 written as 玄); thereafter, the Renzong emperor Zhao Zhen (*zhen* 禎 written as 貞), Qinzong Zhao Huan (*huan* 桓 written as 桓) and Xiaozong Zhao Shen (*shen* 慎 written as 慎). There have also been instances where scribes or calligraphers have inadvertently changed or substituted the incorrect word in an emperor's name. For example, the Taizong emperor, who was known as Kuangyi or Guangyi, sometimes had the character *yi* changed instead of *kuang* or *guang*. Based on the presence of taboo characters, the Beijing scroll has been designated a work of the Southern Song period. The names of Emperor Xiaozong (r. 1163–1190) and his predecessors have been avoided in the rendering of Zhang Hua's admonitory text. However, one should not be too hasty in concluding that the Song version is a work of the Xiaozong reign merely on the absence or presence of taboo characters; a stylistic analysis is even more important.

In the Song version, the calligrapher who wrote the text and the artist who created the illustrations handled the brush very differently. The brush of the former was stiff and angular, while the latter's was gentle and supple. Differences and gradations in the use of ink are even more obvious. The calligraphy of the text is remarkably similar to the style of Emperor Gaozong (r. 1127–1162) as seen in *Yangsheng lun* (fig. 3) or *Binfeng tu (Illustration of the Odes of Bin)* in the Beijing Palace Museum, especially in the execution of the *na* stroke (rightward descending diagonal). According to *Shushi huiyao (Essentials of the History of Calligraphy)* by Tao Zongyi (*c.* 1320–after 1402), Gaozong had 'originally studied the style of Huang Tingjian [1045–1105], but later followed Youjun [Wang Xizhi, 303–365]. It is also said he followed Mi Fu's style and combined it with the bone structure of Six Dynasties [calligraphy] to form his own.'[11]

The *kaishu* is characterized by a compact well-knit structure, inner restraint and a longish form. Many Southern Song courtiers modelled their calligraphy after Gaozong's. Judging from the inscriptions found on works attributed to the court painter Ma Hezhi (act. 1131–1162), there were more than ten people writing in this style. Although the calligraphy of the Song version is of the highest standard, it cannot have been from the hand of Gaozong, as there are taboo characters for Xiaozong present. Even though he had abdicated in 1162 in favour of his son, as retired emperor there would have been no need for Gaozong to avoid the name of his successor. It

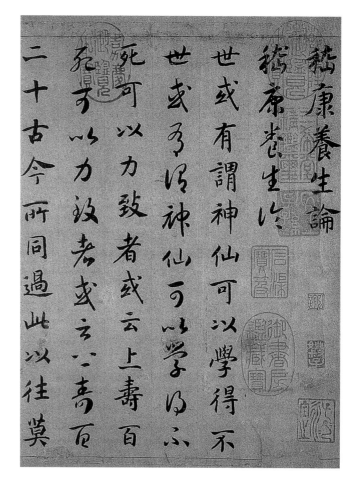

Fig. 3 Song emperor Gaozong (r. 1127–1162), *Yangsheng lun.* Detail of a handscroll; ink on paper. Palace Museum, Beijing.

must therefore have been a work presented by a high-ranking scholar official. The prevalence of the Gaozong style suggests that he was still alive when this was written, so the latest possible date for the Song version would be just before his death in 1187. There is no possibility that the Beijing scroll is of a later date since the seals on the Tang version indicate that by the Mingchang era (1190–1196) of Emperor Jin Zhangzong's reign (1189–1208), the 'mother copy' was already in the Jin (1115–1234) imperial collections.

If the above hypothesis can be established, the artist of the Song version was someone who had access to the private imperial collections and a knowledge of bronze antiquities. The text contained taboo characters and the calligraphy was written in the Emperor Gaozong's style. These are not the usual characteristics of an ordinary artisan painter and his works.

Scene 1 of the Song version contains the introductory text followed by the first illustration, titled 'feminine virtue honours yielding, holding within codes of moral behaviour' (see pl. 23 left).[12] This is a reference to the self-sacrifice of spouses and the aristocratic code of chivalry. The depiction of a prince face-to-face with his lady is a suggestion that the relationship between husband and wife is like that between ruler and subject. The following scene represents how the Lady Fan ate no meat for three years so that she could influence King Zhuang of Chu. The three empty bronze vessels are a symbol of her abstinence (see pl. 24 right). Scene 3 is a depiction of how in order 'to reform [Duke] Huan, the lady of Wei ignored her love for music' (pl. 24 centre).[13] She is shown kneeling with her back upright, quietly listening to the morally uplifting sounds from the bells and stone chimes, thus preventing the Duke from being mesmerized by the licentious music she made.

From the pictorial composition and the placement of text in the Tang version, it can be seen that the images were executed before the text was added. With the Song version, the opposite seems to be the case. The calligrapher did not have a prior arrangement with the artist as to the apportionment of space. There was merely a rough division of twelve spaces to allow for the illustrations. The lack of space at the beginning of the scroll resulted in the first two scenes overlapping. This has consequently created the mistaken impression that the Song version contained two and not three additional scenes.

Based on the organization of pictorial space in traditional narrative handscrolls and the Tang version, the text is usually found on the right and the image on the left. Yet in the Song version, the inscription which identifies Scene 2 can be found squarely in the centre of Scene 1 between the male and female figures, thus creating a discrepancy between image and text (see fig. 1). Since the pictorial space following the introductory text was too narrow and could not accommodate the entire scene, the artist was forced to place the princely figure in Scene 2 after the text. More spatial difficulties confronted the artist further along the scroll: the calligrapher had barely given any thought to the artist's need to contain each scene within the space allotted, forcing the artist to stray onto space for the next scene, which can be seen in Scenes 3 and 6 (see pls 23–25). The painting was made up of six pieces of paper with an average length of 105 cm. There was a need to make the pictorial compositions compact, slightly cutting down the blank spaces around the text. If the scroll had been the work of a single hand, such problems requiring the 'cutting of feet to fit the shoes' would not have arisen. Moreover, the cramped organization at the beginning of the scroll and the immoderate slackening in the middle are considered an extreme violation in the art of copying old masters.

The social status of the calligrapher was far above that of the copyist. From the way in which the text on the Song version was written, it would appear that the writer was someone who was inconsiderate and used to ordering people around. Tradition has it that Gaozong had this attitude towards the writing of inscriptions. According to *Nan Song yuanhua lu (Record of Southern Song Academy Painters)*: 'In Siling's [Gaozong's] *Mao shi* [Mao's annotated edition of the *Shi jing*], spaces were left and orders were given for illustrating the text.'[14] This is the type of attitude that could easily have passed to his officials. Unlike the *Mao shi* scrolls, which have been passed down as specimens of artistic cooperation between Gaozong and Ma Hezhi (figs 4, 5), there is no textual evidence that the Song version is another such example. In the discussion below, the social differences between the calligrapher and the copyist as well as the problems of dating will gradually become clear.

The style of the illustrations in the Song version suggests that the copyist was a literatus. When literati painters copied from old masters, they would unintentionally and in varying measure reveal their individuality. Although the Song version appears to have been copied from the Tang, some of Ma Hezhi's stylistic characteristics may be detected in the former. This is most evident in the copying of the landscape scene (fig. 7, pl. 26). The artist had drawn the outline and then used *cun* (texture) strokes, instead of adding colour, as would have been the case if he were emulating Six Dynasties (265–589) landscape painting. He also changed the style of rendering human figures, using the 'earthworm' and 'locust' techniques of drawing outlines. The brush was used in a manner which was rotating, thick and heavy, thus creating a distinctive contrast between thick and fine lines. Using pale ink and omitting the use of light colour, a dry brush was then employed to create texture. The landscape in the Song version is similar to *Xiaoya Luming zhi shi tu (Odes from the Xiaoya Starting with Deer Cry)* attributed to Ma Hezhi (figs 6, 7). Similarities in the rendering of faces may also be observed by comparing the Song version with the *Binfeng tu* (see fig. 4). Since most of the paintings attributed to Ma are unsigned, Xu Bangda feels that *Xiaoya luming zhi shi tu*, the *Mao shi* scrolls and *Hou Chibi fu tu (Illustration of the Latter Ode of the Red Cliff)* are the most reliably ascribed.[15] Besides these examples, there is also *Chenfeng shipian tu (Ten Episodes from the Odes of Chen)* in the Shanghai Museum. In the 'Beam Gate' (*Hengmen*) episode, the lines used to form the flowing waters of the brook start and end in a manner similar to those on the draperies of the Song version.

One of the earliest references to Ma Hezhi may be found in the *Tuhui baojian (Precious Mirror of Painting)*

Fig. 4 'The wolf's dewlap' (*Lang ba*), from the *Illustration of the Odes of Bin*. Painting attributed to Ma Hezhi (act. 1131–1162). Detail of a handscroll; ink and colour on silk, 25.5 × 557.5 cm. Palace Museum, Beijing.

Fig. 5 'Felling a tree' (*Fa mu*), from *Odes from the Xiaoya Starting with Deer Cry*. Calligraphy attributed to Song emperor Gaozong (r. 1127–1162); painting attributed to Ma Hezhi (act. 1131–1162). Detail of a handscroll; ink and colour on silk, 28 × 864 cm. Palace Museum, Beijing.

Fig. 6 'The beauty of fish' (*Yu li*), from *Odes from the Xiaoya Starting with Deer Cry*. Calligraphy attributed to Song emperor Gaozong (r. 1127–1162); painting attributed to Ma Hezhi (act. 1131–1162). Detail of a handscroll; ink and colour on silk, 28 × 864 cm. Palace Museum, Beijing.

Fig. 7 Detail of the landscape scene from the *Admonitions* scroll in the Palace Museum, Beijing.

by the Yuan historian Xia Wenyan (fourteenth century):

> Ma Hezhi was a native of Qiantang [present day Hangzhou]. During the Shaoxing era (1131–1162), he passed the *jinshi* examination. He excelled at painting. In figures, Buddhist images, and landscapes, he imitated Wu [Wu Daozi, act. *c.* 710–760]. His brushwork was fluttering and unrestrained. He concentrated on eliminating excessive adornment and created his own style. The emperors Gaozong and Xiaozong deeply admired his painting. When they wrote out the three hundred odes of the *Mao shi*, they ordered Hezhi to paint illustrations. He rose to the rank of vice president of the Board of Works.[16]

Hua jian (Mirror of Painting) by Tang Hou (act. early fourteenth century) states:

> Ma Hezhi did figures beautifully. His running brush was fluttering and unrestrained. Contemporaries regarded him as a 'Little Master Wu' [Wu Daozi]. He was able to cast off vulgar habits and concentrate on lofty antiquity. Other men could not easily reach this.[17]

Because his paintings possessed the quality of 'lofty antiquity', Zhou Mi (1232–1298) in his *Wulin jiushi (Reminiscences of Hangzhou)* regarded Ma as foremost among only eleven men in the Imperial Painting Academy.[18]

In actual fact, the 'Academy' that Zhou was referring to was not an institution but a term commonly used to refer to imperial artistic circles. In the lists of artists found in the *Nan Song yuanhua lu*, when the Imperial Painting Academy was reconstituted during the early years of the Shaoxing reign era, there were about twenty-eight names. Of these, sixteen held the lowly appointment of *daizhao* ('compiler'). Ma Hezhi was not included in these lists because he was already vice-president of the Board of Works, a position of the fourth rank. The highest position that an artist could hope to attain as an academician was that of *zhonglang* (painter-in-attendance), a position of the ninth rank. This was the appointment held by the famous landscape painter Li Tang (*c.* 1050–after 1130). According to Zhou Mi, Ma Hezhi was ordered to take charge of the Academy even though he was at the Board of Works, because his painting was the 'choicest of the age'.

From an examination of both stylistic and circumstantial evidence, the Song version may be said to be contemporaneous with Ma Hezhi. Since so many works from this period are attributed to Ma, regardless of whether they are signed or genuine, the Song version probably comes from a group of court artists working in the literati painting style of Ma Hezhi. However, this is merely a proposal for a possible line of enquiry. As the Tang version fell into the hands of the Jin emperor Zhangzong during the early 1190s, the latest possible dating for the Song version would logically be the 1180s, just prior to the departure of the 'mother copy' from the Southern Song imperial collections. The Tang version entered the collection of Jia Sidao (1213–1275) during the reign of the Song Emperor Lizong (1225–1264). It is not possible that the Song version could have been created during this period, as it does not have the personalized collectors' seals found on all works from the Jia family's collection. Moreover, seals were rarely affixed to paintings in the Southern Song imperial collection.

When the Tang version was in the possession of the Jin imperial family in the north, the Song version was the sole remaining copy of a legendary painting in the Southern Song imperial collection. At this time, the Song imperial collections possessed only one work by Gu Kaizhi, *Qingniu daoshi (Daoist Master Riding a Water Buffalo)*.[19] Art historians are still trying to make sense of the rationale behind copies and facsimiles in the Song imperial collections. According to the materials and sources currently available, the Tang version was the only painting which moved from the Palace Treasury (*neifu*) of the Southern Song to the coffers of the Jin during the Mingchang era.[20]

The emergence of the Song version was not the result of an idle brush; there was a motive for its creation. The reason for copying the Tang version was not only artistic, the subject-matter also had a didactic function. There were numerous Southern Song works like the *Admonitions* that illustrated admonitory texts for women and examples of female virtue (*nü de*). Ma Hezhi was said to have painted the story of Lady Xu Mu; Liu Songnian (*c.* 1050–after 1125), the *Gongcan tu (Palace Sericulture)*; Ma Yuan (act. 1090–after 1125), the *Nü xiao jing (Classic of Filial Piety for Women)*; and Mou Yi (b. 1178), *Daoyi tu (Preparing Clothes)*, now in the collection of the National Palace Museum in Taipei. Other unsigned works from this period include versions of the *Nü xiao jing* in the Palace Museum in Beijing and the Liaoning Provincial Museum, the *Xiao jing (Classic of Filial Piety)* in Taipei Palace Museum, and handscrolls and albums on the subject of tilling and weaving, *Gengzhi tu*.

During this period, practice of the Neo-Confucian principles of Zhu Xi (1130–1200) was widespread. Although Zhu had organized the teachings of Confucius into a complex metaphysical cosmology and elevated them to the pinnacle of Chinese philosophy, he did not ignore the traditional Confu-

cian concerns for daily life and social ills. Areas which received unprecedented attention were the thoughts and acts of women. The severe oppression which women were subjected to during this period can perhaps be likened to the intensified tightening of bandages during the foot-binding process.

With the loss of their northern territory and the country in tatters, the Gaozong reign saw a series of virtuous women emerge from within the Song imperial family. Gaozong's mother Lady Wei was one such example. She made the fitting gesture of transferring the bodies of Emperor Huizong (r. 1100–1125), the Dowager Empress Zhang and Gaozong's consort Xing for burial in the south. Empress Xing had been captured by the Jin, but while in captivity she took part in espionage activities and managed to smuggle a letter to her husband about conditions in the north before her death. When a system of governance was being established during the early Southern Song period, the 'three cardinal guides and five constant virtues' (*sangang wuchang*) as specified in the feudal ethical codes also formed the basis of rules of conduct for women. In the light of these circumstances, the purpose of the Song scroll should speak for itself.

In the north, the Jurchen Jin promoted feminine virtue even more vigorously. In 1150 Wanyan Liang, the Prince of Hailing, killed Xizong (r. 1135–1150) and set himself up as emperor. Although he tried hard to rule like a Confucian monarch, life in the palace quarters was dissipated and undisciplined. His successors Shizong (r. 1161–1189) and Zhangzong devoted their energies to re-establishing order and morality. Shizong's consort Wulinda was the most outstanding example of a chaste woman during the Jin period. She had been married to Shizong while he was the Prince of Ge. Though beautiful, Wulinda was also known for her kind and understanding nature. Wanyan Liang coveted her and summoned her to his palace after sending her husband away on a mission. Rather than submit to the attentions of the depraved ruler, Wulinda wrote a declaration of her chastity and committed suicide. Her exemplary action would undoubtedly have had an effect on her husband's respect for Confucian values. Shizong ordered the *Analects of Confucius (Lunyu)* and the writings of *Mencius (Mengzi)* to be translated into Jurchen and presented his personal bodyguards with translations of the *Xiao jing*. During his reign, there was an enthusiastic espousal of feminine ethics and the preservation of chastity, not unlike the Southern Song policies. This was a turning point in the history of Jurchen women. In the *Jin shi (History of the Jin)*, there are twenty-two biographies of Han-Chinese and Jurchen women in the chapters on exemplary women (*lienü zhuan*). Seen in this light, acquiring the Tang version of the *Admonitions* scroll would have been a positive expression of the Jurchen imperial family's yearning for Confucian culture.

The Song version was not only a product of its time but may also be regarded as a new artistic creation. In the copying of old masters, it is necessary to use the same painting materials and to retain the expressive form of the original. However, there are several significant changes in this version: it was painted on paper instead of silk, and rendered in the *baimiao* method without the addition of colour. This suggests that both the artist and its first owner not only attached importance to the contents of the Tang version but were also receptive to new forms of artistic expression. This is an attitude worth noting in the copying of paintings, as it touches on our present-day interest in the painting's history.

The late Northern Song period saw the rise of literati interest in the arts. Just when this was spreading to academic painting, the Jurchen attacked. When the Jin dynasty was established in the north, it became fashionable for the Han-Chinese and Jurchen courtiers to participate in the artistic activities of literati circles. By contrast, the interest of the Southern Song literati in painting was suspended for a time. Consequently the scholarly *baimiao* style of Li Gonglin first took root in the north before travelling south to Lin'an (modern Hangzhou) where it fused with the local Jiangnan style.

When the Imperial Painting Academy resumed its activities in the early Shaoxing era, it comprised mainly court painters who had fled south. The penetration of the literati influence into this domain was gradual. When the Song version appeared, it was a sign that Li Gonglin's *baimiao* style had found favour within the Southern Song Academy. The most accomplished literati who engaged in this sort of artistic activity were notable scholar-officials like Ma Hezhi. They officially introduced Li Gonglin's *baimiao* style into imperial circles, and its practice gradually spread. For example, the aristocratic monk-painter Fanlong (act. early twelfth century) was often summoned to court. According to Zhuang Su in *Huaji bu yi (A Supplement to the Huaji)*, he 'sketched Buddhist icons and his brush technique was very similar to Longmian [Li Gonglin]. Gaozong liked his painting so much that each time he saw one, he immediately inscribed an evaluation.'[21]

Jia Shigu (act. *c.* 1130–1160), who served as painter-in-attendance at the Southern Song Painting Academy during the Shaoxing period, studied *baimiao* and the 'one-stroke method' (*yibi fa*). He taught his skill to Liang Kai (act. late twelfth to early thirteenth century) whose fine-brushed *baimiao* style had its origins in the techniques of Wu Daozi and Li Gonglin. During the mid- to late Southern Song

period, Mou Yi's *Daoyi tu* was representative of the *baimiao* style which dominated court painting. *Nan Song guange xu lu (Supplementary Index of the Southern Song Academy)* refers to an anonymous painting, *Xie Li Gonglin Kongque mingwang (Sketch of Li Gonglin's Peacock King)* and other similar paintings.[22] However, the high standards of the Imperial Painting Academy had obscured the true significance of literati painting styles. For all its grandeur, the *baimiao* works of the Southern Song were no match for those of the Jin. It was not until the unification of northern and southern China during the Yuan period (1271–1368) that divergent paths of development in literati painting came together and acquired an independent artistic standing.

From the colophons and seals, the provenance of the Song version and the path of its transmission can be traced. The geographical origins of its owners can also be determined; as the majority of them were northerners, the Song version must have been spirited away to northern China after the Yuan conquest of the Southern Song. Three centuries later, it passed into the Qing (1644–1911) imperial collection. From 1924 until the end of the Second World War, it passed from hand to hand, before returning in 1953 to the Palace Museum in Beijing after being located by the National Cultural Relics Management Bureau in the Dongbei Museum (now known as the Liaoning Provincial Museum). Although there were probably owners who did not leave their mark on the scroll, a chain of transmission can be seen – Southern Song: Imperial collection; Yuan period: a Mr Li, then Mr Jiang; Ming period: Wu Bocheng, Xiao Shiying, Mr Yan; Ming-Qing transitional period: Liang Qingbiao; and then the Qing imperial collection. It was taken by China's last emperor Puyi (1906–1967) to Manchuria (Manchukuo), and then placed in the Dongbei Museum before its return to the Palace Museum.

Not long after the Song version was completed, its 'mother copy', the Tang version, became part of the Jin imperial collection. After the Yuan conquest of northern China, the Tang version fell into the hands of Jia Sidao. At this point, even though both the Tang and the Song versions were in Lin'an, they had different owners. During the Yuan and Ming periods, they were separated once more, one version ending up in northern China and the other in the south. During the Ming-Qing transition, the two versions were reunited once more in the collection of Liang Qingbiao. As evidenced by the placement of his seals over the joins in the paper, Liang had remounted the Song version. Since he employed Zhang Huangmei, one of the most famous mounters in Yangzhou, it is very likely that the remounting of the Song version is an example of his work. Works mounted by Liang from his collection are distinguished by their brocade wrapper and jade rollers, a style of mounting which the Qianlong emperor emulated. Despite his extensive collection of paintings, Liang regrettably did not make a catalogue. A peculiar characteristic of his collecting was his fascination with early paintings which were facsimiles or had the same subject-matter. Apart from the two *Admonitions* scrolls, Liang also possessed two Song copies of *Luoshen fu tu (Nymph of the Luo River)* which were attributed to Gu Kaizhi (in the collection of the Liaoning Provincial Museum and the Freer Gallery of Art, Washington, DC), a Jin-period painting by Zhang Yu, *Wenji gui Han tu (The Return of Lady Wenji)* (in the Jilin Provincial Museum) and Gong Suran's *Zhaojun chusai tu (Zhaojun Travels North)* (Osaka Municipal Museum of Art). The extent of his interest was such that he left behind a whole series of 'narrative blueprints', unjustly causing art historians of a later generation to mistake him for a master forger of ancient figure painting. Both versions of the *Admonitions* eventually entered the collection of the Qianlong emperor, who regarded them with varying degrees of devotion. However, as part of the Qing imperial collection, both were considered treasures. In 1900 the Tang version came into the possession of Captain Clarence Johnson, who sold it to the British Museum. The two versions have now been apart for a century.

There are many layers of meaning to an ancient painting. Historical and cultural issues can be revealed by analysing a work from different perspectives. However, in the study of an anonymous painting like the Song version, the most obvious difficulty lies in the lack of direct evidence of its creation. To overcome this problem, I have resorted to the extrapolation of circumstantial evidence. By looking for clues in the seals and colophons, a logical hypothesis may now be presented and perhaps the lost history of an early Chinese painting reconstructed.

Translated by Hwang Yin

NOTES

1   Mr Yu's essay was first published in this slightly abridged translation by Hwang Yin in *Orientations* (Yu Hui 2000) and is republished here with minor changes with kind permission of Ms Hwang and the magazine's publisher. The original Chinese, including transcriptions of the Yuan colophons to the 'Song version', has been published in *Gugong Bowuyuan yuankan* (Yu Hui 2002) – editor's note.
2   *SQBJ chubian* 1918, *juan* 32, *xiang* 35.
3   Tang Lan 1961.
4   Xu Bangda 1984, pp. 208–209.
5   Li Yu 1984, p. 445.
6   Kohara 2000 (1967), pp. 36–40.
7   *XHHP, juan* 1 in *HSCS* 1963, vol. 2, p. 3.
8   Mi Fu, *Hua shi* in Lu Fusheng *et al.* (eds) 1992–, vol. 1, p. 978.
9   Zhang Bangji 1986, p. 690 (*juan* 1).
10   Zhang Yanyuan, *Lidai minghua ji, juan* 2; tr. adapted from Bush & Shih 1985, p. 60.
11   Tao Zongyi, *juan* 6, in Lu Fusheng *et al.* (eds) 1992–, vol. 3, p. 54.
12   Tr. Shih, Hsio-yen 1976, p. 12; all translations of the 'Admonitions' text are quoted and adapted from Shih's.
13   Tr. Shih, Hsio-yen 1976, p. 12.
14   *Nan Song yuanhua lu, juan* 3, 'Putian ji', in *HSCS* 1963, vol. 4, p. 49.
15   Xu Bangda 1985.
16   Xu Bangda 1991, pp. 278–279.
17   Ibid., p. 279.
18   Zhou Mi, *Wulin jiushi, juan* 6 (1981, p. 105).
19   Chen Gaohua (ed.) 1984, p. 844.
20   The only other artwork was a piece of calligraphy, a Tang copy of Wang Xizhi's *Kuaixue shiqing tie (Clearing After Sudden Snow)*, now in the National Palace Museum in Taipei.
21   Tr. Bush & Shih 1985, p. 138.
22   Chen Gaohua (ed.) 1984, p. 843.

'Like the gossamer thread of a spring silkworm' – Gu Kaizhi in the Yuan Renaissance

Shane McCausland

From our early twenty-first-century vantage point, the *Admonitions* scroll drops out of clear view in the historical record of the Yuan dynasty (1271–1368), which is to say, during the art-historical moment at which art began no longer to refer primarily to nature but to the self. The implication is that Gu Kaizhi, seen then (as today) as China's 'first painter', and the scroll that best represents him to us today, the *Admonitions*, led separate lives during the Yuan renaissance, as the literati canon took form, before being reunited later on in the Ming (1368–1644), once the literati painting tradition was well underway. Since Yuan art theory and practice are pivotal in Chinese art history, and since we hope with this book to write a history of the *Admonitions* scroll, it is worth trying to chart the paths taken by the scroll and by 'Gu Kaizhi' in this time, so as to understand their possible roles in the Yuan transformation. In part, therefore, this enquiry contributes to the 'cultural biography' of the scroll inscribed in this book. And in part, it seeks to inform the continuing interest in such concepts of painting as 'mind-prints' or 'images of the mind' (*xinyin*), and as self-expression, in modern East Asian art and art historiography.

Seals of the Jin emperor Zhangzong (r. 1190–1208) place the *Admonitions* in the imperial collection of the Jurchen Jin dynasty (1115–1234) in the early thirteenth century. When the Jin fell in 1234 to the Mongol empire established by Chinghiz Khan (r. 1206–1228), it presumably passed from the Jin into the Mongol imperial collection. It may then have passed down the Mongol imperial line to Qubilai (r. 1260–1294) in the mid-thirteenth century, but by the end of the Southern Song (1127–1279), it had come into the hands of the treacherous late Southern Song chancellor Jia Sidao (1213–1275), three of whose seals it bears.[1] After Jia was cashiered in 1275, it should have passed into the Song imperial collection in Lin'an (Hangzhou), and thence almost imme-diately into the Yuan imperial collection in the capital Dadu (Beijing), following Qubilai's invasion of the south in 1276. However, there are no Gu Kaizhis in the surviving inventory of Jia Sidao's collection,[2] and just two, neither an 'Admonitions', in the selection of the Song collection made by Wang Yun (1227–1304) for Qubilai in 1276.[3] One of these two titles, the *Nymph of the Luo River*, is extant in several versions.

Nor was the *Admonitions* subsequently seen in circulation by the late thirteenth- to early fourteenth-century southern Chinese connoisseurs Zhou Mi (1232–1298) and Tang Hou (mid-1250s–mid-1310s), who compiled inventories of their encounters with such scrolls. A painting of the *Nymph of the Luo River* was one of just four Gu Kaizhis recorded by Tang Hou (see below). Zhou Mi records just three attributions in two collections.[4] One of these paintings may be the *Biographies of Exemplary Women* (*Lienü renzhi tu*; Palace Museum, Beijing), a Song copy of an older painting (pls 29–30). The *Admonitions* itself bears a 'Phags-pa-script seal reading 'Ali' that may belong to a late thirteenth-century Uighur official of that name who served in south China. 'Ali' also owned several works of Chinese calligraphy, but his scrolls seem not to have circulated, at least not in this circle of collectors. Another seal has been linked to a fourteenth-century monk. The identity of some of the early and mid-Ming seal owners prior to Yan Song (1480–1562) is also still in doubt.[5]

Even as the *Admonitions* itself was rarely seen by connoisseurs and painters as it passed through state and private collections during the Song-Jin-Yuan period, its general appearance and those of other Gu Kaizhi scrolls were widely known through copies and recensions. These paintings were not immune to historical changes in perception and, therefore, style, as the Song-type hardening and flattening of the line in the Beijing *Biographies* scroll illustrate. Depictions of the 'Admonitions' must have continued to play a didactic role in (presumably) aristocratic households, in colourful images

Fig. 1 (right) 'Lady Feng and the Bear'. Attributed to Gu Kaizhi (*c*.345–406), *Admonitions of the Instructress to the Court Ladies (Nüshi zhen tu)*. Detail of a hand-scroll, now mounted; ink and colour on silk. The Trustees of The British Museum (OA 1903.4-8.1 Chinese Painting 1).

Fig. 2 (right) 'Lady Feng and the Bear'. Southern Song court artists (traditionally attributed to Li Gonglin), later 12th century, *Admonitions of the Instructress to the Court Ladies (Nüshi zhen tu)*. Handscroll; ink on paper. Palace Museum, Beijing.

Fig. 3 (below) *Lady Feng and the Bear*. Mounted album leaf (?); ink and colours on silk, *c*.53 × *c*.93 cm. Song or Yuan period, 12th–14th century. The Trustees of The British Museum (OA 1914.12-19.01).

Fig. 4 Wang Zhenpeng (act. *c*.1280–1329), *Vimalakirti and the Doctrine of Non-Duality*, dated 1308. Detail of Vimalakirti from a handscroll; ink on silk, 39.5 × 218.7 cm. Metropolitan Museum of Art, New York.

with little apparent connection to the art of Gu Kaizhi. The Song- or Yuan-period artisan painting in the British Museum depicting *Lady Feng and the Bear* is an interesting example (compare figs 1, 2 and 3).

More influential, however, would have been the circulation of a *baimiao* or ink-outline copy of the *Admonitions* ascribed to the late Northern Song (960–1127) literatus painter Li Gonglin (*c*.1041–1106). In the early Yuan this painting, which may be the monochrome copy in the Palace Museum in Beijing,[6] was in the collection of Li Ti (*c*.1250–?), a member of the elite collectors' circle (fig. 2, pls 23–28).

A comparison of the stylistic differences between the Beijing *Admonitions*, seen by Yu Hui as a mid-Southern Song work (see pp. 146–148, 161–167), and, say, an actual copy of an early painting by Li Gonglin again highlights these changes. *Pasturing Horses (Muma tu)*, a descriptive and colourful scroll also in the Palace Museum, Beijing, painted after a lost original by the Tang (618–907) painter Wei Yan (active *c*. late seventh to early eighth century), is a good example of one of Li's copies. Placed in chronological order, these facsimiles signal a trend from a pictorial to a schematic drawing style in Song painting, which can be imagined in parallel with the epistemic 'retreat into the object' often observed in Song poetry and philosophy.

While all of this prefigures and conditions the abstract, independent quality of Yuan painting, it does not satisfactorily explain an apparent rupture of the link between artistic

expression and the natural world in it. A look at the court artist Wang Zhenpeng's (act. *c*.1280–1329) 1308 portrayal of the Buddhist layman *Vimalakirti* (Metropolitan Museum of Art; fig. 4), a famous Gu Kaizhi subject, illustrates how we may begin to account for this change. Wang addressed himself to copying an original ink-outline painting in the Chinese literati tradition of Gu Kaizhi and Li Gonglin, but also responded to the Yuan imperial family's esoteric religious interests as well as the Mongol taste for beautifully *crafted* brush painting. He adapted the *baimiao* outline strokes to produce a stylistic hybrid: the brittle, organic Sino-Tibetan style. As a work of court art, it reflected the court's patronage of diverse ethnic, cultural and religious groups within (and indeed outside) its Chinese empire. A similar programme, and one loosely modelled on this one, was the Manchu colonial enterprise involving patronage of international learning and use of hybrid styles in the Qing (1644–1911).

In a study of the calligraphic revival under the Qing regime, Lothar Ledderose, who describes calligraphy as being 'at the core of China's cultural definition' has stressed how the discipline acted not to make Chinese culture more exclusive, but to democratize Chinese values.[7] If we pursue the idea of a further 'retreat into the object' in a diachronic history of the Yuan transformation, therefore, we are likely to see the Yuan reversion to calligraphic values in painting as barring social integration and mobility. But if we conceive of the change as a simplification of culture in a more synchronic model, we may recognize the intent to promote and internationalize Chinese values.

For our narrative in this book, the pivotal master of the early Yuan was not Wang Zhenpeng but the literatus artist and statesman Zhao Mengfu (1254–1322). To counter the displacement of the Chinese tradition by new modes of representation such as the Sino-Tibetan, but in response to the Mongols' predisposition towards fine craft workmanship, Zhao re-evaluated China's artistic legacy, forming a new canon from artworks then in circulation, and reworking the idioms in them in new works. The strikingly modern 'calligraphic' idioms he developed capitalized on his command of the unique technology of the Chinese brush medium. Their appearance marked a decisive break with the past, by causing a disjuncture from the quest for verisimilitude through illusionism, from the medieval concept of the natural order as the image of social transformation. By allying the idea of rectitude, *zheng*, with the rediscovery of personal meaning expressed in the art of the past (*gu yi*), he invested a new authenticity based on human subjectivity into the brush arts. Understanding these changes would throw not just new light on the paradigmatic role of calligraphy in Chinese culture, but also on the modern definition of the literati arts as being *xin yin*, 'mind-prints' or 'images of the mind', that is, idealistic images that reflect and promote self-cultivation as the means to transform society.

The hybrid nature of this renaissance in the arts, its long-ignored imbrication in the realities of Mongol rule, is in fact clear from the outset. In my account, it begins in about 1290, when Zhao Mengfu reinvented a lost portrait by Gu Kaizhi in a new pictorial statement reworked to justify the controversial 1286 decision Zhao took, as a southern Chinese aristocrat, to join the first wave of southern Chinese scholars to serve in Qubilai's government in the capital. In this role, Zhao put new value in art of the past by using it as a resource for self-expression, but also to create an allegory of good government, as well as a model of artistic practice.

Judging by the thin, tensile lineament he employed for the draughtsmanship in his new painting, the *Mind Landscape of Xie Youyu* (The Art Museum, Princeton University; fig. 5, pl. 22), though we have no record of Zhao's having seen the *Admonitions*, he conceptualized the art of Gu Kaizhi in terms of the gossamer-like line in it (pl. 11), giving it an independent, abstract quality in his painting. Zhao Mengfu's translation of Gu's 'naturalism' into the graphic style of the *Mind Landscape* announced the first critical reassessment of China's literary art tradition, and marked the formal end, presaged by Su Shi (1036–1101) and the late Northern Song literati, of the organic development of artistic expression, founded in nature. We ignore at our peril the imprint – on this artistic renaissance – of the new beginning Qubilai had envisioned for China in both his choice of dynastic name, Yuan (primal, original, beginning), and reign name, Zhiyuan (supreme beginning; 1264–1294).

Indeed, the artistic reform began with the earliest artists, in calligraphy with the pioneering regular-script master Zhong You (150–230), and in painting with Gu Kaizhi, and moved, over the 1290s, 1300s and 1310s, through Tang calligraphers and painters, and on to those of the Five Dynasties (907–960), Song and 'recent times'. Over time, each viewing experience of an old work could culminate in a new work in that mode: as old paintings were visualized in terms of their line-idioms, new ones became delineations rather than representations. Outlines still described the forms of horses, figures, trees, mountains, water or rocks in the various genres through which Zhao Mengfu – uniquely – worked. But as schematic marks, they pulsed with a new concern for subjectivity and the expression of personal integrity. Through a new calligraphic disciplining of these marks as abstractions, their immanent qualities could connote the pictorial mode of an old master for rhetorical or discursive purposes. Zhao

Mengfu's reform of Gu Kaizhi offers the first point of insight into the methodology by which this came about.

Before addressing this question in the *Mind Landscape*, it is important to understand the theoretical topography against which we approach it. What, we may ask, was the basis for knowledge about Gu Kaizhi and the function of this learning in the early Yuan? The Gu Kaizhi composition best-known to Zhao Mengfu was probably the *Nymph of the Luo River*. The version in Liaoning Provincial Museum bears a colophon by Zhao's fellow scholar-official, the bamboo painter Li Kan (1245–1320). The version in Beijing (pls 20, 31) bears Zhao's transcription of the ode and a short note dated 1299 in which Zhao describes Gu's *Luoshen* painting as a rare treasure. One or other of these paintings may have been one of the four scrolls that formed the basis for Tang Hou's evaluation of Gu Kaizhi in his book, *Mirror of Painting, Ancient and Modern (Gujin huajian)*, a text long thought to represent many of Zhao Mengfu's views on art.[8] Tang Hou's entry, which begins by identifying Gu's linear idiom as a pioneering mode for expression in art, merits an extensive quote therefore.

> In Gu Kaizhi's painting, [his delineation] is like the gossamer thread of a spring silkworm. At first sight, [the forms] appear very naïve, and indeed sometimes the form-likenesses are deficient. But if you look carefully, [Xie He's] 'Six Laws' [of painting] are all complete; some of the figures have composures and facial expressions that are simply not describable in words. [Here Tang Hou mentions paintings he has seen]. His 'brush conception' recalls spring clouds floating in the void or the flow of water over ground, which is to say that it always emerges from nature. He applied washes to the faces of his figures, and then delicately applied dots [for the eyes] in a dark colour, but not so as to make it look just pretty. As a young man, Wu Daoyuan [Wu Daozi] of the Tang doggedly copied Gu Kaizhi's painting, and Wu's composition and 'brush conception' can to a great extent be likened to Gu's. Many of Wu's works in the Xuanhe [1119–1125] and Shaoxing [1131–1162] collections were given inscriptions calling them the genuine traces of Gu Kaizhi. One must watch out for them![9]

Tang Hou's prime concern was with conveying the fresh, silken quality of Gu's delineation, which gave his art its individual character, and hence authenticity. His metaphor for Gu's linework – 'like the gossamer thread of a spring silkworm' – appears to originate with him, and suggests he had based his judgement on fine paintings.[10] Tang Hou also

referred to the 'summary' quality in Gu's painting, a quality of early painting observed by critics like Zhang Yanyuan, whose *Lidai minghua ji* was evidently an important source. But Gu's primitive technique is redeemed by its conforming to the canonical 'six laws' or 'methods', *liu fa*, of the Southern Qi (479–501) critic Xie He. In his influential treatise *Guhua pinlu,* Xie He had thought Gu Kaizhi highly overrated, and had placed him in only the third of his six classes of painters, which outraged later critics.[11] But Gu's place in the canon had been shored up as much by critics' amusement at his eccentricities as by Mi Fu and Song emperor Huizong's (r. 1101–1125) having recorded the titles of more than half a dozen paintings by Gu Kaizhi.[12] Then Tang Hou gives the brief list of paintings he had seen.

This is followed by literary images of Gu's 'brush conception', *bi yi*, in which Gu's brush is said to proceed with all the unseen auspicious force of scudding clouds or surging water in nature. Tang moves on to reassure readers of Gu's methods in portraiture, in which he loftily avoided making figures look 'just pretty', which was perhaps to put down contemporary professional portraiture. Finally, Tang Hou claims Gu Kaizhi for the literati, by tracing his lineage through the Painting Sage Wu Daozi (689–759), and by warning of the failures of Song imperial connoisseurship. Importantly, this was to insert a literati social agenda into art history, claiming, thereby, autonomy for Yuan literati and Chinese culture from China's changing imperia.

The intriguing title of Tang Hou's book, *Mirror of*

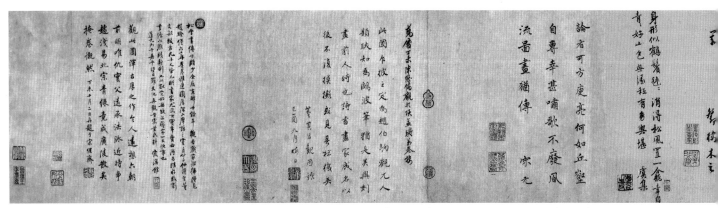

Luo Tianchi (2)   Dong Qichang   Chen Jiru   Song Wu   Yu Ji

Fig. 5 (above and below) Zhao Mengfu (1254–1322), *Mind Landscape of Xie Youyu (Youyu qiuhuo)* (above), and colophons (below). Hand-scroll; the painting, ink and colour on silk, 27.4 × 117.0 cm; the colophons, ink on paper, 27.4 × 214.3 cm. The Art Museum, Princeton University. (Colophons after Fong, Wen C. *et al*. 1984, pp. 282–283.)

Painting, draws from a political and ethical tradition of ministers acting as mirrors to China's rulers by reflecting their true selves back to them, leading them to perfect their kingship. Tang's title suggests that paintings, or delineations, act as agents of change in being mirrors of a truer reality. His book thus asserts the political and ethical role of art. In the case of Gu Kaizhi, his gossamer threads connoted the primordial delicacy of the line, but were also, by way of the indigenous

tradition of sericulture, a metaphor for the beginning of uniquely Chinese order and values; it was the hope to preserve that order which gave Tang Hou both a sense of identity and a *raison d'être* in a Mongol world. Tang Hou's internal art history and class lineage thus put a gloss on self-preservation: the circumstances of the Yuan renaissance evidently called for a pressing of Chinese cultural values, as newly defined, into the wider international debate about the significance of art and culture in Mongol China.

Another problem we may consider about Gu Kaizhi is the apparent contradiction between his status as one of China's first painters of literary accomplishment, which would make him indispensable in any history of literati art or male self-expression, and his reputation as a painter of women,

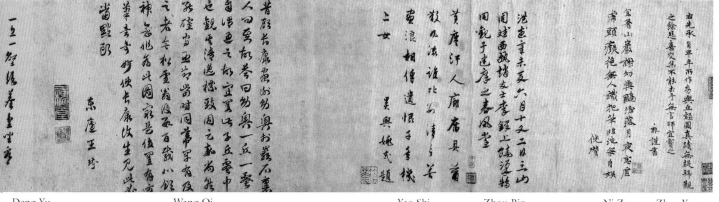

Deng Yu   Wang Qi   Yao Shi   Zhou Bin   Ni Zan   Zhao Yong

Buddhist and Daoist subjects. We would assume that to 'salvage' his art in spite of its obsolete subject-matter and didactic rhetoric, his signature line-idiom was reinvented in modern, meta-representational terms so as to remain relevant to the cultural dilemmas of the Yuan literati class: – dilemmas such as whether male virtue ethics led to social transformation through public-minded service in or cultivated protest against Mongol government of China. With his portrait of a Chinese 'recluse at court', it seems that Zhao Mengfu could decoct the all-important subjectivity of Gu Kaizhi from the female, Buddhist and Daoist figures of the *Nymph, Biographies, Admonitions* and other scrolls he knew. We appear not to have inherited, even in debased form, any of the portraits of courtiers-in-landscapes that Gu Kaizhi is recorded to have painted. In any case, Zhao tailored the Gu Kaizhi idiom in works he did know to his own personal circumstance as a scholar-official when he created a new image of himself in the reinvented portrait of the court recluse.

In late Yuan and indeed early Ming painting and criticism, Gu Kaizhi is largely forgotten, as Stephen Little observes. Cao Zhao's (act. mid- to late fourteenth century) *Gegu yaolun* (Essential Criteria of Antiquities) of about 1387, for instance, merely incorporates Gu Kaizhi as part of the grouping 'Gu, Lu, Zhang and Wu' – referring to the four early masters Gu Kaizhi, Lu Tanwei (act. *c.* 465–472), Zhang Sengyou (act. *c.* 500–*c.* 550) and Wu Daozi – said to be so influential on Li Gonglin, the book's ancestor of literati landscape. In this text, figure painting and aristocratic subjects, Gu Kaizhi's forte, were sidelined; the calligraphic qualities of the male scholar's landscapes and calligraphy had become the prime agents of transformation.

By the time of Dong Qichang's (1555–1636) 'Great Synthesis' (*da cheng*) – focused on an even more narrowly defined transformation of calligraphy and landscape – in the late Ming, the *Admonitions* scroll alternated between being a state treasure and a relic of the calligraphy of Gu Kaizhi or the early cursive master Wang Xianzhi (344–388), as it moved back and forth between the collections of the Ming emperors and the powerful literary elite of the Jiangnan region.[13] The traces of the master's brush, and the scroll's imperial provenance were what mattered, not its subject. By the eighteenth century, on the basis of Dong Qichang's evaluation of it, the *Admonitions* would be repackaged (and regendered) as one of the 'Reunion of Four Beauties', *si mei ju*, the top grouping of Chinese paintings in the Qianlong (1736–1795) emperor's collection. After its arrival at the British Museum in the early twentieth century, its attribution to Gu Kaizhi gave form once again to the beginning of Chinese art, as scholars and painters attempted to define a uniquely Eastern art as opposed to

Western art. More recently, as this binary model for cultures gives ground to concepts of their hybridity, it has become an icon of 'world culture'.

The concern in this paper, then, is not just to examine how Zhao Mengfu's recreation of Gu Kaizhi's *Mind Landscape* in about 1290 marked the beginning of this crucial shift from descriptive and courtly to historical literati art. It is also to see how this new focus on the self in art might inform modern accounts of this same question.

The *Mind Landscape of Xie Youyou (Youyu qiuhuo)* by Zhao Mengfu was inspired by a fabled Gu Kaizhi portrait mentioned in his biographies. In them, Gu Kaizhi was said to have done the original portrait-in-a-landscape out of admiration for a courtier called Xie Kun (280–322), who had lived about a century before him, and advocated an attitude of 'reclusion at court' (*chao yin*) as a solution to the competing responsibilities to state and self. The portrait was inspired by an incident shortly after the founding of the Eastern Jìn (317–419), in around 320 CE, in which Xie Kun was asked by the crown prince Sima Shao (later Mingdi, r. 323–325), to compare himself with a fellow courtier, Yu Liang (289–340), a leader of the powerful Yu faction. Xie Kun's answer was that he was no match for Yu Liang when it came to keeping discipline at court, but that in 'walking on the hill and fishing in the valley' – that is, for his wilderness mentality – he was the better man.[14] The Chinese title, *Youyu qiuhuo*, literally translates as 'Youyu [Xie Kun's *zi* or style name] in hill and valley' – and this was how Gu Kaizhi, and then Zhao Mengfu, chose to portray him.

In a colophon to the painting, the late Yuan master Ni Zan (1301–1374) saw both Gu Kaizhi ('Tiger-head' in Ni's poem) and Zhao Mengfu's ('Gull Wave') paintings as self-portraits (fig. 5 below). Ni Zan supposed that in electing to serve Qubilai, a path only a demented genius would go down, Zhao Mengfu was like Gu Kaizhi, who was famously equal parts 'painter, wit and fool':[15]

> How right that Xie Youyu should have been painted
> amid 'mountain and valley',
> While the moon was setting on Gull Wave Pavilion
> [Zhao Mengfu's home studio], on a night its windows were empty.
> No one quite understood Tiger-head, so mad was he
> As, taking up brush and ink, he painted this for self-amusement.

With a melancholic image of Zhao Mengfu's empty home studio before dawn, Ni's poem evokes the isolation he imag-

Fig. 6 Attributed to Zhan Ziqian (mid- to late sixth century), *Spring Outing (Chunyou tu)*. Detail of a handscroll; ink and colour on silk, 43 × 80.5 cm. Palace Museum, Beijing. (After *MSQJ, Painting*, vol. 2, no. 1.)

covered rocks rendered in green wash bordered by a fine ink-outline, and a valley with a stream flowing through it. A row of young green pines lines the far bank. Two-thirds of the way along the stream, we find a cave entrance or platform for the reclusive figure of Xie Kun, who sits, neatly dressed, on the recluse's tiger skin (pl. 22). His pose recalls the seated postures of the Seven Worthies of the Bamboo Grove in the Jìn dynasty frieze from Nanjing (see p. 58, fig. 9). Near Xie Kun are two deciduous trees that have recently been identified as magnolias.[18] The 'tree orchid' (*mulan*) in Chinese, the magnolia was said to have the scent of an orchid and the flower of a lotus: symbols of virtue and purity. In ancient times it was an imperial tree, and its roots were occasionally bestowed on meritorious courtiers, presumably for cultivation, an appropriate image of Qubilai's favour here, as we shall see. At the end of the painting, in the far distance are some blue-and-green cone-shaped hills. The painting is unsigned, but bears a seal of Zhao Mengfu.

However 'primitive' the formal elements, as they emulate ancient 'clumsiness', they belie the subtle orchestration Zhao sampled from early painting. Though flat and tipped-up, the landscape works as a symbolic stage, intelligible spatially by the archaistic use of trees and rocks as markers. The painting is temporally specific, the magnolias having already flowered, a sign that it is mid- to late summer; and yet it is idealized: the moss-covered rocks suggest the sanctity of a place long undisturbed by humans. This is a place of decorum: the large pine at the beginning 'bows' solicitously in welcome. The rhythmic passages of pines and waterfalls, punctuated by stepping stones and watery inlets, pace a viewing of the scroll in several movements. At a climactic point, the figure appears from behind the trees sheltering in his reclusive niche. After the last pine comes the reverie of a flat-distance view across water to distant blue-green hills, which seems to be at once the view admired by the reclusive Xie Kun and the painting's view of its own wider setting. This is the view referred to in a poem-colophon to the painting by Zhao Mengfu's contemporary Deng Yu (act. early fourteenth century):

On a hill by a valley, beyond dust and earth
He sits watching the Eastern Mountains rising out of
     white clouds.
But this was actually painted by a hand of the Jade Hall
     [Hanlin Academy],
Though one might think it by the Greater or Lesser
     General Li [Sixun and Zhaodao].

Shih Shou-chien has profitably suggested a stylistic comparison of the landscape with that in the Beijing *Nymph of the Luo*

ined Zhao would have felt while serving in the Mongol capital. Only Gu Kaizhi, who lived in eccentric denial of the wrongs done him, seemed to offer a model for his self-reflection in this situation.

The colophon to the painting by Zhao Mengfu's son Yong (*c.*1289–*c.*1362) calls the *Mind Landscape* an 'early work', and the colophons of Ni Zan and others indicate that it was done at court, so we may initially date it to the period of Zhao Mengfu's first series of court appointments between spring 1287 and autumn 1295 (excluding the period between the sixth month of 1292 and early 1295, when Zhao was serving at Ji'nan in Shandong).[16] It would also make sense if the painting had been done after Qubilai's heir apparent, probably Temür (later Chengzong, r. 1294–1307), had asked Zhao to compare himself to a powerful faction leader at the Mongol court – although such a moment is yet to be identified in text.[17]

A self-consciously primitive work, the painting takes the abbreviated form and style of early Chinese painting of the Six Dynasties. We see a long hill composed of smooth moss-

Fig. 7 Zhao Mengfu (1254–1322), *Elegant Rocks, Sparse Forest (Xiushi shulin)*, and artist's inscription. Handscroll; ink on paper, 27.5 × 92.8 cm. Palace Museum, Beijing.

River scroll,[19] but the landscape recalls, for this poet, not Six Dynasties (221–589) painting, but the work of the 'Greater and Lesser Generals Li', referring to the blue-and-green-style landscape painters Li Sixun and Li Zhaodao, members of the Tang imperial family active around 700 CE. Taken up in the Song by imperial clansmen Zhao Boju and Zhao Bosu (late eleventh to early twelfth century), blue-and-green was the aristocratic landscape style in China. 'Until I read the Yuan colophons telling me it was by Gull-wave [Zhao Mengfu]', Dong Qichang would write in his 1609 colophon, overlooking the seal and the painting as a painting, 'I was sure this picture was by Zhao Bosu.' In Dong Qichang's case, however, his silence about Gu Kaizhi and his mention of Zhao Bosu placed Zhao Mengfu in Dong's decorative and inferior 'Northern School' of painting, while not tarring Gu Kaizhi with the same brush.

Deng Yu's invoking this style in his poem was to highlight Zhao Mengfu's own royal pedigree as a descendant of the Song royal family, although this was hardly something a contemporary would have needed reminding. Since the Lis and the Zhaos were all seen to have learned from the early landscapist Zhan Ziqian (mid- to late sixth century),[20] the poem suggests another model for a Gu Kaizhi landscape in the Zhan Ziqian attribution, *Spring Outing* (Palace Museum, Beijing; fig. 6), which in about 1290 belonged to Hu Yong (act. *c.* 1277–after 1295?), a gregarious southern Chinese official.[21]

Mentioning the painting's stylistic connection with the cosmopolitan Tang dynasty was also sympathetic to Zhao Mengfu's position at Qubilai's court. Like the Mongols, the early Tang rulers were not Chinese speaking (they spoke Turkish), and in common with the Tang, the Mongol court was more international and feudal than its Song counterpart, and comprised more aristocrats and non-Chinese and fewer 'meritocrat' academicians. Feigning doubt about Zhao Mengfu's scholar-official status by alluding to his royal heritage thus proposed a double role for him at the Yuan court,

part modelled on the Tang polity and part on present reality. The reference to the 'Jade Hall' (usually Hanlin Academy) also enables us to date the painting to one of Zhao Mengfu's two periods of early service as an imperial academician, in the Jixianyuan or Academy of Worthies between the fifth month of 1290 and the sixth month of 1292, and in the History Office of the Hanlin Academy in the first eight months of 1295.[22]

The first of these periods also coincides with a time of immense pressure on Chinese scholar-officials to justify the terms of their service at court. The nuance of 'reclusion at court', for instance, comes into sharper focus when set beside other 'hermit' ideologies in the public domain in this period. Self-rustication or eremitism was not simply a trans-historical masquerade, but a recognized means to shape the political process as two celebrated cases of about 1290 illustrate. In 1289 the Song loyalist Xie Fangde (?–1289) starved himself to death in protest against being brought from hiding in rural south China to court by Qubilai. In 1291 the prominent northern Chinese scholar Liu Yin (1249–1293) also refused to leave his country home, but was dubbed an 'unsummonable minister' by the khan.[23] Following these refusals, Zhao Mengfu's recreation of Gu Kaizhi's portrait of Xie Kun provided him with a unique justification for service – as a recluse.

Much of the surface of this painting is wash or plain silk; its success depends on calligraphic independence and technical excellence with the brush, the traces of which render the boundaries of the forms, including the hill's arterial structure and emblematic trees. These are transformations of the linear idiom that cannot be simply wished away. Certainly they were present in the minds of the five men whom – I would suggest – Zhao Mengfu invited to comment on the painting in colophons attached to it.[24] For instance, Yao Shi (d. *c.* 1318), who with Zhao Mengfu was one of the 'Eight Talents of Wuxing',[25] uses the flattering term *langmiao ju*, the 'talent to be a great minister'. Famously paid to the 'Calligraphic Sage'

Wang Xizhi,[26] this compliment identifies Zhao Mengfu's calligraphic and ministerial talents with Wang's. Apparently these connections were not self-evident.

More recently, these transformations have been described in terms of the growing presence of the self through calligraphic abstraction in early Chinese painting, that is, late in the development from the naturalistic quality of the line in the pre-Song period (e.g. Gu Kaizhi) to the patternism of the late Northern Song ink-outline (e.g. Li Gonglin), to the fully-theorized calligraphic abstraction in Zhao Mengfu's late work. Wen Fong, for instance, sees the *Mind Landscape* this way: the rock outlines harbour the qualities of tense, pulsating 'iron-wire' strokes (*tiexian miao*) – an idiom learned from Li Gonglin's interpretation of Gu Kaizhi's gossamer-like line; the pines convey the calligraphic aesthetics of ancient seal-script calligraphy (*zhuan shu*).[27]

As the name 'seal' script indicates, it is used in the legends of carved seals, as well as for the titles of engraved stelae. The form of the earliest Chinese writing, it was first executed using a sharp or hard instrument, for instance on soft clay in the moulds for bronze vessels, well before the introduction of the brush, bamboo and later paper for writing. It contrasts flat areas of positive and negative space in a single plane within an imaginary grid. Such design-conscious aesthetics gave the script an archaic flavour once brush and paper became more standard media for calligraphy in the Six Dynasties. Thereafter, seal-script writing could easily be transferred from a wood, metal or stone medium onto paper or silk by ink-rubbing or seal-impression to set up exciting visual tensions and apparent movement among the resulting black and white (or, in the case of a seals, red and white) patterns. This archaic design concept resurfaces in these flat, emblematic forms of trees, bringing them new life and making them resonate with ancient Chinese civilization.

Certainly by the time of his colophon to *Elegant Rocks, Sparse Forest* (*Xiushi shulin*; Palace Museum, Beijing; fig. 7) of about 1314, Zhao Mengfu claimed to be incorporating these abstractions into his landscape forms, in what was the incarnation of a long-held literati ideal. In the poem-colophon to this painting,

> The rocks are like 'flying-white', the trees like 'seal' [script].
> To paint the bamboo, I went back to the 'spreading eight' [later clerical script].
> Only he who has discerned this
> Will know that calligraphy and painting have always been one.

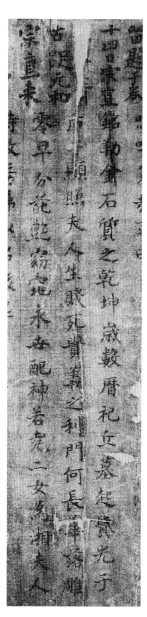

Fig. 8 *Xiaonü Cao E bei (Filial Woman Cao E stele)* (right) and colophon (left) by Zhao Mengfu (1254–1322). Details of a handscroll. Liaoning Provincial Museum.

Zhao remarked that his 'trees [are] like "seal" script', hence the comparison of the trees in the *Mind Landscape* with seal-script characters.

The rocks in the 1314 painting are said to have been done in a full-blown calligraphic script – 'flying white', according to the poem. The 'un-theorized' rocks in the *Mind Landscape*, done in a cross-over idiom, 'iron-wire', which was a patterning of the line that still deferred to Gu Kaizhi's swirling-silk lineament via Li Gonglin's *baimiao*, suggest how this calligraphic disciplining of pictorial abstraction began.

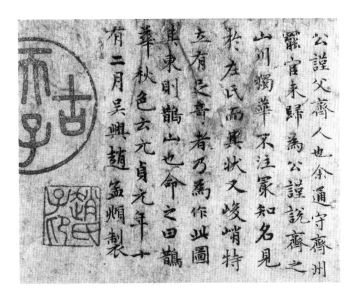

Fig. 9 Zhao Mengfu (1254–1322), *Autumn Colours on the Qiao and Hua Mountains (Qiao Hua qiuse)*, dated 1296. Detail of the inscription on a handscroll; ink and colour on paper, 28.4 × 93.2 cm. National Palace Museum, Taipei.

Zhao Mengfu's earliest works of calligraphy and painting, including the *Mind Landscape*, date to his first stay at court (1287–1295), a time and place when views about the present were commonly expressed vicariously, in anecdotes from the early dynastic history of the Han and Six Dynasties (206 BCE–589 CE). This was the case as much in political and judicial debate as in the literary arts of poetry, calligraphy and painting. For Zhao Mengfu, the decisive break with the Song and the south came now as he exchanged courtly Song modes – the flowers his father had loved – and the blue-and-green landscape mode, for this new official's rhetoric. Encountering fresh material on official travels after 1287 changed the experience and value of past art, and put new emphasis on the choices individuals made. As a leading connoisseur and official, Zhao Mengfu began to append critical remarks to old masterworks written in fine calligraphy in colophons on the backing paper, creating a new space for the display of forms and ideas gleaned from the models.

In about 1287 Zhao Mengfu appended a colophon to a rare manuscript ascribed to Zhong You (150–230), *Stele of Filial Woman Cao E (Xiaonü Cao E bei*; Liaoning Provincial Museum; fig. 8), in which he described the manuscript, already well known through rubbings, as his 'number-one model of regular script'. If brush traces did indeed image the mind, then the style of the inscription became the visual manifestation of the lesson, as the verbal, visual and historical were recast in a new interpretation of the past, in the new space beside the model.

We may better grasp the overall role played by models, as this art revival began, if we understand an intellectual predisposition to blur distinctions between calligraphy and painting. This drew on an existing ideal expressed by the Tang critic Zhang Huaiguan (act. 713–742), which matched calligraphers and painters at comparable stages across time, such as Zhong You and Gu Kaizhi:

If you were to compare them to calligraphers, you would say that Gu Kaizhi and Lu Tanwei were like Zhong You and Zhang Zhi [act. latter half of second century], and Zhang Sengyou was like Wang Xizhi.[28]

Zhao Mengfu's art historical studies and new work of the 1290s mirrored a shift in political rhetoric from the individualist Six Dynasties to a more cosmopolitan model for the Yuan state, the Tang dynasty. This shift also sets in context Deng Yu's affinity for the Tang polity in his poem-colophon, above. In calligraphy, Zhao's studies in the stylish classical Wang tradition[29] were thus tempered with exercises after early Tang calligraphers,[30] and in painting, he studied Tang figures and animals.[31] By the mid 1290s his calligraphy incorporated the perceived discipline and rigour of these Tang models (fig. 9): the characters were square in shape and balanced within an imaginary geometric grid; his brush technique created more rounded, three-dimensional strokes.

In the 1300s his frame of reference shifted forward in time to the art of the late Northern Song literati, including the running-cursive style Su Shi, the figure painting of Li Gonglin,[32] and Song landscape styles. By the 1310s it was the demanding, extreme cursive styles of Huaisu (725–c. 799) and Yang Ningshi (873–954), and in painting, the almost abstract expressionism of the literati genre of 'old trees, bamboo and rocks'. This schematic plan of Zhao Mengfu's artistic development must also allow for returns to brush modes and subjects previously studied, as for instance, with classic brush modes like the running-cursive calligraphy of the Dingwu rubbing of Wang Xizhi's *Orchid Pavilion Preface* and ink-outline figure painting in the Li Gonglin tradition.

Methodologically and stylistically speaking, however, the years 1287–1295 marked the beginning of this 'art-historical art', as Max Loehr (1903–1988) termed it, this process of turning the study of old masterworks to the advantage of self and society. The early standard script of Zhong You, therefore, may be crudely but effectively gauged as being on a historical and calligraphic 'level' with Gu Kaizhi's painting. Finally, we may posit the method by which Zhao Mengfu recreated 'Gu Kaizhi' in the *Mind Landscape*. Studying the pioneering standard-script calligraphy of Zhong You helped

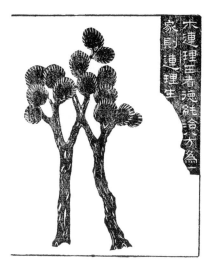

Fig. 10 Attributed to Su Shi (1036–1101), *Withered Tree, Bamboo and Rock (Kumu zhushi)*. Hand-scroll; ink on paper, 23.4 × 50.9cm. Shanghai Museum.

Fig. 11 'Trees of conjoined cosmic pattern' (*lianli mu*). Engraving of an omen. Wu Liang Shrine, Shandong, 2nd century CE. (After Feng & Feng 1906 [1821], *juan* 4.)

him re-imagine and discipline Gu Kaizhi's gossamer-thread line; this he then employed to render 'summary' landscape forms that could be imagined from relics of Gu Kaizhi's paintings and contingent early works.

In order to retain a concept of style as a versatile critical tool, however, we cannot reduce the painting to calligraphy. We should want to recognize further stylistic innovations by exploring genre and narrative structure, for instance. To what extent did the rhetorical function of Gu's paintings as narrative and didactic illustrations of Buddhist, Daoist and Confucian tenets inform, or authenticate Zhao Mengfu's *Mind Landscape*? For another of the colophon writers, Yu Ji (1272–1348), a scholar-official protégé of Zhao Mengfu's, the Gu Kaizhi model did connote religious syncretism, which indicates that the rhetoric of Yuan politics drew not only from history, but also from religion:

> His bodily form is like a crane, his sideburns long and
>   unkempt,
> A pine-wind wafts across him, there in his niche.
> As much as I love the greens and blues of these
>   mountains,
> Luckily I do not bear the responsibilities Youyu held.

Yu Ji reads the forms as symbols of a spiritual wisdom that entitled Xie Kun, and hence Zhao Mengfu, to hold political power. He sees the archaistic 'space cell' as a *kan*, a niche carved into rock in a cave or cliff to house a Buddha figure. He sees the figure as a crane: a form assumed by Daoist immortals. He observes a pine-wind, both a Confucian and a Daoist symbol. It alludes to the classical image of righteous wind – the *junzi* or moral exemplar of the Confucian classics – bending grass (the people) to his will. It also symbolizes longevity to Daoists: the pine-wind at court was famously loved by the Daoist courtier and alchemist Tao Hongjing (456–536).[33] Yu Ji's claim that Xie Kun, and hence Zhao Mengfu, had achieved the goals of the Three Religions – Buddhist enlightenment, Daoist transcendence and Confucian transformation – highlights another dimension of the ideology of 'reclusion at court' in religious syncretism.

We may push this further to argue that what makes Zhao Mengfu's painting historically specific is this multi-dimensional quality, the multiple resonances of the forms across time. Yu Ji's gloss on the pine image, for instance, short circuits the influential but debilitating dialectic between court and exile in the use of this image by the late Northern Song scholar-officials. Huang Tingjian (1045–1105) had written of the great exile Su Shi, for instance, that,

> 'Hill and valley' were naturally in his breast from the
>   beginning
> Hence he made old trees twisted by wind and frost.

The gnarled pines Su Shi painted were thus symbols of his integrity in the face of unjust persecution and exile (fig. 10).[34] The green pines in the *Mind Landscape* ascribe 'wilderness' integrity to the court-recluse's colleagues in the imperial academy.

This rosy view of court politics and of the emperor's judgement of his courtiers' characters is to an extent conventional, but there is yet another dimension to these trees by which Zhao Mengfu invoked classical rhetoric to shape contemporary belief. In the correlative universe of dynastic and pre-dynastic China, omens such as natural disasters and wonders were not dismissed as superstition, but were tangible signs of Heaven's rating of the state of human affairs. The pairs of interlinked pines may be read as auspicious omens, like those at the Han dynasty Wu Liang shrine (fig. 11). An inscription there connects their appearance (they could be pictured growing from the same roots, in a conjugal embrace or simply with interlocking branches) with a ruler's virtue having spread throughout the empire.

That Qubilai himself was a great believer in omens is also surely moot. In the autumn of 1290 a series of disastrous omens – earthquakes – struck the capital region. A devastating quake on 20 September 1290 at Wuping, north of Beijing, unnerved him so much that he demanded an explanation from the state academies. Although widely seen as a signal of government failure, the academicians were afraid to criticise the obvious culprit, the powerful Uighur-Tibetan financier Sangha (?–1291).[35] Hand-picked by Qubilai to provide for the court's staggering expenditure, Sangha and his clique had – and not just in the eyes of Chinese – grossly exceeded their authority by levying crippling taxes on the population and promoting corrupt associates. Zhao Mengfu is said to have linked Sangha's harsh tax regime with the quakes in private to Arghun Sali (?–after 1303), a Uighur minister and Hanlin academician, who then memorialized the khan paraphrasing Zhao Mengfu's denunciation. This led to probably the last and most explosive of Zhao Mengfu's confrontations with Sangha since 1287 over tax and public welfare. On this occasion Zhao Mengfu's arguments prevailed, and mounting charges over the following months eventually led to Sangha's impeachment: on 23 February 1291, he was sacked and, after investigations, he was executed on 17 August.[36] It would make sense if the *Mind Landscape* pines had appeared after Sangha and his cronies had fallen from grace; the 'linked trees' would then have been an appropriate allegory to signal that these men no longer impeded the spread of Qubilai's sagely virtue through the empire, and further, that he could now implement humane tax policies.

Significantly, history records that these *lianlimu* or 'trees of conjoined cosmic pattern' indeed blessed the reign of first Eastern Jìn emperor Yuandi (r. 317–322),[37] when, as Crown Prince, Sima Shao asked his question of Xie Kun. With these interlinked pines, the *Mind Landscape* makes a parallel claim for seeing Qubilai, the first Yuan monarch, as a sagely Chinese emperor.

As well as being a self-portrait in masquerade and an allegory of good government, the *Mind Landscape* also has an autobiographical basis in Yuan politics. It is really tempting to read the ideological distance between Xie Kun and Yu Liang in terms of the rivalry between Zhao Mengfu and Sangha. More than this, the painting is very likely to refer to a specific clash, if only because the hero of the painting, Xie Kun, died soon after the original event of about 320, whereas Yu Liang, his nemesis, lived many more years. This is in fact the reverse of Zhao Mengfu and Sangha's situation. The *Mind Landscape* could date to as early as 1287, as Shih Shou-chien argued, but it seems unlikely, as Zhao Mengfu was then newly arrived at court and unproven, and Sangha only rose to prominence at the end of that year. After this they clashed at court on various occasions, usually about taxation, but on one occasion Sangha almost had Zhao Mengfu flogged for arriving late. Unfortunately, the little we know of Zhao Mengfu's relations with Qubilai's designated heir, probably his grandson Temür, the Sima Shao of the original narrative, throws hardly any light on the matter. Temür knew enough of Sangha to have been impressed by his bureaucratic efficiency,[38] and enough of Zhao Mengfu to engage him in the compilation of Qubilai's 'Veritable Records' in 1295. Certainly Temür would have observed the ideological rivalry between them, having witnessed Zhao Mengfu's objections to his grandfather's appointment of Sangha as chief financial officer as early as the end of 1287.[39] But if and when he questioned Zhao Mengfu about Sangha we do not know.

We also know little of the context of Gu Kaizhi's original painting, like whether it was a self-portrait or a portrait of a patron such as Xie An (320–395), who once was a recluse in the Eastern Mountains.[40] Zhao Mengfu's contemporaries, moved by the narrative content and execution of the painting, related the *Mind Landscape* to Zhao's talent for persuasion in art and politics. Assuming Gu Kaizhi's painting had been a self-portrait, Ni Zan saw Zhao's as the same, hence an expression of his isolation. Dong Qichang was concerned by whether the painting was decorative or scholarly. However, the circumstance of the creation of a parallel early text, the 'Admonitions', and of Gu Kaizhi's illustration of it, offer a way forward here. We see both these as drastic efforts to rectify affairs of state following the disgrace of an overbearing figure at court close to the emperor. In this respect, it is hard to think of a more spectacular parallel event connected to Zhao Mengfu during his term at (or near) the capital from 1287 to 1295 than Sangha's fall from grace.

The last of the colophons by Zhao Mengfu's contemporaries, written by a poet friend from Suzhou called Song Wu (1260–*c*.1340), adopts the language of high political stakes. According to a preface Zhao wrote to a collection of Song's poetry in 1295, the two men shared intimate conversations, often over landscape paintings and poetry, when Song spent the autumn of 1291, in the aftermath of Sangha's execution, in the capital.[41] Written perhaps in return for Zhao's preface when the two met again in Suzhou in the autumn of 1295, Song's poem-colophon ties in nicely with the idea of Zhao Mengfu having painted the *Mind Landscape* under similar conditions to the *Admonitions*:

> Asked 'How do you compare with Yu Liang?'
> His incomparable reply, 'I am at my best in hill and valley'.
> By great fortune this plaintive song is not lost;
> This stylish painting exists for posterity.

The poet refers to some 'great fortune' that enabled Zhao to paint the 'stylish painting'. Without it, it seems there would have been neither 'plaintive song' – his righteous complaint about the wayward Sangha, we wonder? – nor the 'stylish painting' in which the song took pictorial form. This is less melodramatic than it sounds: Song would have known the consequences of an unsuccessful attack on Sangha. He would also have known that from around 1290 on, Zhao Mengfu had genuine fears of attempts on his life by rivals jealous of Qubilai's unguarded favouritism towards him, and that Qubilai had relied very publicly upon Zhao's judgement during and after Sangha's downfall, when Zhao helped to exonerate some of the latter's supporters.[42] Zhao's fears were such that he requested and received a post outside the capital not long after Song Wu's stay, in the sixth month of 1292. He returned only briefly in 1295 at Temür's summons, before leaving for a period of prolonged 'retirement' at home in Wuxing. Both stylistically, as outlined above, and contextually, therefore, we would expect the *Mind Landscape* to date to about 1290–1292, when Zhao Mengfu was also about Xie Kun's age in the picture.

This essay began by exploring the provenance of the *Admonitions* scroll during the later Jin, early Mongol, Southern Song and Yuan periods. It speculated, for lack of evidence, about a possible transmission through state or private collections, and explored the 'consumption' and recension of this and other paintings associated with Gu Kaizhi. It has also explored how Yuan literati construed the painting of Gu Kaizhi, especially through Zhao Mengfu's *Mind Landscape of Xie Youyu*, an early Yuan re-creation of a fabled Gu Kaizhi portrait-in-a-landscape. As well as having been created at the initial moment of Zhao's career, broadly 1287–1295, and probably about 1290–1292, the painting has been seen as pivotal in Chinese art history, having appeared at the inception of a Yuan renaissance in the arts founded on calligraphic revivalism.

This return to Gu Kaizhi's portrait of 'reclusion at court' worked in part to justify Zhao Mengfu's controversial 1286 decision to serve under Qubilai Khan with the aim of representing Chinese civilization at court, and the eccentric but brilliant figure of Gu Kaizhi lent Zhao Mengfu a credible voice for this purpose. In part, Gu Kaizhi also represented the beginning of literary painting, and Zhao's re-evaluation of his art led to a reform of the canon of past styles, visualized and renewed in new works through the discipline of calligraphy, the pre-eminent self-expressive mode in Chinese art history. As Song Wu observed in his colophon to this painting, Gu Kaizhi represented the hope of cultural posterity for Chinese amid the uncertainty of a Mongol world.

Intriguingly, it was this literati mode of subjective expression based on abstract calligraphic values that Chinese and Japanese scholars and painters of the 1920s harked back to as evidence of Eastern 'progress' when they saw European Post-Impressionist painting make a similar cross-over to paradigms beyond representation.[43] The transformations resulting from Zhao Mengfu's service and this painting would appear to lie at the heart of any modern understanding of Gu Kaizhi, of the *Admonitions* scroll and indeed of literati painting in later Chinese art history.

NOTES

1 See pl. 34; Mason 2001, p. 32.
2 Sun Tagong (?attr.) 1962.
3 Wang Yun 1962 (1276), p. 33.
4 Zhou Mi *c.*1296, in Weitz 1994, nos 1.93.1–2 & 36.1.1–2.
5 See Wang Yao-t'ing and Stephen Little's essays in this volume.
6 Zhou Mi *c.*1296, in Weitz 1994, vol. 2, p. 539. For the Beijing painting, see Yu Hui's essay in this volume.
7 Ledderose 2001.
8 A doctoral dissertation about Tang Hou was recently completed by Diana Chou (Chou, Yeongchau 2001).
9 *Hua jian* (*MSCK* 1956 ed.), vol. 1, p. 161.
10 Revived in the early eighteenth century by the collector An Qi (1683–1742?), and again by Kohara Hironobu in 1967 (2000 [1967], p. 44; see also p. 34), this metaphor has become virtually synonymous with Gu Kaizhi's art in late modern scholarship that has stressed the humanist role of Chinese painting.
11 Xie He, *Guhua pinlu* in Acker 1979 (1954), pp. 18–19.
12 *Hua shi*; *XHHP*.
13 See the essays by Stephen Little and Yin Ji'nan in this volume.
14 For Xie Kun's biography, see *Jin shu*, *juan* 49; see also Shih Shou-chien 1984.
15 A similar point is made by Richard Barnhart (1983, p. 116).
16 Shih Shou-chien (1984) dates it to 1287, and Richard Barnhart (1983, pp. 114–115) to before 1287. For Zhao's annotated biography, see Ren Daobin 1984.
17 There is some doubt as to who Qubilai's chosen successor was after 1285. Hsiao Ch'i-ch'ing writes that 'the question [of who would succeed still] hung in the balance at the time of Qubilai's death' in February 1294 (1993, p. 494).
18 Arboriculturalists Reg Maxwell, Alan McHaffie and Conolly McCausland have suggested they may be the tree form, *M. Kobe*.
19 Shih, Shou-chien 1984.
20 *Hua jian* (*MSCK* 1956 ed.), vol. 1, pp. 162–163.
21 Weitz 1994, vol. 2, p. 396.
22 Ren Daobin 1984, pp. 66, 68.
23 For these and other cases, see Mote 1975 (1959).
24 The set currently begins anachronistically with the three later fourteenth-century colophons by Zhao Yong, the late Yuan master Ni Zan and Zhou Bin (act. late fourteenth century). Cary Y. Liu has suggested to me that the original order of the Yuan and early Ming colophons would likely have been: Yao Shi (d. *c.*1318), Wang Qi (act. *c.*1290–1310), Deng Yu (act. early fourteenth century), Yu Ji (1272–1348), Song Wu (1260–*c.*1340), Zhao Yong, Ni Zan and Zhou Bin. Shih (1984) dated Zhao Yong's to about 1360, and Ni Zan's to about the 1360s. They were probably moved up above the five earlier colophons – in the Ming perhaps – because the authors of these, including friends and protégés of Zhao Mengfu, had become comparatively obscure.
25 Li, Chu-tsing 1981.
26 *Jin shu*, quoted in Morohashi 1955 (1984), vol. 4, no. 9436.19
27 Fong, Wen C. *et al.* 1984.
28 Quoted in *LDMHJ*; tr. adapted from Acker 1954, pp. 195–196.
29 E.g. his 1295 colophon to the 'Shenlong' version of Wang Xizhi's *Orchid Pavilion Preface* (*Lanting xu*) in the National Palace Museum, Taipei.
30 Such as Zhao's 1291 colophon to Ouyang Xun's (557–641) *Confucius Making an Offering in a Dream* (*Zhongni mengdian tie*) in Liaoning Provincial Museum, and his 1298 colophon to Lu Jianzhi's (latter half seventh century) *Prose-poem on Literature* (*Wen fu*) in the National Palace Museum, Taipei.
31 E.g. the 1295 colophon to the Han Huang (723–787) attribution, *Five Oxen* (*Wuniu tu*) in the Palace Museum, Beijing.
32 E.g. the *Small Portrait of Su Shi* of 1300, in the National Palace Museum, Taipei.
33 *Nan shi*, *juan* 76, 'Biography of Tao Hongjing', quoted in Morohashi 1955 (1984), vol. 6, no. 14516.271.1.
34 Bush & Shih 1985, p. 212
35 Biography in de Rachewiltz 1993, pp. 558–583.
36 Ren Daobin 1984, p. 54; de Rachewiltz 1993, p. 573.
37 *Jin shu*, 'Annals of Yuandi', *juan* 6.
38 De Rachewiltz 1993, p. 581.
39 See Zhao Mengfu's stele for Danba (d. 1303), *Danba bei*.
40 'Biography of Xie An': *Jin shu* 1999, *juan* 79, pp. 1379–1382. In his essay in this volume, Yin Ji'nan notes that Zhan Jingfeng (1519–1600) recorded a painting ascribed to Gu Kaizhi entitled *Xie Taifu Dongshan* (*Grand Tutor Xie in the Eastern Mountains*), which may have been similar to his portrait of 'Xie Kun in hill and dale'.
41 Zhao Mengfu, 1295 preface to Song Wu 1981 (1295), quoted in Ren Daobin 1984, p. 68.
42 *Yuan shi*, *juan* 172: Ren Daobin 1984, pp. 42, 55.
43 The topic of a recent study by Aida Yuen Wong (2001).

The Evolving Significance of Gu Kaizhi and the *Admonitions of the Court Instructress*

Maxwell K. Hearn

The four papers discussed here address three of the most vexing questions surrounding the pictorial theme known as the 'Admonitions of the Court Instructress': the date of its creation, its relation to Gu Kaizhi (*c.* 344–*c.* 406), and the impact that this theme and Gu Kaizhi have had on artists and collectors of the Tang (618–907) and later periods.

Chen Pao-chen's study offers carefully researched and reasoned answers to the first two of these questions. Chen concludes that the British Museum scroll is a faithful copy based on a late fourth- or early fifth-century original, most likely by Gu Kaizhi. But this summary hardly does justice to all that Chen accomplishes. By first drawing attention to the abstract nature of Zhang Hua's (232–300) rhymed prose-poem – a concise text that she transcribes and translates on pp. 15–17 – Chen makes clear that the visual interpretation of such a poem required an exceptionally talented and knowledgeable artist, one who could draw upon other textual sources to illustrate the historical figures mentioned in the text as well as imaginatively illustrate those passages where specific historical references do not exist. In scene four, for example, which depicts Lady Feng protecting Emperor Han Yuandi from a bear (the first scene preserved in the British Museum scroll), Chen shows that the artist based his illustration not on Zhang Hua's poem, but on Lady Feng's biography in the *Han History (Han shu)*. This enables Chen to identify the leftmost figure in this scene as Lady Fu, one of Han Yuandi's favourites, convincingly clearing up a misreading of this figure by some scholars (including the person who inscribed the Beijing copy – see below), as an attendant of Lady Ban in the subsequent scene. This misunderstanding has led some scholars to view the text passages on the British Museum scroll as later interpolations – an interpretation that Chen convincingly refutes.

As to the date of the British Museum scroll, Chen uses archaeologically recovered works to demonstrate that the prototype for the British Museum scroll must date to the fourth or fifth century and that the artist's skilful use of scale, costume and facial expressions to convey social distinctions reveals him to be a master. But Chen also points out misunderstandings in the rendering of the palanquin and costumes that identify the British Museum scroll as a copy. But how early could the copy be? Chen notes that meaningless elaborations in the scarves and ribbons of Wei-Jin era (220–420) costumes are already apparent on the decorated ceramic tiles from Dengxian, Henan, that are datable to the early sixth century. Yet Chen reasons that the British Museum scroll must be later. Noting that the earliest reliable seal ('Ruisi Dongge') on the painting dates to around 1075, she concludes that the scroll was made before that date, but after 847, the year Zhang Yanyuan completed his *Record of Famous Paintings in Successive Dynasties (Lidai minghua ji)*, which does not mention the scroll.

This is the weakest point in Chen's argument. If the copy post-dates 847, then the original must still have existed at that time, in which case it, too, escaped the notice of Tang writers. Following Chen's logic, we would have to conclude that the original could not have been created until the late Tang dynasty – a possibility that Chen's stylistic evidence refutes. Given the absence of any Tang record linking Gu with the *Admonitions* theme, one must presume either that the authorship of the original *Admonitions* composition was already unclear by that time or that such a small-scale work was simply overlooked by Zhang Yanyuan and other Tang critics – the likelihood of which would be even greater if the composition only survived as a copy.

If one accepts Chen's conclusion that the texts inscribed on the British Museum scroll are contemporaneous with the painting, then the calligraphic style of the texts presents another means of determining its date, as has been suggested by Wen Fong.[1] Chen's discovery of two scribal errors in the text accompanying the tenth scene, which shows a lady being rebuffed by the emperor, not only confirms the pictorial evidence that the British Museum scroll is a copy, but shows that the calligrapher was not an erudite scholar, but a lowly scribe. Since the calligraphy does not reflect a fourth-fifth century style, the calligrapher clearly did not imitate the style of an earlier text – if there was one. Establishing the period style of the calligraphy, therefore, would offer an important means for dating the British Museum scroll. Given Chen's excellent stylistic analysis of the painting, one hopes that she will undertake a similarly detailed analysis of the calligraphy.

In an effort to attach a name to the *Admonitions* composition, Chen points to two events that occurred during Gu Kaizhi's lifetime (in 375 and 396) that might have motivated a ruler to commission such a work. Chen concludes that Gu, as a leading artist already famous by 363–365, when he painted a depiction of Vimalakirti on the wall of the newly built Waguan Temple in the capital, would have been an obvious choice for such a commission. But the *Admonitions* composition, like those of the *Nymph of Luo River* and *Biographies of Exemplary Women*, only attracted attention as a work of Gu Kaizhi in the Song dynasty (960–1279), when the rise of scholar-official painting may have made it attractive to identify such antique compositions with the earliest-recorded literary artist. That such disparate paintings could all be associated with Gu should add to our sense of caution when trying to go beyond defining period styles to specify a single artist.[2]

In her paper, Alfreda Murck investigates the apparent anonymity of the *Admonitions* composition and the obscurity of the British Museum scroll's history prior to the eleventh century. In so doing, she highlights the importance of the Song literatus Mi Fu (1052–1107) in associating Gu's name with this composition. Prior to Mi Fu, Murck finds no evidence linking Gu with illustrations of Zhang Hua's 'Admonitions' text; indeed, references to Gu and Zhang never appear in the same poem. Not only is the *Admonitions* theme not mentioned in connection with Zhang Hua, but it seems not to have been mentioned at all prior to Mi Fu, perhaps, as Murck suggests, because of the inordinate power that female regents exercised during more than one-quarter of the eleventh century, when the *Admonitions* scroll would have been regarded as 'the visual equivalent of a hot potato' (as described by Murck at the 2001 colloquy).

Murck goes on to show that Tang and Song poets usually refer to Gu Kaizhi in connection with his 'pure foolishness' or his literary accomplishment. The only painting by Gu that is mentioned is his depiction of Vimalakirti at the Waguan Temple. Murck suggests that the notoriety of this painting was enhanced in Song times because Du Fu (712–770)

admired it. Since Du Fu was 'rediscovered' in the Song, Murck points out that his appreciation of Gu's painting would have counted for a lot among Song scholars, even though, as she notes, Shen Gua (1031–1095) had early on commented on the absence of authentic works by Gu.

Murck next examines Mi Fu's record of an *Admonitions* scroll in his *History of Painting* of 1103 and the identity of the scroll's owner at the time: Liu Youfang, a highly regarded eunuch in the Palace Domestic Service. Murck's analysis of Mi's text reveals that while he may not have made the attribution to Gu himself, he clearly found it plausible enough to record. Murck stops short of linking Mi and Liu to the British Museum scroll, but thanks to her research, it is tempting to do so. Since the scroll bears the genuine seal of the Ruisi Palace, which was built around 1075, it was already in the palace during Liu's lifetime. Indeed, it is not difficult to surmise that such a sensitive 'hot potato' might be bestowed upon this loyal eunuch sometime after the seal was impressed on the scroll – perhaps at his retirement in 1099. Presumably the same scroll then returned to the palace after Liu's death but prior to 1120, when it was catalogued in Emperor Huizong's (r. 1101–1125) collection. If this were the case, one would still have to account for the absence of genuine Huizong-era seals on the British Museum scroll – either through later loss or intentional removal.

Because Gu Kaizhi was known for his literary accomplishments, Murck points out that Song literati would have found him an attractive artist to promote. She observes that Mi Fu's identification of the *Admonitions* scroll with Gu makes sense in the context of the Northern Song (960–1127), when a leading circle of literati intersected with an inner court dominated by powerful palace women and eunuchs. In such an environment, linking the *Admonitions* scroll with Gu would have given it new layers of meaning and relevance. It seems entirely likely, Murck concludes, that Mi Fu was the first to publish the *Admonitions* scroll as Gu's work. When the scroll was recorded in Huizong's *Catalogue of the Imperial Painting Collection during the Xuanhe Era (Xuanhe huapu)* of 1120, Mi's tentative identification of the scroll's authorship was already viewed as authoritative. Building on Murck's findings, one might further suggest that it was also at this period – a time when, as Wen Fong has pointed out, men such as Su Shi (1037–1101) articulated a new, 'scholar-official aesthetic' that sought for 'renewal through the revival of ancient styles'[3] – that other antique compositions, such as the *Nymph of the Luo River* and *Biographies of Exemplary Women*, were also attributed to Gu Kaizhi.

After its mention in Huizong's catalogue, the *Admonitions* scroll again drops out of the textual record until Ming times. Yu Hui, in 'The *Admonitions* Scroll: A Song Version', introduces possible evidence for tracking the scroll's whereabouts during the early Southern Song period (1127–1279) by identifying a *baimiao* copy of the British Museum scroll, formerly attributed to Li Gonglin (*c.* 1041–1106), as the work of a Southern Song academy painter active in the 1180s. This scroll, now in the Palace Museum, Beijing, presents a complete composition with no missing sections. Thus, establishing the date of the Beijing scroll and assessing the reliability of its opening sections would have important implications for our understanding of the British Museum scroll.

Yu Hui argues convincingly that while the Beijing scroll is not an exact tracing copy, it is clearly based on the British Museum painting except for the opening three scenes (now lost from the British Museum scroll), which he demonstrates are fanciful creations. Yu notes that the presence of several archaic bronze vessels in the scene showing Lady Fan abstaining from eating meat are an anachronism: a fourth-century artist would have depicted lacquer or pottery dishes not archaic bronzes, which only became an important pictorial motif in Song times.

Yu has a harder time trying to explain the misplacement of the texts for scenes two (Lady Fan abstaining from meat) and four (Lady Feng and the bear) in the Beijing scroll. He comes to the somewhat forced conclusion that the texts were written first and the paintings were added afterwards – a sequence that might have pertained had the texts been written out by an emperor or high official, but that is otherwise contrary to logic. The fact that the breaks between sheets of paper often bisect a scene (as in scenes three and six) also suggests to Yu that the artist was forced into this spacing by the pre-existence of the texts. But if the texts were inscribed prior to the execution of the paintings, one must wonder why the calligrapher twice chose to place inscriptions at the end of a sheet of paper. It would seem more logical to assume that the artist painted the scenes first, and that the calligrapher then added the texts, but misunderstood their placement, erroneously inserting the text for Lady Fan between the two figures intended to accompany the introductory passage and adding the text for scene five, which illustrates Lady Ban refusing to sit in the palanquin, to the right of Lady Fu, who belongs with the preceding scene.

The majority of Yu Hui's paper is given over to an analysis of the evidence for dating the Beijing scroll to the late twelfth century. Yu first takes note of the seals on the painting, including those of the Qianlong emperor (r. 1736–1795), Liang Qingbiao (1620–1691) and a Mr Yan, whose two seals along the front edge of the painting are identified as Ming (1368–1644) in date. Yu next discusses the four colophons

attached to the scroll, dated from 1345 to 1392, which attribute the scroll to Li Gonglin.[4] Next, Yu examines the texts inscribed on the scroll and notes that the taboo against writing the characters of the Song emperors' personal names has been observed through Emperor Xiaozong (r. 1163–1189). He also points out that the calligraphy, which he believes to be by a different hand than the painting, shows the influence of Emperor Gaozong (1107–1187, r. 1127–1162). This leads him to speculate that the text was written when Gaozong was still alive. Yu also suggests that the Beijing scroll could not post-date the 1190s because of seals on the British Museum scroll belonging to the Jin emperor Zhangzong (r. 1189–1208), but this conclusion is invalidated by the fact that those seals have been shown to be spurious (see Wang Yao-t'ing in this volume, pp. 192–218). Finally, Yu likens the Beijing scroll's style to that of Ma Hezhi (act. *c.* 1130–*c.* 1170). All of these factors lead Yu Hui to conclude that the Beijing scroll was the work of a court artist active in the 1180s.

But colophons and seals can be forged or added later and pictorial references to archaic bronzes and the style of Ma Hezhi need not be limited to the Southern Song period. The fact that both the Beijing and British Museum scrolls were in Liang Qingbiao's collection provides another time frame in which the British Museum scroll was available for copying.[5] Could the Beijing scroll be a seventeenth-century copy created as an intentional forgery of a Li Gonglin? Yu Hui himself notes that Liang has been mistaken by later generations as a master forger. Might this be the case here?

In dating the Beijing scroll, one might do well to consult the work of Thomas Lawton, who considered a similar problem when seeking to date a *baimiao* version of the *Nymph of the Luo River* now in the Freer Gallery of Art.[6] Lawton lists a sequence of relevant comparisons and eloquently characterizes the stylistic shift documented by such a sequence as 'the gradual transformation of the austere, unadorned Northern Song *baimiao* figure painting tradition towards an increasingly more relaxed, ornamental interpretation ...'[7] A similar sequence of comparisons sheds light on the Beijing scroll's date. In Li Gonglin's illustration to chapter sixteen of *The Classic of Filial Piety*, datable to about 1085 (fig. 1), one sees ritual vessels, bells and chimes similar to those in the Beijing scroll (pl. 24). When one examines the style of the figures, however, the drapery lines in Li's painting are simpler, fewer in number, and more varied – alternating between angular and round forms, while those in the Beijing scroll show a proliferation of rhythmically repeated curving lines that reveal a delight in linear elaboration and abstract pattern (see pls 23–28).[8] The *Biographies of Exemplary Women* (fig. 2), a Song-era copy of an antique composition attributed to Gu –

Fig. 1 Li Gonglin (*c.*1041–1106), Chapter 16, 'The Influence of Filial Piety and the Response to It', from *The Classic of Filial Piety*. Datable to about 1085. Detail of a handscroll; ink on silk, 21.9 × 475.5 cm. The Metropolitan Museum of Art, New York. Ex coll. C. C. Wang Family, from the P. Y. and Kinmay W. Tang Family Collection, Promised and Partial Gift of Oscar L. Tang, 1996 (1996.479).

also owned by Liang Qingbiao – provides a possible prototype for this mannerism, but the lines in that painting are weightier, more varied and more descriptive.[9] A similar disparity is evident when one compares the Beijing scroll to Wei Jiuding's *Nymph of the Luo River* of around 1368 (fig. 3). The Freer's copy of the *Nymph of the Luo River* composition (fig. 4), dated by Lawton to the sixteenth century, exhibits linework that begins to approximate the weightless, decorative lines in the Beijing scroll, but for an even closer parallel one might point to the rhythmically patterned draperies in *Sixteen Views of Living in Seclusion* (fig. 5) painted in 1651 by Chen Hongshou (1598–1652).

To doubt a Southern Song date for the Beijing scroll would seem to fly in the face of an impressive array of Chinese scholarly opinions (and also contradicts my earlier acceptance of this dating when I delivered my remarks on this paper at the colloquy). As Yu Hui points out, both Tang Lan and Xu Bangda have published this scroll as a Southern Song copy.[10] But I believe than neither Yu Hui nor these earlier scholars paid adequate attention to the painting's style. Tang Lan only mentions the scroll in passing, noting that it preserves the opening scenes that are lost from the British Museum scroll. Xu Bangda treats the scroll in a discussion of attributions to Li Gonglin, pointing out the stylistic reasons why such an attribution is implausible: 'The [Beijing] picture is a figural work in *baimiao* and the brushwork used to describe the draperies is fluid, but the facial expressions are wanting in spirit and emotion and it would be difficult to call it a beautiful work … As to its method of painting, it lacks Li Gonglin's sense of antiquity, ease, and lofty elegance.'[11]

While Xu dismisses the painting as the work of Li Gonglin, he does not reflect further on the painting's date.

Fig. 2 (above left) Unidentified artist (11th–12th century?; formerly attributed to Gu Kaizhi), *Biographies of Exemplary Women*. Detail of a handscroll; ink on silk, 25.8 × 470.3 cm. Palace Museum, Beijing. (After *Zhongguo lidai huihua* 1978–, vol. 1, p. 32.)

Fig. 3 (left) Wei Jiuding (act. later 14th century), *Nymph of the Luo River*. Inscription by Ni Zan (1306–1374) dated 1368. Detail of a hanging scroll; ink on paper, 90.8 × 31.8 cm. National Palace Museum, Taipei. (After *Gugong shuhua tu lu* 1989–, vol. 5 [1990] p. 107.)

Fig. 4 (top) Unidentified artist (16th century?), *Nymph of the Luo River*. Detail of a handscroll; ink on paper, 24.1 × 527.4 cm. Gift of Eugene and Agnes E. Meyer, The Freer Gallery of Art, Smithsonian Institution, Washington, DC (68.12). (After Lawton 1973, no. 2, p. 30.)

Fig. 5 (above) Chen Hongshou (1598–1652), 'Studying Buddhist Sutras', from the album, *Sixteen Views of Living in Seclusion*. Dated 1651. Leaf 16 of an album of 16 paintings; ink and light colour on paper, 21.4 × 29.8 cm. National Palace Museum, Taipei.

Accepting the colophons as integral to the painting, he concludes that the work is Southern Song. He finds support for this theory in his analysis of the texts accompanying the illustrations. Appreciating the calligraphy, which he describes as lean and strong, Xu observes that the Song taboo against using the personal names of Song emperors has been observed (although not consistently). After pointing out that this fact was overlooked by the fourteenth-century colophon writers, he concludes that the avoidance of taboo characters indicates that the writing and painting must date to the Xiaozong era or later. But while Xu takes evident pleasure in debunking the attribution to Li Gonglin and showing how the fourteenth-century writers neglected the evidence of the taboo characters, his willingness to assign the Beijing scroll to the Southern Song reflects our field's inadequate knowledge or interest in this period, which has long languished in the shadow of earlier and later literati-dominated eras.

The sixteenth and seventeenth centuries witnessed a major revival of figure painting, when artists as diverse as Wang Shanggong (act. late sixteenth century), Ding Yunpeng (1547–*c.*1621), Wu Bin (act. *c.*1583–1626), Chen Hongshou and Shitao (1642–1707) all executed works in the *baimiao* manner associated with Li Gonglin. The Beijing scroll would have been a highly marketable object in this context. For Liang Qingbiao, its existence would also have added significantly to the value and credibility of the British Museum scroll in his possession, providing compelling evidence of its importance as a model for Li Gonglin. Might the coincidence of Liang's simultaneous ownership be too good to be true?

Shane McCausland's study of 'Gu Kaizhi in the Yuan (1271–1368) renaissance' provides an exciting new perspective on the significance of Gu Kaizhi to Zhao Mengfu (1254–1322), the pre-eminent literati artist of the early Yuan.

McCausland begins by noting that the *Admonitions* scroll drops out of sight during the Yuan and its transmission is uncertain until the sixteenth century. He might have added that if any Yuan artist was likely to have seen the *Admonitions* scroll it would have been Zhao, who was a leading figure both at the Yuan court and in Hangzhou, the regional centre of southern literati culture. The fact that neither Zhao nor his colleagues ever remarked on this scroll underscores how easy it is for even major works of art to escape the notice of commentators or artists for extended periods of time.

McCausland states that the only attribution to Gu Kaizhi that Zhao knew was the *Nymph of the Luo River*, now in Beijing, as evidenced by Zhao's colophon, dated 1299, which includes a transcription of Cao Zhi's poem and a short note praising the painting 'as a rare treasure by Gu'. But Xu Bangda has identified the Beijing colophon as a tracing copy

of a calligraphy now in the Tianjin Municipal Art Museum.[12] On the Tianjin original, Zhao makes no mention of having seen any painting, so his transcription of Cao Zhi's poem cannot be taken as evidence that he knew the Beijing scroll or any other version of this composition. Yet this point is not crucial to McCausland's argument, since he makes clear that, even before 1299, Gu Kaizhi played a pivotal role in Zhao Mengfu's revolutionary translation of naturalism into a graphic style.

That Gu was important in this process is underscored by the attention he receives in *Mirror of Painting (Gujin huajian)* by Tang Hou, a close follower of Zhao. In that text the calligraphic quality of Gu's linear drawing style is likened to 'the gossamer thread of a spring silkworm', a description that, McCausland notes, appears to originate with Tang Hou. This is an important point to emphasize. Although Tang Hou apparently never saw the *Admonitions* scroll, his evocative description of Gu's brushwork seems to match the lineament in the British Museum painting precisely – far better than it does any other extant attribution to Gu. Nevertheless, we should be wary of adopting fourteenth-century terminology in attempting to define a fifth-century style. Because Tang's characterization shifts attention from the descriptive function of brushwork to more abstract, expressive qualities, it would be anachronistic for scholars today to use Tang's term to describe the archaic linear drawing style of Gu Kaizhi, which Zhang Yanyuan described quite differently as 'firm, muscular, and continuous … complete and precise [because] one cannot see the ends [of the strokes]'.[13] But Tang Hou's metaphor for Gu's brushwork may be pertinent in evaluating later evocations of Gu's style. In the Beijing copy of the *Admonitions* scroll, for example, the fluid, curving lines float weightlessly across the paper as if spun from a silkworm yet, significantly, they no longer perform the same descriptive function that they do in the British Museum scroll.

The vehicle for Zhao's foray into calligraphic abstraction is his reinvention of Gu Kaizhi's lost portrait of Xie Kun, the *Mind Landscape of Xie Youyu* of around 1290–1292. The majority of McCausland's paper presents an insightful reading of the many layers of meaning embedded in this painting. I think McCausland correctly identifies the painting as a self-portrait done in defence of Zhao's problematic choice to serve at court rather than observe self-rustication. McCausland also identifies references in the painting to Zhao's royal pedigree, his laudatory view of Khubilai's rule, his intense rivalry with the powerful courtier Sangha (?–1291), and his desire to celebrate the longevity and durability of Chinese culture through a conscious revival of an archaic style associated with an early representative of the scholar class. By situating this work at the starting point of Zhao's methodical study of calligraphy and painting, McCausland demonstrates the painting's pivotal importance to Zhao's revolutionary transformation of art and art history so that, even today, our view of Gu Kaizhi and the British Museum scroll are coloured by the literati ideal that Gu came to embody.

The four papers discussed above enrich our understanding of both the British Museum scroll and the evolving significance of Gu Kaizhi among later Chinese painters and collectors. Chen Pao-chen confirms the British Museum scroll's status as a copy, but more significantly, clarifies the early date of its composition and underscores its importance as the closest approximation of Gu Kaizhi still extant. Alfreda Murck demonstrates that the transformation of Gu into a 'literati' painter began in Tang and Song times, particularly with the rise of scholar painting in the late Northern Song. Shane McCausland shows how the notion of Gu as 'China's first painter of literary accomplishment' made him an important source of inspiration for Zhao Mengfu. Yu Hui draws attention to the increasing number of antique figural compositions that were copied during the Song. Often these earlier models were reinterpreted as *baimiao* compositions. This

reinterpretative process, which began with Li Gonglin, reveals how expressive, calligraphic brushwork became increasingly important to scholar-artists until, in McCausland's words, Zhao Mengfu transformed painting into 'fully-theorized calligraphic abstraction'.

Ironically, Gu Kaizhi had little significance as an artistic model after the thirteenth century when, increasingly, he was displaced by Li Gonglin. But Gu's revival among Song and Yuan literati artists and connoisseurs as the patriarch of literary figure painting ensured his lasting cultural significance. During the Ming and Qing dynasties, as scholars increasingly sought to create encyclopaedic stylistic lineages that traced artistic schools back to their roots, interest in Gu revived. In the sixteenth and seventeenth centuries, when figure painting was enjoying a renaissance, identifying examples of Gu's work must have been particularly urgent. It is probably no coincidence, therefore, that it was during this period that new attributions to Gu Kaizhi, Li Gonglin and other early masters appeared on the burgeoning art market and that the British Museum's *Admonitions* scroll was embellished with a spurious signature, fake imperial seals, and other attributes that made it an even more marketable commodity.

NOTES

1 See Wen C. Fong's essay in this volume, pp. 23–26.
2 Thomas Lawton sounds a similar note of caution in his discussion of a version of the *Nymph of Luo River* now in the Freer Gallery of Art (1973, p. 27).
3 See Wen C. Fong's essay in this volume, p. 32.
4 For a reproduction of the colophons see *Zhongguo gudai shuhua mulu* 1986–2000, vol. 19 (1998), Jing 1–275, pp. 67–68, where the scroll is grouped with other attributions to Li Gonglin and is listed as 'anonymous Song'.
5 Kohara Hironobu suggested in 1967 that the Beijing scroll was a copy made by Liang Qingbiao (2001 [1967], p. 40). In note 6 of her paper, Chen Pao-chen suggests that the Beijing scroll is a Ming painting. Her note also provides a list of modern bibliographic references to the scroll (although it omits Xu Bangda's discussion – see below, note 10).
6 Lawton 1973, pp. 30–31.
7 Ibid., p. 30.
8 For a discussion of Li Gonglin's *Classic of Filial Piety* see Fong, Wen C. 1992, pp. 46–65; see also Barnhart *et al.* 1993.
9 For a reproduction of this scroll and documentation of Liang's ownership see *Zhongguo lidai huihua* 1978–, vol. 1, pp. 20–32.
10 Tang Lan 1961, p. 7; Xu Bangda 1984, vol. 1, pp. 208–209.
11 Xu Bangda 1984, vol. 1, p. 209. See also *Zhongguo lidai huihua* 1978–, vol. 1, catalogue section p. 3, where all of the early colophons appended to this scroll are rejected as forgeries.
12 For Xu's evaluation, see Xu Bangda 1984, vol. 1, p. 22. For the Tianjin version of Zhao's text, see *Zhongguo gudai shuhua mulu* 1986–2000, vol. 9 (1992), Jin 7-0035, pp. 21–22.
13 Tr. after Acker 1954, pp. 177, 183.

Part 3
The Treasure of Empires

Beyond the *Admonitions* Scroll: A Study of its Mounting, Seals and Inscriptions

Wang Yao-t'ing

Introduction

The *Admonitions of the Instructress to the Court Ladies* scroll has passed through the hands of many collectors over the centuries, and in that time it has become tattooed with impressions of their many seals; it has also been remounted many times. My concern in this paper is not with the artist or his style, but with these collecting activities beyond the painting itself, as the title indicates, up to about the beginning of the Qianlong period (1736–1795).

1 The Tang Imperial Collection

It has been argued in the past that the *Admonitions* scroll was once in the Tang (618–907) imperial collection on the basis of a seal with the legend 'Hong wen zhi yin' ('seal of Hongwen', or 'seal [of] Hong Wenzhi') at the end of the painting (fig. 3, seal 1.1 – see pp. 205–210). Now, in his *Lidai minghua ji (Record of Painters Through the Ages*, 847), the ninth-century critic Zhang Yanyuan writes that these 'were old seals from the Dongguan (Eastern Tower), [and that] those used for stamping books are very small'.[1] It has thus long been understood – wrongly – that the *Admonitions* was in the collection of the Hongwenguan or Office for the Dissemination of Culture, part of the Tang state academy, the Hanlin Academy.[2] There are in fact a number of similar seals on Song dynasty (960–1279) scrolls, such as the one on the calligraphy piece *Mid-Autumn (Zhongqiu tie)* (seal 1.2), attributed to Wang Xianzhi (344–388) but actually by Mi Fu (1051–1107) or one of his contemporaries.[3] Zhang Yanyuan's description of these seals as 'very small' provides faint hope of these two examples really being seals of the Tang imperial collection: the 'Hong wen zhi yin' seal is 2.6 by 2.6 cm, and hardly what one would call 'very small',[4] especially when com-

pared to the genuinely small 'Zhen-guan' linked seal[5] (of the Zhenguan reign, 627–649) and the 'Kaiyuan' seal (of the Kaiyuan reign, 713–741) that appear in extant calligraphy copybooks. The 'name' portion of the seal legend (i.e. Hong Wen, Hongwen or Hong Wenzhi) is also a common enough name or part name. It could just as well refer to the prestigious Hongwenguan as be the name of some post-Song collector; it could even be an out-and-out forgery. Whatever the case, the *Admonitions* scroll did, of course, only enter the literary record in the late eleventh century, when it was noted by Mi Fu, in his *Hua shi (History of Painting*, 1103), as being in the collection of the eunuch Liu Youfang.[6]

2 The *Admonitions* in Song Imperial Collections

A scroll entitled *Admonitions of the Instructress to the Court Ladies (Nüshi zhen tu)* was again recorded soon after that in about 1120 in *Xuanhe huapu (Xuanhe [1119–1125] Painting Manual)*, the catalogue of the Northern Song (960–1127) emperor Huizong's (1082–1135; r. 1101–1125) painting collection.[7] But it is as well to remember that in pre-modern times copies of pictures like this abounded. In 1966, for instance, a Northern Wei (386–533) lacquer screen depicting 'Ancient Worthies and Exemplary Women' (*Guxian lienü tu*) and bearing similar images to the *Admonitions* was discovered in the tomb of Sima Jinlong (484 CE) in Shanxi Province. It would therefore require visual evidence (from seals, etc.) that does not exist on the British Museum painting in its present form to prove that the painting recorded by Mi Fu in his *History of Painting* was also the painting in Emperor Huizong's collection, known as the 'Xuanhe collection'.

2a The Xuanhe collection seals

The impression of seals and the mounting of scrolls in the Xuanhe collection tend to follow an established pattern,[8] and there are in fact plenty of extant works that can be compared with the *Admonitions* scroll in this regard. As far as the mounting of the *Admonitions* scroll itself is concerned, the main sections are (as if unrolling from right to left): the front border-panel (*geshui*) of yellow silk brocade (fig. 1); the painting itself; the two end border-panels of yellow silk brocade (figs 3–4); and finally, in the colophon section in the tail, the transcription of part of Zhang Hua's 'Admonitions' text by the Jin (1115–1234) emperor Zhangzong (r. 1190–1208) (figs 5–7). Various seals on the scroll suggest it was in Huizong's collection. On the front border-panel (right below the half accession number – for which see below, Part 6) there is a rectangular 'Zhenghe' seal (of Huizong's Zhenghe reign period, 1111–1117; seal 2.1). At the top of the opening passage of the painting itself are a double-gourd-shaped seal 'Yu shu' (imperially inscribed; seal 3.1), and another, 'Xuan-he', below and to the right of the last (seal 4.1). Then, towards the top of the painting at the end is a 'Xuanhe' seal (seal 5.1). Finally, at the top of the rear border-panel there is a large seal in 'nine-wiggle' seal script (*jiudiewen*) which reads 'Neifu tushu zhi yin' ('seal of calligraphy and painting in the inner palace'; square, *relievo*; seal 6.1).

As is well known, the extant painting is missing the opening section of admonitions, but we cannot tell whether it was already truncated when Huizong owned it. However that may be, the *Admonitions* does not have the full complement of seven imperial seals usually impressed on the mountings of scrolls in the Xuanhe collection; and, the arrangement of what seals there are differs clearly from that on other well-known examples. With the exception of Huizong's large 'Neifu tushu zhi yin' seal, which was usually stamped on the Song 'plain paper' mounted at the end of a scroll (i.e. in the colophon section or backing), Xuanhe seals were either bridging seals, or they appeared on yellow brocade panels beside the silk or paper medium on which the actual artwork, whether painting or calligraphy, was executed. In some cases, such as when old scrolls had irregular old mountings, the standard procedure could not be followed. Old artworks did not always come in the standard shapes and sizes that would allow the collector to arrange his seals the same way every time. The mountings of extant scrolls once in Huizong's collection certainly do not display this kind of consistency, which means we cannot expect his seal arrangements to be entirely consistent either.

However, something like the standard layout of Huizong's mounting and seals may be gauged from the following three examples known to me: Wang Xizhi's *Ritual to Pray for Good Harvest* (*Xingrang tie*; The Art Museum, Princeton University); Wang Xizhi's *Distant Official Service* (*Yuanhuan tie*); and Sun Guoting's (646–691) *Essay on Calligraphy* (*Shupu*), both in National Palace Museum, Taipei.[9] In each case, the front and rear border-panels are of yellow silk brocade, while the seal paste appears to be 'water-based vermilion' (*shuitiao zhuyin*). Furthermore, the layout is consistent, as follows:

- *Xingrang tie*, on the front border-panel: there is a 'slender-gold' script (*shoujin*) imperial inscription of the title in the upper left corner, an impression of the circular double-dragon seal below this (seal 7.1), and an impression of the 'Xuan-he' linked seal below that in the lower left corner (seal 4.2). On the rear border-panel: there is an impression of a 'Zhenghe' seal in the upper right corner (seal 2.3), one of a 'Xuanhe' seal in the lower right (seal 5.3), and in the centre at the left edge of this panel, in the position of a bridging seal (i.e. over the seam), is an impression of a 'Zheng-he' linked seal (seal 8.1).
- *Yuanhuan tie*, on the yellow brocade border-panel: a title, 'Jin Wang Xizhi Yuanhuan tie', is written directly onto the panel, and an impression of a square double-dragon seal lies over the first two characters ('Jin Wang') (seal 7.2); in the lower left corner is a 'Xuanhe' seal (seal 5.2). On the rear border-panel, there is a 'Daguan' seal (of the Daguan reign period, 1107–1110) in the upper right corner (seal 9.1), and a 'Xuan-he' seal in the lower left corner (seal 4.3); but there is no impression of a 'Zheng-he' linked seal bridging the seams at the left edge.
- *Shupu* (consistent with *Xingrang tie*), on the front border-panel: there is a 'slender-gold' script inscription of the title in the upper left corner, an impression of the circular 'double-dragon' seal below this (seal 7.3), and an impression of a 'Xuan-he' linked seal below that in the lower left corner (seal 4.4). On the rear border-panel is a 'Zhenghe' seal in the upper right corner (seal 2.2), a 'Xuanhe' seal in the lower right (seal 5.4), and in the centre at the left edge of this panel, bridging the seam, is a 'Zheng-he' linked seal (although only its enclosing frame is visible today).

How do the seals and their placement on these three examples compare with those on the *Admonitions*?

At the beginning of the *Admonitions* painting itself we find a 'Xuan-he' linked seal (seal 4.1), and at the end of it, a

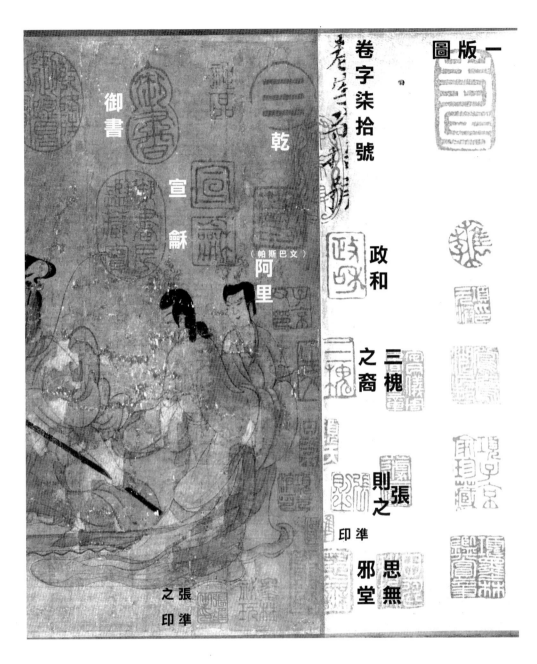

Fig. 1 Seals, etc. along the left edge of front border-panel (top to bottom): *Juan* series, no. 70 (half accession number); Zhenghe (rectangular, *relievo*); Zhang Zezhi (square, *relievo*).
Bridging the panel and painting: Sanhuai zhi yi (square, *relievo*); Zhun yin (small square, *relievo*); Siwuxietang (square, *relievo*).
Along the right edge of the painting: *qian*-trigram (three horizontal lines; circular, *relievo*); Ali ('Phagspa script; square, *relievo*).
Second column: Xuan-he (linked seal; squares, *relievi*); Zhang Zhun zhi yin (small square, *relievo*)
Third column: Yu shu (double gourd, *relievo*).

'Xuanhe' rectangular seal (seal 5.1), which is obviously quite different. Also, in the 'Yu shu' ('imperial calligraphy') gourd-shaped seal (seal 3.1), the *yu* has a 'single person' radical (*ren*; radical 9), which differs from the 'double-person' radical (*chi*; radical 60) (seal 3.2) in the *yu* in the 'Yu shu' seal on *Pasturing Horses (Muma tu)* attributed to Han Gan (*c.* 715– after 781; but thought to have been painted by Huizong), for instance. The 'Zhenghe' seal on the front border-panel (seal 2.1) is also quite different from the 'Zhenghe' seal on the *Shupu* (seal 2.2). We can also see that the 'Neifu tushu zhi yin' square seal in 'nine-wiggle' script (seal 6.1) on the second of the rear border-panels corresponds exactly with the same seal

on the painting of *Monkey and Cats (Houmao tu)* by Yi Yuanji (latter half of eleventh century) (seal 6.2) in Taipei Palace Museum.[10] If we compare the seal pastes, we find that the paste of the 'Zhenghe' (seal 2.1) and 'Neifu tushu zhi yin' (seal 6.1) seals at each end of the scroll has quite obviously faded. By contrast, the paste of three seals on the *Admonitions* painting itself (the 'Xuan-he' linked seal [seal 4.1] and 'Xuanhe' [seal 5.1] and 'Yu shu' seals) has hardly faded at all. At the same time, the definition of these seal legends is sharper. What conclusions should we draw from such differences within a set of seals supposedly belonging to one collector on one painting?

Fig. 2 Top right: Ruisi Dongge
(square, *relievo*).
Bottom left: Xianzhitang yin
(square, *intaglio*).

圖版二

睿思
東閣

賢志
堂印

Still more interesting is the fact that Wang Xizhi's *Three Passages of Calligraphy: Ping'an, Heru and Fengju* in Taipei Palace Museum has a front border-panel of flower-patterned yellow brocade. This and the form of its Xuanhe seals differ from what we find on the yellow brocade border-panels in the three scrolls of calligraphy listed above. However, the 'Xuanhe' linked seal on the patterned border-panel (seal 4.5) tallies with the 'Xuan-he' linked seal on the *Admonitions* scroll. The 'Xuanhe' seals on the actual painting and calligraphy in these two scrolls are also quite close (seals 5.1, 5.5), whereas the 'Zhenghe' seals on the front border-panel are very different in each case (seals 2.1, 2.4). So what does this all mean?

Does Huizong's calligraphy catalogue, *Xuanhe shupu* (*c.* 1120), provide evidence of his having owned the *Three Passages of Calligraphy*? In the *Three Passages* scroll as we see it today, the emperor's title-slip reads 'Jin Wang Xizhi Fengju tie' (*Presenting Oranges* by Wang Xizhi of the Jin'), but, intriguingly, *Fengju tie* is the last of the three passages in the current mounting. *Xuanhe shupu* only lists a work entitled *Ping'an tie*,[11] but if these three passages were already mounted in one scroll at that time, surely the title-slip of that scroll would have been inscribed with the title of the first passage, or else would have listed all three? These inconsistencies make one doubt whether this *Three Passages* scroll was after all

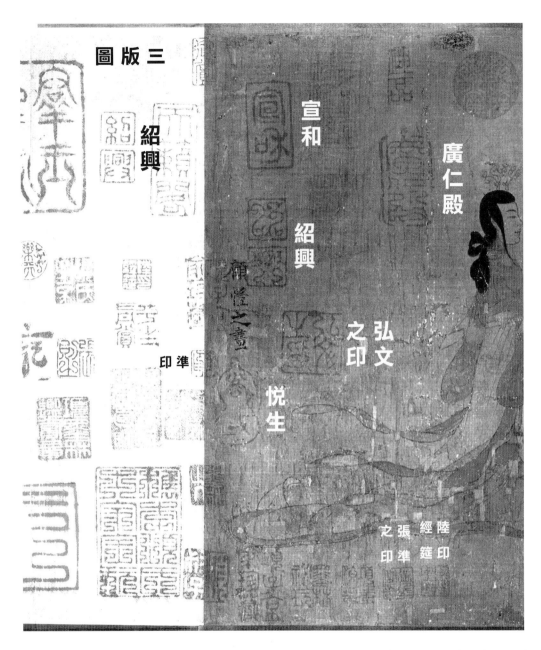

Fig. 3 Upper right: Guangrendian (rectangle, *relievo*).
Second column to last on the painting: Xuanhe (rectangular, *relievo*); Shao-xing (linked seal; squares, *relievo*); Hongwen zhi yin (rectangular, *relievo*).
Along the left edge of the painting: Gu Kaizhi hua ('signature'); Yue sheng (double gourd shape, *relievo*).
Bridging seal: Zhun yin (rectangular, *relievo*).
Second column on end-panel: Shao-xing (linked seal; squares, *relievo*).

in Huizong's collection. A closer look at its 'slender-gold' title-slip, and a comparison with the relaxed naturalism of the strokes on *Yuanhuan tie*, shows the characters of the *Fengju tie* title-slip to be so forced and 'hard' that they cannot have come from Huizong's hand.[12] This leads to the conclusion that the showcase of Xuanhe seals on *Ping'an tie* was also added later. We may envision a similar scenario for the *Admonitions* scroll.

2b The 'Ruisi Dongge' seals

There are eight oversize seals with the legend 'Ruisi Dongge' ([Palace of] Sagacious Contemplation, East Wing) stamped on the body of the painting itself (fig. 2, seal 10.1).[13] As one

might expect with eight very large seals all on the same work, the spacing between and placement of them is not uniform. The top of the sixth, for instance, is not even on the painting, making it very hard to decipher, and impossible to compare with other examples. But the real question is, is the 'Ruisi Dongge' seal a seal of Huizong as is widely thought, or of his son, the first Southern Song (1127–1279) emperor Gaozong (1107–1187; r. 1128–1162)?[14]

Let us look first at the use of three Southern Song imperial seals: 'Neifu shu yin' (Seal of calligraphy of the inner palace), which appears on *Caoshu si tie (Four Passages in Cursive Script)* by Mi Fu in Osaka Municipal Museum of Art; 'Ruisidian yin' (Seal of the Palace of Sagacious Contempla-

Fig. 4 Bridging the end-panels (right): Qun yu zhong mi (rectangle, *relievo*); Yong (?) (monogram seal, *relievo*); Chang (square, *relievo*).
Middle column: Neifu tushu zhi yin (square, *relievo*); An Yizhou jia zhencang (rectangular, *relievo*); Jiaolin Yuli shi tushu (square, *relievo*); Qiuhuo tushu (square, *relievo*).
Along left edge: Jiangshang Da shi tushu yin (rectangular, *relievo*).
Bridging seals (left edge): Bin chen (square, *intaglio* [right half] and *relievo* [left half]).
First column: Shiqi zhi yin (square, *relievo*).

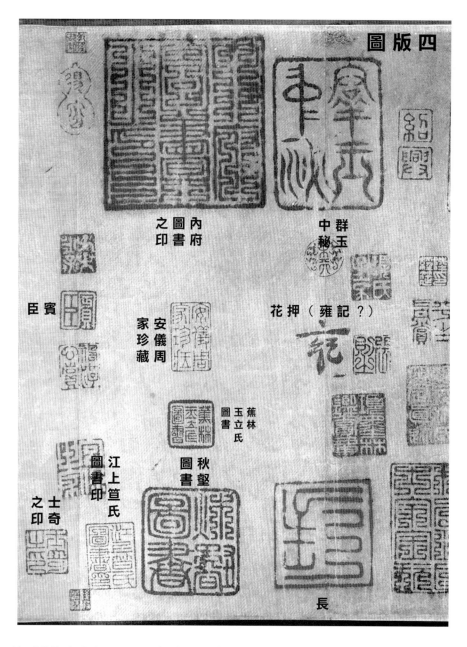

tion) on *Tiaoxi shi tie (Poem on Tiao Streams)* by Mi Fu in Beijing Palace Museum; and 'Jixidian bao' (Treasure of the Palace of Bright Countenance) on *Qiyan shi (Seven-character line verse)* by Huang Tingjian (1045–1105) in Taipei Palace Museum. These are all works on paper, and the seals were used to bridge the seams of the sheets. In the case of artworks on silk, however, lengths of silk were of course far longer than lengths of paper, so there was not much need for bridging seals. A unique explanation for the multiple impressions of the 'Ruisi Dongge' seal on the *Admonitions* scroll is Kohara Hironobu's theory that it was originally impressed once in each scene.[15]

The condition of these large seal impressions has deteri-

orated substantially, but it is still worth comparing them with similar examples such as those on important scrolls like the Han Huang (723–787) attributions, *Five Oxen (Wuniu tu)* and *Four Scholars in a Garden Collating Old Writings (Wenyuan tu)*, and *Studies of Birds and Insects (Xiesheng juan)* attributed to Huang Quan (903–968), all in the Peking Palace Museum; and *Blue Magpie and Thorny Shrubs (Shanzhe jique)* attributed to Huang Jucai (933–after 993) (seal 10.2), and *Pasturing Horses (Muma tu)* attributed to Han Gan (seal 10.3), both in the Taipei Palace Museum.

The large 'Ruisi Dongge' seal on Huang Jucai's *Blue Magpie and Thorny Shrubs* measures 7.4 cm across, which tallies with the diameter of the impressions on the *Admonitions*.

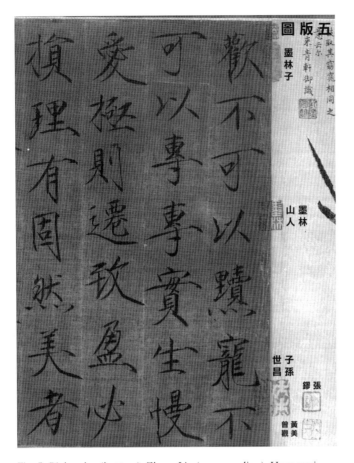

Fig. 5   Right edge (bottom): Zhang Liu (square, *relievo*); Huangmei zeng guan (square, *intaglio*).
Bridging seals: Molinzi (rectangular, [blurred]); Molin shanren (square, *intaglio*); Zisun shichang (square, *intaglio*).

Not only is a painting of this title recorded in *Xuanhe huapu*, but its mounting is also typical of scrolls in the Xuanhe collection. At the same time, there are no seals of Song Gaozong on the *Blue Magpie*, which leaves little doubt that all examples of the 'Ruisi Dongge' seal are Huizong's.

Furthermore, we find that Han Huang's *Five Oxen* is also to be found in the *Xuanhe huapu*, and *Pasturing Horses*, attributed to Han Gan, was actually painted by Huizong himself. All of this proves that the extant *Admonitions* was already in existence at least as early as the Northern Song period. More specifically, we know that the Ruisidian (Palace of Sagacious Contemplation) was founded in the eighth year of Xining (corresponding to 1075 CE).[16] We also know from a recorded anecdote that at some point in the latter half of the eleventh century, the collector-connoisseur Xue Shaopeng (latter half eleventh century) 'acquired the original "Dingwu" stone engraving of Wang Xizhi's calligraphic masterpiece, *Orchid Pavilion Preface (Dingwu Lanting)*.' This anecdote

continues, 'In the Zhenghe period the stone was appropriated by Youling [i.e. Huizong], who installed it in the Ruisi Dongge [the eastern wing of the (Palace of) Sagacious Contemplation].'[17] Here is evidence that this wing did indeed house works of calligraphy. Another of its functions in Huizong's reign was as an incense manufactory.[18]

2c Provenance from Song Huizong to Song Gaozong

If we were to suppose for a moment that the 'Ruisi Dongge' seal did belong to Song Gaozong, Zhou Mi's (1232–1298) study of 'Works of Calligraphy and Painting in the Shaoxing [1131–1162] Imperial Collection' (i.e. Gaozong's) comes to mind as a useful source:

> Siling [i.e. Gaozong] had a profound understanding of calligraphy and adored fine antiques. Although his reign was marred by constant warfare, he still made strenuous efforts to purchase all the major works of painting and calligraphy he could find. A tireless individual, he took them out to enjoy them whenever he had a free moment. In fact, because of his passion for painting and calligraphy, he had no reservations about spending enormous amounts of money and time to acquire them. As a result, he was presented works of painting and calligraphy from all over the empire every day. He even bought back in the market objects lost up north [i.e. following the Jin invasion in 1126–1127]. Song Gaozong's Shaoxing collection was, therefore, not inferior to his father's Xuanhe and Zhenghe collection.[19]

This gives a clear idea of the continuity between Huizong's Xuanhe and Gaozong's Shaoxing collections. Zhou Mi also records:

> The title-slips and inscriptions on old paintings that had come from Huizong's Xuanhe collection were removed and discarded. The emperor instructed Cao Xun and others to examine these works, to select and add new title-slips, and to submit their list to the emperor for approval.[20]

If the *Admonitions* scroll passed from Huizong's collection directly into his son Gaozong's, this might explain why the Xuanhe seals are all awry, and why there are no Xuanhe seals on the front or rear border-panels. It would also indicate that the later, spurious Xuanhe collection seals we see now had to have been added after the scroll left the Southern Song palace. It is also possible the opening scenes of the painting were lost in the Huizong-Gaozong transition. Before we proceed to look at the typical arrangement of Gaozong's seal set, we should take a closer look at the seals themselves. Zhou Mi tells us that

> When a handscroll entered Gaozong's imperial palace, various seals were impressed on it: a round *qian*-trigram [three horizontal lines] seal was used (not on a seam) at the head of the painting itself; and a small square seal reading 'Xishi cang' appeared below it. At the very end of the painting, they used a linked pair, 'Shao-xing'. The bridging seals were not used on the 'ink traces' [the body of the painting or calligraphy itself] at the top. Only the small 'Xishi cang' seal was used at the bottom. The small 'Shaoxing' seal was used at the end.[21]

The Shaoxing collection seals on the *Admonitions* scroll are as follows:

- a *qian*-trigram seal at the head of the painting (seal 11.1; cf. seals 11.2–11.4 and fig. 8);
- a 'Shao-xing' linked seal in bird-and-insect script (*niao-chongshu*) at the end of the painting (seal 13.1);
- and a 'Shao-xing' linked seal in small-seal script (*xiaozhuan*) on the rear border-panel (seal 13.9).

The 'Shao-xing' linked seal in bird-and-insect script also appears at the end of *Mid-Autumn* (seal 13.10), on the work of calligraphy itself. In fact, this seal was usually impressed in this position, in the lower left corner of a work. (NB This placement *should* have been possible with the *Admonitions* scroll, but seals of the sixteenth-century collector Xiang Yuan-bian [1525–1590] occupy that corner of the painting.) *Mid-Autumn* itself is generally considered to be by Mi Fu, and the Huizong and Gaozong seals on it later forgeries.

The 'Shao-xing' small-seal-script linked seal on the rear border-panel is the same as the examples seen on Wang Xizhi's *Three Passages of Calligraphy: Ping'an, Heru and Fengju* (seal 13.12); *Bitter Bamboo Sprouts (Kusun tie)* by Huaisu (725–after 777) (seals 13.13, 13.15); and *Tang Rhymes in Small Standard Script* by Wu Cailuan (seal 13.14). In fact, this whole group is thought to be fake.[22] The situation with the *qian*-trigram seal (seal 11.1) is similar, and it too may be considered fake.

2d The 'Xianzhitang yin' seal and the Song Empress Wu

The presence of a seal at the bottom of scene 1 with the legend 'seal of the Hall of Virtuous Ambition' ('Xianzhitang yin'; fig. 2, seal 14.1) suggests that the *Admonitions* scroll was once in the collection of Song Gaozong's empress, Wu

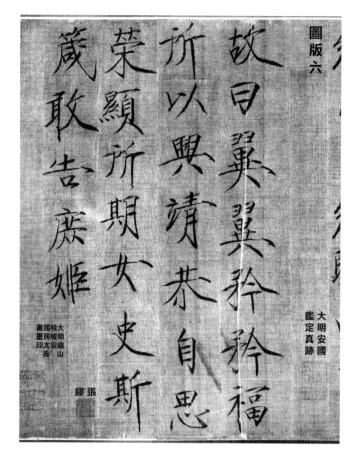

Fig. 6 Jin Zhangzong, transcription of the 'Admonitions' text. Seals along bottom edge (right to left): Daming An Guo jianding zhenji (rectangle, *intaglio*); Zhang Liu (square, *intaglio*); Daming Xishan Guipo An Guo Mintai shi shuhua yin (square, *intaglio*).

(1115–1197). The *History of the Song (Song shi)* provides the link:

> The Wise, Sagely, Benevolent and Upright Empress Wu was from Kaifeng. After becoming empress, she studied classical literature and history. She was also a skilled calligrapher. She once painted pictures of *Exemplary Women of the Past (Gu lienü tu)*, which she placed to the right of her throne as a 'mirror' [i.e. caution]. She named her hall of residence Xianzhi ('virtuous ambition') after the use of the term in the preface to the *Shi jing (Book of Poetry)*.[23]

As didactic illustrated texts, *Exemplary Women of the Past* and *Admonitions of the Instructress (Nüshi zhen)* are, of course, two of a kind. Based on the late Western Han (206 BCE–9 CE) imperial librarian Liu Xiang's (77–6 BCE) *Biographies of Exemplary Women (Lienü zhuan)*, the *Admonitions* was not only

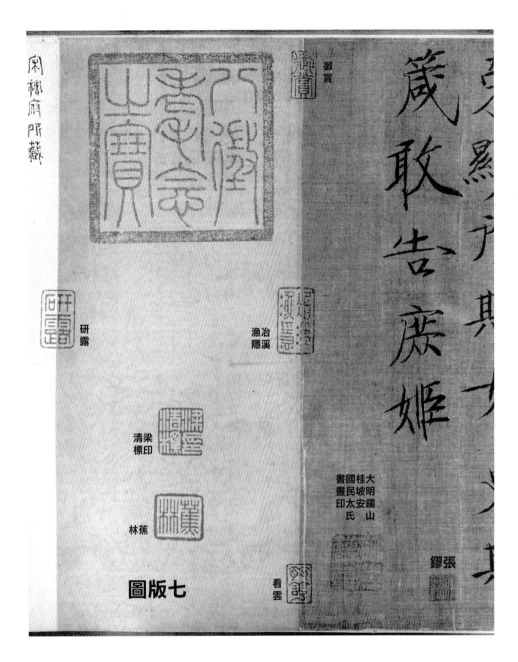

圖版七

about exemplary women, but about some of the same women. In Liu Xiang's case, he believed that the way to educate a ruler was to begin at home, as it were, so he selected as his standard-bearers worthy concubines from poetry and history who had elevated the state or distinguished their household. He compiled some eight chapters of exemplary biographies as a powerful warning to emperor Chengdi (r. 32–7 BCE) and his favourites, Empress Zhao and her sister, consort Zhao. So his *Biographies* was an admonition to them all. Not long after he had written this book, we learn of the Eastern Han (25–220) empress Liang (106–150) having had illustrations of his *Biographies* placed around her as a cau-

tion.[24] It is reasonable to suppose that the Song empress Wu could have had the *Admonitions* scroll in her collection for the same reason.

What story do the seals and inscriptions on the scroll itself tell of the object's possible provenance from a Southern Song palace into the Jin imperial collection? The kind of circumstance under which it left the Song would surely have been a major event such as bestowal on a minister or subject, or presentation as a diplomatic gift. Wu Ju (1173–1202), for instance, was a nephew of Empress Wu and a famous calligrapher and diplomat who led a number of visits to the Jin as an ambassador. The official Song history records that 'the Jin

Fig. 8 Dai Song (attr.), *Cow and Calf (Runiu tu)*. Leaf of the *Minghui jizhen* album; ink on silk, 21.4 × 45.9 cm. National Palace Museum, Taipei.

praised him for his sincerity … and said that of all the southern ambassadors they trusted the words of none but him'.[25] It is tempting to speculate that the *Admonitions* scroll could have come to the Jin through this channel, for the purpose of maintaining or improving foreign relations.

3 The *Admonitions* Scroll and Jin Zhangzong

What is known about the acquisition of the *Admonitions* scroll for the imperial collection of the Jurchen Jin dynasty? Three pieces of evidence in the scroll provide clear links to the Jin emperor Zhangzong (1168–1208): a seal of the Palace of Widespread Humanity ('Guangrendian'; seal 15.1) at the end of the painting itself; a 'Qun yu zhong mi' bridging seal (seal 16.1) between the two rear border-panels; and a colophon-transcription of the 'Admonitions' text in Zhangzong's calligraphy at the end of the scroll (figs 5–7).

3a Jin Zhangzong's calligraphy and his art collection
The Jin emperor Taizong (r. 1123–1134) initially acquired works of calligraphy and paintings from the Song imperial collection during the 1126–1127 invasion of north China (the so-called 'Jingkang crisis'), when the Jin captured the North-ern Song capital Bianjing (modern Kaifeng, Henan Province). After the fall of the city, one of their top priorities was the removal of this collection from the imperial city.[26] This much is clear: although everyone knew that Emperor Huizong had always been an ardent lover of art treasures, the Jin units charged with the task of recovering them had no idea where they were kept. In an attempt to curry favour with the Jin, Liang Ping, a eunuch inside the Jin garrison (who had presumably accompanied members of the Song imperial family into captivity) disclosed the location of the storage vaults. Jin forces were then able to enter the court precincts and carry off all the Song treasures, including pearls, jade, crystals, textiles, rare books, and all the great works of calligraphy and painting. They also got hold of the emperor's seals, including fourteen of white jade, two of green jade (one a Qin, 221–206 BCE, imperial seal), nine in gold and one in silver, as well as those of his empress and crown prince.[27] We may gauge what Zhangzong inherited of this collection by the fact that in 1192 (the third year of his Mingchang reign, 1190–1195) he instructed Wang Tingyun (1151–1202), 'together with secretary of state Zhang Rufang, to grade the finer works of calligraphy and painting; accordingly, they divided a total of 550 scrolls into different categories'.[28]

We have seen how the admonitions genre was often put to good use in the court context, so we may wonder whether Zhangzong had any ulterior motive in writing the transcription of Zhang Hua's 'Admonitions' text that is now part of the scroll. We may suppose that he did, and that it concerned the behaviour of one of his concubines, Li Shier (Yuanfei, act. late twelfth to early thirteenth century). Although she came

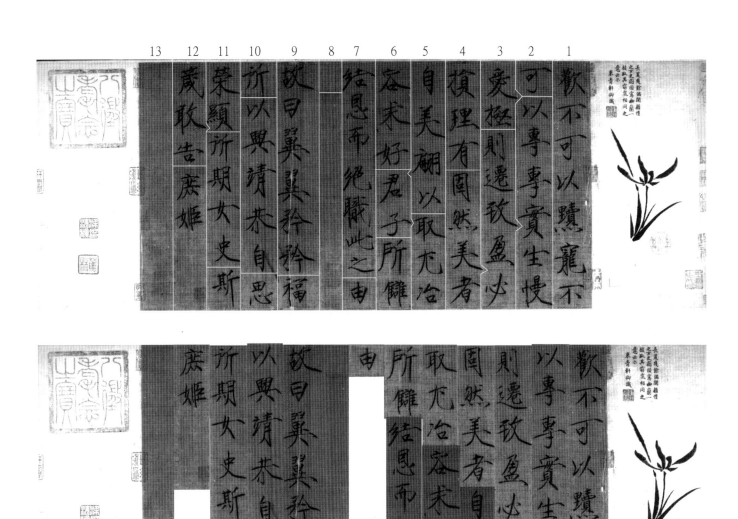

Fig. 9 (top) The 'Admonitions' transcription.

Fig. 10 (above) Reconstruction of the 'Admonitions' transcription.

from humble stock, the Jin dynastic history relates, the emperor doted on her. As a result, her brothers were ennobled, and court officials struck alliances with them in the hope of promotion to ministerial posts. She schemed to have the Prince of Wei (thirteenth century) invested as crown prince, but before long was handed her own death sentence by him.[29] We will recall that Zhang Hua's (232–300) 'Admonitions of

the Instructress' had been composed under very similar circumstances and for a similar reason, after a woman in the Western Jìn (265–316) imperial harem had taken politics into her own hands. After Jìn emperor Huidi (r. 290–306) ascended the throne, his empress, Jia (256–300), had begun to monopolize government, and it became fairly obvious that the dynasty was headed for ruin. Zhang Hua's official biography in the *Jin shu* records that he was 'a loyal imperial servant', and while there were even by then upright officials who advocated actually deposing the empress, he worked to repair the damage to the imperium. The purpose of Zhang's 'Admonitions' was simply to admonish her.[30]

The level of Zhangzong's integration into Han-Chinese culture was fairly deep, and his ties with the Song imperial line quite close. Zhou Mi tell us that

> Jin Zhangzong's mother was the daughter of one of Huizong's daughters [whom the Song emperor had married to Jin princes], which explains why Zhangzong was obsessed with calligraphy and always tried to measure himself up to the Xuanhe emperor [i.e. Huizong]. His painting and calligraphy was very faithful [to his great grandfather's]. Consequently, the institutions and culture of his Mingchang reign were the finest of the Jin dynasty.[31]

This reasoning is clearly skewed, but it is true that Huizong did marry quite a few of his daughters to Jurchen princes,[32] and Zhangzong is said to have been deeply moved whenever he was reminded of Huizong, like when he encountered works of art that Huizong had owned.[33]

There are a number of extant examples of Huizong's calligraphy, including signed inscriptions, title-slips, and so on, so that we may readily distinguish his hand. The same is not true of Jin Zhangzong: I have yet to come across even one signed inscription by him. This is puzzling, but there is an explanation. Huizong's painting *Court Ladies Preparing Newly Woven Silk (Daolian tu)* has a title-slip reading: 'Zhang Xuan's [mid-eighth century] *Court Ladies Preparing Newly Woven Silk* copied by Tianshui' (*Tianshui mo Zhang Xuan Daolian tu*). A colophon at the end of the scroll by the collector-connoisseur Zhang Shen (late fourteenth century) states:

> To the right is Xuanhe's [i.e. Huizong's] copy of Zhang Xuan's *Ladies Preparing Newly Woven Silk*. Mingchang [i.e. Jin Zhangzong] respectfully referred to [his great grandfather Huizong] in the title-slip by his place of origin [*junwang*], and also impressed [a full complement of] seven imperial seals on the scroll. The depth of his respect gives us to understand that his ancestry through the Song female line still counted for something in his own generation. What else could it be?

Following Zhang Shen's use of this term *junwang* (which means something like 'respect for a person's native place'), people have come to accept that it was Zhangzong who in fact

wrote this title-slip in Huizong-style 'slender gold' (*shoujin*) script.

We have a second example of this with another of Huizong's copies of a Tang painting, *Lady Guoguo on a Spring Outing (Guoguo furen youchun tu)* in Liaoning Provincial Museum. It is similarly labelled: *Tianshui mo Zhang Xuan Guoguo furen youchun tu* (Zhang Xuan's picture of Lady Guoguo going on a spring outing copied by Tianshui). The problem with Zhangzong's calligraphy being modelled so closely on Huizong's is telling them apart. One difference I have noted is in the way the character *tu* (picture) is written. Huizong wrote the small square 'mouth' radical (*kou*) within the larger one as a square, whereas Zhangzong wrote it as a small triangle. The *tu* characters in the title-slips to these two paintings illustrate this difference.[34] There are other examples.[35]

3b The 'Guangrendian' seal

We return to the *Admonitions* scroll, and the seal mentioned above reading 'Guangrendian' (Palace of Widespread Humanity; seal 15.1). Now we know the building itself was in Shangjing (the Jin 'upper capital'),[36] and we have records of some of the activities held in it during Zhangzong's reign,[37] but is there any way of authenticating this seal? It also appears on two extant works of calligraphy: Wu Cailuan's *Tang Rhymes* (seal 15.2), and *Mid-Autumn* (seal 15.3) attributed to Wang Xianzhi. What could be telling here is a comparison of the collectors' seals on all three scrolls.

I reckon the Xuanhe and Shaoxing seals (both full and linked) on all three scrolls are forgeries, so I suspect the 'Guangrendian' seals are too. We can determine that the 'Guangrendian' seal on the Zhang Zeduan attribution *Spring Mountains (Chunshan tu)* in the Taipei Palace Museum, which I have seen and know to be similar to the one on the *Admonitions*, is fake (seal 15.4), simply because *Spring Mountains* is a Ming (seventeenth-century) forgery. So until further evidence appears, I think we can take it that the one on the *Admonitions* is also a fake.

With the exception of this seal, there do not appear to be any other seals on the *Admonitions* painting itself that are linked to the Jin court or to Zhangzong. According to the *History of the Jin (Jin shi)*, the Guangrendian was built to the south-east of the Liang Palace (Liangdian) in the second year of Huangtong (1142 CE),[38] which would have been in the lifetime of Song Gaozong's empress, Wu (1115–1197). Even if we had thought the seal genuine, this would have raised a few doubts on our part as we would have had to wonder whether the scroll could really have made its way from the Jin to the Southern Song and back again to Zhangzong in such a short space of time.

We may now draw the following conclusion. If, as I have argued, the Xuanhe and Shaoxing seals on the *Admonitions* scroll are fake, then only the 'Ruisi Dongge' seal remains as a credible seal of Huizong, and we may therefore suppose that the Jin pillaged the scroll during the 'Jingkang crisis' of 1126–1127. Unfortunately, this still leaves us without a satisfactory explanation for the seal of Song Gaozong's empress, Wu.

3c The 'Qun yu zhong mi' seal

We come now to the seal reading 'Qun yu zhong mi' ('secreted among collected jades'; seal 16.1) on the rear border-panel, which is widely accepted as being one of Jin Zhangzong's set of seven Mingchang imperial seals. Its usual placement may be determined by looking at two scrolls impressed with the full set – Huizong's *Court Ladies Preparing Newly Woven Silk* in Boston, and Zhao Gan's *Early Snow along the River* in Taipei.[39] The mounting and placement of the seven seals are consistent in both. The 'Qun yu zhong mi' seal impression on the *Admonitions* scroll is basically consistent with the same seal on them also (seals 16.3, 16.2).[40] Another example of this seal is on the album *Tangren shieryue pengyou xiangwen shu (Calligraphy by the Tang dynasty 'Friends of the Twelve Months')* in the Taipei Palace Museum (seal 16.4). Note how the 'sign' radical (*shi*) of the character *mi* (in the lower left quadrant) has just one horizontal stroke at the top in each case.

In addition, we may say that the application of the set of seven Mingchang imperial seals is consistent on these three scrolls, *Court Ladies, Early Snow* and the calligraphy. Even though the calligraphic works by the Friends of the Twelve Months are mounted as album leaves, and are missing the first, second and fifth months, the placement of four of the Mingchang seals – 'Yufu baohui' (Treasured painting of the imperial palace); 'Neidian zhenwan' (Precious trinket of the inner palace); 'Qun yu zhong mi'; and 'Mingchang yulan' (Mingchang imperial viewing [seal]) – is consistent with the other examples, and as it should be. Something else that tallies is that all the right halves (*qun yu*) of these 'Qun yu zhong mi' bridging seals lie over a tortoiseshell-patterned silk panel.

We should also note that in two further examples, Huaisu's *Autobiography Scroll (Zixu tie)* in Taipei (seal 16.5) and Wang Xizhi's *Yuanhuan tie* (seal 16.6), the *shi* radical of the *mi* character has not one but two horizontal strokes, indicating that these two impressions are from another copy of the seal.

The standard placement of the seal is thought to be that on Zhao Gan's *Early Snow* and *Court Ladies Preparing Newly Woven Silk*, where it is impressed as a bridging seal on the rear border-panel in the middle of the scroll. On the *Admonitions*, however, it is at the top. This slightly different placement is also seen on the *Autobiography Scroll*, where it also appears toward the top of the scroll (but on the front border-panel). Its position seems to have varied, therefore, since on Wang Xizhi's *Yuanhuan tie*, it appears once again as a bridging seal on the rear border-panel in the middle. How do we explain this, and determine which of these is genuine? The large 'Mingchang yulan' seal provides a parallel here, since its use obviously varied too: the version of this seal impressed on *Yuanhuan tie* is clearly not the one impressed on the Zhao Gan and other scrolls. The simple explanation for 'Qun yu zhong mi' would seem to be that there were two seals in use, one with one horizontal stroke in the *shi* radical of the character *mi*, the other with two. This use of two variant copies of the same seal is not so uncommon: a third case is the use of two different 'Shiqu baoji' (Precious cabinet of the stony gully) seals on scrolls in the Qianlong imperial collection.

4 The *Admonitions* Scroll and the 'Admonitions' Transcription

Before we consider the authenticity of this unusually positioned 'Qun yu zhong mi' seal any further, we must first decide whether it relates to the painting itself or to Zhangzong's calligraphic transcription of the 'Admonitions' text in the colophon section, or whether it was imported into the scroll from an unrelated artwork. If we look at the seals on the painting and the transcription, we find that with the exception of Xiang Yuanbian's, collectors' seals are found on *either* the painting *or* the transcription, but not both. There are only three seals on Zhangzong's transcription: one, 'Zhang Liu', of a well-known late seventeenth-century scroll mounter; and two of the early Ming collector An Guo (1418–1534), 'Daming An Guo jianding zhenji' (Genuine traces authenticated by An Guo in the Great Ming), and 'Daming Xishan Guipo An Guo Mintai shi shuhua yin' (Seal on the calligraphy and painting of Master An Guo, [*zi*] Mintai, [*hao*] Guipo, of Xishan in the Great Ming) (figs 6–7).[41]

Several points may be made: the seals Xiang Yuanbian liked using do not appear equitably on the two sections; there are no seals of the early Ming (1368–1644) collector An Guo on the painting itself; and while there are numerous seals of late Ming–early Qing (seventeenth-century) collectors on the painting itself, they do not reappear on the transcription. This must mean that the *Admonitions* painting and the transcription were separate objects before being mounted together in this scroll.

1.1 Hongwen zhi yin
2.6 × 2.6 cm
Admonitions scroll

1.2 Hongwen zhi yin
2.6 × 2.6 cm
Wang Xianzhi, *Mid-Autumn*

2.1 Zhenghe
2.7 × 1.6 cm
Admonitions scroll

2.2 Zhenghe
3 × 1.3 cm
(incomplete)
Sun Guoting, *Shupu*

2.3 Zhenghe
3 × 1.7 cm (incomplete)
Wang Xizhi,
Xingrang tie

2.4 Zhenghe
2.7 × 1.6 cm
Wang Xizhi,
*Ping'an Heru
Fengju tie*

2.5 Zhenghe
(impressed upside down)
2.7 × 1.6 cm
Wu Cailuan, *Tang Rhymes*

3.1 Yu shu
4.2 × 2.2 cm
Admonitions scroll

3.2 Yu shu
4.2 × 2.5 cm
Han Gan, *Pasturing
Horses*

3.3
Yu shu
4.4 × 2.3 cm
Wu Cailuan, *Tang Rhymes*

4.1
Xuan-he
4.3 × 1.9 cm
Admonitions scroll

4.2
Xuan-he
4 × 2 cm
Wang Xizhi,
Xingrang tie

4.3
Xuan-he
4.2 (incomplete) ×
2 cm Wang Xizhi,
Yuanhuan tie

4.4
Xuan-he
4.1 × 2.1 cm
(incomplete)
Sun Guoting, *Shupu*

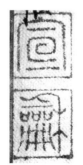

4.5
Xuan-he
4.3 × 1.9 cm
Wang Xizhi, *Ping'an
Heru Fengju tie*

4.6
Xuan-he
4.4 × 1.9 cm
Wu Cailuan, *Tang
Rhymes*

5.1
Xuanhe
3.5 × 1.9 cm
Admonitions scroll

5.2
Xuanhe
3.5 (incomplete) × 2 cm
Wang Xizhi,
Yuanhuan tie

5.3
Xuanhe
3.5 (incomplete) × 2 cm
Wang Xizhi,
Xingrang tie

5.4
Xuanhe
3.5 × 2 cm
Sun Guoting, *Shupu*

5.5
Xuanhe
3.5 × 1.9 cm
Wang Xizhi, *Ping'an Heru
Fengju tie*

6.1
Neifu tushu zhi yin
7 × 7 cm
Admonitions scroll

6.2
Neifu tushu zhi yin
7 × 7 cm
Yi Yuanji, *Monkey and Cat*

6.3
Neifu tushu zhi yin
7 × 7 cm
Wu Cailuan, *Tang Rhymes*

7.1
double dragon seal
3.2 × 3.2
Wang Xizhi, *Xingrang tie*

7.2
double dragon seal
3.3 × 3.2 cm
Wang Xizhi, *Yuanhuan tie*

7.3
double dragon seal
3.3 × 3.2 cm
Sun Guoting, *Shupu*

8.1
Zheng-he
h. 4.4 cm
Wang Xizhi,
Xingrang tie

8.2
Zheng-he
h. 4.4 cm
Wu Cailuan,
Tang Rhymes

9.1
Daguan
2.7 × 1.5 cm
Wang Xizhi, *Yuanhuan tie*

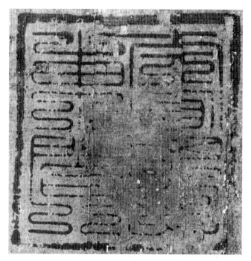

10.1
Ruisi Dongge
7.4 × 7.4 cm
Admonitions scroll

10.2
Ruisi Dongge
7.4 × 6.9 (incomplete) cm
Huang Jucai, *Blue Magpie*

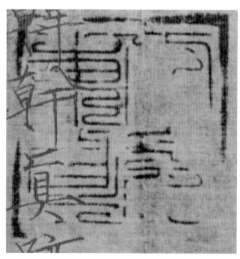

10.3
Ruisi Dongge
7.4 × 7.4 cm
Han Gan (attr.), *Pasturing Horses*

11.1
qian-trigram seal
2.8 × 2.8 cm
Admonitions scroll

11.2
qian-trigram seal
2.8 × 2.8 cm
Wu Cailuan, *Tang Rhymes*

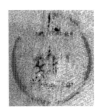

11.3
qian-trigram seal
2.8 × 2.8 cm
Wang Wei (attr.),
Fu Sheng

11.4
qian-trigram seal
2.8 × 2.8 cm
Dai Song (attr.),
Cow and Calf

12.1
Xishi cang
1.4 (incomplete) ×
1.4 cm
Dai Song (attr.),
Cow and Calf

12.2
Xishi cang
1.4 × 1.4 cm
Wang Xizhi,
*Kuaixue shiqing tie
(Clearing After
Sudden Snow)*

13.1
Shao-xing
3.6 × 1.7 cm
Admonitions
scroll

13.2
Shao-xing
Wang Wei (attr.),
Fu Sheng

13.3
Shao-xing
Anon. Song,
*Sailing to a
Mountain Market
(Jiangfan shanshi)*

13.4
Shao-xing
3.5 × 1.5 cm
Wang Xizhi,
*Kuaixue shiqing
tie*

13.5
Shao-xing
3.4 × 1.4
Xu Hao, *Shu Zhu
Juchuan gaoshen*

13.6
Shao-xing
2.1 × 1 cm
Huang Tingjian,
*Hanshan zi Pang
jushi shi*

13.7
Shao-xing
3.1 × 1.6 cm
Xue Shaopeng,
*Various Writings
(Za shu)*

13.8
Shao-xing
3 × 1.5 cm
Mi Fu, *Letter*

13.9
Shao-xing
3 × 1.6 cm
Admonitions scroll

13.10
Shao-xing
Wang Xianzhi,
Mid-Autumn

13.11
Shao-xing
3 × 1.5 cm
Wang Xizhi,
*Ping'an Heru
Fengju tie*

13.12
Shao-xing
3 × 1.6 cm
Wang Xizhi,
*Ping'an Heru
Fengju tie*

13.13
Shao-xing
3 × 1.6 cm
Huaisu, *Bitter
Sprouts*

13.14
Shao-xing
3 × 1.5 cm
Wu Cailuan, *Tang
Rhymes*

13.15
Shao-xing
3 × 1.5
Huaisu, *Bitter Sprouts*
(lower seal)

14.1
Xianzhitang yin
2.7 × 2.7 cm
Admonitions scroll

15.1
Guangrendian
3.8 × 2.2 cm
Admonitions scroll

15.2
Guangrendian
3.8 × 2.1 cm
Wu Cailuan, *Tang Rhymes*

15.3
Guangrendian
Wang Xianzhi, *Mid-Autumn*

15.4
Guangrendian
3.8 × 2 cm
Zhang Zeduan (attr.), *Spring Mountains* (17th century)

16.1
Qun yu zhong mi
6.3 × 4.6 cm
Admonitions scroll

16.2
Qun yu zhong mi
6.2 × 4.4 cm
Zhao Gan, *Early Snow along the River*

16.3
Qun yu zhong mi
6.3 × 4.7 cm
Huizong, *Ladies Preparing Newly Woven Silk*

16.4
Qun yu zhong mi
6.2 × 4.4 cm
Tang 'Friends of the Twelve Months' album

16.5
Qun yu zhong mi
6.2 × 4.7 cm
Huaisu, *Autobiography*

16.6
Qun yu zhong mi
6.2 × 4.7 cm
Wang Xizhi, *Yuanhuan tie*

17.1
Juan series, no. 70,
half accession number,
Admonitions scroll

17.2
Juan series, no. 67,
half accession number on
Xie Yuan, *Peach Blossoms*

17.3
Juan series, no. 2,
half accession number on
Wang Wei (attr.), *Fu Sheng*

18
si yin ('half seal')
6.1 × (incomplete) cm
Fachang, *Scenes from Life*
(*Xiesheng juan*)

19
Zhang Liu
1.1 × 1.1 cm
*Calligraphy by Four Song
Masters* (Taipei Palace
Museum)

20.1
Daming Xishan Guipo
An Guo Mintai shi
shuhua yin
Zhao Mengfu, *A Person
Riding* (*Renqi tu*;
Beijing Palace Museum)

20.2
Daming An Guo
jianding zhenji
Zhao Mengfu, *A Person
Riding* (*Renqi tu*;
Beijing Palace Museum)

The extant scroll is, of course, a relic of numerous remountings and internal reconfigurations.[42] But according to An Qi (1683–1742), who owned the scroll in the first half of the eighteenth century, it was not until the intervention of Liang Qingbiao (1620–1691) that Jin Zhangzong's calligraphy became part of it. In *Moyuan huiguan lu* (preface dated 1742), An Qi writes:

> This painting was authenticated by Minister of State Liang [Qingbiao, when in his collection] … The passage on silk at the end, comprising eleven lines of the 'Admonitions' text beginning *Huan bu ke yi du, chong bu ke yi zhuan*, and written in 'slender-gold' script in characters about an inch high, must have been inserted there by him.[43]

If we check this against the historical record, we indeed find no evidence of any transcription by Jin Zhangzong associated with the scroll before this. Mi Fu's record in *Hua shi* is no help, of course, since he lived a century before Zhangzong. But the late Ming connoisseur Chen Jiru's (1558–1639) *Nigu lu* notes, 'I viewed the *Admonitions* scroll in Wumen [i.e. Suzhou]. It is said to be by Gu Kaizhi, but is in fact an early Song copy. The inscriptions [apparently referring to those on the painting] are written by Song Gaozong, not by Wang Xianzhi.'[44] Then, Zhu Yizun's (1629–1709) book of his colophons, *Pushuting shuhua ba (Colophons to Calligraphy and Painting of the Pavilion of Sunning Books)*, merely states: 'In the spring of Kangxi *renzi* [corresponding to 1672 CE], I viewed the *Admonitions* at the house of Mr Wang of Jiangdu.'[45] Bian Yongyu's (1645–1712) *Shigutang shuhua huikao (Studies in Calligraphy and Painting of the Hall of Investigating Antiquity*; preface dated 1682) also records just the painting and no passage of calligraphy after it.[46]

Prior to the twentieth century, this transcription was always attributed to Song Huizong and not Jin Zhangzong. So, after the calligraphy and painting were mounted together by Liang Qingbiao (presumably between 1682 and his death in 1691), the written records begin to note this. First, Wu Sheng, in his *Daguan lu (Record of Great Views*; preface dated 1712): 'Song Youling [i.e. Huizong] transcribed some words from the "Admonitions" text on silk, in all eleven lines.'[47] Then, the Qianlong imperial catalogue *Shiqu baoji chubian* (1745–1747) stated: 'The final section of the scroll, on plain paper [*sic!*, it is on silk], comprises a section of Song Huizong's transcription of the "Admonitions" text totalling seventy-six characters of standard script in eleven rows.'[48] In Hu Jing's (1769–1845) *Xiqing zhaji*, we find the same record repeated.[49] The first to ascribe this transcription to Jin Zhang-

zong were, of course, the Japanese scholars Yashiro Sachio and Toyama Gunji in the twentieth century.[50]

What light can an examination of the extant scroll itself throw on An Qi's claim that Liang Qingbiao inserted 'the inscription in "slender-gold" script' (i.e. Jin Zhangzong's transcription of the 'Admonitions' text)? We note first that on the middle border-panel (below and to the left of Qianlong's orchid painting) are two seals, 'Zhang Liu' (*relievo*, old-seal script) and 'Huangmei ceng guan' ('viewed by Huangmei' [?]), one above the other (fig. 5). Another seal of Zhang Liu appears on Zhangzong's transcription (*intaglio*, small seal script; fig. 6; cf. seal 19), as noted. It seems possible that it was Liang Qingbiao who engaged Zhang Liu, the well-known Yangzhou painter, mounter, authenticator and dealer in Song painting, to mount the painting and calligraphy together in a single scroll.[51]

So, was An Qi right about Liang Qingbiao's remounting of the scroll? The bridging seals at the head of the transcription comprise (in descending order) one of Qianlong, 'Neifu zhencang' (Treasure of the inner-palace collection), and three of Xiang Yuanbian: 'Molinzi' (Master of Ink Forest); 'Molin shanren' (Ink Forest Mountain Man); and 'Zisun shichang' (sons and grandsons prospering for generations) (fig. 5). Bridging the transcription and the end border-panel in the middle, there is one seal of Liang Qingbiao, 'Yexi yuyin' (Fisher-recluse of Ye stream; fig. 7). The difficulty here is how to explain the three seals of Xiang Yuanbian at the beginning, when Xiang lived a century before Liang Qingbiao. Could An Qi, who owned the scroll, simply not have noticed these three seals? Or, were the left halves of the three added later? (The latter seems more likely: 'Molinzi' is deliberately blurry, while 'Molin shanren' differs from other examples. They all appear to have been re-stamped, which is suspicious.) Even if An Qi did suffer a momentary lapse of concentration, and the Xiang Yuanbian seals are genuine, this still proves that the painting and the transcription were two separate objects prior to Xiang Yuanbian's owning the scroll.

Physical evidence from Zhangzong's calligraphy shows clearly that the calligraphy and painting portions in this handscroll originally were unrelated. The calligraphy, originally mounted in a taller scroll, was cut up and reassembled in the current arrangement. Close examination reveals a horizontal cut mark below the first character in the second line (*ke*), the second character in the third line (*ji*), the third character in the fourth line (*you*), the fourth character in the fifth line (*yi*), the fifth character in the sixth line (*zi*), the seventh character in the seventh line (*zhi*), the first character in the tenth line (*suo*), the second character in the eleventh line (*xian*), and the third character in the twelfth line (*gao*) (fig. 9). This odd 'saw-tooth' pattern of cuts across the silk indicates that each full line of the original scroll contained eight characters (with the exception of one that had nine, due to the slightly smaller size of the characters). In order to reduce the height of the inscription to that of the painting, the calligraphy was cut up and arranged into columns seven characters in height (except for one that has eight). In other words, the height of the calligraphy scroll was formerly greater than that of the painting. This technique of cutting up calligraphic inscriptions to fit smaller formats is not unusual, and was commonly used, for instance, to reduce large ink-rubbings to small album leaves. We would have to conclude, therefore, that if Zhangzong's 'Admonitions' text was originally done for this painting, its height would have matched – and that it would not have been cut to fit.

The horizontal cut marks allow us to reconstruct the original form of the inscription (fig. 10), but the vertical cut marks also attest to the care that went into preserving the integrity of the characters. Look, for example, at the lower right diagonal stroke in the fifth character of the third line (*zhi*), the lower right diagonal stroke in the sixth character of the fourth line (*mei*), the lower left diagonal stroke in the third character of the fifth line (*pian*), the right end of the horizontal stroke in the fifth character of the sixth line (*zi*), and the lower right diagonal stroke in the second character in the twelfth line (*gan*). In each case there is a kink in the vertical cut, where the mounter cut around the stroke so as not to slice the character apart.

What about the 'signature' of Gu Kaizhi at the end of the painting (fig. 3)? Unfortunately, written records prior to the sixteenth century are hardly effusive. We have Mi Fu's attribution, and the *Xuanhe huapu*'s mention of just the painting's title under the heading 'Gu Kaizhi', but we would certainly not expect an ancient painting such as this to bear an artist's signature. Indeed, scholars have observed that the so-called signature, 'painted by Gu Kaizhi', is a later forgery.[52] We may note that after Dong Qichang (1555–1636) viewed the scroll at the house of Xiang Yuanbian in about 1582, he did not refer to any signature: 'Some years ago, I saw a hand-scroll painting by a Jin artist, which was said to be by Hutou ['Dragon-head', referring to Gu Kaizhi] …'[53] He seems not to have seen a 'signature'. In fact, the first person to record these four-characters was Zhang Chou (1577–1643), in his *Qinghe shuhua fang* (preface dated 1616),[54] but he did not record the presence of any 'Admonitions' text transcription accompanying the painting. It is only at this point, in the late Ming–early Qing period, that records such as these begin to provide relatively complete descriptions of the scroll's contents.

It is worth noting that not long before this time, at the end of the Jiajing reign (1522–1566) in 1565, the Suzhou connoisseur Wen Jia (1501–1583) took part in inventorying the disgraced minister Yan Song's (1480–1565) collection, and noted the contents in his *Qianshantang shuhua ji* of 1568. In the 'Song dynasty' entry in the 'Calligraphy' section of this title, Wen Jia recorded a work entitled *Huizong shu Nüshi zhen* ('"Admonitions of the Instructress to the Court Ladies" transcribed by Song Huizong', with a note: 'in "slender-gold" script on silk').[55] Under the 'Jin dynasty' in the 'Painting' section, we find a work entitled *Jinren hua Zhang Maoxian Nüshi zhen tu* ('a picture of Zhang Maoxian's [Hua] "Admonitions of the Instructress to the Court Ladies" by a Jìn artist').[56] Obviously, the painting and the transcription were then separate objects. Further, under 'Song Huizong' in the more detailed inventory of property confiscated from Yan Song in *Tianshui Bingshan lu*, we find an entry reading: 'two scrolls of passages of calligraphy from the "Admonitions of the Instructress to the Court Ladies"' (*Nüshi zhen deng tie liangzhou*).[57] The existence of two scrolls explains that Song Huizong – which is to say Jin Zhangzong – had in fact transcribed the entire 'Admonitions' text. Only the final part of this transcription is extant today.

5 Yuan and Ming collections

Two sources, Wen Jia's *Qianshantang shuhua ji*, and *Tianshan Bingshan lu*, tell us that Yan Song had owned the *Admonitions* painting, and that the painting and transcription were separate objects. If this is true, then the 'Guangrendian' seal cannot prove whether or not Zhangzong owned the *Admonitions* painting. Also, we still haven't ruled out the possibility that Zhangzong's 'Qun yu zhong mi' seal on the rear border-panel came from another scroll.

We know that the *Admonitions* scroll was owned by the Southern Song statesman Jia Sidao (1213–1275) from his three seals, 'Yue sheng', a double-gourd-shaped seal at the end of the painting below the signature (fig. 3); 'Chang' (at the bottom, bridging the end-panels in fig. 4); and 'Qiuhuo tushu' (to the left of the last). These three are identical to comparable examples on two calligraphic works in the Taipei Palace Museum, Huang Tingjian's (1045–1105) *Songfengge shi (Pine-wind Tower Poem)*; and *Song sijia zhenji (Genuine Traces by Four Song Masters)*.

The gap between the lifetimes of Jin Zhangzong and Jia Sidao make it possible that the scroll moved from north China (under Jurchen or, after 1234, Mongol rule) to south China (under Han-Chinese rule) in the mid-thirteenth century.[58]

Even if both Huizong's 'Neifu tushu zhi yin' and Zhang-zong's 'Qun yu zhong mi' seals (on the rear border-panel) are genuine, the question still remains as to whether they 'belong' to the painting owned by Huizong or to the transcription by Zhangzong. An Qi opined that the rear border-panel was of 'Song dynasty silk brocade',[59] and considered the rear border-panel of the Huaisu *Autobiography Scroll* to be, similarly, of a '[stitched] gold phoenix-patterned Song dynasty silk brocade'.[60] The 'Qun yu zhong mi' seals were placed where we would not expect them on the *Admonitions* and the *Autobiography Scroll*. Besides this, the seals bridging the end of the *Admonitions* painting and the border-panel following it post-date 'Xiang Yuanbian'. Therefore, we cannot but conclude that originally, the painting and the text had to have been two separate objects, and hence that the latter part of this scroll was inserted in remounting. One wonders whether the rear brocade border-panel was not also brought in from some other scroll.

The earliest bridging seals on the current mounting would seem to be two over the seam of the front border-panel and the beginning of the painting, 'Sanhuai zhi yi' (Descendants of the three scholar trees, i.e. sons of the Wang family) in the middle; and 'Siwuxietang' (Hall of 'No evil thoughts') at the bottom (fig. 1). (The next in date are those of Xiang Yuanbian.)

In the fourteenth century, a 'Sanhuai zhi yi' seal belonged to a famous Daoist master (*daoshi*) called Wang Shouyan (1273–1353).[61] But during the Ming, the statesman Wang Ao (1450–1524) had the same seal, which means that it could have been impressed as late as the fifteenth or sixteenth century. The owner or owners of the 'Siwuxietang' seal are still unidentified. The phrase *siwuxie* (literally, thoughts without evil) is a quote from the *Book of Odes*.[62] The term *xianzhi* ('worthy ambition') in the name of Empress Wu's 'Xianzhi Hall' also came from the *Odes* (the 'Odes of Mao'), which suggests the 'Siwuxietang' seal could be another one of hers, although this is hardly conclusive evidence.

We have not yet resolved the question of how the *Admonitions* scroll could have passed from the Song to the Jin (or Zhangzong's) imperial collection in such a short period of time during the twelfth century. We have taken the 'Ruisi Dongge' seals to be genuine, and the Xuanhe and Shaoxing seals to be fake, and we have argued that the scroll passed directly from Huizong's collection into the Jin imperial collection, following the capture of the Northern Song capital Bianliang (modern Kaifeng) in 1126. The problem is still how to explain the 'Xianzhitang yin' seal (seal 14.1) of the Southern Song empress Wu?

The first to claim that this was a seal of the empress Wu was Feng Fang (1492–1563?) in the Ming. In 1549, Feng wrote a prose-poem entitled 'Zhenshangzhai fu' (Prose-poem of the Studio of True Appreciation) for the collector-connoisseur Hua Xia (*c.*1465–1566), in which he mentions some old seals belonging to Hua Xia, including one that read 'Sanhuai zhi yi' in *relievo*, and two he said were of Gaozong's empress Wu, 'Xianzhitang yin' in *intaglio* ('in silken lines'), and 'Xianzhi zhuren'.[63] If Hua Xia possessed the 'Sanhuai zhi yi' and 'Xianzhitang yin' seals, could *he* not have impressed them on the *Admonitions* scroll?[64] The only thing is that there are no collector's seals of Hua Xia on the *Admonitions* scroll today, so we can only observe at this point that the actual 'Xianzhitang yin' and 'Sanhuai zhi yi' seals were still in circulation in the sixteenth century.

The *Admonitions* also has an unusual monogram seal (*huaya*), which resembles the running-cursive form of the character *yong* (harmony) (fig. 4, in the middle, bridging the end-panels). It also appears on the scroll of *Three Passages of Calligraphy*. Its owner(s) is yet to be identified. Finally, at the head of the *Admonitions* painting itself, there is a 'Phags-pa-script seal, 'Ali' (below the trigram seal, fig. 1), which has been identified as the name of a Uighur collector active in the late thirteenth century.[65] One might think that the configuration of Song, Jin and Yuan collectors' seals on the *Admonitions*, *Three Passages*, *Mid-Autumn* and Wu Cailuan's *Rhymes*, is unnaturally repetitive,[66] but whereas the Xuanhe and Shaoxing seals probably are fake, the Yuan seals seem genuine. Interestingly, in the Yuan, all four scrolls were owned by the Uighur 'Ali'.

6 The 'Half' Inventory Number, Juan zi qishi hao

In the top left corner of the front border-panel of the *Admonitions* is inscribed half of an accession or inventory number, which reads 'Juan zi qishi hao' ('*Juan* series, no. 70') (fig. 1, seal 17.1). (The left half is on the painting; the right half would presumably have been entered on a ledger.) What does it signify? Several other paintings have numbers within the same series or classification. The Wang Wei (699–759) attribution *Fu Sheng Teaching the Classic* (*Fu Sheng jiao jing tu*) in Osaka Municipal Museum of Art has one that reads 'Juan zi er hao' ('*Juan* series, no. 2') (seal 17.3). The Song painter Xie Yuan's *Peach Blossoms* (*Zheji bitao tujuan*) in a private collection in Taipei has one that reads 'Juan zi liushiqi hao' (*Juan* series, no. 67) (seal 17.2). And, in the Palace Museum in Peking is a painting entitled *Song Zhao Chang bi Jiadie tujuan* ('a handscroll painting, "Butterflies", painted by Zhao Chang [*c*. 960–after 1016] of the Song dynasty'), which is recorded in *Shiqu baoji chubian* as having the accession mark 'Juan zi shi hao' (*Juan* series, no. 10).[67]

The two (half) accession numbers on the *Admonitions* and Xie Yuan's *Peach Blossoms* are written in an identical hand, while, though damaged, the traces of the number on the front border-panel of the Wang Wei *Fu Sheng* are just clear enough for this inscription to be identified with the same hand. This would confirm their having once been part of a series.

The scroll of Wang Wei's *Fu Sheng*, which is recorded in the *Xuanhe huapu*[68] as well as in *Zhongxingguange chucang tuhua ji* (*Record of Paintings in the Collection of the Zhongxing Academy*) (*c*. 1095–1124),[69] is generally agreed to be the most typical extant example of Song Gaozong's Shaoxing imperial scroll mounting. On the front brocade border-panel we still see his small standard-script title, 'Wang Wei xie Ji'nan Fu Sheng' (Wang Wei's painting of Fu Sheng from Ji'nan), in one line in the upper left corner; his round *relievo* qian-trigram seal impressed at the head of the painting; and the *relievo* 'Shao-xing' linked seal in the lower left corner of the painting itself. With the exception of the presence of one seal, 'Xishi cang', this tallies with Zhou Mi's description of Gao-zong's mounting in his *Qidong yeyu*, discussed above.

Based on the dates of these scrolls, the 'half' accession numbers – reading 'X zi X hao' (X-series, X number) – were first used either in or before Gaozong's reign. Now, the most commonly used serial 'numbering' system in Gaozong's time was the 'thousand-character system' (*Qianwen bianhao*; a series of one thousand unique characters). Zhou Mi describes how after authentication, palace scrolls 'were given a number using the thousand-character system, as well as an authentica-tion seal' before imperial inspection and remounting.[70] Else-where in Zhou Mi's writings, he reminisces about being taken on an inspection tour of the Song Directorate of the Palace Library (Mishusheng) in the spring of 1275. 'The scrolls', he writes, 'were divided among more than fifty vermilion lacquer chests, which were all full of works of calligraphy and painting. On that day, I viewed only the scrolls kept in chests 'qiu', 'shou', 'dong', and 'cang'.[71] The series *qiu* (autumn), *shou* (receive), *dong* (winter) and *cang* (store) come from the 'thousand-character numbering system', and confirm its use there. Zhou Mi goes on to note that although 'he saw over one hundred and sixty scrolls [in these four chests], not ten of them were excellent'. His comments are evidence of how many scrolls were stored in each chest, that is, how many numbers there were per category, or series, of the numbering system (160+ ÷ 4 = 40+). Unfortunately, the character *juan*, which happens to mean 'handscroll', does not appear in this system, which convinces me that 'half' accession numbers

containing the series *juan* do not refer to the Southern Song imperial collection inventory.

Something else that needs an explanation is another inventory number, this time in full not half, in the corner at the end of the scroll of Xie Yuan's *Peach Blossoms*. It reads, 'Wen zi qi hao' (*Wen* series, no. 7). A similar example is in the lower right corner of the first leaf of the album of *Sixteen Arhats* attributed to the Tang painter Lu Lengjia (act. *c*. 730–760) in the Peking Palace Museum: '[?] zi yi hao' ([?] series, no. 1). In the 'Huachanshi' (Painting Chan Hall) sec-tion of Qianlong's *Shiqu baoji chubian*, the lower left edge of Juran's *Jiangshan wanxing* (*Evening Elation Amid Rivers and Mountains*) is said to have had the number: 'Wen zi ershiwu hao' (*Wen* series, no. 25).[72] The previous two examples, *Peach Blossoms* and the *Sixteen Arhats*, have not half, but whole accession numbers. They also both have a seal over their char-acters, reading 'Libu pingyan shuhua guanfang' (Board of Rites bonded warehouse for accredited works of calligraphy and painting), as well as having the so-called 'si yin' half-seal (of the early Ming imperial collection). The Juran landscape does not have the 'Libu pingyan shuhua guanfang' seal, but it does have a half-seal reading '… dusheng shuhua zhi yin' (Seal of calligraphy and painting of the Ministry/Department of …) (and there is another illegible half-seal below it). The usual explanation that these are official Ming accession or inventory numbers is therefore probably correct.

In the Yuan palace collections there were well over a thousand scrolls, and it is logical they too would have had accession numbers. An entry in 'Annals of the Directorate of the Imperial Library' (*Mishujian zhi*) in the *Yuan shi*, dated the fifth month of the second year of Zhizheng (1354 CE), goes as follows:

> The collection of the Directorate comprises all items inherited from the Jin and Song, as well as objects offered to the throne and/or purchased. There is a large number of ancient records and fine paintings, exclusively there for the emperor to view or read. From the Zhiyuan period (1264–1294) to now, there has been no assigned storage area, and the subject categories were rather basic, with the result that everything is chaotic. If both the historical books and works of calligraphy and paint-ing are not classified into the categories 'Classics, His-tory, Philosophy and Collectanea' (*jing shi zi ji*), but are arbitrarily classified, and if objects are not divided into categories and properly numbered …, how can they be located and presented to the emperor when required?[73]

The orderly way for the scrolls to be 'divided into categories and properly numbered' would have been to use the 'thousand-character essay' numbering system. It seems, however, that extant works formerly in the Yuan imperial collection – such as the *Scroll of the Thirteen Emperors (Lidai diwang tujuan)* by Yan Liben (*c.* 600–674); *Longlin kaiyun* by Wu Cailuan; *Essay on Calligraphy (Shupu)* by Sun Guoting; *Scroll for Zhang Datong (Zeng Zhang Datong juan)* by Huang Tingjian; *Lian Po Lin Xiangru zhuan* by Huang Tingjian; *Nymph of the Luo River (Luoshen fu)* attributed to Gu Kaizhi; and *Portraits of Song Emperors (Song zhudi yurong)* – have since been remounted so many times that any class marks have been lost.

We identified above three artworks with inventory numbers beginning '*juan* series… ' written by the same hand. If they are not Song, could they be Jin or Yuan imperial serial numbers? We know that Jin Zhangzong owned some 'five hundred and fifty scrolls', but we do not know what kind of serial numbers he used. By coincidence, the four scrolls with the character *juan* on them (if we now include Zhao Chang's *Butterflies*) are all mounted as *juan*, handscrolls. This may mean that *juan* was in fact a formal category into which these scrolls were placed. Although this may have been a Yuan category, there are no surviving accession numbers extant that would enable us either to confirm or deny that it was the system used for the Yuan imperial collection. Obviously, Liang Qingbiao also owned the four scrolls in question in the late seventeenth century, but, again, although there are numerous other examples of scrolls formerly in his collection extant today, no one has yet been able to suggest whether he used this taxonomy.

My own feeling is that these probably are court designations of certain similar or collective items. For instance, after the Southern Song minister Jia Sidao was disgraced and cashiered, the Southern Song government listed all his chattels, and his painting and calligraphy scrolls were all impressed with a seal reading 'Taizhou fangwu didang kui yin' (Seal of the Taizhou Service Depository). Yuan palace inventory numbers are little understood, as has been indicated, but, as pre-Yuan artworks, it is possible the inscriptions on them are such marks.[74] We know that the difficulty of recording half accession numbers was sufficient to make the eldest Yuan princess (Princess Dazhang, Xiangge Laji; *c.* 1283–1331) dispense with this procedure for her own collection. From the Ming, there are plenty of extant examples of the use of the thousand-character numbering system, for instance by collectors like Xiang Yuanbian, but they did not use 'half' accession numbers. However, there are examples of half accession numbers figured according to this system by the Ming 'Libu pingyan shuhua guanfang', so cases of an individual's property having

been confiscated and inventoried by the Ming government become moot here.

Two important early Ming cases are those of Hu Weiyong (?–1380) and Lan Yu (?–1393). It is quite likely, for instance, that the Ming official 'si yin' half-seal was impressed on Hu Weiyong's collection of scrolls after confiscation.[75] It is a pity we do not know the full extent of his collection: I know of only two of his seals, 'Haoliang Hu shi' and 'Xiangfu tushu', on just one painting, *Emperor Minghuang's Flight to Shu (Minghuang xin Shu tu)* in the Taipei Palace Museum. While there are many masterworks extant today that do have the 'si yin' half-seal on them, it is odd that only these two seals of Hu Weiyong survive.

Another well-known case is that of Yan Song. An account of the fate of his collection is found in Shen Defu's (1578–1642) *Wanli ye huo bian*, under the title, 'Confiscation of antiquities':

When Mr Yan was cashiered [late in Jiajing, 1522–1566], other art aficionados never got to see his property. His collection of calligraphy and painting was kept in the Inner Palace. In the first year of Emperor Muzong's reign [1567 CE], the state was suddenly unable to pay the army officers' annual salaries. Every last handscroll and hanging scroll of Yan's was valued – but for not more than a few strings of cash, even for famous Tang and Song works. Now the imperial princes of the blood (Prince of Cheng, surnamed Zhu, and his brothers) obtained them for a good price. The eldest brother Xizhong got the most, and impressed them with a seal of the Baoshantang [Hall of Treasuring the Good]. When he later became seriously ill, he gifted his collection to the chief minister Zhang Juzheng [1525–1582]. Zhang was ennobled as the Prince of Dingxiang, but was brought down not long later. Since he too was cashiered, the collection returned to the Ming government. Within a few years, corrupt eunuchs in charge of the official collections began stealing and selling off their contents. All of a sudden art lovers like Prefect Han Jingtang [Han Shineng, act. 1567–1619] and Grand Scholar Xiang Molin [Xiang Yuanbian] were competing to buy these pieces. They accumulated only the finest things, but the prices were still modest, not like today, when prices have increased tenfold. Objects that had been in Mr Yan's collection had been impressed with the half-seal of the Yuanzhou Prefecture Government Office (Yuanzhoufu jingli si); those that had been in Master Zhang's had a half-seal of the Xingzhou Prefecture Government Office (Xingzhoufu jingli si) impressed on them. These two prefectural seals used during the making of property records and registration numbers are still visible on the scrolls at the head of the work of painting or calligraphy. In the space of about two decades, these objects were twice officially confiscated, transferred to the imperial palace, and then sold off to collectors outside the palace. Whenever I am viewing works of calligraphy and painting in a grand household, I often come across these scrolls. Just recently, swindlers have been faking the half-seals to trick anyone who wants to hear about them. People from Suzhou and Huizhou are turning out fakes by the hundred. You don't want to know![76]

One would think that even a few characters would survive from these 'property records and registration numbers' on extant artworks, but to date I have not come across either of the half-seals, 'Yangzhoufu jingli siyin' or 'Xingzhoufu jingli siyin'. It could be that, like the early Ming 'Dianli jicha siyin' seal, one would see only the last two characters, *si yin* at the left side of the seal (the rest to the right having been impressed in the ledger). Perhaps when we come across a 'si yin' part seal, we too readily take it for the early Ming 'si yin' half-seal (seal 18), and do not appreciate that it could be part of one of these two late Ming official seals.

The passage quoted above suggests a scenario in which the *Admonitions* scroll could have been acquired by Xiang Yuanbian following the government's confiscation of Yan Song's property. The inventory of property confiscated from

Yan Song recorded in the *Tianshui Bingshan lu* totalled '3,201 handscrolls, hanging scrolls and albums containing famous works of calligraphy and painting from ancient to modern',[77] which indicates that his possessions were classified by format into 'handscrolls, hanging scrolls, and albums' (*juan, zhou, ce*). Of the four scrolls with '*juan* ...' inventory numbers identified above, two – the *Admonitions* and *Fu Sheng Teaching the Classic* attributed to Wang Wei – are recorded as having belonged to Yan Song.[78] But, as *Tianshui Bingshan lu* may not record the whole of Yan Song's collection, we cannot confirm that the other two – the Xie Yuan and Zhao Chang – were as well. We may like to suppose that the half accession numbers on the *Admonitions* and *Fu Sheng* were inscribed after this particular incident, but clearly other cases of mighty officials being cashiered, such as that of Zhang Juzheng, are also possible.

Conclusion

The aim of this paper has been to discuss the 'frame' around the *Admonitions* painting, rather than the painting itself – and I have not commented here on the authenticity or the date of the painting. Although there are still many things we do not understand about the *Admonitions* scroll, I do believe that the more we study this long-treasured artefact, the better we will come to know it.

Translated by Shane McCausland

NOTES

1   *LDMHJ* (*HSCS* 1955, vol. I, *juan* 3, p. 99; tr. Acker 1954, p. 232).
2   Tang Gaozong (r. 650–683) mentions the officials and collection of the Hongwenguan in his inscription in the Song (960–1279) rubbing version of Wang Xizhi's (303–361) *Letters of the Seventeenth (Shiqi tie)*. Zhou Mi (1232–1298) records a seal reading 'Hong wen guan' on Sun Guoting's (646–691) *Caoshu Qianwen (Thousand-character Essay in Cursive Script)*; see Zhou Mi, *ZYTZC* (*MSCS* 1975, vol. XII, pt. 3, sect. 3, p. 1834).
3   See Xu Bangda, 'Wang Xianzhi Zhongqiutie' (Wang Xianzhi's *Mid-Autumn*) (Xu Bangda 1984, pp. 12–14).
4   Huang Weizhong 1994.
5   The term 'linked seals' denotes a seal comprising two characters, each enclosed within its own boundary.
6   Mi Fu, *Hua shi* (*MSCS* 1975, vol. X, pt. 2, sect. 9, p. 4).
7   *XHHP* 1120 (*HSCS* 1955, vol. I, *juan* 1: 'Gu Kaizhi', p. 3).
8   See also Xu Bangda 1981.
9   *Yuanhuan tie* and *Shupu* are recorded in Huizong's calligraphy

catalogue, *Xuanhe shupu* (*XHSP*; *HSCS* 1955, vol. II, *juan* 15, p. 347 and *juan* 18, p. 403, respectively).
10   Another example of this seal may be found on *Buddha Preaching the Law (Rulai shuofa tu)* in the same museum. This painting was clearly in Huizong's collection from the whole and part seals on it (Li Yumin 1996).
11   *XHSP* (*HSCS* 1955, vol. II, *juan* 15, p. 345).
12   Mr Xu Bangda believes the Xuanhe seals are fake, the Shaoxing ones genuine, and that the pre-Northern Song inscriptions and records have been inserted from another source; see his 'Jin Wang Xizhi Fengju tie' (*Presenting Oranges* by Wang Xizhi of the Jin) in 1987, pp. 23–34.
13   Six of the eight are easily legible; a seventh has had a large seal belonging to the Qianlong emperor, 'Bazheng maonian zhi bao', impressed over it; the eighth at the very end of the painting is now very indistinct.
14   It is generally thought that the seal belongs to Huizong; see *Jin-Tang yilai shuhuajia jiancangjia kuanyin pu*, vol. I, p. 77; and

Songhua jinghua. For the view that it is Southern Song, see Kohara 1967, pt. 1, pp. 24–26.

15 Kohara 1967, pt. 1, pp. 24–26.

16 *Song shi, juan* 85 (*Zhi* 38: *Dili*) (1985, p. 2099).

17 See Wang Mingqing 1966, *juan* 3, p. 117.

18 Zhou Mi, *ZYTZC* (*MSCS* 1975, vol. XII, pt. 3, sect. 3, p. 200).

19 Zhou Mi, *QDYY, juan* 6 (*BJXSJG* 1977, ser. 13, pt. 4, p. 2115).

20 Ibid., pp. 2122–2123.

21 Zhou Mi, *YYGYL, juan xia* (*MSCS* 1975, vol. 6, pt. 2, sect. 2, p. 110). This is one of the few records of the 'Xishi cang' seal. See examples in seals 12.1–12.2.

22 Xu Bangda, 'Shi Huaisu Kusun tie' (On Huaisu's *Bitter Sprouts*, 1987, pp. 82–84). In the case of the *Bitter Sprouts* scroll, there was no need to impress two 'Shao-xing' linked seals close to each other on the same scroll: only the lower one is in the correct position (seal 13.15). We also find this lower seal on a letter by Mi Fu (seal 13.8), which pre-dates Gaozong's reign by not very long. If we had to choose between the two, we would have to take the lower one to be the more 'correct'.

23 *Song shi, juan* 243 (*Liezhuan* 2: *Houji, xia*: 'Wu Huanghuo zhuan') (1985, pp. 8646–8647).

24 See Wu Zhuo 1977.

25 *Song shi, juan* 465 (*Liezhuan* 224) (1985, p. 592).

26 *Song shi, juan* 23 (*Ji* 23: 'Qinzong') (1985, p. 436).

27 *Sanchao beimeng huibian*, pt. *yi*: 'Zhongzhi' 54, p. 226.

28 *Jin shi, juan* 126 (*Liezhuan* 64) (1970, p. 2731).

29 *Jin shi, juan* 64 (*Liezhuan* 2: *Houji, xia*: 'Yuanji') (1970, pp. 1527–1531).

30 Wu Zhuo 1977.

31 Zhou Mi, *GXZSXJ* (*xia*: 'Zhangzong xiao Huizong') (*BBCSJC* 1969, pp. 41ff).

32 See also Tao Jinsheng 1981, p. 93, n. 2, and pp. 106–108, n. 103.

33 In the spring of 1198, for instance, Zhangzong 'was greatly moved and turned pale' when shown a collection of jades and other arte-facts from the Southern Song and Xuanhe collections. 'An imperial concubine, Chenfei, tried to soothe him with the words: "Those who make things do not necessarily use what they make; those who use things do not necessarily make what they use. The southern emperors can only have made these things for Your Majesty's use."' In the winter of the same year, he came across a screen painting of Huizong's beloved 'Gen' mountain ['Gen' is one of the eight tri-grams from the classic *Book of Changes (Yi jing)*, and can sometimes take the form of a mountain]. A eunuch, Yu Wan, provided him with an explanation: Huizong had built a Gen mountain on this spot out of ornate rocks brought from the south-east, and that this profligacy had brought about the demise of the Northern Song regime. Zhangzong's predecessor had ordered a picture made of it as a warning not to repeat the mistake.' See *Da Jin guo zhi, juan* 19, (*BBCSJC* 1969, p. 5).

34 Xu Bangda 1981.

35 The Southern Tang (923–935) painter Zhao Gan's *Early Snow along the River (Jiangxing chuxue)* has a title-slip on the front border-panel by the Qianlong emperor (r. 1736–1795) that reads, *Zhao Gan Jiangxing chuxue tu*. According to An Qi's (*c.*1683–*c.*1744) *Moyuan huiguan lu* (1742) there was an imperial double-gourd-shaped seal and Jin Zhangzong's title in ink, reading *Zhao Gan Jiangxing chuxue tu* on the front yellow brocade border-panel. See An Qi, *MYHGL, juan* 3 (Wang Yunwu [ed.] 1970, pp. 128–129). The *tu* (picture) character in Qianlong's title evidently imitated the 'slender-gold' style of Jin Zhangzong because the mouth radical is written as a triangle. Zhou Fang's (780–804) *Barbarians Presenting Tribute (Manyi zhigong tu)* in the Taipei Palace Museum also has the triangle. Finally, through comparison with the calligraphy on these title-slips reckoned to be by Zhang-

zong, scholars now believe the title-slip reading *Xueji jiangxing tu Guo Zhongshu zhenji* to Guo Zhongshu's (*c.*910–977) *Sailing on a River After Snow (Xueji jiangxing tu)* to be by his hand too. See Ho, Wai-Kam *et al.* 1980, p. 97.

36 *Jin shi, juan* 24 (*Zhi* 5, *Dili shang*) (1970, p. 550).

37 E.g. an official parade in 1207; see *Jin shi, juan* 12 (*Benji* 12: 'Zhangzong' 4) (1970, pp. 279–280).

38 *Jin shi, juan* 24 (*Zhi* 5, *Dili shang*) (1970, p. 550).

39 After the Qianlong emperor removed the front border-panel from this scroll, the missing parts of the seal legends were reconstruc-tively written in red ink.

40 Professor Yashiro Sachio has said the two seals are different, but has given no further explanation; Toyama 1964, pp. 671–675.

41 Cf. Zhang Liu's seal with the one in seal 19, and An Guo's with those in seals 20.1–20.2.

42 Kohara 1967, pt. I, pp. 24–26.

43 An Qi, *MYHGL, juan* 3 (Wang Yunwu [ed.] 1970, pp. 128–129).

44 Chen Jiru, *Nigu lu, juan* 4 (*MSCS* 1975, vol. 5, pt. 1, sect. 10, p. 286).

45 Zhu Yizun, *Pushuting shuhua ba* (*MSCS* 1975, vol. 5, pt. 1, sect. 9, p. 166).

46 Bian Yongyu 1682 (*Huakao, juan* 8) (1958, p. 349).

47 Wu Sheng 1713 (1970, vol. 11, pp. 1, 1309).

48 *SQBJ chubian* 1971, p. 1047.

49 Hu Jing 1971 (1816), *juan* 3, p. 22.

50 *SDQJ* 1980, Song II, pp. 159–160.

51 On Zhang Liu, see Wu Qizhen 1971, *juan* 5, p. 607; *juan* 6, pp. 683–689. Wu viewed Song and Yuan paintings at Zhang's house in Yangzhou on the 28th day of the 7th month of 1675. On Zhang's relations with Liang Qingbiao, see Chen Yaolin 1988, pp. 56–57.

52 Kohara 1967.

53 Dong Qichang 1968, *juan* 4, p. 1954.

54 Zhang Chou 1616 (*zi ji*) (1975, pp. 35b–36a).

55 Wen Jia 1568, 'Huizong shu Nüshi zhen' (*MSCS* 1975, vol. 6, pt. 2, sect. 6, p. 43).

56 Ibid, p. 48.

57 *Tianshui Bingshan lu* (*CSJCXB* 1985, vol. 48, p. 481). These scrolls are referred to in the entry by the word *zhou*, but in the past, connoisseurs did not always differentiate between *zhou*, 'hanging scrolls', and *juan*, 'handscrolls', as we do today. E.g. Huaisu's *Autobiography Scroll*, which is indubitably a handscroll, is referred to as *Huaisu Zishu xu deng liangzhou* ('two *zhou* scrolls of Huaisu's *Autobiography Preface*').

58 Huaisu's *Autobiography Scroll*, for instance, also has both Zhang-zong's 'Qun yu zhong mi' and Jia Sidao's 'Qiuhuo tushu' seals.

59 An Qi, *MYHGL, juan* 3 (1970, p. 123).

60 An Qi, *MYHGL, juan* 3 (1970, p. 123).

61 See his colophon to the Yuan painter Li Shixing's (1283–1328) *River Country in Late Autumn (Jiangxiang qiuwan)* in the Taipei Palace Museum.

62 *Shijing*: 'Lu song, Jiong': (in James Legge's translation) 'In the Book of Poetry are three hundred pieces, but the design of them all may be embraced in one sentence: "Having no depraved thoughts".'

63 *SQBJ chubian* 1971, p. 611.

64 Interestingly, a 'Zhenshangzhai yin' seal (square, *intaglio*) also appears on the rear border-panel of *Three Passages of Calligraphy: Ping'an, Heru, Fengju*, as do 'Xianzhi zhuren' and 'Sanhuai zhi yi'. On the rear border-panel of Yan Zhenqing's (709–785) *Epitaph for My Nephew (Jizhi wengao)* we find a seal reading 'Zhenshangzhai' (rectangular, *relievo*), as well as 'Xianzhitang yin'. The second is in the lower left corner, which means it must pre-date the first. In the lower right and upper left corners of this border-panel is another bridging seal, 'Ruiwen tushu' (Auspicious design on calligraphy and

painting). This is the seal of Gaozong's favourite concubine Liu Niangzi, and indicates that Yan Zhenqing's *Epitaph* was indeed part of the Southern Song palace collection. The 'Zhenshangzhai yin' seal (square, *intaglio*) on *Three Passages* bridges the rear border-panel and colophon section, meaning that the scroll was obviously remounted by Hua Xia. It is certainly possible the 'Xianzhi zhuren' and 'Sanhuai zhi yi' seals above it were impressed by him.

65   Zhaona Situ 1998, pp. 87–90.

66   These are:
- *Admonitions*: *qian*-trigram, Guangrendian, Ali, Siwuxiezhai, yuanya, Sanhuai zhi yi;
- *Three Passages*: *qian*-trigram, Ali, Siwuxiezhai, yuanya, Sanhuai zhi yi, Xianzhi zhuren;
- *Mid-Autumn*: Guangrendian, Ali, Hong wen zhi yin, Xianzhi zhuren,
- *Tang Rhymes*: *qian*-trigram, Guangrendian, Ali, Xianzhitang yin, Xianzhi zhuren.

67   *SQBJ chubian* 1971, p. 955.

68   *XHHP* 1120 (*HSCS* 1955, vol. 1, *juan* 10, pp. 101–104).

69   *Zhongxingguange* (*MSCS* 1975, vol. 18, pt. 4, sect. 5, p. 208.

70   Zhou Mi, *QDYY, juan* 6 (*BJXSDG* 1977, ser. 13, pt. 4, p. 2122).

71   Zhou Mi, *YYGYL, juan xia* (*MSCS* 1975, vol. 6, pt. 6, sect. 2, p. 28).

72   The Juran landscape is leaf 7 of the album, *Highlights of Tang, Song and Yuan Painting (Tang Song Yuan minghua daguan ce)*. See *SQBJ chubian* 1971, p. 1224. Kohara Hironobu has stated that these are Ming imperial inventory marks but without further explanation (Kohara 1985, p. 145).

73   *Yuan shi* (*Mishujian zhi* 6) (1985, p. 6).

74   Fu Shen 1981, p. 82.

75   Ding Xiyuan 2001.

76   Shen Defu (*BJXSDG* 1976, vol. 8, p. 211).

77   *Tianshui bingshan lu* (*CSJCXB* 1985, p. 501).

78   *Tianshui bingshan lu* (*CSJCXB* 1985, p. 494).

A 'Cultural Biography' of the *Admonitions* Scroll:
The Sixteenth, Seventeenth and Early Eighteenth Centuries

Stephen Little

Admired for his scholarship, his love of jokes, and his brilliance as a master of religious and secular figure painting, Gu Kaizhi had attained a mythical status long before the beginning of the Ming dynasty (1368–1644).[1] Nonetheless, it was during the late Ming and early Qing (1644–1911) dynasties that Gu Kaizhi's *Admonitions of the Court Instructress* first attained the degree of fame it enjoys today.

Very little is known of the *Admonitions* scroll's provenance during the early Ming dynasty. Early Ming texts are silent with regard to the *Admonitions* scroll, and indeed close to silent regarding Gu Kaizhi himself. Gu is not mentioned at all, for example, in Cao Zhao's (later fourteenth century) manual of collecting, the *Gegu yaolun* of 1388. Charles Mason has recently suggested that in the late fifteenth or early sixteenth century the *Admonitions* scroll entered the collection of the scholar-official Wang Ao (1450–1524; fig. 1).[2] Wang was a renowned poet and calligrapher, and served as Grand Secretary from 1506 to 1509. Evidence for Wang's ownership of the scroll consists of a single square seal that overlaps the first yellow damask border and the first section of the painting. The seal reads 'Sanhuai zhi yi' and is identical to a seal on a handscroll of Wang Ao's calligraphy dated 1520 in the Shanghai Museum.[3]

It is generally assumed from Wen Jia's (1501–1583) *Qianshantang shuhua ji* of 1569 that in the mid-sixteenth century the *Admonitions* scroll was owned by Yan Song (1480–1565), a powerful and corrupt official who served as Grand Secretary at the court of the Jiajing emperor from 1542–1562.[4] Although Yan Song left no seals on the *Admonitions* scroll, and even though the scroll is mentioned in Wen Jia's catalogue not as by Gu Kaizhi but as by a 'Jin dynasty artist', most modern scholars have assumed that the scroll in Yan Song's collection was the same as the *Admonitions* scroll in the British Museum.[5] Yan Song's extraordinary collection was confiscated by the Ming government in 1562, and Wen

Fig. 1 Anonymous, *Portrait of Wang Ao (1450–1524)*, Ming or Qing dynasty (16th–17th century). Hanging scroll; ink and colour on paper, 161.4 × 95.6 cm. Nanjing Museum. (After *Nanjing Bowuguan cang Zhongguo xiaoxiang hua xuanji* [1993], pl. 21).

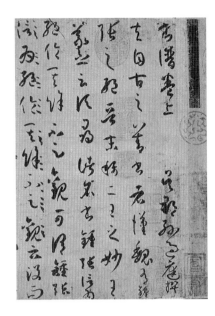

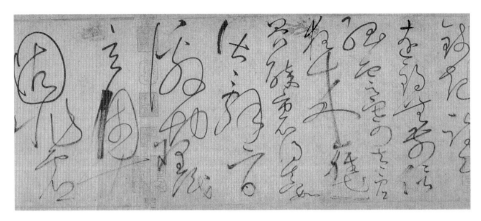

Fig. 2 (left) Sun Guoting (646–691), *Shu pu (Essay on Calligraphy)*. Tang dynasty, dated 687. Detail of a handscroll; ink on paper, 26.5 × 900.8 cm. National Palace Museum, Taipei.

Fig. 3 (above) Huaisu (725–after 777), *Autobiography Scroll (Zishu tie)*. Tang dynasty, dated 777. Detail of a handscroll; ink on paper, 28.3 × 755 cm. National Palace Museum, Taipei.

Jia was commissioned to make a list of the works it contained. Among other famous works, Yan Song owned Sun Guoting's *Shu pu* (fig. 2), Huaisu's *Autobiography* (fig. 3), Zhan Ziqian's *Travelling in Spring* (Palace Museum, Beijing), Wang Shen's *Misty River and Layered Peaks* (Shanghai Museum), Zhang Zeduan's *Going Up the River at the Qingming Festival* (fig. 4), a Song dynasty *baimiao* (ink-outline) copy of the *Admonitions* scroll attributed to Li Gonglin (possibly the Southern Song scroll now in the Palace Museum, Beijing),[6] and Gong Kai's *Zhong Kui Accompanying his Sister* (Freer Gallery of Art), in addition to many other important works of the Yuan and Ming dynasties.[7]

In Yan Song's collection was also a transcription of the *Admonitions* text by Emperor Huizong (r. 1101–1125).[8] This is listed in Wen Jia's *Qianshantang shuhua ji* as 'Huizong's Transcription of the Admonitions of the Court Instructress', on silk, in slender gold script'.[9] It is possible that this scroll (or a fragment thereof) and the transcription of Zhang Hua's text in 'slender gold' script now appended to the *Admonitions* scroll (possibly inscribed by Jin Zhangzong, r. 1190–1208) were one and the same thing.[10]

Sometime between 1562 and about 1570 the *Admonitions* scroll entered the collection of the scholar-official Gu Congyi (1523–1588), a native of Shanghai.[11] Gu served as an official during the reigns of Jiajing (1522–1566) and Longqing (1567–1573); his posts included Drafter in the Secretariat and Case Reviewer in the Court of Judicial Review. He had a tremendous reputation as a connoisseur of painting. That Gu owned the *Admonitions* scroll is known from a brief reference to the painting in the *Siyouzhai hualun* by the late

Ming scholar He Liangjun (1506–1573), in which he mentions seeing the *Admonitions* scroll at Gu's home. He Liangjun writes:

> Recently I again saw the *Admonitions of the Court Instructress* at the home of Gu Yanshan [Gu Congyi]. It is by Gu Kaizhi, and has only figures [i.e. no background]. The women are a little more than three inches in height. All [the figures] have a lifelike spirit, seemingly wanting to walk; they are divine but have not lost their naturalness. Is it not the kind of thing one calls 'superior beyond superior'? Furthermore, the silk and colours look like new, yet it is a divine object and must be carefully protected.[12]

It would appear that Gu Congyi owned the *Admonitions* scroll for only a short time, for it soon entered the collection of Xiang Yuanbian (1525–1590), a native of Huating near Shanghai in Jiangsu province. Gu Congyi's ownership of the *Admonitions* scroll is also confirmed in Dong Qichang's (1555–1636) colophon on the twelfth century handscroll entitled *Dream Journey on the Xiao and Xiang Rivers* in the Tokyo National Museum (fig. 5). Part of this colophon reads:

> Secretariat [Drafter] Gu of Haishang [Shanghai] owned four famous handscrolls: Gu Kaizhi's *Admonitions of the Court Instructress*, Li Boshi's [Li Gonglin's] *The Yangzi River in Shu*, the *Nine Songs*, and this *Xiao and Xiang Rivers*. The *Admonitions of the Court Instructress* is [now] in the home of Xiang Zuili [Xiang Yuanbian] ...[13]

Fig. 4 Zhang Zeduan, *Going up the River at the Qingming Festival (Qingming shanghe tu)*. Late Northern Song dynasty, *c*.1100. Detail of a handscroll; ink and colour on silk, 24.8 × 528 cm. Palace Museum, Beijing.

Fig. 5 Li of Shucheng, *Dream Journey on the Xiao and Xiang Rivers*. Southern Song dynasty, late 12th century. Detail of a handscroll; ink on paper, 30.4 × 400.4 cm. Tokyo National Museum.

Fig. 6 Wang Wei (699–759), *Fu Sheng of Ji'nan*. Tang dynasty, 8th century. Handscroll; ink and colour on silk, 34 × 47.6 cm. Osaka Municipal Museum of Art, Abe Collection.

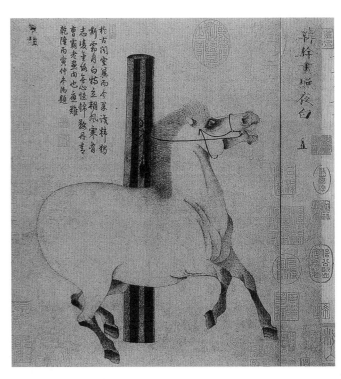

Fig. 7 Han Gan (act. *c.*742–756), *Night-shining White*. Tang dynasty, 8th century. Handscroll; ink on paper, 30.8 × 34 cm. Metropolitan Museum of Art, New York, The Dillon Fund Gift, 1977.78.

Xiang Yuanbian, a pawnbroker, was the most famous owner of the *Admonitions* scroll in the late sixteenth century. Xiang's collection of painting and calligraphy was only surpassed in size by that of the Qianlong emperor (r. 1736–1795).[14] Xiang Yuanbian's astonishing collection also included calligraphic works by Wang Xizhi (for example, the *Fengju tie* now in the National Palace Museum, Taipei, which was also owned by Wang Ao), Ouyang Xun, Chu Suiliang, and Huaisu (the *Autobiography* in Taipei), and such paintings as Wang Wei's *Fu Sheng of Ji'nan* (fig. 6), Lu Lengjia's *Six Luohans* (Palace Museum, Beijing), Han Gan's *Night-shining White* (fig. 7), Emperor Huizong's *Finches and Bamboo* (Metropolitan Museum of Art, New York), Ma Yuan's *The Four Sages of Mount Shang* (fig. 8), and many paintings by masters of the Yuan dynasty.[15] Over fifty of Xiang Yuanbian's seals can be found on the British Museum scroll.[16]

As he did on many of the handscrolls in his collection, Xiang Yuanbian inscribed a short colophon following the *Admonitions* painting (pl. 38 right):[17]

A treasure of the Song inner palace, by Gu Kaizhi of the Jin dynasty, painting of the *Admonitions of the Court Instructress*, with text in small standard script. A divine object; genuine. Now the highly prized possession of Xiang Yuanbian of the Ming dynasty, called also Molin Shanren.[18]

The great painter, calligrapher, and scholar-official Dong Qichang's first-hand knowledge of the *Admonitions* scroll began during Xiang Yuanbian's ownership of the painting. Beginning in the late 1570s, until he obtained the *jinshi* degree in 1589, Dong Qichang spent many hours with Xiang Yuanbian studying the latter's collection.[19] Dong's colophon on the *Nymph of the Luo River* handscroll traditionally attributed to Gu Kaizhi in the Freer Gallery of Art, Washington, DC (figs 9, 10), includes the lines:

Of Gu Changkang's [Gu Kaizhi's] paintings, only this and the *Nüshi zhen* [the *Admonitions* scroll] in the collection of Xiang [Yuanbian] are extant. They are indeed a pair of treasures.[20]

It was not the *Admonitions* scroll's painting that Dong Qichang so admired, however, but the calligraphy. Given his penchant for landscape painting, this should not be surprising. Kohara Hironobu has written, 'Late in the Wanli period (1573–1620), the *Admonitions* scroll contained a colophon by the pre-eminent connoisseur and artist Dong Qichang.'[21] This colophon, however, was not originally inscribed on the *Admonitions* scroll, but was written as a colophon to a reproduction of the scroll's inscriptions, included in Dong's compendium of ancient calligraphic models illustrated with ink rubbings, the *Xihongtang fashu* of 1603 (fig. 11).[22] Here, in

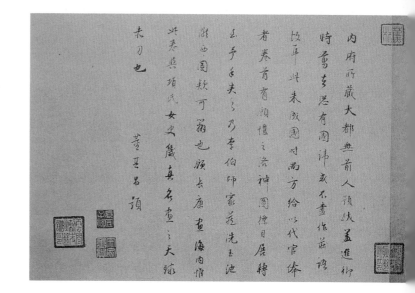

Fig. 8 (top) Ma Yuan (act. *c.*1190–*c.*1225), *The Four Sages of Mount Shang*. Southern Song dynasty, *c.*1225. Detail of a handscroll; ink and light colour on paper, 33.6 × 307.3 cm. Cincinnati Art Museum, Anonymous gift (1950.77).

Fig. 9 (above) Gu Kaizhi (attr.), *Nymph of the Luo River*. Song dynasty, 12th–13th century. Detail of a handscroll; ink and colour on silk, 24 × 310 cm. Freer Gallery of Art, Smithsonian Institution, Washington, DC.

Fig. 10 (right) Dong Qichang (1555–1636), colophon on Gu Kaizhi (attr.), *Nymph of the Luo River*. Freer Gallery of Art, Smithsonian Institution, Washington, DC. (After Lawton 1973, p. 23.)

Fig. 11 Reproduction of the calligraphic inscriptions on Gu Kaizhi's *Admonitions of the Court Instructress*. From Dong Qichang (1555–1636), *Xihongtang fashu*. Ming dynasty, dated 1603. Detail from an album of ink rubbings. Freer Gallery of Art Library, Smithsonian Institution, Washington, DC.

Fig. 12 (below) Colophon by Dong Qichang (1555–1636) to the reproduction of the calligraphic inscriptions on Gu Kaizhi's *Admonitions of the Court Instructress*. From Dong Qichang (1555–1636), *Xihongtang fashu*. Ming dynasty, dated 1603. Detail from an album of ink rubbings. Freer Gallery of Art Library, Smithsonian Institution, Washington, DC.

Fig. 13 (below left) Wang Xianzhi (344–388), *Thirteen Lines of the Nymph of the Luo River*. Ink rubbing. (After *SDZS* 1970–, vol. 4, pls. 90–91.)

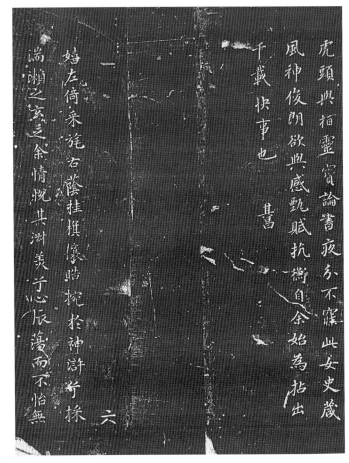

Plate 32 Brocade protective wrapper from the Qianlong (1736–1795) imperial scroll mounting of *c*.1746
(missing the title-slip by the Qianlong emperor).

Plates 32–40 Passages from the *Admonitions of the Instructress to the Court Ladies (Nüshi zhen tu)* scroll,
painting attributed to Gu Kaizhi (*c*.345–406). Handscroll mounted on a panel; ink on paper and silk,
25 × 329 cm (sections in pls 32 and 40 are mounted separately). The Trustees of The
British Museum (OA 1903.4–8.1 Chinese Painting 1).

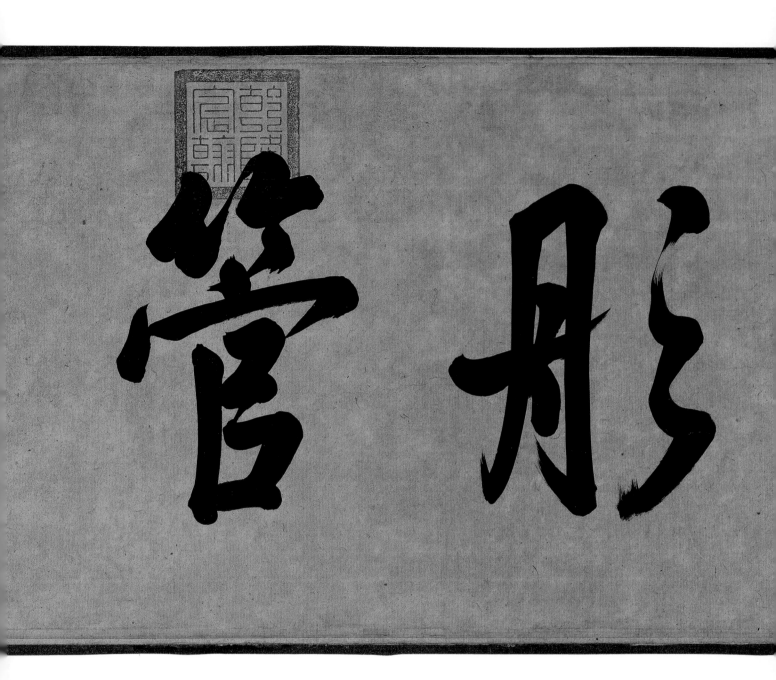

Plate 33 Right: Silk embroidery (*kesi*) depicting a peony, a protective wrapper preserved from a Song (960–1279) period mounting of the scroll.
Left (continued to pl. 34 right): 'Tong guan fang' (fragrance of a red tube), title-piece by the Qianlong emperor (r. 1736–1795), *c*.1746.

228

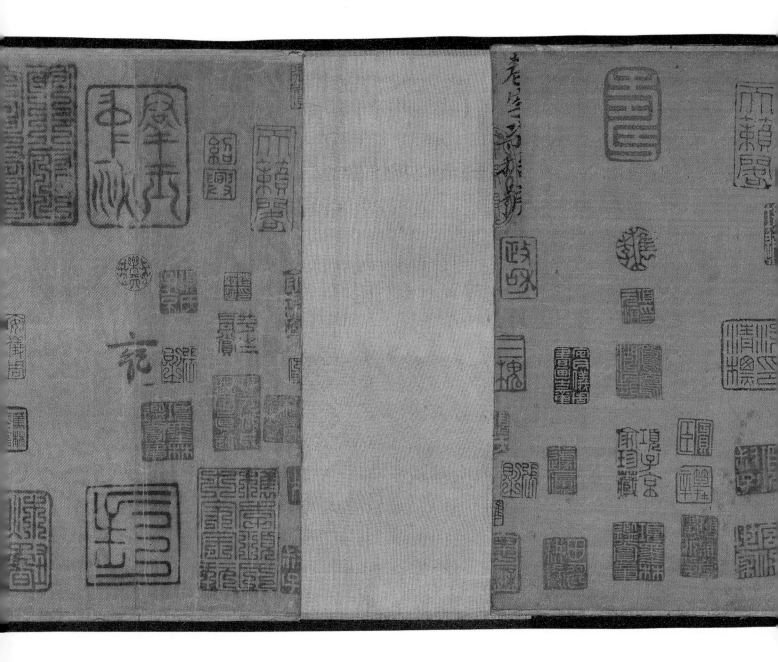

Plate 34 Right (continued from pl. 33 left): 'Tong guan fang' (fragrance of a red tube), title-piece by the Qianlong emperor (r. 1736–1795), *c.*1746.
Left: Silk end-panels formerly mounted at either end of the *Admonitions* painting.

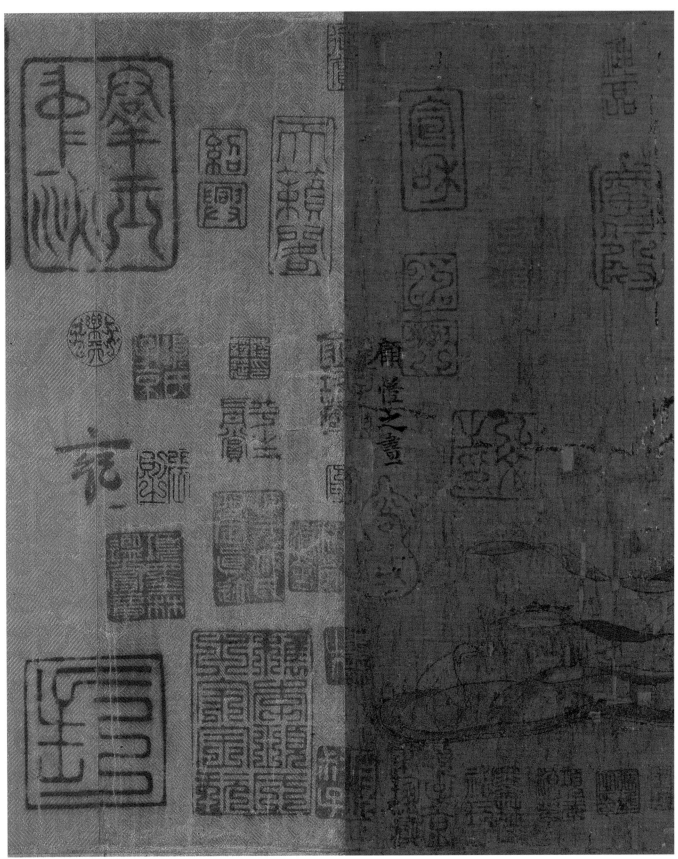

Plate 35 Digital recreation of the end of the painting and the adjoining rear end-panel.

Plate 36 Digital recreation of the front of the painting and the adjoining front end-panel.

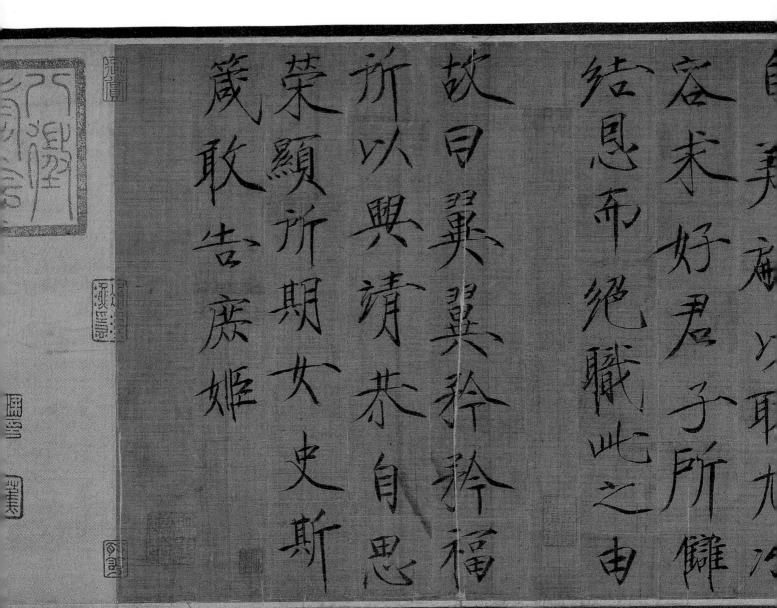

容未好君子所雖

結恩而絕職此之由

故曰翼翼矜矜福

所以興靖恭自思

榮顯所期女史斯

箴敢告庶姬

Plate 37 Right: Painting of an orchid by the Qianlong emperor (r. 1736–1795).
Centre and left: Partial transcription in 'slender gold' script of the 'Admonitions' text by Zhang Hua, attributed to the Jin emperor Zhangzong (r. 1190–1208), traditionally attributed to the Song emperor Huizong (r. 1101–1125).

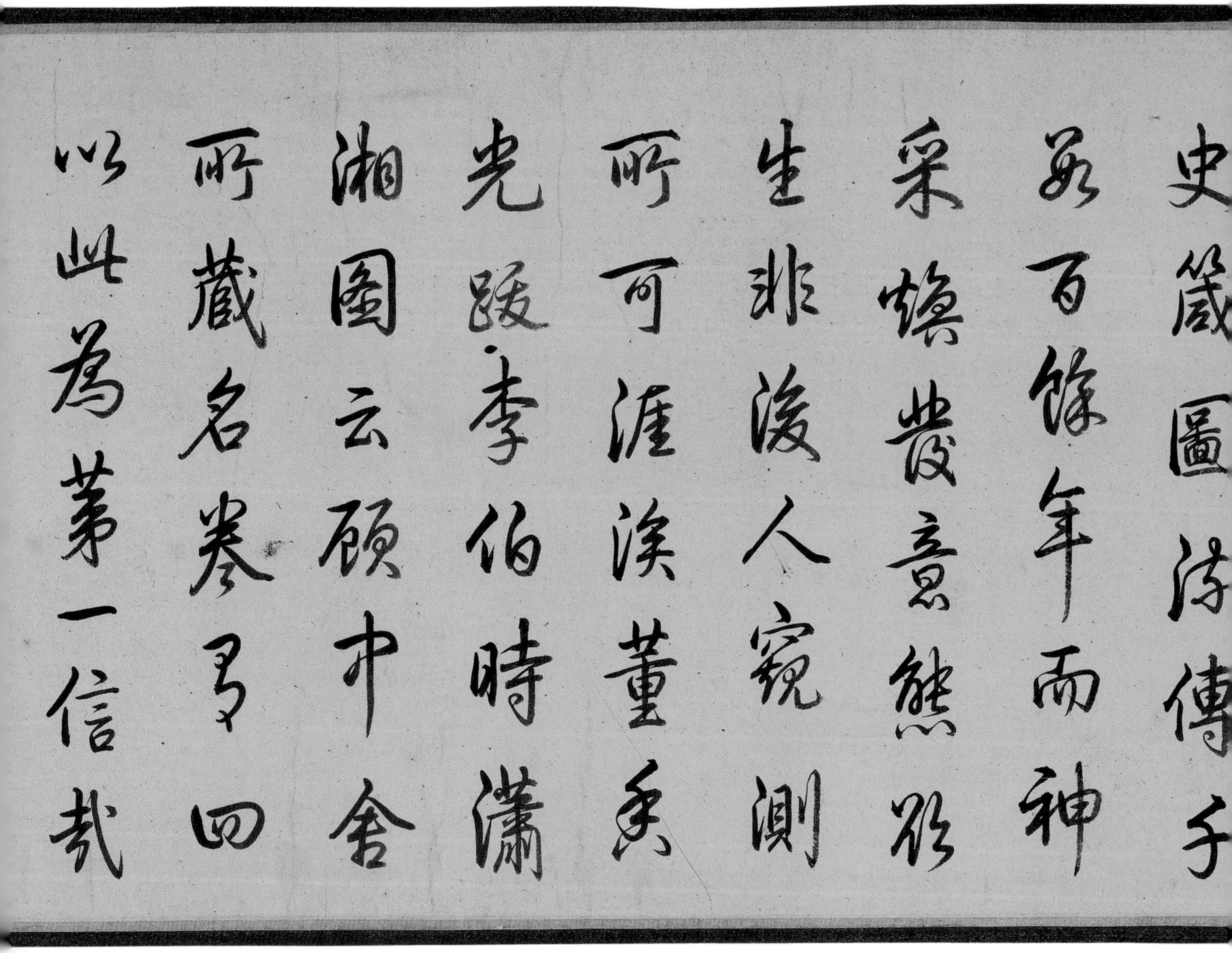

史箴圖浮傳于

世百餘年而神

采煥發意態熊形

生非後人窺測

所可涯涘董其

光跋李伯時瀟

湘圖云碩中舍

所藏名卷弓四

以此為第一信哉

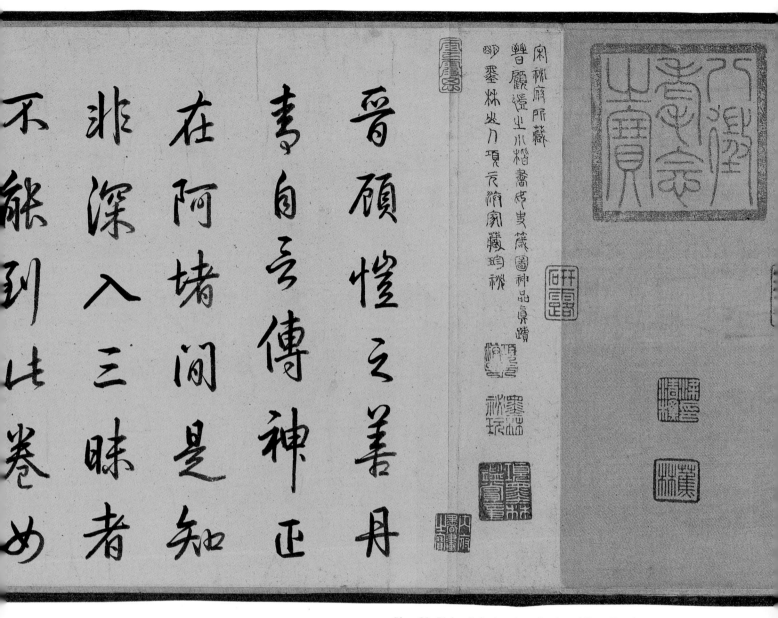

Plate 38 Right: Colophon in seal script of Xiang Yuanbian (1525–1590).
Centre (continued to pl. 39): Colophon of the Qianlong emperor (r. 1736–1795), dated 1746.

正復不可思議

率紀弟亏亦為

是卷慶創合也

乾隆丙寅夏至

前五日靜怡軒

御筆

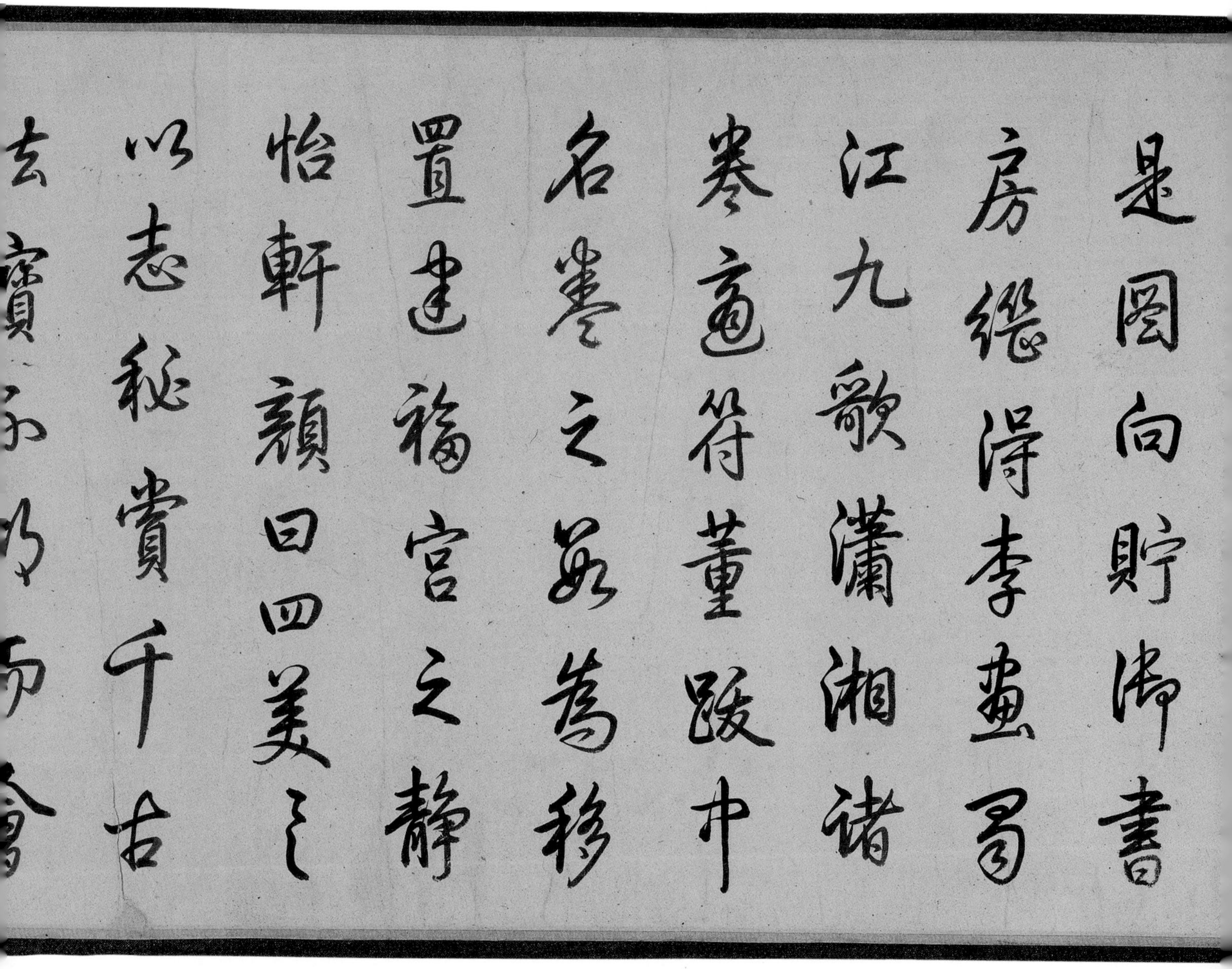

是圖向貯御書
房繼得李畫昌
江九歌瀟湘諸
棗童符董跋卅
名畫之安為移
置建福宮之靜
怡軒頴曰四美之
以志秘賞千古
去寶不乃而會

Plate 39 (continued from pl. 38) Colophon of the Qianlong emperor (r. 1736–1795), dated 1746.

Plate 40 Zou Yigui (1686–1772), *Pine, Bamboo, Rock and Spring (Songzhu shiquan)*, colophon-painting in ink on paper for the Qianlong imperial mounting of *c*.1746.

240

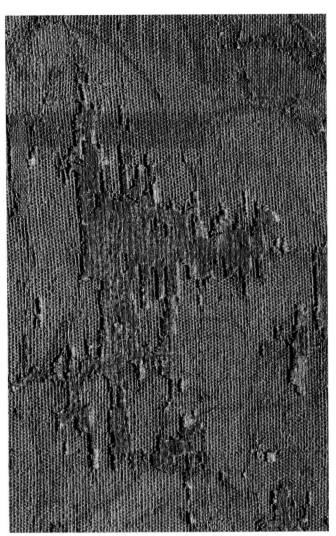

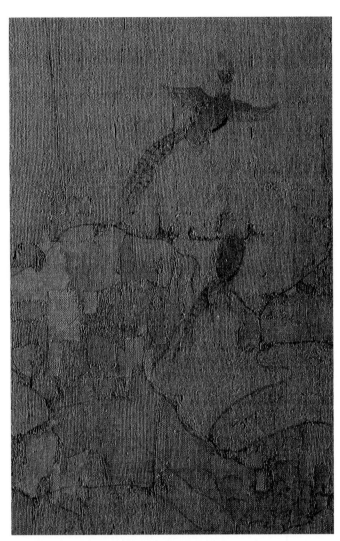

Plate 41 Close-up detail of the silk from scene 2
(Lady Ban, pl. 3).

Plate 42 Close-up detail of the silk from scene 3
(the landscape and archer, pl. 5).

the very first *juan* of the compendium, the *Admonitions* text from the British Museum scroll directly follows Yang Xi's *Huangting jing*, Wang Xizhi's *Yue Yi lun*, and Wang Xianzhi's *Thirteen Lines of the Nymph of the Luo River*. Dong's colophon (fig. 12) to the Gu Kaizhi calligraphy reads:

When Hutou [Gu Kaizhi] discussed calligraphy with Huan Lingbao [Huan Xuan; 369–404], they stayed up until midnight before going to bed.[23] In this [scroll] of the *Admonitions of the Court Instructress*, the spirit [of the calligraphy] is refined, and it contends with the *Ganzhen fu* [the *Nymph of the Luo River* calligraphy in standard script by Wang Xianzhi (344–388)]. Since I first took this up, it has been the happiest thing in a thousand years. Qichang.[24]

Dong Qichang so admired the calligraphy of the *Admonitions* scroll that he not only had it reproduced as a calligraphic model in the *Xihongtang fashu*, but at least once copied it with his own brush as well, adding the following colophon to one of his copies (this text is recorded in Dong's *Huachanshi suibi*):

Colophon to my copy of the [calligraphy on the] *Admonitions of the Court Instructress*

In the past those who examined the Jin dynasty painting of the *Admonitions of the Court Instructress* said, 'This is Hutou's [Gu Kaizhi's] brush.' [In attempting] to classify the inscriptions of the Admonitions attached to the side of the paintings, [they] said that it was Daling's [Wang Xianzhi's] calligraphy. I have no idea where [the idea] of Daling writing the Admonitions came from. Sun Guoting's *Shu pu* mentions 'Youjun's [Wang Xizhi's] *Admonitions of the Grand Preceptor*[25] – is this how the [idea that Wang Xianzhi was the calligrapher of the] [*Admonitions of the*] *Court Instructress* was falsely transmitted to later [generations]? While its characters completely embody the style of the *Thirteen Lines* [Wang Xianzhi's *Nymph of the Luo River* calligraphy], it is certainly not by Wang Youjun [Wang Xizhi]. On a leisurely day, in a moment of inspiration, I decided to write, and thereupon copied it [the text of the *Admonitions of the Court Instructress*]. If one had not seen the original, one might think that its spirit had been attained [in my copy], yet it does not resemble [the original].[26]

Dong Qichang's deep admiration for the elegant standard-script transcription of Zhang Hua's 'Admonitions of the

Court Instructress' on the British Museum scroll is noteworthy for several reasons. First, Dong clearly believed that the *Admonitions* scroll – both painting and calligraphy – were authentic works by Gu Kaizhi. This is indicated in his inclusion of the word *zhenji* ('authentic work') at the end of the title of the reproduction of the 'Admonitions' calligraphy in the *Xihongtang fashu*. Second, his comparison of the 'Admonitions' calligraphy with the calligraphy of Wang Xianzhi's *Nymph of the Luo River* (fig. 13), as stated in the *Huachanshi suibi*, reveals that he was an astute scholar of early calligraphy, and recognized in the *Admonitions* text a calligraphic structure and style consistent with that of the most sophisticated Eastern Jin masters of standard script in Jiankang (Nanjing) during the second half of the fourth century – particularly Wang Xianzhi (344–388). The *Nymph of the Luo River*, also known as the *Thirteen Lines*, was Wang Xianzhi's most famous work of standard script, and has been widely admired as such since the Tang dynasty (618–906), as has been shown by Lothar Ledderose and others.[27]

An interesting footnote to Xiang Yuanbian's ownership of the *Admonitions* scroll is that the 'slender gold' script transcription of the 'Admonitions' text, now attached to the scroll (pl. 37) and originally attributed to Song Huizong, probably had a separate history of ownership prior to the early sixteenth century. This is suggested by the presence of two seals belonging to the Ming dynasty collector An Guo (1481–1534) on the same piece of silk as the calligraphy.[28] These seals appear nowhere else on the *Admonitions* scroll, suggesting that the *Admonitions* painting attributed to Gu Kaizhi and the 'slender gold' transcription of the text attributed to Huizong were only joined together sometime between 1569 (the date of Wen Jia's *Qianshantang shuhua ji*) and 1590 (the date of Xiang Yuanbian's death). Significantly, today both sections of the scroll bear the seals of Xiang Yuanbian.[29]

After Xiang Yuanbian's death in 1590 the transmission of the *Admonitions* scroll becomes somewhat hazy. A brief account of the *Admonitions* scroll in the scholar and connoisseur Chen Jiru's (1558–1639) *Nigulu* of *circa* 1635 states that he saw the painting in Wumen (Suzhou). Chen writes, 'Hitherto [this] was said to be by Gu Kaizhi, but it is truly a copy of the early Song dynasty, and the 'Admonitions' text was written by [Song] Gaozong – not by Wang Xianzhi.'[30] Assuming that Chen was speaking of the British Museum scroll (and not the *baimiao* copy in the Palace Museum, Beijing, which is of Song date[31]), it is noteworthy that none of his contemporaries who commented on the *Admonitions* scroll agreed with his assessment of the painting's date.[32]

In the seventeenth century the *Admonitions* scroll began to be increasingly recorded in Chinese painting catalogues. It appears, for example in the late Ming scholar Zhang Chou's *Qinghe shuhua fang* of 1616.³³ Zhang Chou (1577–1643) was a native of Kunshan in Jiangsu province.³⁴ His father, Zhang Yingwen, was a wealthy scholar and art collector. When he was eleven (1588) Zhang Chou's family moved to Suzhou. In 1594 Zhang acquired one of his first works of art as a gift from his father – a painting by Tang Yin.³⁵ Zhang Chou eventually owned an excellent collection of nearly one hundred ancient paintings and calligraphies. These included one of the versions of Gu Kaizhi's *Nymph of the Luo River* (it is not clear which), Wang Xianzhi's *Zhongqiu tie*, a copy of the *Nymph of the Luo River* composition by Zhao Boju, and Song Gaozong's transcription of the *Nymph of the Luo River* poem in running script.³⁶ After the *Qinghe shuhua fang* was completed, Zhang's reputation as a connoisseur of ancient painting and calligraphy spread far and wide, and it was said that 'people flocked to Zhang Chou to show him their treasures'.³⁷

Zhang Chou's record of the *Admonitions* scroll transcribes the sections of Zhang Hua's 'Admonitions' text that are inscribed on the painting itself, transcribes Dong Qichang's colophon on the *Admonitions* calligraphy reproduced in the *Xihongtang fashu* (1603), and quotes the discussion of the scroll in Mi Fu's (1051–1107) *Hua shi*.³⁸

The fate of the *Admonitions* scroll during the transition from the Ming to the Qing dynasties is unclear. At some point during the Ming Chongzhen (1628–1644) and Qing Shunzhi (1644–1661) reigns, the *Admonitions* scroll entered the collection of Zhang Xiaosi, a native of Dantu (Zhenjiang, Jiangsu province), about whom little is known.³⁹ Zhang's collection contained many important works, some of them from Xiang Yuanbian's collection. Two of Zhang's seals appear on the *Admonitions* scroll, on the first yellow silk damask border (*geshui*), and on the blue silk *geshui* after the painting, next to an unidentified Mongol script seal.

During the late Shunzhi or early Kangxi (1662–1722) period, the *Admonitions* scroll entered the collection of Da Zhongguang (1623–1692). Da, like Zhang Xiaosi a native of Zhenjiang, Jiangsu, is best known today as a landscape painter and calligrapher.⁴⁰ He obtained the *jinshi* degree in 1652, and rose to the rank of Censor at the early Qing court. As a painter he excelled at landscapes and depictions of orchids and bamboo.⁴¹ He was famous as a connoisseur, and was often visited by the painters Yun Shouping (1633–1690) and Wang Hui (1632–1717). At the end of his life he retired to Mao Shan near Nanjing and became a Daoist adept. While his collection was not large, it included a copy of the *Dingwu* rubbing of Wang Xizhi's *Orchid Pavilion Preface*, a calligraphy by Su Shi, paintings by Zhao Mengfu and Ni Zan, and works by Wang Shimin, Zha Shibiao, Wang Hui, and Yun Shouping.⁴²

Two of Da Zhongguang's seals appear on the *Admonitions* scroll: on the yellow damask *geshui* preceding the painting, and on the second (beige) damask border following the painting, situated immediately next to the 'Qiuhe tushu' seal of the Southern Song Prime Minister Jia Sidao (1213–1275). That Da Zhongguang was not the only owner of the *Admonitions* scroll in the early Kangxi period is indicated by a note in the scholar Zhu Yizun's *Pushuting shuhua ba*, which states that in 1672 Zhu saw the scroll in the Wang family collection in Jiangdu, Jiangsu province.⁴³

Ten years later, in 1682, the *Admonitions* scroll was recorded in Bian Yongyu's (1645–1712) *Shigutang shuhua huikao*.⁴⁴ Like Zhang Chou's *Qinghe shuhua fang* of 1616, this work transcribes the *Admonitions* text as it appears on the painting, and quotes the references to the scroll in Mi Fu's *Hua shi* and Dong Qichang's colophon in the *Xihongtang fashu*. It is possible, judging from the similarity of Bian Yongyu's entry to that in Zhang Chou's *Qinghe shuhua fang*, that he merely copied the record of the *Admonitions* scroll from Zhang's catalogue of 1616.

During the early Kangxi period the scroll entered the collection of Liang Qingbiao (1620–1691), one of the greatest collectors of the early Qing dynasty. Liang was a native of Zhengding, Hebei province.⁴⁵ He received the *jinshi* degree in 1643, and in 1645, a year after the Manchu conquest of the north, entered the service of the Qing government. Liang had an illustrious career as an official in the courts of Shunzhi and Kangxi. In 1656 he was appointed Minister of Military Affairs, in 1666 Minister of the Board of Rites, in 1672 Lecturer on Confucian Classics in the Imperial Presence, and in 1688 Grand Secretary. Liang Qingbiao owned over two hundred and fifty paintings that survive today, among them the *Admonitions* scroll and three other paintings attributed to Gu Kaizhi (the *Nymph of the Luo River* scrolls in the Liaoning Provincial Museum [fig. 14] and the Freer Gallery of Art [fig. 9], and the *Biographies of Exemplary Women* in the Palace Museum, Beijing [pls 29–30]), Wang Wei's *Fu Sheng of Ji'nan* (fig. 6), the *Five Planets and Twenty-eight Lunar Mansions* attributed to Zhang Sengyou (Osaka Municipal Museum), the *Night Revels of Han Xizai* in Beijing, Zhou Wenju's *Playing Weiqi in Front of a Double Screen* in Beijing, Zhao Gan's *Early Snow on the River* in Taipei, Fan Kuan's *Travellers among Streams and Mountains* in Taipei, three paintings by Ma Yuan (*A Daoist Immortal on a Dragon* in Taipei, *Four Sages of Mount Shang* in Cincinnati, and *Sketches of Water* in Beijing), the Southern Song *baimiao* copy of the *Admonitions* scroll traditionally attributed to Li Gonglin (Palace Museum, Beijing), and many works by masters of the Yuan and Ming dynasties.⁴⁶ After his death in 1691, many of the paintings in

Liang Qingbiao's collection entered the collection of the Tianjin salt merchant An Qi. Unlike An, however, Liang left no catalogue of his collection.

Professor Kohara has also suggested that during the Kangxi reign the *Admonitions* scroll was seen by the scholar-official and collector Gao Shiqi (1645–1704). A single seal of Gao Shiqi appears on the second damask border following the painting (which also bears the small painting of an orchid by the Qianlong emperor), but it does not correspond to any of Gao's known seals. Furthermore, the *Admonitions* scroll is not listed in either of Gao Shiqi's primary texts on painting, the *Jiangcun xiaoxia lu* or the *Jiangcun shuhua mu*.[47]

In the late Kangxi period the *Admonitions* scroll was recorded in Wu Sheng's *Daguan lu*, a catalogue that has a preface written by Song Luo (1643–1713) in 1712.[48] While little is known of Wu Sheng, he was a sophisticated connoisseur, and was acquainted with the painter Wang Shimin (1592–1680) and his son Wang Shan (1645–1728).[49] Wu Sheng was a native of Suzhou. Wang Shan, in his preface to the *Daguan lu*, states that Wu Sheng was already fond of ancient ritual bronze vessels as a child, while Song Luo, in his preface, writes of Wu's 'craving for antiquity', and compares him with the seventeenth century collectors and connoisseurs Sun Chengze (1592–1676) and Liang Qingbiao (1620–1691).[50]

Wu Sheng's account of the *Admonitions* scroll begins with a record of its materials and dimensions, followed by a listing of the individual scenes depicted in the painting. Among his comments on the painting, Wu wrote,

At the end of the painting is the signature in four characters, 'Painted by Gu Kaizhi.' Song Youling [Emperor Huizong] added extracts from the 'Admonitions' text, which are inscribed in eleven columns on silk that is one foot four inches in length.

The best known of Hutou's [Gu Kaizhi's] paintings are the *Luoshen fu* and this painting [the *Admonitions* scroll]. The brush and ink of the *Luoshen*, however, is rather weak, and the poem's text is not inscribed [on the painting]. [In] this painting, the 'Admonitions' [text] of high antiquity, in small standard script, has a refined subtlety. Some who came before considered this to be Daling's [Wang Xianzhi's] calligraphy. Dong Zongbo [Dong Qichang] mentions the story of Hutou [Gu Kaizhi] and Huan Lingbao [Huan Xuan] discussing calligraphy until midnight, precisely to settle [the fact] that [this] is by Changkang [Gu Kaizhi]. He [Dong] had it [the 'Admonitions' text] carved in the *Hongtang* [i.e. copied into the *Xihongtang fashu*], which has

Fig. 14 Gu Kaizhi (attr.), *Nymph of the Luo River*. Song dynasty (960–1279). Detail of a handscroll; ink and colour on silk, 26 × 646 cm. Liaoning Provincial Museum, Shenyang.

consequently [put such] unreliable criticisms to rest.

At the beginning and end of the painting are borders [*geshui*] of yellow damask. The 'Xuanhe', 'Shaoxing', and other assorted collectors' seals are all intact.

The *Daguan lu* account ends with transcriptions of the 'Admonitions' text from the painting, the 'Huizong' inscriptions, and Xiang Yuanbian's colophon. Wu Sheng's record is significant for its attempt to describe the key aspects of the scroll and its documentation, and for its critical commentary with regard to the attribution to Gu Kaizhi. Wu Sheng criticizes (unnamed) earlier scholars who thought that the calligraphy was by Wang Xianzhi, and cites Dong Qichang's opinion regarding Gu Kaizhi's authorship of the calligraphy as powerful evidence for the authenticity of the *Admonitions* scroll as an Eastern Jin dynasty work.

Fig. 15 Wen Zhengming (1470–1559), *Goddess and Lady of the Xiang River*. Ming dynasty, inscription dated 1517. Detail of a hanging scroll; ink and light colour on paper, 100.8 × 35.6 cm. Palace Museum, Beijing.

Noteworthy in Wu Sheng's 1712 account is his mention of the 'Xuanhe' seal at the beginning of the painting. Because its actual position on the scroll violates Huizong's established protocols of seal placement (as have been demonstrated by Xu Bangda[51]), the 'Xuanhe' seal was clearly added after Huizong's lifetime (this is also true of the 'Zhenghe' seal on the yellow damask border immediately preceding the painting, and possibly true of the 'Yushu' ('Imperially inscribed') seal that appears in the upper right corner of the painting as well).[52] Wu Sheng makes no mention of the one seal of Jin Zhangzong still clearly visible on the scroll (the 'Qun yu zhon gmi' ['Central Treasure of Accumulated Jades'] seal that overlaps two silk damask borders following the painting).[53]

In the early eighteenth century the *Admonitions* scroll entered the collection of the wealthy Korean salt merchant An Qi (1683–c. 1746).[54] In 1742 An Qi completed the catalogue of his collection, entitled *Moyuan huiguan*.[55] An Qi's record of the *Admonitions* scroll begins, like Wu Sheng's, by listing the painting's materials and dimensions. An then states that the scroll had previously been owned by Liang Qingbiao (1620–1691), and remarks on the size of its figures, its 'rich colouring', and 'divine spirit'. Then comes a detailed description of each scene, followed by these comments:

The brushwork's rank is the fullest expression of high antiquity, and the application of ink truly resembles spring silkworms spitting silk threads. It is truly not the

Fig. 16 Chen Hongshou (1598–1652), 'Scholar Under a Pine Tree', from an album of *Figures in a Landscape*. Early Qing dynasty, mid-17th century. Album leaf; ink and light colour on paper, 33.5 × 27.3 cm. Freer Gallery of Art, Smithsonian Institution, Washington, DC.

kind of thing the Tang [618–906] artists could possibly reach. Each painting is matched with its corresponding 'Admonitions' text, in eight sections. The standard script technique is genuinely antique, grave and serious [in style]. At the end of the painting is the signature, reading 'Painted by Gu Kaizhi.' The text has already been carved into stone and [recorded] in the *Xihongtang [fashu]*, so is not recorded again [here]. On the yellow damask *geshui* border at the beginning of the scroll is a single column inscribed in ink with 'half-characters', belonging to an earlier inventory system.[56] On the Song dynasty damask *geshui* at the end of the scroll is stamped a seal with red [characters] which is very strange.[57] On the painting are seals reading 'Zheng[he]', 'Xuan[he]', 'Shaoxing', and 'Mingchang,' and various other seals. At the end is an inscription in slender-gold script, beginning with the lines 'Favour must not be abused, and love must not be exclusive',[58] comprising a section of the 'Admonitions' text, written in eleven columns on silk, with characters [each] bigger than an inch. This inscription [in slender gold script] was definitely added by Xiangguo [Liang Qingbiao].[59] Follow-

Fig. 17 Dong Qichang (1555–1636), *Landscape Inspired by a Wang Wei Poem*. Ming dynasty, dated 1621. Hanging scroll; ink on paper, 109 × 49 cm. Private Collection.

ing that are three columns in small characters, inscribed by Xiang Molin [Xiang Yuanbian; 1525–1590]. [Xiang's colophon is then transcribed.] The scroll has many seals of Master Xiang. The outer wrapper is a piece of Song dynasty *kesi* silk tapestry, and an ancient jade holds the scroll shut – it is glossy jade like a tally seal. Truly a beautiful sight!

An Qi is the only commentator to mention a 'Mingchang' seal of Jin Zhangzong (r. 1190–1208). The seal is not mentioned in the record of the *Admonitions* scroll in the Qianlong imperial catalogue of 1745 (*Shiqu baoji*), and is not visible on the scroll today.[60]

Many of the paintings in An Qi's collection passed into the collection of the Qianlong emperor (r. 1736–1795), who so valued the *Admonitions* scroll that it was elevated to a previously unmatched status as a work of art (see Nixi Cura's paper in this volume, pp. 260–276).

To conclude, then, what did the *Admonitions* scroll signify for collectors and critics of the Ming and early Qing dynasties? Most commentators of the sixteenth, seventeenth, and early eighteenth centuries, including Xiang Yuanbian, He Liangjun, Dong Qichang, Zhang Chou, Wu Sheng, and An Qi, believed (and stated unequivocally) that the *Admonitions* scroll was an original work by Gu Kaizhi. Wen Jia and Chen Jiru proposed different ideas – the former that it was by an anonymous Jìn dynasty artist, the latter that it was a Song dynasty copy with calligraphy by Emperor Gaozong. The prevailing view, however, was that the scroll was a rare and genuine work of the Eastern Jìn. The notion that the *Admonitions* scroll was a copy of the Tang dynasty has only became widespread since the late Qing dynasty (it is first mentioned in Hu Jing's *Xi Qing zhaji* of 1816[61]).

As pointed out by Dong Qichang in his colophon to the Freer Gallery version of the scroll cited above, the works best taken to reflect Gu Kaizhi's original style in the late Ming were the *Nymph of the Luo River* and the *Admonitions* scrolls. In contrast to the surviving copies of the *Nymph of the Luo River* composition attributed to Gu Kaizhi now in the Palace Museum, Beijing, the Liaoning Provincial Museum, Shenyang, the Freer Gallery of Art, and the British Museum, several of which appear to have been recognized since at least the seventeenth century as Song dynasty (960–1279) copies, the *Admonitions* scroll enjoyed a special status. Certainly in terms of its representation of the archaic landscape style of the Eastern Jìn dynasty, the *Nymph of the Luo River* composition was accorded great honour in the Ming and Qing dynasties. In the *Dongtu xuanlan bian* of 1591, the painter Zhan

Jingfeng (1520–1602), in discussing a version of the *Luoshen fu* composition owned by Han Shineng (1528–1598),[62] emphasized those aspects of the composition that for him typified painting of the pre-Tang period – particularly the 'iron-wire' lines and lack of ink wash in the rocks and hills, features that, in his words, 'the likes of Zhang Xuan and Zhou Fang could not even imagine'.[63] It is significant here that among the surviving works attributed to Gu Kaizhi in the Ming and early Qing, the *Admonitions* scroll was most often accorded consideration as a 'genuine work'.

At the same time, it is worth noting that despite the high regard in which the *Admonitions* scroll was held in the late Ming and early Qing dynasties, as a work of art it had little impact on figure painting of the period, with the possible exception of the occasional work of Wen Zhengming (1470–1559; fig. 15), or such artists as Chen Hongshou (fig. 16), and it is unknown whether Chen ever even saw the *Admonitions* scroll. Even in an age (the late Ming and early Qing) in which landscape painting predominated in importance, the archaic landscape of the *Nymph of the Luo River* cannot have been seen as particularly relevant to the kind of creative and expressive transformations envisaged and carried out by such artists as Dong Qichang (fig. 17).

Instead, in this period the *Admonitions* scroll appears to have been perceived as a kind of talismanic relic of a long-lost golden age of Chinese painting and calligraphy, the Eastern Jin (317–420) – the period of Wang Xizhi, Wang Xianzhi, and Gu Kaizhi, and one in which artists like Gu were revered by politicians and generals. By the Ming and Qing dynasties, to be able to own or see such a work was considered nothing less than astonishing. As Cao Zhao, the author of the collecting manual *Gegu yaolun* wrote in 1388, 'Dong Yuan and Li Cheng were painters of comparatively recent date, yet their works are already as rare as stars [at dawn], or as phoenixes, not to speak of authentic paintings by famous artists of the Jin and Tang dynasties.'[64] In a similar vein, the early Ming calligrapher Shen Du wrote in 1408:

Paintings by Jin dynasty artists are rarely seen in the world. How much more so is this the case for a brilliant light like Hutou [Gu Kaizhi]? Looking at these strangely archaic trees and rocks, and elegant figures, he should be treasured as the ancestor of the Six Laws [of painting]. Of the Heavenly Talents praised by [various] compendia, he alone has survived, with a marvellous creativity, refined and subtle.[65]

NOTES

1 Chen Shih-hsiang 1953, pp. 12–17.
2 Mason 2001, p. 32. On Wang Ao, see *Mingren* 1978, p. 78; also Goodrich & Fang (eds) 1976, pp. 1343–1346.
3 See Shanghai (ed.) 1987, vol. 1, p. 116, no. 6. Wang Ao's calligraphic handscroll of 1520 is published in *Zhongguo gudai shuhua tumu* 1986–, vol. 2 (1987), p. 241, no. 1-0431. The same seal appears on Wang Xizhi's *Fengju tie* in the National Palace Museum, Taipei; see *Gugong lidai fashu quanji*, vol. 1 (1976), p. 4. Due to the British Museum's early twentieth century remounting of the *Admonitions* scroll, Wang Ao's 'Sanhuai zhi yi' seal is now cut in half.
4 On Yan Song see Goodrich & Fang (eds) 1976, vol. 2, pp. 1586–1591.
5 Yu Jianhua cautiously states, 'it is possible that this is [the work] painted by Gu Kaizhi' (Yu Jianhua *et al.* [comps] 1962, p. 210).
6 See the paper by Yu Hui in this volume on the *baimiao* copy in Beijing.
7 Wen Jia 1992– (1569), pp. 832–834.
8 Ibid., p. 830.
9 The *Yishu congbian* (*YSCB*) edition has 'slender sinew' for 'slender gold'; both are pronounced *shoujin*.
10 It is significant that this 'slender gold' script transcription of the 'Admonitions' text is published as being by Jin Zhangzong in *SDZS* 1970–, vol. 16, pp. 159–161 & pls 89–90.

11 See *Mingren* 1978, pp. 954–955.
12 He Liangjun 1992– (*c.*1570), p. 869.
13 The text of Dong's colophon is transcribed in *SQBJ chubian* 1971 (1745), p. 1203. See also Gray 1985 (1966), pp.185–186.
14 For a study of Xiang Yuanbian's collection, see Zheng Yinshu 1984. For a biography of Xiang Yuanbian, see Goodrich & Fang (eds) 1976, vol. 1, pp. 539–544.
15 Wong, K. S. 1989, pp. 156–158; for a reconstructed list of the paintings in Xiang Yuanbian's collection, see Zheng Yinshu 1984, pp. 140–192.
16 Zheng Yinshu 1984, p. 140. Xiang's ownership of the painting is corroborated in the *Wuzazu* by the late Ming author Xie Zhaozhe (1567–1624); see Oertling 1997, pp. 132.
17 See, for example, Xiang's colophon on Huaisu's *Autobiography*, transcribed in *SQBJ xubian* 1971 (1793), p. 2628.
18 Adapted from the translation in Kohara 2000 (1967), p. 56.
19 During this period Dong served as a private tutor in Jiaxing, Jiangsu province; see Riely 1992, pp. 394–395.
20 Translated in Lawton 1973, p. 24. The Chinese text is transcribed in Xu Bangda 1984, vol. 1, p. 24.
21 Kohara 2000 (1967), p. 22.
22 On the *Xihongtang fashu* see Riely 1992, p. 399. See also Wang Qingzheng 1992, pp. 337–338, and Qi Gong 1998.

23 Gu Kaizhi and the politician Huan Xuan were good friends who had frequent discussions about works of art; for other stories regarding their relationship, see Mather 1976, p. 366. On Huan Xuan's calligraphy, see Wang Shizhen's *Gujin fashu yuan* (1992–), p. 205.

24 I am grateful to Stephen Allee for his help in translating the last line of Dong's colophon, the complete text of which is also recorded in Zhang Chou 1992– (1616), p. 142, and in Bian Yongyu 1992– (1682), p. 896.

25 Dong Qichang refers here to Wang Xizhi's *Admonitions of the Grand Preceptor*, mentioned in a list of Wang's calligraphy in Sun Guoting's *Shu pu* of 687; see *Gugong lidai fashu quanji*, vol. 1 (1976), p. 174. See also Chang & Frankel (trs) 1995, p. 10.

26 Dong Qichang 1992– (*Huachanshi suibi*), p. 1008.

27 On Wang Xianzhi's *Nymph of the Luo River* calligraphy, see *SDZS* 1970–, vol. 4, pp. 191–192, and pls 90–91; also Zhang Qiya (ed.) 1996, pl. 158, and Ledderose 1979, pp. 14, 84 n. 117.

28 On An Guo, see Goodrich & Fang (eds) 1976, vol. 1, pp. 9–12. An Guo and Gu Kaizhi came from the same home town (Wuxi in Jiangsu province). One of An Guo's seals is recorded and transcribed in *SQBJ chubian* 1971 (1745), p. 1074; for a variant transcription see Zhang Heng 2000, 'Painting' vol. 4, part 1, p. 8. An Guo also owned Liang Kai's *Liberating the Soul from the Netherworld* now in the Wan-go H. C. Weng collection; see Little *et al.* 2000, cat. no. 30.

29 Wang Yao-t'ing, however, has suggested in his colloquy paper that the Xiang Yuanbian seals on the 'slender gold' script transcription of the 'Admonitions' text are forgeries.

30 Chen Jiru 1992– (*c*.1635), p. 1055 (*juan* 4); cited in Yu Jianhua *et al.* (comps) 1962, p. 156.

31 Published in Ma Cai 1958, pl. 5.

32 On Chen Jiru's reputation as a connoisseur, see Ren Daobin 1991, p. 9.1–26.

33 Zhang Chou 1992– (1616), pp. 141–142.

34 On Zhang Chou, see Goodrich & Fang (eds) 1976, vol. 1, pp. 51–53.

35 Ibid., p. 51.

36 See Zhang Chou 1992– (n.d.), pp. 125–126.

37 Goodrich & Fang (eds) 1976, vol. 1, p. 52.

38 For Mi Fu's brief mention of Gu Kaizhi's *Admonitions* handscroll see Mi Fu 1992– (1103), p. 978; also Yu Jianhua *et al.* (comps) 1962, p. 155. It is conceivable that Zhang Chou never actually saw the *Admonitions* scroll, for, as Hin-cheung Lovell has shown, the *Qinghe shuhua fang* includes works that Zhang had seen, and others that he had not. For those that he had seen he generally mentioned the collection in which he saw it, which is not true of his account of the *Admonitions* scroll.

39 On Zhang Xiaosi, see Yu Jianhua (ed.) 1980, p. 824.

40 Yu Jianhua (ed.) 1980, p. 927.

41 For a landscape painting by Da Zhongguang, see Osaka 1975, pl. 141.

42 See Shanghai (ed.) 1987, vol. 2, pp. 900–901.

43 Yu Jianhua *et al.* (comps) 1962, p. 156.

44 Bian Yongyu 1992– (1682), p. 896.

45 For a study of Liang Qingbiao as a collector, see Lee & Ho 1981, pp. 101–157.

46 Ibid., pp. 114–146, for a reconstructed list of Liang Qingbiao's collection.

47 Gao Shiqi 1992– (1639) and 1992– (n. d.).

48 Wu Sheng 1992– (1712), p. 372.

49 Lovell 1973, pp. 44–45.

50 Wu Sheng 1992– (1712), p. 124.

51 Xu Bangda 1981, p. 37.

52 Lee & Ho 1981: 107. In the early eighteenth century the collector An Qi (1683–*c*.1746) accused Bian Yongyu (1645–1712) of adding false seals of Emperor Huizong to the paintings he had owned, and it is conceivable that these seals were added to the *Admonitions* scroll by Bian (although it is not known whether or not Bian actually owned the scroll, despite its being listed in his *Shigutang shuhua huikao* of 1682).

53 As pointed out by Wang Yao-t'ing, however, this seal exists in several versions, and it is not clear whether the impression on the *Admonitions* scroll is genuine or not. For another example see *Signatures* 1964, vol. 1, p. 166.

54 For a biography of An Qi see Hummel 1943, vol. 1, pp. 11–13. A portrait of An Qi, dated 1715, by Wang Hui, Yang Jin, and Tu Luo, is in the Cleveland Museum of Art; see Ho, Wai-kam, *et al.* 1980, cat. no. 259.

55 See Lovell 1973, pp. 47–49. See also Lawton 1970, pp. 191–215.

56 This consists of five 'half-characters' reading 'Juan zi qishi hao' ('The character *juan*, number seventy'). These characters are clearly visible on the scroll. This inventory label is first mentioned (and recognized as significant) in An Qi's 1742 catalogue; the characters are transcribed in *SQBJ chubian* 1971 (1745), pp. 1074–1075. This inventory tally, which may date to the Southern Song dynasty, can be closely matched by similar inventory labels on the Tang painter Wang Wei's *Fu Sheng of Ji'nan* (or *Fu Sheng Expounding the Classics*) in the Osaka Municipal Museum of Art (Osaka 1994, pl. 3), and the Northern Song painter Xie Yuan's *Peach Blossoms*, now in a private collection in Taiwan (recorded in *SQBJ chubian* 1971 [1745], p. 620, and published in National Museum of History 1995, pl. 5).

57 This almost certainly refers to the Mongol-script seal on the same silk border at the end of the painting that bears the 'Neifu tushu zhi yin', 'Qun yu zhon gmi', and Jia Sidao seals. The same seal appears on Wang Xizhi's *Fengju tie* in the National Palace Museum, Taipei; see *Gugong lidai fashu quanji*, vol. 1 (1976), p. 4; see also *Signatures* 1964, vol. 1, p. 370, no. 579.

58 The translation is from Shih, Hsio-yen 1976, p. 11. It is noteworthy that An Qi does not attribute the calligraphy to Emperor Huizong.

59 As pointed out above, this is unlikely given Xiang Yuanbian's seals on the 'slender gold' script calligraphy and the painting.

60 For a genuine example of the 'Mingchang' seal, see *Signatures* 1964, vol. 1, p. 166.

61 Cited in Yu Jianhua *et al.* (comps) 1962, pp. 159–160.

62 On Han Shineng see Riely 1992, p. 397. Han was Dong Qichang's professor at the Hanlin Academy. According to Xu Bangda, the scroll owned by Han corresponds to the Liaoneng Provincial Museum version of the *Nymph of the Luo River* (Xu Bangda 1984, vol. 1, p. 26). Han's painting collection is listed in Zhang Chou's *Nanyang minghua biao* (1992– [*c*.1598]).

63 Zhan Jingfeng 1992– (1591), p. 22.

64 David 1971, p. 15.

65 See *Zhongguo gudai huihua* 1978, pp. 2–3, pls 2–19; see also Yu Jianhua *et al.* (comps) 1962, p. 176.

Late Ming Collectors and Connoisseurs, and the Making of the Modern Concept of 'Gu Kaizhi'

Yin Ji'nan

Such is the complexity of research into early Chinese history that any argument concerned with the historicity of a particular artist proceeds with the possibility that whatever is said may be deeply flawed.[1] That Gu Kaizhi (*c*. 345–406), for instance, was by nature 'half man, half immortal' (*ban ren ban xian*) – as has been recently pointed out by Professor Wu Hung[2] – has actually made the process by which history shaped 'Gu Kaizhi' a good deal more complicated than the process by which 'Gu Kaizhi' created works of art. It is natural that the legendary Gu Kaizhi and the creation of the Gu Kaizhi legend have been intimately connected and mutually influential; indeed, the 'history of the art of Gu Kaizhi' can also be understood as an 'art history overgrown with the legends of Gu Kaizhi'. If, therefore, we are to really understand what Gu Kaizhi represents within the complex and polysemic world of the spirit, we must begin by moving beyond the concept we have of Gu Kaizhi today.

We might say there are three Gu Kaizhis of textual significance. The first is the literary image of Gu Kaizhi, which was put into words by Liu Yiqing (403–444) in the Southern Dynasties (420–589). Then, Fang Xuanling (578–648) and other Tang (618–907) historians created his historical image. Finally, his art-historical image was created later in the Tang by the art historian Zhang Yanyuan (*c*. 815–after 875). He fused the literary with the historical image of 'Gu Kaizhi', but also gave us the concept of a Gu Kaizhi who expounded the theory of 'transmitting the spirit' (*chuan shen lun*) in his art. In fact, the Gu Kaizhi of art-historical significance outlined by Zhang Yanyuan was a learned discourse of a complexity not sustainable beyond his contemporary horizon. The numerous Six Dynasties (220–589) paintings he recorded represent, for us, an irrecoverable 'cultural imagining', for it seems he was not given to describing the content or style of ancient paintings: his passion was for transmitting the historical literature he encountered, and for drawing pithy conclusions.

The contents of Song dynasty (960–1279) court and private collections indicate a growing rift between them and those works recorded by Zhang Yanyuan and the earlier Tang critic Pei Xiaoyuan (act. *c*. 627–650). It was, by Song times, extremely difficult for collectors and connoisseurs to see genuine works by Gu Kaizhi, making it effectively impossible for them to formulate any concept of Gu Kaizhi on the basis of his oeuvre. Of course, the Northern Song (960–1127) literatus Li Gonglin (1049–1106) is a quite unique case of a true spiritual torch-bearer in that he was acknowledged in his own time as the heir to Wu Daozi (act. *c*. 710–760), who was in turn regarded by both Song and Tang connoisseurs as the heir to Gu Kaizhi. In the Song, the orthodoxy of imperial absolutism and patriarchal society, which has long been forcefully expressed within the ideological structure of art history as a discipline, did indeed take shape in the orthodox views of Song critics. For them, as far as figure painting went, 'the modern did not measure up to the ancient', and as far as landscape painting went, 'the ancient did not measure up to the modern'. The centrality and orthodoxy of landscape painting within the tradition became further established in the following centuries and was basically complete by the time of Dong Qichang (1555–1636) in the late Ming dynasty (1368–1644).

The literary and historical writings of the Southern Dynasties and Tang critics had created a textual 'Gu Kaizhi', whereas in inventories, collections and connoisseurship, men of the Song created a 'Gu Kaizhi' who had painted scrolls. A powerful overlapping of these two figures of 'Gu Kaizhi' would give collecting practices among late Ming and early Qing (1644–1911) collectors and connoisseurs an even more sharply focused bias. Intriguingly, the three compositions ascribed to Gu Kaizhi today all first appeared in the literary record during the Song dynasty. The *Admonitions of the Instructress to the Court Ladies (Nüshi zhen tu)* scroll is seen in

Mi Fu's (1052–1107) *History of Painting (Hua shi; c.*1103) and the *Catalogue of the Xuanhe [1119–1125] Imperial Painting Collection (Xuanhe huapu;* preface 1120) edited at the late Northern Song court. *Biographies of Exemplary Women (Lienü zhuan)* also appears in *History of Painting.* The *Nymph of the Luo River* appears in the Southern Song (1127–1279) writer Wang Zhi's *Snow Stream Collection (Xuexi ji).* To apply the sceptical thinking of the 'Discrimination in Ancient History' movement,[3] any attempt to rely on these works as a basis from which to study the historical Gu Kaizhi, would end up destroying the current concept of Gu Kaizhi constructed with them.

Historically, it only took the overlapping of the concept of Gu Kaizhi built up by Zhang Yanyuan with works later ascribed to Gu Kaizhi to produce an effective learning about Six Dynasties painting that was quite real, and this process took place from the Song to the Ming. Owing to the more widespread use of print technology and the new vogue for collecting old books, there was no difficulty finding histories of early painting and critical literature on individual works to read. We may certainly say that Ming 'men of culture' (*wenren*) preserved for posterity the print and manuscript editions of ancient records that had come down to them from former dynasties. Woodblock-printed compendia (*congshu*) were major sources of learning and information about the calligraphers and painters of the Six Dynasties. The official Tang-edited histories of the Six Dynasties, and Liu Yiqing's *New Tales of the World (Shishuo xinyu)* were easily acquired in the Ming period, as were such texts as Xie He's (act. *c.* 500–535?) *Classification of Paintings (Guhua pinlu);* Zhang Yanyuan's *Lidai minghua ji;* Pei Xiaoyuan's *Record of Paintings in Public and Private Collections in the Zhenguan Era (Zhenguan gongsi hua shi);* Mi Fu's *History of Painting* and the *Xuanhe huapu;* and Tang Hou's (act. early fourteenth century) *Mirror of Painting (Hua jian).* This network of literary texts played an important role in the construction of Ming collectors' and connoisseurs' basic conception of Six Dynasties painting. Indeed, the broad circulation of history books and painting texts meant that textual learning about Six Dynasties painting was far more widespread than learning conveyed through old paintings, or 'tracing copies' (*moben*) of them.

We can clearly see the influence of the ancient painting literature on the late Yuan–early Ming critic Tao Zongyi (*c.*1316–1402), for instance. Under the heading, 'Preface, painting' (Xuhua), in *juan* 18 of his collection of notes, *Record of My Ploughing (Nancun chuogeng lu),* he quotes from the major Tang, Song and Yuan classic records on painting, including the following – Tang: Zhang Yanyuan's *Lidai minghua ji;* Song: Guo Ruoxu's (act. latter half eleventh century) *Record of Paintings that I have Seen and Heard About*

(Tuhua jianwen zhi), Deng Chun's (twelfth century) *Painting, Continued (Hua ji;* 1167), and the anonymous *Supplement to 'Painting, Continued' (Huaji buyi;* 1298), Chen Dehui's *Further Record of Paintings (Xu hua ji),* and Zhao Xigu's (act. *c.*1195–*c.*1242) *Collection of Pure Earnings in the Realm of the Immortals (Dongtian qinglu ji; c.*1242); Yuan (1271–1368): Tang Hou's *Hua jian,* and Xia Wenyan's (fourteenth century) *Precious Mirror of Painting (Tuhui baojian;* 1365). He also mentions the *Xuanhe Painting Manual.*[4] This is more or less the bibliography of primary sources that students of Chinese painting history consult today. What made it even easier still for late Ming and early Qing 'men of culture' to obtain the classic texts on painting listed above was the publication of such woodblock-print compendia as Wang Shizhen's (1526–1590) *Master Wang's Garden of Calligraphy and Painting (Wangshi shuhua yuan),* Mao Jin's (1599–1659) *Jintai bishu* and Zhan Jingfeng's (1519–1600) *Supplement to Master Zhan's Garden of Calligraphy and Painting (Zhanshi shuhua yuan buyi).*

Late Ming Collectors and Connoisseurs

Not only are men who may be called collectors and connoisseurs in the late Ming actually quite small in number, but they were also all congregated in three neighbouring regions: Suzhou, Songjiang and Jiaxing Prefectures (west of Shanghai). Xiang Yuanbian (1525–1590), Li Rihua (1565–1635), and Yu Fengqing (seventeenth century) were all Jiaxing men, and Wang Keyu (1587–1645), although from Huizhou, lived there for a long time. The brothers Wang Shizhen and Shimou were Taicang men; Wen Zhengming (1470–1559) and his sons Peng (1489–1573) and Jia (1501–1583), as well as Han Shineng (1528–1598) and Zhang Chou (1577–1643) were men of Changzhou and Wu County (the Suzhou area). In Huating there were He Liangjun (1506–1573), Dong Qichang (1555–1636), and Chen Jiru (1558–1639). Shanghai had Gu Congyi (1523–88). Wuxi had Hua Xia (act. 1567–1619). Zhan Jingfeng was from Xiuning, but was able to encounter many works of ancient painting and calligraphy in the Zhejiang area. The top echelon of collectors and connoisseurs were not just gathered in this region, but relations between them were also very intimate. Works of painting and calligraphy in Hua Xia, Han Shineng, and Xiang Yuanbian's collections, in particular, established connections between collectors of different calibre in this one region, so that from the perspective of later art and collecting history, this must be considered an area in which cultural power was richly concentrated.

What early paintings did these men actually own? The only work of Six Dynasties painting in Wang Shizhen's collection was one said to be Shi Daoshi's (later fourth to mid-fifth century) *Eight Thoroughbreds (Bajun tu)*, the subject of an essay by Wang entitled 'Record of the Jin painter Shi Daoshi's *Eight Thoroughbreds*'.[5] In it, he managed to quote Xie He's *Classification of Painters*, Li Sizhen's (d. 696) *Continuation of the 'Classification of Painters' (Xu hua pin)*, Pei Xiaoyuan's *Zhenguan gongsi hua shi*, Guo Ruoxu's *Tuhua jianwen zhi*, and the *Xuanhe Painting Manual* – the very same core of important old texts that Wang Shizhen published in his wood block-printed compendium on painting, *Master Wang's Garden of Painting (Wangshi huayuan)*. Wang Shizhen certainly did not believe the painting to be by the hand of Shi Daoshi, since he also wrote: 'Today, this scroll does not have the small "Zhenguan" [627–649] seal; this indicates that it is a "tracing copy" made outside the court.' But we have no way of knowing whether he and his brother Shimou ever saw any other attributions to Six Dynasties painters.

Six Dynasties paintings acquired by Xiang Yuanbian included the *Admonitions* scroll in the British Museum,[6] and Zhang Sengyou's (act. late fifth to mid-sixth century) *Cloudy Mountains, Red Trees (Yunshan hongshu tu)* in the National Palace Museum in Taipei. However, we have little idea what Xiang Yuanbian considered important or reliable criteria in authenticating old scrolls. He had close links with his peers, including Hua Xia, Wen Zhengming and his son Jia, Wang Jimei and his son Keyu, Chen Jiru, Li Rihua and Dong Qichang.[7] But Xiang Yuanbian also criticised the connoisseurship of other collectors – for instance, when he heaped scorn upon 'eyes' of Wang Shizhen and his brother, and Gu Congyi and his brother. He considered the finest connoisseurs to be Zhan Jingfeng and himself.[8]

The 'tracing copies' of Eastern Jin and Six Dynasties paintings that Zhan Jingfeng saw would basically have been those in the private collections of his peers, such as that of Han Shineng, to which he often referred in his *Dongtu xuanlan bian (Book of My Abstruse Reading)*. Records indicate that copies of old paintings that Han Shineng owned included:

- Cao Buxing (third century), *Bingfu tu (Military tallies)*
- Gu Kaizhi, *Luoshen tu (Nymph of the Luo River)*
- *Shezhi tu (Shooting pheasants)*
- *Youjun jia yuanjing (Scenery around Wang Xizhi's house)*
- Zhang Sengyou, *Wuxing ershiba xiu tu (The Five Planets and Twenty-eight Lunar Mansions)*

Zhan Jingfeng saw another Gu Kaizhi *Nymph of the Luo River*[9] and a Cao Buxing *Landscape* scroll at Han Shineng's

house, and he saw, with Guo Hengzhi, yet another Gu Kaizhi *Nymph* scroll owned by an antique dealer they visited in the capital Chang'an. Judging by Zhan Jingfeng's colophons, he seems also to have seen Wang Shizhen's *Eight Thoroughbreds* by Shi Daoshi. At the mansion of Grand Preceptor Liu he saw and inscribed Zhang Sengyou's *Reading a Stele (Guanbei tu)*. In *juan* one of his *Dongtu xuanlan bian*, he also refers to a painting ascribed to Gu Kaizhi entitled *Grand Tutor Xie in the Eastern Mountains (Xie Taifu Dongshan)*. Zhan Jingfeng's criteria in connoisseurly judgement seem to have been based upon the brushwork in painting. When he appraised the *Nymph of the Luo River* scroll belonging to the Chang'an antique dealer, he wrote: 'the layout of the shorelines, trees and rocks, and plants and grasses recalls pre-Tang methods, and not the handling of a Five Dynasties or Northern Song hand. Only the texturing of the rocks is a very practised, hard scraping, which does indeed resemble the work of a Northern Song hand.' His final judgement is: 'I do think it is not a Northern Song "tracing copy" of a Tang scroll, but a preliminary sketch [*fenben*] by Li Xu, the Prince of Jiangdu (later seventh century).' Moreover, in his colophon, Zhan Jingfeng referred to the 'gossamer thread of a spring silkworm' (*chun can tu si*) – the phrase the Yuan critic Tang Hou had used to describe Gu Kaizhi's painting. To be sure, this phrase also had a certain influence over the later collector-connoisseur An Qi (1683–1742?), who similarly repeated it in his own record of the *Admonitions* scroll.

He Liangjun and Zhang Chou both saw the so-called Gu Kaizhi *Biographies of Exemplary Women*. Han Shineng, Zhan Jingfeng, Dong Qichang, Zhang Chou and Wang Keyu all saw versions of Gu Kaizhi's *Nymph of the Luo River*. Yan Song (1480–1567) and his son Yan Shifan (?–1565), Gu Congyi and Xiang Yuanbian all owned the *Admonitions* scroll at one time or another, and it was also seen by Wen Jia and Dong Qichang.

In spite of the considerable cultural power that collectors and connoisseurs from this region held, they made absolutely no new contribution to the development of the orthodox tradition of *figure* painting, and it becomes clear that this tradition, which had been established over the Tang-Song transition, could only ever have been literary in nature in the Ming. The Tang and Song art historians and critics that late Ming collectors and connoisseurs incessantly quoted had already constructed a ready-made knowledge system, but at the same time, in their colophons we often find the Ming men remarking of Jin and Tang paintings and works of calligraphy that there are 'not many seen nowadays'. The task that fell to them, it would seem, was simply to use the pithy descriptions from early painting literature to 'authenticate' the Six Dynasties paintings they encountered. They were not in the habit of using the literature to investigate the subjects and titles of extant paintings critically: although the Tang dynasty *Zhenguan gongsi hua shi* and *Lidai minghua ji* were among their most easily obtained painting texts, none of these connoisseurs questioned Gu Kaizhi's authorship of the *Nymph*, *Admonitions* and *Biographies* scrolls. Even the otherwise brilliant Dong Qichang said nothing remarkable. It is only with the advent of textual criticism by Qing dynasty scholars like Sun Xingyan (1753–1818) that we begin to find clear doubts being expressed about the link between Gu Kaizhi and the scroll of *Benevolent and Wise Women* from the *Biographies of Exemplary Women (Lienü zhuan renzhi tu)*. Sun wrote: 'If you look in *Zhenguan gongsi hua shi* and *Lidai minghua ji* you will find they do not record [this] painting by Gu Hutou [Kaizhi].'[10] The learning most influential among these late Ming collectors and connoisseurs, therefore, was that which drew from collectible objects. Hence, the colophons and seals already on their scrolls were what constituted the experience and learning of most of these men.

The *Admonitions*, *Biographies* and *Nymph of the Luo River* Scrolls

As has just been indicated, it is far from clear whether late Ming collectors and connoisseurs believed that Gu Kaizhi painted the *Nymph*, *Admonitions* and *Biographies* scrolls. Let us consider each case, beginning with the *Biographies of Exemplary Women*.

A study of the extant writings of these late Ming men suggests three possible reasons why they could have believed Gu Kaizhi painted the *Biographies*. The first is that Liu Xiang's (77?–6? BCE) text, *Biographies of Exemplary Women*, may be said to be one of the earliest subjects to have passed through the historical record – from the Eastern Han (25–220) to the Ming and Qing – and was painted by many Six Dynasties artists. The second is that Gu Kaizhi praised his predecessor Wei Xie's (act. late third to early fourth century) paintings of seven Buddhas and the 'greater heroines' (*da lienü*), the latter comprising illustrations of the *Biographies*, calling them 'mighty, and yet still full of emotive force'.[11] Third, *Lidai minghua ji* records that Gu Kaizhi painted a picture of the *Chaste Woman Agu (Agu chunü tu)*. The narrative behind this illustration comes from the section of Liu Xiang's *Biographies of Exemplary Women* entitled *Biographies of the Eloquent and Erudite (Lienü zhuan: Biantong zhuan)*, where the original title is 'Chaste Woman Agu' ('Agu chunü'), which is the same as the title of the recorded painting. As well as Gu Kaizhi, Shi

Daoshi and Dai Kui (?–396) each painted a *Picture of Chaste Woman Agu (Agu chunü tu)*. As noted, this comes from the section of Liu Xiang's *Biographies of Exemplary Women* entitled *Biographies of the Eloquent and Erudite*, a subject also painted by both Xie Zhi (later third century) and Pu Daoxing (420–478). Historically, the *Biographies* has long figured in China's politics and society: 'female virtue' (*nü de*) and 'female ethical conduct' (*nü jiao*), the designs of absolutist and patrician Confucian ideology, were not only in vogue in the Han (206 BCE–220 CE), Wei (386–533) and Six Dynasties, but also between the Song and the Ming.

The *Nymph of the Luo River* – the second case – is a subject that the Jin emperor Mingdi (r. 323–325) painted, and would have been recognized as a Six Dynasties painting subject in the critical writings of Tang collectors and connoisseurs. According to Mr Xu Bangda, extant versions of the *Nymph* scroll connected to Gu Kaizhi comprise one in the Beijing Palace Museum, another in Liaoning Provincial Museum, and a third in the Freer Gallery in Washington, DC. However, the only instances of this composition in the literary record are one mentioned by Han Shineng and one by An Qi (with the 'Mingchang' [1190–1195] seal). Besides these, there are several versions of the *Nymph of the Luo River* that are anonymous or attributed to Tang or Song painters. One is the Lu Tanwei (act. 465–472), *Nymph of the Luo River (Luoshen fu tu)*, in ink outline (*baimiao*), now in the Freer Gallery, which Xu Bangda believes is a replica copy done by a Ming or Qing forger. Another is the *Nymph of the Luo River (Luoshen fu quan tu)* by an unknown Tang painter recorded in the first catalogue of the Qianlong (1736–1795) imperial collection, *Shiqu baoji chubian* (in *juan* 35). A third is the Li Gonglin ink-outline version of the *Nymph of the Luo River (Luoshen tu)*, recorded in the 'Ningshougong' (Ningshou Palace) section of the second Qianlong catalogue, *Shiqu baoji xubian*, where it is described in an inscription by the Qianlong emperor as 'the third *Nymph of the Luo River* scroll' (*di san juan*). Thus all the various copies labelled Gu Kaizhis played a part in building Ming and Qing collectors' and connoisseurs' understanding of Six Dynasties painting; Han Shineng, Zhan Jingfeng, Xiang Yuanbian, Dong Qichang, Liang Qingbiao (1620–1692) and An Qi all had a hand in this process.

In actual fact, Dong Qichang's attention was not entirely on the *Nymph of the Luo River* scroll he owned (Freer Gallery), in spite of his having appraised it with the words: 'Of Gu [Kaizhi's] paintings, only this and the *Admonitions of the Instructress to the Court Ladies* scroll in the collection of Xiang [Yuanbian] are extant. They are indeed a pair of treasures.'[12] He intended to swap it with a work of calligraphy by Chu Suliang (596–658; *Xishengjing*, 'Scripture of Western Ascension'), which suggests how highly he esteemed Jin and Tang calligraphy. Indeed, if the *Nymph* paintings had any spiritual connections, they were with the masterpieces of calligraphy by the great calligraphers upon which quite a few late Ming collectors and connoisseurs had focused their interest. While the 'Nymph of the Luo River Ode' (Luoshen fu) was a celebrated work of Chinese literature in its own right, it was perhaps more important that the Calligraphic Sage Wang Xizhi's (303–361) son Wang Xianzhi (344–388) had once transcribed it. This transcription, which survives only in part, is known in the history of calligraphy as the *Commander's Thirteen Lines (Daling shisan hang)*. In the Ming, versions of Wang Xianzhi's *Thirteen Lines* of the *Nymph* ode were in the collections of Han Shineng and Xiang Yuanbian, and Wen Zhengming's family owned a copy by Li Gonglin. Dong Qichang wrote numerous colophon-transcriptions to these, and when Xiang Yuanbian's version was to be printed in Dong's *Xihongtang fatie (Calligraphy Copybook of the Hall of Playing Geese)*, Dong prepared a freehand transcription (*linben*) to be included in it. Dong Qichang did this in the knowledge that the great literati artists Li Gonglin and Zhao Mengfu (1254–1322) had both transcribed the *Nymph* ode before him. Zhan Jingfeng saw just one of Zhao Mengfu's transcriptions of the *Commander's Thirteen Lines*, but today we know of no less than three of Zhao Mengfu's transcriptions of the *Nymph* ode in small block script:

1) Dated Dade third year (1299 CE), written for Yu Zijia. This manuscript was in the collection of Wu Rongguang in the Qing Daoguang period (1831–1850), but is today lost.

2) Dated Dade fourth year (1300 CE), written for 'loyalist Sheng' (Sheng *yimin*), a genuine work, now in Tianjin Art Museum.

3) Dated Yanyou sixth year (1319 CE), a genuine work with a colophon by Zhang Tianyu (b. 1270). Formerly in Xiang Yuanbian's 'Hall of Heavenly Music' (Tianlaige) collection; later in the Qing imperial collection; then in Huang Zhongming's collection. Photographic reproduction by Shangwu yinshuguan.

The cultural significance of Cao Zhi's (192–232) 'Nymph of the Luo River Ode' has been reduplicated again and again by the transcriptions of calligraphers through history. This layering process and the so-called Gu Kaizhi paintings that illustrate it are intimately linked: we can easily imagine, then, how owning a single work comprised of Cao Zhi's ode, Wang Xianzhi's calligraphy and Gu Kaizhi's painting must have been something a collector wished for in his wildest dreams. The

Qing collector Gu Fu, who recorded a version of the *Nymph* painting in his *Greatest Views in My Life (Pingsheng zhuangguan)*, is an interesting case here. After describing the painting, Gu wrote: 'Then follows a transcription of the 'Nymph of the Luo River Ode' in block script, which has been attributed to Daling [i.e. Wang Xianzhi]. I can confirm, however, that it is by Hutou [i.e. Gu Kaizhi], and uphold the view of Wenmin [i.e. Dong Qichang].' While this illustrates how the views of the great Dong Qichang became mixed up with any later so-called Gu Kaizhi version of the painting, the real point is that it was the calligraphy which basically guaranteed the preservation of Gu Kaizhi's *Nymph of the Luo River* in the Ming period. In the case of the *Admonitions*, it is the same scenario: Xiang Yuanbian believed that the calligraphic inscriptions in block script on the painting were written by Gu Kaizhi; Dong Qichang believed they were by Wang Xianzhi.[13]

Dong Qichang may have appeared profoundly knowledgeable about the historical origins of Wang Xianzhi's *Thirteen Lines*, but he in fact knew very little about either the *Nymph* or the *Admonitions* paintings. He was far from being alone in what was a situation common to all the late Ming collector-connoisseurs. Their main collecting interests, after all, were Song and Yuan editions of printed or manuscript books, works of Jin and Tang calligraphy, and landscapes by literati of the Five Dynasties and Northern Song up to the Yuan.

We turn now to the third case, the *Admonitions* scroll. Finding early literary material or indirect evidence to link it to Gu Kaizhi has proven extremely difficult, not just because there simply is no record in the Tang literature of Gu Kaizhi's having painted this subject, but also because there are no records in the Tang literature of any Six Dynasties figure painter having done it. We can only wonder if this owes anything to the 'anti-northern, pro-southern' bias of the writer of one of our most important sources – *Lidai minghua ji* by Zhang Yanyuan. Quite how skewed this book is is evident from the following comparison: far fewer Northern Dynasties painters are recorded (thirteen, compared to seventy-four southerners), and far fewer works by them – only Yang Zihua's (act. mid- to late sixth century) and Cao Zhongda's (act. 550–577).

Since the Song dynasty, these three sets of copies – the *Biographies, Admonitions* and *Nymph* scrolls – have borne the nominal title of Gu Kaizhi's oeuvre through the collecting world and the critical process. They have shaped people's 'learning' about Gu Kaizhi and his works so powerfully that this 'learning' still exerts great influence on contemporary art-historical research and connoisseurship. To this extent we are still compelled to use the words Gu Kaizhi and Six Dynasties painting in order to discuss the *Admonitions* scroll.

Basis for a Concept of 'Gu Kaizhi'

It is my belief that we need to effect a more reflexive critical approach to the 'concept of Gu Kaizhi' in cultural history. As it stands today, this concept may be roughly summed up as follows. First, we see Gu Kaizhi as an exponent of the theory of 'transmitting the spirit'. Second, we see him as a scroll-painter of female subjects. Third, we see him as a wall-painter of Buddhist subjects. However, the idea of creating a post-facto concept of 'Gu Kaizhi' on this third basis is meaningless since the murals he limned in Eastern Jin (317–419) temples have long been, as it were, historically 'extinct'. A concept of Gu Kaizhi as a painter of female subjects is, I would say, the most objective, since we may depend upon paintings of these three main subjects – the *Biographies*, the *Admonitions* and the *Nymph* – to create a concept of him based upon actual images.

Benevolent and Wise Women (Lienü zhuan renzhi tu) and the *Admonitions of the Instructress to the Court Ladies* were categorized by the Song critic Guo Ruoxu as figural works in which one 'regards virtue' (*guan de*). There is some overlapping in the subject matter of these two scrolls, for instance, with the scenes of 'Lady Feng intercepting the bear' and 'Lady Ban refusing to ride in the imperial palanquin'. The Ming painter Ding Yunpeng (act. 1584–1618) and the Qing painter Jin Tingbiao (act. *c.* 1727–d. 1767) both painted the story of 'Lady Feng intercepting the bear', and their paintings, *Feng Wan Confronts the Bear (Feng Wan dang xiong tu)* and *Concubine Confronting a Bear (Jieyu dang xiong tu)*, in the Beijing Palace Museum collection, illustrate how the basic ideology behind stories and paintings like these was still being carried forward in the Ming and Qing. The intensity of the relationship between the actual virtuous and chaste women of Ming and Qing history, and past learning and its attendant beliefs must have been well beyond the influence of connoisseurly learning. While most women would have had absolutely no knowledge of Gu Kaizhi, they were very likely to know Liu Xiang's *Biographies of Exemplary Women*, a conclusion we may draw from some of the model lives recounted by Qing historians in the official *Ming History (Ming shi)*:

Tang Huixin, from Shanghai. She mastered the *Classic of Filial Piety (Xiao jing)* and *Biographies of Exemplary Women*. She was married to Deng Lin of Huaxiang.

Ouyang Jinzhen, from Jiangxia. Her father was called Wu. She gave instruction in the *Classic of Filial Piety* and *Biographies of Exemplary Women*.

Two women *nées* Fan, from Kuaiji. From an early age they enjoyed studying, and both mastered the *Biographies of Exemplary Women*.

A woman called Madam Xiang, from Xiushui ... She was expert in women's craftwork, mastered the *qin* and *se* [seven- and twenty-five-stringed zithers], as well as the *Biographies of Exemplary Women*. She served her paternal grandmother and stepmother with extreme filial piety.[14]

Liu Xiang's *Biographies* was reprinted many times in the Song to Ming period. In the thirty-first year of the Ming Jiajing reign (corresponding to 1552 CE), for instance, Huang Luceng published a print edition of *Biographies of Exemplary Women of the Past (Gu lienü zhuan, 7 juan)*. But the same period also saw the publication of *Biographies of Exemplary Women Ancient and Modern, Newly Engraved, and Augmented and Expanded with a Complete Set of Portraits and Appraisals (Xinjuan zengbu quanxiang pinglin gujin lienü zhuan)*, a block-print edition in eight *juan*.[15] A third publication was the *Illustrated Biographies of Exemplary Women (Lienü zhuan tu)*, a print edition in sixteen *juan*.[16] The Ming dynasty witnessed a wholesale revival of the Song-period Confucian (feudal) ethical code, and especially the code of female ethical conduct.

The Ming empress Renxiao (1360–1407), wife of the Yongle emperor (r. 1403–1424) and eldest daughter of Wang Xuda from Zhongshan, was an avid reader of Liu Xiang's *Biographies*, and also wrote a book entitled *Lessons for the Inner Quarters (Nei xun)*. During the Yongle reign, the prominent minister Xie Jin (1369–1415) and others were instructed by the emperor to make selections for a book entitled *Biographies of Exemplary Women Ancient and Modern* in three *juan*, which was to be published throughout the country. Later, in the Qing dynasty, Wang Xiang put together a new book called the *Four Books for Women (Nü si shu)*, comprising the Han scholar Ban Zhao's (49–*c.* 120) *Precepts for Women (Nü jie)*, the Tang writer Song Ruohua's (?–820) *Analects for Women (Nü lunyu)*, the Ming empress Renxiao's *Lessons for the Inner Quarters*, and his mother Madam Liu's *Models for Women: a Quick Record (Nü fan jie lu)*. Wang Xiang's compilation was highly influential in Qing society. The modern scholar Chen Dongyuan has calculated that:

If we put together 'Biographies of Exemplary Women' sections and other biographical appendices, we find no more than sixty women per dynastic history prior to the

Yuan History (Yuan shi). The *Song History (Song shi)* has the most, with just fifty-five; the *Tang Histories (Tang shi)* have fifty-four; with the *Yuan History* we finally reach 187 women. The *Yuan History* was edited by Song Lian and others, men of the Ming dynasty who advocated female chastity or virginity [i.e. remaining chaste and faithful to one's husband or betrothed, even after his death, as demanded by the Confucian moral code]. For this reason, they and later Ming historians collected information on quite a lot of chaste women and female martyrs. They collated the veritable records and annals of the Ming reigns at the same time as keeping note of tales of the dynasty's chaste women and female martyrs. Thus, when it came to the time for Qing historians to edit the *Ming History*, the number of biographies of chaste women and female martyrs that they had assembled came to be 'about ten thousand women'. The most outstanding of the chaste women selected for inclusion in the history numbered 308.[17]

This was not just the cultural background for exemplary and chaste women, it was also the cultural background for Ming collector-connoisseurs.

If we have resolved that there is an 'expressive causality' between the *Biographies* and the *Admonitions* on one hand, and society, on the other, we are still faced with the problem of explaining the *Nymph* paintings in the late Ming and subsequent periods, for there is a certain contradiction between these two types of female subject, the *Nymph* and the *Biographies*. Unlike the *Biographies* and *Admonitions*, the *Nymph of the Luo River* does not grind any moral-didactic axe; it emphasizes how unattainable a bewitching and beautiful woman is from a man's perspective. It is basically about beauty, desire and yearning, a theme that comes fairly close to what Guo Ruoxu called the 'carefree beauty' (*mili*) type of figure paint-

ing. The two quite unrelated figures of 'Gu Kaizhi' that we find here – one didactic, and one 'carefree' – were never remarked upon by our Ming collector-connoisseurs.

To put this in perspective, however, we may try to gauge the speed and frequency at which old scrolls circulated as commodities in late Ming society from the records of men like Li Rihua. Some collectors held onto scrolls for long periods of time, like Hua Xia, Han Shineng, and Xiang Yuanbian; generally speaking, they were not scholars renowned for their insights into the spiritual dimensions of art history, nor were they critical literary scholars. Others, who were such scholars, like Zhan Jingfeng, Dong Qichang, Li Rihua, and Chen Jiru took a relatively short time to appreciate and digest copies of Six Dynasties paintings – just like in the old saying that scrolls pass 'like clouds and mists before one's eyes' (*yunyan guo yan*). We should also bear in mind that the old paintings in question had long been kept out of general view in society, and this lack of long-term 'publicity' resulted in many would-be researchers being unable to participate in debate about them in any kind of meaningful way. For all these reasons, there is no way we can demand that late Ming collectors, connoisseurs or 'men of culture' should have possessed clear and precise knowledge of Six Dynasties painting.

There are those who even today still take Gu Kaizhi to be an irreducible entity in their discourse about him, but this essay has shown that the present unified concept of Gu Kaizhi results from a historical process involving the compounding the three textual 'Gu Kaizhis' and the 'Gu Kaizhis' of the three scroll paintings. This compounding was carried out in the late Ming by collectors and connoisseurs when they constructed the coercive 'learning' about Six Dynasties painting that we inherit today. The reality is that the compounded 'Gu Kaizhi' never existed in the Eastern Jìn, but came to exist in the historical process since the Song dynasty.

Translated by Shane McCausland

NOTES

1   Professor Yin's title, 'Mingdai houqi jiacangjia guanyu Liuchao huihua zhishi de hecheng yu zuoyong: yi "Gu Kaizhi" de gainian wei xiansuo', literally reads, 'Late Ming collectors and connoisseurs, and their compounding and use of learning about Six Dynasties painting: the case of the concept of "Gu Kaizhi"' (translator's note).

2   Wu Hung 1997, p. 47.

3   In the 1920s and 1930s, the 'Discrimination in Ancient History' movement (Gushibian pai), led by scholars including Gu Jiegang (1893–1980), sought to question Chinese culture and identity with a new critical approach to traditional Chinese historiography, and discovered tensions and contradictions between Chinese nationalism and culture (translator's note).

4   Tao Zongyi 1959 (1366), *juan* 18.

5   'Jin Shi Daoshi Bajun tu ji', in *Yanzhou shanren sibu gao* (*SKQS*), *juan* 137. Also in *Peiwenzhai shuhua pu*, *juan* 81.

6   Xiang Yuanbian's inscription reads: 'The *Admonitions of the Instructress to the Court Ladies* painting and small block-script [inscriptions] by Gu Kaizhi of the Jin, formerly in the Song imperial collection.'

7   Zheng Yinshu 1984.

8   *Mingshi jishi* (Chen Tian 1993), part *geng*, *juan* 7: 'Zhan Jingfeng', quoting *Dongtu ji*: 'Xiang once said to me, "Who today has a proper pair of eyes? [The Wang brothers] are blind men, and the eyes of [the Gu brothers] are dim. Only Wen Zhengming had a pair of eyes, but he is long dead." What he really wanted was for me to say he had a pair of eyes, but I looked at him and finally replied: "The world is such a big place that you could never hope to meet all the worthy people in it, let alone be certain which of them has a pair of eyes." Xiang therefore said: "The only ones who have a pair of eyes in the world today are you and me."' (The manner of Xiang Yuanbian's retort clearly recalls the well-known reply of Cao Cao [155–220] to Liu Bei [r. as Shu emperor Zhaolie, 221–223]: 'The only heroes in the world today are you and me.' See *San guo zhi*, *juan* 32 (1999, p. 652). It is also possible that Xiang's reply was fashioned by Zhan Jingfeng.)

9   Zhan Jingfeng, *Dongtu xuanlan bian* (1992 [1591], vol. 4, *juan* 2).

10 Sun Xingyan 1841?

11 'Wei er you qing shi', quoted from Gu Kaizhi's 'Lun hua' (Discussion of painting) by Zhang Yanyuan in *Lidai minghua ji* (*HSCS*), *juan* 5, p. 65.

12 Tr. Lawton 1973, p. 24.

13 Dong Qichang, *Huachanshi suibi*: 'In the past those who examined the Jin dynasty painting of the *Admonitions of the Instructress to the Court Ladies* said, "This is Hutou's [Gu Kaizhi's] brush". [In attempting] to classify the inscriptions of the "Admonitions" attached to the side of the paintings, [they] said that it was Daling's [Wang Xianzhi's] calligraphy. I have no idea where [the idea] of Daling writing the "Admonitions" came from.' (Tr. Stephen Little, in this volume.)

14 *Ming shi*, *juan* 301–302 (Biographies of Exemplary Women, chapters 1 and 2; 1974).

15 Text by Liu Xiang of the Han; addenda by Mao Kun (1512–1601) of the Ming; appraisals by Peng Yang of the Ming.

16 Text by Liu Xiang of the Han; edited by Wang Daokun of the Ming; illustrations by Qiu Ying (*c.*1495–1552) of the Ming.

17 Chen Dongyuan 1937, pp. 180–181.

The *Admonitions* Scroll in the Context of Ming Aesthetics and Collecting: Material Artefact, Cultural Biography and Cultural Imagining

Cary Y. Liu

I want to focus my comments on trying to place the papers by Wang Yao-t'ing, Stephen Little and Yin Ji'nan into the larger context of the aesthetic and cultural discourse concerning ownership, collecting, and connoisseurship in the Ming period (1368–1644). As a framework, I will try to expand on the notion of 'boundaries' introduced by Wang Yao-t'ing.

In his paper, Wang Yao-t'ing goes beyond the boundaries of the *Admonitions* painting alone, and enlarges his attention to the collector seals, inscriptions, and physical mounting in order to raise important questions, not so much about authorship, authenticity, or style, but about the scroll's history and transmission as a cultural artefact. Here, later alterations, losses, and other changes to the scroll are as important as what survives from an original. The approach, however, is keyed to what is found within the physical boundaries of the scroll itself, which then dictates, yet also limits, possible avenues of investigation. As a result certain aspects of the scroll's history remain unexplained, and the aesthetic values and collecting practices during the Ming period remain unexplored.

Still, Wang Yao-t'ing's meticulous investigations raise a number of important issues. For example, concerning the Northern Song (960–1127) emperor Huizong (r. 1101–1125) seals on the *Admonitions*, by noting 1) their non-standard placement on the scroll, 2) the difference from similar seal impressions on other works, and 3) the difference in seal paste (or seal ink) of the impressions on the front and back borders from those on the actual painting, he concludes that there are many questions that need to be resolved concerning these seals. Through careful comparison he shows that the same Huizong seals are impressed on the Wang Xizhi (303–361), *Ping'an tie* calligraphy scroll in the collection of the National Palace Museum, Taipei. His analysis shows that the Huizong seals on the calligraphy scroll, and consequently those on the *Admonitions* scroll, are later additions.

This concurs with the opinion of many scholars, and builds on Kohara Hironobu's judgement that the Tang dynasty (618–907) and many of the Song dynasty (960–1279) seals on the *Admonitions* are incorrect or irresolvable.[1] It is interesting to note that concerning the weak four-character signature-line 'Painted by Gu Kaizhi' (*Gu Kaizhi hua*) at the end of the scroll, Kohara dates its later addition to the scroll to between 1582 and 1616 during the Ming dynasty. One of the Song seals may actually be impressed over this added signature, indicating that the seal would have been stamped afterwards.[2] For Kohara, consequently, the Song seals were added in the Ming dynasty while the *Admonitions* scroll was in the possession of the famed collector Xiang Yuanbian (1525–1590). When Dong Qichang (1555–1636) viewed this scroll in Xiang Yuanbian's collection in 1582, he did not make any mention of the signature, and the first mention of the signature-line is only recorded in 1616. This has interesting ramifications for our understanding of the scroll's history and about the nature and practice of Ming collecting.

The implication is that Xiang Yuanbian – whose numerous seals appear on the *Admonitions* and on many important works that later entered the Qing (1644–1911) imperial collection – or some other Ming collector-connoisseur, added, or arranged to have added, the fake Song seals. Was this an act of restoration, an effort to enhance the value of the scroll, or an attempt to configure a personal sphere through ownership? If true, what does this say about other painting and calligraphy scrolls that passed through Xiang Yuanbian's collection? For example, we have already mentioned that some of the added Huizong seals on the *Admonitions* match seals found on the *Ping'an tie* calligraphy scroll. This would suggest that Xiang Yuanbian may have also been responsible for adding the Song seals on the latter work, and indeed, Xiang Yuanbian's seals are also found on this calligraphy scroll.

Besides Wang Xizhi's *Ping'an tie*, in comparison with the *Admonitions* scroll, Wang Yao-t'ing also calls our attention to the more than coincidental appearance of similar fake Song imperial seals and the same Ming collector seals (including those of Xiang Yuanbian) that are duplicated on two other well-known early calligraphies: the *Zhongqiu tie (Mid-Autumn)* attributed to Wang Xianzhi (344–388), and Wu Cailuan's (ninth century) *Tang yun (Tang Rhymes)*. So how are we to understand what is happening in the Ming practice of collecting and ownership? We will return to this issue below.

To begin to delve further into these questions, we need again to expand our boundaries, and in the papers presented by Stephen Little and Yin Ji'nan we see related but different approaches to viewing the Ming situation. Stephen Little concentrates on reconstructing the history and provenance of the scroll between the sixteenth and early eighteenth centuries, developing a 'cultural biography'. Beyond using evidence found on the actual scroll, textual sources in the form of recorded colophons and contemporary descriptions are relied upon to give flesh to details concerning the scroll's transmission from collector to collector. In his conclusion Little asks, 'What did the *Admonitions* scroll signify for the collectors and critics of the Ming and early Qing dynasties?' In his judgement, authorship and connoisseurship concerns were central.

This same consideration is approached from a very different and surprising angle in the paper by Yin Ji'nan who seems to ask what *could* the *Admonitions* scroll signify for Ming collectors and connoisseurs. Yin Ji'nan questions the limited sources of knowledge available to Ming collectors and connoisseurs in making critical determinations about the authenticity of Six Dynasties (265–589) art. Besides questioning the basic authority of late Ming connoisseurs, however, Yin Ji'nan also points out that this was the moment when the corpus of textual criticism and visual materials that came to comprise the legend or 'concept of Gu Kaizhi' in later times was formulated. In this sense he has not traced a distilled 'cultural biography'; instead what he has outlined is a concocted 'cultural imagining' (*wenhua xiangxiang*).

As I read these three papers, I was struck by how well they complement each other by approaching the Ming situation with differing sets of boundaries. It is also important to note that in each paper, directly or indirectly, there is a recognition of the fundamental role of collecting in China; that is, 'to assemble a world', an exercise in 'cultural imagining'.[3] This is the territory of leisurely aesthetic sensibilities occupied by the collector-connoisseur – to assemble 'useless things' (*wu yi*), and by ordering them to find 'uses in the uselessness' (*wu yong zhi yong*), which has Daoist undercurrents.

I want now to try to place these three papers into this larger territory involving a discourse that tries to balance the pursuit of pleasure in useless things and leisurely activities (*xian shi*), on the one hand, with their usefulness in guiding social propriety, moral education, and spiritual enlightenment, on the other. Historically such a discourse stems from as far back as the *Book of Documents (Shang shu)*, and on the imperial stage is most familiar in the dictum that sees a direct correspondence between excess indulgence in pleasure with moral and dynastic decline.[4] When Zhang Yanyuan (*c.*815–after 875) in the Tang dynasty 'writes about the "fortunes of painting", the connection between dynastic decline and a ruler's excessive interest in art and/or collecting is implied'.[5] In this discourse, as defined by Zhang Yanyuan, art works such as the *Admonitions* are viewed ideally as 'useless' (*wu yi*) or as 'superfluous things' (*zhang wu*). In this scenario, the age-old task has been to justify the collecting of 'useless' things. A careful equilibrium must be maintained where usefulness is to be found in the uselessness. Art for self-cultivation or moral instruction is just such a justifying excuse, and is often seen in past descriptions of the *Admonitions*.

In a must-read article on Ming aesthetics and collecting by Wai-yee Li entitled 'The Collector, the Connoisseur, and Late-Ming Sensibility', a wide spectrum of Ming writings about things are used as source materials.[6] Li identifies two groups of texts. The first group includes treatises and manuals that treat things in a generic fashion as material, social, and political commodities; where private and public value is determined by aesthetic taste and style, balanced appropriately between the freedom to pursue individual pleasure and concerns for social and moral propriety. Seen in this way, the gathering and ordering of things, serves, on one hand, to define private realms of inner freedom and significance. On the other hand, such boundaries of selfhood need to strike a balance with arenas in public life, and for this purpose, material things can help to present an image of an outer self for social consumption. Here we must pause to acknowledge the influential work on this category of writings that has already been done by Craig Clunas in his 1991 book *Superfluous Things: Material Culture and Social Status in Early Modern China*.

The second group of late Ming writings about things identified by Wai-yee Li, takes on a more radical sensibility. Instead of trying to balance the extremes of personal freedom versus social responsibility, these writings – often in the form of personal accounts – give free rein to the pursuit of private pleasure in leisurely activities and collecting useless things. Material things become a medium through which immaterial things take form by way of personal desires, experiences, memories, and nostalgia. Instead of being treated in a generic or normative fashion, each object is viewed as a unique experience that gains value through intense possession, radical subjectivity, or obsession. A collector's obsession becomes a 'useless' thing's greatest source of value from which an empathetic bond comes into being. This bond can be understood as a 'union of the thing and self' (*wu wo he yi*) and allows for the definition of a private realm of significance.[7] It is through this relationship between thing and self that boundaries are redrawn and a new inner world is discovered or unearthed, and it is in this context that we should understand the term 'extraordinary' or 'unusual' (*qi*) that is encountered in Ming dynasty critical, literary, and artistic theory.[8] On this notion of the 'extraordinary' in calligraphy, the late Ming artist Wang Duo (1592–1652) wrote:

It is like excavating an ancient artefact that has never been seen or heard of before from an ancient tomb – it is extraordinary, odd, and shocking – truly bizarre. But what one does not realize is that this ancient artefact had always been in the tomb. Other people have dug two to three feet ... and then have stopped. Today I have dug deep and drawn it out to show ...'[9]

Both the balanced and radical sensibilities in Ming collecting that we have just tried to outline, have as their role an aim to assemble and order 'things' to establish the boundaries of selfhood, a private realm or extraordinary world. It is with this in mind that we now return to consider the three papers. Getting back to the earlier question raised in an analysis of Wang Yao-t'ing's paper, If it is true that many of the Song seals and the signature-line on the *Admonitions* painting were added in the Ming period by Xiang Yuanbian or some other collector, what were they trying to do? Remember, Dong Qichang, and certainly others, had viewed and recorded the scroll while it was in Xiang Yuanbian's collection prior to the addition of the fake seals and signature. If this was the case, under such scrutiny, can it simply be assumed that the false seals and signature were added to increase the commercial value of the handscroll, or to increase its value as a social commodity for its owner? Another possible explanation asks us to expand upon the personal and social relationships among the circle of Ming patrons, collectors, and connoisseurs outlined in the cultural biography developed by Stephen Little. More than shared friendships and interests, in some instances elements of gamesmanship may have come into play. Identifying forgeries and intentionally added false seals and colophons on scrolls may have served as the focus of contests to test friends or trick rivals. It is almost inconceivable for us to imagine today, but some valuable scrolls, such as the *Admonitions*, may have been embellished in the Ming period for use in such connoisseurial duels involving 'useless things'. Recognizing a deceptive fabrication demonstrated the viewer's talent, while the failure of others to notice only highlighted the collector's mastery, erudition, and wit.[10] Alternatively, one must also consider the possibility that Ming collectors who possessed this scroll, recognized this painting as something 'extraordinary' and proceeded to assemble, order, and define a private realm in which Gu Kaizhi came to life as a mythic concept that was half obsession and half intelligence.[11] By analogy, such enhancements added by Ming collectors to ancient scrolls, may be likened to Wang Duo's quest for the 'extraordinary' in calligraphy: 'Today I have dug deep and drawn it out to show.' It is this sensibility in the late Ming that may underlie Yin Ji'nan's discussion of an irrecoverable 'cultural imagining' around the 'concept of Gu Kaizhi'.

NOTES

1   See Kohara 2000 (1967), pp. 22–25.
2   Kohara 2000 (1967), p. 44.
3   For a detailed examination of collecting as a means 'to assemble a world', see Li, Wai-yee 1995, pp. pp. 275–286. Much of my following discussion on Ming collecting is based on this article.
4   Li, Wai-yee 1995, p. 273, note 6.
5   Li, Wai-yee 1995, p. 272. On the difficulties of enjoying leisure as reflected in Tang dynasty literature, see Owen 1998.
6   Li, Wai-yee 1995.
7   Li, Wai-yee 1995, p. 295.
8   See Ching, D. C. Y. 1999.
9   Modified translation follows Ching, D. C. Y. 1999, p. 351.
10   More than just playing, such contests can be seen as flights of obsessive egoism, and instances of such game playing are difficult to document. The notion of game playing among Ming and later artists, connoisseurs, and collectors was brought to my attention in discussions during the colloquium with Arnold Chang.
11   Huan Wen (fifth century) characterized Gu Kaizhi's being as half obsession and half intelligence. See Li, Wai-yee 1995, p. 288.

A 'Cultural Biography' of the *Admonitions* Scroll: The Qianlong Reign (1736–1795)

Nixi Cura

The 'cultural biography' of the Admonitions scroll through the eighteenth century is inextricably linked with the most prominent owner of the scroll, the Manchu Qing emperor Qianlong (fig. 1), who ruled from 1736 to 1795. By most prominent, I also mean most visually prominent, in reference to the large quantity of marks left by the emperor on the body of the scroll over a period spanning almost the entire duration of his reign. And the Qianlong emperor does loom large in the history of late imperial China. Heir to the Qing (1644–1911) dominion, a flourishing multi-ethnic empire first established in 1644 and subsequently stabilized by three capable Manchu rulers before him, he eschewed the role of mere caretaker and expanded the Qing rulership to encompass all things under heaven. Some have called his governance despotic,[1] and some prefer the more neutral term 'universal',[2] but his command over all aspects of the Qing realm remains undisputed. In the production of art and in the construction of artistic canons, as well as in politics, the Qianlong emperor strove for comprehensiveness, clarity, and control. Perhaps the most revered painting in his collection, the *Admonitions* scroll, as reconfigured in the eighteenth century, embodies the ideals and ideologies of the Qianlong emperor.

Throughout this paper, I will often refer to the scroll in terms of the body, for, like a body, it can breathe the very air of antiquity, it can grow and shrink with the passage of time, and it can elicit desirous thoughts from its viewers. It is not just one work but a body of several works in the forms of painting, calligraphy, and seal carving. And as a figure paint-ing, it is a painting of bodies: fighting (pl. 1) and heaving (pl. 3), but, primarily, admonished bodies. The bodies of palace women depicted are docile, regulated, manipulable. Just as the poem by Zhang Hua (232–300) counsels self-regulation among court women and implies the controlling gaze of the emperor, so too does the painter wield the power to idealize and deploy their bodies (fig. 2). The artist, perhaps Gu Kaizhi

Fig. 1 Giuseppe Castiglione (Lang Shining, 1688–1766), *Portrait of Emperor Qianlong in Court Dress.* Hanging scroll; colour on silk, 271 × 142 cm. Palace Museum, Beijing. (After Nie Chongzheng [ed.] 1996, p. 150.)

 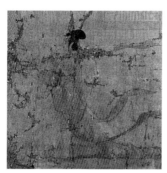 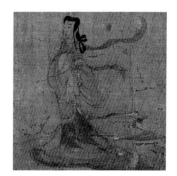 

Fig. 2 Details of palace ladies from the *Admonitions* scroll; from left to right: scenes 1, 2, 6 and 9.

(*c.* 345–*c.* 406), recurrently painted the prescribed body of a palace lady: controlled yet poised for transformation to suit the needs of her master. The themes of control – self-control, imperial control – resurface in the eighteenth-century config-uration of the *Admonitions* scroll.

Authors in this volume have proposed various dates for the *Admonitions* scroll, ranging from the Six Dynasties (220–586) to the Song (960–1279). In this paper, I propose that the *Admonitions* scroll is an eighteenth-century object or, rather, that it *was* an eighteenth-century object. I can make this ludicrous claim because my inquiry proceeds outward from the 'original' *Admonitions* scroll to the total material object after it was remounted at the command of the Qian-long emperor. The few who saw the *Admonitions* scroll in the eighteenth century may have held as lively a debate over its dating as took place at the '*Admonitions*' colloquy. Today we use essentially the same techniques of authentication – analysis of style, composition, iconography, and so on. Alas, the eigh-teenth-century debate did not enter the historical record, as Stephen Little[3] and Yin Ji'nan[4] have explained in this volume. So in this paper I assume the Qianlong emperor's 'subject-position': an unproblematic acceptance of the *Admonitions* scroll as a genuine original work by Gu Kaizhi. This is not to say that the issue of authenticity is irrelevant; on the contrary, the scroll's putative authenticity helped pre-determine its fate at the hands of its imperial keeper.

My discussion of the Qianlong reception of the *Admo-nitions* scroll unfolds in three sections. First, I outline the position of the *Admonitions* scroll within the larger body of knowledge as interpreted and clarified during the Qianlong reign. Here, the scroll is but one of many manipulable objects that constituted a comprehensible and categorizable Qing dominion. To glean the full extent to which the scroll could be reshaped, the second section involves an examination of Qianlong-period accretions: the seals, the emperor's orchid painting (pl. 37) and his colophon (pls 38–39). Close read-

ings of the iconography and texts reveal the emperor's corre-lation of the scroll to his ideology of rulership. The third sec-tion focuses on the thematic correspondence between the painting and the Qianlong-commissioned colophon-painting by Zou Yigui (1686–1772), delving into issues surrounding the emperor-subject relationship.

I A Comprehensive Body of Knowledge

The *Admonitions* scroll was co-opted into a body of knowl-edge categorized and rearranged for optimal clarity, in accor-dance with the Qianlong emperor's 'encyclopaedic approach to art'[5] and to all matters pertinent to his vision of enlightened Manchu rule. The *Shiqu baoji* (Precious Case of the Stone Gully) inventory of the imperial art collection commissioned in 1745, with two subsequent revisions in 1793 and 1815, is merely one example of the many Qianlong-era cataloguing and collecting projects. Another edict in 1771 initiated the massive empire-wide text compilation project, the *Siku quan-shu* (Complete Library of the Four Treasuries).[6] The pur-ported comprehensiveness – all writings in the empire – of the final product came about through a blatantly ideological weeding out of texts with anti-Manchu content. Many of the authors of these 'treasonous' writings, along with their families, were ultimately weeded out during this literary inquisition.

The myriad classification projects undertaken during the Qianlong reign are far too many to enumerate here. But rele-vant to the current topic is a cluster of projects aimed at laying down Manchu origin-myths as history and at clarifying Manchu elite lineages from ancient times on. These include, among others, *Baqi Manzhou shizu tongpu* (Collective Genealogies of the Eight-Banner and Manchu Lineages, 1745), *Manzhou jishen jitian dianli* (Rituals for the Manchu Worship of the Spirits and of Heaven, 1781) and *Manzhou yuanliu kao* (Researches in the Origins of the Manchus, 1783).[7] These seem to bear little relationship to the *Four Treasuries* or to the *Shiqu baoji*, but, taken as a whole, they formed the basis for countering the argument that the Manchus were itinerant barbarians without mercy and without a history, and laid to rest any doubts about the ability of the Manchus to be just, capable, and virtuous rulers of the empire. Beyond that, the Qianlong emperor set out to prove that the Manchu Qing dynasty was more just, more capable, and more virtuous than any dynasty before it. This systemic 'more is more' mentality is one important factor underlying the physical expansion of the *Admonitions* scroll in the Qianlong reign.

II The Qianlong Imperial Body and the *Admonitions* Scroll

Prior to any discussion of the individual Qianlong-era additions to the scroll, we must first identify its form during that time. During the 2001 colloquy, one gallery case held two discrete segments, with the section containing the Gu Kaizhi figure painting on the old silk displayed below the non-figurative elements of the scroll (fig. 3). This is the current incarnation of the *Admonitions* scroll, but this was not the form in which the British Museum acquired it in 1903; it was then a handscroll modestly identified as an 'old Chinese painting' brought back from China after the Boxer Rebellion.[8] After having ascertained its identity as possibly the only genuine extant work by Gu Kaizhi, at some point, probably the 1910s, the Keepers decided to dismantle its handscroll mounting and remount the scroll in separate portions on a stiff frame. Perhaps this was in the interest of preservation, for several passages of the painting appear to have suffered damage from the stress of repeated unrolling and re-rolling. Whatever the reasons, the resultant format has optimized viewing of this masterpiece and distilled it down to its essence – the canonical painting by Gu Kaizhi.

In order to view this work in the handscroll format in which it entered the British Museum collection, one must consult the woodblock reproduction of the scroll published in 1912, shortly before this reformatting is thought to have been carried out. Or one can visualize the eighteenth-century scroll, using contemporary technology, by re-inserting the old painting back into its place indicated by the arrow in fig. 3.[9] Even so, our digitally reconstructed scroll still lacks Zou Yigui's colophon-painting (pl. 40) that had been mounted at the very end, and was exhibited in 2001 in a separate gallery case altogether. We may now proceed backwards in time, as it were, to reassemble the sundry parts of an eighteenth-century body that remained intact until the early twentieth century. Reconstituted, the scroll would have unrolled as follows.[10]

Fig. 3   The *Admonitions* scroll. Above: the painting panel, the portions attributed to Gu Kaizhi. Top: the colophons panel, the non-figurative sections mounted separately to the original work. The arrow below the colophons panel (right) indicates the position of the painting in the Qianlong handscroll mounting.

The exterior of the scroll was mounted with a patterned blue brocade protective outer-wrapper (pl. 32), with its label inscribed by the Qianlong emperor. He wrote: '*Admonitions of the Court Instructress* painted by Gu Kaizhi, together with calligraphy; a genuine treasure in the divine class from the Inner Palace.'[11] Inside, the scroll opened to a fragment of old *kesi* silk tapestry with flowers on a blue ground , followed by a panel of yellow silk impressed with a large square Qianlong seal (pl. 33). Then came a three-character title in the Qianlong emperor's calligraphy (pls 33 left–34 right). It translates as 'Fragrance of the Red Tube' and refers to the instrument of authority belonging to the Instructress and symbol of moral virtue in the *Book of Poetry (Shi jing)*.[12] Next was an older band of yellow brocade containing seals dating from the Song dynasty on.

Then there is the painting itself, followed by first a pale blue then a buff-coloured strip of silk brocade, both imprinted with seals ranging in date from the Song to the Qing dynasties. Another panel of the same old yellow brocade comes afterwards, upon which the Qianlong emperor directly painted an orchid and added an inscription and several of his seals. Next is another length of Song-period silk mellowed with age and bearing an eighteen-line colophon in 'slender gold' calligraphy, which, according to the *Shiqu baoji* catalogue entry, is by the Song emperor Huizong (1082–1135; r. 1101–1125).[13] It is bracketed to the left by a pale blue border

panel marked with seals, and this is followed by a greyish white slip inscribed with the Ming (1368–1644) collector Xiang Yuanbian's (1525–1590) assessment of the scroll as a genuine work by Gu Kaizhi (pl. 38 right). The last two sections of the scroll were both added during the Qianlong reign: first, a colophon written in 1746 by the emperor, who in it echoes earlier attributions of the painting to Gu Kaizhi (pls 38–39); and, finally, the colophon-painting of pines, bamboo, rocks and a spring by the Qing court official Zou Yigui.[14]

In the twelfth month of 1746, the emperor commissioned eight of his favourite painters – Zou Yigui, Zhang Ruoai (1713–1756),[15] Dong Bangda (1713–1756),[16] Li Shizhuo (*c.*1690–1770),[17] and the four court painters Cao Kuiyin, Zhang Yusen, Zhou Kun, Yu Sheng[18] – each to paint two works apiece. Later these were affixed to the outer box(es) containing the 'Four Beauties' (*si mei ju*)[19] – that is, the *Admonitions* scroll and three paintings then ascribed to the Northern Song (960–1127) master Li Gonglin (*c.*1041–1106).[20] These paintings were not subsequently recorded as integral parts of these scrolls in the second or third editions of the *Shiqu baoji*.[21] The box(es) either remain in the palace collections in Beijing or Taipei, or have long been removed by pilferers.[22] On one of the Four Beauties, the *Shu River* scroll in the Freer Gallery (fig. 11), the Qianlong emperor explains in one of his four colophons that he kept the scrolls in a pavilion in the Palace of Established Happiness

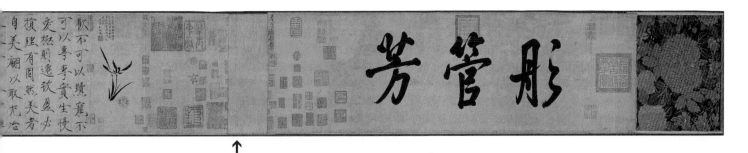

(Jianfugong), and that he personally wrote a three-character inscription, *si mei ju* ('Reunion of Four Beauties'), for the pavilion door tablet.[23] The remnants of Gu Kaizhi's work essentially formed the nucleus of an elaborate eighteenth-century framework constructed around it by the Qianlong emperor.

A. The emperor's seals

The Qianlong additions act not as a mere frame for the treasure inside, but also as an armature that the emperor linked with seals and inscriptions displayed throughout the older body of the scroll. The opening passage of the painting already contained Song palace seals stamped on each scene and each section of the mounting.[24] Likewise, Xiang Yuanbian so effusively pressed his seals on each scene that one cannot doubt his genuine delight and pride in ownership.[25] By comparison, the Qianlong seals seem small in number and size. In 1746, the year of his colophon, the emperor effected rules to keep the number of all his official seals down to twenty-five,

and demanded standardized carving styles for seals in both Chinese characters and Manchu writing.[26] Though the emperor's personal seals numbered in the hundreds over the duration of his reign, the use of standard seals proclaimed an individual style.

Thirty-seven Qianlong seal impressions appear along the length of the *Admonitions* scroll, though only four more than once (Table 1). The variety of seals has the unexpected effect of diffusing the imperial presence throughout the scroll, while enhancing the ornamentality of the field of seals. Aside from their role as markers of possession tattooed, as it were, on the surface of the scroll, the seals also provide a temporal dimension to the emperor's viewing and inscription of the scroll. For example, in scene 1, directly above the head of Lady Feng as she leaps in front of the bear (pl. 2), the *Shiqu baoji* inventory seal (fig. 4) was affixed in or shortly after 1745, not too long after the scroll had entered the palace.[27] In the next scene, above and to the right of the figure of Lady Ban refusing to ride in the emperor's carriage, a large square seal datable to

Fig. 4 (left) *Shiqu baoji* inventory seal, scene 1 of the *Admonitions* scroll, above the head of Lady Feng.

Fig. 5 (below right) Qianlong seal in scene 2 of the *Admonitions* scroll: 'Hall of five blessings in five generations, a treasure of the seventy-year-old heir apparent.'

Fig. 6 (below centre) Qianlong seal in scene 8 of the *Admonitions* scroll: 'Treasure of an eighty-year-old remembering the eight phases of life.'

Fig. 7 (below left) Qianlong seal after the Gu Kaizhi composition in the *Admonitions* scroll: 'Treasure of an eighty-year-old remembering the eight phases of life'.

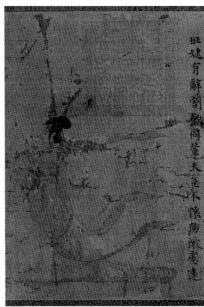

Table 1: The Quianlong emperor's seals

Seal	Position	Pinyin	Translation	Format
	Label of the blue patterned brocade cover	Yu shang	Imperial appreciation	relief
	Label: over the characters *shen* and *nei*	illegible		relief
	Label: over the characters *pin* and *fu*	illegible		relief
	Label	Qianlong chen han	Qianlong imperial signature	relief
	Label	[Xian] wen zhi xi	Imperial seal of burnished refinement	relief
	Yellow patterned silk panel	Wu fu wu dai tang gu xi tian zi bao	Hall of five blessings in five generations, a treasure of the seventy-year-old son of heaven	relief
	Bridging the border between yellow panel and title page	Guang pi xin men cong	Listening at the gate of a wide open heart	relief
	Bridging the border between yellow panel and title page	Qin shu dao qu sheng	Drawing life from the path of the *qin* and literature	relief
	Fragrance of the Red Flute (above the character *guan*)	Qianlong chen han	Qianlong imperial signature	relief
	Title page	Chun xin [?] [?] zhi [?]	Pure heart ...	relief
	Title page	Qing xin [ju] xue	Clear heart collecting snow	intaglio

Seal	Position	Pinyin	Translation	Format
	Bridging the border	[?] yao tian ji di	Surpassing [?] reaching nature	intaglio
	Yellow brocade protective wrapper (*ge shui*); upper left border	Si mei ju	Four beauties	relief
	Scene 1: above and slightly to the the right of emperor's head	Qianlong yu lan zhi bao	Treasure under Qianlong's imperial gaze	relief
	Scene 1: just left of 'Ruise Dongge' seal	Shi qu bao ji	Precious case of the stone gully	relief
	Scene 2: above Lady Ban	Wu fu wu dai tang gu xi tian zi bao	Hall of five blessings in five generations, a treasure of the seventy-year-old son of heaven	relief
	Scene 8: above and right of seated woman	Ba zheng mao nian zhi bao	Treasure of an eighty-year-old remembering the eight phases of life	relief
	Scene 9: between and above the two figure groupings	Tian zi gu xi	Seventy-year-old son of heaven	relief
	Scene 9: directly above head of last figure	Qianlong jian shang	Examined and appreciated by Qianlong	intaglio
	Scene 9: upper left, second row from left	San xi tang jing jian xi	Seal for treasure examined in the Hall of Three Rarities	relief

Seal	Position	Pinyin	Translation	Format
	Scene 9: upper left, second row from left	Yi zi sun	Fitting for sons and grandsons	intaglio
	Bridging the border between buff and yellow brocades	Qianlong yu shang	Qianlong imperial signature	relief
	Bridging the border between buff and yellow brocades	Ji xia yi qing	Deep leisure harmonious feeling	intaglio
	Epidendrum	Qianlong chen han	Qianlong imperial signature	relief
	Epidendrum	Yi tai he	Bright dawn great peace	relief
	Epidendrum	illegible		relief
	Epidendrum	illegible		intaglio
	Bridging the border between brown silk and grey brocade	Yu shang	Imperial appreciation	relief
	Grey brocade	Ba zheng mao nian zhi bao	Treasure of an eighty-year-old remembering the eight phases of life	relief
	Bridging the border between Xiang Yuanbian's and Qianlong's colophons	Yun xia si	Contemplating clouds and mist	relief
	Bridging the border between Xiang Yuanbian and Qianlong's colophons	Neifu shu hua zhi bao	Treasure among the books and paintings in the imperial household	intaglio
	Qianlong's colophon	Qian (trigram)	Qian[long]	relief

Seal	Position	Pinyin	Translation	Format
	Qianlong's colophon	Long	[Qian]long	relief
	Qianlong's colophon	Yu shu	Imperially written	relief
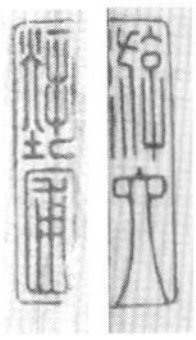	Bridging the border between Qianlong's colophon and Zou Yigui's colophon-painting	You liu yi bu	Garden of roaming the six arts	relief
	Zou Yigui's colophon-painting	Tai shang huang di zhi bao	Treasure of the supreme emperor	relief
	Zou Yigui's colophon-painting	Qianlong yu lan zhi bao	Treasure under Qianlong's imperial gaze	relief

1787 reads 'Hall of five blessings in five generations, a treasure of the seventy-year-old son of heaven' (fig. 5),[28] celebrating the expansion of the emperor's living lineage to five generations in 1784. Commemorating his eightieth birthday in 1790 is another large bordered square seal, 'Treasure of an eighty-year-old remembering the eight phases of life,'[29] which appears twice on the scroll: once in scene 8, looming over a palace lady 'reflecting upon her duties' (fig. 6); and again on the blue strip after the Gu Kaizhi painting, where it dwarfs the Xiang Yuanbian colophon to its left (fig. 7). Read in conjunction with the dated Qianlong inscriptions and additions, the seals evoke the emperor's physical presence in front of the *Admonitions* scroll from his youth to old age.[30]

B. The emperor's painting

Let us move on to another evocation of the emperor's body: his orchid painting and accompanying inscription at upper left (pl. 37 right), which reads:

One summer's day in a moment of leisure I chanced to examine Gu Kaizhi's picture of the Instructress. Accordingly I drew a spray of epidendrum, with no other intent but to illustrate the idea of beauty in chaste retirement. Written by the Emperor in the Laiqing Pavilion.[31]

By writing this directly upon the old yellow silk mounting after the Gu Kaizhi painting, the emperor displays a self-confidence in his painting skill that may be unwarranted. The brushwork is clumsy, hesitant, and utterly lacking in depth. But that really is not the point. This assertive act marks the emperor not just as owner of and commentator on the scroll, but also as an artist who ranks alongside Gu Kaizhi. Furthermore, the choice of the orchid signifies the Qianlong emperor's co-optation of this icon's associations with eremitic painters and poets in the wild.[32] More pertinently, the choice of the orchid demonstrates the emperor's appropriation and effective cancellation of its symbolism of loyalty to a fallen dynasty.

While the iconography of the orchid expropriates notions of political loyalty, choice words in the accompanying inscription underline the emperor's belief in his enlightened rule. Gray translated the phrase *yaotiao* as 'beauty in chaste retirement'; in the opening poem of the *Book of Poetry (Shi jing)*, the Confucian classic dating around 600 BCE, *yaotiao* refers to a demure and captivatingly beautiful woman.[33] The 'Little Preface', an influential Han dynasty (*c.*150 BCE) exegesis of the *Shi jing*, advocates the sage-king's selection of this ideal mate as the 'foundation of royal transformation' (*wang hua zhi ji*).[34] Reinforcing the classical associations between exemplary rulers and their virtuous wives, the Qianlong emperor consciously quotes the 'Little Preface' in his title 'the beginning of royal transformation' (*wang hua zhi shi*) for the Song copy of the *Admonitions* scroll in the Palace Museum (pl. 23 right).[35] Presumably, the Qianlong emperor's perfect mate might be found among the archetypically beautiful and virtuous ladies depicted in the *Admonitions* scrolls. The Qing rulers often chose consorts to forge political alliances, but, as a matter of policy, they completely severed the relationship between their wives and their natal families, thereby reducing potential influence-peddling by distaff kin. By treating them as imperial property and controlling every aspect of their lives, the Qianlong emperor could effectively remould each of his forty-one empresses and consorts to the desired ideal.[36] The allusions in both versions of the *Admonitions* scroll to the most oft-cited ode in the Confucian didactic tradition correlates his possession of the scrolls and the palace women depicted within to the possession of kingly attributes extolled from ancient times.

The lopsided dynamic of power between male viewer and female subjects also functions as a metaphor for Manchu-Chinese relations during the Qing. The political, social, and sexual regulation of palace women was but one microcosm of (male) Manchu domination over (female) China, with any latent subversion kept in check by effective bureaucracies and physical threat. Continual admonitions to the Manchu elite to uphold martial values during the Qianlong reign were reinforced by representations of the emperor as martial exemplar, as in a court painting of him demonstrating his archery prowess (fig. 8). As early as 1636, the Manchu regent Hong Taiji (r. 1627–1635) had expressed his anxiety over the ineluctable '"Chinese Way" of liquor, leisure, and riding in sedan chairs'.[37] Through his connoisseurship of Chinese painting – which can be seen as a form of active mastery or even condescension – the Qianlong emperor could alleviate the ongoing Manchu anxiety over the powerful seduction of Chinese culture.

The Qing emperors' preoccupation with traditional Chinese art forms and classical political theory has been interpreted as signalling the Sinicization of the Manchus, since they did adapt Chinese modes of representation in art and in the art of governance. But as Pamela Crossley argues, any essentialized 'Chinese' representation is but one of many simultaneous self-expressions formulated for different constituencies under Qing rule.[38] Just as the *Admonitions* scroll or any other recognizable Chinese artefact could be refashioned to suit the emperor's ideological requirements, so too did the Qianlong emperor willingly submit his own body to compartmentalization and manipulation. To his Manchu constituency, he was the able warrior and military leader (fig. 8). To his Mongol constituency, he was the guiding principle of their Buddhist faith.[39] To his Han constituency, particularly the Chinese bureaucracy on which he so relied, he was a scholar at ease with the Three Perfections of poetry, calligraphy, and painting (fig. 9). His ostensible submission to the classical Chinese ideal of the sage-king would also have appealed to the Confucian constituency. The Qianlong emperor's unremitting control can be seen to originate, paradoxically, from his apparent surrender to his role within each group's cultural order.

C. The Qianlong colophon

The Qianlong emperor's colophon of 16 June 1746 proves instructive in gauging his sentiments on the *Admonitions* scroll (pls 38–39). I reproduce it in its entirety:

> Gu Kaizhi of the Jin dynasty was skilful at painting in colour. He said himself that the power to express a man's soul in a portrait depended entirely on the pupils of the eyes; and he knew that without entering deeply into *samādhi* this power could not be attained. This scroll, illustrating the *Admonitions of the Instructress*, has been handed down for more than a thousand years. Yet the radiance of genius shines forth from it; every expression and attitude is full of life; an art not to be measured by the compasses and plumb-lines of later men. Dong Qichang says in his inscription on Li Gonglin's picture of the *Rivers Xiao and Xiang*: 'Mr. Secretary Gu [Gu Congyi, *c.*1520–*c.*1580] was the owner of four famous scrolls, and in enumerating them he mentions this one first'. This is true! This picture had always been kept in the Imperial Library, but subsequently, having acquired the *Shu River*, *Nine Songs* and *Xiao-Xiang* scrolls by Li Gonglin, I had it shifted to the Jingyi Pavilion of the Jianfu Palace, so that together they might correspond exactly to the famous group mentioned in Dong's note. The inscription says: 'The Four Beauties are brought

Fig. 8 Wang Zhicheng (Jean-Denis Attiret, 1702–1768), *Emperor Qianlong Shooting an Arrow*. Detail of a screen; oil on paper, 95 × 213.7 cm. Palace Museum, Beijing. (After Nie Chongzheng [ed.] 1996, pp. 211–213.)

Fig. 9 Anonymous, *Portrait of Emperor Qianlong in Ancient Costume*. Detail of a hanging scroll; colour on silk, 100.2 × 63 cm. Palace Museum, Beijing. (After Nie Chongzheng [ed.] 1996, p. 200.)

together to express profound admiration'. Deeply impressed by the unexpected reunion of these ancient and classical treasures, I have hastily scribbled these words, to show that I regard this scroll as 'a sword reunited with its fellow'. Written by the Emperor in the Jingyi Pavilion, five days before the summer solstice of the year *bingyin* (1746) in the reign of Qianlong.[40]

The emperor makes three salient points. First, he implicitly accepts the attribution of the scroll to Gu Kaizhi and panegyrises the 'radiance of genius' emanating from Gu's work. Second, he places himself within a lineage of distinguished collectors, most prominently the late Ming calligrapher, painter, and theorist Dong Qichang (1555–1636), whose works he avidly collected and emulated. Finally, he informs the reader where in the Forbidden City the scroll was kept along with other high-pedigree scrolls.

His remarks prove equally instructive for what he does not address. He provides no critical evaluation of the painter's brushwork or compositions. There is a generic quality to his praise – 'every expression and attitude is full of life; an art not to be measured by the compasses and plumb-lines of later men' – that indicates an awareness of Gu Kaizhi's place in the canon, but does not reveal a passionate regard for the painting itself. Nor does he comment on the subject matter, the seals, or the earlier colophons. That tedious job he left to the compilers of the catalogue of the imperial painting collection, the *Shiqu baoji*.

In essence, the Qianlong emperor shows greater concern for the act of collecting than for the individual art works. His name-dropping demonstrates his connoisseurship of connoisseurs, and even this is very selective in that he refers to only one person who actually owned the *Admonitions* scroll and gives greater attention to Dong Qichang, who had only mentioned it in passing while commenting on another painting entirely. By ordering the *Admonitions* scroll to be stored as one of the Four Beauties, along with three paintings by Li Gonglin, he pays tribute to Gu Congyi's acuity as a collector, and at the same time affirms his own status as a discriminating collector in his own right. The phrase 'a sword reunited with its fellow' ostensibly celebrates the reunion of the Four Beauties, but also alludes to the rejoining of the swords of *Admonitions* author Zhang Hua and his friend Lei Huan (act. third

century), signifying the triumph of virtue over political machinations.[41] Following this analogy, we must then infer that the emperor saw the re-assemblage of this group of paintings in his possession as proof of his own virtue and righteousness.

The other three 'Beauties' are now generally regarded as copies of or misattributions to Li Gonglin, just as the *Admonitions* scroll can only be attributed as a composition by Gu Kaizhi.[42] Regardless, while perceived as genuine works in the eighteenth century, these three paintings – the *Dream Journey on the Xiao and Xiang Rivers* (fig. 10), now in the Tokyo National Museum and designated a 'National Treasure' in Japan; the *Shu River* (fig. 11; Freer Gallery, Washington, DC); and the *Nine Songs* (fig. 12), in the collection of the Palace Museum, Beijing – were systematically lavished with seals and colophons by the Qianlong emperor. Each of the three, like the *Admonitions* scroll, contains a small composition by the emperor: bamboo; plum blossoms; and orchid and chrysanthemum, respectively. In addition, each contains a painting by a different court artist/official mounted at the end of each scroll: Dong Bangda's painting of *Su Shi's Poetic Intent* on the *Xiao and Xiang Rivers* scroll; a portrait of the Warring States (475–221 BCE) martyr Qu Yuan (340?–278 BCE) by Zhang Ruoai on the *Nine Songs* scroll; and Ding Guanpeng's painting after a Du Fu (712–770) poem on the

Shu River scroll.[43] Let us now turn to Zou Yigui's painting (pl. 40), made at the Qianlong emperor's command for the *Admonitions* scroll.

III Zou Yigui, Bureaucrats and the Body Politic

Zou Yigui, who lived from 1686 to 1772, attained his highest post, Vice-Minister of Rites, between 1750 and 1753, concurrently serving in the Grand Secretariat. Later the emperor awarded him the honorary title of Minister of Rites. Earlier in his career, in the Provincial Administration and Provincial Surveillance Commissions, as the Education Commissioner in Guizhou, and as governor of Hubei, he gained a reputation for rooting out corruption and exposing fraud. His honesty and uprightness made him an appropriate choice of artist-official to paint a picture-colophon for the *Admonitions* scroll. What better way to demonstrate the emperor's virtue but through his virtuous officials, his eyes and ears, as well as his hand-servants in the implementation of policy?

Jiang Baoling (1781–1840) in his *Molin jinhua*, or *Current Discourses on the Ink Forest*, stated that Zou Yigui painted 'landscapes in the styles of Ni [Zan (1301–1374)] and Huang [Gongwang (1269–1354)] which were strangely cold, but

Fig. 10 (right) Attributed to Li Gonglin (*c*.1041–1106), *A Dream Journey on the Xiao and Xiang Rivers*. Detail of a handscroll; ink on paper, 30.3 × 400.4 cm. Tokyo National Museum.

Fig. 11 (below) *Shu River*, or *Panoramic Landscape: 'The Painting of the River Szechuan'*. Song dynasty (960–1279), 13th century. Details of a handscroll; ink on paper, 32.8 × 1426.5 cm. Freer Gallery of Art, Smithsonian Institution, Washington, DC: Gift of Charles Lang Freer, F1916.539.

Fig. 12 (right) Attributed to Li Gonglin (*c*.1041–1106), *Illustrations to the Nine Songs of Qu Yuan*. Details of a hand-scroll; ink on paper. Palace Museum, Beijing.

Fig. 13 (below) Zou Yigui (1686–1772), *Studio amid Pine Cliffs and Rocks*. Hanging scroll; ink on paper, 145.9 × 73.9 cm. National Palace Museum, Taipei. (After *Gugong shuhua tu lu* 1989–, vol. 11 [1993], no. 243.)

not inferior'.[44] Stripping away the critical hyperbole stemming from Zou's status at court, Qin Zuyong (1825–1884) concurs with Jiang in writing that Zou's landscapes, though 'generally pleasing, lacked spirit resonance'.[45] In other words, Zou was a competent but not brilliant painter of trees and rocks in the manner of the two Yuan (1271–1368) masters, who employed a monochrome, calligraphic style. A hanging scroll painting of a studio amid pines and rocks in the National Palace Museum, Taipei, is his rendition of the standard eighteenth-century idea of a Ni Zan composition (fig. 13). Although the overall composition lacks coherence, the trees are drawn with sensitivity and delicacy, much as they are in his painting on the *Admonitions* scroll. We see that Zou Yigui could proficiently paint a graceful stately pine.[46]

Qing critics agreed, however, that Zou Yigui truly excelled in painting flowers. His most famous work, a long handscroll of a hundred flowers, was painted for the emperor and graced with imperial poetry.[47] Jiang praised it as 'truly a life's masterpiece of colour', with 'each leaf and each petal mutually interlocked'.[48] The nineteenth-century commentators Dou Zhen[49] and Lu Jun[50] claimed that only he painted in a manner worthy of his teacher Yun Shouping (1633–1690). In fact, Zou married Yun's daughter, Yun Lanxi (eighteenth century), a noted flower painter in her own right. In his *Manual on Painting (Xiaoshan hua pu)*, Zou meticulously described how to depict 115 varieties of flowers using eleven mineral pigments.[51] Elsewhere in the text he stated that a truly marvellous flower painting relies on transmitting 'a spiritual effect'.[52]

By contrast, landscape constitutes a small percentage of his works commissioned by the emperor and listed in the three editions of the *Shiqu baoji*. He expended little ink on discussing pines and bamboo in his *Manual on Painting*.[53] This excursus on Zou Yigui's preoccupation with and exper-

I believe the answer to the choice of Zou Yigui's landscape lies in juxtaposing his work with the only other landscape scene in the *Admonitions* scroll, in scene 3: 'to rise to glory is as hard as to build a mountain out of the dust; to fall into calamity is as easy as the rebound of a tense spring' (pl. 5). Michael Nylan has commented that beyond a merely literal rendering of the 'mountain' and the 'tense spring', as Kohara Hironobu argued, this scene, by virtue of its inclusion in a scroll full of remonstrances, signifies the peril of not maintaining virtue and upright conduct.[55] Although no mountain is depicted in the Zou Yigui composition, it is evoked by association with the landscape genre, defined in the eighteenth century by trees and rocks; but a large Qianlong seal also seems to stand as visual proxy for the absent mountain peak. Zou Yigui, renowned for his scrupulous incorruptibility, and the Qianlong emperor, virtuous by virtue of his continued peaceful rule, together demonstrate the tranquillity and bliss of heeding this admonition. Restoring Zou Yigui's painting to its position within the Qianlong scroll (fig. 14) helps to reanimate this interpretive framework.

Up to this point, I have argued that the *Admonitions* scroll in many ways embodied the Qianlong emperor's control and manipulation of representational forms to reflect and effect his ideological position. But his subjects were not mute objects, and were not always the docile bodies depicted in the scroll. Zou Yigui does not lose his agency by dint of incorporation into the emperor's refashioning of the *Admonitions* scroll. He painted twisted pines, for instance, which have stood for the long-suffering official who perseveres in adversity. From the emperor's point of view, this was a desirable

tise in flower painting brings us to the question of why the Qianlong emperor would have had a flower painter submit a picture of pines, bamboo, and rocks; and why this subject matter in juxtaposition with the figures on the *Admonitions* scroll?

The choice of subject matter for the paintings attached to the other three of the 'Four Beauties' bear discernible relationships to the Li Gonglin scrolls: a portrait of Qu Yuan for the *Nine Songs* written by Qu; a painting illustrating a Du Fu poem on the *Shu River* in Sichuan, upon which Du Fu and many other Tang poets had versified; and an evocation of the poet Su Shi (1037–1101) for the *Xiao and Xiang Rivers*, a common lyrical pairing in the Song.[54] Zou Yigui's untitled rendering of pine trees contains no figures, no colour, and no ostensible reference to the *Admonitions* subject matter.

Fig. 14 Reconstructed order of the *Admonitions* scroll (from top to bottom and right to left), including the colophon-painting by Zou Yigui.

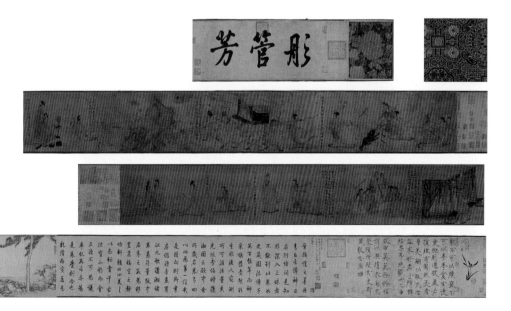

Fig. 15 (far left) Luo Guanzhong (*c*.1330–*c*.1400), *Romance of the Three Kingdoms*, detail of caning. Qing dynasty. Woodblock print on paper. (After McKnight 1992, p. 338.)

Fig. 16 (left) Li Baojia (1867–1906), *Guanchang xianxing ji*, detail of caning. Qing dynasty. Woodblock print on paper. (After McKnight 1992, p. 339.)

Fig. 17 (below left) Detail of death by slicing from the records of Jinshan County (*Jinshan xian baojia zhangcheng*). Qing dynasty. Woodblock print on paper. (After McKnight 1992, p. 451.)

Fig. 18 (below) Detail of death by strangulation from the records of Quanshan County (*Quanshan xian baojia zhangcheng*). Qing dynasty. Woodblock print on paper. (After McKnight 1992, p. 450.)

trait in a subject. But I would venture to say that an official would rather avoid adversity. An anecdote about Zou Yigui recounts a time when there was great demand – presumably imperial demand – for his painting. He grumbles that, although a high official, his true status was no better than that of a slave.[56] His servitude could only be alleviated by retirement from office, freedom from a mercurial and demanding ruler.

Zou Yigui was well acquainted with the notion of slavery, and the corporal and capital punishment of imperial subjects. He did not live to see the completion of the *Siku*

quanshu compilation project and its physical effects: both texts and people were wiped off the record. However, as a high official, he was fully aware of the consequences of the Qianlong emperor's wrath. He would have been privy to details of the queue-cutting scare of 1768, when rumours abounded of itinerant sorcerers cutting off people's queues without their knowledge, then using the hair to bewitch their victims. It was feared that any attack on the queue, the physical representation of the Manchu rulers' ability to tame and reshape Chinese bodies, might point to a widespread anti-

Manchu sentiment in the south. In his quest for clarification, the Qianlong emperor found no satisfaction. What started out as a search for the definitive roots and causes of the queue-cutting phenomenon, developed into a large-scale chastisement and banishment of many officials deemed negligent in handling the case.[57]

It is noteworthy, then, that in or shortly after 1746, the year after the Qianlong emperor wrote his colophon to the *Admonitions* scroll, Zou Yigui, in his capacity as governor of Hubei province, was instrumental in helping two accused criminals to escape capital punishment. In his memorial to the emperor, he wrote: 'The laws regarding prisons are comprehensive and consistent. But more and more prison wardens these days use unlawful punishments.'[58] Traditional Chinese jurisprudence allowed for torture, with recalcitrant defendants caned bloody until a confession issued forth. Scenes from the *Romance of the Three Kingdoms* (fig. 15) by Luo Guanzhong (*c*.1330–*c*.1400) and a nineteenth-century account of an official's duties (fig. 16) vividly illustrate the spectacle of these proceedings. In his memorial, Zou Yigui continued:

> Certainly a prisoner should receive his punishment. The government sometimes has its methods, but these methods should not be unlawful, for this cannot be considered law. If this is the case, how then can we command the prisoner's death through unlawful punishment?[59]

He defended the use of cruel punishment, knowing, probably through having witnessed many of these tortures, that the gruesome spectacle of public execution was a much worse fate. Images of death by slicing (fig. 17), strangulation (fig. 18) and other physical bodily mutilation were the all too true-to-life manifestations of the imperial prerogative.

We are thus reminded of Chen Zi'ang (658?–699?), the Tang dynasty official who dared send a memorial to Empress Wu Zetian (627?–705) censuring the harsh punishments given her political enemies, and of Chen Zi'ang's exemplar of virtue, Zhang Hua, the poet of the 'Admonitions of the Court Instructress'.[60] Although it is tempting to see Zou Yigui as a Qing-period Zhang Hua, who carried out his duty as a forthright official despite the possibly fatal consequences, Zou did not suffer for having criticized the emperor's laws. In his case, the emperor handed reprieves to the accused and in 1750 awarded Zou Yigui by inviting him to take prestigious posts in Beijing. Before his death at the age of eighty-seven, he even managed to fulfil his wish to retire, which he spent painting flowers at leisure.

The Qianlong emperor's reframing of the *Admonitions* scroll effected symbolic control over the physical and abstract bodies under his command – the body of the scroll, the abstract body of the empire, and the individual bodies of his subjects. However, the self-discipline inherent in the Qianlong emperor's study and application of classical Chinese conceptions of the sage-king and, in particular, his controlled appreciation of the *Admonitions* scroll suggest an underlying anxiety. The lissom figures in the *Admonitions* scroll belie the brute consequences of those who dared counter the imperially ordained order of things. But the emperor himself was subordinate to this order. His portrait as an archer (fig. 8), echoing the figure of the archer in scene 3 of the *Admonitions* scroll (pl. 5 left), indicated that, as emperor, he exercised supreme control formed through systematic practice; and yet, as subject, he had it all to lose in the 'rebound of a tense spring'.

NOTES

1   Lord Macartney, ambassador of Great Britain to China from 1792 to 1794, described Qianlong as 'despotic, and decorated with all the titles and epithets of oriental hyperbole', but 'who tempered the despotism he introduced with so much prudence and policy that it seemed preferable to the other evils which [his subjects] had so recently groaned under ...' (quoted in 'China and the eighteenth-century world: Macartney in China' <http://www.stanford.edu/class/history92a/readings/macartney.html>; cited 12 June 2002). See also Hevia 1995. This depiction of Qianlong became pabulum after Wittfogel 1957.

2   Kahn 1971. Re-interpretations of Qing universal rule appear in Rawski 1998, Crossley 1999 and Elliott 2001.

3   See Stephen Little, pp. 219–224, 241–248, in this volume.

4   See Yin Ji'nan, pp. 249–256, in this volume.

5   Hearn 1996, p. 176.

6   See Guy 1987.

7   Crossley 1987.

8   Binyon 1912, p. 3; Mason 2001, p. 33.

9   As I demonstrated in digital form when giving this paper at the 2001 colloquy.

10 With guidance from Kohara 2000 (1967).

11 Binyon 1912, p. 4.

12 Kohara 2000 (1967), pp. 9–10, n. 11.

13 *SQBJ chubian* 1971 (1745), p. 1074.

14 The title assigned to the colophon-painting, *Pine, Bamboo, Rock, Spring (Song zhu shi quan)*, appears in *SQBJ chubian* 1971 (1745),

p. 1198, but not on the work itself.

15   Son of Grand Secretary Zhang Tingyu (1672–1755); see Hummel 1943, p. 55, and Yu Jianhua (ed.) 1992, p. 839.

16   He received the *jinshi* degree in 1733, was a Hanlin Academician, and member of the Grand Secretariat; Hummel 1943, p. 792; Yu Jianhua (ed.) 1992, p. 1225.

17   Attained the post of Vice-Censor. Li Fang 1919, pp. 9a–9b; Ruitenbeek 1992, pp. 274, 312; Ho, Wai-kam *et al.* 1980, no. 277.

18   Yu Jianhua (ed.) 1992, pp. 903, 834, 903, 263. For Yu Sheng, see also Nie Chongzheng 1987, pp. 75–77.

19   Imperial Household archives, *Neiwufu huoji dang* 86/3412, QL11.12.9. The emperor's commission of these boxes does not appear in the *Shiqu baoji* in the entries of either the *Admonitions* scroll or any of the four artists' works.

20   Each of the 'Four Beauties' contains an oval relief seal with the characters 'Si mei ju' flanked by facing dragons (see Table 1, p. 266).

21   No such box(es) accompany the *Admonitions* scroll and *Shu River* (fig. 11) in the Freer Gallery, Washington, DC. I am unaware of a box accompanying the *Dream Journey over the Xiao and Xiang Rivers* (fig. 10), Tokyo National Museum, or the *Nine Songs* (fig. 12), Palace Museum, Beijing.

22   The entry for *Shu River* (fig. 11) in Charles Freer Lang's art inventory indicates that in 1900 the 'painting was stolen from the Imperial collection at Pekin [*sic*] and was later owned by the late Viceroy Tuan Fang [Duanfang (1861–1911)]'. 'Catalogue of kakemono by Japanese and Chinese artists', Charles Lang Freer's Papers, Freer Gallery of Art, Arthur M. Sackler Gallery Archives, L. 1139.

23   The hall is identified as the Jingyixuan (Pavilion of Quiet Harmony) in the emperor's 1746 *Admonitions* colophon (see n. 40 below), although its retranscription in *SQBJ chubian* 1971 (1745), p. 1198, diverges from the actual colophon, merely identifying the location of the pavilion as a 'room in the western part' (*xi bian zhi shi*) of the Jianfu Palace.

24   On the authenticity of these seals, see Wang Yao-t'ing, pp. 192–218, in this volume.

25   A total of thirty-three seal impressions by Xiang Yuanbian are listed in Kohara 2000 (1967), pp. 52–56.

26   Xu Qixian 1995, p. 63.

27   Prior to its acquisition by the Imperial Household, the *Admonitions* scroll belonged to the connoisseur An Qi (1683–1742?), whose seals appear on the yellow brocade preceding the scroll and on the buff brocade after the end of the painting; Kohara 2000 (1967), pp. 52, 55. Through connections with the high minister Mingju (1635–1708), An Qi's family became wealthy by manipulating the Tianjin salt monopoly. Some profits were funnelled into his collection of old paintings and calligraphy, but costly lawsuits and political intrigues relating to the succession of the Yongzheng emperor (r. 1723–1735) forced cessation of new acquisitions and eventual sale of the collection; Hummel 1943, pp. 11–13, 577–578. Historical sources do not mention how the *Admonitions* scroll landed in the Qing palace. An Qi may or may not have still owned the scroll when he published his catalogue *Moyuan huiguan* in 1742. The lack of Yongzheng-period seals seems to indicate the transfer of the scroll to the palace in the first ten years of the Qianlong reign, some time between 1736 and 1746.

28   *Wu fu wu dai tang gu xi tian zi bao*. See Table 1, p. 266.

29   *Ba zheng mao nian zhi bao*. See Table 1, pp. 266–267.

30   This meticulous documentation is part of Qing archival thoroughness established during the Kangxi reign. See Crossley 1999,

pp. 9–36 and Rawski 1998, pp. 11–13, 179–181.

31   Kohara 2000 (1967), p. 55, after Gray 1966. The emperor's colophon-painting dates to between the acquisition of the scroll and its 1745 entry in *SQBJ chubian* 1971 (1745), p. 1198.

32   Lee & Ho (eds) 1968, pp. 97–101.

33   From 'At the pass, gazing' (*Guan sui*), 'Odes of Zhou and the South' (*Zhou nan*). Alternately translated as 'the beautiful and good girl' (Karlgren [tr.] 1950, p. 2), 'the modest, retiring, virtuous young lady', (Legge [tr.] 1960, pp. 183–184), and 'shy was/is this noble lady' (Waley [tr.] 1996, pp. 5–6).

34   Waley (tr.) 1996, p. 37.

35   Traditionally attributed to Li Gonglin; *SQBJ chubian* 1971 (1745), pp. 963–965. Based on stylistic and other evidence, Yu Hui dates its production to the time of Ma Hezhi (act. 1131–1162); 2001, and pp. 146–167 in this volume. I gratefully acknowledge the Editor for bringing my attention to the 'Li Gonglin' title inscription, its classical allusions, and possible implications.

36   Rawski 1998, pp. 127–159.

37   Elliott 2001, p. 276ff.

38   Crossley 1999, pp. 3–9.

39   Elverskog (forthcoming). Stuart & Rawski 2001 (p. 120) illustrates an unmounted thangka entitled *The Qianlong Emperor as the Bodhisattva Manjusri* in ink and colour on silk done in the Qianlong imperial workshop with face by Giuseppe Castiglione (Lang Shining, 1688–1766) (collection of the Freer Gallery of Art, Washington, DC). See Nie Chongzheng (ed.) 1996, pp. 202–204, for three further examples of thangkas with the Qianlong emperor as the central deity, in the Palace Museum.

40   Kohara 2000 (1967), p. 57, after Gray 1966, pp. 8–9 (amended).

41   Ferguson 1918, p. 107; Alfreda Murck, pp. 138–145 in this volume.

42   Unlike the Li Gonglin attributions, there survive no genuine works by Gu Kaizhi with which to compare the British Museum scroll.

43   *SQBJ chubian* 1971 (1745), pp. 1198–1206; Kohara 2000 (1967), p. 35, n. 37.

44   Jiang Baoling 1985 (1853), p. 47.

45   Qin Zuyong 1967 (1866), *juan* 2, p. 5.

46   See also another Zou Yigui *Landscape*, with inscription by the Qianlong emperor dated 1770 (*gengyin*) (hanging scroll; ink on paper, 167.8 × 83.9 cm in the National Palace Museum, Taipei), illustrated in *Gugong shuhua tu lu* 1989–, vol. 11 (1993), no. 239.

47   *SQBJ chubian* 1971 (1745), pp. 630–631.

48   Jiang Baoling 1985 (1853), p. 47.

49   Dou Zhen 1985, *juan* 1, p. 45a.

50   Lu Jun 1830, *juan* 21, p. 29a.

51   Zou Yigui 1937 (18th c.), pp. 5–27. A separate section deals exclusively with Western-style chrysanthemum paintings.

52   Hirth 1905, p. 29.

53   Zou Yigui 1937 (18th c.), pp. 40–41.

54   Murck 2000.

55   See Michael Nylan, pp. 122–124 in this volume.

56   Feng Jinbo 1985 (1796), p. 674. Feng's account reprises a similar complaint by the Tang artist Yan Liben (d. 673), as recorded in Zhang Yanyuan's *Lidai ming hua ji* (Record of Famous Painters of Successive Dynasties); see Acker 1974, vol. 2, pt. 1, p. 214.

57   Kuhn 1990.

58   Li Yuandu 1985 (1866), pp. 503–504.

59   Ibid.

60   See Alfreda Murck, pp. 138–145, in this volume.

The Nineteenth-Century Provenance of the *Admonitions* Scroll: A Hypothesis

Zhang Hongxing

From the time of its acquisition by the British Museum from a private source in London in 1903, it has been a well-known fact that in the second half of the eighteenth century, the *Admonitions of the Instructress to the Court Ladies* scroll was stored in a special place in the Forbidden City.[1] This fact was documented both by the Emperor Qianlong (1711–1799; r. 1736–1795) in his 1746 colophon to the painting (pls 38–39), and by his courtiers in *Shiqu baoji chubian (Precious Cabinet of the Stony Gully, First Edition)*, the first catalogue of the imperial collection of calligraphy and painting, completed in 1747.[2] Equally clear are the details of the British Museum's acquisition of the scroll. A letter from its owner, Captain C. Johnson, dated 7 January 1903, suggests that the Museum and the owner had reached an agreement concerning its purchase: the Museum would offer to pay Capt. Johnson a sum of £25.[3] On 8 April of the same year, the scroll was given its present accession number.[4]

By contrast, the scroll's immediate past, or its exact whereabouts for most of the nineteenth century, is obscure. It is certain that the scroll remained in the Qing imperial collection in the fifteen years after Qianlong's death in 1799, for Hu Jing (1769–1845), chief compiler of *Shiqu baoji sanbian (Precious Cabinet of the Stony Gully, Third Edition*; 1815), recorded in his *Xiqing zhaji (Records of Xiqing)* that he viewed it on 31 August 1815.[5] It has thus been assumed that the scroll remained in the Qing imperial collection for the rest of the nineteenth century, despite the fact that there are no seals or colophons of the later Qing emperors or empresses on it, until the Boxer Rebellion (1989–1901),[6] when it was removed from the imperial collection and somehow made its way into Capt. Johnson's possession. This assumption was never a subject of scrutiny until the 2001 colloquium, when the vagueness of the scroll's nineteenth-century history became suddenly unacceptable, particularly when this blank period is set against studies of other detailed episodes in its

eventful history before and after the nineteenth century. As far as the provenance of the scroll is concerned, how can we claim, without proof, that it was kept permanently in the imperial collection until 1900, rather than coming out of the imperial palace at some point prior to that date?[7] If the scroll remained in the imperial collection up to 1900, was it kept in the same place as in the eighteenth century, or was it removed to another place or places within the palace? If the scroll did somehow find its way outside the palace collection prior to this date, under what conditions did this happen? Was it a case of an emperor or an empress giving it as a gift to a member of the royal family; or was it looted from the Summer Palace in 1860,[8] after which it drifted onto the art market; or did a eunuch take it out of the imperial collection illicitly and sell it to a collector or a dealer? Finally, how exactly did the scroll come into Capt. Johnson's possession during the Boxer Rebellion, and to what degree was his presence in China as a military officer connected with his acquisition of the *Admonitions* scroll?

None of these questions derives from empty speculation. To begin with, the dispersal of the Qing imperial collection is known to have occurred for a variety of reasons. For instance, some pieces left the palace when they were given as gifts by an emperor to members of the royal family. *Pingfu tie* or the *Letter of Recovery from Illness* (fig. 1) by Lu Ji (261–303), allegedly the earliest surviving masterpiece of calligraphy (currently in the Palace Museum, Beijing), was bestowed by Qianlong upon Yongxing (1752–1823), his twelfth son, in 1777. According to Wang Shixiang,[9] the scroll remained with the prince's family for another three generations until the 1880s, when another prince, Yixin (1832–1898), assumed ownership of it when he was put in charge of the affairs of the princes' residences in the capital. It was eventually offered for sale by Yixin's descendant Puru (1896–1963) in 1937, and was acquired by Zhang Boju (1898–1982), a wealthy collector

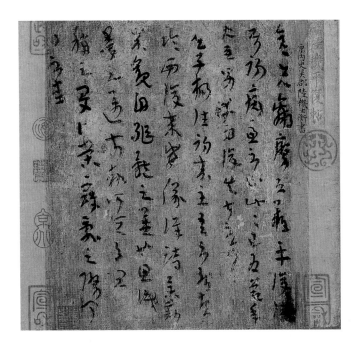

Fig. 1 Lu Ji (261–303), *Pingfu tie (Letter of Recovery from Illness)*.
Second half of the 3rd century. Handscroll; ink on paper,
23.8 × 20.5 cm. Palace Museum, Beijing.

Fig. 2 Attributed to Song Huizong (r. 1101–1125), *Five-Coloured Parakeet (Wuse yingwu)*. First half of the 12th century. Detail of a handscroll; ink and colour on silk, 53.3 × 125.1 cm. Museum of Fine Arts, Boston: Maria Antoinette Evans Fund (33.364).

from a banking family. Using the palace collection as a source for gift giving was indeed a common practice among the later Qing emperors after Qianlong. *Wuse yingwu* or *Five-Coloured Parakeet* attributed to Song Huizong (1082–1135; r. 1101–1125) in the Boston Museum of Fine Arts (fig. 2), for example, was probably given by one of the later emperors to Yixin, as his seal on the scroll suggests. Another familiar case is the famous *Jiulong tu* or *Nine Dragons* by Chen Rong (first half of the thirteenth century) in the same museum.[10] But to propose that the *Admonitions* scroll was given away like this invites difficulties.

These difficulties are essentially iconographic, by which term I refer to the special meaning that an emperor assigned to individual pieces in his collection through placing, grouping, naming, and augmenting. Let us return to the example of Lu Ji's *Recovery from Illness*. Although this work of calligraphy was in the Forbidden City before being given away, it had been kept in a palace of Qianlong's mother, and had thus always been treated as in a sense her own property. It was only after her death in 1777 that Qianlong gave it to Yongxing as a souvenir. Gift giving thus became an expression of shared grief among the members of the royal family.[11] When we consider the position of the *Admonitions* scroll at the Qianlong court, we are confronting a completely different situation. In the early years of his reign, Qianlong seemed to follow the conventional and indiscriminate way in which the majority of

works of art had been stored in previous reigns. Thus he kept the *Admonitions* scroll in the Yushufang or Imperial Study (see pl. 39), one of the four main storehouses for the imperial collection.[12] Yet, as the *Shiqu baoji* catalogue project approached completion in 1746, Qianlong decided to have the scroll stored separately. He had it removed from the Imperial Study and placed together with three other scrolls, all today attributed to Li Gonglin (1049–1106): *Xiao and Xiang Rivers (Xiao-Xiang tu)* in Tokyo National Museum, *Shu River (Shuchuan tu)* in the Freer Gallery of Art in Washington DC, and *Nine Songs (Jiuge tu)* in the Chinese History Museum (see pp. 271–272, figs 10–12). The four scrolls were rehoused in a west chamber exclusively dedicated to them in the Jingyixuan, or Verandah of Delightful Serenity, in the garden of the newly built Jianfugong (Palace of Established Happiness) compound, Qianlong's official and residential area (figs 3, 4), which was second in status only to the Hall of the Nourished Mind (Yangxindian).[13] In so doing, as his colophon on the scroll explains, the emperor intended to mark the unusual reunion of the four scrolls in his palace after a two-hundred-year separation (pls 38–39).[14]

He named the event *si mei ju* or the 'Union of the Four Beauties', a phrase borrowed from *Tengwangge shi xu (Preface*

Fig. 3 Dong Hao (18th century), *Flowering Plum at the Veranda of Delightful Serenity (Jingyixuan meihua)*, dated 1774. Hanging scroll; ink and colour on paper, 80.6 x 121 cm. National Palace Museum, Taipei. (After *Gugong shuhua tu lu* 1989–, vol. 12 [1994], p. 29.)

to *Collected Poems of the Gathering at the Tengwang Pavilion)* by the genius Tang poet Wang Bo (650–675), who refers to the rare union of good weather, beautiful scenery, a gay mood and a joyful event.[15] Furthermore, the emperor wrote the three characters *si mei ju* on a plaque which he had hung in the room,[16] and also had them carved on a seal which he had impressed on the four scrolls (fig. 6). Moreover, he added to each scroll one or more cross-referential commemorative inscriptions (pls 38–39), as well as four paintings by himself: the fitting subjects were bamboo (for the *Xiao-Xiang* scroll; fig. 7), plum-blossom (for the *Shu River* scroll), orchid (for the *Admonitions*; pl. 37), and chrysanthemum (for the *Nine Songs*). Finally, he had the scrolls remounted in an identical format and with the textile pieces for the outer wrappers (mounted on the 'back' at the beginning of the scrolls) cut from the same piece of silk brocade, as seen in illustrations

from the *Admonitions* and *Xiao and Xiang* scrolls in pl. 32 and fig. 8,[17] and he commissioned works from his court artists to commemorate the event.

To place this special treatment of the *Admonitions* (and other three scrolls) in context, we will observe that the bestowal of such prestige occurred only twice more in the Qianlong reign, and was confined to only six further scrolls. These included the well-known *san xi* or Three Rarities: *Clearing after the Sudden Snow (Kuaixue shiqing tie)* attributed to Wang Xizhi (303–361) in the Taipei Palace Museum, *Mid-Autumn (Zhongqiu tie)* by Wang Xianzhi (344–386) in Palace Museum, Beijing, and *Letter to Bo Yuan (Bo Yuan tie)* by Wang Xun (350–401) in the same museum, all of which were placed in the The Hall of the Nourished Mind, in the spring of 1746.[18] The remaining scrolls included the little-known *san you* or Three Friends, namely *Eighteen Noblemen (Shiba gong tu)* attributed to Cao Zhibai (1272–1355) in the Palace Museum, Beijing, *Gentlemen's Grove (Junzi lin tu)* by various Yuan and Ming painters in the same museum, and *Plum Blossoms (Meihua hejuan)* by various Song, Yuan and Ming artists (Liaoning Provincial Museum), all of which were

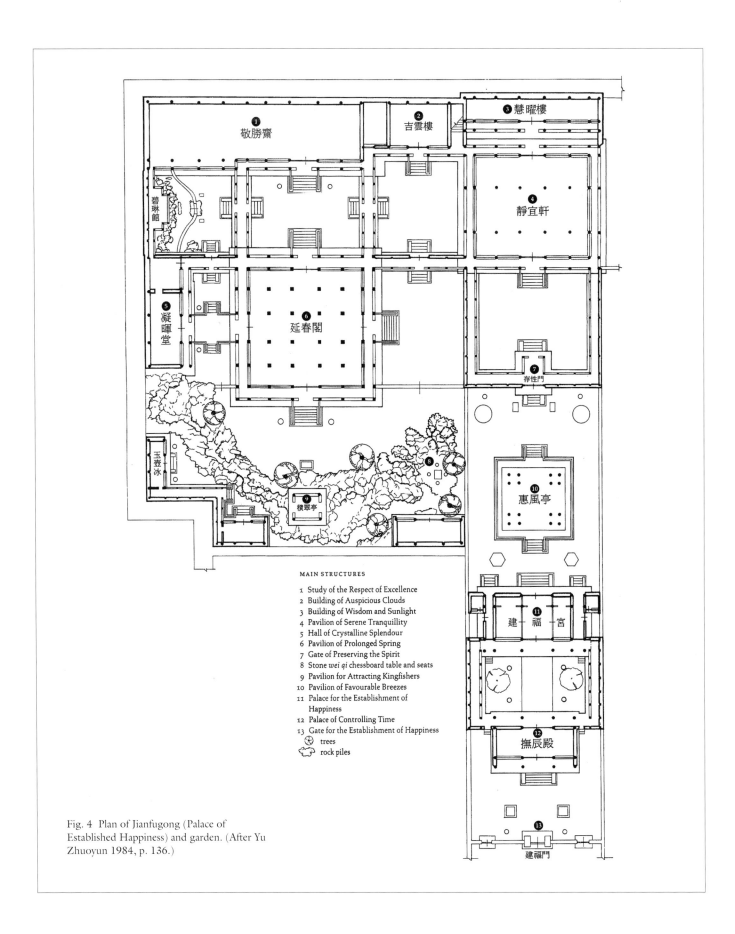

敬勝齋

吉雲樓

慧曜樓

碧琳館

靜宜軒

凝暉堂

延春閣

存性門

玉壺冰

惠風亭

積翠亭

建　福　宮

撫辰殿

建福門

MAIN STRUCTURES

1 Study of the Respect of Excellence
2 Building of Auspicious Clouds
3 Building of Wisdom and Sunlight
4 Pavilion of Serene Tranquillity
5 Hall of Crystalline Splendour
6 Pavilion of Prolonged Spring
7 Gate of Preserving the Spirit
8 Stone *wei qi* chessboard table and seats
9 Pavilion for Attracting Kingfishers
10 Pavilion of Favourable Breezes
11 Palace for the Establishment of
   Happiness
12 Palace of Controlling Time
13 Gate for the Establishment of Happiness
   trees
   rock piles

Fig. 4 Plan of Jianfugong (Palace of
Established Happiness) and garden. (After Yu
Zhuoyun 1984, p. 136.)

Fig. 5 Photograph of Jianfugong (Palace of Established Happiness) after the fire of 1923. (After Johnston 1934, facing p. 336.)

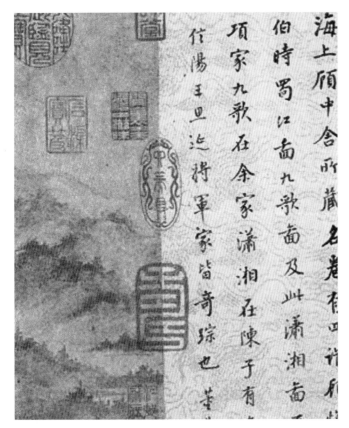
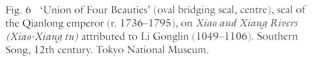

Fig. 6 'Union of Four Beauties' (oval bridging seal, centre), seal of the Qianlong emperor (r. 1736–1795), on *Xiao and Xiang Rivers (Xiao-Xiang tu)* attributed to Li Gonglin (1049–1106). Southern Song, 12th century. Tokyo National Museum.

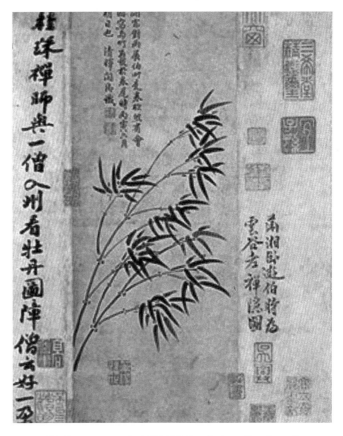

Fig. 7 Qianlong emperor (r. 1736-1795), painting of bamboo, for *Xiao and Xiang Rivers (Xiao-Xiang tu)* attributed to Li Gonglin (1049–1106). Southern Song, 12th century. Tokyo National Museum.

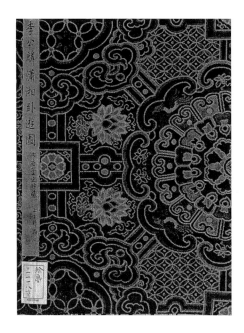

Fig. 8 Brocade outer wrapper for *Xiao and Xiang Rivers (Xiao-Xiang tu)*, attributed to Li Gonglin (1049–1106). Qing dynasty, Qianlong period, *c.*1746. Tokyo National Museum.

moved to the Ninghuitang or Hall of the Congealed Sunset, also in the Palace of the Established Happiness, in the following year (i.e. 1747).[19] Together they constituted the top ten 'star' pieces in the entire palace collection of calligraphy and paintings.

For Qianlong, the significance of these pieces was more profound than is commonly understood. As far as the Three Rarities scrolls are concerned, as the emperor himself explained, the phrase 'three *xi*' connoted not only the rarity of the three Wangs' calligraphic pieces, but also the 'three admirations' of the Song philosopher Zhou Dunyi (1017–1073):

士希賢   *shi xi xian*
賢希聖   *xian xi sheng*
聖希天   *sheng xi tian*

A gentleman admires a worthy;
a worthy admires a sage;
a sage admires Heaven.[20]

In the light of this, the term Four Beauties must have referred to sources other than Wang Bo's 'union of the four beauties',

Fig. 9 Dong Bangda (1699–1769), *Union of Four Beauties (Simei ju hefu)*, dated 1746. Pair of hanging scrolls; ink on paper, the right scroll 171.7 × 111.8 cm, the left 172 × 111.6 cm. National Palace Museum, Taipei. (After *Gugong shuhua tu lu* 1989–, vol. 12 [1994], p. 121, and vol. 14 [1995], p. 343.)

Table 1: Various listings of *si mei* (Four Beauties)

Jia Yi's *si mei*	*zhi*, ruling	*ping*, tranquillizing	*xian*, manifesting	*rong*, glorifying
Wang Bo's *si mei*	fine weather	beautiful scenery	good mood	joyful event
Neo-Confucian *si mei*	*ren*, kindness	*yi*, righteousness	*zhong*, loyalty	*xin*, trustworthiness
Qianlong: *si mei ju* Qianlong title-piece:	*Admonitions* *tong guan fang* (fragrance of red tube)	*Shu River* (not recorded)	*Nine Songs* *jin bian ji yan*	*Xiao-Xiang* *qi tun yun meng*
Qianlong painting:	wild orchid	plum blossom	orchid and chrysanthemum	bamboo in rain
Courtier painter:	Zou Yigui	Ding Guanpeng	Zhang Ruoai	Dong Bangda
Subject:	*Songzhu shiquan* (landscape)	*Du Fu shi yi* (landscape)	*Qu Zi xing yin tu*	*Su Shi shi yi* (landscape)
Qianlong title-piece	Li Gonglin *Admonitions* *wanghua zhi shi* (beginnings of kingship)			

and would have plumbed deep levels of Confucian political and moral teaching. Several interpretations are possible here. For instance, Qianlong could have drawn on the Han scholar Jia Yi (201–169 BCE) who used the phrase *si mei* to refer to four qualities of a good ruler, namely:

治平顯榮
zhi ping xian rong
Ruling, tranquillizing, manifesting and glorifying.[21]

Or Qianlong could have been more interested in the Neo-Confucian interpretation, which usually associated the phrase with four personal qualities of the gentleman (see table 1):

仁義忠信
ren yi zhong xin
kindness, righteousness, loyalty and trustworthiness.[22]

It is, therefore, crucial to realize that the *Admonitions* scroll differed from most artworks in the imperial collection in many respects. For Qianlong, it was a jewel of his collection; it was stored deep in his living quarters in the Forbidden City; it was an integral part of a core group of scrolls; and above all, it was closely linked to his life and thought.

After Qianlong's death, the palaces in which he had lived and the things he had used were left as they were by his successors. According to the Last Emperor Puyi's (1906–1967; r. Xuantong, 1909–1911) memoirs, the entire Palace of Estab-

lished Happiness, in which the *Admonitions* scroll had been stored, was sealed off in the reign of the Emperor Jiaqing (r. 1796–1821).[23] The practice of sealing off areas in the Forbidden City in the nineteenth century perhaps derived from late Qing emperors' sense of filial piety, rather than having been impelled by the court's worsening financial situation, as one may be tempted to suspect. Indeed, even in the case of the Hall of the Nourished Mind, which continued to be used as a main audience hall throughout the century, the room for storing the Three Rarities was by and large kept as it was in the Qianlong reign, and the three scrolls no doubt remained there for many decades untouched. The Three Rarities did not leave the imperial collection, nor did the Three Friends scrolls, until around 1921 to 1924, when Puyi, faced with the depleted financial situation of the royal household, disposed of them, as *Gugong yiyi shuhua mulu (Catalogue of Calligraphy and Paintings Missing from the Old Imperial Palace)*, published in 1925, suggests.[24] According to Yang Renkai,[25] two of the Three Rarities, namely Wang Xianzhi's *Mid-Autumn* and Wang Xun's *Letter to Bo Yuan*, were sold by Puyi in Tianjin, and subsequently went into the collection of Guo Baochang (1889–?), best known in the West as the supervisor of the manufacture of the official Hongxian (1915–1916) ceramic ware at Jingdezhen during the administration of Yuan Shikai (1859–1916), and as the author of the introduction to the catalogue of the international exhibition of Chinese art held at the Royal Academy in London in 1935. The Three Friends scrolls were taken by Puyi to Changchun, and then became

Fig. 10 Attributed to Wang Xizhi (344–386), *Xingrang tie (Ritual to Pray for Good Harvest)*. Tang (618–907) tracing copy. The Art Museum, Princeton University.

dispersed at the end of World War II. Thus it seems very unlikely that any later emperor other than Puyi would have ventured to separate Qianlong's Four Beauties, and give the *Admonitions* scroll as a gift to a prince or princess, courtier, or high official at a time when the imperial system had not quite collapsed, when filial piety was still a prime obligation, and when the sanctity of the imperial art collection had not been tarnished.

Using similar reasoning, we can also dismiss the speculation that the *Admonitions* scroll disappeared from the Summer Palace in 1860 when the place was sacked and burnt down by French and British troops and that the part of the imperial collection deposited there was dispersed. In addition, contemporary diaries, which contain a substantial amount of information about the objects dispersed from the Summer Palace, do not lend themselves to such a theory. Weng Tonghe (1830–1904), a senior court minister and one of the best-informed collectors in the capital between the late 1850s and the 1890s, recorded in his diary several pieces that had found their way out of the palace collection and had surfaced on the Liulichang art market in the capital. These included the famous *Xingrang tie* (fig. 10) by Wang Xizhi, currently in the Princeton University Art Museum, which Weng knew to have passed through the Liulichang market in 1865.[26] But nowhere in his diary is any one, let alone all of the Four Beauties scrolls mentioned.

Furthermore, my own research among the court archives concerning the Verandah of the Delightful Serenity has uncovered no evidence to support the contention that the *Admonitions* scroll was removed from the Forbidden City and transferred to the Summer Palace prior to 1860. In fact, the surviving documents regarding the building are so scanty that

they do not support the supposition that the scrolls remained in the building either. Nevertheless, a record of the Zaobanchu (Imperial Workshop in the Forbidden City), dated 25 January 1870, is worth noting. This record is short, consisting of only three sentences, but it documents an order from one of the two dowager empresses, probably Cixi (1835–1908), regarding repair-work on the building. Of importance is the last sentence, which reads:

> As to the six calligraphy pieces and the four paintings in the room, Union of the Four Beauties, remove and transfer them to the Maoqindian (Hall of Diligence) [a hall near the main audience hall, Qianqinggong (Palace of Heavenly Tranquillity)], and store them there.[27]

Because the record does not give details such as the titles of the four paintings, we are in no position to claim that the four paintings must infallibly be the four scrolls in question. Yet there is a high degree of probability that this is indeed the

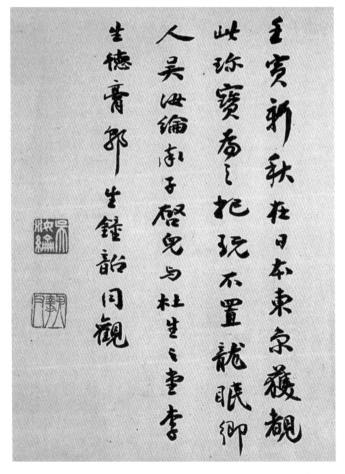

Fig. 11 Wu Rulun (1840–1903), colophon, dated 1902, to *Xiao and Xiang Rivers (Xiao-Xiang tu)*, attributed to Li Gonglin (1049–1106). Tokyo National Museum.

Fig. 12 Duanfang (1861–1911). (After Martin 1907, facing p. 243.)

case, for we already know that the room was reserved exclusively for the Four Beauties.

Even if the four paintings mentioned in the archive do not necessarily refer to the Four Beauties, the presumption that the *Admonitions* scroll remained in the palace collection until 1900 corresponds to our present knowledge of the provenance of three other scrolls in its group. While *Nine Songs* (see p. 272, fig. 12), currently in the Chinese History Museum in Beijing,[28] remained in the palace collection until the early Republican period as suggested by *Gugong zhoukan*, the weekly bulletin of the then newly-established Palace Museum, in 1934,[29] neither of the other two scrolls is known to have entered any collection outside the palace prior to the Boxer Rebellion.[30] As far as the *Xiao and Xiang Rivers* scroll,

Fig. 13 Major Noel du Boulay (1861–1949) in the Yiheyuan Summer Palace in 1900. (After du Boulay 1990–1991, p. 84.)

currently in the Tokyo National Museum, is concerned, the first colophon (fig. 11) of the post-Qianlong period was written in Tokyo by Wu Rulun (1840–1903), a noted Chinese scholar and official of the late Qing, and is dated to 1902.[31] The *Shu River* scroll in the Freer Gallery is reported to have once been in the collection of Duanfang (1861–1911; fig. 12), a well-known high official and art collector in late nineteenth- and early twentieth-century China.[32] Judging from Duanfang's catalogue *Renyin xiaoxia lu*, in which it is mentioned, the scroll could have been acquired by Duanfang sometime around 1902 when the catalogue was compiled.[33]

What conclusions can be reached from the evidence presented above? First, it has become possible to hypothesize that the *Admonitions* scroll was dispersed as a consequence of the Boxer Rebellion in the year 1900, rather than at some time before that date. But the information so far uncovered by my research does not provide sufficient evidence to suggest with a similar degree of confidence the exact circumstances under which Capt. Johnson acquired the scroll in China. In the first place, we do not know exactly where in the palace collection the *Admonitions* scroll was just before the crisis broke out. Certainly, according to *Gugong zhoukan* the *Nine Songs* scroll was in the Summer Palace in 1934, and therefore arguably Cixi may have had it moved there from the Verandah of Delightful Serenity prior to 1900. This in turn leads to another possible argument based on the group to which it belonged, namely that the *Admonitions* and the other two Beauties could have been moved there together with the *Nine Songs*. But this argument cannot rule out the possibility that the *Nine Songs* could have been moved to the Summer Palace after 1900.

Secondly, we have insufficient information to clarify the circumstances of Capt. Johnson's acquisition of the *Admonitions* scroll in China. Capt. Johnson's personal details are straightforward: he was born at Madras in India on 6 April 1870;[34] his father, Samuel Maurice Johnson, worked for an engineer's office as an accountant in that area.[35] His first military commission was as a second lieutenant in a British Army regiment in India, the Royal Welch Fusiliers, on 21 September 1889. He was then promoted to the rank of lieutenant on 21 September 1891, and transferred to the First Bengal Lancers in the Indian Army a year later. He was promoted again, to captain, in command of one of the four squadrons in September 1900. He remained in the Indian Army and received several further promotions, retiring as a colonel in 1912.[36] He moved to England, first living in Beches Manor Hotel at Wokingham, Berkshire, and then at 6 Bentinck Street, London W1, by Regent's Park. He died there on 17 November 1937.[37]

Equally clear is his having been in China in 1900. Johnson's regiment, the First Bengal Lancers, was among the units selected to participate in the 'Relief of Pekin' operation.[38] This cavalry regiment set off on 1 July from Lucknow, and travelled by train to Calcutta, where it embarked on the 6 and 7 July, reached Hong Kong, and finally arrived at Dagu, near Tianjin, probably on 20 July, by which time the area had already come under allied control.[39] The regiment reached the city of Tianjin on 2 August, approached Beijing on 14 August and had entered the city by the following day.[40] The regiment stayed in Beijing for the next two months, and the main body left on 26 October, travelling via Hong Kong for India.[41]

The Indian Army units' occupation of Beijing is well documented in the archive of the India Office, according to which they were stationed in the following areas of the city: the east part of the Chinese City, the Legations,[42] and the Yiheyuan Summer Palace north-west of the city after a Russian troop had evacuated it suddenly in early October.[43] But, curiously enough, Capt. Johnson's name does not appear in any documents of the expedition. Although promoted to squadron commander, he was not cited for distinguished ser-vice. Nor was he listed as being among the company of Bengal Lancers in the parade that marched through the Forbidden City on 28 August. When a detachment of British troops under the command of Major Noel du Boulay (1861–1949; fig. 13) took possession of the Yiheyuan Summer Palace following the Russians' sudden evacuation and handover to the Imperial Household 'without giving any warning of their intentions to their allies',[44] twelve mounted troopers from the First Bengal Lancers reportedly assisted in the occupation.[45] But Capt. Johnson was possibly not present on this occasion either.[46]

When we next come across his name, Capt. Johnson was already back in India, where he obtained permission to live outside the country for half a year between July 1901 and December 1902, to allow him to recover from ill health and to resolve other private matters.[47] Counterchecking his letter to Mr Sydney Colvin of the British Museum,[48] we know that Capt. Johnson did stay in London during that period and that he eventually sold the *Admonitions* scroll to the Museum shortly before he was called back to India. The question of how he got his hands on it remains, for now, a mystery.[49]

NOTES

1   See, for instance, Waley 1923, p. 59.
    I am grateful to the Exchange Program of the British Academy and Chinese Academy of Social Sciences for funding my research trip to Beijing. Special thanks are due to my colleagues in the Department of Fine Art, University of Edinburgh, and in the National Museums of Scotland in Edinburgh, for supporting this project throughout; to the curators of the Palace Museum, Chinese First Historical Archives, Tokyo National Museum, Freer Gallery, British Museum and British Library, for their generous assistance; and to Mark Jones, Craig Clunas, Robert Hillenbrand, David Caldwell, Yang Xin, Yu Hui, Shane McCausland, Robert Knox, Frances Wood, Ian Baxter, Thomas Lawton, Roderick Whitfield, Wang Tao and Charles Mason, for their helpful comments.

2   *SQBJ chubian* (*SKQS* 1991, vol. 825) 1747, *juan* 36 & 44, pp. 429–430. The date for the completion of the *Siqu baoji* is given here as 1747, rather than the commonly cited date of 1746, because the last three paintings to be included bear colophons by the Qianlong emperor dated 1747.

3   C. Johnson's letter to Mr Sydney Colvin, Keeper of the Prints and Drawings, reads: 'Dear Sir, I will accept your offer of £25 (twenty-five pounds) for my Chinese scroll. Will you please send me an i.o.u. for that amount payable about April next, as I propose to pay a tradesman's bill with it. Yours truly, (Cap.) C. Johnson.' I am grateful to the Department of the Oriental Antiquities for allowing me to read the Museum's papers concerning the scroll's acquisition (*Admonitions* scroll file).

4   See *Admonitions* scroll file, Department of Oriental Antiquities.

5   Hu Jing 1934 (1866), p. 22b, where Hu erroneously recorded that the painting was on paper.

6   Waley 1923, p. 59; Fu Baoshi 1958, p. 32; Pan Tianshou 1958, p. 21; Ma Cai 1958, pp. 21–22; Yang Renkai 1991, p. 57.

7   Zheng Zhenduo believed the scroll was taken from the Yuanmingyuan Summer Palace in Beijing at the time the Anglo-French allied armies sacked and burned the palace in 1860 (1951, p. 87 & 1958, p. 217).

8   Ibid.

9   Wang Shixiang 1998, p. 70.

10 These three examples are cited in Yang Renkai 1991, p. 55–57. Other paintings given out as gifts are recorded in the works of courtiers such as Ruan Yuan (1842, *juan* 8, p. 21).

11 Wang Shixiang 1998, p. 70.

12 The other three were Qianqinggong (Palace of Heavenly Tranquillity), Yangxindian (Hall of the Nourished Mind), and Chonghuagong (Palace of Continuous Glory), in the Forbidden City, as indicated in *Shiqu baoji*.

13 The Palace of the Established Happiness itself has a dramatic history. Built by the Qianlong emperor in the 1740s, the majority of the buildings in this compound, including the Verandah of Delightful Serenity, were burnt to ashes in a disastrous fire on the evening of 27 June 1923 (fig. 5). According to the memoirs of Puyi, the last emperor who then still lived with his deposed court in the Forbidden City, the fire was not an accident but was probably started by the eunuchs in an attempt to cover up their theft of numerous treasures stored in the palace. Since then this area has remained a ruin, although recently the Palace Museum authorities have launched a multimillion-pound project to rebuild the entire compound. For the 1923 incident, see Puyi 1979, pp. 133–136; Johnston 1934, pp. 335–337. For the history and architectural

reconstruction of the palace compound, see Fu & Bai 1980, pp. 14–16; Gugong 2000, pp. 26–37.

14 Tr. in Gray 1966, pp. 8–9; quoted in Kohara 2000 (1967), pp. 56–57.

15 *QTW* 1961–1965 (1814), *juan* 181, pp. 2327–2328.

16 *Guochao gongshi* 1987 (1769), *juan* 13, p. 245.

17 According to a court document discovered in the Chinese First Office of Historical Archive, Beijing, by Nixi Cura, the four scrolls were further stored in a specially made box. See Nixi Cura's article in the present volume.

18 See Qianlong's colophons to the three scrolls in *SQBJ chubian* (*SKQS* 1991, vol. 824) 1747, *juan* 19, pp. 545, 548–550.

19 See Qianlong's colophons to two of the three scrolls in *SQBJ chubian* (*SKQS* 1991, vol. 825) 1747, *juan* 44, pp. 662, 664. This catalogue also records that like the Four Beauties, the Three Friends scrolls were placed in a case (p. 666).

20 *Guochao gongshi* 1987 (1769), *juan* 13, pp. 255–256.

21 *Xinshu, juan* 9, in *SKQS*, vol. 695, p. 453.

22 Liu Zongyuan (773–819), 'Tianjue' (Nobility), *QTS* 1960, vol. 12, *juan* 582, pp. 7465–7466. As Harold L. Khan (1971, pp. 160–162) has observed, both Jia Yi and Liu Zongyuan's works were part of the future Qianlong emperor's core reading before he ascended the throne in 1735.

23 Puyi 1979, p. 133.

24 Yang Renkai 1991, catalogue, pp. 540, 553, 559.

25 Ibid., pp. 82–83.

26 Weng Tonghe 1989 (1925), p. 403.

27 *Neiwufu huojidang*, 37, no. 3115–3125, Chinese First Office of Historical Archives.

28 I am indebted to Thomas Lawton for this information.

29 *Gugong zhoukan* (1934, no. 357).

30 The conclusion is drawn after checking the index to the major catalogues edited by John C. Ferguson (1994 [1933]).

31 Wu Rulun's visit to Japan is recorded in his journal 'Dongyou conglu' 198[?] [1902], although his encounter with the scroll is not mentioned. According to Mr Tsuruta Takeyoshi's research into the early provenance of the scroll in Japan (1992), it was acquired by Mr Harada Gorō (1893–1980), a noted Japanese art dealer, from a relative of Guo Baochang (1867–1940) at Liulichang in Beijing. After Harada returned to Japan with the scroll, he contacted Kikuchi Seido (1852–1920), a well-known banker, and sold it to him. The scroll remained in the Kikuchi family through the first half of the twentieth century, until 1951, when it was acquired by the National Commission for Protection of Cultural Properties (now the Agency for Cultural Affairs of the Ministry of Education, Science and Sports). It was designated a National Treasure in March 1953, and was transferred to the Tokyo National Museum in August 1961 under the present accession number TA-161. I am indebted to Messrs Dainobu Yuji and Minato Nobuyuki of Tokyo National Museum for this information. For this writer, however, there is a serious mismatch between the above account and that suggested by Wu Rulun's colophon. There being no reason to challenge the authenticity of Wu's colophon, the scroll must have been in Japan by 1902. Yet, Harada Gorō, the alleged dealer of the work, was only ten years old at that time, and was surely too young to have executed this transaction.

32 Personal communication from Thomas Lawton. *Shu River* scroll was acquired by Charles Lang Freer (1854–1919) in New York in 1916 from Pang Yuanji (ca. 1865–1949), a well-known Shanghainese collector of the time. As Lawton suggests, the scroll may have entered Pang's collection after Duanfang was assassinated in 1911. It is puzzling, however, that it is not recorded in Pang's catalogue of his collection, *Xuzhai minghua lu* (1925).

33 See Duanfang 1995 (1902), pp. 336–344. How Duanfang acquired this scroll is unknown, but we should be able to rule out the possibility that he received it as a gift from the Empress Dowager Cixi for his service while she was a refugee in north-west China in 1900–1901, when the western allies occupied the capital. See *Duanzhongminggong zhougao*, which contains 532 of his memorials written between 1899 and 1909, including several acknowledging receipt of gifts from Cixi.

34 Baptisms Solemnized at Vespery Saint Matthias, 1870, *Index to Madras Baptisms*, The British Library, Oriental & India Office Collection.

35 Marriage Solemnized at Madras Saint George's Cathedral, 1869, *Index to Madras Church Marriages*, The British Library, Oriental & India Office Collection.

36 *Indian Army List*, vols 1889–1912, The British Library, Oriental & India Office Collection. See also Daniels 1925, p. 52.

37 Grants of Probate and Administration during the quarter ending the 30th day of September 1938, folio 226, i., *Grants of Probate*, The British Library, Oriental & India Office Collection. See also Deaths Registration in Oct. Nov. & Dec. 1937, *Index of Deaths in England and Wales since 1837*, microfilm in the National Library of Scotland.

38 For a general account of the Indian Army's involvement in the 'Relief of Pekin' operation see Harfield 1990, pp. 158–167; for that of Johnson's regiment, see Daniels 1925, pp. 54–59.

39 The manuscripts in The Military Collection 402, L/MIL/7/16676, The British Library, Oriental & India Office Collection.

40 Norie 1903, p. 65–68; The Military Collection, L/MIL/17/20/12, The British Library, Oriental & India Office Collection; Daniels 1925, p. 55.

41 Norie 1903, pp. 138, 150.

42 Ibid., map, pp. 92–93.

43 Ibid., p. 137.

44 Ibid.

45 For Noel du Boulay's involvement in the British occupation of the Yiheyuan Summer Palace, see Anthony du Boulay 1990–1991, pp. 83–102.

46 This is inferred purely from a bureaucratic point of view. Johnson was promoted to captain in September, obviously in Beijing. However, in Mr du Boulay's letter of 7 October to the Chief of Staff reporting the composition of the British Troops stationed in the Summer Palace, Johnson's name does not appear, although a different captain is mentioned. See du Boulay 1990–1991, pp. 86–87.

47 *Indian Army List*, 1903, The British Library, Oriental & India Office Collection.

48 See n. 3.

49 At the time of revising this paper, new information from Capt. Johnson's daughter concerning the circumstances of his acquisition of the scroll came to my attention. In a note by Mrs Betty Manzano recently brought into the Museum, she writes: 'In 1900 my father the late Capt C. A. K. Johnson of the 1st Bengal Lancers was stationed in the Summer Palace in Peking during the Boxer Rebellion. He had occasion to find a high born Chinese lady with her family in great distress in a dangerous plight and he was able to guide them to safety. In gratitude for his help and protection this lady presented him with the Scroll which on his return to England he donated to the British Museum on 9 October 1902' (note written following a visit to the Museum on 7 January 1985). As this family tradition requires corroboration, I decided not to incorporate it into the paper at this stage of research. Re-reading the essay, it appears that my overall hypothesis, that the scroll came out of the palace during the Boxer Rebellion, will remain valid should the Johnson family's story be verified in future.

The *Admonitions* Scroll in the Twentieth Century

Charles Mason

The twentieth century marked one of the most eventful periods in the long history of the *Admonitions* scroll. Removed from China by a British soldier at the beginning of the century, the painting was brought to England where it entered the collection of the British Museum in 1903. At the British Museum the scroll was studied for the first time by Western scholars, and received its first exposure to a mass audience in a 1910 exhibition. Reproduced and remounted to encourage even greater public visibility during the early 1910s, the scroll then underwent a long period of critical scrutiny and conflicting interpretation before scholars finally reached a consensus opinion about it in the late 1950s and 1960s. Having at last achieved a secure position in the Western canon of Chinese art history, the painting ended the century locked away in the storerooms of the British Museum as one of its greatest but least often seen treasures. This essay traces the progress of the scroll through each of these various stages so that we may better understand how and why the painting has come to be where and what it is today.

From China to the British Museum

While the general sequence of events by which the *Admonitions* scroll left China and ended up in the British Museum is known, many details of the story are not entirely certain. As the preceding essays by Nixi Cura and Zhang Hongxing have shown, the *Admonitions* scroll was a treasured part of the Qing (1644–1911) imperial collection during the latter half of the eighteenth and nineteenth centuries. However, at some point around the time of the Boxer Rebellion in 1900, under circumstances that are still unclear, the scroll was removed from the imperial collection and found its way into the hands of a British army officer named Captain Clarence Johnson (1870–1937). When Capt. Johnson's tour of duty in China ended, he returned to England taking the scroll with him. For the next several years the scroll remained in Johnson's possession in London. Then in early 1903, faced with mounting debts, Johnson decided to sell the painting and contacted the British Museum about purchasing it.

One version of what happened next says that Capt. Johnson, believing the scroll's jade fastening toggle to be its most valuable component, first showed the painting to the Museum's Keeper of British and Medieval Antiquities, Sir Hercules Read, who was then the Museum's resident expert on Chinese decorative arts. After examining both the toggle and the painting, Read decided that the latter looked more interesting than the former, so he referred Johnson to his colleagues in the Museum's Department of Prints and Drawings, which at the time was also in charge of its Asian painting collection. There, the story continues, the painting was inspected by the department's keeper and assistant keeper, Sir Sidney Colvin (1845–1927) and Laurence Binyon (1869–1943). Although neither Colvin nor Binyon had any formal training in Chinese culture or art history, they instinctively recognized the quality of the painting, and thus agreed to buy it for the Museum without knowing exactly what it was.[1]

As stirring as this tale of serendipitous discovery is to the romantic imagination, however, internal Museum documents paint a rather different picture of events. Those records indicate that Capt. Johnson contacted Colvin directly in January 1903 to propose the sale of the scroll. Colvin then arranged for a number of experts from outside the Museum to examine the painting for the purpose of identifying its subject, author, date and provenance prior to its arrival in England. Having learned from these experts that the painting was at least potentially a very important work of art, Colvin subsequently secured approval from the Museum trustees to purchase the scroll for the relatively modest sum of twenty-five pounds, and the painting formally entered the collection on 8 April 1903.[2]

Regardless of how it occurred, the relocation of the *Admonitions* scroll from the Qing imperial collection to the collection of the British Museum was a momentous event in the painting's history. Although the scroll had changed hands many times previously in its existence, this was the first time (as far as is known) that it left Chinese soil. Moreover this was also the first time that it became part of a public rather than a private collection. The radical change in context had profound implications for the scroll's significance as a cultural object. Within China, the painting had been a familiar masterpiece, an organic part of a living artistic and intellectual tradition with roots stretching back to the time of the scroll's creation. In England, by contrast, the scroll became an exotic curiosity, a metaphorical symbol of a foreign civilization within an institution that was devoted to glorifying the far-reaching power of the imperialist British state. Although the scroll later recovered some of its original connotations as Western understanding of China and Chinese culture improved, it has never entirely lost its status as an alien object even to this day.

Early Scholarship and Exhibition

At the time the British Museum purchased the *Admonitions* scroll in 1903, the basic facts about its subject, authorship, and provenance were already known. However, further research was needed to confirm and refine this information, and to determine the scroll's place within the broader history of Chinese painting. Consequently, as news of the acquisition spread, a number of scholars in England and Europe began to study the scroll more intensively, and over the next five or six years the first wave of Western writing about the painting appeared in various books and journals. By the end of the decade, these writings had made the scroll so famous that in 1910 the Museum decided to showcase the painting for the first time in a major public exhibition. This event elevated the scroll's reputation even further, and secured its position as one of the most celebrated Chinese paintings in the Western world.

Among the first scholars to begin researching the *Admonitions* scroll after its acquisition by the British Museum was one of its new custodians, Laurence Binyon. In January 1904, he published an article in the *Burlington Magazine* that provided Western audiences with the first detailed account of the painting's contents, attribution, condition, and provenance.[3] Reading this article today, one is struck by how much Binyon had learned about the scroll within just nine months of its acquisition. Although the essay contains some minor factual errors (for example, it misidentifies the author of the paint-

ing's textual inscriptions as Ban Zhao [*c.* 45–*c.* 120] instead of Zhang Hua [232–300], and confuses some of the seals of the Ming [1368–1644] collector Xiang Yuanbian [1625–1690] with those of a tenth-century collector named Song Qi), nevertheless the information it presents is largely accurate and surprisingly comprehensive. Perhaps the most interesting aspect of this article is the argument it makes for the scroll's historical importance. At the time the essay was published, many Western scholars believed that Chinese painting was essentially a debased form of Indian art whose chief merit was that it had provided a foundation for the development of Japanese painting. In this article, however, Binyon uses the early date and high quality of the *Admonitions* painting to refute that belief, and to make the case that Chinese painting should be considered an independent tradition worthy of study in its own right. This was the first time any Western scholar had made such an argument in print, and thus Binyon's 1904 essay stands as a landmark not only in the history of Western scholarship on the *Admonitions* scroll specifically, but also in the history of Western scholarship on Chinese painting more generally.

For the next several years, Binyon's *Burlington Magazine* article remained the primary scholarly work on the *Admonitions* scroll in the Western world. Then, in 1908, Binyon published his book *Painting in the Far East*, which contained an entire chapter devoted to Gu Kaizhi (*c.* 345–406) and the *Admonitions* painting.[4] Although the discussion of the scroll in this book was similar in substance to the 1904 article, its descriptions of the painting's contents and style were more detailed, and its contextualization of the painting within the broader history of Asian art more nuanced. Consequently, *Painting in the Far East* quickly became the new definitive source of information about the scroll. As the book was reprinted in a number of new and expanded editions over the next several decades, it brought tremendous public exposure to the painting. Indeed, *Painting in the Far East* became so widely circulated that it, more than any other single publication, may be credited with transforming the *Admonitions* scroll from a little-known curiosity into one of the most renowned Chinese paintings during the first few decades of the twentieth century.

Apart from Binyon, a second scholar who played a major part in early Western efforts to research the *Admonitions* scroll was Cambridge University professor Herbert Giles (1845–1935). Giles had been one of the external experts invited by the British Museum to help evaluate the scroll when it was initially being considered for purchase in 1903, and he continued to assist Colvin and Binyon with their research efforts after the acquisition was completed. It was

Giles who was mainly responsible for identifying the stories behind many of the scenes in the painting, and he who provided much of the biographical information about the painting's attributed author, Gu Kaizhi. Despite all his work on the scroll, however, Giles' only significant publication related to the *Admonitions* painting was a chapter in his 1905 book *An Introduction to the History of Chinese Pictorial Art*, in which he translated a number of anecdotes from early Chinese texts about Gu's life.[5] Although none of these stories was directly connected to the *Admonitions* painting itself, nevertheless the book significantly advanced Western understanding of the scroll by providing the first account of the cultural milieu in which the painting had originally been created and viewed. Sadly for him, Giles' work on the *Admonitions* scroll was largely superseded and forgotten by later scholars, but at the time his part in the initial research effort was almost as great as Binyon's and helped enormously to improve the overall state of Western knowledge about the painting during those early years.

Lastly, a third important early Western scholar of the *Admonitions* scroll was Professor Édouard Chavannes (1865–1918) of the Collège de France in Paris. As has already been suggested, one of the major questions about the scroll which was still unsolved during the first few years after its acquisition was the exact source of the inscriptions that appear between the scenes throughout the painting. Although scholars were able to read these inscriptions and to identify some of the stories they described, the specific text from which the passages were taken was unknown. Therefore, it was a great breakthrough when, in a 1909 issue of the journal *T'oung Pao*, Chavannes finally revealed that the inscriptions came from a treatise by a third century courtier named Zhang Hua.[6] The identification of the painting's textual basis had an immediate impact on Western understanding of the scroll in a number of important ways. First, it revealed (as some scholars had already suspected) that a segment of the painting was missing from the beginning of the scroll. Second, it clarified what was happening in some of the painting's more obscure passages (particularly the landscape passage). And third it placed the scroll in a more specific historical context and provided some insight into the possible circumstances of its creation. Like Giles' work, Chavannes' discovery eventually became so much a part of the common knowledge that most people forgot where the information had originated. But there is no doubt that like Giles, Chavannes made a tremendous contribution to the evolution of *Admonitions* scroll scholarship in the West and should be credited accordingly.

By the end of the first decade of the twentieth century, the books and articles mentioned above had made the *Admonitions* scroll so famous that its custodians at the British Museum decided to show it for the first time in a major public exhibition. The opportunity for this exhibition came in 1910 when the British Museum purchased the Wegener collection of Chinese paintings. To celebrate this new acquisition, the Museum organized a large public display of its best Chinese and Japanese paintings, including the *Admonitions* scroll. Unfortunately, there are no attendance records from this exhibition, so we cannot be sure how many people saw the *Admonitions* scroll at that time. But whatever the number was, it was surely larger than had ever seen the painting on any single occasion in China. The exposure of the painting to a mass audience in this exhibition helped to enhance still further the fame and reputation the scroll had achieved in print, and ensured that for the next fifty or sixty years it would be one of the most visible and most talked about Chinese paintings in the world.

Reproduction and Remounting

Following the success of the 1910 exhibition, interest in the *Admonitions* scroll reached unprecedented heights. An internal British Museum memo written by Colvin in late 1910 reveals that the Museum had received numerous requests for photographs or other illustrations of the scroll from scholars and institutions all over Europe, America, and Asia.[7] In response to the painting's increasing popularity, the Trustees of the British Museum made two major decisions that had far-reaching consequences for the scroll. First they decided to commission a facsimile reproduction of the painting that would enable scholars around the world to study the work without having to come to England to see it. And second they decided to have the scroll cleaned and remounted to make it more attractive for public display. Both actions had the effect of further transforming the painting from a private into a public object, and together they changed the way the scroll would be seen and experienced forever.

Given the limits of the technologies available at the time, the decision to reproduce the *Admonitions* scroll was not a simple proposition. The first challenge was to find a publishing firm capable of handling such a difficult task. Initially Museum officials intended to hire the Oxford University Press, but after some debate, they eventually followed Colvin's recommendation and gave the job instead to a Japanese publisher who was then living in London named K. N. Ohashi.[8] Ohashi in turn employed an expert Japanese draughtsman to prepare a series of full-scale drawings of the painting complete with its seals and inscriptions. These drawings were then used to cut a set of wood-blocks from which multiple colour facsimiles of the painting could be taken. After the prints were completed, they were turned over to yet another Japanese craftsman to be mounted together in a handscroll format. Altogether including the preparation of the drawings, the carving of the wood-blocks, the printing, and the mounting, the reproduction project took approximately two years (from 1911 to 1913) to complete and yielded one hundred copies of the painting. Although the process was laborious and time consuming, the results justified the effort, for the finished product was an extraordinarily faithful facsimile of the painting that captured its aesthetic qualities far more accurately than would have been possible with any other printing processes available at the time.[9]

To accompany the Ohashi reproduction of the *Admonitions* scroll the British Museum also published a short catalogue containing yet another essay about the painting by Laurence Binyon.[10] Drawing upon all previous scholarship on the scroll, this essay provided the most detailed account of the painting written anywhere up to that point. Although its descriptions of the scroll's contents, style, and history are all informative and worth reading, the catalogue is chiefly interesting to readers today for what it has to say about the painting's attributed authorship and date. For many years, Binyon had been concerned that some sceptics would not believe the painting was a genuine original work by Gu Kaizhi. Therefore, he took the opportunity in this catalogue to present four reasons why he believed the traditional attribution of the *Admonitions* scroll should be accepted.

Binyon's first reason for accepting the painting's traditional attribution was the superior quality of its drawing. According to Binyon, only a master responding to a powerful inner vision could have produced the expressive, subtly modulated lines of the *Admonitions* painting. Therefore, it was inconceivable to him that the painting could be (as some people suggested) a later copy or forgery. His second reason for accepting the traditional attribution was the painting's primitive style. To Binyon's eyes, the awkward, naïve style of the landscape passage in particular clearly pre-dated the landscape styles seen in Tang and later paintings. Thus, while he could not say with certainty that the style was that of Gu Kaizhi, the fact that he could at least say it was consistent with Gu's period of activity again strongly inclined him toward the traditional attribution. Binyon's third argument in favour of the scroll's traditional attribution rested on the painting's long traceable history. He was much impressed by the fact that the painting was recorded as a work of Gu Kaizhi in at least two Song dynasty texts, and he gave special weight to the fact that the painting had also been included as such in two

Chinese imperial collections. As Binyon saw it, if the painting's traditional attribution had been accepted by the best connoisseurs a Chinese emperor could muster, then it was only right that he and other Westerners should accept that attribution as well. Finally, Binyon's fourth reason for accepting the scroll's attribution to Gu Kaizhi was its dilapidated condition. Although Binyon acknowledged the fact that Chinese forgers sometimes deliberately distressed paintings to make them appear older than they really were, the numerous signs of remounting and restoration on the *Admonitions* scroll indicated to Binyon a genuinely long history of respect and veneration. When the painting's condition was added to all of the other factors mentioned above, it convinced Binyon even more that the traditional attribution was correct.

Binyon's 1912 catalogue essay was an impressive piece of scholarship, and might have become the new definitive work on the subject. However, as will be discussed further below, his vigorous defence of the painting's authenticity had the unintended consequence of provoking scholars around the world to examine this issue more closely. Consequently, rather than fixing the scroll's place in Chinese art history once and for all, Binyon's essay instead initiated a new period of debate and controversy over the painting that would last for more than five decades.

Once the reproduction project was completed, the British Museum turned its attention to improving the scroll's condition and appearance. At that time, the scroll was still in the mounting that had been created for it during the reign of the Qianlong emperor (r. 1736–1795) in the eighteenth century. This mounting consisted of a number of different elements: an exterior silk wrapper and title slip; an interior frontispiece of Song dynasty (960–1279) silk brocade; a prefatory inscription written by the Qianlong emperor; an old silk border strip covered with collector's seals; the painting itself; several more silk border strips with collector's seals, an inscription by Xiang Yuanbian, and an orchid painting by Qianlong; a piece of calligraphy attributed to the Song emperor Huizong (r. 1101–1125) re-inscribing several of the textual passages from the original Zhang Hua text of 292; a lengthy colophon of appreciation written by Qianlong; and a painting of pine trees, rocks, and bamboo that was created especially for the *Admonitions* scroll by an eighteenth-century court artist named Zou Yigui (1686–1774) following an imperial command. Because many of the scroll's components were quite old and fragile, and because their organization in the handscroll format made them difficult to study and display, Museum officials decided to have the scroll disassembled and remounted in more manageable units. Ideally, they would probably have liked to have given this work to a specialist Chinese or Japanese mounter. However, since they did not want to send the painting back to Asia for an extended period, the Museum instead entrusted the job to one of its staff conservators, a man named Stanley W. Littlejohn (d. 1916).[11]

Unfortunately, there are no detailed records of the work that Littlejohn performed on the scroll, so we do not know exactly what he did or when he did it. However, judging from the scant evidence that does exist, it seems that he took the scroll apart, cleaned and relined it, and then remounted it as four separate flat panels. He divided the different components of the scroll among these panels in such a way that the painting formed one unit; the silk brocade frontispiece, prefatory inscription, border strips with collector's seals, Huizong calligraphy, and Qianlong colophon formed a second unit; the Zou Yigui painting formed a third unit; and the exterior wrapper and title strip formed a fourth unit. A somewhat ambiguous reference in the Museum records suggests that Littlejohn began work on the scroll in 1914, and he is presumed to have finished it before he enlisted in the British army in 1917. He was later killed at Ypres in 1918, and no additional physical changes were made to the scroll after that date.

Apart from its removal from China, the remounting of the scroll was one of the key moments in the painting's history during the twentieth century. By radically changing its physical format, the remounting also completely changed the way the scroll was seen and experienced by Western audiences. For example, whereas in its original format the painting had been viewed sequentially one or two scenes at a time, after remounting all of the scenes were visible at once. And whereas in its original format the painting had been seen in the context of its former owners' seals and inscriptions, after remounting it became more of an isolated object. Although the remounting did have some beneficial effects (like making the painting easier to display, and protecting it from the stresses of rolling and unrolling), these were more than offset by various negative consequences (like the loss of cultural integrity, and the increased exposure to light and dust). Of course it is not fair to judge past actions by contemporary values, and no doubt at the time the remounting was undertaken, it was seen as the best way to enhance the scroll's appearance and accessibility to the public. Nevertheless, while the decision to remount the *Admonitions* scroll may be historically understandable, it is still in many ways highly regrettable. Thus it is to be hoped that in the future the British Museum will consider reversing the process, if not physically on the scroll itself, then virtually on a digital image of the scroll. Doing this would thus allow audiences once again to see and experience the painting in the way that was originally intended.

The Attribution Controversy

The first decade or so after the British Museum acquired the *Admonitions* scroll was a period of tremendous excitement when many people were captivated by the romantic notion that a great and rare masterpiece had just been discovered. But as so often happens in the art world, once the initial wave of enthusiasm faded, people began to look at the painting more critically. In particular they began to look more closely at its attribution, and whether or not it could really be what it purported to be. As was noted earlier, this period of scrutinizing the painting's authenticity began shortly after the publication of Binyon's 1912 catalogue essay and continued into the 1960s. During those fifty-odd years, scholars from all over the world joined the debate and expressed many different opinions about the painting's possible authorship and date. Although by the late 1960s a majority of those scholars had settled on a consensus opinion regarding the scroll's attribution, the issue was never fully resolved and continued to be a contentious subject right up to the end of the century and beyond, as several of the other papers in this volume make abundantly clear.

So many different scholars participated in the debate over the *Admonitions* scroll's attribution between the 1910s and 1960s that it is impossible to summarize all of their views here. However, if minor discrepancies are ignored, then a majority of the opinions that were expressed about the painting's authorship and date during those five decades can be categorized into three major schools of thought.

The first school of thought on the *Admonitions* scroll's attribution held that the painting was an original work of art from the hand of Gu Kaizhi himself. Following Binyon's lead, subscribers to this school supported their views by citing the superior quality of the painting's drawing and composition, and by noting the fact that its ascription to Gu dated back at least nine hundred years. Until some incontrovertible evidence was discovered to prove otherwise, scholars in this camp believed that respect for the scroll and the culture that produced it demanded that its traditional attribution be maintained. Apart from Binyon, some notable adherents to this point of view included Raphaël Petrucci (1872–1917) and Soame Jenyns (1904–1976).[12]

The second major school of thought on the *Admonitions* scroll's attribution held that the painting was an original work of art, but did not necessarily accept the association with Gu Kaizhi. The scholars who subscribed to this view believed that the style of the calligraphy used to write the inscriptions on the painting as well as the style of the figure drawing itself indicated a date later than Gu's period of activity. Accordingly, they ascribed the painting to the hand of an unidentified master of the Sui or early Tang period (*c.* seventh century), and sought to understand the scroll within the context of the courtly art traditions of those two dynasties. Two of the leading proponents of this opinion about the *Admonitions* scroll's attribution were Naitō Torajirō (1866–1934) and Basil Gray (1904–1989).[13]

Lastly, the third major school of thought on the *Admonitions* scroll's attribution held that the painting was not an original but a copy, and maintained that while it might have some connection to the style of Gu Kaizhi or another pre-Tang painter, it was definitely Tang or later in date. Followers of this school typically supported their views by citing several passages in the scroll (for example, the construction of the litter in scene 2, or the drawing of the male figure's body in scene 5) where visual inconsistencies suggest the hand of someone imitating a design rather than painting a picture. They also argued that the psychological characterizations of the figures and the ways the figures related to one another through gestures and glances were too sophisticated for the fourth or fifth century, and could only have been done after the start of the Tang dynasty, either in the seventh or eighth century, or, according to some, even as late as the ninth or tenth century. Among the many influential scholars who subscribed to this school of thought were Taki Seiichi (1873–1945), Arthur Waley (1880–1966), John Ferguson (1866–1945), Michael Sullivan and Kohara Hironobu.[14]

Although for the first few decades of the attribution debate no single school of thought had the upper hand, by the late 1950s and 1960s it was clear that most scholars had sided with the third school and believed the painting to be a Tang copy of a pre-Tang original that was probably close to the style of Gu Kaizhi. At least, this is the opinion that appeared in most textual references to the painting published from the mid-1950s onwards. However, the establishment of a consensus opinion did not mean that the issue was fully resolved, and the attribution problem remained a matter of concern through and past the end of the century, to re-emerge as one of the central points of discussion at the 2001 symposium.

'Canonization'

As we have seen, the *Admonitions* scroll was celebrated as an important masterpiece in the West almost from the moment the British Museum acquired it. Yet despite the efforts of early scholars like Binyon to establish the painting as an iconic work of Chinese art, it was not until after the Second World War that the painting really became a standard part of the art his-

torical canon. From the mid-1950s onwards, the *Admonitions* scroll was included in virtually every general history of Chinese art and Chinese painting published in the Western world. Paradoxically, however, the more visible the painting became in print, the less visible it became in real life. Concerned about its safety and preservation, the British Museum gradually reduced its exhibition exposure during the 1970s and 1980s, eventually removing it from display altogether and placing it in storage.

The formation of a more-or-less standardized canon of Chinese art in the West was a gradual process. As Western scholars learned more about how Chinese art evolved, they were better able to discern which works of art were truly important in that history. Although men like Binyon contributed enormously to the early stages of this process, the greatest advances ocurred after the Second World War, when improved access to information and images revolutionized the field and led to a significant increase in the overall quality of Western scholarship on Chinese art.

Two books in particular from the early post-war period stand out for helping to clarify the position of the *Admonitions* scroll as one of the true milestones of Chinese painting. The first of these books was Osvald Sirén's (1879–1966) 1956 magnum opus *Chinese Painting: Leading Masters and Principles*.[15] Published in seven volumes, this monumental work chronicled the entire history of Chinese painting from the pre-imperial age up to the end of the Qing dynasty. It identified all of the major artists who had been active at any given time and discussed selected examples of their major surviving works. Because this book was so comprehensive, the paintings it discussed naturally assumed the status of important icons. Therefore, it was extremely significant that it not only included the *Admonitions* scroll as one of its example paintings but also declared it to be one of the finest and most important Chinese paintings from the entire Six Dynasties period. Considering the fact that the scroll's attribution was still being hotly debated at the time, this declaration was an extraordinarily strong affirmation of the painting's art historical importance, and in fact may have been one of the major catalysts that caused scholars in the 1960s and 1970s to refocus their attention away from the question of the painting's authorship and toward the question of its historical contextualization.

A second post-war book that helped tremendously to cement the *Admonitions* scroll's place in the pantheon of Chinese art was James Cahill's 1960 book *Chinese Painting*.[16] This book was quite different from Sirén's work in a number of important respects. Much more intimate and more narrative, it focused on the development of Chinese painting as an evolutionary process. It drew out the connections between works of art and between works of art and their historical contexts to create a sense of an organic visual culture unfolding over time. Because each of the paintings included in this book therefore seemed to be role players in a larger plot, they too were charged with extra importance. In the case of the *Admonitions* scroll, for instance, the painting was presented as a key element in the evolution of Chinese secular figure painting. This was the first time that the painting had been discussed in such a context, and thus *Chinese Painting* not only enhanced the *Admonitions* scroll's status, but also inspired people to see it in a fresh way.

From the mid-1960s onwards, virtually every general history of Chinese art and Chinese painting published in the West included some mention of the *Admonitions* scroll. For the most part, these later publications did not add significantly to the general state of knowledge about the painting. A few books, however, did occasionally manage to present the painting in a new light. One example from the end of the century is the collaboratively authored book *Three Thousand Years of Chinese Painting*, which included a chapter by Wu Hung.[17] In this essay, Wu situated the painting much more specifically within the context of southern Chinese painting during the Six Dynasties period (265–589). By comparing the *Admonitions* scroll to a broad range of visual materials from the

period, he gave readers a more complex sense of how the painting fitted into its original historical environment. Although in some ways Wu's treatment of the scroll made it seem less singular and less uniquely important than had earlier books, nevertheless it still reaffirmed the painting's central status in the world of early Chinese art.

Conclusion

Viewed from our own chronologically proximate vantage point, the experiences the *Admonitions* scroll underwent during the twentieth century certainly seem momentous. However, when those same experiences are viewed in the context of the painting's entire 1500-year history, they suddenly do not seem quite so significant. Throughout its long life, the *Admonitions* scroll has belonged to many different owners, been subjected to many physical alterations, and had many different meanings imposed upon it. Yet despite all this, it has always endured and outlasted those who sought to control it. Therefore, for all the seeming permanence of its current situation, the scroll's history suggests that in another hundred years, or perhaps only another fifty or even twenty years, it will somehow be re-invented once again and embark on a whole new phase of what is sure to remain an eventful existence.

NOTES

1   Hatcher 1995, p. 166.
2   Museum file (the curatorial file for the scroll in the Department of Oriental Antiquities, which contains various letters, notes, and memos related to the history of the painting since it entered the Museum collection).
3   Binyon 1904.
4   Binyon 1908, pp. 37–50.
5   Giles 1905, pp. 17–21.
6   Chavannes 1909.
7   Museum file.
8   Museum file.
9   Indeed, the Ohashi reproduction even compares favourably with later reproductions of the scroll that were produced in 1925 and 1966 using photographic technologies; see Fukui 1925a (reproduction in 1925b, pl. 1) and Tsujimoto 1966.
10 Binyon 1912.
11 Museum file; also Binyon & Colvin 1918.
12 Petrucci 1920; Jenyns 1935.
13 Naitō 1926; Gray 1966.
14 Taki 1915; Waley 1923; Ferguson 1927; Sullivan 1954; and Kohara 1967.
15 Sirén 1956.
16 Cahill 1960.
17 Wu Hung 1997.

The *Admonitions* Scroll in the Eighteenth, Nineteenth and Twentieth Centuries: Discussant's Remarks

Craig Clunas

Art history was relatively new as a discipline when the *Admonitions* scroll attributed to Gu Kaizhi came to the British Museum in 1903. It is tempting to see the shape of the symposium and this resulting volume dedicated to the scroll nearly a century later in 2001 as mirroring the shape of the discipline over that century; it began with the questions (which are still vitally important) 'when was this made and by whom?', moved through 'what forces within Chinese culture, what broader cultural contexts, exercised agency in bringing it into being?', before ending with issues of reception, where what the work *is* matters less immediately than what people have historically *thought* it to be. This shift in view from one where meaning inheres in objects at the point of making to one where meaning is seen as constantly contingent and revised – a move in art historical terms from an overwhelming concern with the hand of the artist to one for the eye of the beholder – has happened right across the humanities. Such a development, at least in the visual arts, owes much to anthropology, a discipline which, particularly in the work of Igor Kopytoff, has given us the concept of the 'biography' of the object,[1] so effectively deployed by several of the scholars (Nixi Cura, Zhang Hongxing and Charles Mason) whose contributions will be examined here. This notion of the 'cultural biography' will be returned to later in this paper, specifically as it bears on the material substance of the object.

Part of the biography of the *Admonitions* scroll obviously lies in this history of the object in the centuries after its production, whenever that may have been. But one recent and unignorable part (or at least a part which we will ignore at our peril) is that of its dissemination, in the age of mechanical reproduction, through technologies of printing and publishing. It is surely one of the most published Chinese paintings of all time. But for all that the term has been used here rather loosely, the *Admonitions* scroll itself is never 'reproduced' as such, except in the two facsimiles produced by the British

Museum, themselves a fascinating topic for further research which is addressed to an extent in the paper by Charles Mason in this volume. It is for a start the wrong shape for the technologies of reproduction which we have had until very recently (the technology of 35 mm slides, and of pictures in rectangular books), which instead favour attention to detail. This is not simply a technical issue, since the mechanics of the slide lecture, of left screen/right screen, compare and contrast, are deeply implicated in some of the most ingrained philosophical habits of the discipline, and in particular in its implicit Hegelianism, where left screen/right screen implies the thesis/antithesis/synthesis model of that beguiling system of thought.[2] A brief census of *which* preferred details have been used in publication to stand for the scroll as a whole is therefore not without interest. The following list of English-language examples is entirely unscientific, and based on what came immediately to hand at the time of writing:

- Stephen Bushell, *Chinese Art* (1904): scene 9, Instructress, (detail) entitled 'Pan Chao, Lady Historian and Superintendent of the Court, writing her Book'
- Laurence Binyon, *Painting in the Far East* (1908): scene 4, Toilette scene (detail)
- Soame Jenyns, *A Background to Chinese Painting* (1935): scene 9, Instructress
- Ludwig Bachhofer, *A Short History of Chinese Art* (1946): scene 2, Palanquin
- William Cohn, *Chinese Painting* (1948): scene 3, Mountain
- Lawrence Sickman and Alexander Soper, *Art and Architecture of China* (1956): scene 5, Bedroom, and scene 7, Rejection
- James Cahill, *Chinese Painting* (1960): scene 7, Rejection
- Michael Sullivan, *A Short History of Chinese Art* (1967): scene 5, Bedroom

- Mario Bussagli, *Chinese Painting* (1966): scene 9, Instructress
- Mary Tregear, *Chinese Art* (1980): scene 7, Rejection
- Jessica Rawson (ed.), *British Museum Book of Chinese Art* (1992): scene 7, Rejection
- Robert Thorp and Richard Vinograd, *Chinese Art and Culture* (2001): scene 7, Rejection, but only the female figure

We thus have what looks very much like a progressive narrowing of the range of scenes which stand for the scroll, and a situation where some of them (the family group, Lady Feng and the bear, the meditating lady) *never* do duty in standing for the scroll in its entirety.

This list, drawn as it is from works which all explicitly have the discursive object 'Chinese art' or 'Chinese painting' as their focus, makes the assumption that the *Admonitions* scroll has been and remains part of a private conversation which specialist historians of Chinese art have among themselves. But this is not the case. If one scene can stand for the *Admonitions*, then the *Admonitions* can be made to stand for 'Chinese art'. It was one of only seven works of art to be spotted when Ernst Gombrich (1909–2001) 'cast a glance at what happened in other parts of the world' in the chapter entitled 'Looking Eastwards' in *The Story of Art* (first published in 1950, but continuously in print since then). There, as many readers of this canonical work will surely remember, 'There really is no such thing as Art. There are only artists.'[3] Gu Kaizhi (*c.*345–*c.*406) thus takes his place alongside Ma Yuan (act. *c.*1190–1230), Gao Kegong (1248–1310) and Liu Cai (d. after 1123) as the only four Chinese artists readers of *The Story of Art* will ever hear about, a pretty idiosyncratic canon by any standards. Under the (romanticized and wholly inaccurate) title 'Husband reproving his wife', Gombrich illustrates scene 7, the Rejection, using it to characterize Chinese art as a whole as above all didactic, and as proof that 'the Chinese artist had mastered the difficult art of representing movement'.[4] By its appearance in Gombrich, the *Admonitions* acquires a heavy burden of metonymy, as standing for 'Chinese art', and a much heavier one than (say) Botticelli's *Birth of Venus* must carry, as one European oil painting out of hundreds in the book. It seems highly likely that if one checked other totalizing 'world histories' of art the *Admonitions* would appear there too. Part of this ubiquity surely stems from the work's stable presence in a metropolitan centre of publishing and scholarship, with the consequent accessibility of images for reproduction. But if scholars in the field of Chinese art had a choice of just seven objects to stand for that object of study, and could start from a blank slate, i.e. if there were no precon-

ceptions as to the shape of the canon already in place, would the *Admonitions* still inevitably be one of them? Perhaps it would, but this heretical thought bears raising. It seems hard to escape the relatively banal conclusion that the *Admonitions* is not just published because it is famous but famous because it is published, even if this does deflate still further the now surely exhausted claim made by Walter Benjamin (1892–1940) in 1936 that 'that which withers in the age of mechanical reproduction is the aura of the work of art'.[5] Quite the reverse seems to have happened here.

The paper by Nixi Cura on the cultural biography of the scroll in the Qianlong reign clearly shows that, whatever the Qianlong emperor thought the *Admonitions* to be, its significance did not lie in the fact that it was part of something called 'Chinese art'. It was too important for that, as a celebrated physical monument to 'this culture of ours' (*si wen*). Cura's paper includes so much that it provokes yet more questions; for example, how often was the scroll handled and/or viewed? Is it one viewing, one seal, giving us at least a minimum number? The colophon begins, 'One summer's day in a moment of leisure I chanced to examine ...' This is the elegant and time-sanctioned nonchalance of the connoisseur in the Chinese tradition, but it in turn raises many questions about the degree of spontaneity involved. What, for example, was the emperor doing just before and just after he 'chanced to examine' the work and experience sequentially the body of framing material which the paper so meticulously reconstructs? Importantly, in an aspect of the presentation of her paper in London which unfortunately cannot be reproduced in printed form, the author showed us how new technology, properly deployed, can enable us to go beyond the left screen/right screen type of argument and make new types which are better suited to the material with which art historians of China deal.

Zhang Hongxing's paper opens up in an exemplary fashion work on the nineteenth century imperial court, which until so recently was one of the last great no-go areas of Chinese art. In 1967 Michael Sullivan could write of post-Qianlong court artists, 'Even their names are not known.'[6] They are known to Dr Zhang, whose current work on nineteenth century court patronage ought to alter completely the way we think about late Qing court culture. Visual imagery of imperial power retained compelling importance at court right through the prolonged crisis of revolt and imperialism. If the Dowager Empress Cixi (1835–1908) cared so much about the power of new images, it is hard to believe that she cared not at all for the power of the old ones. Particularly interesting therefore is the 1870 notice of the empress' order to move the 'four pictures'; in the light of this it seems unlikely that the

Admonitions was not one of them. The paper also casts a new light on Western fetishization of the imperial collection, so much more permeable in Dr Zhang's description than we thought. Instead of a black hole into which things disappeared, never to emerge except in moments of national chaos, he shows us in passing the collection as part of an imperial economy of the gift. He stresses too the political and moral force of terms like *simei* – this is not dilettantism, but a form of seemly amusement, the concept of *wan*, which is so closely connected to power, and rulership.[7]

Finally, Charles Mason's paper serves as a deft reminder that controversies over the *Admonitions* did not begin with the symposium of which this volume is the record, but themselves have a history of which it is but the latest chapter. His work suggests at least the possibility that the differing views of Laurence Binyon (1869–1943) and Arthur Waley (1889–1968), the authority of the 'eye' versus the authority of the text, recapitulate the old Sinology versus Art History debate of John Pope's celebrated essay,[8] as well as the formalism versus contextualization debate which to an extent superseded it. He underscores the inescapable fact that the range of options as to the date of the *Admonitions* scroll has in fact not altered substantially since the decade immediately following its acquisition. Are we then just back where we started? If we are not, it is because the precision and the resources with which contemporary scholarship now addresses the second and third of the three areas of enquiry raised in the opening paragraph above have continued to intensify and enlarge the scope of our engagement with the work. It cannot be that the date of the scroll no longer matters, but on the basis of the evidence here it certainly does not seem to matter so *much*, and scholars have other ways of fruitful engagement with the work to set alongside issues of date and authorship.

Both Nixi Cura's paper and that of Charles Mason draw attention to the work's framing in the British Museum. By this is meant, on one level, framing in the institutional sense, the way in which an artefact is re-inscribed with new meanings when it crosses cultural and institutional frontiers, but at least as much it must mean framing in the literal sense, since although in the course of the symposium the work was repeatedly referred to as the 'handscroll', that is precisely the form the *Admonitions* does not at present take.[9] The work, as Cura and Mason remind us, has been framed, mounted, and physically restructured, so that the important part (the pictures) is no longer headed and tailed by 'all that writing' in Chinese. One section of it has been removed from the frame and remounted separately. It should be made explicit that this is mentioned not out of any sense that the British Museum has been remiss in its custodianship of the work. It has not. It is

rather raised in order to insist that a cultural-biography approach must be precisely about training ourselves to see those things we have learned 'do not matter', and to do this by granting *practices* as much status in our enquiry as *statements*. A cultural biography approach is of necessity a materialist one, which addresses issues of where and when (and who), which in the case of a work in a Museum above all addresses display, and its opposite, storage. We badly need a history of looking, of viewing practices for Chinese painting in general, a field where there has been little work since that of Robert van Gulik nearly fifty years ago.[10] How many of the scenes into which we divide the picture were to be viewed at a single opening? Did that change over time? And who got to look at it, in the Qing collection, beyond the Qianlong emperor himself? What were its audiences, how big and of what social composition, when it was in other collections, including its present institutional home? In this respect all three papers begin the process of assembling both the archive of statements by writers self-identified as historians of Chinese art and that much harder-to-research archive of practices surrounding the work. All three authors have rightly realized that discourse is not just statements; it is practices also, right up to and including devices like the push-button timed lighting which formed part of the conditions of viewing when the present writer first saw the *Admonitions* 'for real' thirty years ago. Students coming to the British Museum to see Chinese scrolls have something which is arguably closer to a 'Ming' experience of viewing than the experience of going to the National Gallery approaches an Italian Renaissance engagement with an altarpiece. The practices of viewing today, in a context where objects necessarily cannot be seen simply by arriving at the institution where they are held (in contrast to something like *The Birth of Venus*), still involve the mobilization of the right kinds of social and cultural capital; they take social interactions and negotiation, and they are bounded in time. When looking is over, the pictures go away. These things are hard to research, but highly important to Chinese painting studies, where the fact that no work is on permanent display is a determining characteristic of the field of practices in which the study of Chinese painting must necessarily operate.

It is thus extremely valuable to have available the very brief catalogue accompanying the exhibition (alluded to by Charles Mason) of *Chinese and Japanese Paintings (Fourth to Nineteenth Century A.D.)* held in the Print and Drawing Gallery of the British Museum in 1910, an exhibition in which the Museum first showed off the *Admonitions* to the world.[11] The preface to this pamphlet sets the exhibition in the context of a collection much developed since the Museum's last significant display of similar material in 1888, when 273 pictures, mostly Japanese but some Chinese, from the collection of William Anderson had been displayed.[12] It speaks of significant acquisitions since then, under three categories: the first of these contains 'fortunate single purchases, of which the most memorable is the unique scroll by Ku K'ai-chih'; the second group stems from the 'very important and varied collection' of Frau Olga-Julia Wegener, wife of a German diplomat in late Qing Beijing; and the third is made up of the Buddhist material acquired in the course of his second expedition by Sir Marc Aurel Stein (1862–1942), objects then very newly (in fact as recently as August 1909) arrived from Dunhuang. A map in the pamphlet shows that the *Admonitions* was the first item the visitor to the exhibition saw, confronting them as they entered the gallery. It was mounted on slope 1, the other side of which was occupied by six of the Dunhuang painted banners. These make very different companions for the *Admonitions* from the three works by Li Gonglin with which it had so recently shared a space, physical *and* conceptual, in the imperial collections in Beijing. In his lengthy catalogue entry, writing it into a narrative of history, Binyon corrects some of the mistakes he had made in earlier descriptions of the work, ascribing the text correctly to Zhang Hua on the authority of Édouard Chavannes (1865–1918), here given the central role in the identification of the scenes. He goes on, 'The painting is signed, but the signature is of later date. The texts between the pictures seem also to have been added ...' He dates these, on the basis of unnamed 'Japanese palaeographers' to no later than the eighth century. He draws attention to the seals, and ends with the Qianlong colophon. The work is thus linked to the court milieu of the Qianlong emperor in more than one way. The great French sinologue Édouard Chavannes died in 1918 at the age of only fifty-three. He in turn had been taught by Stanislas Julien (1797–1873), a man of the late enlightenment whose understanding of China's culture came directly from the Jesuit presence at the imperial Qing court.[13] The chain of transmission in the orientalist field can be quite short.

One area in the history of reception of the *Admonitions* scroll which still remains to be fully explored is that of Chinese (and Japanese) views of it in the twentieth century. The presence at the symposium of so many distinguished colleagues testified to the place which the picture *now* holds in the field for all of us, but what was the attitude of the pioneers of art history in China itself to the picture? How does it feature in the construction of histories of Chinese art by such writers as Huang Binhong (1864–1955), Pan Tianshou (1897–1971), and Zheng Zhenduo (1897–1958). What do they have to say about it? If we looked in the writings of Xu Beihong (1895–1953), would we find he mentions it? We know he obtained permission to paint in London galleries, since he made a small oil copy of one of the Raphael cartoons from the Royal Collection on display in the Victoria and Albert Museum. Did he even see the *Admonitions* in the course of his trips to London, and if he didn't, who else did? It is a measure of the success of the symposium that at its end one feels compelled to address a whole new set of questions. The *Admonitions* scroll has generated new questions about itself for a very long time now, for nearly a millennium at even the most pessimistic view of its age. We make the field, but the field also makes us, and it may well be that this is one of those great works, where every generation not so much gets the *Admonitions* it deserves as feels compelled to reinvent it. The work demands our attention, and enables us to sustain through it conversations about culture which have no point of closure in sight. That is as good a definition of the truly pre-eminent work as any.

NOTES

1   Kopytoff 1986.
2   Nelson 2000.
3   Gombrich 1972, p. 4.
4   Gombrich 1972, p.108.
5   Benjamin 1992, p. 215.
6   Sullivan 1967, p. 260.
7   Stuart 1998.
8   Pope 1947.
9   On the wider framing context of Chinese art studies in Britain see Clunas 1994.
10   Van Gulik 1958.
11   *Guide to an Exhibition of Chinese and Japanese Paintings (Fourth to Nineteenth Century A.D.) in the Print and Drawing Gallery*, Second Edition, Revised (London, 1910). The fact that a second edition was necessary says something about the success of the exhibition.
12   Anderson 1886.
13   Gernet 1995.

The Conservation History and Condition of the *Admonitions* Scroll

Sydney Thomson

The *Admonitions* scroll was dismantled about the time of the First World War (1914–1918) and is likely to have been mounted in its current form by S. W. Littlejohn (d. 1916), who was working with or under Mr Urushibara, the Japanese mounter at the British Museum. During this period, the painting was separated from its frontispiece and colophons, presumably for ease of display and storage, but also to prevent further damage from rolling and unrolling.

There are tantalizing references to the painting in Museum records, which in 1911 refer to it as being rolled, and by 1914 as having been cleaned and backed; by January 1918, it is described as 'mostly mounted and framed'. Recently, further treatment has come to light with a reference in the records, dated 3 September 1923, to the painting being coated with a transparent protective solution under the supervision of Dr Alexander Scott. In the same year Dr Scott, who was a scientist working in the British Museum, published an article recommending the use of cellulose acetate for the consolidation of pigments on Asian paintings.[1]

Today the scroll is housed in a purpose-made case and stored vertically in an environmentally controlled atmosphere where temperature, humidity and light levels are regulated. Blinds are fitted in front of the case to provide further protection from light.

There are two other components separately mounted in acid-free board to consider. The first is a fine ink painting on paper by Zou Yigui (1680–1766) depicting a landscape of pine and juniper trees (h. 24.8 cm × w. 74.0 cm), which was formerly mounted at the end of the scroll (pl. 40). It shares a seal with the end of the colophon section, which confirms its previous location. The second is the geometric and floral Chinese-patterned cover silk, which, like the Zou Yigui painting, is in good condition (pl. 32). The colours are vivid blue, green, orange/red and yellow/gold, and it measures h. 24.5 cm × w. 25.5 cm. There is no title inscription on the original.

However, a replica of the handscroll (*c.*1913) was made on paper and includes identical copies of the inner and outer cover silks (the peony and the blue geometric and floral designs). These were painted on silk – they are *not* woven textiles – and the blue geometric and floral design does contain a title inscription.

Description of the Mounting

The scroll has been divided into two parts, with the painting itself mounted on a separate panel from the frontispiece, calligraphy and colophons. These panels are identical in size: h. 42.5 cm × w. 374.0 cm.

The mounting in each case seems to combine a Japanese-style support with Chinese mounting silk. A wooden lattice core was used for the construction of the panels, which were then covered with layers of Japanese paper. A combination of Chinese silks has been used in the mounting. A strip of purple silk creates a narrow border to frame each object. Interestingly, different mounting silks have been used for the outer borders. Although the mounting silks are of the same colour, the silk surrounding the painting is of a plain weave, whereas the silk which surrounds the calligraphy and colophons is patterned.

Dimensions

The silk painting dimensions are: h. 25.0 cm × w. 348.5 cm. Mounting silk dimensions, including the narrow silk strip to the panel edge, are top 9.5 cm, bottom 8.4–8.7 cm, right margin 13.1 cm and left margin 13.1 cm. The calligraphy dimensions are h. 25.0 cm × w. 329.0 cm. Mounting silk dimensions, as above, are top 8.8 cm, bottom 8.6 cm, right

Fig. 1   Detail of silk under raking light.

margin 22.5 cm and left margin 22.5 cm. NB the narrow silk strip measures *c.* 5 mm in each case; it is variable.

Condition of the Painting Silk

The scroll is painted on one long continuous piece of silk, with the images divided visually by passages of calligraphy. There is no evidence of the silk ever having been cut into sections.

The silk support is very dark in colour with a brown/green hue. It is certain to have discoloured with age and inevitably it must be anticipated that there will also be surface dirt ingrained into the silk weave. The condition of the silk is extremely weak but supported as it is, remains stable. An alum/glue size is likely to have been used, and as this is inherently acidic, it would have contributed to the degradation of the silk still further.

There are many silk repairs, with at least four different episodes of repair being evident throughout the long history of the scroll. Repairs have been made from both the front and the back. There are long sections of repair silk which have been applied to the top and bottom to compensate for uneven edges. Whilst it would appear that care has been taken to align the silk weave in most cases, some repair silk attached from the back has a more open weave than the original and consequently appears much more noticeable.

Most of the retouching carried out to the repairs is of a very high quality indeed. This is evident on one particular period of repair where the technique used for the in-painting line subtly compliments the original. There is, however, one particular sequence of repair where the pigment used has darkened and is now visually distracting.

Technical Examination of the Painting

The painting has been examined and photographed using raking light, and under ultraviolet and infrared light sources. The UV light source especially highlights the areas of damage and may assist in the identification of some pigments, while the IR light source accentuates the subtleties of brushwork and some of the silk repair.

In raking light, some lifting areas of silk and silk repair were highlighted (fig. 1, pls 41–42). The entire surface of the painting displays many vertical rolling creases and areas of weakness, and there are many fine, hair-like fractures and splits. In some places there is an obvious contrast is between the silk support and the areas of repair which appear dark and beneath the substrate, suggesting that they had been applied from the reverse.

Ultraviolet light reveals clearly the damage to the silk painting which cannot be seen under normal lighting conditions (fig. 2). The irregular patches of repair silk are easily identified. On close examination there appear to be several major areas of repair: for example, the large section located at the bottom right-hand corner of the opening passage of the painting, the canopy of the palanquin and most of the upper part of the mountain. Interestingly, the red pigment seals are clearly evident under UV, whereas they are invisible in IR. In addition, gamboge (yellow), for example, absorbs rather than reflects UV, and consequently appears dark.

Infrared is best known for revealing under-drawing that is carbon based. In this case, the subtleties of brushwork and silk repair are more easily read, with the background appearing lighter in tone (fig. 3). Sometimes IR helps in distinguishing pigments. For example, the carbon-based pigments such

as lamp black are not penetrated and show dark on the photo-graphic image (see the women's hair), as does azurite, which can be differentiated from cobalt blue or ultramarine, which are nearly transparent in IR.

Pigments

This palette is limited; nonetheless, the colours here are fairly standard and commonly used in Chinese painting.

Chinese ink (*mo*) has been the favourite writing and painting material of the Far East for centuries. This is prepared by burning oil in earthenware lamps. The soot formed on the inside of the lamp is collected and mixed with fish glue size – the pigment binder. It is scented with musk or camphor before being moulded into sticks and dried. The fine lines are drawn with black ink.

Fig. 2 The *Admonitions* painting photographed under UV light.

Fig. 3 Detail of *Admonitions* painting under IR light.

Fig. 4 Detail of silk mounting under raking light.

Vermilion (*dansha*) is mercuric sulphide. It is found in nature as the mineral cinnabar, which is the principal ore of the metal mercury. Chinese vermilion is rather coarsely crystalline and slightly violet/red in colour compared with English vermilion, due mainly to its dry method of production. Vermilion is used to colour swathes of drapery, utensils and other objects depicted within the painting. The many seals on the painting are most likely to be vermilion.

Malachite (*shilü*) is the natural basic copper carbonate, a crystalline pigment. In spite of its ready decomposition, it has remained unchanged in many paintings for centuries. It is unaffected by light.

Azurite (*shiqing*) appears, under good conditions, a remarkably stable pigment. It is a natural copper carbonate. A subdued blue-green (azurite and malachite) mineral pigment is used to illustrate the mountain and scudding cloud images.

Gamboge (*tenghuang*) is a yellow gum resin.

The mineral pigments are considerably more stable than the organic colours, and are much less sensitive to damage from exposure to light.

Frontispiece and Colophons

This panel consists of a frontispiece and subsequent sections of calligraphy and seals. The silk textile depicts a peony and foliage; it appears in a stable condition, but there are some visible areas of loss and abrasion.

Fig. 5 Detail of 'Admonitions' inscription under UV light.

There are ten sections of calligraphy and seals, and in some cases seals overlap silk joints. The painting was originally contained in a space between the fourth and fifth sections from the right, prior to dismantling.

Interestingly, the sixth section from the right shows clear evidence of the type of damage caused by over-tightening of a tying braid, which suggests that this part was once much nearer the front of the scroll, if not the inside of a cover silk (fig. 4).

All the colophon sections are on silk apart from two parts, the title-piece (section 3 below) and the colophons in sections 11 and 12, which are on paper. From right to left, the order of sections is as follows:

1. Peony silk (textile) frontispiece (pl. 33 right): this is the elaborate inside of the cover silk. (NB the outer blue silk cover in pl. 32 is mounted separately in an acid-free window mount.)
2. Yellow crane-patterned silk (pl. 33 centre).
3. Title-piece on paper, reading *tong guan fang* ('fragrance of a red reed'; pls 33 left–34 right).

4. Yellow crane-patterned silk (pl. 34).
5. The same mounting silk used to in-fill the gap when the painting was removed (pl. 34).
6. Pale blue silk with seals in red ink with evidence of tying braid marks (fig. 4, pl. 34 left).
7. Very pale-blue silk with seals in red ink.
8. Yellow silk with ink drawing of an orchid (pl. 37 right).
9. Calligraphy in 'slender-gold' script on silk. In ultraviolet light, horizontal joins are evident indicating that the calligraphy has been cut into vertical strips and replaced side by side (fig. 5, pl. 37).
10. Pale blue silk with seals in red ink (pl. 38 right).
11. White paper with seals in red ink (pl. 38 right).
12. Calligraphy on paper support (pls 38–39).

The jade toggle is supposedly missing.

On detailed inspection, the *Admonitions* scroll appears to be in a stable condition. The linings are somewhat rudimentary but they are effective, and the value of this should be gauged against the inherent dangers of any major interventional conservation programme.

NOTE

1 Scott 1923. Additional sources for this report are van Gulik 1958; Gettens & Stout 1966; March 1969.

Chronology of Chinese Dynasties

EARLY DYNASTIES

Shang	*c.*1500–1050 BCE
Western Zhou	1050–771 BCE
Eastern Zhou	
Spring and Autumn	770–475 BCE
Warring States	475–221 BCE

IMPERIAL CHINA

Qin	221–207 BCE
Han	
Western Han	206 BCE–9 CE
Xin	9 CE–25
Eastern Han	25 CE–220
Three Kingdoms	
Shu (Han)	221–263
Wei	220–265
Wu	222–280
Southern dynasties (Six Dynasties)	
Western Jin	265–316
Eastern Jin	317–420
Liu Song	420–479
Southern Qi	479–502
Liang	502–557
Chen	557–589

Northern dynasties	
Northern Wei	386–533
Eastern Wei	534–550
Western Wei	535–557
Northern Qi	550–577
Northern Zhou	557–581
Sui	589–618
Tang	618–906
Five Dynasties	907–960
Liao	907–1125
Song	
Northern Song	960–1127
Southern Song	1127–1279
Jin	1115–1234
Yuan	1271–1368
Ming	1368–1644
Qing	1644–1911

REPUBLICAN CHINA

Republic	1912–1949
People's Republic	1949–

Note: Dates given here are generally accepted. The dates, titles, readings, translations of terms, etc., provided by individual contributors have, wherever possible, been preserved in their texts.

Chronology of the *Admonitions* Scroll in the British Museum

Names in brackets refer to publications in the bibliography.

1903 8 April: Acquired from Capt. C. A. K. Johnson (1st Bengal Lancers) for £25 0s 0d. Signature of Gu Kaizhi authenticated as genuine by Mr Kohitsu, Arthur Morison, Herbert Giles.

1904 (Binyon)

1905 (Giles)

1908 (Binyon)

1909 (Chavannes)

1910 First public showing of the scroll in exhibition to celebrate acquisition of Wegener collection.
5 November–10 December: In response to international requests from the Continent, America and China, Sydney Colvin initiates project to make facsimile copies of scroll. He recommends K. N. Ohashi and his workmen, who are in Europe for a Japanese-British exhibition, over Oxford University Press.

1912 (Binyon)
4 October: Facsimile prints are completed under direction of Ohashi and his chief workman Mr Sugusaki; woodblocks handed back.
12 October: Mr Urushibara mounts 100 facsimiles; Laurence Binyon given leave to take a copy to America for his lectures.

1913 5 April: Selling price of replica agreed at £7 7s 0d.
14 June: Total cost of replicas is £454 15s 8d (original estimate £160).
4 July: Copies presented to Édouard Chavannes and Taki Sei'ichi, who had agreed to write reviews.
4 December: Trustees reject Ohashi's demand for £100 to cover 'losses' incurred in the making of the replica and ignore his threats to disseminate reproductions in Japan to recoup the money.

1914 (Taki)
4 April: The painting is cleaned and backed.
3 July: A translation is to be made of the Qianlong colophon.
10 October: Photographic negatives presented to Bernard Berenson Esq.

1915 (Giles)
Following Laurence Binyon's request, Herbert Giles and his son Lionel publish a translation of the Qianlong colophon.

1914?–1918? S. W. Littlejohn remounts the scroll on stretchers.

1918 (Ferguson, Binyon & Colvin)
11 January: Scroll is referred to as 'smartly mounted and framed'.
23 September: S. W. Littlejohn, Japanese-speaking staff conservator who had assisted with the 1912 replica, is killed at Ypres.

1920 (Petrucci)

1921 2 July: Museum document refers to 'the long frame containing the Ku K'ai-chih painting'.

1922 September–October: Nihonga painters Maeda Seison and Kobayashi Kokei create a meticulous copy of the scroll under the direction of Fukui Rikichirō, who makes a map of damage and repairs (both in the collection of Tōhoku University, Sendai, Japan).

1923 (Waley)
3 September: Scroll is coated with a transparent protective solution under Dr Scott's supervision.

1925 (Fukui)
Tōhoku University, Sendai, Japan: Fukui Rikichirō exhibits a collotype facsimile of scroll, made from photographs obtained during his 1922 visits to Museum (?), together with the copy made by Maeda Seison and Kobayashi Kokei.

1926 (Naitō)

1927 (Ferguson)

1928 3 November: A new curtain is fitted to shield the painting from light.

1930 4 October: *Nymph of the Luo River* attributed to Gu Kaizhi is offered to Museum by Messrs Yamanaka for £3500; dated by Binyon to Song (10th–13th century).

1933 12 December: Museum document refers to 'the Ku K'ai-chih: this is mounted on a stretcher 12 ft long'.

1934 1 May: Prof. Paul Pelliot gives a lecture on the scroll's authenticity to a small, select audience.

1935 (Jenyns, Liu Haisu)

[Sino-Japanese War, World War II, Chinese Civil War]

1951 (Sullivan)

1954 (Maeda, Sullivan)

1955 (Toyama, Wen Zhaotong)

1956 (Ma Cai, Sirén)

1958 (Fu Baoshi, Jin Weinuo, Ma Cai, Pan Tianshou)

1960 (Cahill)

1961 (Tang Lan, Zi Zheng)

1962 (Yu Jianhua *et al.*)

1966 (Gray)
February: Kyoto publishing house Benridō produce a colour collotype replica, sold with a new essay on the scroll by Basil Gray.

1967 (Kohara)

1976 (Shih, Hsio-yen)

1985 (Gray, reprint of 1966)

1990 (Farrer)
Scroll has been on permanent exhibition in the King Edward VII Wing (North Wing), viewable by push-button timed lighting.
6 September–4 November: Scroll goes into storage at BM while pick of Chinese calligraphy and painting collection travels to Hayward Gallery for the exhibition *The Brush Dances and the Ink Sings*.

1995 (Whitfield)

1997 (Wu Hung)

2000 (Kohara, tr. of 1967)

2001 (Mason, McCausland, Murck, Murray, Yu Hui)
18–20 June: 'The *Admonitions* Scroll – Ideals of Etiquette, Art And Empire', international colloquium held at BM in conjunction with Percival David Foundation.
16 June–12 August: Scroll is exhibited in *Emperors and Court Ladies: Chinese Figure Painting* with other works from the Museum collection.

Bibliography

Acker 1954, 1974, 1979: William R. B. Acker (tr. and annot.). *Some T'ang and Pre-T'ang Texts on Chinese Painting. Sinica Leidensia*, vol. 8. 2 vols. Leiden: E. J. Brill, 1954. Vol. 2, reprint, Leiden: E. J. Brill, 1974. Vol. 1, reprint, Westport, Connecticut: Hyperion, 1979.

Ackerman & Carpenter 1963: James S. Ackerman & Rhys Carpenter. *Art and Archaeology*. Englewood Cliffs, N. J.: Prentice-Hall, Inc., 1963.

Akiyama *et al.* (eds) 1966–: Akiyama Terukazu 秋山光和 *et al.* (eds). *Genshoku Nihon no bijutsu* 原色日本の美術. 30 vols. Tokyo: Shōgakkan, 1966–1972.

An Qi 1970, *MYHGL* (1742): An Qi 安岐 (An Yizhou 儀周; 1683–1742?). *Moyuan huiguan* 墨緣彙觀 (Viewing Records; completed 1742). Wang Yunwu 王雲五 (ed.). *Renren wen kui te sanqi* 人人文庫特三七. Taipei: Shangwu, 1970. Also, reprint, Lu Fusheng *et al.* (eds) 1992–, vol. 10 (1996), pp. 315–416.

Anderson 1886: William Anderson (1842–1900). *Descriptive and Historical Catalogue of a Collection of Japanese and Chinese Paintings in the British Museum*. London: Longmans & Co.; etc., 1886.

Anhui (Ma'anshan) 1986: Anhui sheng wenwu kaogu yanjiusuo, Ma'anshan shi wenhuaju 安徽省文物考古研究所, 馬鞍山文化局. 'Anhui Ma'anshan Dong Wu Zhu Ran mu fajue jianbao' 安徽馬鞍山東吳朱然墓發掘簡報 (Excavation report on the Dong Wu Zhu Ran tomb at Ma'anshan, Anhui Province). *Wenwu*, 1986.3, pp. 3–15.

Ayers 1963: John Ayers. 'Ku K'ai-chih'. *Encyclopaedia of World Art*, vol. 3 (1963), pp. 1037–1042. London: McGraw-Hill, 1959–1967.

Bachhofer 1946/1947: Ludwig Bachhofer (1894–1976). *A Short History of Chinese Art*. New York: Pantheon, 1946. London: Batsford, 1947.

Ban Zhao 班昭 (*c.*45–*c.*120 CE). *Nü jie* 女誡 (Precepts for Women).

Bao Zhao 1980: Bao Zhao 鮑照 (414–466). *Bao Canjun jizhu* 鮑參軍集注 (Collected Works of Bao Zhao, Annotated). Shanghai: Guji chubanshe, 1980.

Baptisms Solemnized at Vespery Saint Matthias, 1870. Index to Madras Baptisms. The British Library, Oriental and India Office Collection.

Baqi manzhou shizu tongpu 八旗滿洲氏族通譜 (Collective Genealogies of the Eight-Banner and Manchu Lineages; 1745).

Barnhart 1972: Richard M. Barnhart. 'Survival and revival, and the classical tradition of Chinese figure painting'. *Taipei International Symposium 1970* 1972, pp. 143–210.

Barnhart 1983: Richard M. Barnhart. *Along the Border of Heaven*. New York: Metropolitan Museum of Art, 1983.

Barnhart *et al.* 1993: Richard M. Barnhart *et al. Li Kung-lin's 'Classic of Filial Piety'*. New York: Metropolitan Museum of Art, 1993.

BBCSJC 1969: *Baibu congshu jicheng* 百部叢書集成 series. Taipei: Yiwen, 1969.

Belting 1987: Hans Belting. Christopher Wood (tr.). *The End of the History of Art?* Chicago: University of Chicago Press, 1987.

Benjamin 1992: Walter Benjamin (1892–1940). 'The work of art in the age of mechanical reproduction'. Walter Benjamin, edited and with an introduction by Hannah Arendt, translated by Harry Zohn. *Illuminations*, pp. 211–244. London, 1992.

Berkowitz 2000: Alan J. Berkowitz. *Patterns of Disengagement: The Practice and Portrayal of Reclusion in Early Medieval China*. Stanford, Calif.: Stanford University Press, 2000.

Bian Yongyu 1958, 1991, 1992– (1682): Bian Yongyu 卞永譽 (1645–1712). *Shigutang shuhua huikao* 式古堂書畫彙考 (Studies of Calligraphy and Painting of the Hall of Testing Antiquity; preface dated 1682). Reprints, Taipei: Zhengzhong shuju, 1958. Shanghai: Shanghai guji, 1991. Lu Fusheng *et al.* (eds) 1992–, vol. 6, pp. 1–1081.

Binyon & Colvin 1918: Laurence Binyon (1869–1943) & Sir Sidney Colvin (1845–1927). 'The late Stanley William Littlejohn'. *The Burlington Magazine*, vol. 32, no. 178 (January 1918), pp. 16–19.

Binyon 1904: Laurence Binyon. 'A Chinese painting of the fourth century'. *The Burlington Magazine*, vol. 10, no. 4 (January 1904), pp. 39–44.

Binyon 1908: Laurence Binyon. *Painting in the Far East*. London: E. Arnold, 1908.

Binyon 1912: Laurence Binyon. *Admonitions of the Instructress in the Palace. A Painting by Ku K'ai-chih in the Department of Prints and Drawings, British Museum, Reproduced in Coloured Woodcut*. Text by Laurence Binyon; woodblock engraving by S. Sugisaki; colour printing by Y. Urushibara. London: Trustees of the British Museum, 1912.

Birrell (tr.) 1982: Anne Birrell (tr.). *New Songs from a Jade Terrace*. London: George Allen & Unwin, 1982.

Birrell 1993: Anne Birrell. *Chinese Mythology: An Introduction*. Baltimore & London: The Johns Hopkins University Press, 1993.

BJXSDG: *Biji xiaoshuo daguan* 筆記小説大觀. Taipei: Xinxing, 1976–.

Bokenkamp 1996: Stephen Bokenkamp. 'Declarations of the perfected'. Donald S. Lopez, Jr (ed.). *Religions of China in Practice*, pp. 166–187. Princeton, N. J.: Princeton University Press, 1996.

Bol 1992: Peter Bol. *This Culture of Ours: Intellectual Transitions in T'ang and Sung China*. Stanford, Calif.: Stanford University Press, 1992.

Boltz 1993: William G. Boltz. 'Chou li'. *Early Chinese Texts: A Bibliographical Guide* 1993, pp. 24–32.

British Museum 2001: http://www.thebritishmuseum.ac.uk/compass/ixbin/hixclient.exe?_IXDB_=compass&_IXFIRST_=1&_IXMAXHITS_=1&_IXSPFX_=graphical/full/&$+with+all_unique_id_index+is+$=OBJ2100&submit-button=summary

Bunjin-ga suihen 文人畫粹編 (Literati Painting, Essential Works). 20 vols. Tokyo: Chūō-kōron-sha, 1974–1979. Vol. 1, Ō E 王維 (Wang Wei) (reprint) 1985.

Bush & Shih 1985: Susan Bush & Hsio-yen Shih. *Early Chinese Texts on Painting*. Published for the Harvard-Yenching Institute: Cambridge, Mass.: Harvard University Press, 1985.

Bush 1971: Susan Bush. *The Chinese Literati on Painting: Su Shih (1037–1101) to Tung Ch'i-ch'ang (1555–1636)*. Harvard-Yenching

Institute Studies, no. 27. Cambridge, Mass.: Harvard University Press, 1971.

Bushell 1904: Stephen Bushell (1844–1908). *Chinese Art*. London: H. M. Stationery Office, 1904.

Bussagli 1966: Mario Bussagli. *Chinese Painting*. London: Hamlyn, 1966.

Cahill 1960: James Cahill. *Chinese Painting*. Geneva: Skira, 1960.

Cahill 1980: James Cahill. *An Index of Early Chinese Painters and Paintings*. Berkeley, Calif.: University of California Press, 1980.

Cahill 2001: James Cahill. 'Symposia, conferences and colloquies … the last word?'. *Orientations*, vol. 32, no. 8 (October 2001), p. 118.

Cao Zhao 曹昭 (later 14th century). *Gegu yaolun* 格古要論 (Essential Criteria of Antiquities). See David 1971.

Cao Zhi 曹植 (192–232). 'Luoshen fu' 洛神賦 (Ode of the Nymph [or Goddess] of the Luo River).

Cao Zhi. 'Huazan xu' 畫贊序 (Preface to the 'Eulogies on Painting').

Carlitz 1991: Katherine Carlitz. 'The social uses of female virtue in late Ming editions of Lienü zhuan'. *Late Imperial China*, vol. 12, no. 2 (1991), pp. 117–148.

Chang & Frankel (trs) 1995: Chang Ch'ung-ho & Hans Frankel (trs). *Two Chinese Treatises on Calligraphy*. New Haven: Yale University Press, 1995.

Chavannes 1909: Édouard Chavannes (1865–1918). 'Notes sur la peinture de Kou K'ai-tche conservée au British Museum'. *T'oung Pao*, vol. 10 (1909), pp. 76–86.

Chaves 2000: Jonathan Chaves. *The Chinese Poet as Painter*. New York: China Institute, 2000.

Chen Bangzhan (comp.) 1977: Chen Bangzhan 陳邦瞻 (d. 1623) (comp.). *Song shi jishi benmo* 宋史記事本末. Beijing: Zhonghua shuju, 1977.

Chen Dazhang 1958: Chen Dazhang 陳大章. 'Henan Dengxian faxian Beichaoqi secai huihuaxiang zhuanmu' 河南鄧縣發現北朝期色彩繪畫像磚墓 (A Northern Dynasties polychrome-painted brick tomb discovered in Deng County, Henan Province). *Wenwu cankao ziliao* 文物參考資料, 1958.6, pp. 55–56.

Chen Dehui 陳德輝 (Song, 960–1279). *Xu hua ji* 續畫記 (Painting Records, Continued).

Chen Dongyuan 1937: Chen Dongyuan 陳東原. *Zhongguo funü shenghuo shi* 中國婦女生活史 (History of the Lives of Women in China). Shanghai: Shangwu, 1937.

Chen Gaohua (ed.) 1984: Chen Gaohua 陳高華 (ed.). *Song Liao Jin huajia shiliao* 宋遼金畫家史料 (Historical Materials on Song, Liao and Jin Painters). Beijing: Wenwu chubanshe, 1984.

Chen Jiru 1975, 1992 (*c*.1635): Chen Jiru 陳繼儒 (1558–1639). *Nigu lu* 妮古錄 (*c*.1635). Reprints, *MSCS* (1975), part 5. Lu Fusheng *et al.* (eds) 1992–, vol. 3, pp. 1038–1059.

Chen Pao-chen 1987: Pao-chen Chen 陳葆真. 'The Goddess of the Lo River: A study of early Chinese narrative handscrolls'. Ph. D. diss., Princeton University, 1987.

Chen Pao-chen 1995: Chen Pao-chen. 'Time and space in Chinese narrative paintings of Han and the Six Dynasties'. Chun-chieh Huang & Erik Zürcher (eds) *Time and Space in Chinese Culture*, pp. 239–268. Leiden: E. J. Brill, 1995.

Chen Pao-chen 2000: Chen Pao-chen. 'Three representational modes for text/image relationships in early Chinese pictorial art'. *Taida Journal*, no. 8 (March 2000), pp. 87–135.

Chen Pao-chen 2002: Chen Pao-chen. 'From text to images: a case study of the *Admonitions* scroll in the British Museum'. *Taida Journal*, no. 12 (March 2002), pp. 35–51.

Chen Tian 1993: Chen Tian 陳田 (1849–1921). *Mingshi ji shi* 明詩紀事 (Events in Ming Poetry). Shanghai: Shanghai guji chubanshe, 1993.

Chen Yaolin 1988: Chen Yaolin 陳耀林. 'Liang Qingbiao congtan' 梁清標叢談 (On Liang Qingbiao). *Gugong Bowuyuan yuankan*, 1988.3, pp. 56–57.

Chen Zengbi 1979: Chen Zengbi 陳增弼. 'Han, Wei, Jin duzuo shi xiaota chulun' 漢魏晉獨坐式小榻初論 (Preliminary discussion of the single-seat stool in Han, Wei and Jin). *Wenwu*, 1979.9, pp. 66–71.

Chen, Shih-hsiang 1953, 1961: Chen Shih-hsiang (tr. & annot.). *Biography of Ku K'ai-chih*. Chinese Dynastic Histories Translations, no. 2. Berkeley & Los Angeles: University of California Press, 1953, 1961.

Chen, Yu shih 1996: Yu-shih Chen. 'The historical template of Pan Chao's Nü chieh'. *T'oung Pao*, vol. 82, fasc. 4–5 (1996), pp. 229–257.

Chhae Pyeong-seo 1959: Chhae Pyeong-seo 蔡秉瑞. 'Anak-kunbang pyokhwa kobunpalgul surok' 安岳沂傍壁畫古墳發掘手錄. *Asea Yon'gu* 亞細亞研究 (Seoul), vol. 2, no. 2 (1959), pp. 109–130.

Ching, D. C. Y. 1999: Dora C. Y. Ching. 'The aesthetics of the unusual and the strange in seventeenth-century calligraphy'. Harrist & Fong 1999, pp. 340–359.

Chou, Yeongchau 2001: Diana Yeongchau Chou. 'Reexamination of Tang Hou and his *Huajian*'. Ph. D. diss., University of Kansas, 2001.

Chu ci 楚辭 (Songs of Chu). Attributed to Qu Yuan 屈原 (*c*.343–*c*.277 BCE) *et al.* Including 'Jiu ge' 九歌 (Nine Songs).

Chung, P. C. 1981: Priscilla Ching Chung. *Palace Women in the Northern Sung, 960–1126*. Leiden: E. J. Brill, 1981.

Clunas 1994: Craig Clunas. 'Oriental Antiquities/Far Eastern Art'. *positions: east asia cultures critique*, vol. 2, no. 2 (1994), pp. 318–355.

Cohn 1948: William Cohn (1880–1961). *Chinese Painting*. London: Phaidon, 1948.

Contag & Wang 1982: Victoria Contag & Wang Chi-ch'ien. *Seals of Chinese Painters and Collectors of the Ming and Ch'ing Periods*. 2nd edition; Hong Kong: Hong Kong University Press, 1982.

Crossley 1987: Pamela Kyle Crossley. '*Manzhou yuanliu kao* and the formalization of Manchu heritage'. *Journal of Asian Studies*, vol. 46, no. 4 (November 1987), pp. 761–790.

Crossley 1999: Pamela Kyle Crossley. *A Translucent Mirror: History and Identity in Qing Imperial Ideology*. Berkeley, Los Angeles & London: Berkeley University Press, 1999.

CSJCCB: *Congshu jicheng chubian* 叢書集成初編 series. Shanghai: Shangwu yinshuguan, 1937.

CSJCXB: *Congshu jicheng xubian* 叢書集成續編 series. Taipei, 1985.

Da Jin guo zhi: *Da Jin guo zhi* 大金國誌 (Annals of the Great Jin State). *BBCSJC* 1969.

Daniel 1925: A. M. Daniel. *Skinner's Horse: The History of The 1st Duke of York's Own Lancers (Skinner's Horse) & The 3rd Skinner's Horse*. London: Hugh Rees, 1925.

Dao de jing 道德經. Tr. Arthur Waley (1889–1966). *The Way and Its Power: A Study of the Tao Tê Ching and Its Place in Chinese Thought*. London: Mandala Books, 1977.

Datong 1972: Datong City Museum 大同市博物館. 'Shanxi Datong Shijiazhai Beiwei Sima Jinlong mu' 山西大同石家寨北魏司馬金龍墓 (Northern Wei tomb of Sima Jinlong at Shijiazhai, Datong, Shanxi). *Wenwu*, 1972.3, pp. 20–33.

David 1971: Sir Percival David, Bart. (1892–1964). *Chinese Connoisseurship: The Ko Ku Yao Lun. A translation made and edited by Sir Percival David, with a facsimile of the Chinese text of 1388*. London: Faber & Faber; New York: Praeger, 1971.

Davis 2001: Richard L. Davis. 'Chaste and filial women in Chinese historical writings of the eleventh century'. *Journal of American Oriental Studies*, vol. 121, no. 2 (April–June 2001), pp. 204–218.

de Rachewiltz 1993: Igor de Rachewiltz (ed.). *In the Service of the Khan:*

Eminent Personalities of the Early Mongol-Yüan Period, 1200–1300. Wiesbaden: Harrassowitz, 1993.

Deaths Registration in Oct., Nov. & Dec., 1937. *Index of Deaths in England and Wales since 1837.* Microfilm, National Library of Scotland.

Deng Chun 1963 (1167): Deng Chun 鄧椿 (act. 1127–1167). *Hua ji* 畫繼 (Painting, Continued; 1167). Beijing: Renmin meishu chubanshe, 1963. Also, *HSCS* edition.

DGL: Da guan lu. See Wu Sheng 1712.

Diao Yong 刁雍 (390–484). 'Xing xiao lun' 行孝論 (On Filial Piety). *Wei shu* 1974, *juan* 84, p. 1858.

Ding Xiyuan 2001: Ding Xiyuan 丁羲元. 'Dianli jicha siyin kao' 典禮紀察司印考 (A study of the 'Dianli jicha siyin' official seal). *Gugong wenwu yuekan*, vol. 214 (2001 1), pp. 64–78.

Dong Qichang 1968: Dong Qichang 董其昌 (1555–1636). *Rongtai bieji* 容臺別集. In *Mingdai yishujia ji huikan* 明代藝術家集彙刊 (Literary Collections of Ming Artists): *Rongtai ji*. Taipei: Zhongyang tushuguan, 1968.

Dong Qichang 1992–: Dong Qichang. *Huachanshi suibi* 畫禪室隨筆 (Jottings of the Hall of Painting Chan; n.d.). Reprint, Lu Fusheng *et al.* (eds) 1992–, vol. 3, pp. 999–1033.

Dong Qichang. *Xihongtang fashu/tie* 戲鴻堂法書 (Calligraphy Copybook of the Hall of Playful Geese). 4 vols. Huating: Dongshi lecheng, 1603.

Dongguan Han ji 東觀漢記. Cited in *YWLJ, juan* 21, pp. 388–89.

Dou Zhen 1985: Dou Zhen 竇鎮 (b. 1847). *Guochao shuhuajia bi lu* 國朝書畫家筆錄 (Record of Writings by Calligraphers and Painters of the Qing Dynasty). *Qingdai zhuanji congkan, yilin lei* 1985, vol. 22.

DSXZ 1980 (1703): Qiu Zhao'ao 仇兆鰲 (ed.). *Du shi xiangzhu* 杜詩祥注 (The Poetry of Du Fu, Annotated; 1703). Reprint, 5 vols, Beijing: Zhonghua, 1985.

du Boulay 1990–1991: Anthony du Boulay. 'The Summer Palace 1900: an inventory by Noel Du Boulay'. *Transactions of the Oriental Ceramic Society,* vol. 55 (1990–1991), pp. 83–102.

Duanfang 端方 (1861–1911). *Duanzhongmingong zougao* 端忠敏公奏稿 (Memorials of Duanfang). N.p., 1909.

Duanfang 1995 (1902): Duanfang. *Renyin xiaoxia lu* 壬寅消夏錄 (Catalogue to Pass Away the Summer of the Renyin Year). Facsimile in *Xuxiu siku quanshu,* vol. 1089. Shanghai: Shanghai guji chubanshe, 1995.

Eagleton 1990: Terry Eagleton. *The Ideology of the Aesthetic.* Cambridge, Mass.: Basil Blackwell, 1990.

Early Chinese Texts: A Bibliographical Guide 1993. Michael Loewe (ed.). Early China Special Monograph Series No. 2. Berkeley: The Society for the Study of Early China & The Institute of East Asian Studies, University of California-Berkeley, 1993.

Ebrey 1992: Patricia Buckley Ebrey. 'Women, money, and class: Ssu-ma Kuang and Neo-Confucian views on women'. *Papers on Society and Culture of Early Modern China,* pp. 613–669. Taipei: Institute of History and Philology, Academia Sinica, 1992.

Elderfield 2000: John Elderfield. *Henri Matisse: A Retrospective.* New York: The Museum of Modern Art, 1992.

Elliott 2001: Mark Elliott. *The Manchu Way: The Eight Banners and Ethnic Identity in Late Imperial China.* Stanford, Calif.: Stanford University Press, 2001.

Elman 2000: Benjamin A. Elman. *A Cultural History of Civil Examinations in Late Imperial China.* Berkeley, Calif.: University of California Press, 2000.

Elverskog (forthcoming): Johan Elverskog. *Things and the Qing: Mongolian Visual and Material Culture.* Forthcoming.

Fan Zuyu: Fan Zuyu 范祖禹 (1041–1098). *Fan Taishi ji* 范太史集 (Collected Works of Fan Zuyu). In *SKQS*, vol. 1100.

Fashu yaolu: Zhang Yanyuan 張彥遠 (*c.*815–874) (comp.). *Fashu yaolu* 法書要錄 (Essential Record of Calligraphy). Lu Fusheng *et al.* (eds) 1992–.

Feng & Feng 1906 (1821): Feng Yunpeng 馮雲鵬 & Feng Yunyuan 馮雲鵷 (19th century). *Jinshi suo* 金石索 (Index of Carvings on Metal and Stone). Shi yin ben 石印本, 1821. Reprint, Shanghai: Wenxinju shiyin, 1906.

Feng Jinbo 馮金伯 (fl. 1788). *Moxiangju hua shi* 墨香居畫識 (Knowledge of Painting from the House of Ink Fragrance; 1796). Series *Qingdai quanji congkan, yilin lei* 1985, vol. 72.

Ferguson 1918: John C. Ferguson (1866–1945). 'Ku K'ai-chih's scroll in the British Museum'. *Journal of the North China Branch of the Royal Asiatic Society*, vol. 49 (1918), pp. 101–110.

Ferguson 1927: John C. Ferguson. *Chinese Painting.* Chicago: University of Chicago Press, 1927.

Ferguson 1994 (1933): John C. Ferguson. *Lidai zhulu huamu* 歷代著錄畫目 (Catalogue of Painting Records through the Ages; 1933). Yangzhou: Jiangsu guangling gujukeyinshe, 1994.

Fong & Watt 1996: Wen C. Fong & James C. Y. Watt. *Possessing the Past: Treasures from the National Palace Museum, Taipei.* New York: Metropolitan Museum of Art, 1996.

Fong, Wen C. 1976: Wen C. Fong. 'Archaism as a "Primitive" Style'. Christian F. Murck (ed.). *Artists and Traditions: Uses of the Past in Chinese Culture*, pp. 89–109. Princeton, N. J.: Princeton University Press, 1976.

Fong, Wen C. 1981: Wen C. Fong. '"Receding-and-Protruding Painting" at Tun-huang'. *Proceedings of the International Conference on Sinology: Section on Art History*, pp. 73–94. Taipei: Academia Sinica, 1981.

Fong, Wen C. 1992: Wen C. Fong. *Beyond Representation: Chinese Painting and Calligraphy 8th–14th Century.* New York: The Metropolitan Museum of Art, 1992.

Fong, Wen C. 1999: Wen C. Fong. 'Chinese Calligraphy: Theory and History'. Harrist & Fong 1999, pp. 28–84.

Fong, Wen C. 2001: Wen C. Fong. *Between Two Cultures: Late-Nineteenth- and Twentieth-Century Chinese Paintings from the Robert H. Ellsworth Collection in The Metropolitan Museum of Art.* New York: Metropolitan Museum of Art, 2001.

Fong, Wen C. 2002: Wen C. Fong 方聞. 'Chuan Gu Kaizhi *Nüshi zhen tu* yu Zhongguo yishushi' 傳顧愷之《女史箴圖》与中國藝術史 (The *Admonitions* scroll and Chinese art history). *Taida Journal*, no. 12 (March 2002), pp. 1–34.

Fong, Wen C., *et al.* 1984: Wen C. Fong *et al. Images of the Mind: Selections from the Edward L. Elliott Family and John B. Elliott Collections of Chinese Calligraphy and Painting at The Art Museum, Princeton University.* Princeton, N. J.: The Art Museum, Princeton University, 1984.

Foucault 1972, 2001 (1969): Michel Foucault (1926–1984). *The Archaeology of Knowledge (L'Archéologie du savoir).* First published 1969. Tr. A. M. Sheridan Smith. London: Tavistock, 1972. Reprint, London: Routledge, 2001.

Foucault 1973: Michel Foucault. *The Order of Things: An Archaeology of the Human Sciences.* New York: Vintage Books, 1973.

Franke & Twitchett (eds) 1993: Herbert Franke & Denis Twitchett (eds). *The Cambridge History of China. Vol. 6, Alien Regimes and Border States, 710–1368.* New York: Cambridge University Press, 1993.

Franke 1976: Herbert Franke (ed.). *Sung Biographies.* Wiesbaden: Steiner, 1976–.

Frazer 1913: Sir James G. Frazer. *The Golden Bough,* part 1, *The Magic Art and the Evolution of Kings.* London: Macmillan, 1913.

Freedberg 1989: David Freedberg. *The Power of Images: Studies in the History and Theory of Response.* Chicago: The University of Chicago Press, 1989.

Freer: 'Catalogue of kakemono by Japanese and Chinese artists'. Charles Lang Freer's Papers. Freer Gallery of Art, Arthur M. Sackler Gallery Archives, Washington, DC.

Fu & Bai 1980: Fu Lianxing 傅連興 & Bai Lijuan 白麗娟. 'Jianfugong huayuan yizhi' 建福宮花園遺址 (Site of the Palace of Established Happiness). *Gugong Bowuyuan yuankan,* 1980.3, pp. 14–16.

Fu Baoshi 1958: Fu Baoshi 傅抱石 (1904–1965). *Zhongguo de huihua* 中國的繪畫 (Chinese Painting). Beijing: Zhongguo gudian yishu chubanshe, 1958.

Fu Shen 1981: Fu Shen 傅申. *Yuandai huangshi shuhua shoucang shilue* 元代皇室書畫收藏史略 (A Brief History of the Yuan Imperial Collection of Calligraphy and Painting). Taipei: National Palace Museum, 1981.

Fukui 1925a: Fukui Rikichirō 福井利吉郎 (1886–1972) (supervisor). Monochrome collotype reproduction of the *Admonitions* scroll. Sendai University, 1925.

Fukui 1925b: Fukui Rikichirō. *Short Notes on the Tohoku Imperial University Copy of the Ku K'ai-chih's Scroll in the British Museum and a Sketch-book of Korin, Forming a Collection of Life-studies from the Birds of Japan, and Certain Exotic Species.* Reprinted from *Guide to an Exhibition in the Tohoku Imperial University.* Sendai, 1925.

Fukui Rikichirō. *Fukui Rikichirō bijutsushi ronshū* 福井利吉郎芸術史論集 (Anthology of Essays on Art History by Fukui Rikichirō). 3 vols. Tokyo: Chūō-kōron bijutsu shuppan, 1998–2000.

Furuta 1992: Furuta Shin'ichi 古田真一. 'Rikucho kaiga ni kansuru ichi kosatsu – Shiba Kinryu ba shuddo no shitsuga byobu o meggute' 六朝絵画する一考察 – 司馬金龍墓出土の漆画屏風をめぐって (An investigation of the Six Dynasties paintings – surrounding the lacquer paintings on the screen excavated from the tomb of Sima Jinlong)'. *Bigaku* 美學, no. 168 (Spring 1992), pp. 57–67.

Gan Bao 1999 (*c.*322): Gan Bao 干寶 (act. 317–322). *Soushen ji* 搜神記 (In Search of the Supernatural). *Han Wei Liuchao biji xiaoshuo daguan* 漢魏六朝筆記小說大觀 series, vol. 11, pp. 362–363. Shanghai: Guji chubanshe, 1999.

Gansu Provincial Institute 1989: Gansu Provincial Institute of Cultural Relics and Archaeology 甘肅省文物考古研究所. *Jiuquan Shiliuguo mu bihua* 酒泉十六國墓壁畫 (Murals in a Sixteen-Kingdom Period Tomb at Jiuquan). Beijing: Wenwu chubanshe, 1989.

Gao Shiqi 1992– (1639): Gao Shiqi 高士奇 (1645–1704). *Jiangcun xiaoxia lu* 江村銷夏錄 (Record of Whiling Away the Summer; 1639). Reprint, Lu Fusheng *et al.* (eds) 1992–, vol. 7, pp. 988–1039.

Gao Shiqi 1992– (n.d.): Gao Shiqi. *Jiangcun shuhua mu* 江村書畫目 (Catalogue of Calligraphy and Painting). Reprint, Lu Fusheng *et al.* (eds) 1992–, vol. 7, pp. 1068–1078.

Gao Wen *et al.* 1996: Gao Wen 高文 *et al. Zhongguo huaxiang shiguan yishu* 中國畫像石棺藝術 (Art of Pictorially Engraved Sarcophagi in China). Taiyuan: Shanxi renmin chubanshe, 1996.

Gernet 1995: Jacques Gernet. 'Henri Maspero and Paul Demiéville: Two Great Masters of French Sinology'. Wilson & Cayley (eds) 1995, pp. 45–47.

Gettens & Stout 1966: R. J. Gettens & G. L. Stout. *Painting Materials: A Short Encyclopaedia.* New York: Dover Publications, Inc., 1966.

Giles 1905: Herbert Giles (1845–1935). *An Introduction to the History of Chinese Pictorial Art.* Shanghai: Kelly and Walsh, 1905.

Giles 1915: Herbert A. Giles (1845–1935). 'An emperor on Ku K'ai-chih'. *Adversaria Sinica,* ser. 2, no. 1 (1915), pp. 45–52. Shanghai: Kelly & Walsh, 1915.

Gombrich 1960: E. H. Gombrich (1909–2001). *Art and Illusion: A Study in the Psychology of Pictorial Representation.* Washington, D.C. and New York: Pantheon Books, 1960.

Gombrich 1972a (1950): E. H. Gombrich. *The Story of Art.* First published 1950; 12th edition, enlarged and revised. London: Phaidon, 1972.

Gombrich 1972b: E. H. Gombrich. *Symbolic Images: Studies in the Art of the Renaissance.* London: Phaidon, 1972.

Gong Dazhong 1984: Gong Dazhong 宮大中. 'Mang-Luo Beiwei xiaozi huaxiang shiguan kaoshi' 邙洛北魏孝子畫像石棺考釋 (A study of the pictorial engravings of the Northern Wei filial-piety sarcophagi from Mangshan, Luoyang). *Zhongyuan wenwu* 中原文物 vol. 28, no. 2 (1984), pp. 48–53.

Goodman 1983: Nelson Goodman. 'Art and authenticity'. Dennis Dutton (ed.). *The Forger's Art: Forgery and the Philosophy of Art,* pp. 93–114. Berkeley, Calif.: University of California Press, 1983.

Goodrich & Fang (eds) 1976: L. Carrington Goodrich & Chao-ying Fang (eds). *Dictionary of Ming Biography.* 2 vols. New York: Columbia University Press, 1976.

Graham-Dixon 2001: Andrew Graham-Dixon. 'The Admonitions (*c.*400) attributed to Gu Kaizhi'. *Sunday Telegraph Magazine,* June 10, 2001, p. 74.

Grants of Probate 1938: 'Grants of Probate and Administration made in the estates of all persons of European extraction whether British subjects or not by the High Court, Calcutta, in the Province of Bengal during the quarter ending the 30th day of September 1938'. Grants of Probate, folio 226, i. The British Library, Oriental & India Office Collection.

Gray 1966: Basil Gray (1904–1989). *Admonitions of The Instructress of The Ladies in the Palace – A Painting Attributed to Ku K'ai-chih.* London: Trustees of the British Museum, 1966. Published together with a colour collotype reproduction of the *Admonitions* scroll; colour photography by Tsujimoto Yonesaburo *et al.*, for Benridō, Kyoto: Asahi shimbunsha, 1966.

Gray 1985 (1966): Basil Gray. '"Admonitions of the Instructress of the Ladies in the Palace": A Painting Attributed to Ku K'ai-chih'. *Studies in Chinese and Islamic Art, Vol. 1: Chinese Art,* pp. 166–195. London: The Pindar Press, 1985.

Gu Fu 顧復 (Qing, 1644–1911). *Pingsheng zhuangguan* 平生壯觀 (Great Views of a Lifetime).

Gu Kaizhi 顧愷之 (*c.*344/345–405/406); attributed to. 'Hua Yuntaishan ji' 畫雲臺山記 (Note on the painting of Cloud Terrace Mountain). Quoted in *LDMHJ, juan* 5: *HSCS* 1962, pp. 71–72.

Gu Kaizhi. 'Qimeng ji' 啟蒙記 (Memoirs for Enlightening the Purblind).

Gu Kaizhi; attributed to. 'Lun hua' 論畫 (On painting). *LDMHJ.*

Gu Kaizhi; attributed to. 'Wei-Jin shengliu huazan' 魏晉勝流畫贊 (Comments on paintings of worthies by Wei and Jin artists). *LDMHJ.*

Gugong 2000: Gugong Bowuyuan gujianbu 故宮博物院古建部. 'Gugong Jianfugong huayuan fuyuan sheji yanjiu' 故宮建福宮花園复原設計研究 (Research on the restoration of the Palace of Established Happiness and its garden). *Gugong Bowuyuan yuankan,* 2000.5, pp. 26–37.

Gugong Bowuyuan (ed.). *Ming Qing di hou bao xi* 明清帝后寶璽 (Treasured Seals of Ming and Qing Emperors and Empresses). Beijing: Zijincheng chubanshe, 1996.

Gugong Bowuyuan yuankan: Gugong Bowuyuan yuankan 故宮博物院刊 (Palace Museum Journal). Beijing: Wenwu chubanshe, 1958–.

Gugong lidai fashu quanji 1976–: National Palace Museum. *Gugong lidai fashu quanji* 故宮歷代法書全集 (Compendium of Calligraphy through the Ages in the Palace Museum). Taipei: National Palace Museum; vol. 1, 1976.

Gugong shuhua tu lu 1989–: Qin Xiaoyi 秦孝儀 (ed.). *Gugong shuhua tu lu* 故宮書畫圖錄 (Illustrated Catalogue of Painting and Calligraphy in the National Palace Museum). Taipei: National Palace Museum, 1989–. Vol. 11, 1993.

Gugong wenwu yuekan: *Gugong wenwu yuekan* 故宮文物月刊 (National Palace Museum Monthly of Chinese Art). Taipei: National Palace Museum, 1983–.

Gugong yiyi shuhua mulu 故宮已佚書畫目錄 (Catalogue of Calligraphy and Paintings Missing from the Old Imperial Palace). Beijing, 1925.

Gugong zhoukan: *Gugong zhoukan* 故宮周刊 (Palace Museum Weekly). Beiping: Guoli Beiping Gugong Bowuyuan, 1929–1936.

Guide to an Exhibition of Chinese and Japanese Paintings (Fourth to Nineteenth Century A.D.) in the Print and Drawing Gallery. Second Edition, revised. London: Trustees of the British Museum, 1910.

Gujin tushu jicheng 古今圖書集成 (Ancient and Contemporary Documents, Classified). Shanghai: Shanghai wenyi chubanshe, 1991.

Guo Ruoxu 1974: Guo Ruoxu 郭若虛 (act. 1070–after 1080). *Tuhua jianwen zhi* 圖畫見聞誌 (Account of Paintings Seen and Heard of *or* Experiences in Painting). *HSCS.*

Guochao gongshi 1987 (1769): *Guochao gongshi* 國朝宮史 (History of the Palaces of the Present Dynasty; 1769). Beijing: Beijing guji chubanshe; vol. 1, 1987.

Guy 1987: R. Kent Guy. *The Emperor's Four Treasuries: Scholars and State in the Late Ch'ien-lung Era.* Cambridge, Mass., & London: Council on East Asian Studies, Harvard University; Harvard University Press, 1987.

Guyuan 1984: Guyuan Cultural Relics Institute 固原文物研究所. 'Ningxia Guyuan Beiwei mu qingli jianbao' 寧夏固原北魏墓清理簡報 (Excavation report of the Northern Wei tomb at Ningxia, Guyuan). *Wenwu*, 1984.6 (no. 337), pp. 46–55.

Han shu 1962: Ban Gu 班固 (32–92), Ban Biao 班彪 (3–54) *et al.* (comps). *Han shu* 漢書 (History of the Former Han). *SKQS*, vol. 251. Also, punctuated & annotated edition, Beijing: Zhonghua shuju, 1962.

Handler 1992: Sarah Handler. 'A little world made cunningly: the Chinese canopy bed'. *Journal of the Chinese Classical Society*, no. 2 (spring 1992), pp. 4–27.

Handler 1993: Sarah Handler. 'The Chinese screen: movable walls to divide, enhance, and beautify'. *Journal of the Chinese Classical Furniture Society*, no. 3 (summer 1993), pp. 4–31.

Harada 1937: Harada Yoshito 原田淑人 (1885–1974). *Kan Rikuchō no fukushoku* 漢六朝の服飾 (Fashion in the Han and Six Dynasties). Tokyo: Tōyō bunko, 1937.

Harfield 1990: Alan Harfield. *The Indian Army of the Empress 1861–1903.* Speldhurst: Spellmount, 1990.

Harrist & Fong 1999: Robert E. Harrist, Jr, Wen C. Fong *et al. The Embodied Image: Chinese Calligraphy from the John B. Elliott Collection.* Princeton, N. J.: The Art Museum, Princeton University, 1999.

Harrist 1999: Robert E. Harrist, Jr. 'Connoisseurship: Seeing and believing'. Smith & Fong (eds) 1999, pp. 293–309.

Hatcher 1995: John Hatcher. *Laurence Binyon: Poet, Scholar of East and West.* New York: Oxford University Press, 1995.

Hawkes 1974: David Hawkes. 'The Quest for the Goddess'. Cyril Birch (ed.). *Studies in Chinese Literary Genres*, pp. 42–68. Berkeley and Los Angeles: University of California Press, 1974.

He Liangjun 1992 (*c*.1570): He Liangjun 何良俊 (1506–1573). *Siyouzhai hualun* 四友齋畫論 (Essays on Painting of the Studio of the Four Friends; *c*.1570). Reprint, Lu Fusheng *et al.* (eds) 1992–, vol. 3.

Hearn & Fong 1999: Maxwell K. Hearn & Wen C. Fong. *Along the Riverbank: Paintings from the C. C. Wang Family Collection.* New York: Metropolitan Museum of Art, 1999.

Hearn & Smith (eds) 1996: Maxwell K. Hearn & Judith G. Smith (eds). *Arts of the Sung and Yuan.* New York: Metropolitan Museum of Art, 1996.

Hearn & Smith (eds) 2001: Maxwell K. Hearn & Judith G. Smith (eds). *Chinese Art: Modern Expressions.* New York: Metropolitan Museum of Art, 2001.

Hearn 1996: Maxwell K. Hearn. 'The Qing synthesis'. Richard M. Barnhart *et al.* (eds). *Mandate of Heaven: Emperors and Artists in China: Chinese Painting and Calligraphy from The Metropolitan Museum of Art, New York*, pp. 113–185. Zürich: Museum Rietberg Zürich, 1996.

Hebei Provincial Institute 2000: Hebei Provincial Institute of Cultural Relics 河北省文物研究所. *Hebei gudai muzang bihua* 河北古代墓葬壁畫 (Ancient Tomb Murals from Hebei). Beijing: Wenwu chubanshe, 2000.

Hevia 1995: James Louis Hevia. *Cherishing Men from Afar: Qing Guest Ritual and the Macartney Embassy of 1793.* Durham, N. C.: Duke University Press, 1995.

Hightower 1957: James R. Hightower. 'The Wen Hsuan and genre theory'. *HJAS*, vol. 20 (1957), pp. 512–533.

Hirth 1905: Friedrich Hirth (1845–1927). *Scraps from a Collector's Note Book: Being Notes on some Chinese Painters of the Present Dynasty with Appendices on Some Old Masters and Art Historians.* Leiden: E. J. Brill; Leipzig: Otto Harrassowitz; New York: G. E. Stechert & Co., 1905.

HJAS: *Harvard Journal of Asiatic Studies.* Cambridge, Mass.: Harvard-Yenching Institute, 1936–.

Ho, R. M. W. 1993: Richard M. W. Ho. *Ch'en Tzu-ang: Innovator in T'ang Poetry.* Hong Kong: Chinese University Press, 1993.

Ho, Wai-kam, *et al.* 1980: Wai-kam Ho *et al. Eight Dynasties of Chinese Painting: The Collections of the Nelson Gallery-Atkins Museum, Kansas City, and the Cleveland Museum of Art* (Badai yizhen 八代遺珍). [Exh. cat.] Cleveland: Cleveland Museum of Art with Indiana University Press, 1980.

Ho, Wai-kam, *et al.* 1992: Wai-kam Ho *et al. The Century of Tung Ch'i-ch'ang 1555–1636.* 2 vols. [Exh. cat.] Kansas City, Missouri: Nelson-Atkins Museum, 1992.

Hou Han shu 1965: Fan Ye 范曄 (398–445) (comp.). Hou Han shu 後漢書 (History of the Later Han). Punctuated and annotated edition, Beijing: Zhonghua shuju, 1965.

Hou, Sharon 1986: Sharon Shih-jiuan Hou. 'Women's literature'. *Indiana Companion to Traditional Chinese Literature* 1986, pp. 175–194.

HPCS 1982: Yu Anlan 于安瀾 (ed.). *Huapin congshu* 畫品叢書 (Compendium of Painting Criticism). Shanghai: Shanghai renmin meishu chubanshe, 1982.

HSCS 1955, 1962, 1963, 1974, 1982: Yu Anlan (ed.). *Huashi congshu* 畫史叢書 (Compendium of Painting Histories). 5 vols. Shanghai: Shanghai renmin meishu chubanshe, 1955, 1962, 1963, 1982. Also, Taipei: Wenshizhe chubanshe, 1974.

Hsiao Ch'i-ch'ing 1993: Hsiao Ch'i-ch'ing. 'Mid-Yüan politics'. Franke & Twitchett (eds) 1993, pp. 490–560.

Hsieh Cheng-fa 2001: Hsieh Cheng-fa 謝振發. 'Beiwei Sima Jinlong mu de qihua pingfeng shixi' 北魏司馬金龍墓的漆畫屏風試析 (A study of the painted lacquer screen from the Northern Wei tomb of Sima Jinlong). *Taida Journal*, no. 11 (2001.9), pp. 1–56.

Hu Jing 1934, 1971 (1816): Hu Jing 胡敬 (1769–1845). 'Xiqing zhaji' 西清劄記 (Records of Xiqing). *Hushi shuhua kao san zhong* 胡氏書畫考三種 (Three Studies on Calligraphy and Painting by Mr Hu; 1816). Beiping: Caixunge, 1934. Taipei: Hanhua chubanshe, 1971.

Hua jian: Tang Hou 湯垕 (mid-1250s–mid-1310s). *[Gujin] hua jian* 古今畫鑒 (Mirror of Painting [Ancient and Modern]). *MSCK* (1956), vol. 1, pp. 159–178.

Hua shi (1103): Mi Fu 米芾 (1052–1107). *Hua shi* 畫史 (History of Painting; 1103). *MSCS* (1947). Also, Yang Jialuo (ed.) 1962, vol. 624.

Huaji buyi 畫繼補遺 (Supplement to 'Painting, Continued'; 1298). Also attributed to Zhuang Su 莊肅 (late 13th century). Deng Chun 1963.

Huang Bosi 黃伯思 (1079–1118). *Dongguan yulun* 東觀餘論 (*c*.1110). Reprint of 1584 edition; Taipei: National Central Library, 1984.

Huang Luceng 黃魯曾 (mid-16th century). *Gu lienü zhuan* 古列女傳 (Biographies of Exemplary Women, the Ancients; 1552).

Huang Miaozi 1991: Huang Miaozi 黃苗子. *Wu Daozi shiji* 吳道子事輯 (Research Materials on Wu Daozi). Beijing: Zhonghua shuju, 1991.

Huang Tingjian 1979: Huang Tingjian 黃庭堅 (1045–1105). *Shan'gu shi neiwai jizhu* 山谷詩內外集注 (Annotated Collection of Huang Tingjian's Poetry). Reprint, Taipei: Xuehai chubanshe, 1979.

Huang Tingjian 2001: Huang Tingjian. *Huang Tingjian quanji* 黃庭堅全集 (Complete Literary Works of Huang Tingjian). Chengdu: Sichuan University, 2001.

Huang Weizhong 1994: Huang Weizhong 黃緯中. 'Guanyu Gu Kaizhi "Nüshi zhen tujuan" shang de "Hongwen zhi yin" qiangai shijian zhi taolun' 關於顧愷之《女史箴圖卷》上的『弘文之印』鈐蓋時間之討論 (A discussion of the dating of the 'Hongwen zhi yin' seal on the *Admonitions of the Instructress to the Court Ladies* picture-scroll by Gu Kaizhi). *Gugong wenwu yuekan*, vol. 12, no. 5 (no. 137; August 1994), pp. 88–93.

Hucker 1985: Charles O. Hucker. *A Dictionary of Official Titles in Imperial China*. Stanford, Calif.: Stanford University Press, 1985.

Hummel 1943: Arthur W. Hummel. *Eminent Chinese of the Ch'ing Period (1644–1912)*. 2 vols. Washington, DC: U. S. Government Printing Office, 1943.

Hwang Yin 2001: Hwang Yin. 'Symposium report'. *Orientations*, vol. 32, no. 8 (October 2001), pp. 97–103.

Imperial Household archives: *Neiwufu huoji dang* 內務府活計檔. No. 1 Historical Archives, Beijing.

Indiana Companion to Traditional Chinese Literature 1986: William H. Nienhauser, Jr (comp.). *Indiana Companion to Traditional Chinese Literature*. 2nd rev. edn. Taipei: SMC Publications Inc., 1986.

Ise 1922–: Ise Senichirō 伊勢專一郎 (1891–1948). *Shina no kaiga* 支那の繪画 (Chinese Painting). Kyoto: Naigai shuppan kabushiki kaisha, 1922, 1929.

Ise 1934: Ise Senichirō. *Shina sansui gashi* 支那山水画史 (History of Chinese Landscape Painting). Kyoto: Tōhō bunka gakuin Kyōto kenkyūjo, 1934.

Jao Tsung-i 1986: Tsung-I Jao. 'Wen hsuan'. *Indiana Companion to Traditional Chinese Literature* 1986, pp. 891–893.

Jenner 1981: William J. F. Jenner. *Memories of Loyang: Yang Hsuan-chih and the Lost Capital (493–534)*. Oxford: Clarendon Press; New York: Oxford University Press, 1981.

Jenyns 1935: Soame Jenyns (1904–1976). *A Background to Chinese Painting*. London: Sidgwick & Jackson, Ltd., 1935.

Jia Yi 1991: Jia Yi 賈誼 (201–169 BCE). *Xin shu* 新書 (New Book). *SKQS* (1991), vol. 695.

Jiang Baoling 1985 (1853): Jiang Baoling 蔣寶齡 (1781–1840). *Molin jinhua* 墨林今話 (Current Talk on the Forest of Ink; 1853). Series *Qingdai quanji congkan, yilin lei* 1985, vol. 9.

Jin shi 1970, 1975: Tuotuo 脫脫 (1313–1355) *et al.* (eds). *Jin shi* 金史

(History of the Jin). Taipei: Guofang yanjiu yuan, 1970. Also, Beijing: Zhonghua shuju, 1975.

Jin shu 1930, 1974: Fang Xuanling 房玄齡 (578–648) & Chu Suiliang 褚遂良 (596–658) (comps). *Jin shu* 晉書 (History of the Jìn; 646). *SKQS*, vol. 255. Also, Bona edition, Shanghai, 1930–1937. Also, punctuated & annotated edition, Beijing: Zhonghua shuju, 1974.

Jin Weinuo 1958: Jin Weinuo 金維諾. 'Gu Kaizhi de yishu chengjiu' 顧愷之的藝術成就 (Gu Kaizhi's artistic achievement). *Wenwu cankao ziliao*, 1958.6, pp. 19–24.

Jin Weinuo 1984: Jin Weinuo. 'Caojiayang yu Yang Zihua fengge' 曹家樣與楊子華風格 (The 'Cao' School and the Style of Yang Zihua). *Meishu yanjiu*, 1984.1, pp. 37–51.

Jin Weinuo 2000: Jin Weinuo. 'Artistic achievements of Buddhist sculpture from the Longxingsi in Qingzhou—On the Qingzhou style and the Northern Qi "Cao" School'. Wu Hung (ed.) 2000, pp. 377–396.

Jin-Tang yilai shuhuajia jiancangjia kuanyin pu 晉唐以來書畫家鑑藏家款印譜 (Index of Seals of Artist and Collectors Since the Jin-Tang Period). Hong Kong: Yiwen chubanshe, 1964.

Jiu Tang shu 1975: Liu Xu 劉昫 (887–946). *Jiu Tang shu* 舊唐書 (Old History of the Tang). 16 vols. Beijing: Zhonghua shuju, 1975.

Johnson 1903: Clarence K. Johnson (1870–1937). Letter to Mr. Sydney Colvin, dated 7 January 1903. Photocopy, *Admonitions* scroll file, Department of Oriental Antiquities, British Museum.

Johnston 1934: Reginald Johnston (1874–1938). *Twilight in the Forbidden City*. London: Victor Gollancz Ltd, 1934.

Juliano 1980: Annette L. Juliano. *Teng-hsien: An Important Six Dynasties Tomb*. Ascona, Switzerland: Artibus Asiae Publishers, 1980.

Kahn 1971: Harold L. Kahn. *Monarchy in the Emperor's Eyes: Image and Reality in the Ch'ien-lung Reign*. Cambridge, Mass.: Harvard University Press, 1971.

Karetzky & Soper 1991: Patricia E. Karetzky & Alexander Soper. 'A Northern Wei painted coffin'. *Artibus Asiae*, vol. 51, no. 1/2 (1991), pp. 5–20.

Karlgren (tr.) 1950: Bernhard Karlgren (1889–1978) (tr.). *The Book of Odes*. Stockholm: Museum of Far Eastern Antiquities, 1950.

Kinney, Anne Behnke. *Lienü zhuan* website. ‹http://www.etext.lib.virginia.edu/chinese/lienu/browse/html›.

Knechtges 1982–: David R. Knechtges (tr. & annot.). Xiao Tong 蕭統 (501–531). *Wen xuan* 文選 (Literary Anthology). Princeton, N. J.: Princeton University Press; vol. 1, 1982; vol. 2, 1987; vol. 3, 1996.

Kohara 1967 (a, b): Kohara Hironobu 古原宏伸. 'Joshi shin zukan' 女史箴圖卷 (The *Admonitions of the Instructress to the Court Ladies* picture-scroll). *Kokka*, no. 908 (Nov. 1967), pp. 17–31 (pt. 1); no. 909 (Dec. 1967), pp. 13–27 (pt. 2). Also, tr. in Kohara 2000 (1967).

Kohara 1985: Kohara Hironobu. 'Ō E oyobi sono denshō sakuhin' 王維及其傳稱作品 (Wang Wei and his attributed works). *Bunjinga suihen*, vol. 1 Ō E, pp. 125–145.

Kohara 1991: Kohara Hironobu. 'Narrative illustration in the handscroll format'. Murck & Fong (eds) 1991, pp. 247–266.

Kohara 1997: Kohara Hironobu. 'Ga Undai-san ki' 畫雲臺山記 ('Note on the Painting of Cloud Terrace Mountain'). *Yamato bunka* 太和文華, no. 97 (1997), pp. 7–29.

Kohara 2000 (1967): Kohara Hironobu. Shane McCausland (tr. & ed.). *The* Admonitions of the Instructress to the Court Ladies *Scroll*. (Revision of Kohara 1967.) *Percival David Foundation of Chinese Art Occasional Papers 1*. London: School of Oriental and African Studies, 2000.

Kokka: *Kokka* 国華. Tokyo: Kokka-sha, 1889–.

Komai 1974: Komai Kazuchika 駒井和愛 (1905–1971). 'Joshi shin zukan ko' 女史箴圖卷考 (An examination of the *Admonitions of the*

Instructress to the Court Ladies picture-scroll). *Chūgoku kokogaku ronso* 中國考古學論叢 (Collected Essays on Chinese Archaeology), pp. 382–399. Tokyo: Keiyusha, 1974.

Kong Yingda 1968: Kong Yingda 孔穎達 (574–648). *Mao shi zhengyi* 毛詩正義 (*Mao shi zhu shu* 毛詩注疏). *Sibu beiyao* 四部備要 edition. Reprint, Taipei: Taiwan Zhonghua shuju, 1968.

Kopytoff 1986: Igor Kopytoff. 'The cultural biography of things: commoditization as process'. Arjun Appadurai (ed.). *The Social Life of Things: Commodities in Cultural Perspective*, pp. 64–94. Cambridge: Cambridge University Press, 1986.

Kroll & Knechtges (eds) 2003: Paul Kroll & David R. Knechtges (eds). *Studies In Early Medieval Chinese Literature And Cultural History, in Honor of Donald Holzman and Richard B. Mather*. Provo, Utah: T'ang Studies Society, 2003.

Kuhn 1990: Philip A. Kuhn. *Soulstealers: The Chinese Sorcery Scare of 1768*. Cambridge, Mass.: Harvard University Press, 1990.

Laing 1974: Ellen Johnston Laing. 'Neo-Taoism and the Seven Sages of the Bamboo Grove in Chinese painting'. *Artibus Asiae*, vol. 36, nos 1/2 (1974), pp. 5–54.

Lang 1984: Berel Lang. *The Death of Art*. New York: Haven, 1984.

Lang Shaojun 1995a: Lang Shaojun 郎紹君. 'Lin Fengmian yishu de jingshen neihan' 林風眠藝術的精神內涵 (The spirit and content of Lin Fengmian's art). Zheng Chao (ed.) 1995, p. 95–113.

Lang Shaojun 1995b: Lang Shaojun. 'Chuangzao xinde shenmei jigou— Lin Fengmian dui huihua xingshi yuyan de tansuo' 創造新的審美機構 — 林風眠對繪畫形式語言的探索 (Creating a new aesthetic structure: Lin Fengmian's exploration of a formal language). Zheng Chao (ed.) 1995, pp. 188–218.

Lawton 1970: Thomas Lawton. 'Notes on five paintings from a Ch'ing dynasty collection'. *Ars Orientalis*, vol. 12 (1970), pp. 191–215.

Lawton 1973: Thomas Lawton. *Freer Gallery of Art Fiftieth Anniversary Exhibition, II: Chinese Figure Painting*. [Exh. cat.] Washington, DC: Smithsonian Institution, Freer Gallery of Art, 1973.

LDMHJ: Zhang Yanyuan 張彥遠 (*c*.815–after 875). *Lidai minghua ji* 歷代名畫記 (Record of Famous Paintings through Successive Ages; completed 847). See also Zhang Yanyuan (847).

Ledderose 1973: Lothar Ledderose. 'Subject matter in early Chinese painting criticism'. *Oriental Art*, no. 19 (spring 1973), pp. 69–83.

Ledderose 1979: Lothar Ledderose. *Mi Fu and the Classical Tradition of Chinese Calligraphy*. Princeton, N. J.: Princeton University Press, 1979.

Ledderose 2001: Lothar Ledderose. 'Aesthetic appropriation of ancient calligraphy in modern China'. Hearn & Smith (eds) 2001, pp. 212–245.

Lee & Ho (eds) 1968: Sherman E. Lee & Wai-kam Ho (eds). *Chinese Art under the Mongols: The Yuan Dynasty (1279–1368)*. Cleveland: Cleveland Museum of Art, 1968.

Lee & Ho 1981: Sherman E. Lee & Wai-kam Ho. 'The nature and significance of the collection of Liang Ch'ing-piao'. *Proceedings of the International Conference on Chinese Studies*, pp. 101–157. Taipei: Academia Sinica, 1981.

Legge 1861–: James Legge (1815–1897). *The Chinese Classics*. 5 vols. Hong Kong: the author; London: Trübner, 1861–1872.

Legge 1935, 1960 (1893): James Legge. *The Chinese Classics. Vol. 4: She King, or the Book of Poetry*. 2nd edition. Oxford: Clarendon Press, 1935. Also, Hong Kong: Hong Kong University Press, 1960.

Legge 1967: James Legge (tr.). *Li Chi, Book of Rites*. New York: University Books, 1967.

Li Baoxun 1909: Li Baoxun 李葆恂 (1859–1915). *Wuyiyouyizhai lunhua shi* 無益有益齋論畫詩 (Poems on Paintings from the Lodge of No Use is of Use). N.p., 1909.

Li Fang 1919: Li Fang 李放 (b. 1883/4). *Baqi hua lu* 八旗畫錄 (Record of Painting in the Eight Banners). [Tianjin], 1919.

Li Fengmao 1996: Li Fengmao 李豐楙. *Wuru yu diejiang* 誤入與謫降 (Chance Entrance and Earthly Deposition). Taipei: Xuesheng shuju, 1996.

Li ji 禮記 (Book of Rites). Beijing: Zhonghua shuju, 1992.

Li Lian 1922: Li Lian (1488–1566) 李濂. *Bianjing yiji zhi* 汴京遺蹟志. 6 vols. Henan: Gu'an shuju, 1922.

Li Lian. *Hua pin* 畫品 (Paintings graded).

Li Shan 李善 (d. 689) (annot.). *Wen xuan Li Shan zhu* 文選李善注 (Wen xuan, Annotated by Li Shan). Facsimile of the recut of a Southern Song (1127–1279) edition of the *Wen xuan* published by Hu Kejia 胡克家 (1759–1816) in 1809. Taipei: Wenyi shuguan, 1967.

Li Sizhen 李嗣真 (d. 696). *Xu hua pin lu* 續畫品錄 (Continuation of the 'Classification of Painters').

Li Yaobo 1973: Li Yaobo 黎瑤渤. 'Liaoning Beipiao xian Xiguanjianzi Bei Yan Feng Sufu mu' 遼寧北票縣西官營子北燕馮素弗墓 (Tomb of Feng Sufu of Bei Yan at Xiguanjianzi, Beipiao County, Liaoning Province). *Wenwu*, 1973.3, pp. 2–28.

Li Yu 1984: Li Yu 李浴. *Zhongguo meishu shi gang* 中國美術史綱 (The Web of Chinese Art History). Shenyang: Liaoning meishu chubanshe, 1984.

Li Yuandu 1985 (1866): Li Yuandu 李元度 (1821–1887). *Qingchao xian zheng shi lue* 清朝先正事略 (Summary of Key Matters in the Qing Dynasty). Published as *Guochao xian zheng shi lue* 國朝先正事略 (Summary of Key Matters in the Qing Dynasty; 1866). Series *Qingdai quanji congkan, yilin lei* 1985, vols 192–193.

Li Yumin 1996: Li Yumin 李玉珉. 'Rulai shuofa tu' 如來說法圖 (Buddha Preaching the Law). *Gugong shuhua jinghua* 故宮書畫菁華 (Treasured Paintings and Calligraphic Works in the National Palace Museum), p. 151. Taipei: National Palace Museum, 1996.

Li, Chu-tsing 1981: Chu-tsing Li. 'The role of Wu-hsing in early Yüan artistic development under Mongol rule'. John D. Langlois (ed.). *China Under Mongol Rule*. Princeton, N. J.: Princeton University Press, 1981.

Li, Wai-yee 1995: Wai-yee Li. 'The collector, the connoisseur, and late-Ming sensibility'. *T'oung Pao*, no. 81 (1995), pp. 269–302.

Lienü zhuan jiaozhu 1983: Attributed to Liu Xiang 劉向 (77–6 BCE). Liang Duan 梁端 (ed.). *Lienü zhuan jiaozhu* 列女傳校注 (Biographies of Exemplary Women, Annotated). Taipei: Zhonghua shuju, 1983.

Liji jijie 1989: Sun Xidan 孫希旦 (1736–1784) (ed.). *Liji jijie* 禮記集解 (Annotated Book of Rites). Beijing: Zhonghua shuju, 1989.

Lim, Lucy 1990: Lucy Lim. 'The Northern Wei tomb of Ssu-ma Chin-lung and early Chinese figure painting'. Ph. D. diss., New York University, 1990.

Little, *et al.* 2000: Stephen Little *et al. Taoism and the Arts of China*. [Exh. cat.]. Chicago: Art Institute of Chicago, 2000.

Liu Xiang 劉向 (77–6 BCE). *Lienü zhuan* 列女傳 (Biographies of Exemplary Women). Series *SBCK* (1937), no. 060. *SKQS* (1991), vol. 695. Also, see O'Hara 1971.

Liu Xiang. *Lienü zhuan tu* 列女傳圖 (Illustrated Biographies of Exemplary Women). Edited by Wang Daokun 汪道昆 (Ming, 1368–1644), illustrated by Qiu Ying 仇英 (*c*.1495–1552).

Liu Xiang. *Xinjuan zengbu quanxiang pinglin gujin lienü zhuan* 新鐫增補全像評林古今列女傳 (Biographies of Exemplary Women Ancient and Modern, Newly Engraved, and Augmented and Expanded with a Complete Set of Portraits and Appraisals). Addenda by Mao Kun 茅坤 (1512–1601), appraisals by Peng Yang 彭烊 (Ming, 1368–1644).

Liu Yiqing 1982, 1984: Liu Yiqing 劉義慶 (403–444) (comp.). *Shishuo xinyu* 世説新語 (New Tales of the World). Shanghai: Shanghai guji chubanshe, 1982. Also, Taipei: Hanxue chubanshe, 1984. Tr. Mather 1976.

Liu Zongyuan 1961– (1814): Liu Zongyuan 柳宗元 (773–819). 'Tianjue' 天爵 (Nobility). *QTW* 1961– (1814), vol. 582.

Liu, James J. Y. 1975: James J. Y. Liu. *Chinese Theories of Literature*. Chicago: University of Chicago Press, 1975.

Liu, James T. C. 1973: James T. C. Liu. 'How did a neo-Confucian school become the state orthodoxy?' *Philosophy East and West*, vol. 23, no. 4 (October 1973), pp. 483–505.

Liu, Madam 劉氏 (Qing, 1644–1911). *Nü fan jie lu* 女范捷錄 (Models for Women: a Quick Record). In Wang Xiang, *Nü si shu*.

Loehr 1964: Max Loehr (1903–1988). 'Some fundamental issues in the history of Chinese painting'. *The Journal of Asian Studies*, vol. 23, no. 2 (February 1964), pp. 185–193.

Loehr 1972: Max Loehr. 'Phases and content in Chinese painting'. *Taipei International Symposium 1970* 1972, pp. 285–311.

Loehr 1980: Max Loehr. *The Great Painters of China*. New York: Harper and Row, 1980.

Loewe 2000: Michael Loewe. *Biographical Dictionary of the Qin, Former Han, and Xin Periods, 221 BC–AD 24*. Handbuch der orientalistik, Vierte Abteilung, China, 16 Bd. Leiden: E. J. Brill, 2000.

Lovell 1973: Hin-cheung Lovell. *An Annotated Bibliography of Chinese Painting Catalogues and Related Texts*. Ann Arbor: Center for Chinese Studies, University of Michigan, 1973.

Lu Fusheng *et al.* (eds) 1992–: Lu Fusheng 盧輔聖, Cui Erping 崔爾平 & Jiang Hong 江宏 (eds). *Zhongguo shuhua quanshu* 中國書畫全書 (Compendium of Chinese Calligraphy and Painting). 13 vols. Shanghai: Shanghai shuhua chubanshe, 1992–.

Lu Jun 1830: Lu Jun 魯駿 (1774?–1840?). *Song Yuan yilai huaren xingshi lu* 宋元以來畫人姓氏錄 (Record of Painters from the Song and Yuan by Surname; 1830).

Lun yu: Confucius (Master Kong) 孔子 (551–479 BCE). *Lunyu* 論語 (Analects of Confucius). Beijing: Zhongguo shudian, 1992. Tr. Legge 1960.

Luo Feng 1990: Luo Feng. 'Lacquer painting on a Northern Wei coffin'. *Orientations*, vol. 21, no. 7 (July 1990), pp. 18–29.

Luo Guanzhong 羅貫中 (c.1330–c.1400). *Sanguo zhi yanyi* 三國志演義 (Romance of the Three Kingdoms).

Luoyang Museum 1980: Luoyang Museum 洛陽博物館. 'Luoyang Beiwei huaxiang shiguan' 洛陽北魏畫像石棺 (Northern Wei engraved sarcophagi at Luoyang). *Kaogu* 考古, 1980.3, p. 230.

Luoyang qielan ji: Zhou Zumo 周祖謨 (ed. & annot.). *Luoyang qielan ji jiaoshi* 洛陽伽藍記校釋 (Record of the Monasteries of Luoyang: Annotations). Beijing: Zhonghua shuju, 1963.

Ma Cai 1956: Ma Cai 馬采. 'Gu Kaizhi de yishu chengjiu' 顧愷之的藝術成就 (Gu Kaizhi's artistic achievement). *Xin jianshe* 新建設, 1956.10.

Ma Cai 1958: Ma Cai. *Gu Kaizhi yanjiu* 顧愷之研究 (Research on Gu Kaizhi). Shanghai: Shanghai renmin meishu chubanshe, 1958.

Macartney, Lord. 'China and the eighteenth century world: Macartney in China' website: ‹http://www.stanford.edu/class/history92a/readings/macartney.html›; cited 12 June 2002.

McCausland 2000: Shane McCausland. 'Zhao Mengfu (1254–1322) and the revolution of elite culture in Mongol China'. Ph. D. diss., Princeton University, 2000.

McCausland 2001: Shane McCausland. 'The *Admonitions* scroll: Ideals of etiquette, art and empire from early China'. *Orientations*, vol. 32, no. 6 (June 2001), pp. 22–29.

McCausland 2003: Shane McCausland. 'The history and historicity of a Chinese handscroll painting'. *East Asia Journal: Studies in Material Culture*, vol. 1, no. 1 (2003/1), pp. 71–84.

McCausland, Shane (tr. & ed.). Kohara Hironobu. *The* Admonitions *of the Instructress to the Court Ladies Scroll*. See Kohara 2000 (1967).

McKnight 1992: Brian E. McKnight. *Law and Order in Sung China*. Cambridge: Cambridge University Press, 1992.

Maeda 1954: Maeda Seison 前田青村 (1885–1971). 'Joshi shin zukan no mosha' 女史箴図卷の模寫 (The replica of the *Admonitions* scroll). *Geijutsu Shincho* 芸術新潮, 1954.12, pp. 70–72.

Mann 2000: Susan Mann. 'Presidential address: Myths of Asian womanhood'. *Journal of Asian Studies*, vol. 59 (2000), pp. 835–862.

Manzhou jishen jitian dianli 滿洲祭神祭天大典禮 (Rituals for the Manchu Worship of the Spirits and of Heaven; 1781).

Manzhou yuanliu kao 滿洲源流考 (Researches in the Origins of the Manchus; 1783).

Mao Jin 毛晉 (1599–1659). *Jintai bishu* 津逮秘書. N.p., 1922.

March 1969: Benjamin March (1899–1934). *Some Technical Terms of Chinese Painting*. Baltimore: Waverly Press, 1935; reprint, New York, 1969.

Marriages Solemnized at Madras Saint George's Cathedral, 1869. *Index to Madras Church Marriages*. The British Library, Oriental and India Office Collection.

Martin 1907: W. A. P. Martin. *The Awakening of China*. New York: Doubleday, Page & Co., 1907.

Mason 2001: Charles Q. Mason. 'The British Museum *Admonitions* scroll: a cultural biography'. *Orientations* vol. 32, no. 6 (June 2001), pp. 30–34.

Mather 1964: Richard Mather. 'Chinese letters and scholarship in the third and fourth centuries: Wen-hsueh p'ien of the *Shih-shuo hsin-yü*'. *Journal of the American Oriental Society*, vol. 88, no. 4 (1964), pp. 348–391.

Mather 1976: Richard B. Mather (tr.). *Shih-shuo Hsin-yü: A New Account of Tales of the World by Liu I-ch'ing with Commentary by Liu Chün*. Minneapolis: University of Minnesota Press, 1976.

Meishu yanjiu: Meishu yanjiu: Zhongyang meishu xueyuan xuebao 美術研究：中央美術學院學報 (Research in the Fine Arts: Journal of the Central Academy of Fine Arts). Beijing: Renmin meishu chubanshe, 1979–.

Mengzi: Mencius (Mengzi 孟子; 372–289 BCE). *Mengzi* (Mencius). Beijing: Zhongguo shudian, 1992.

Mi Fu 1947, 1973, 1975, 1982, 1992– (1103): Mi Fu 米芾 (1052–1107/8). *Hua shi* 畫史 (History of Painting; 1103). MSCS editions (1947, 1975). Also, reprint of Ming edition by Mao Jin, Taipei: Shangwu, 1973. Also, HPCS edition (1982). Also, Lu Fusheng *et al.* (eds) 1992–, vol. 1, pp. 978–989.

Miao Yue 1947: Miao Yue 繆鉞. 'Wen xuan fujian (4)' 文選賦箋 (Notes on rhapsodies in *Wen xuan*, part 4). *Zhongguo wenhua yanjiu huikan* 中國文化研究彙刊, no. 7 (1947), pp. 66–72.

Ming shi 1974: Zhang Tingyu 張廷玉 (1672–1755) (ed.). *Ming shi* 明史 (History of the Ming). 20 vols. Beijing: Zhonghua shuju, 1974.

Mingren chuanji ziliao suoyin 明人傳記資料索引 (Index to Sources for Ming Biographies; 1964). Reprint, Taipei: Wenshizhe chubanshe, 1978.

Morohashi 1955, 1960, 1984–: Morohashi Tetsuji 諸橋轍次 (1885–1984). *Dai Kan-Wa jiten* 大漢和辭典 (Large Chinese-Japanese Dictionary). 13 vols. Tokyo: Taishūkan shoten, 1955, 1960; 1984–1986.

Mote 1975 (1959): Frederick W. Mote. 'Confucian eremitism in the Yüan period'. Arthur F. Wright (ed.). *Confucianism and Chinese Civilization*, pp. 252–290. Stanford, Calif.: Stanford University Press, 1959; reprint, 1975.

MSCK: *Meishu congkan* 美術叢刊 (Collected Texts on the Arts). Taipei: Taiwan shudian, 1956.

MSCS 1947, 1962, 1975: Huang Binhong 黃賓虹 (1864–1955) & Deng Shi 鄧實 (comps). *Meishu congshu* 美術叢書 (Compendium of the Arts). Shanghai: Shenzhou guo guang she, 1947. Also, Taipei: Shenzhou guo guang she, 1962. Also, Taipei: Yiwen, 1975.

MSQJ, Painting: Zhang Anzhi 張安治 *et al.* (eds). *Zhongguo meishu quanji: huihua bian* 中國美術全集・繪畫編 (Compendium of the Arts of China, Painting). [Various publishers], 1984–. Beijing: Renmin chubanshe, 1986.

Murck & Fong 1991: Alfreda Murck & Wen C. Fong (eds). *Words and Images: Chinese Poetry, Calligraphy and Painting*. New York: Metropolitan Museum of Art; Princeton, N. J.: Princeton University Press, 1991.

Murck 2000: Alfreda Murck. *Poetry and Painting in Song China: The Subtle Art of Dissent*. Cambridge, Mass.: Harvard University Press, 2000.

Murck 2001: Alfreda Murck. 'Images that admonish'. *Orientations*, vol. 32, no. 6 (June 2001), pp. 52–57.

Murray 1988: Julia K. Murray. 'The *Ladies' Classic of Filial Piety* and Sung textual illustration: problems of reconstruction and artistic context'. *Ars Orientalis*, vol. 18 (1988), pp. 95–129.

Murray 1990: Julia K. Murray. 'Didactic art for women: The *Ladies' Classic of Filial Piety*'. Marsha Weidner (ed.). *Flowering in the Shadows: Women in the History of Chinese and Japanese Painting*, pp. 27–53. Honolulu: University of Hawaii Press, 1990.

Murray 1995: Julia K. Murray. 'Buddhism and early narrative illustration in China'. *Archives of Asian Art*, vol. 48 (1995), pp. 17–31.

Murray 1998: Julia K. Murray. 'What is 'Chinese Narrative Illustration'?' *Art Bulletin*, no. 80 (Dec 1998), pp. 602–615.

Nagahiro 1969: Nagahiro Toshio 長廣敏雄. *The Representational Art of the Six Dynasties Period* (Rikuchō jidai geijutsu no kenkyū 六朝時代芸術の研究). Tokyo: Bijutsu Shuppansha, 1969.

Naitō 1926: Naitō Torajirō 内藤虎次郎 (Konan 湖南; 1866–1934). 'History of Chinese Paintings' (2). *Bukkyō bijutsu* 仏教美術, vol. 7 (July 1926), pp. 12–16.

Naitō 1927, 1939: Naitō Konan 内藤湖南 (Torajirō 虎次郎). *Shina kaiga shi* 支那絵画史 (A History of Painting in China). Tokyo: Kōbundō 1927, 1939.

Nakamura 1913: Nakamura Fusetsu 中村不折 (1866–1943). *Shina kaiga shi* 支那絵画史 (History of Chinese Painting). Tokyo: Genkōsha, 1913.

Nan Qi shu 1972: Xiao Zixian 蕭子顯 (489–537). *Nan Qi shu* 南齊書 (History of the Southern Qi). Beijing: Zhonghua shuju, 1972.

Nan shi 1975: Li Yanshou 李延壽 (7th century). *Nan shi* 南史 (History of the Southern Dynasties). Beijing: Zhonghua shuju, 1975.

Nan Song guange xu lu 南宋館閣續錄 (Supplementary Index of the Southern Song Academy). In Chen Gaohua (ed.) 1984.

Nan Song yuanhua lu: Li E 厲鶚 (Qing, 1644–1911) (ed.). *Nan Song yuanhua lu* 南宋院畫錄 (Record of Southern Song Academy Painters). *HSCS* 1963, vol. 4.

National Museum of History 1995: *The Exquisite Chinese Artifacts: Collection of Ching Wan Society*. [Exh. cat.] Taipei: National Museum of History, 1995.

Needham 1956: Joseph Needham (1900–1995), with Wang Ling. *History of Scientific Thought. Science and Civilization in China*, vol. 2. Cambridge: Cambridge University Press, 1956.

Neiwufu huoji dang: jishi lu 內務府活計檔：計事錄 (Archives of the Imperial Household Department: Records of Palace Works). No. 1 Historical Archives, Beijing.

Nelson 2000: Robert S. Nelson. 'The slide lecture, or the work of art

history in the age of mechanical reproduction'. *Critical Inquiry*, 26 (Spring 2000), pp. 414–434.

Nie Chongzheng (ed.) 1996: Nie Chongzheng 聶崇正 (ed.). *Qingdai gongting huihua* 清代宮廷繪畫 (Qing Court Painting). Hong Kong: Commercial Press, 1996.

Nie Chongzheng 1987: Nie Chongzheng. 'Qingdai gongting huajia xutan' 清代宮廷畫家續談 (Continued discussion of court painters of the Qing dynasty). *Gugong Bowuyuan yuankan*, 1987.4, pp. 72–87.

Nienhauser *et al.* (eds & trs) 1994: William Nienhauser, Jr, *et al.* (eds & trs). *The Grand Scribe's Records*. Bloomington: Indiana University Press, 1994.

Noel 1995: William Noel. *The Harley Psalter*. Cambridge: Cambridge University Press, 1995.

Norie (ed.) 1903: E. W. M. Norie (ed.). *Official Account of the Military Operations in China 1900–1901*. N.p.: Middlesex Regiment, 1903.

Nylan 2001: Michael Nylan. 'The legacies of the Chengtu plain'. Robert W. Bagley (ed.). *Ancient Sichuan: Treasures from a Lost Civilization*, pp. 309–328. Seattle, Wash.: Seattle Art Museum, 2001.

O'Hara 1945, 1971: Albert R. O'Hara (1907–). *The Position of Women in Early China*. Washington DC: Catholic University of America Press, 1945. Reprint, Taipei: Mei Ya Pubs, 1971.

Oertling 1997: Sewall Oertling. *Painting and Calligraphy in the Wu-tsa-tsu*. Ann Arbor: Center for Chinese Studies, The University of Michigan, 1997.

Okumura 1939: Okumura Ikurō. *Uri-nasu* (Essays on Far Eastern Art). Kyoto: n.p., 1935–1939.

Osaka 1975: Osaka Municipal Museum of Art. *Chūgoku kaiga* 中国絵画 (Chinese Painting). 2 vols. Osaka: Osaka Municipal Museum of Art, 1975.

Osaka 1994: Osaka Museum of Art and Shanghai Museum. *Chūgoku shoga meihin zuroku* 中国書画名品図録 (Masterworks of Chinese Calligraphy and Painting). [Exh. cat.]. Osaka: Osaka Municipal Museum of Art, 1994.

Otto 2001: Beatrice K. Otto. *Fools Are Everywhere: The Court Jester around the World*. Chicago: University of Chicago Press, 2001.

Owen (ed. & tr.) 1996: Stephen Owen (ed. & tr.). *Anthology of Chinese Literature: Beginnings to 1911*. New York & London: W. W. Norton, 1996.

Owen 1998: Stephen Owen. 'The difficulty of pleasure'. *Extrême-Orient, Extrême-Occident*, no. 20 (1998), pp. 9–30.

Pan Tianshou 1958: Pan Tianshou 潘天壽 (1897–1971). *Gu Kaizhi* 顧愷之. Shanghai: Shanghai renmin meishu chubanshe, 1958.

Pang Yuanji 1925: Pang Yuanji 龐元濟 (ca. 1865–1949). *Xuzhai minghua lu* 虛齊名畫錄 (Masterpieces of the Empty Studio). Shanghai, 1925.

Panofsky 1939: Erwin Panofsky (1892–1968). *Studies in Iconology: Humanistic Themes in the Art of the Renaissance*. New York: Harper Torchbook, 1939.

Panofsky 1955: Erwin Panofsky. *Meaning in the Visual Arts*. Garden City, N. Y.: Doubleday Anchor Book, 1955.

Pei Jingfu 裴景福 (1855–1926). *Zhuangtaoge shuhua lu* 壯陶閣書畫錄. 22 vols. Shanghai: Zhonghua shuju, 1937.

Pei Xiaoyuan 1992– (639): Pei Xiaoyuan 裴孝源 (act. *c.*627–50). *Zhenguan gongsi huashi* 真觀公私畫史 (History of Painting, Public and Private, of the Zhenguan Era, 627–649; 639). Lu Fusheng *et al.* (eds) 1992–, vol. 1.

Peiwenzhai shuhua pu 佩文齋書畫譜 (Manual of Calligraphy and Painting of the Studio of Admiring Culture). *Yingyin Wenyuange Siku quanshu* 影印文淵閣四庫全書 series, 5 vols. Taipei: Taiwan shangwu, 1983–.

Petrucci 1920: Raphaël Petrucci (1872–1917). *Chinese Painters: A Critical Study*. New York: Brentano's, 1920.

Pope 1947: John Pope. 'Sinology or art history'. *Harvard Journal of Asiatic Studies*, vol. 10 (1947), pp. 388–417.

Preminger & Brogan (eds) 1993: Alex Preminger & T. V. F. Brogan (eds). *The New Princeton Encyclopedia of Poetry and Poetics*. Princeton, N. J.: Princeton University Press, 1993.

Puyi 1979: Puyi 溥儀 (1906–1967). *From Emperor to Citizen: the Autobiography of Aisin-Gioro Pu Yi*. Beijing: Foreign Languages Press, 1979.

Qi Gong 1998: Qi Gong 啟功. 'Cong "Xihongtang tie" kan Dong Qichang dui fashu de jianding' 從《戲鴻堂帖》看董其昌對法書的鑒定 (Dong Qichang's connoisseurship of calligraphy as seen in the *Copybook of the Hall of Playful Geese*). Duoyun Publishing House (ed.). *Dong Qichang yanjiu wenji* 董其昌研究文集 (Essays on Dong Qichang), pp. 624–631. Shanghai: Shanghai shuhua chubanshe, 1998.

Qian, Nanxiu 2003: Nanxiu Qian. 'Women's role in Wei-Chin character appraisal as reflected in the Shih-shuo hsin-yu'. Kroll & Knechtges (eds) 2003.

Qin Xiaoyi (ed.) 1993: Qin Xiaoyi 秦孝儀. *Gugong shuhua tulu*

Qin Zuyong 1967 (1866): Qin Zuyong 秦祖永 (1825–1884). *Tong yin lun hua* 桐陰論畫 (Discussing Painting in the Shade of a Tong Tree; 1866). 3 vols. Taipei: Wenguang tushu gongsi, 1967.

Qingdai quanji congkan, yilin lei 1985: *Qingdai quanji congkan, yilin lei* 清代全集叢刊藝林類, (Qing Dynasty Compendium: Forest of Arts). Reprint, Taipei: Mingwen shuju, 1985.

QSS 1992: *Quan Song shi* 全宋詩 (Complete Poetry of the Song Dynasty). 72 vols. Beijing: Peking University, 1992–2000.

QTS 1960: Cao Yin 曹寅 (1658–1717) *et al.* (comps). *Quan Tang shi* 全唐詩 (Complete Poetry of the Tang dynasty). 25 vols. Beijing: Zhonghua shuju, 1960.

QTW 1961–1965 (1814): *Qinding quan Tang wen* 欽定全唐文 (Imperially Sanctioned Complete Tang Prose; 1814). Taipei: Huawen shuju, 1961–1965.

Raphals 1998: Lisa Raphals. *Sharing the Light: Representations of Women and Virtue in Early China*. Albany: State University of New York Press, 1998.

Rawski 1998: Evelyn Rawski. *The Last Emperors: A Social History of Qing Imperial Institutions*. Berkeley, Los Angeles, & London: University of California Press, 1998.

Rawson (ed.) 1992: Jessica Rawson (ed.). *British Museum Book of Chinese Art*. London: British Museum Press, 1992.

Reily 1992: Celia Carrington Reily. 'Tung Ch'i-ch'ang's life (1555–1636)'. Wai-kam Ho *et al.* 1992, vol. 2, pp. 394–395.

Ren Daobin 1984: Ren Daobin 任道斌. *Zhao Mengfu xinian* 趙孟頫系年 (Compiled Biography of Zhao Mengfu). Henan: Henan remin meishu chubanshe, 1984.

Ren Daobin 1991: Ren Daobin. 'Ch'en Chi-ju as critic and connoisseur'. Wai-ching Ho (ed.) *Proceedings of the Tung Ch'i-ch'ang International Symposium*, pp. 9.1–25. Kansas City, Missouri: Nelson-Atkins Museum of Art, 1991.

Renxiao Wen huanghou 仁孝文皇后 (Empress Renxiao, 1360–1407). *Nei xun* 內訓 (Lessons for the Inner Quarters).

Robinet 1979: Isabelle Robinet. 'Metamorphosis and deliverance from the corpse'. *History of Religions*, vol. 19, no. 1 (1979), pp. 57–70.

Ruan Yuan 1965 (1842): Ruan Yuan 阮元 (1764–1849). *Shiqu suibi* 石渠隨筆 (1842). *Yueyatang congshu* 粵雅堂叢書 (Compendium of the Yueya Hall), vol. 15. Taipei: Taiwan huawen shuju, 1965.

Ruitenbeek 1992: Klaas Ruitenbeek. *Discarding the Brush: Gao Qipei 1660–1734*. Amsterdam: Rijksmuseum Amsterdam; Gent: Snoeck-Ducaju & Zoon, 1992.

Runan xianxian zhuan 汝南先賢傳. Cited in *YWLJ, juan* 35.

Safford 1891: A. C. Safford. *Typical Women of China*. Shanghai: Kelly & Walsh, 1891.

San guo zhi 1971, 1999: Chen Shou 陳壽 (223–279). *San guo zhi* 三國誌 (History of the Three Kingdoms). Taipei: Chengwen chubanshe, 1971. Also, Beijing: Zhonghua shuju, 1999.

Sanchao beimeng huibian: Xu Mengxin 徐夢莘 (1126–1207). *Sanchao beimeng huibian* 三朝北盟彙編. Taipei: Wenhai chubanshe, 1962. Also, Taipei: Dahua shuju, 1979.

Sargent 1992: Stuart H. Sargent. 'Colophons in countermotion: Poems by Su Shih and Huang T'ing-chien on paintings'. *HJAS*, vol. 52, no. 1 (June 1992), pp. 263–302.

SBCK: *Sibu congkan [chubian]* 四部叢刊 [初編] (Collectanea of Books in Four Bibliographic Categories). First series, reduced edn. Shanghai: Shangwu, 1937.

Schneider 1980: Laurence Schneider. *A Madman of Ch'u: The Chinese Myth of Loyalty and Dissent*. Berkeley, Calif.: University of California Press, 1980.

Scott 1923: Alexander Scott. 'The cleaning and restoration of museum exhibits 2d report'. British Museum, Department of Scientific and Industrial Research. London: H. M. Stationery Office, 1923.

SDQJ 1980–: *Shudao quanji* 書道全集 (Anthology of [Chinese] Calligraphy). 16 vols. Taipei: Dalu shudian, 1980–. Chinese tr. of *SDZS*.

SDZS 1954–, 1970–: *Shodō zenshū* 書道全集 (Anthology of [East Asian] Calligraphy). 26 vols. Tokyo: Heibonsha, 1954–68. Also, 24 vols, Tokyo: Chūōkōron-sha, 1970–73.

Sekai bijutsu zenshū: *Sekai bijutsu zenshū* 世界美術全集 (Anthology of World Art) 14, *Chūgoku* 中国 (China). N.p.: Heibonsha, 1952. Tokyo: Kadokawa shoten, 1963.

Shanghai (ed.) 1987, 1995: Shanghai Museum (ed.). *Zhongguo shuhuajia yin jian kuan shi* 中國書畫家印鑒款識 (Seals and Signatures of Chinese Calligraphers and Painters). 2 vols. Beijing: Wenwu chubanshe, 1987. Shanghai: Wenwu chubanshe, 1995.

Shen Congwen 1981: Shen Congwen 沈從文. *Zhongguo gudai fushi yanjiu* 中國古代服飾研究 (A Study of Ancient Chinese Costumes). 2 vols. Taipei: Longtian chubanshe, 1981.

Shen Defu 1976: Shen Defu 沈德符 (1578–1642). *Wanli yehuo bian* 萬曆野獲編. Series *BJXSDG* (1976–), vol. 15.

Shi ji: Sima Qian 司馬遷 (c.145–c.86 BCE) (comp.). *Shi ji* 史記 (Historical Records). Beijing: Zhonghua shuju 1999 (1959).

Shi jing 詩經 (Book of Odes [*or* Poetry *or* Songs]): 'Bei feng' 邶風 (Odes of Bei); 'Bin feng' 豳風 (Odes of Bin); 'Chen feng' 陳風 (Odes of Chen).

Shih Shou-chien 1984: Shou-chien Shih. 'The *Mind Landscape of Hsieh Yu-yü* by Chao Meng-fu'. Fong, Wen C., *et al.* 1984, pp. 238–254.

Shih Shou-chien 1996: Shih Shou-chien 石守謙. *Fengge yu shibian* 風格與世變 (Style and Changing Contexts). Taipei: Yunchen Cultural Enterprise, 1996.

Shih, Hsio-yen 1976: Hsio-yen Shih. 'Poetry illustration and the works of Ku K'ai-chih'. James C. Y. Watt (ed.). *The Translation of Art: Essays on Chinese Painting and Poetry*, pp. 6–29. *Renditions* special issue no. 6. Hong Kong: The Chinese University of Hong Kong, 1976.

Sickman & Soper 1956, 1971: Lawrence Sickman & Alexander Soper. *The Art and Architecture of China*. Baltimore: Penguin Books, 1956. Reprint, Harmondsworth: Penguin, 1971.

Sickman 1984: Laurence Sickman. 'The sarcophagus of filial piety: its date and iconography'. Edward Chaney & Neil Ritchie (eds). *Oxford, China and Italy: Writings in Honour of Sir Harold Acton on his Eightieth Birthday*, pp. 71–79. London: Thames and Hudson, 1984.

Signatures 1964: *Signatures and Seals on Painting and Calligraphy*. 5 vols. Hong Kong: Cafa Co., 1964.

Silbergeld 1999a: Jerome Silbergeld. 'The referee must have a rule book: modern rules for an ancient art'. Smith & Fong (eds) 1999, pp. 149–169.

Silbergeld 1999b: Jerome Silbergeld. *China into Film: Frames of References in Contemporary Chinese Cinema*. London: Reaktion Books, 1999.

Sima Qian 司馬遷 (*c*.145–*c*.86 BCE). 'Taishigong zixu' 太史公自序 (Self-statement of the Grand Historian). *Shi ji* (1999), *juan* 130, pp. 2483–2509.

Sirén 1956: Osvald Sirén (1879–1966). *Chinese Painting: Leading Masters and Principles*. 7 vols. London: Lund Humphries; New York: The Ronald Press, 1956–1958.

SKQS 1983, 1991: Ji Yun 紀昀 (1724–1805) *et al.* (eds). *Siku quanshu* 四庫全書 (The Complete Books of the Four Libraries; 1772–1781). Wenyuange 文淵閣 edition, Taipei: Shangwu yinshuguan, 1983–86. Also, Shanghai: Shanghai guji chubanshe, 1991.

Smith & Fong (eds) 1999: Judith G. Smith & Wen C. Fong (eds). *Issues of Authenticity in Chinese Painting*. New York: Metropolitan Museum of Art, 1999.

Song Ruohua 宋若華 (?–820). *Nü lunyu* 女論語 (Analects for Women). In Wang Xiang, *Nü si shu*.

Song shi 1977, 1985: Tuo Tuo 脱脱 (1313–1355) *et al.* (eds). *Song shi* 宋史 (History of the Song). Beijing: Zhonghua shuju, 1977. Also, Taipei, 1985.

Song Wu 1981 (1295): Song Wu 宋無 (1260–*c*.1340). *Cuihan ji* 翠寒集 (Azure Cold Collection; preface dated 1295). *Siku quanshu zhenben 11 ji* series, vol. 172. Taipei: Shangwu, 1981.

Songhua jinghua: National Palace Museum (ed.). *Gugong Songhua jinghua* 故宮宋畫精華 (Masterpieces of Song Painting in the Palace Museum). Taipei: National Palace Museum, 1975–1976.

Songhuiyao jigao 宋會要輯稿 (Collected Essentials of Song Government, Edited Draft). Xu Song 徐松 (1781–1848) (comp.). 8 vols. Taipei: Xinwenfeng, 1976.

Soper (tr. & annot.) 1951: Alexander C. Soper (tr. & annot.). *Kuo Jo-hsu's 'Experiences in Painting' (T'u-hua chien-wen chih): An Eleventh Century History of Chinese Painting Together with the Chinese Text in Facsimile*. Washington, DC: American Council of Learned Societies, 1951.

Soper 1948: Alexander C. Soper. 'Life motion and the sense of space in early Chinese representational art'. *Art Bulletin*, vol. 30, no. 3 (1948), pp. 167–86.

Soper 1958: Alexander C. Soper. 'T'ang Ch'ao Ming Hua Lu: Celebrated Painters of the T'ang dynasty by Chu Ching-hsuan of the T'ang'. *Artibus Asiae*, vol. 21, nos 3–4 (1958), pp. 204–230.

Soper 1960: Alexander C. Soper. 'South Chinese influence on the Buddhist art of the Six Dynasties period'. *Bulletin of the Museum of Far Eastern Antiquities, Stockholm*, no. 3a (1960), pp. 47–112.

Spade 1979: Beatrice Spade. 'The education of women in China during the Southern Dynasties'. *Journal of Asian History*, vol. 13, no. 1 (1979), pp. 15–41.

Spiro 1988: Audrey Spiro. 'New light on Gu Kaizhi'. *Journal of Chinese Religions*, vol. 16 (1988), pp. 1–17.

Spiro 1990: Audrey Spiro. *Contemplating the Ancients: Aesthetic and Social Issues in Early Chinese Portraiture*. Berkeley: University of California Press, 1990.

Spiro 2003: Audrey Spiro. 'Of noble ladies and notable conventions: the search for Gu Kaizhi'. Kroll & Knechtges (eds) 2003, pp. 213–257.

SQBJ chubian [various editions] (1745–1747): Zhang Zhao 張照 (1691–1745), Liang Shizhen 梁詩正 *et al.* (comps & eds). *[Midian zhulin] Shiqu baoji [chubian]* 石渠寶笈初編 (Precious Cases of the Stone Gully, First Edition; 1745–1747). Originally published:

Wenyuange Siku quanshu, zi bu. SKQS (1991), vols 824–825. Also, Hanfen lou, 1918. Also, reprints, 2 vols, Taipei: National Palace Museum, 1971. *Siku yishu congshu* edition, 2 vols, Shanghai: Shanghai guji chubanshe, 1991.

SQBJ sanbian: *Shiqu baoji sanbian* 石渠寶笈三編 (Precious Cases of the Stone Gully, Third Edition; 1815). 10 vols. Taipei: National Palace Museum, 1969.

SQBJ xubian 1971 (1793): *Shiqu baoji xubian* 石渠寶笈續編 (Precious Cases of the Stone Gully, Second Edition; 1793). 8 vols, Taipei: National Palace Museum, 1971.

Straughair 1975: Anna Straughair. *Chang Hua: A Statesman-Poet of the Western Chin Dynasty*. Occasional Paper 15, Australian National University, Faculty of Asian Studies. Canberra: Australian National University, 1975.

Stuart 1998: Jan Stuart. 'Imperial pastimes: Dilettantism as statecraft in the eighteenth century'. Chuimei Ho & Cheri A. Jones (eds) *Life in the Imperial Court of Qing Dynasty China*. Proceedings of the Denver Museum of Natural History, Series 3, No. 15 (1998), pp. 55–66.

Stuart & Rawski 2001: Jan Stuart & Evelyn Rawski. *Worshiping the Ancestors: Chinese Commemorative Portraits*. Washington, DC: Smithsonian Institution, 2001.

Su Bai (ed.) 1989: Su Bai 宿白 (ed.). *Zhongguo meishu quanji. Huihua bian 12* 中國美術全集、繪畫編 12 (A Comprehensive Collection of Chinese Art, Painting 12), 'Mushi bihua' 墓室壁畫 (Tomb murals). Beijing: Wenwu chubanshe, 1989.

Su Shi 蘇軾 (1037–1101). *Hou Chibi fu* 後赤壁賦 (Latter Ode of the Red Cliff).

Su Shi shiji: Su Shi. *Su Shi shiji* 蘇軾詩集 (Collected Poetry of Su Shi). Beijing: Zhonghua shuju, 1996.

Su Shi wenji: Su Shi. *Su Shi wenji* 蘇軾文集 (Collected Prose of Su Shi). Beijing: Zhonghua shuju, 1986.

Sui shu 1973: Wei Zheng 魏徵 (580–643) *et al.* (comps). *Sui shu* 隋書 (History of the Sui). 6 vols. Beijing: Zhonghua shuju, 1973.

Sullivan 1954: Michael Sullivan. 'A further note on the date of the Admonitions scroll'. *The Burlington Magazine*, vol. 96, no. 619 (July 1954), pp. 307–309.

Sullivan 1962: Michael Sullivan. *The Birth of Landscape Painting in China*. Berkeley & Los Angeles: University of California Press, 1962.

Sullivan 1967: Michael Sullivan. *A Short History of Chinese Art*. Berkeley: University of California, 1967.

Sullivan 1996: Michael Sullivan. *Art and Artists of Twentieth-Century China*. Berkeley & Los Angeles: University of California Press, 1996.

Sun Chengze 孫承澤 (1592–1676). *Gengzi xiaoxia ji* 庚子銷夏記 (Whiling away the Summer). 4 vols. China: s.n., 1761.

Sun Guoting 孫過庭 (648?–703?). *Shu pu* 書譜 (Manual on Calligraphy; 687).

Sun Ji 1996: Sun Ji 孫機. *Zhongguo shenghuo* 中國聖火 (Sacred Fire of China). Shenyang: Liaoning jiaoyu chubanshe, 1996.

Sun Tagong (?attr.) 1962: Sun Tagong 孫鼛公 (attr. to; also 'anon.'). *Yuesheng suozang shuhua bielu* 悦生所藏書畫別錄 (Excerpted Record of the Calligraphy and Painting Collection of Jia Sidao). *MSCS* (1962), vol. 20.

Sun Xingyan 1841?: Sun Xingyan 孫星衍 (1753–1818). *Pingjinguan [jiancang shu]hua ji* 平津館鑒藏書畫記 (Collected [Works of Calligraphy and] Painting in [the Collection of] the Hall of the Level Ford; 1841?).

Suzuki 1966: Suzuki Kei 鈴木敬. *Daiei Hakubutsukan* 大英博物館 1 (The British Museum 1). N.p.: Kodansha, 1966.

Swann 1932: Nancy Lee Swann. *Pan Chao: Foremost Woman Scholar of China*. New York: Century Company, 1932.

Taida Journal: *Guoli Taiwan daxue meishushi yanjiu jikan*

國立臺灣大學美術史研究集刊 (Taida Journal of Art History). Taipei: Guoli Taiwan daxue yishushi yanjiusuo, 1994–.

Taipei International Symposium 1970 1972: National Palace Museum (ed.). *Proceedings of the International Symposium on Chinese Painting, National Palace Museum, Taipei, June 18–24, 1970.* Taipei: National Palace Museum, 1972.

Taiping guangji 1994: Li Fang 李昉 (925–996) *et al.* (eds). *Taiping guangji* 太平廣記. 5 vols. Tianjin: Tianjin guji chubanshe, 1994.

Taiping yulan 1960: Li Fang 李昉 (925–996). *Taiping yulan* 太平御覽 (Imperially Reviewed Encyclopaedia of the Taiping Era). Beijing: Zhonghua shuju, 1960.

Taki 1911: Taki Seiichi 瀧精一 (1873–1945). 'Ku K'ai-chih's illustrations of the Poem of Lo-shén'. *Kokka*, no. 253 (June 1911), pp. 349–357.

Taki 1914: Taki Seiichi. 'Eikoku Hakubutsukan Ko Gaishi no Joshi shin zukan' 英國博物館顧愷之の女史箴図卷 (The *Admonitions of the Instructress to the Court Ladies* by Gu Kaizhi in the British Museum). *Kokka*, no. 287 (April 1914), pp. 259–265.

Taki 1915: Taki Seiichi. 'Landscape painting under the Six Dynasties'. *Kokka*, no. 297 (February 1915), pp. 183–186 & no. 298 (March 1915), pp. 211–213.

Tanaka 1936: Tanaka Toyozō 田中豐藏 (1881–1948). 'Chūgoku bijutsu shisō' 中国芸術思想 (Thought in the arts of China; 1936). *Tōyō bijutsu dansō* 東洋美術談叢 (Collected Discourses on East Asian art). N.p.: Asahi shimbunsha, 1949.

Tang Hou 湯垕 (mid-1250s–mid-1310s). *[Gujin] Hua jian* 古今畫鑒 (Mirror of Painting [Ancient and Modern]; *c.*1310?).

Tang Lan 1961: Tang Lan 唐蘭. 'Shilun Gu Kaizhi de huihua' 試論顧愷之的繪畫 (On the painting of Gu Kaizhi). *Wenwu*, 1961.6, pp. 7–12.

Tao Jinsheng 1981: Tao Jinsheng 陶晉生. *Nüzhen shilun* 女真史論 (Studies in Jurchen History). Taipei, 1981.

Tao Zongyi 1959 (1366): Tao Zongyi 陶宗儀 (*c.*1316–1402). *Nancun chuogeng lu* 南村輟耕錄 (Record of Fitful Ploughing; 1366). Beijing: Zhonghua shuju, 1959.

Tao Zongyi 1992–: Tao Zongyi. *Shushi huiyao* 書史會要 (Essentials of the History of Calligraphy). Lu Fusheng *et al.* (eds) 1992–.

THBJ: Xia Wenyan 夏文彥 (14th century). *Tuhui baojian* 圖繪寶鑑 (Precious Mirror of Painting; preface dated 1365). *HSCS*.

Thompson 1998: Lydia Thompson. 'The Yi'nan tomb: narrative and ritual in pictorial art of the Eastern Han (25–220 C.E.)'. Ph. D. diss., New York University, 1998.

Thorp & Vinograd 2001: Robert L. Thorp & Richard Ellis Vinograd. *Chinese Art and Culture.* New York: Harry N. Abrams, Inc., 2001.

Tianshui Bingshan lu: Anon. *Tianshui Bingshan lu* 天水冰山錄. Zhou Shilin edition, compiled latter half 17th century. Series *CSJCXB* (1985), vol. 48.

Toyama 1955: Toyama Gunji 外山軍治. 'Joshi shin' 女史箴 (Nüshi zhen; Jin Zhangzong's inscription in the *Admonitions* scroll; 1955). *SDZS, Sō*, vol. 1, no. 89, p. 259. Chinese tr., *SDQJ, Song*, vol. II, nos. 89–91.

Toyama 1964: Toyama Gunji. 'Shoshu sho "Joshi shin" – den Ko Kaishi "Joshi shin" zukan' 章宗書「女史箴」－傳顧愷之《女史箴》図卷 ('The "Admonitions of the Instructress to the Court Ladies" transcribed by Emperor Jin Zhangzong – the "Admonitions of the Instructress to the Court Ladies" picture-scroll attributed to Gu Kaizhi). *Kinchō shi kenkyū* 金朝史研究 (Studies in Jin History), pp. 670–678. Kyoto: Tōyōshi kenkyūkai, 1964.

Tregear 1980: Mary Tregear. *Chinese Art.* New York: Oxford University Press, 1980.

Tsujimoto 1966: Tsujimoto Yonesaburō *et al.* Colour collotype reproduction of the *Admonitions* scroll. Kyoto: Benridō, 1966. See Gray 1966.

Tsuruta 1992: Tsuruta Takeyoshi 鶴田武良. 'Harada Gorō shi kikigaki: Taishō Shōwa shoki ni okeru Chūgoku ga korekushion no seiritsu' 原田悟郎氏聞書：大正昭和初期における中国画コレクションの成立 (Interview with Mr Harada Goro on the creation of Chinese painting collections in Japan during the Taisho and early Showa periods). In *Nichū kokkō seijōka 20 shunen: Chūgoku Min-Shin meiga ten* 日中国交正常化20周年：中国明清名画展 (Exhibition to Commemorate the 20th Anniversary of the Normalisation of China-Japan Diplomatic Relations – Masterpieces of Ming and Qing Paintings). N.p.: China-Japan Friendship Foundation, 1992.

Twitchett and Loewe (eds) 1979: Denis Twitchett & Michael Loewe (eds). *The Cambridge History of China, vol. 3: Sui and T'ang China, 589–906, Part I.* Cambridge: Cambridge University Press, 1979.

Umezawa 1926: Umezawa Waken 梅澤和軒 (1871–1931) & Nakamura Fusetsu 中村不折 (1866–1943). *Rikuchō jidai no geijutsu* 六朝時代の芸術 (Art of the Six Dynasties). N.p.: Arts Ltd, 1926.

van Gulik 1958: R. H. van Gulik (1910–1967). *Chinese Pictorial Art as Viewed by the Connoisseur; notes on the means and methods of traditional Chinese connoisseurship of pictorial art, based upon a study of the art of mounting scrolls in China and Japan.* Rome: Istituto italiano per il Medio ed Estremo Oriente, 1958.

Waley 1923, 1958: Arthur Waley (1889–1966). *Chinese Painting.* London: Ernest Benn; New York: Grove Press & Charles Scribner, 1923. Reprint, New York: Grove Press, 1958

Waley (tr.) 1937, 1996: Arthur Waley (tr.). *The Book of Songs.* London: George Allen and Unwin, 1937. Joseph R. Allen (ed. & additional tr.). New York: Grove Press, 1996.

Wang 1999: Eugene Y. Wang. 'Coffins and Confucianism – The Northern Wei sarcophagus in the Minneapolis Institute of Arts'. *Orientations*, vol. 30, no. 6 (June 1999), pp. 56–64.

Wang Bo 1961–1965 (1814): Wang Bo 王勃 (647–675). 'Tengwangge shi xu' 滕王閣詩序 (Preface to the poetry collection of the Tengwang Pavilion). *QTW* 1961–1965 (1814), vol. 4.

Wang Cheng-hua 2001: Wang Cheng-hua 王正華. 'Chen Hung-shou's "On Painting": A study of stylistic net-working and regional competition in late-Ming Chiang-nan'. Hsieh Ming-liang 謝明良 (ed.). *Quyu yu wangluo* 區域與網絡 (Regions and Connections), pp. 329–380. International Symposium. Taipei: Graduate Institute of Art History, National Taiwan University, 2001.

Wang Mingqing 1966: Wang Mingqing 王明清 (1127–about 1215). *Huizhu houlu* 揮塵後錄. *Sibu congkan xubian, zibu.* Taipei, 1966.

Wang Qingzheng 1992: Wang Qingzheng 汪慶正. 'Dong Qichang fashu ketie jianshu' 董其昌法書刻帖簡述 (An overview of Dong Qichang's woodblock-printed copybooks). Ho, Wai-kam, *et al.* 1992, vol. 2, pp. 337–348.

Wang Sengqian 王僧虔 (426–485). 'Lunshu' 論書 (On calligraphy). Cited in *Fashu yaolu*.

Wang Shixiang 1998: Wang Shixiang 王世襄. 'Xi Jin Lu Ji "Pingfu tie" liuchuan kaolüe' 西晉陸機《平復帖》流傳考略 (A study of the provenance of *Pingfu tie* by Lu Ji of the Western Jin). *Zhang Boju Pan Su juanxian shouchang shuhua ji* 張伯駒・潘素捐獻收藏書畫集 (Collection of Calligraphy and Painting Donated by Zhang Boju and Pan Su). Beijing: Zijincheng chubanshe, 1998.

Wang Shizhen 1992–: Wang Shizhen. *Gujin fashu yuan* 古今法書苑 (Garden of Ancient and Modern Calligraphy; n.d.). Reprint, Lu Fusheng *et al.* (eds) 1992–, vol. 5, pp. 1–612.

Wang Shizhen 王世貞 (1526–1590). *Yanzhou shanren sibu gao* 弇州山人四部稿 (Four Part Draft by the Mountain Man of Yanzhou; 1573). *SKQS*. Also, *Peiwenzhai shuhua pu* edition.

Wang Shizhen. *Wangshi shuhua yuan* 王氏書畫苑 (Master Wang's Garden of Calligraphy and Painting).

Wang Xiang 王相 (Qing, 1644–1911). *Nü si shu* 女四書 (Four Books for Women).

Wang Yao-t'ing 2001: Wang Yao-t'ing 王耀庭. 'Beyond the *Admonitions* scroll: a study of the mounting, seals, and calligraphy'. Paper given at the conference, 'The *Admonitions* Scroll – Ideals of Etiquette, Art, and Empire from Early China', *Percival David Foundation Colloquies on Art & Archaeology in Asia, No. 21*. The British Museum, 18–20 June, 2001.

Wang Yun 1962 (1276): Wang Yun 王惲 (1227–1304). *Shuhua mulu* 書畫目錄 (Catalogue of Calligraphy and Painting; preface dated 1276). *MSCS* (1962), vol. 18, IV/6, pp. 21–39.

Wang Zhi 王銍 (12th century). *Xuexi ji* 雪溪集 (Snow Stream Collection).

Wang Zhongluo 1980: Wang Zhongluo 王仲犖. *Wei Jin Nanbeichao shi* 魏晉南北朝史 (History of the Wei, Jin, and Southern and Northern Dynasties). Shanghai: Shanghai renmin chubanshe, 1980.

Wang, Yi-t'ung (tr.) 1984: Yi-t'ung Wang (tr.). *A Record of Buddhist Monasteries in Lo-Yang*. Princeton, N. J.: Princeton University Press, 1984.

Watson 1965: Burton Watson. *Su Tung-p'o: Selections from a Sung Dynasty Poet*. New York & London: Columbia University Press, 1965.

Wei shu 1930, 1974: Wei Shou 魏收 (506–572). *Wei shu* 魏書 (History of the Wei). Bona edition, Shanghai, 1930–1937. Beijing: Zhonghua shuju, 1974.

Weitz 1994: Ankeney Weitz. 'Collecting and connoisseurship in early Yuan China: Zhou Mi's Yunyan guoyan lu'. Ph. D. diss., Kansas University, 1994.

Wen Jia 1975, 1992– (1568/9): Wen Jia 文嘉 (1501–1583). *Qianshantang shuhua ji* 鈐山堂書畫記 (Records of Calligraphy and Painting of Qian Mountain Hall; 1568/9). *MSCS* (1975), part 6. Also, reprint, Lu Fusheng *et al.* (eds) 1992–, vol. 3, pp. 829–833. Also, *YSCB*.

Wen xuan 文選 (Anthology of Literature). Reprint of 1809 recutting of 1181 edition in 60 *juan*. Taipei: Zhonghua, 1977. See also Xiao Tong 1936.

Wen Yiduo 1949: Wen Yiduo 聞一多 (1899–1946). *Wen Yiduo quanji* 聞一多全集 (Complete Works of Wen Yiduo). Shanghai: Kaiming shudian, 1949.

Wen Zhaotong 1955: Wen Zhaotong 溫肇桐. 'Shitan Gu Kaizhi de Nüshi zhen tujuan' 試探顧愷之的女史箴圖卷 (An inquiry into Gu Kaizhi's *Admonitions* scroll). *Zhongguo huihua yishu* 中國繪畫藝術 (Chinese Pictorial Art). Shanghai: Shanghai chubanshe, 1955.

Wen Zhaotong 1985: Wen Zhaotong. *Gu Kaizhi xinlun* 顧愷之新論 (New Research on Gu Kaizhi). Chengdu: Sichuan meishu chubanshe, 1985.

Weng Tonghe 1989 (1925): Weng Tonghe 翁同龢 (1830–1904). *Weng Tonghe riji* 翁同龢日記 (Diary of Weng Tonghe). Vol. 1, 1925. Beijing: Zhonghua shuju, 1989.

Wenley 1947: A. G. Wenley. *The Grand Empress Dowager Wên Ming and the Northern Wei Necropolis at Fang Shan. Freer Gallery of Art Occasional Papers, vol. 1, no. 1*. Washington, DC: Freer Gallery, 1947.

Wenwu cankao ziliao: Wenwu cankao ziliao 文物參考資料 (Museums and Library Journal). Peking: Ministry of Fine Arts, 1950–1958.

Wenwu: Wenwu 文物 (Cultural Relics). Beijing: Wenwu chubanshe, 1959–.

West 1977: Stephen H. West. *Vaudeville and Narrative: Aspects of Chin Theater*. Wiesbaden: Franz Steiner Verlag, 1977.

Whitfield 1995: Roderick Whitfield. 'Landmarks in the collection and study of Chinese art in Great Britain – Reflections on the centenary of the birth of Sir Percival David, Baronet (1892–1967)'. Wilson & Cayley (eds) 1995, pp. 202–214.

Wilson & Cayley (eds) 1995: Ming Wilson & John Cayley (eds). *Europe Studies China – Papers from an International Conference on the History of European Sinology*. London: Hanshantang Books; Taipei: Chiang Ching-kuo Foundation for International Scholarly Exchange, 1995.

Wittfogel 1957: Karl A. Wittfogel (1896–1988). *Oriental Despotism: A Comparative Study of Total Power*. New Haven: Yale University Press, 1957.

Wong 2000: Aida-Yuen Wong. 'A new life for literati painting in the early twentieth century: Eastern art and modernity, a transcultural narrative?' *Artibus Asiae*, vol. 60, no. 2 (2000), pp. 297–326.

Wong, K. S. 1989: Kwan S. Wong. 'Hsiang Yüan-pien and Suchou artists'. Chu-tsing Li (ed.). *Artists and Patrons: Some Social and Economic Aspects of Chinese Painting*, pp. 155–163. Lawrence, Kansas: University of Kansas Press, 1989.

Wu Guanzhong 1992: Wu Guanzhong 吳冠中. Chen Ruixian 陳瑞獻 (ed.). *Yitu chunqiu: Wu Guanzhong wenxuan* 藝途春秋：吳冠中文選 (Collection of Wu Guanzhong's Writings). River Edge, N. J.: Global Publishing, 1992.

Wu Hung (ed.) 2000.7: Wu Hung 巫鴻 (ed.). *Proceedings of the International Conference on Cultural and Artistic Interaction between Han and Tang*. Beijing: Center for the Study of Chinese Archaeology, Peking University, July 2000.

Wu Hung (ed.) 2000: Wu Hung (ed.). *Between Han and Tang: Religious Art and Archaeology in a Transformative Period*. Beijing: Cultural Relics Publishing House, 2000.

Wu Hung 1989: Wu Hung. *The Wu Liang Shrine: The Ideology of Early Chinese Pictorial Art*. Stanford, Calif.: Stanford University Press, 1989

Wu Hung 1994a: Wu Hung. 'Transparent stone: Inverted vision and binary imagery in medieval Chinese art'. *Representations*, no. 46 (Spring 1994), pp. 58–86.

Wu Hung 1994b: Wu Hung. 'Three famous stone monuments from Luoyang: 'Binary' imagery in early sixth century Chinese pictorial art'. *Orientations*, vol. 25, no. 5 (May 1994), pp. 51–60.

Wu Hung 1995: Wu Hung. *Monumentality of Early Chinese Art and Architecture*. Stanford, Calif.: Stanford University Press, 1995.

Wu Hung 1996a: Wu Hung. *The Double Screen: Medium and Representation in Chinese Painting*. London: Reaktion Books; Chicago: University of Chicago Press, 1996.

Wu Hung 1996b: Wu Hung. 'Screen images: three modes of "painting-within-painting" in Chinese art'. Hearn & Smith (eds) 1996, pp. 319–337.

Wu Hung 1997: Wu Hung. 'The origins of Chinese painting (paleolithic period to Tang dynasty)'. Yang Xin, Richard M. Barnhart, Nie Chongzheng, James Cahill, Lang Shaojun & Wu Hung. *Three Thousand Years of Chinese Painting*, pp. 15–86. New Haven: Yale University Press; Beijing: Foreign Languages Press, 1997.

Wu Qizhen 1971: Wu Qizhen 吳其貞 (act. 1635–1677). *Shuhua ji* 書畫集. Taipei: Wenshizhe, 1971.

Wu Rulun 198[?] (1902): Wu Rulun 吳汝綸 (1840–1903). 'Dongyou conglu' 東遊叢錄 (Journal of my travels in Japan; 1902). *Tongcheng Wu xiansheng quanshu* 桐城吳先生全書 (Literary Works of Mr Wu of Tongcheng). Beijing: Beijingshi Zhongguo shudian, 198[?].

Wu Sheng 1920, 1970, 1992– (1712/1713): Wu Sheng 吳升 (act. early 17th century). *Daguan lu* 大觀錄 (Great Vista of Colophons; prefaces dated 1712/1713). Wujin: Lishi shengyilou, 1920. Reprints, Taipei: Guoli Zhongyang tushuguan & Hanhua wenhua, 1970. Lu Fusheng *et al* (eds) 1992–, vol. 8, pp. 124–582.

Wu Zhuo 1977: Wu Zhuo 吳焯. 'Cong Zhang Hua de Nüshi zhen tan Nüshi zhen tujuan' 從張華的女史箴談女史箴圖卷 (Zhang Hua's 'Admonitions' text and the *Admonitions* scroll). *Meishu yanjiu,* 1977.2, pp. 78–80.

XCB 1986 (1174): Li Tao 李燾 (1115–84). *Xu zizhi tongjian changbian* 續資治通鑑長編 (Comprehensive Mirror for Aid in Government, Continued; 1174). 34 vols. Beijing: Zhonghua shuju, 1986.

XHHP 1955, 1982, 1992– (1120): *Xuanhe huapu* 宣和畫譜 (Xuanhe [1119–1125] Painting Manual; catalogue of the Song emperor Huizong's painting collection, preface dated 1120). *HSCS* (1955), part I, vol. 1; (1982), vol. 2. Lu Fusheng *et al.* (eds) 1992–, vol. 2, pp. 60–131.

XHSP 1955 (*c*.1120): *Xuanhe shupu* 宣和書譜 (Xuanhe [1119–1125] Calligraphy Manual; catalogue of Song emperor Huizong's calligraphy collection, *c*.1120). *HSCS* 1955.

Xi sheng jing 西升經 (Scripture of Western Ascension).

Xia Wenyan 夏文彥 (14th century). *Tuhui baojian* 圖繪寶鑒 (Precious Mirror of Painting; 1365). In *Shufa zhengzhuan, Tuhui baojian*. N.p.: Shijie shuju, 1937; reprint, Beijing: Xinhua shudian, 1983. Also, see *THBJ*.

Xian Qin 1988: Lu Qinli 逯欽立 (comp.). *Xian Qin Han Wei Jin Nanbeichao shi* 先秦漢魏晉南北朝詩 (Poetry of the Pre-Qin, Han, Wei-Jin, and Northern-and-Southern Dynasties). 3 vols. Reprint, Taipei: Muduo, 1988.

Xiang Yuanbian 項元汴 (1525–90). *Tianlaige guanhua ji* 天籟閣觀畫記 (Viewing Records of the Hall of Heavenly Music).

Xiao jing 孝經 (Classic of Filial Piety).

Xiao Tong 1936: Xiao Tong 蕭統 (501–531). *Wen xuan* 文選 (Literary Anthology). Commentary by Li Shan 李善 (*c*.658). *Guoxue jiben congshu jianbian* 國學基本叢書簡編 edition. Shanghai: Shangwu yinshu guan, 1936.

Xiao Tong 1964: Xiao Tong. *Liuchen zhu wen xuan* 六臣注文選 (*Wen xuan* [Literary Anthology], with Commentaries by Six Early Tang Scholars). Reprint, Taipei: Guangwen shuju, 1964.

Xie He 謝赫 (act. *c*.479–535). *[Gu] huapin [lu]* 古畫品錄 ([Old Record of the] Classification of Paintings). Text & tr. in Acker 1954, 1979, pp. 1–32.

Xie Jin 謝縉 (1369–1415) *et al. Gujin lienü zhuan* 古今列女傳 (Biographies of Exemplary Women, Ancient and Modern).

Xie Zhaozhe 謝肇淛 (1657–1624). *Wu za zu* 五雜組.

Xin Tang shu: Ouyang Xiu 歐陽修 (1007–72) & Song Qi 宋祁 (998–1061) (eds). *Xin Tang shu* 新唐書 (New History of the Tang; 1060). 20 vols. Beijing: Zhonghua shuju, 1975.

Xu Bangda 1981.1: Xu Bangda 徐邦達. 'Song-Jin neifu shuhua de zhuanghuang biaoti cangyin hekao' 宋金內府書畫的裝潢標題藏印合考 (A study of the mountings and collectors' seals on works of calligraphy and painting in the Song and Jin imperial collections). *Meishu yanjiu*, 1981.1, pp. 83–85.

Xu Bangda 1981: Xu Bangda. *Gu shuhua jianding gailun* 古書畫鑑定概論 (Introduction to the Connoisseurship of Ancient Chinese Painting). Beijing: Wenwu chubanshe, 1981.

Xu Bangda 1984: Xu Bangda. *Gu shuhua wei'e kaobian* 古書畫偽訛考辨 (Studies on Forgeries in Ancient Calligraphy and Painting). 2 vols. Jiangsu: Jiangsu guji chubanshe, 1984.

Xu Bangda 1985: Xu Bangda. 'Chuan Song Gaozong Zhao Gou Xiaozong Zhao Shen shu Ma Hezhi tu *Mao shi* juan kaobian' 傳宋高宗趙構孝宗趙眘 (慎) 書馬和之《毛詩》卷考辯 (A study of the inscriptions to Ma Hezhi's *Mao Odes* attributed to Song Gaozong and Xiaozong). *Gugong Bowuyuan yuankan*, 1985.3, pp. 69–78.

Xu Bangda 1987: Xu Bangda. *Gushuhua guoyan yaolu* 古書畫過眼要錄

(Essential Record of Works of Ancient Calligraphy and Painting Viewed by the Author). Changsha: Hunan meishu, 1987.

Xu Bangda 1991: Xu Bangda. Robert E. Harrist, Jr (tr.). 'The Mao shi scrolls: Authenticity and other issues'. Murck & Fong (eds) 1991, pp. 267–288.

Xu Beihong 1983: Xu Beihong 徐悲鴻 (1895–1955). 'Dangqian Zhongguo zhi yishu wenti' 當前中國之藝術問題 (Problems facing art in China today). *Xu Beihong danchen jiushi zhounian jinianji* 徐悲鴻誕辰九十週年紀念集 (Collection Commemorating Xu Beihong's Ninetieth Birthday), pp. 217–218. Beijing: Xu Beihong Memorial Museum, 1983.

Xu Qixian 1995: Xu Qixian 徐啟憲. 'Qingdai baoxi luetan' 清代寶璽略談 (A brief account of the imperial seals of the Qing dynasty). *Gugong Bowuyuan yuankan*, 1995.3, pp. 62–66.

Xu Song 許嵩 (8th century). *Jiankang shilu* 建康實錄. *SKQS*. 8 vols. Beijing: Zhonghua shuju, 1984.

Xuanhe huapu: See *XHHP*.

Xunzi: Xunzi 荀子 (340–245 BCE). *Xunzi*. Beijing: Zhongguo shudian, 1992.

Yang Jialuo (ed.) 1962: Yang Jialuo 楊家駱 (ed.). *Songren huaxue lun* 宋人畫學論 (Essays on Painting by Song Writers). *Yishu congbian* 藝術叢編 edition. Taipei: Shijie shuju, 1962.

Yang Renkai 1991: Yang Renkai 楊仁愷. *Guobao chenfulu: gugong sanyi shuhua jianwenlu* 國寶沉浮錄：故宮散佚書畫見聞錄 (Record of the Fate of National Treasures: Calligraphy and Paintings Seen and Heard of Missing from the Old Imperial Palace). Shanghai: Shanghai renmin meishu chubanshe, 1991.

Yang Xin 1989: Yang Xin 楊新. 'Shangpin jingji, shifeng yu shuhua zuowei' 商品經濟，世風與書畫作偽 (The commodity economy, the spirit of the age and the forgery of calligraphy and painting). *Wenwu*, 1989.10, pp. 87–94.

Yang Xin 2001: Yang Xin. 'Cong shansui huafa tansuo "Nüshi zhen tu" de chuangzuo shidai' 從山水畫法探索《女史箴圖》的創作時代 (The date of creation of the *Admonitions of the Instructress to the Court Ladies* painting in the light of landscape painting technique). *Gugong Bowuyuan yuankan*, 2001.3, pp. 17–29.

Yang Xiong 楊雄 (53 BCE–18 CE). *Fa yan* 法言. Chengdu: Bashu shushe, 1988.

Yang Xiong. 'Ganquan fu' 甘泉賦 (Rhapsody of the Sweet Spring). *Wen xuan*, vol. 1, juan 7, pp. 321–332.

Yang Xiong. *Shier zhou, ershiwu guan zhen* 十二州，二十五官箴 (Admonitions to the Twenty Provinces and Twenty-five Officials).

Yao Zui 姚最 (act. 557–589). *Xu huapin* 續畫品 (Classification of Painters, Continued). Acker 1954, pp. 33–58.

Ye Dehui 葉德輝 (1864–1927). *Guanhua baiyong* 觀畫百詠 (One Hundred Poems with Notes and Comments on Famous Chinese Paintings). China: Yeshi Guangutang, 1918.

Yi jing 易經 (Book of Changes).

Yi li 儀禮. Beijing: Zhongguo shudian, 1990.

Yonezawa 1952: Yonezawa Yoshiho 米澤嘉圃. Explanatory texts to illustrations. *Sekai bijutsu zenshū, Chūgoku 1* 世界美術全書, 中国 1. Tokyo, 1952.

Yonezawa 1961: Yonezawa Yoshiho. 'Ko Gaishi no "Ga Undai-san ki"' 顧愷之の《画雲臺山記》 (Gu Kaizhi's 'Record of Painting Cloud Terrace Mountain'). *Tōkyō Daigaku Tōyō Bunka Kenkyūjo kiyō bessatsu* 東京大學東洋文化研究所紀要別冊 (Bulletin of the East Asian Cultures Research Institute of Tokyo University, Supplement), *Chūgoku kaigashi kenkyū sansuiga ron* 中国绘画史研究山水画論 (Research on the History of Painting in China, Essays on Landscape).

YSCB: *Yishu congbian* 藝術叢編 series.

Yu Anlan (ed.). *Huashi congshu* (Compendium of Painting Histories). See *HSCS*.

Yu Hui 2000: Yu Hui. 'The *Admonitions* scroll: A Song version'. *Orientations*, vol. 32, no. 6 (June 2001), pp. 41–51.

Yu Hui 2002: Yu Hui 余輝. 'Songben *Nüshi zhen tu* juan tankao' 宋本《女史箴圖》卷探考 (A study of the Song version of the *Admonitions of the Instructress to the Court Ladies* picture-scroll). *Gugong Bowuyuan yuankan*, 2002.1 (no. 99), pp. 6–16.

Yu Jianhua (ed.) 1980, 1992: Yu Jianhua 俞劍華 (1895–1979) (ed.). *Zhongguo meishujia renming cidian* 中國美術家人名辭典 (Dictionary of Chinese Artists). Shanghai: Shanghai renmin meishu chubanshe, 1980; rev. edn, 1992.

Yu Jianhua 1986: Yu Jianhua. *Zhongguo hualun leibian* 中國畫論類編 (Texts on Chinese Painting, Edited by Category). 2 vols. Beijing: Renmin meishu chubanshe, 1986.

Yu Jianhua et al. (comps) 1961/1962: Yu Jianhua, Luo Shuzi 羅叔子, & Wen Zhaotong 溫肇桐 (comps). *Gu Kaizhi yanjiu ziliao* 顧愷之研究資料 (Research Materials on Gu Kaizhi). Beijing: Renmin meishu chubanshe; Hong Kong: Nantong tushu, 1962 (preface dated 1961).

Yu Zhuoyun 1984: Yu Zhuoyun. *Palaces of the Forbidden City*. London & New York: Allen Lane & Viking Press, 1984.

Yuan shi 1976, 1985: Song Lian 宋濂 (14th century) et al. *Yuan shi* 元史 (History of the Yuan). 15 vols. Beijing: Zhonghua shuju, 1976. Taipei: Dingwen, 1985.

Yunji qiqian: Zhang Junfang 張君房 (11th century) (comp.). *Yunji qiqian* 雲笈七籤. Beijing: Huaxia chubanshe, 1996.

YWLJ: Ouyang Xun 歐陽詢 (557–641) (comp.); Wang Shaoying 汪紹楹 (ed. & annot.). *Yiwen leiju* 藝文類聚 (Literary Anthology, Assembled by Category). 2 vols. Shanghai: Shanghai guji chubanshe, 1965.

Zeng Zhaoyu et al. 1956: Zeng Zhaoyu 曾昭燏 et al. *Yi'nan guhuaxiang shimu fajue baogao* 沂南古畫像石墓發掘報兑 (Excavation Report on the Ancient Painted Stone Tomb at Yi'nan). Shanghai: Wenwu chubanshe, 1956.

Zhan Jingfeng 1992– (1591): Zhan Jingfeng 詹景鳳 (1519–1600). *Dongtu xuanlan bian* 東圖玄覽編 (Book of my Abstruse Reading; 1591). Reprint, Lu Fusheng et al. (eds) 1992–, vol. 4, pp. 1–59.

Zhan Jingfeng. *Zhanshi shuhua yuan buyi* 詹氏書畫苑補益 (Supplement to Master Zhan's Garden of Calligraphy and Painting).

Zhang Bangji 1986: Zhang Bangji 張邦基 (act. c.1131). *Mozhuang man lu* 墨庄漫錄. *Congshu jicheng xinbian* series, vol. 86. Taipei: Xinwenfeng chuban gongsi, 1986.

Zhang Chou 1888, 1975, 1994 (1616): Zhang Chou 張丑 (1577–1643). *Qinghe shuhua fang* 清河書畫舫 (preface dated 1616). [China]: Chibei caotang, 1888. Also, Taipei: Xuehai, 1975. Also, Lu Fusheng et al. (eds) 1992–, vol. 4, pp. 127–384.

Zhang Chou 1992– (c.1598): Zhang Chou. *Nanyang minghua biao* 南陽名畫表 (c.1598). Reprint, Lu Fusheng et al. (eds) 1992–, vol. 4, pp. 123–125.

Zhang Chou 1992– (n.d.): Zhang Chou. *Qinghe miqie shuhua biao* 清河祕篋書畫表 (n.d.). Reprint, Lu Fusheng et al. (eds) 1992–, vol. 4, pp. 125–126.

Zhang Heng 2000: Zhang Heng 張珩. *Muyanzhai shuhua jianshang biji* 木雁齋書畫鑑賞筆記 (Connoisseur's Notes on Calligraphy and Painting of the Muyan Studio). 8 vols. Beijing: Wenwu chubanshe, 2000.

Zhang Hua 張華 (232–300 CE). 'Nüshi zhen' 女史箴 (Admonitions of the Instructress to the Court Ladies; 292). *Wen xuan*.

Zhang Huaiguan 張懷瓘 (8th century). *Shu duan* 書斷. Zhang Yanyuan (comp.). *Fashu yaolu*.

Zhang Huaiguan. *Shu gu* 書估 (Calligraphy Dealer). Zhang Yanyuan (comp.). *Fashu yaolu*.

Zhang Qingjie 2000: Zhang Qingjie 張慶捷. 'Suidai Yu Hong mu shiguo fudiao de chubu kaocha' 隋代虞弘墓石椁浮雕的初步考察 (Preliminary Investigation of Bas-relief Carvings on Yu Hong's Stone Sarcophagus of the Sui Dynasty). Wu Hung (ed.) 2000.7, pp. 1–24.

Zhang Qiya (ed.) 1996: Zhang Qiya (ed.). *Zhongguo shufa meishu, vol. 3: Wei Jin Nanbeichao* 中國書法美術 3：魏晉南北朝 (The Art of Chinese Calligraphy, vol. 3: the Wei, Jin and Northern and Southern Dynasties). Beijing: Wenwu chubanshe, 1996.

Zhang Yanyuan (comp.). *Fashu yaolu* 法書要錄 (Essential Record of Calligraphy). Shanghai: Shanghai shuhua, 1986.

Zhang Yanyuan 1962, *LDMHJ*, etc (847): Zhang Yanyuan 張彥遠 (c.815–after 875). *Lidai minghua ji* 歷代名畫記 (Record of Famous Paintings through Successive Ages; completed 847). *HSCS* 1962, 1974, 1982, vol. 1. Also, Shanghai: Shanghai renmin meishu, 1964. Also, Lu Fusheng et al. (eds) 1992–, vol. 1. Also, tr. in Acker 1954.

Zhao Mengfu 趙孟頫 (1254–1322). *Luoshen fu* 洛神賦 (Transcription of the 'Ode of the Nymph of the Luo River'). N.p.: Shangwu yinshuguan, n.d.

Zhao Xigu 趙希鵠 (act. c.1195–c.1242). *Dongtian qinglu ji* 洞天清祿集 (Collection of Pure Earnings in the Realm of the Immortals; c.1242).

Zhaona Situ 1998: Zhaona Situ 照那斯圖 (Junast). 'Yuandai fashu jianshangjia Huihuiren Ali de tushu yin' 元代法書鑑賞家回回人阿里的圖書印 (Seal of calligraphy and painting of the Uighur Ali, connoisseur of calligraphy in the Yuan dynasty). *Wenwu*, 1998.9, pp. 87–90.

Zheng Chao (ed.) 1995: Zheng Chao 鄭朝 (ed.). *Lin Fengmian yanjiu wenji* 林風眠研究文集 (Collected Essays on Lin Fengmian). Hangzhou: Zhongguo Meishu Xueyuan chubanshe, 1995.

Zheng Yinshu 1984: Zheng Yinshu 鄭銀淑. *Xiang Yuanbian zhi shuhua shoucang yu yishu* 項元汴之書畫收藏与藝術 (Xiang Yuanbian's Calligraphy and Painting Collection and Art). Taipei: Taiwan wenshizhe, 1984.

Zheng Zhenduo 1951: Zheng Zhenduo 鄭振鐸 (1897–1958). 'Weida de yishu chuantong' 偉大的藝術傳統 (The great artistic tradition; 1951). In Zheng Zhenduo 1985, pp. 81–87.

Zheng Zhenduo 1958: Zheng Zhenduo. 'Zhongguo lidai minghuaji xuyan' 中國歷代名畫集序言 (Preface to the collection of masterpieces of Chinese painting through the ages; 1958). In Zheng Zhenduo 1985, pp. 206–220.

Zheng Zhenduo 1985: Zheng Zhenduo. Zhang Qiang 張薔 (ed.). *Zheng Zhenduo meishu wenji* 鄭振鐸美術文集 (Essays on the Arts by Zheng Zhenduo). Beijing: Renmin meishu chubanshe, 1985.

Zhi Gong 1972: Zhi Gong 志工. 'Lüe tan Beiwei de pingfeng qihua' 略談北魏的屏風漆畫 (A brief discussion of the lacquer painting on a Northern Wei screen). *Wenwu*, 1972.8, pp. 55–59.

Zhongguo gudai huihua 1978: *Zhongguo gudai huihua. Gugong Bowuyuan canghua ji. 1, Dong Jin, Sui, Tang, Wudai bufen* 中國古代繪畫. 故宮博物院藏畫集. 1, 東晉・隋・唐部分 (Ancient Chinese Painting: Collection of the Palace Museum. 1, Eastern Jin, Sui and Tang Section). Beijing: Renmin meishu chubanshe, 1978.

Zhongguo gudai shuhua mulu 1986–2000: *Zhongguo gudai shuhua mulu* 中國古代書畫目錄 (Illustrated Catalogue of Selected Works of Ancient Chinese Painting and Calligraphy). Compiled by the Group for the Authentification of Ancient Works of Chinese Painting and Calligraphy. 23 vols to date. Beijing: Wenwu chubanshe, 1986–2000. Vol. 2, 1987; vol. 19, 1998.

Zhongguo lidai huihua 1978–: *Zhongguo lidai huihua: Gugong bowuyuan cang huaji* 中國歷代繪畫. 故宮博物院藏畫集 (Chinese Painting of Successive Dynasties: Selected Paintings from the Collection of the Palace Museum). Beijing: Renmin meishu chubanshe, 1978–. Vol. 1:

Dong Jìn, Sui, Tang, Wudai bufen (Eastern Jìn, Sui, Tang, Five Dynasties Section; 1978).

Zhongxingguange: *Zhongxingguange chucang tuhua ji* 中興館閣儲藏圖書記 (Record of Paintings in the Collection of the Zhongxing Academy). *MSCS* 1975, part 18.

Zhou li 周禮 (Rites of Zhou). Beijing: Zhonghua shuju, 1992.

Zhou Mi, *GXZSXJ* 1969: Zhou Mi 周密 (1232–1298). *Guixin zashi xuji* 癸辛雜識續集. Series *BBCSJC* (1969).

Zhou Mi, *QDYY* 1977: Zhou Mi. *Qidong yeyu* 齊東野語. *BJXSDG* series (1977), 13, part 4.

Zhou Mi, *Wulin jiushi*: Zhou Mi. *Wulin jiushi* 武林舊事 (Reminiscences of Hangzhou). Hangzhou: Xihu shushe, 1981.

Zhou Mi, *YYGYL* 1975 (*c*.1296): Zhou Mi. *Yunyan guoyan lu* 雲煙過眼錄 (Record of Things That Have Passed Before My Eyes Like Clouds and Mists; *c*.1296). *MSCS* 1975. Text in Weitz 1994.

Zhou Mi, *Zhiyatang zachao* (*ZYTZC*): Zhou Mi. *Zhiyatang zachao* 志雅堂雜鈔 (Notes of Hall of Ambitious Elegance). *Biji xubian* series, vol. 31, Taipei: Guangwen, 1969. Also, *MSCS* 1975.

Zhu Jingxuan 1992–: Zhu Jingxuan 朱景玄 (fl. 841–6). *Tangchao minghua lu* 唐朝名畫錄 (Celebrated Painters of the Tang Dynasty). Lu Fusheng *et al.* (eds) 1992–, vol. 1, pp. 161–169.

Zhu Xi 1970: Zhu Xi 朱熹 (1130–1200). *Shi ji zhuan* 詩集傳. Zhengzhi daxue zhongwen yanjiusuo 政治大學中文研究所 (comps). *Guoxue yaoji congkan* 國學要籍叢刊 edition. Taipei: Xuesheng shuju, 1970.

Zhu Yizun 1975, 1991: Zhu Yizun 朱彝尊 (1629–1709). *Pushuting shuhua ba* 曝書亭書畫跋 (Colophons to Paintings and Calligraphies of the Pavilion of Sunning Books). *MSCS* 1975, part 5. Also, Taipei: Mingwen, 1991.

Zhu Yizun. *Pushuting ji* 曝書亭集 (Collected Works from the Pavilion of Sunning Books; 1705). Shanghai: Shangwu, 1935. Basic Sinological Series edition.

Zhuang Shen 1986: Zhuang Shen 莊申. 'Gu Changkang zhushu kao' 顧長康著述考 (Study of the literary works of Gu Kaizhi). *Zhongyang yanjiu yuan lishi yuyan yanjiusuo jikan* 中央研究院歷史語言研究所集刊 (Bulletin of the Institute of History and Philology, Academia Sinica), vol. 58 (1986), part 2, pp. 447–483.

Zhuang Su 莊肅 (late 13th century) (also unattributed). *Huaji buyi* 畫繼補遺 (Supplement to 'Painting, Continued'). *Zhongguo meishu lunzhu congkan* edition. Beijing: Renmin meishu chubanshe, 1963.

Zizhi tongjian: Sima Guang 司馬光 (1019–1086). *Zizhi tongjian* 資治通鑒. Shanghai: Shanghai guji chubanshe, 1987.

Zou Yigui 1937 (18th century): Zou Yigui 鄒一桂 (1686–1772). *Xiaoshan huapu* 小山畫譜 (Zou Yigui's Manual of Painting; 18th century). Series *CSJCCB* (1937).

Zürcher 1955: E. Zürcher. 'Imitation and forgery in ancient Chinese painting and calligraphy'. *Oriental Art*, n. s., vol. 1 (1955), pp. 141–146.

ZZJC: *Zhuzi jicheng* 諸子集成 (Philosophers). Shanghai: Shanghai shudian, 1986.

Index and Glossary

Qu Yuan 屈原 (343–278 BCE) 36–37, 271, *272–273*
Qu Yuan (Yokoyama Taikan) *37*
Qu Zi xing yin tu (Zhang Ruoai) 271, 273, 283
Quanshan xiao baojin zhangcheng 274
Qubilai Khan 元世祖忽必烈 (Yuan Shizu; r. 1260–1294) 168ff
Qun yu zhong mi 群玉中秘 (seal legend, Jin Zhangzong) *197, 201ff, 209,* 244
Quyang (Hebei) 河北曲陽 (tomb at) 97

Raphael 37, 298
Rawson, Jessica 296
Read, Sir Hercules 288
Red Bird 111, 119
Red Brow insurgency 117
Regent's Park 285
rejection scene in *Admonitions* 13, 19, 22, *49, 49–50, 59, 78, 80,* 95, *96,* 100, 108, *109,* 122, 128, 133, 146, *158, 261,* 295, 296
  calligraphy of *25,* 183–184
Rembrandt 37
ren yi zhong xin 仁義忠信 283
renwu 人物 (figure) 54
Renxiao (Ming empress, 1360–1407) 254
Renyin xiaoxia lu (Duanfang) 285
Renzong 北宋仁宗趙禎 (Northern Song emperor, r. 1022–1063) 34, 142, 161
Republic of China 36
Romance of the Three Kingdoms (Luo Guanzhong) *274,* 275
Royal Academy 283
Royal Collection 298
Royal Welch Fusiliers 285
Ru 儒 (Confucian) 122, 123
ruan 阮 (guitar) 97
Ruan Ji 阮籍 (4th century) 141
Ruan Xian 阮咸 (4th century) 141
Rubens 37
Ruisi Dongge 睿思東閣 (palace, seal legend) 18, 46, 132, 134, 183, 184, *195,* 196ff, 207
Ruisidian (palace) 63, 134, 198
Ruisidian yin 睿思殿印 (seal legend) 196–197
Runiu tu 傳戴嵩乳牛圖 (*Cow and Calf,* attr. Dai Song) *201*
Runzhou 潤州 (Zhenjiang) 148

Saduo bensheng 薩埵本生 (*Jātaka of Prince Sudāna*) *45*
samghati 29
San xi 三希 (Three Rarities) 279, 282, 283
San you 三友 (Three Friends) 279, 283
sangang wuchang 三網五常 (three cardinal guides and five constant virtues) 165
Sangha 桑哥 (?–1291) 180–181, 188
Sanhuai zhi yi 三槐之裔 (seal legend) *194,* 213, 219
Sanqi changshi (Cavalier attendant-in-ordinary) 136
schema and correction 31
Schneider, Laurence 37

scientific realism 36
Scott, Dr Alexander 299
se 瑟 (twenty-five-stringed zither) 254
sei 靜 (Jap., stillness) 58
Shandong 山東 46
Shang 商 (dynasty, *c.*1500–*c.*1030 BCE) 105, 122
Shang shu 尚書 (*Book of Documents*) 258
Shangguan Zhou 上官周 (1665–*c.*1750) 2, 4, 7, 35
Shanghai 上海 220, 250, 254
Shangjing 上京 (Jin capital) 203
Shangshan 商山 222, 242
Shangyao sarcophagus *113*
Shanzhe jique 山鷓棘雀 (*Blue Magpie and Thorny Shrubs,* Huang Jucai) 197
Shaoxing 紹興 (Southern Song reign, 1131–1162) 164, 166
  Shaoxing collection 171, 198ff
  Shaoxing seals *196,* 196ff, *208,* 243, 245
Shaoxing (Zhejiang) 浙江紹興 148
shen 神 (divine/spirit) 19, 20, 21
Shen Defu (1578–1642) 215
Shen Du 沈度 (1357—1434) 247
Shen Gua 沈括 (1031–1095) 140, 184
sheng 笙 (mouth-organ) 43
Sheng *yimin* 盛逸民 (*c.*1300) 253
Shengjiao xu 聖教序 (Chu Suiliang) 24
shenqi 神氣 (spiritual air) 20
shensi 神似 (supernatural realism) 21, 31
Shenyang (Liaoning) 遼寧沈陽 148
shenyun 神韻 (sprit resonance) 36
Shenzong 北宋神宗 (Northern Song emperor, r. 1067–1085) 34, 139, 142, 143
Shezhi tu 射雉圖 (*Shooting Pheasants*) 251
Shi Daoshi 史道碩 (later 4th–mid-5th century) 251, 252
Shi ji 史記 92
Shi jing 詩經 (*Book of Poetry* or *Odes*) 9, 36, 37, 101–102, 199, 213, 268
shi ping xian 視平線 (horizon) 44
shi qi rong, xiu qi rong 飾其容、修〔脩〕其容 (variant characters in 'Admonitions', line 39) 104, 107 n. 50
shi xi xian, xian xi sheng, sheng xi tian 士希賢，賢希聖，聖希天 (A gentleman admires a worthy; a worthy admires a sage; a sage admires Heaven) 282
shi yan zhi 詩言志 (poetry speaks intent) 33
Shiba gong tu 十八公圖 (*Eighteen Noblemen,* Cao Zhibai) 279
shidafu hualun 士大夫畫論 (scholar-official painting) 32
Shier zhou, ershiwu guan zhen 十二州二十五官箴 ('Admonitions to the Twelve Provinces and Twenty-five Officers') 106 n. 14
Shigutang shuhua huikao (Bian Yongyu) 211, 242
Shih Shou-chien 石守謙 31, 175, 180
Shijiali fokan 釋迦立佛龕 (*Śākyamuni Stele*) *44*
shijie 尸解 (escape from the corpse) 117
shilü 石錄 (malachite) 301

Shinü tu 仕女圖 (*Female Attendant*) 132, *133*
Shiqi tie 十七帖 (*Letters of the Seventeenth,* Wang Xizhi) 216 n. 2
Shiqi zhi yin 士奇之印 (seal legend, Gao Shiqi) *197*
shiqing 石青 (azurite) 301
Shiqu baoji 石渠寶笈 (catalogues, Qianlong) 146, 211, 214, 246, 252, 261ff, 277ff
Shiqu baoji 石渠寶笈 (seal legend, Qianlong) 204, *266*
Shishuo xinyu (Liu Yiqing) 20, 123, 135, 250
Shitao 石濤 (1642–1707) 188
Shizong 金世宗、葛王 (Prince of Ge, later Jin emperor, r. 1161–1189) 165
Short History of Chinese Art (Ludwig Bachhofer) 295
Short History of Chinese Art (Michael Sullivan) 295
shoujin 瘦筋 (slender-sinew) 247 n. 9
shoujin 瘦金 ('slender-gold' script) 193, 196, 203, 211, 212, 220, 241, 245, 247 n. 9, 263, 303
Shu 蜀 (one of Three Kingdoms, 220–264)
Shu pu 書譜 (*Essay on Calligraphy,* Sun Guoting) 193ff, 215, *220,* 241
Shu Zhu Juchuan gaoshen 唐徐浩書朱巨川告身 (calligraphy by Xu Hao)
Shuchuan tu 蜀川圖 (*Shu River,* attr. Li Gonglin) 220, 263, 269, *270–271,* 273, 278, 279, 283, 285
shuitiao zhuyin 水調朱印 193
Shun 舜 (sage-king) 34, 93, *94, 109, 112, 113,* 114, 116, 123, 124, *150*
Shun, wives of *56; see also* Yao's daughters
Shunzhi 順治 (Qing reign period, 1644–1661) 242
Shuren Li Sheng 蜀人李昇 (act. 908–925) 47
Shushi huiyao 161
si mei ju 四美具 (Union of Four Beauties) 7, 174, 263, 264, *266,* 269–270, *271,* 273, 278–279, *281, 282,* 284–285, 296–297
Si mei ju hefu (Dong Bangda) *282*
si shen 四神 (animals of the four directions) 44ff, 108ff, *110*
si wen 斯文 ('this culture of ours') 296
si yin 司印 (part seal legend) *210,* 214, 215, 216
Sichuan 四川省 273
Sickman, Lawrence 295
Siku quanshu 四庫全書 261–262, 274
Silbergeld, Jerome 37, 60
Siling 思陵 (Song emperor Gaozong) 162, 198
Silk Route 28, 29
Sima Guang 司馬光 (1019–1086) 63
Sima Jinlong 司馬金龍 (d. 484) screen 22, 54, 57, 58, 59, 86, 87, 90, 93, *94,* 95ff, *96,* 98, 114, 124, 132–133, 134, *149–151,* 192
Sima Qian 司馬遷 (*c.*145–*c.*86 BCE) 91, 92
Sima Shao 司馬紹 (Jin emperor Mingdi, r. 323–325) 115, 174, 180